W9-CVO-370

THE ILLUSTRATED ENCYCLOPEDIA OF WORLD HISTORY

The Illustrated Encyclopedia of World History

K. Donker van Heel, Editor

SHARPE REFERENCE

An imprint of M.E. Sharpe, INC.

1997 Library Reference Edition published by Sharpe Reference

Sharpe Reference is an imprint of M.E. Sharpe, Inc.

M.E. Sharpe INC.
80 Business Park Drive
Armonk, NY 10504

Editor: Koen Donker van Heel
Executive Editors: Paulien Retèl & Lisette van Meurs
Revision Editor American Edition: Michael Weber
Art Director: Henk Oostenrijk, Studio 87, Utrecht, The Netherlands
Picture research: Image Select International, London, U.K.

The Illustrated Encyclopedia of World History is a completely revised
and updated edition of the encyclopedic volume of *The Adventure of Mankind*,
edited by Henk Dijkstra.
Copyright 1997 by H.D. Communication Consultants B.V.,
Hilversum, The Netherlands

Library of Congress Cataloging-in-Publication Data

The illustrated encyclopedia of world history /
K. Donker van Heel, editor.
p. cm.
Summary: Alphabetical entries examine the major people, places,
and events of world history as well as movements, organizations, and books.
ISBN 1-56324-805-0
I. History—Dictionaries. 2. World History—Juvenile literature.
(1. History—Dictionaries. 2. World History. 3. Encyclopedias and dictionaries.)
Donker van Heel, K.
D9.145 1996
96-30544
CIP

Printed and bound in Spain.

The paper used in this publication meets the minimum requirements
of American National Standards for Information Services—Permanence of
Paper for Printed Library Materials,
ANSI Z 39.48-1984.

On the facing page:
At medieval universities lectures were hold not only on theology but on law
and medicine as well. The lecturing at the Faculty of Medicine was fully theorethical
and based on the ancient works of the philosopher physicians Galen and
Hippocrates as well as on their Arabian commentator Avicenna.
These three authorative authors are depicted here on the right-hand side of the
lecture room.

On the following page:
The storming of Jerusalem, a miniature from the *Chronique de Jérusalem*,
made around 1450 by Girart de Roussillon for Philips the Good, duke of Burgundy.
The fear that existed in the Christian West in the 15th century of the Turkish
advance in Asia Minor and Eastern Europe gave rise to a renewal
of the crusaders' spirit.

On page 8:
Small and large lakes yielded plenty of fish and were popular hunting
grounds for the hunt for waterfowl. Large quantities of rushes and reeds were cut here
for house building. Detail of the 16th century Brussels tapestry 'Otter, Swans and
Salamanders,' commissioned by King Sigismund II August of Poland.

Os qꝫ. pꝛius
exteꝛo deo
omnipotenti vitam
ppetuam dꝯ et
sanitatem coꝛpoꝛꝫ
medicanti aoꝛbos
magnos per eum
quꝯobtul ꝯi cū
ex virtutibus sanitate ꝗseruantibꝰ
et ptentibus alanctore ꝶSanti
Antesliteꝛ arte mediaē ꝫ Intreuū sāita
diuinis et aoꝛsis Intelligetenabꝰ Alto
opeꝛam ad ꝗmentans et assumens
ꝶIn pmis Iterꝰ agꝛediens quādem
ꝗmentatcoēm seu coliectoem artis cyrur
gie Alto ꝗtus deo vuo ꝫ veꝛo ꝗ omībꝰ
tribuit esse fine ꝗ millū rite fundatꝰ
exoꝛdium. Ad eū deuotissime traꝰ
rendo totis viribꝰ coꝛdie mei suꝑlicando
ꝫ In hoc opeꝛe et In cūctis aliis mittat
michi auxiliū de scto ꝫ de syon tueatur

me felix pnapui tribuendo ꝫ feliciuꝯ
medūū gubernando Et Iubeat qpseꝛe
ꝗ fiat vale ad fine optūuū ducendo·
ꝶ Ratio huiusmodi cōmentatcoīs seu
collectoīs non fuit sibꝛoꝛ defect ꝴ pꝛoꝑ
vmitas et pfectus·Non em quilꝫ omꝰ
sibꝛos habere potest·et si hret tcdiū esset
senteꝛe·ꝫ foꝛaꝰ omīa In mente retineꝛe
ꝶuria lectio delectat certa pꝛest·Et In
astrutatoꝛibus semper occurrunt melio
rameta faenae eꝰ pꝛ additamenta
fuit ꝶPueri em sumus In collo
mutantis ꝗ vide possumꝰ ꝗꝗd mittas
et aliꝗtulum plus ꝶEst erto In
astrutatoꝛibus et assumatoꝛomībꝰ vmitas
ꝫpfectꝰ·Veꝛ ꝗ ut ait plato eꝛthmꝰ
ea que scribuntur breuꝰ ꝗ expediat
diuūta sut et obseruat ea veꝛo que
sonttius vitentes fasas sud·Vne est
sibeꝛ qui vpꝛehentatoīm effumiat·
ꝶEt pꝛopteꝛ hoc ni ad solacium

La noble cite de Jherusale fu prinse lan: mil· iiiixx· ccccxdix le vedredi· xv jour de mois de Jullet

Introduction

The knowledge of history is essential for anyone who wants a better understanding of contemporary global developments.
The Illustrated Encyclopedia of World History was designed to guide you through the seventy centuries of world history that have shaped the world as we know it today.

This book is unique: it offers a broad view of all the important people, events, wars, treaties, and places that truly made history... all in one volume. The easy-to-use A-Z format of this encyclopedia facilitates any search and enables the reader to compare important historical figures and events. Cross-references allow easy access to further information that helps broaden the reader's insight into a particular event, period, or personality. *The Illustrated Encyclopedia of World History* is written in clear, accessible language, offering readers concise information on a variety of subjects at a single glance.

The nearly 5,000 entries vary from explanations of historical events to biographical details on political leaders, revolutionaries, scientists, and other important figures, from ancient history up to the present. Influential writers, composers, philosophers, and artists are also included to further enrich the historical tapestry. The book highlights the ancient civilizations of Egypt and Greece, Rome, and Persia; the Middle Ages, The Renaissance, the Age of Exploration; and the Industrial Revolution, right up to today's ever changing events, from assassinations and acts of terrorism to elections and revolutions.

This richly illustrated work includes a variety of color and black-and-white images that complement the text. The portraits and artifacts depicted include treasures from the world's most important museums and collections. In addition, maps from the specific time periods help provide readers with a clear idea of the strategic importance of various locations of events in the context of the time when they occurred.

A unique feature of this book are full-color thematic pages that illustrate great historical events, topics, people, and places; these thematic pages provide a broader view of a particular subject and include additional cross-references to related topics throughout the volume. Representative themes are: Medieval Castles; Japan's Early History; Presidents Of The United States; Important Women; The Berlin Wall; and The Abolishment of Apartheid.

The Illustrated Encyclopedia of World History provides quick-and-easy access in a single volume to the widest possible range of information on the history of humankind. In clear language and vibrant pictures, it leads the inquisitive reader and researcher on an exciting journey from the dawn of civilization to the present day.

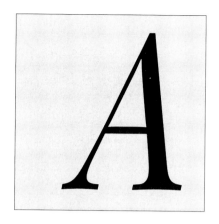

Aachen City in western Germany, also known as Aix-la-Chapelle. Famous in Roman times for its natural springs, A. later served as the seat of the Carolingian dynasty. Each successive Carolingian emperor was crowned there until 1531. The Treaty of Aachen (1688) ended the war between France and Spain over the Spanish Netherlands. The Second Treaty of Aachen (1748) ended the War of Austrian Succession.

Abbas, el (564-c.652) Uncle of Muhammad and initially his adversary. A.'s descendants founded the Abbasid dynasty.

El Abbas

Abbasid Caliph dynasty (749-1258) The second caliph, Al-Mansur, moved the court from Damascus to Baghdad. The caliphate reached its height under Haroun ar-Rashid. The dynasty ended after Baghdad's conquest by the Mongols (1258).

Abd el-Krim (1882-1963) Leader of the rebel Riffins in Morocco. From 1921 until 1926, he battled against Spanish and French rule with limited success.

Abd el-Kadir (1808-1883) Algerian emir who from 1832 to 1847 led a revolt against the French regime. Imprisoned, he was released in 1852 by Louis Napoleon.

Abdallah ibn-Hussein (1882-1951) King of Jordan, 1946-1951. He was assassinated in Jerusalem in 1951.

Abdr el-Rahman I (d.788) First Umayyed emir of Cordoba, 756-788. A. fled to Syria and then Spain after his family was killed in Damascus by the Abbasids (750). In Spain, he seized power over Cordoba in 756.

Abdr el-Rahman III (891-961) Greatest Ummayed emir of Cordoba, 912-929, and first caliph of Cordoba, 929-961. Under A., Arab culture in Spain reached its zenith.

Abélard, Pierre (1079-1142) French theologian and philosopher, known principally today for his tragic affair with his pupil Heloise.

Abercromby, Sir Ralph (1734-1801) English field marshal. In the Napoleonic Wars, he led the successful English landing at Abukir, where he died.

ABM Treaty (Anti-Ballistic Missile) Treaty concluded in 1973 between the U.S. and the Soviet Union. Its goal was to prevent each country from developing a missile system that would render it impervious to nuclear attack by missile. In 1974 it was decided that each country could install a single ABM system.

Abolitionism The movement begun in the 18th century in western Europe and the U.S. to abolish the slave trade and slavery.

Abraham Biblical figure. The name Abraham means "father of many peoples" (Gen. 17:4-6). He was the first of three forefathers of the Jewish people.

Absolutism Political theory that maintains that the power of the state rests in the monarch. It was formulated by the French philosopher Bodin (1529-1596), among others. The English thinker Thomas Hobbes (1588-1679) proposed that absolutism was the only alternative to anarchy.

Abu Bakr (c.572-634) Adherent of Muhammad, who married his

daughter Aisha. After the death of Muhammad (632), A. became the first caliph.

Abu Bakr

Abu Simbel (Egyptian-Nubian) Location on the Nile River where Ramses II built (c.1250 BC) a stone temple in honor of various gods including Amen, Rae, and himself. During the construction of the Aswan Dam (1964-1968), this temple was dismantled and reconstructed 60 meters upstream.

Abukir Port city near Alexandria, Egypt. In 1798, the British Admiral Nelson defeated the French fleet at A.,

Abraham

Abu Simbel

while on land Napoleon Bonaparte defeated Britain's allies, the Turks.

Abydos 1. One of the oldest cities of Egypt. The kings of the first two dynasties are buried there. Known throughout Egyptian history as an important religious center, A. was dedicated to the god of death, Osiris. 2. Ancient city on the Hellespont in Asia Minor. In 480 BC it was the starting point for the Persian expedition led by Xerxes against the Greeks. The Persians built a bridge at A. across the Hellespont. In 411 BC a Spartan fleet was defeated at A. by Athens.

Academy School of the Greek philosopher Plato near Athens, dedicated to the demigod Academos. Initially teaching Platonism, the Academy later adopted a more skeptical philosophy. In 529 AD the school was closed by the Roman Emperor Justinian.

Achaea Region of ancient Greece in the northern Peloponnesus on the Gulf of Corinth.

Achaemenids Ancient Persian royal family named for its patriarch, Achaemenes. The last A. was Darius II, who was defeated by Alexander the Great.

Achaean League Founded in 280 BC by the ten cities of Greek Achaea. Later it came to include other cities in and around the region. Originally aligned against Macedonia, it later opposed Sparta. It was disbanded in 146 BC after its defeat at the hands of the Romans.

Achaeans Ancient Greek people of unknown origin. The name was used by Homer to refer to the Greeks who besieged Troy.

Acropolis Greek name for an elevated citadel. The most celebrated acropolis is the one in Athens dedicated to the goddess Athena.

Acta Diurna ("Daily Acts") Official texts of ancient Rome, carved on stone or metal. First posted c.130 BC, they have been compared to the modern newspaper.

Act of Settlement 1701 resolution of the English Parliament that excluded the male Stuarts from succession to the English throne. Instead, it was

Acropolis

decreed that after the deaths of William III and Anne, the crown would pass to Electress Sophia of Hannover and her descendants.

Act of Supremacy English law enacted in 1534 wherein King Henry VIII and his successors were empowered as head of the Church of England. This act marked a clear break with the Roman Catholic Church and the founding of the Anglican Church.

Action Directe French right-wing terrorist organization that committed various attacks in the 1980's.

Action Français French Conservative political movement founded in 1898 at the time of the Dreyfus Affair. The A. was antidemocratic and anti-Semitic. During World War II, it supported the Vichy government and some of its members were later tried as collaborators.

Actium Mountain range on the west coast of Greece. It was near A. that Marc Antony was defeated in a naval battle by Octavian in 31 BC.

Adad Mesopotamian god of rain and weather.

Adad Niari Name of three kings of Assyria, the last of whom reigned between c.809-782 BC after a period in which his mother, Semiramis, served as regent. He undertook campaigns against Syria and Phoenicia.

Adams, Abigail (1744-1818) Wife of John Adams and mother of John Quincy Adams, both presidents of the U.S.. John and Abigail Adams were the first couple to live in the White House. A. was a formidable figure in her own right, whose correspondence shows her to have had strong views on public issues.

Adams, Henry (1838-1918) American writer. The grandson of John Quincy Adams, A. was a distinguished historian. Among his historical works are *The History of the United States During the Administrations of Jefferson and Madison*, (1889-1891), *Albert Gallatin* (1879), and *Mont-Saint-Michel and Chartres* (1904). He also wrote *The Education of Henry Adams* (1906) and two novels.

Adams, John (1735-1826) 2nd presi-

John Adams

dent of the U.S., 1797-1801. Born in Massachusetts, A. was one of the leaders of the resistance against Britain that culminated in the American Revolution and a member of the committee that drafted the Declaration of Independence. He was the first vice president of the U.S. (1789-1797). During his presidency, an undeclared naval war was fought with France and the Alien and Sedition Acts were passed.

Adams, John Quincy (1767-1848) 6th president of the U.S., 1825-1829. Son of Abigail and John Adams, after studying in Leiden and Amsterdam while his father represented the U.S. in Europe, he too entered the diplomatic service. A. was secretary of state under President Monroe and was influential in the formulation of the Monroe Doctrine. His presidency was unsuccessful and wracked by political squabbling. He later served in Congress.

Adenauer, Konrad (1876-1967) German statesman. A. served as mayor of Cologne (1917-1933) but lost his position when Hitler came to power. He returned to politics in 1945 and became one of the founders of the Christian Democratic Party. From 1949 to 1963, he served as chancellor of the Federal Republic of Germany and was the force behind its postwar reconstruction.

Ader, Clément (1841-1926) French aviation pioneer. On October 9, 1890,

A. made a flight of 50 meters in the steam powered flying machine, the *Eole*.

Adhémar of Monteil (d.1098) French bishop. He represented Pope Urban II at the Council of Clermont (1095) and led the First Crusade (1096-1099).

Adherbal (d.112 BC) King of Numidia, 118-112 BC. He battled with his brother, Jugurtha, and despite the support of the Romans was eventually defeated and killed.

Adler, Alfred (1870-1937) Austrian psychoanalyst. According to A., every person struggles to overcome an inferiority complex. This struggle could cause disturbances that require treatment through psychoanalysis.

Adolf of Nassau (c.1255-1298) Holy Roman Emperor. Elected in 1292, he was defeated and killed in 1298 by Albrecht of Hapsburg.

Adopted Emperors Four successive unrelated Roman emperors, each adopted as heir to the throne. The first, Trajan (d.117), was named as heir by Nerva under pressure of the army. He was succeeded by Hadrian (117-138), Antonius Pius (138-161), and Marcus Aurelius (161-180). Marcus Aurelius's natural son Commodus (180-192) succeeded him.

Alfred Adler

Adria Conflict Conflict between Italy and Yugoslavia over the northwest coast of the Adriatic Sea. The Treaty of St. Germain (1919) gave Italy part of this region (including Trieste) in keeping with its support of Great Britain and France during World War I, although Yugoslavia also claimed it. During World War II, Italy under Mussolini occupied large parts of Yugoslavia but was forced to cede these territories in 1945. A final settlement was not made until 1975.

Adrian I (d. 795) Pope, 772-795. He supported Charlemagne's conquest of Italy and built a great Roman water system.

Adrian IV (d. 1159) Pope, 1154-1159. Born Nicholas Breakspear, A. was the only English pope. He came into conflict with Frederick Barbarossa, who forced him out of Rome.

Adrian VI (1459-1523) Pope, 1522-1523. Born Adriaan Florisz, A. was the only Dutch pope.

Adrianople City in Turkey named for the Roman Emperor Hadrian, who founded it c.125. The Emperor Valens was defeated by the Visigoths there in 378. In 1205 Boudouin I, emperor of the Romanic kingdom of Constantinople, was defeated there by the Bulgars.

Adrianople, Treaty of Concluded in 1829, it ended the Russo-Turkish War (1828-1829). Russia gained the mouth of the Danube, a portion of Armenia, and a protectorate over Serbia and Greece. Turkey was forced to recognize Greek independence.

Aduatuci Belgian tribe from the Meuse valley that vigorously opposed Caesar's Roman legions.

Aedeurs Gallic tribe that inhabited the region between the Loire and the Saône. Because of their loyalty to their Roman rulers, they became, under Claudius, the first Galls to be granted full Roman citizenship.

Adrian IV

Konrad Adenauer

Adrian VI

Aedile Minor official in the Roman Republic who superintended the markets and feasts and maintained public order.

Aegatic Islands Islands in the Mediterranean Sea west of Sicily. In 241 BC the First Punic War was decided there, when a Roman fleet defeated the Carthaginians.

Aegina Island southeast of Greece. In the 6th century BC, A. was Athens' most important trade competitor. The first Greek coins were struck there. In 431 BC all the inhabitants of the island were deported by the Athenians.

Aegir Norse sea god to whom sailors taken prisoner were sacrificed.

Aelia capitolina The name of Jerusalem after the city was rebuilt in 135 BC under Emperor Hadrian.

Aeneid *See* Vergil.

Aeolians The Greek inhabitants of the Lipari islands north of Sicily in the Tyrrhenian Sea.

Aequi Mountain-dwelling tribe from the middle of Italy. They were not subdued by the Romans until 304 BC.

Aeschines (c.390-314 BC) Attic orator and supporter of Philip II of Macedonia. He opposed Demosthenes.

Aeschines

Aesculapius Greek: Asklepios. The Greek god of medicine.

Aethelbert (d.616) King of the Anglo-Saxon kingdom of Kent, 560-616. He was the first British monarch who converted to Christianity, and he married a Merovingian princess. Aethelbert initiated the first Germanic code of laws in a Germanic language.

Aethelstan (d.939) King of England, 925-939. Grandson of the Anglo-Saxon King Alfred the Great, A. subdued the Danelaw region. As a result, he is considered the first king of England.

Aetius, Flavius (d.454) Roman general who succeeded in keeping the barbarians outside the borders of the West Roman Empire. Helped by the Visigoths and the Burgundians, he defeated an attack on Gaul by Attila. Emperor Valentinian, who feared his power, killed him with his own hands.

Aetolian League Federation of Aetolian tribes founded in the 4th century BC. Initially allied with Rome against Macedonia, they later came into conflict with the Rome, leading to their subjugation in 189 BC.

Afghan War In December 1979, Soviet troops invaded Afghanistan and installed Karmal as president but were unable to quell the Western-backed Muslim resistance. In 1986, Karmal was succeeded by Najibullah, who declared a unilateral truce. In 1988-1989, the Soviet Union withdrew its troops. In 1992, Najibullah resigned, after which an Islamic republic was declared. The new regime, however, soon became mired in internal difficulties.

Afghan-British Wars The wars that Great Britain waged against Afghanistan in 1839-1842, 1878-1880, and 1919. Britain's purpose was to incorporate Afghanistan into the British Empire, for it was a buffer-state between British India and Russia. This plan failed, however, due to nationalist resistance. In 1919, the British accepted the country's autonomy.

African National Congress (ANC) Largely black liberation organization and political party that works for a democratic South Africa. The ANC

Aethelbert

was founded in 1912. After the Sharpville massacre (1960), the ANC went underground and began a campaign of armed resistance. The reconciliation reached between the ANC and the South African government under De Klerk brought rapid change in South African politics. The ANC took power in 1994. See Mandela, Tambo.

Aga Khan Title given to the leader of an Islamic sect residing principally in Pakistan. Although this sect has existed since the 14th century, the title was first conferred in this century (1957) by the shah of Persia who bestowed it upon the grandfather of Aga Khan Karim.

Aga Muhammad Khan (1742-1797) Shah of Persia, 1784-97. In 1784, he took Georgia and Khurasan from the Russians. He died by assassination.

Agathokles (361-289 BC) Hellenic adventurer and statesman. A. became autocrat of Syracuse, but conflict with Carthage brought about his political downfall.

Age of Reform Era of political and social reform in the 19th century, especially in Britain. It was precipitated by the process of industrialization and urbanization. The 1832 Reform Bill reformed Parliament. It was followed by numerous labor reforms, including the restriction of child labor.

Agesilaos II (c.444-360 BC) King of Sparta from 399 BC. A. liberated the Greek cities of Asia Minor from Persian rule. In 399 BC, he defeated the combined armies of Athens, Thebes, Corinth, and Argos. At Leuctra and Mantinea (371 BC), he was defeated by the Theban general Epaminondas.

Aggiornamento (modernization) Reform program initiated by Pope John XIII with the aim of overcoming the isolation of the church in the secular world. It reached its zenith with the Second Vatican Council (1962).

Agiedes Oldest of two ancient Spartan royal houses See Agis, Euryponiedes.

Agilulf (d.616) King of the Lombards, 560-616. Based in Northern Italy, he expanded his kingdom considerably and laid the foundations of Christianity.

Agincourt, Battle of Battle in the Hundred Years War. In 1415, the French cavalry was defeated at Agincourt, a village in northern France, by the English longbow archers of Henry V.

Agis Name of several kings of ancient Sparta. Agis IV (d. 240 BC) thought to revive the glory of Sparta through social reform. He was executed by his opponents.

Agnew, Spiro Theodore (1918-) Vice president of the U.S., 1969-1973. A. was governor of Maryland when Richard Nixon picked him as his running-mate in 1968. Elected vice president that year and again in 1972, A. was charged with having accepted bribes while governor, pleaded "no contest," and resigned in 1973.

Agora Open square that served as a central meeting point in ancient Greek cities. Lecturing, deliberation, and trade took place there.

Agrarian Revolution Introduction of production enhancing techniques in European agriculture before the Industrial Revolution (c.1750-1850). The A.R. began in northern Italy and the Low Countries. It featured row cultivation and the breeding of cows for greater milk production.

Agricola, Gaius Julius (40-93) Roman field marshal. In c.80, A. brought virtually all of Britain under Roman rule. His biography was written by his son-in-law Tacitus.

Agrippa, Marcus Vipsianus (c.63-12 BC) Roman field marshal. Through

Agrippina Vipsiana Major

his reorganization of the fleet, A. was responsible for Octavian's victory at Actium.

Agrippa (10 BC-44 AD) Roman reared Jewish king. In 41 BC he was installed by Claudius as king of Judah.

Agrippina, Julia Minor "the Younger" (15-59) Roman matron. The oldest daughter of Agrippina Major and the general Germanicus, she married (49) her uncle Claudius, who adopted her son, Nero, as heir to the throne. Nero, fearful of her machinations, had her murdered.

Marcus Vipsianus Agrippa

Agrippina Vipsiana Major "the Elder" (14 BC-3 AD) Roman matron. Daughter of Agrippa and wife of the general Germanicus, whose sons claimed the throne, she was exiled by Emperor Tiberius and died as the result of a hunger strike.

Ahab King of Israel (c.874-853 BC) A. was the son and successor of Omri.

Ahaz King of Judea (c.735-720 BC) A. became a vassal of the Assyrian king Tiglatpileser III.

Aigiospotamoi River in Thrace. It was the scene of the decisive Spartan naval victory (405 BC) over Athens in the Peloponnesian War.

Aisha (614-678) Daughter of Abu Bakr and favorite wife of Muhammad.

Aizawa, Yasuyi (1782-1863) Japanese nationalist whose writings contributed to the downfall of the Tokugawa shoguns and the restoration of the monarchy in 1868.

Ajanta Village in west central India. A. is the site of Buddhist monastic caves. The oldest of these date from c.200 BC. The most well known contain wall paintings from the 6th and 7th centuries that depict the life of Buddha.

Ajjubids Dynasty of potentates that

ruled over Egypt, Syria, Mesopotamia, and South Arabia, mainly in the 12th century. The founder of this dynasty was Saladin, a feared fighter against crusaders. After Saladin's death (1193), the power of his family declined.

Akbar (1542-1605) Third and greatest Mogul emperor of India, 1556-1605. A. expanded his domain to encompass all of northern India and reorganized the domestic administration. He was supported by Muslims and Hindus alike. He propagated his own religion, "The Divine Belief," which, however, did not survive after his death.

Akhenaton (d.c.1354 BC) King of Egypt, c.1372-c.1354. The son and successor of Amenhotep III, A. was first known as Amenhotep IV, but changed his name when he abandoned polytheism to worship the sun, Aton, alone. He built a new capital, Akhetaton, and tried to obliterate all traces of the worship of Amon, the chief god in the traditional Egyptian pantheon. His innovations were highly unpopular. The bust of his wife, Nefertete, is a prized work of Egyptian art.

Akhetaton (Tell el Amarna) Ancient Egyptian city. A. was built by Akhenaton as the new site of his court but was abandoned after his death (1354 BC).

Akhetaton

In 1877 a great collection of cuneiform tablets was discovered there that contain diplomatic correspondence between the Egyptian king and his vassals in Palestine and Syria.

Akbar

Akihito (b.1933) Japanese emperor. A. was the fifth son of Hirohito and succeeded him as emperor (1989). His motto is *heisei*, "the attainment of peace."

Akkad The first Semitic kingdom of Mesopotamia. A. was founded by Sargon I and flourished between c.2300-2150 BC. The state was centrally organized and contained an extensive bureaucracy. The king was considered divine.

Akko Originally a Canaanite port city. After its conquest by Richard the Lionheart in 1191, A. became the capital of the kingdom of Jerusalem. A century later, A. was retaken by the Muslims.

Aksum Capital of an Ethiopian realm with the same name. It flourished in the 3rd-6th centuries and had trade contacts with Egypt, Arabia, and India.

Al-Fatah Palestinian political movement led by Yasser Arafat. It is the

Alaric

most important movement within the Palestine Liberation Organization.

Alabama-Claims A diplomatic dispute between the U.S. and Britain arising from incidents during the American Civil War. The *Alabama* was a ship built in Britain and used by the Confederacy as a privateer against Union merchant shipping. After the war (1872), it was decided that neutral governments could not allow privateers to be sold to belligerent nations.

Alaca Hüyük Archaeological site situated east of Ankara, Turkey. Excavators have discovered that the place was inhabited around 4000 BC. A more recent layer contains the remnants of a Hittite city that dates from the second millennium BC and includes a gate with sphinxes.

Alalach (Tell Atchana) Ancient city in northern Syria. From c.1900-1200 BC, A. was the capital of a realm that became a buffer-state between Egypt and the Hittites. The Phoenicians destroyed Alalach around 1200 BC.

Alamans Nomadic Germanic tribe. They moved west starting in the 1st century and crossed the borders of the Roman Empire regularly in the 3rd century. Eventually, they settled near the Rhine River. The Franks, led by Chlodovech, subdued them.

Alamein, Al- Town in northern Egypt and site of an important battle in World War II. On October 23th, 1942, the British led by Montgomery defeated the German Field Marshal Rommel's Africa Korps there. The battle is considered one of the turning points of the war.

Alamo Mission in Texas, now within the city of San Antonio. The A. was the site of a famous battle in the Texan War of Independence. Starting on February 23th, 1836, Mexican forces under Santa Anna besieged it. All the defenders, who included Jim Bowie and Davy Crockett, were killed.

Alans Indo-Germanic nomadic people that originally came from the region north of the Black Sea. The tribe was subdued by the Avars around 370 AD.

Alaric (c.370-410) King of the Visigoths. After the death of Emperor

Theodosius in 395, A. plundered Greece and Illyria. In 402 he was temporarily stopped in Italy by the Roman general Stilicho, but after Stilicho died, Alaric conquered Rome. Later, Rome turned against him, and the Visigoths besieged the city. In 410 the inhabitants capitulated, and the city was plundered. Alaric died in the south of Italy, on his way to Africa.

Alawites Islamic Shiite sect. The Shiites consider Ali, not Abu Bakr, as Muhammad's successor. Through the Baath Party, the Alawites have great influence on the Syrian government.

Alawites Moroccan dynasty, founded by Moelai Rashid (1666-1672). The Alawites succeeded the Sadides. In 1912 their power was confirmed when Morocco became a French protectorate.

Alba Longa Home city of Romulus, the legendary founder of Rome. Around 600 BC, Alba Longa was destroyed by the Romans and they never rebuilt it.

Albert, Leopold Clement (1875-1934) King of Belgium, 1909-1934.

Leopold Clement Albert

He led his country's army throughout World War I. A. died while climbing a mountain in Switzerland.

Albert or Albrecht (1559-1621) Arch-

duke of Austria and son of Emperor Maximilian II of Germany. In 1595 he became governor general of the Netherlands. In 1591 he married Isabella of Spain, daughter of Philip II, who had been given sovereignty over the Southern Netherlands by her father. In 1609 he concluded the Twelve-Year Truce as a result of deteriorating economic conditions in Spain.

Albert, prince of Saxony-Coburgh-Gotha (1819-1861) Husband of Queen Victoria of Britain, his cousin, whom he married in 1840.

Albertus Magnus (c.1200-1280) German theologian and one of the most important scholastic philosophers. He taught in German monasteries and at the universities of Paris and Cologne. From 1260-1262 he was Bishop of Regensburg. Afterwards he devoted himself to scientific work. In 1931, he was canonized.

Albigensians Members of a heretical Christian sect that developed around Albi in southern France. The A. joined forces with the Cathars in the 12th and 13th centuries. Under Pope Innocent III, the struggle to suppress these heretics began. The Albigensians were led by the Count of Toulouse, who in the end was subdued by King Louis VIII. (1229, Treaty of Paris).

Albion Name for England or Britain, probably derived from *Alba*, the Celtic name for Scotland. The Romans understood this as "the white island" (*albus* is Latin for "white") because of the white cliffs on the southeast coast. "Perfidious Albion" was Frederick the Great's term for Britain as an untrustworthy power.

Albizzi Noble family that had great influence in Florence during the 14th and 15th centuries. They were, however, overruled by their most important opponents, the Di Medici family.

Albornoz, Aegidius (1310-1367) Archbishop of Toledo and cardinal. He was appointed papal ruler over Italy by Pope Innocent VI and prepared the return of the popes from Avignon to Rome. For nearly 500 years, his *Constitutiones Aegidianae* remained the code of civil law for the ecclesiastical state.

Albertus Magnus

Albrecht of Brandenburg (1490-1545) German monarch who, because of his financial obligations to the pope, was forced to borrow large sums of money from the Fugger family of merchants. In order to absolve his debts, he commissioned the monk Tetzel to sell indulgences. This indirectly spurred the protest of Martin Luther that resulted in the Protestant Reformation.

Albrecht of Hapsburg (1255-1308) Son of the Holy Roman Emperor Rudolph I. After his father's death, he was not elected emperor. In his place, Adolph of Nassau was chosen, but the latter was deposed in 1298, and then Albrecht was elected after all.

Albrecht of Saxony the Courageous (1443-1500) Waged war against Charles the Bold, the Hungarians, the Flemish, and the "Hoeken" in Holland for the Hapsburg Emperors Ferdinand III and Maximilian I

Albrecht of Wittelsbach (1528-1579) Count of Bavaria, 1550-1579. His support of the Counter-Reformation made Bavaria the center of the movement.

Albuquerque, Alphonso de (1453-1515) Portuguese admiral. After 1509 he became viceroy of the Portuguese possessions in India. In that position

Albrecht of Hapsburg

he acquired Goa, Malacca, and Ceylon.

Alphonso de Albuquerque

Alcazar Arabian word meaning stronghold or fort. The alcazar of Toledo is well-known for its important role during the Spanish Civil War in 1936.

Alcibiades (c.450-404 BC) Athenian general and political leader. Around 420 BC he became the leader of the radical democrats in Athens. During the Peloponnesian War, he persuaded his fellow citizens to go on an expedition to Sicily in 415 BC. After its disastrous failure, Alcibiades went over to

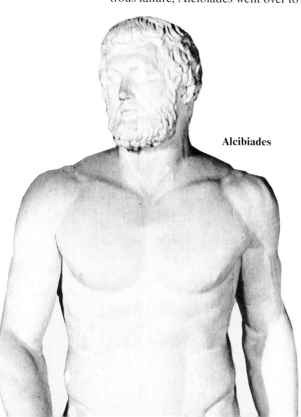

Alcibiades

the Spartans, with whom he later quarrelled. After he had returned to Athens he was appointed admiral and had some successes, especially in 410 BC near Cyzicus. Afterwards he was exiled again. He was killed by political opponents.

Alcuin, Flaccus Albinus (c.732-804) Anglo-Saxon scholar. After 793, A. became one of Charlemagne's most important advisors in nonpolitical matters. In 801 he founded a school in Tours that became greatly important for the revival of spiritual life in Western Europe.

Aleander, Hieronymus (1480-1542) Archbishop of Brindisi and cardinal. He was an important humanist and opponent of the Reformation and also the drafter of the Edict of Worms.

Aleksey Mikhailovich (1629-1676) Second czar of Russia of the House of Romanov. A. was the father of Peter the Great. He won the Russian-Polish war of 1654-1667.

Aleksey Petrovich (1690-1718) Peter the Great of Russia's eldest son. A. quarrelled with his father and fled to Austria. After his return to Russia, he was tortured to death.

Alekseyev, Mikhail Vassilyevich (1857-1918) Russian general. During World War I, he commanded the General Staff. After the abdication of Nicholas II (1917), he was appointed commander-in-chief. In the civil war that broke out shortly afterwards, A. fought against the Bolsheviks.

Aleppo City in the north of Syria. In the second millennium BC. it was an important junction for caravan-routes. After the fall of Palmyra to the Romans (273 AD), its importance increased. A. remained an important center of trade until after the Crusades.

Alesia (Alise-Ste-Reine) Ancient city in France near modern Dijon. It was the center of Gallic resistance, led by Vercingetorix, to the Romans. After a lengthy siege, the Romans captured the city in 52 BC.

Alexander II Pope, 1061-1073. Born Anselmo da Baggio, A. was a strong opponent of ending the requirement of priestly celibacy and of lay-investi-

Flaccus Albinus Alcuin

ture. A. supported William the Conqueror in his conquest of England.

Alexander VI (1431?-1503) Pope, 1492-1503. Born Rodrigo Borgia, A. was a typical Renaissance potentate who encouraged the arts and sciences. He was also, however, notorious for his immorality. A. divided the New

Alexander VI

World between Spain and Portugal in the Treaty of Tordesillas (1494) by drawing a demarcation line west of the Azores.

Alexander I (1777-1825) Czar of Russia, 1801-1825. A. was the son of Paul I. He was at various times both an ally and an opponent of Napoleon. Domestically he began his rule as a reformer but became increasingly conservative later on. He was influen-

Alexander the Great

The son of Philip II of Macedonia, Alexander became king when he was only 22 years old. He died young too, at 33, but in those 11 years he conquered a huge empire.

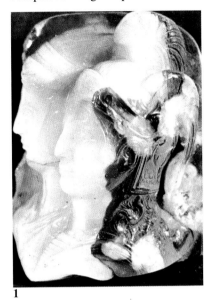

1

2

5

3

4

1. Cameo showing Alexander and his mother Olympias. *See* Olympias.

2. Alexander was tutored by the greatest teacher of his time, the famous philosopher Aristotle. *See* Aristotle.

3. Map of the territories that Alexander conquered in only 11 years' time. *See* Greek-Persian Wars.

4. Mosaic showing Alexander the Great on the left during the Battle of Issus against the Persians. *See* Persians; Darius III; Greek-Persian Wars.

5. Tomb of Alexander the Great, found in Sidon.

6. Bronze statue of Alexander the Great during the Battle of Granicus against the Persians. *See* Persians; Darius III; Greek-Persian Wars.

6

tial in forming the Holy Alliance in 1815.

Alexander II (1818-1881) Czar of Russia, 1855-1881. The son of Nicholas I, A. ended the Crimean War and abolished serfdom (1861). A reformer, he was assassinated on the very day that his important local government reforms were to take effect.

Alexander III (1845-1894) Czar of Russia, 1881-1894. A. was the son of Alexander II. Unlike his father's, his government was reactionary, and he persecuted Jews and Catholics.

Alexander IV (323-?310 BC) King of Macedonia. The son of Alexander the Great. After his father's death, A. nominally ruled the Empire. In reality, he was only a pawn in the political games of the Diadochi.

Alexander (1888-1934) King of Yugoslavia, 1921-1934. A. was the son of Peter I of Serbia. In 1929 he became a dictator. He was assassinated by Croatian separatists in Marseilles.

Alexander, Lord Harold (1891-1969) English field-marshal, who played important roles at Dunkirk, in Burma, and in North Africa during World War II.

Alexander Nevsky (1220-1263) Russian hero. In 1236 A. became monarch of Novgorod. In 1240, he defeated the Swedes near the Neva River, and in 1242 he won a victory over the German Knights on Lake Pskov. He became subordinate to the Tatars c.1250.

Alexander Severus (208-235) Roman Emperor, 222-235. At an early age, A. was adopted by Emperor Elagabalus. He ruled the empire after the latter's death, supervised by his mother, Julia Mamaea, and the praetorian prefect Ulpianus. He fought against the Persians and the Alamans. In 235 he and his mother were murdered by the troops of his successor Maximinus.

Alexander the Great (356-323 BC) King of Macedonia, 336-323 BC, and one of the great conquerors in history. A. was the son of Philip II and Olympias. After succeeding his father, he began war in the spring of 334 BC against the Persians with a huge army.

Alexander
King of Yugoslavia

Alexander the Great

The next year he defeated the Persian King Darius III near the Issus River in Asia Minor. In 332 BC and 331 BC, he conquered Egypt and Phoenicia, after which he again entered the Persian Empire. Darius III was defeated near Gaugamela in 331 BC, and in the years that followed, A. conquered the entire Persian Empire. After returning to Babylon from an expedition to India, A. died in 323 BC. A. was a pupil of Aristotle, and his campaigns helped to spread Greek culture, forming the basis for Hellenistic civilization. After his death, his empire was divided among the Diadochi.

Alexandra Fiodorovna (1872-1918) Wife of Russian Czar Nicholas II. A. was strongly influenced by Rasputin. That and her German birth made her very unpopular during World War I. After the Revolution, she was executed (1918) with her husband and children.

Alexandria Name of a number of cities founded by Alexander the Great. The most important city with this name is in Egypt (founded in 332 BC) and was the capital of the country during the Ptolemaic dynasty. The city was renowned for its library.

Alexis The name of nine Byzantine Emperors between 1081 and 1429. They first ruled from Constantinople, and after 1204 from Trebizond.

Alfonso XIII (1186-1941) King of Spain, 1886-1931. The posthumous son of Alfonso XII, A. married (1906) Victoria Eugenie, granddaughter of

Victoria of Britain. He declined to oppose General Primo Rivera, who established a dictatorship (1923-1930). When the Republicans won the election of 1931, he went into exile.

Alfonsus The name of eleven kings of Asturia, León, and Castille. Among them was Alfonsus VI (c.1042-1109), who fought against the Moors during the Reconquista. He captured Toledo

Alfonsus

in 1085, but he was defeated in 1086 near Zalaka and in 1108 near Uclès.

Alfonsus The name of five kings of Aragon. Among them was Alfonsus V (1396-1458), who was also king of Sicily and heir to Navarre. One of the first Renaissance kings, A. had a splendid court in Naples, a city he had conquered himself.

Alfonso XIII

Alfred the Great (849-899) King of Wessex, 871-899. In 871 he succeeded his brother Aethelred, who had been killed in a battle against the Danes. Eventually he defeated the Danes and later became renowned for his cultural activities, such as having Latin manuscripts translated by the scholars of his court school.

Algeciras City in southern Spain. In 1906 an international conference was held there to consider the Moroccan question. The sultan of Morocco tried in vain to avoid further French penetration of his country.

Algerian War (1954-1962) War of Independence of the Algerian National Liberation Front against the French colonial government. When in 1958 an Algerian government was formed in Cairo, a French coup d'état took place in Algiers, followed by a political crisis in France. The Fourth French Republic fell, and De Gaulle came to power. Algeria remained the scene of heavy fighting. At the Conference of Evian in March 1962, the country became independent.

Alhambra Palace in Grenada (Spain), built during the 13th and 14th centuries under Moorish occupation. It has many pillared halls and inner courts (such as the Court of the Lions) and is a superb example of Moorish architecture.

Ali Bey (1728-1773) Egyptian ruler, 1763-1773. He managed to become

Ali Bey

independent from Turkish domination in 1768 but was defeated by a rival in 1773.

Ali ibn Hussein (c.1500-1562) Turk-

ish admiral under Suleyman I ("the Magnificent"). He lost a naval battle against the Portuguese and afterwards retired to India. There he wrote his great geographical work *The Ocean.*

Ali ibn Abu Talib (c.600-661) Son-in-law and cousin of the prophet Muhammad. In 656 he became the fourth caliph, although he was not universally accepted as such. He was assassinated by fanatics while praying.

Alijah Biblical expression for a pilgrimage to Jerusalem. Later it became the word for the Jewish immigration to Israel. There have been four major waves of immigration between 1882 and 1928. Each consisted mainly of Eastern European Jews. The fifth alijah took place between 1933 and 1948 and consisted of refugees from Nazi Germany and survivors of the concentration camps.

Allenby, Sir Edmund Henry Hynman (1861-1936) British general. He served in Africa, during World War I in France, and in 1917-1918 in Palestine against the Turks. He was promoted to the position of field-marshal and was High Commissioner for Egypt and the Sudan (1919-1925).

Allende Gossens, Salvador (1908-1973) Chilean political leader and one of the founders of the Chilean Socialist Party (1933). He became president in 1970 and struggled against the country's economic malaise and for a socialist Chile. He died during a military coup.

Allia Tributary of the Tiber River, near which the Romans were beaten by the Gauls in 387 BC.

Allied Powers The countries opposed to the Central Powers in World War I and the Axis Powers in World War II.

Allobroges Gallic tribe. Subdued by the Romans (121 BC), they remained loyal, even during the great Gallic revolt of 58-51 BC.

Almagro, Diego de (1475-1538) One of Francisco Pizarro's pqrtners during the conquest of Peru (1530s). He quarreled with Hernando Pizarro and was accused of high treason and strangled. In revenge, his son Diego (1520-1542) killed Francisco Pizarro and was afterwards executed.

Almohades Muslim sect that produced a dynasty (1130-1269) that conquered Morocco, Algiers, Tunis, and Spain. They displaced the Almoravids in Spain (1174). In 1212 their armies were defeated by a confederation of Christian armies led by Alfonso VII of Castille.

Almoravids Muslim sect, founded in West Africa during the 11th century. They ruled a powerful empire centered around Marrakesh. Later they governed Morocco and part of Spain as well as Ghana. Eventually they were defeated by the Almohads.

Altamira, Cave of, Discovered in 1868 in Northwestern Spain near Santillana, the cave in which paintings from the Early Stone Age were found.

Sir Edmund Henry Hynman Allenby

Altdorfer, Albrecht (c.1480-1538) German painter and graphic artist. A member of the Danube school, he worked in Regensburg. Among his works are *Rest during the Flight from Egypt* and *The Birth of Christ.*

Althing The Icelandic Parliament, which is the oldest of Europe. It met for the first time in 930. In 1800 it was abolished under pressure of the Danes, but 43 years later it was reestablished.

Altranstadt, Treaty of 1706 pact between Charles XII of Sweden and Augustus the Strong of Saxony and Poland. It forced Augustus to break his alliance with Russia and to abdicate the Polish throne.

Alva *See* Toledo.

Alva

Alvarado, Pedro de (c.485-1541) Spanish conquistador. He aided Cortés in the conquest of Mexico (early 1520s) and himself conquered Guatemala (1523-1524). He later died in combat against the Indians.

Alvarez de Toledo, Francisco (1515-1584) Viceroy of Peru. He brutally put down a revolution of the Peruvians led by the Inca Tupac Amaru (1572) and was later forced to resign by Philip II of Spain.

Alvarez, Juan (1790-1867) Mexican general. He fought in the Mexican War of Independence from Spain (1810-1824) the war with the United States (1846-1848). A. was elected president of Mexico in 1855, but shortly afterwards resigned in favor of his fellow-soldier Comonfort.

Alyattes (d. c.560 BC) King of Lydia who quarrelled with the Medes. He made a treaty with them after the eclipse started on May 28, 585 BC which Thales of Miletos had predicted.

Amadeus Name of seven counts and two dukes of the House of Savoy.

Amalaric (d.531) King of the Visigoths, 526-531. He was the son of Alaric I. A. lived in Narbonne. A religious conflict with his brother-in-law, the King of the Franks, led to a battle in which he was killed.

Aman-Oellah (1892-1960) King of Afghanistan, 1919-1929. He instituted many reforms, including the abolition of polygamy. The people revolted, and he had to flee.

Amarna, Tell al- *See* Akhetaton.

Amasis I (1570-1546 BC) King of Egypt and founder of the 18th dynasty. He drove the Hyksos from the country, which he expanded in the south.

Amasis II (570-526 BC) King of Egypt. One of the last kings from the House of Saït, he was a great lawyer.

Amaterasoe Japanese sun-goddess, from whom the Japanese imperial family is supposed to be descended.

Amati Family of violin makers from Cremona (Italy) that prospered during the 16th and 17th centuries. The

Francisco Alvarez de Toledo

violins crafted by Nicolo Amati (1596-1684) are world-renowned. The great violin-makers Guarneri and Stradivarius were his pupils.

Ambiorix (mid-1st century BC) King of the Eburones, who fled after an insurrection against Julius Caesar had failed in 54 BC. He waged a bitter guerilla-war for several years but was never caught.

Amendola, Giovanni (1882-1926) Italian liberal political leader and the most important opponent of Mussolini. He organized the so-called Aventine Revolt in 1926 and was beaten so severely by Fascists that he died in Cannes.

American Civil War (1861-1865) Civil war between the Northern and Southern states of the U.S.. Slavery, which was widespread in the South but considered a moral evil by many in the North, was the root cause of the war. It led to widely differing economic and social systems in the two regions and clashing attitudes on many public issues. The North was far more industrialized than the agrarian South. The South claimed the constitutional right to spread slavery into new territories, a claim increasingly denied by the North. Following the election of Abraham Lincoln as president in 1860, Southern states began seceding from the U.S., often called "the Union." The 11 seceding states – Virginia, North Carolina, South Carolina, Georgia, Florida, Alabama, Mississippi, Tennessee, Arkansas, Louisiana, and Texas – formed the Confederate States of America. The

war began when Confederate forces fired on Fort Sumter, off the coast of South Carolina, in April 1861. It effectively ended four years later in April 1865, when Confederate General Lee surrendered to Union General Grant at Appomattox in Virginia. About 600,000 men died during the war. Within a few years, the 11 Southern states were restored to the Union.

American Revolution also known as the **American War of Independence** (1775-1783) Struggle for independence from Britain of the 13 North American colonies that became the U.S.. The conflict was caused by questions of political and economic power. Fighting began at Lexington and Concord, in Massachusetts, in spring 1775. George Washington was chosen by the American Continental Congress to lead the main American army. Independence was proclaimed on July 4, 1776 in a Declaration written mainly by Thomas Jefferson. After the American victory at Saratoga, New York, in 1777, France extended vital aid to the Americans. The final battle of the war took place at Yorktown in Virginia in 1781, where French and American forces captured a British army led by Cornwallis. In the Treaty of Paris (1783), Britain recognized the independence of the U.S.

Amiens, Peace of 1802 peace treaty concluded between Britain on one side and France, Spain, and the Batavian Republic (the Netherlands) on the other. France regained various colonies but had to leave Naples, Rome, and Elba. The Batavian Republic gave Ceylon to England.

Amin Dada, Idi (1925-) Ugandan soldier and political leader. A. came to

Idi Amin Dada

power in Uganda in 1971. In 1972 he expelled all British-Asians and Israelis, which had a disastrous effect on the economy of the country. After years of violent rule, he was forced to flee the country (1979).

Amon Egyptian deity, the head of the pantheon during the New Empire. An enormous demple was built in Karnak for the god of Creation, Amon-Re.

Amon

Amonemhat Name of two Egyptian kings. Amonemhat I was a general who came to power by a coup d'état c.1990 BC. He founded a new residence in Lisjt and made the frontiers stronger by building forts and defensive walls. He also invented the device of co-regency in order to guarantee the stability of government. After a thirty-year rule, he was assassinated.

Amonhotep I (late 16th-early 15th centuries BC) Egyptian king, 1514-1493 BC. He was a son of Amasis I, who liberated Egypt from the rule of the Hyksos. A. extended Egyptian territories up to the third cataract of the Nile River and changed the country into a military state governed by civil servants.

Amonhotep II (15th century) Egyptian king, 1426-1400 BC. Son of the great conqueror Tutmoses III; he expanded the realm into Asia.

Amonhotep III (14th century BC) Egyptian king, 1390-1352 BC. He mainly occupied himself with the construction of massive temples near Thebes. During his reign, decadent trends developed in the arts and foreign policy was neglected.

Amonhotep IV *See* Akhenaton.

Amorites Originally a Semitic, half-nomadic tribe. They are mentioned several times in the Bible. The A. entered Syria from Mesopotamia around 2000 BC. and from c.1600-1300 BC held power there. Their best-known monarch was Hammurabi. The tribe's power was ended by Cassite and Hittite attacks.

Amritsar Massacre Incident in Amritsar, a city in Punjab, India. On April

Amonhotep II

13, 1919, British General Dyer ordered troops to fire without warning on a crowd of people holding an illegal nationalist meeting. Hundreds were killed and thousands wounded. The slaughter was a turning-point in the relations between the British government in India and the nationalists.

Anarchism Political philosophy advocating a society in which no forms of authority exist. This would supposedly result in the most extensive

Amonemhat

freedom and social righteousness possible for everyone.

Anasazi culture Early Native American civilization in North America. Extensive sites have been found in Arizona, Colorado, and New Mexico. An important phase of this civilization was the Classic Pueblo culture (1050-1300), during which dwellings sometimes consisting of as many as 1000 rooms were cut out of steep cliffs.

Anatolia Asian region of Turkey extending to the Euphrates River; also often called Asia Minor. Circa 2000 BC, A. was invaded by the Hittites, who founded a kingdom there. Contemporaneously, on the west coast, the Greeks established themselves. In the interior, Phrygia was founded (800 BC) only to be destroyed by the Cimmerians in the 7th century BC. Later the kingdoms of Lydia and Media were established in the east and west respectively. These were destroyed, successively, by Cyrus II in the 6th century BC and by Philip II of Macedonia in the 4th century BC. In the 1st century BC, A. was annexed by the Romans. It became the crossroads of Hellenism and Christianity.

Ancient Régime Name for the social and political order in France before the French Revolution.

Andernach City in western Germany. In 876 Louis of Saxony defeated Charles the Bald there.

Andersonville Village in southwest Georgia and site of a notorious Confederate prison camp during the American Civil War. Conditions were so bad that 12,000 Union prisoners died there.

Andráda e Silva, José Bonifacio de (c.1763-1838) Brazilian patriot and political leader. He became prime minister in 1822, but a year later he was exiled.

Andrussovo, Treaty of Treaty in 1667 in which Poland ceded eastern Ukraine and Smolensk to Russia.

Anglican Church Name of the Protestant English national church, founded by Henry VIII in 1534 as a result of a dispute with the Pope (*see* Act of Supremacy).

Anglo-Afghan Wars *See* Afghan-British Wars.

Anglo-Saxons Germanic tribes (Angles, Saxons, and Jutes) that dominated England between the 5th and the 11th centuries. The Anglo-Saxon kingdom came to its full power during the reign of King Edgar (959-975). In 1066 the Anglo-Saxons were defeated by the Normans led bi William the Conqueror at the Battle of Hastings.

Ankara, Battle of Battle of 1402 near Ankara in modern Turkey in which the Ottoman Sultan Bajezid I was defeated by the Mongol Tamerlane. Bajezid died in prison in 1403.

Anna of Austria (1601-1666) Daughter of Philip III of Spain and mother of King Louis XIV of France, for whom she was regent between 1643 and 1651.

Anna of Austria

Anne (1665-1714) Queen of England, 1702-1714. The last Stuart ruler, A. was the daughter of James I and Anne Hyde. She married Prince George of Denmark in 1683. A. succeeded William III. She took an active part in British politics.

Anschluss Unification of Germany and Austria, brought about under great German pressure in March 1938. Hitler had made Anschluss one of his goals. He was aided by the Austrian Nazi and Minister of Internal Affairs Seys-Inquart.

Susan Brownell Anthony

Anthony, Susan Brownell (1820-1906) American women's rights activist. A. was a main force behind the woman suffrage movement and also a dedicated abolitionist. She was one of the founders of the Council of Women (1888).

Anti-Comintern-Pact 1936 treaty between Germany and Japan that formed the basis of later agreements among Germany, Japan, and Italy. The purpose of the treaty was to fight communism. After the Hitler-Stalin Pact of 1939, Germany changed the alliance into a pact of the three states against the United States. After Germany invaded Russia in June 1941, the Anti-Comintern-Pact was restored.

Anti-Corn-Law League British movement, founded in 1839 by Richard Cobden, whose purpose was to repeal the 1815 Corn Law that restricted the import of corn. The restrictions raised the prices of corn and bread, causing hardship for many working-class people. After the bad harvest of 1838 caused prices to rise further, workers rioted. The Corn Law, however, was not abolished until 1846.

Antialkidas Spartan leader. After the Peloponnesian War (404 BC), he tried with the aid of Persia to bring the Greek states under the rule of Sparta. He succeeded in 387 BC with the so-called King's Peace. In 371 BC, after the Battle of Leutica, Thebes ended the Spartan hegemony.

The *Ancient Régime*

The term *Ancient Régime* refers
to the way of life and government in
Western Europe before the
French Revolution destroyed it.
Monarchs and aristocrats held power
and dominated society. They
lived lives of great luxury that was
ultimately supported by the labor
of poor working people.

2

1

1. During the *Ancient Régime*,
the first signs of the
Industrial Revolution began to appear.
This is the interior of a 18th-century
textile factory.
See Industrial Revolution.
2. "*Les Grands*," the very rich,
led highly luxurious lives
in their splendid homes and palaces.
Here a play by Voltaire is read to
a gathering in a Paris salon.
See Voltaire, François Marie
Arouet de.
3. Among the European
aristocracy, garden parties were
a popular way of spending one's time.

3

4. The interior of a Rococo
18th-century salon.
5. In rural areas an age-old way of life
persisted in which peasants
performed backbreaking labor

and lived in great poverty. The
great contrast between the lives of the
peasants and those of the rich was one
reason for the French Revolution.
See French Revolution.

4

5

Antietam, Battle of September 17, 1862 battle during the American Civil War. Fought near Antietam Creek in Maryland, it was the bloodiest single day of the war. Union forces under General McClellan defeated the Confederates under Lee, although McClellan failed to follow up his victory.

Antigonus I Monoftalmos ("the one-eyed") (382-301 BC) King of Macedonia, c.316-301 BC. One of Alexander the Great's generals, he became governor of part of Asia Minor after Alexander died (323 BC) and, later, king of Macedonia. He was killed at the Battle of Ipsus during the wars of the Diadochi.

Antigonus II (c.319-239 BC) King of Macedonia, 276-239 BC. Grandson of Antigonus I, he became king after winning a long battle against the Gauls.

Antigonus III Dosos (d.221 BC) King of Macedonia, 227-221 BC. He restored Macedonian hegemony in Greece and captured Sparta in 222 BC.

Antinoös A favorite of the Roman Emperor Hadrian. He was said to be exceptionally handsome. After A. drowned in the Nile (130), Hadrian had him deified and renamed his birthplace in Asia Minor Antinoöpolis.

Antioch I Soter ("the Saviour") (324-262 BC) King of Syria, 280-261? BC. Son of Seleukos I, A. defeated the Egyptians in 276 BC but lost other lands, including Phoenicia, to them in 273-272 BC. A. founded many cities.

Antioch III the Great (242-187 BC) King of Syria, 223-187 BC. A. revived the fortunes of the Seleucid dynasty. He led an expedition to the east that went as far as India. His contacts with Philip V of Macedonia and Hannibal of Carthage led to conflict with Rome. After being defeated by the Romans at Thermopylae (191 BC) and Magnesia (190 BC) and in several naval battles, he accepted the Peace of Apamea in 188 BC, which reduced his empire to inland Asia Minor.

Antoninus Pius (86-161) Roman emperor, 138-161. A. was Hadrian's adopted successor. Under his rule, the

Antioch I Soter

Marc Anthony

Empire had a period of relative rest and prosperity.

Antony, Marc (82-30 BC) Roman soldier and political leader. A. was a follower of Julius Caesar and fellow-consul in 44 BC. After Caesar's assassination that year, he aroused popular sentiment against the killers. He quarrelled with Octavian and in 43 BC was defeated by the Senate's armies. After a reconciliation, A. took control of Rome's eastern possessions. He became (37 BC) the lover of Cleopatra. He quarrelled again with Octavian and was defeated by him at the Battle of Actium (31 BC), after which he committed suicide.

Anubis Egyptian jackal god who protected the necropolis (city of the dead) and watched over the process of mummification.

Antioch III the Great

Apache Native Americans who live in the southwest U.S. and northern Mexico. Most A. were nomads, though some practiced agriculture. Skilled fighters and riders, using horses they acquired from the Spanish, they strenuously resisted the encroaching white settlements. *See* Cochise, Geronimo.

Apartheid *See* De Klerk, Lutuli, Mandela.

Aphrodite Greek goddess of beauty and love.

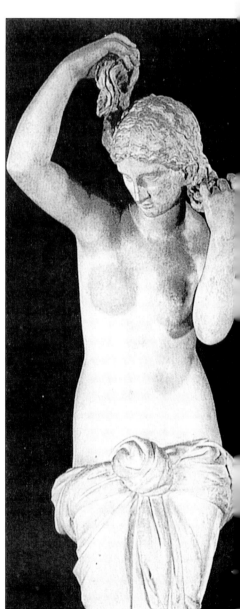

Aphrodite

Apocrypha (Greek: "obscure" or "hidden") Various sacred texts not accepted by all Western religions as part of the Bible.

The Abolishment of Apartheid

1

Starting in 1948, South Africa maintained an official policy of racial segregation called *apartheid*. Whites and nonwhites were separated in many aspects of society, with whites having the privileged position even though they were only a small minority of the population. The system of apartheid also provided for different treatment for South Africa's various nonwhite groups. Over time, protests against apartheid mounted, both in South Africa, led by the African National Congress, and abroad. By the 1980's an international boycott of the South African regime was in effect. Finally, in 1994, South Africa ended apartheid became a multiracial democracy.

2

1. African National Congress leader Nelson Mandela and his wife Winnie Mandela celebrating his release from prison after 27 years. *See* African National Congress; Mandela, Nelson.
2. A demonstration against apartheid in Cape Town, South Africa.
3. Signs like these, stating that only white people were allowed in specific train compartments, were common under the apartheid regime. Apartheid meant that nonwhites were second-class citizens.
4. A demonstration in the Netherlands against apartheid: ANC members wrapping the South-African embassy in an enormous ANC flag.
5. Nelson Mandela, the president of South Africa, and Frederik Willem de Klerk, vice-president, receiving the Nobel Peace prize in 1993 for their efforts for the abolishment of apartheid. *See* Klerk, Frederik Willem de.

3

4

5

Apollo Greek god of prophecy, medicine, herding, music, and the arts. In his temple at Delphi, oracles were pronounced by the Pythia, a priestess sitting on a golden tripod.

Apollo

Appeasement Foreign policy practiced in the 1930's, notably by Britain's Prime Minister Neville Chamberlain. The territorial demands of Hitler were repeatedly acceded to as the best way to preserve peace in Europe at a time when Britain was not prepared to go to war. When Germany occupied all of Czechoslovakia in March 1939, several months after the Munich Conference, appeasement was discredited.

Apraksin, Feodor Matveyevich (1661-1728) Russian admiral. Under Peter the Great, he captured Viborg and Helsingfors from Sweden in 1710 and 1713 respectively.

April Theses Plans formulated by Lenin in the spring of 1917 to gain power for his Bolshevik Party during the Russian Revolution.

Apu Illapu Inca rain god.

Arab League Organization founded in Cairo (1945) as a league of Arab unity. Initially, the member states were Egypt, Lebanon, Transjordan (later Jordan), Saudi Arabia, Syria, and Yemen. These were later joined by Algeria, Bahrain, Kuwait, Libya, Mauritania, Morocco, Oman, Qatar, the Sudan, the United Arab Emirates, and the Yemen Arab Republic. The A. mediates conflicts among members and between members and nonmembers.

Arab Legion Military force created in 1921 to protect the British mandate of Transjordan. After Jordan became independent (1946), the A. played a major role on Jordan's side in the Arab-Israeli War of 1948.

Arabs Formerly the name applied to the Arabic-speaking nomads of the Arabian peninsula, it now is used to refer to all the people whose native language is Arabic, most of whom live in the Middle East. The Arabs were united for the first time in the 7th century by Muhammad. Starting in the 13th-14th centuries, the Arabs were ruled by others: the Turks, British, and French. After World War II, the Arab states became independent.

Arafat, Yasser (1929-) Palestinian leader. Born in Jerusalem, he served in the Egyptian army. In 1964 A. became leader of the Palestinian guerrilla group Al-Fatah, the main constituent of the Palestinian Liberation Organization, or PLO, which he has also headed since 1968. In 1988 A. recognized Israel and renounced terrorism. In 1993 he reached an agreement with the Israeli Prime Minister Rabin concerning Palestinian home rule. That year he, Rabin, and Israeli Foreign Minister Peres received the Nobel Peace Prize. Elections in 1995 formally made A. the leader of the semi-autonomous Palestinian regions on the West Bank of the Jordan River.

Arausio, Battle of In 105 BC a Roman army led by Caius Mallius Maximus was beaten by the Cimbres and the Teutons near Arausio (now Orange, France).

Arbeus, Pedro de Epila (1442-1485) Head of the Spanish Inquisition. He was appointed by Ferdinand II of Aragon in 1484 but was murdered a year later.

Archbishop A clergyman at the head of a bishopric that contains several dioceses. In the Roman Catholic Church, the A.'s authority is directly subordinate to the pope. In the Anglican Church, it is subordinate to the British monarch.

Archimedes (c.285-212 BC) Greek mathematician and physician. A. lived most of his life in Syracuse, on Sicily. He made contributions in the fields of geometry, physics, mechanics, and hydrostatics. According to legend, he discovered the principle of the lever. Thanks to machines he invented, the Roman siege of Syracuse was defended against for several years. When the city was finally taken, Archimedes was killed.

Ardashir I (d.241) King of Persia, 226?-240. A. defeated the Parthian king Artabanus IV and founded the Sassanid Empire (224-650). He established Zoroastrianism as the state religion.

Ardennes Offensive (1944-1945) The last major German offensive of World War II, begun in December 1944. It is also known as the Battle of the Bulge. The Germans' primary aim was to cut the Allied armies off from their ports, particularly Antwerp. Aided by bad flying weather, which nullified the Allies' control of the air, some initial successes were gained, but they were rolled back and by January the offensive had clearly failed.

Areopagus Hill in Athens, Greece, famous as the place where the council of the ancient city-state met. The

Yasser Arafat

Great Archaeological Discoveries

Occasionally archaeologists
make discoveries so interesting and
significant that they result
in headlines all around the world.
These illustrations offer some
examples.

1

2

3

4

5

1. In 1871 the archaeologist
Heinrich Schliemann excavated the
ancient city of Troy. This drawing
shows his wife wearing the
golden jewelry found in one of
the tombs. *See* Schliemann, Heinrich;
Trojan War.
2. The remains of houses
in Pompeii, a Roman city that was
destroyed by a volcanic
eruption in 79 AD.
3. The body of a prehistoric
man found in 1995 in the Swiss Alps.
4. The recently discovered life-size
sculptures of an army that was
a funerary gift for the first Chinese
emperor.
5. The tomb of Tutankhamen
in Karnak, Egypt. It was discovered
in 1922.

Ares

council was named after the hill. In the mid-5th century BC, the council, which represented the aristocracy, lost much of its power.

Ares (Roman: Mars) Greek war god.

Aretas Name of several kings that ruled the Nabatean Empire in present-day Jordan and Syria between the first century BC and the first century AD. Their capital was the city of Petra.

Argenlieu, Georges-Thierry (1889–1964) French naval commander. After serving in World War II, he resigned in 1945 because he failed to achieve peace in Indochina.

Arginuasi Small islands in the Aegean Sea near Lesbos. An Athenian fleet beat the Spartans there in 406 BC.

Ares

Argonaut In Greek mythology, the companions of Jason in his search for the Golden Fleece. Also, the first submarine that could operate in open water. It was built in 1897 by the American Simon Lake.

Arianism The Christian theology of Arius of Alexandria (d. 336). Arius denied the fully divine nature of Jesus since only God could be God. Arianism was declared a heretical doctrine at the Councils of Nicaea (325) and Constantinople (381).

Ariovistus King of the Germanic Sueves. In 71 BC he attacked Gaul to help the Sequani against the Aedni. In 59 BC he was recognized as a king by the Romans, but his power threatened the Romans and Caesar defeated him a year later.

Aristides (c.530-468 BC) Athenian general, known as "the Just." He was one of the Athenian commanders in the Battle of Marathon (490 BC). In 482 BC he was ostracized for opposing Themistocles's naval policy, but he returned a few years later. A. played a leading part in the Battles of Salamis (480 BC) and Plataea (479 BC).

Aristogiton (6th century BC) Athenian hero. He and Harmodius killed the tyrant Hippias in 541 BC.

Aristophanes (5th-4th centuries BC) Greek comic playwright. A.'s plays, written in beautiful Greek, satirize various aspects of Athenian society.

Aristophanes

His most well-known works include The Wasps (422 BC), which mocked the Athenian tendency toward litigation, and *Lysistrata* (411 BC), in which the Athenian women refuse to engage in sex with their husbands as a protest against war.

Aristotle (384-322 BC) Greek philosopher. Together with Socrates and Plato, A. is considered the most important thinker of the ancient world. His works on law, politics, poetics, ethics and other subjects have had a profound influence on Western civilization. A. taught Alexander the Great for several years in Macedonia. Together with Theofrastos, A. founded a philosophical school in Athens around 335 BC, in which a lobby (Greek: *peripatos*) was built. Their students were taught while walking in this lobby and the school acquired the name Peripatetic.

Aristotle

Arius (d.336) Christian theologian and founder of Arianism. He was declared a heretic by the Council of Nicaea (325), excommunicated, and banished from Alexandria but permitted to return.

Armada Enormous military operation, sent out by Philip II of Spain in 1588 to destroy the Dutch and English fleets and then invade England. The 130 ships, carrying 30,000 troops, failed in their attempts to destroy the English and Dutch navies, however. Damaged further by storms, only a small proportion of the Armada managed to return to Spain.

Armenians Indo-Germanic people who in the 6th century BC founded the state of Uratu in Asia Minor. In the 1st century BC, that state was annexed by the Romans. It was later ruled by the Persians, Arabs (7th century) and Turks (10th century). In the 16th century, Armenia was incorporated into the Ottoman Empire. Early in the 20th century, more than one million Armenians were killed or deported by the Turks. After World War I, Armenia was incorporated into the Soviet Union. The dissolution of the Soviet Union in 1991 permitted the revival of an independent Armenia.

Armentières Village in northwestern France. It was the site of the last German offensive (April 1918) against the French and British armies and is named in the popular song of World War I "Mademoiselle from Armentière."

Arminius

Arminius (d.29) Leader of the Germanic Cherusks, whose armies, led by Varo, defeated three Roman legions in 9 AD in the Teutoburg Forest.

A Thousand Years of Western Architecture

Periods in western architecture since the Middle Ages:
Romanesque, until the end of the 12th century
Gothic, from the 12th to the 16th centuries
Renaissance in the 16th century
Baroque, from 1600 to 1700
Neoclassical and Romantic, from 1700 to 1900

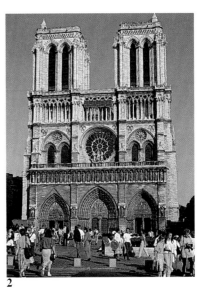

1. The Romanesque cathedral in Durham, England.
2. The Cathedral of Notre-Dame in Paris, an example of the Gothic style.
3. St. Peter's in Rome, a masterpiece of Renaissance architecture.
4. The Melk Monastery in Austria, a typical Baroque structure.
5. The neoclassical Houses of Parliament in London.
6. The Paris Opera, an example of Romantic architecture.

Armstrong, Louis (1901-1971) American jazz musician. Born in New Orleans, A. became an international celebrity and perhaps represents jazz better than any other individual. A Dixieland cornet and trumpet player, he also became famous for his singing. A. played with many bands. He first became well-known from his work with Kid Oliver (early 1920s). His recordings with his own Hot Five and Hot Seven groups (1925-1929) are legendary. In his last years, he toured with his All Stars band.

Arnhem, Battle of World War II action (September 1944) in the east of the Netherlands. The Allies aimed at capturing intact bridges over the Rhine (Operation Market Garden). The operation failed completely, mainly because of a much stronger German resistance than expected.

Arnold, Benedict (1741-1801) American general and traitor. A. served with distinction in the American Revolution. Personal jealousies and problems, however, led him to go over to the British late in the war. He led British raids in Virginia and Connecticut in 1781.

Arnulf of Carinthia (d.899) Carolingian king. The bastard son of Carloman, A. became ruler of the East Frankish kingdom in 877. He was consecrated in Rome as the last Carolingian Emperor in 896.

Benedict Arnold

Arpad (d.907) Hungarian hero. A. was the leader of the Hungarian tribes when they entered the plains of Pannonia from South Russia at the end of the 9th century.

Arras (Atrecht), Battle of World War I action. British troops failed to break through German defenses in April 1917;--**Peace of** 1482 treaty between Maximilian of Austria and Louis XI of France. It reaffirmed Burgundy's status as part of France.

Arsacids Parthian dynasty. The dynasty was founded by Arsaces, who defeated the Seleucids around 250 BC and founded the Parthian Empire in Persia. Ecbatana was its capital. The Arsacids fought against Rome for centuries.

Arsinoe IV (d.41 BC) Queen of Egypt. Daughter of Ptolemy XII, A. became queen in 48 BC. Some years later she was deposed by Caesar, who put her sister Cleopatra VII on the throne. The latter had Arsinoe killed.

Artabazus Persian general. In 480-479 BC, he and Mardonius led the Persian expedition against Greece. See also Plataea, Salamis.

Artafernes Persian general. A. was a cousin of the Persian King Darius and one of the leaders of the Persian army during an expedition against Greece in 490 BC.

Artaxerxes I Makrocheir ("the Big-Handed") (d. 425 BC) King of Persia, 465-425 BC. Favorably mentioned in the Biblical books of Ezra and Nehemia because he permitted the revival of Judaism.

Artaxerxes II (436-358 BC) King of Persia, 404-358 BC. He succeeded Darius II, his father. A. put down a revolt led by his brother Cyrus the Younger at the Battle of Cunaxa (401 BC), during which Cyrus was killed. During his reign, Persia gained great influence in Greece (Treaty of Antalcidas, 387 BC).

Artaxerxes III (d.338 BC) King of Persia, 358-388 BC. The son of Artaxerxes II, he reconquered Egypt after the Battle of Pelusium in 343 BC. A., a bloody ruler, was poisoned by one of his ministers.

Artemis (Roman: Diana) Greek goddess of hunting.

Artemisia I (5th century BC) Ruler of Caria in Asia Minor. She personally participated in the expedition of the Persian King Xerxes against Greece and also fought in the Battle of Salamis (both 480 BC).

Artemisia II (4th century BC) Queen of Caria. She was the successor (c.353 BC) and also both the wife and sister of Mausolus, for whom she built a monument at Halicarnassus. The so-called Mausoleum of Halicarnassus was considered to be one of the seven Wonders of the World.

Artemision Cape, situated north of Euboea in Greece, where the Greek fleet defeated a Persian naval force in 480 BC.

Arthur

Arthur (c.6th century AD) Legendary king of Britain. The historical Arthur may have been a Celtic king who did battle against the Angles and the Saxons. The numerous legends about him and the knights of his Round Table started to appear with frequency in literature of the 11th and 12th centuries. Great works telling the Arthur legend have been written by Malory, Tennyson, Swinburne, William Morris, Edwin Arlington Robinson, and others.

Arthur, Chester Alan (1830-1886) 21st president of the U.S., 1881-1885. Elected vice president in 1880, Arthur succeeded to the presidency upon the death by assassination of President Garfield. He supported civil service reform.

Artemis

Articles of Confederation Document that set forth the powers of the U.S. central government that existed before the government set up by the U.S. Constitution began in 1789. The A. were adopted by the Continental Congress in 1777 but not ratified by all the states until 1781. They established a weak central government consisting of a single-house legislature with no independent executive or judiciary. The government was dependent on the states for revenue and the enforcement of its laws. The weakness of the government led to calls for the revision of the A.. As a result, a convention met in 1787 in Philadelphia and drafted what became the U.S. Constitution.

José Gervasio Artigas

Artigas, José Gervasio (1764-1850) Uruguayan national hero. He led the early independence movement (1811-1820) against Spain. He died during a forced exile in Paraguay.

Arverni Gallic people that was subdued by the Romans in 121 BC. Under Vercingetorix and others, they later revolted against the Romans and were eventually crushed by Caesar in 52 BC.

Aryans Indo-Germanic people that settled in modern Iran around 2000 BC. In modern times, the term has been used by racists, notably Adolf Hitler, to refer to a supposedly superior race of non-Jewish and non-Slavic people.

Asam Bavarian family of Baroque artists. The best-known are the architect and painter Cosmas Damian (1686-1739) and the sculptor Egidius Quirinus (1692-1750). One of their main works is the Nepomuk Church in the city of Munich (1733-1746).

Asgard In Norse mythology, the place where the gods have their palaces and where Valhalla, the hall for slain heroes, is located as well.

Ashanti Former kingdom in West Africa, now part of Ghana. The Ashanti people, one of Ghana's major ethnic groups, migrated into the area before the 13th century. The kingdom was founded as a confederation c.1700. It was conquered by the British and annexed to their Gold Coast colony (1901).

Asher *See* Israel, Tribes of.

Ashkenazim The collective name for the Jewish people who lived in Germany and France before they were expelled in the Middle Ages. It is derived from the Hebrew word for Germany, *Askenaz.* The term distinguished these Jews from the Sephardim, the Jews from Spain and Portugal.

Ashur City on the Tigris River and also the name of the chief Assyrian god. A. was the residence of the Assyrian kings up to the reign of Assurbanipal (669-633 BC). In 614 BC the Medes and the Babylonians destroyed the place.

Asia Minor Common term for Anatolia or Asiatic Turkey.

Asiago City in nortxern Italy. During World War I, in May and June 1916, a fierce but eventually inconclusive battle took place there between the Austrians and the Italians.

Asiento Agreements between Spain and other European states concerning the importation of black slaves into the Spanish colonies. At various times, the right to do so was sold to the Dutch, Genoans, Portuguese, French, and English.

Asoka (d.232 BC), Emperor of India, c.265-238 BC. A member of the Mauryan dynasty, A. united nearly all of India for the first time. After c.261 BC, however, he regretted the bloodshed he had caused and converted to Buddhism, making it the state religion.

Aspasia (5th century BC) Mistress of the Athenian political leader Pericles.

Aspasia

Ashur

Aspern Now a part of Vienna, where in May 1809, the armies of Napoleon were defeated by the Austrians for the first time.

Asquith, Herbert Henry (1852-1928) English liberal political leader and Prime Minister, 1908-1916. During his ministry, the House of Lords lost its veto power and Ireland was granted self-government (Home Rule Act).

Assassins Sect of Ismailites, founded by Hassan as-Sabbah in the 11th century in Persia and Syria, who fought bitter wars against the Crusaders. The word "assassin" is still used in some languages to denote a murderer, especially one with political motives.

Assurnasirpal II

Assemblé Législative French legislative council during the French Revolution (1791-1792). It consisted of 745 representatives of the wealthier citizens. The right wing was called Feuillants, the left wing Jacobins, and the more moderate revolutionaries called themselves Girondins. The Assembly was dissolved in 1792.

Assignats Paper-money, printed during the French Revolution. First issued

in 1789, they soon lost their value because of inflation. In 1797 they were declared void, and France returned to a currency based on gold.

Assurballit II Last king of the Assyrians, who waged war unsuccessfully against the Medes and the Babylonians between 612 and 609 BC. The Assyrian cities of Ashur and Nineveh were destroyed by his enemies.

Assurbanipal (d.626 BC?) King of Assyria, 668-626 BC. Son of Esarhaddon, A. was Assyria's greatest king. He repressed revolts in Egypt, captured Babylon in 648 BC, and destroyed the city of Susa in Elam (639). In his capital, Nineveh, he collected a huge library of tablets in cuneiform writing.

Assurnasirpal II (9th century BC) King of Assyria, 883-859 BC. Using new military tactics, he managed to expand his realm up to the shores of the Mediterranean.

Assuruballit I (14th century BC) Early king of Assyria who laid the foundations of the Middle Assyrian Empire (14th-12th century BC).

Assyria Ancient empire in modern Iraq, centered on the Tigris River. A. began in the third millennium BC and reached its peak in the 9th-7th centuries BC. The capital was Ashur and, under their greatest ruler, Assurbanipal (d.626 BC?), Nineveh. The Assyrians were incessant fighters. Eventually, they were conquered by Medes and Babylonians in the late 7th century BC.

Astor, John Jacob (1763-1848) American merchant. German born, A came to America in 1784. Active in the china and fur trade, he became a successful merchant and died the wealthiest man in America.

Astor, Nancy Witcher (1879-1964) British politician. A great activist for women's rights, she was the first woman to sit in the British Parliament (1919). In the 1930s she was pro-Fascist.

Astyages (6th century BC) King of the Medes, 585-c.550 BC. He was dethroned by his grandson Cyrus the Great, who founded the Persian Empire.

Asuka period Period in Japanese history between 552 and 645, during which Buddhism was introduced in Japan.

Atahualpa (c.1502-1533) The last independent Inca (ruler) of Peru. A. was the son of Huayna Capac and had just defeated his brother Huascar in a civil war when the Spanish, led by Francisco Pizarro, arrived (1532). Through trickery, Pizarro captured A. and had him killed a year later.

Ataman Honorary title of the leaders of the Cossacks in Russia between the 16th and the 20th centuries.

Atatürk See Kemal Pasha

Atatürk

Athanasius, Saint (c.297-373) Patriarch of Alexandria, 328-373. A strong opponent of the teaching of Arius, A. petitioned the Council of Nicaea (325) to accept the orthodox teachings concerning the nature of the relationship between the Father and the Son.

Athaulf (d.415) King of the Visigoths, 410-415. The successor of Alaric I, A. was elected King of the Visigoths in 410 and married a daughter of the Roman Emperor Honorius. After a quarrel with the Roman authorities in Barcelona, Athaulf was killed in 415.

Athena (Roman: Minerva) Greek goddess of wisdom but also of the arts, cities, and of war.

Athens Greek city. The capital of modern Greece, in ancient times it was the capital of the region of Attica. A. was inhabited as early as the Bronze Age. It first flourished under the tyrant Peisistratos and his sons (6th century BC). Athens's most prosperous and powerful time, however, was in the 5th century BC, under Pericles. The Peloponnesian War (431-404 BC) ended the hegemony of the city in Greece. Ancient Athens's cultural legacy has enormously enriched Western civilization.

Athos Peninsula in northeast Greece. The Persian fleet was wrecked there when it was on its way to Athens in 492 BC. A. is best-known today for the Christian religious communities that have lived there since the 10th century onwards.

Atlantic, Battle of the *See* Submarine War.

Atlantic Charter (August 14, 1941) Declaration made by the British Prime Minister Churchill and U.S. President Roosevelt concerning the common political principles of their two countries and their goals for the postwar world following the defeat of the Axis Powers in World War II.

Atlantis Mythical island or continent. First mentioned by Plato, it most likely refers to the island of Thira (Santorini) in the Aegean Sea where, in the 15th century BC, a volcanic eruption brought an end to a sophisticated society.

Aton *See* Akhenaton.

Atrebates Celtic tribe in northern France whose capital was Nemetacum (Arras). A portion of the tribe left for Britain when Caesar went on his campaign in Gaul (c.58 BC).

Atreus, Treasure of Grave, shaped as a bee-hive (tholos), built in Mycenae (Greece) around 1250 BC. The grave measures 15 meters, and the doorstep is made of one piece of stone weighing 120 tons.

Athena

Attica Peninsula in eastern Greece that includes the region around Athens.

Attila (d.453) King of the Huns, 445-453. A. murdered his brother to become sole ruler in 445. He led the Huns on raids against the Eastern and Western Roman Empires. In 451 he invaded Gaul with about 500,000 men but was turned back by the Visigoths and the Romans in a battle fought near Troyes. After Attila's death in 453, the Huns retreated from Western Europe. In legends A. is often called the "Scourge of God."

Attila

Attlee, Clement Richard (1883-1967) British political leader and prime minister. A. entered Parliament as a Labour Party member in 1922. He became leader of the Labour Party in 1935. In 1945, A. replaced Churchill as Prime Minister and served until 1951. During this time, much welfare legislation was enacted and India became independent.

Atum Egyptian creator-god, who engendered the world of gods.

Auchinleck, Sir Claude (1884-1981) English field-marshal. In World War II, he was defeated in North Africa in 1942 by the German general Field Marshal Rommel. He was commander-in-chief in India 1943-1947.

Auden, W. H. (Wynstan Hugh) (1907-1973), British poet. One of the most highly regarded poets of the 20th century.

Auduatuci Belgian tribe that offered stiff resistance against Julius Caesar's Roman legions.

Audubon, John James (1785-1851) American ornithologist and artist. A. was born in Santo Domingo (now Haiti) and educated in France. He came to the U.S. in 1803 and began observing birds. His major work of drawings and descriptions, *The Birds of America,* was first published 1827-1838.

Auerstadt Village in Saxony (Germany) where the Prussian army was defeated by Napoleon in 1806.

Augsburg, League of Treaty between the Holy Roman Emperor and the main cities of Germany, Spain, and Sweden in 1686 intended to sabotage the expansionist policy of Louis XIV of France.

Augsburg, Peace of In 1555, a temporary settlement of religious differences within the Holy Roman Empire. Princes could decide whether their lands would be Lutheran or Catholic.

Augurs Priests in the Roman Empire who predicted the future by observing the behavior of birds.

Clement Richard Attlee

33

Augustine, Saint (354-430) Born Aurelius Augustinus, he is one of the most important church-fathers of the Roman Catholic Church. A. was born in Tagaste (North Africa) and became Bishop of Hippo in 396. He lived in Italy after 376. In his *Confessions* (c.400), he repents of his unchristian, licentious youth. One of his most important books is *De civitate Dei* (*The City of God*), written in 413-426 after the sack of Rome by Alaric. He died in 430 during a siege of the city by the Vandals. Many Christian theologians consider A. the founder of theology.

Saint Augustine

Augustovo City in Poland, near which in World War I the Russians were defeated decisively by German troops in February 1915.

Augustus (63 BC-14 AD) The first Roman Emperor, 29 BC-14 AD. Born Caius Octavius (Octavian), he was raised by his great-uncle, Julius Caesar, and became Caesar's official son and heir. After Caesar's assassination, Octavian formed a triumvirate

Augustus

with Antony and Lepidus, among whom he proved to be the strongest. In 31 BC, he defeated Antony and Cleopatra at the Battle of Actium. In 29 BC, the Senate granted him the title "emperor." A. consolidated Roman rule within the border Caesar had established. He was an efficient administrator and patron of the arts. He was succeeded by Tiberius.

Augustus I, or Sigismund II Augustus (1529-1572) King of Poland, 1548-1572. He expanded Polish rule over Lithuanian territories.

Augustus II the Strong (1670-1733) Elector of Saxony, 1694-1733, and king of Poland, 1697-1733. A. succeeded his brother John George IV as elector. After Jan Sobieski died, he was elected king of Poland. Forced to abdicate in 1706 by the Treaty of Altranstadt in favor of Stanislaus Leszczynski, he regained the throne in 1709. He is best known for his large number of illegitimate children.

Augustus III (1696-1763) Elector of Saxony, 1733-1763, and king of Poland, 1735-1763. Son of Augustus II, he became Polish king with the support of Russia and Austria. His death ended the union of Saxony and Poland.

Aurangzeb (1618-1707) Mogul Emperor of India, 1658-1707. A. succeeded his father Shah Jahan, whom he imprisoned in 1658. His hostility to the Hindus led to the dissolution of his realm after his death.

Aurelian (Lucius Domitius Aurelianus) (c.215-275) Emperor of Rome, 270-275. One of the greatest emperors, A. restored many regions to the empire, including Britain, Gaul, Spain, Egypt, and Syria. He destroyed Palmyra and captured its queen, Zenobia. He also built a 12-mile, 40-foot wall around Rome that still remains in places. A. was assassinated during a campaign in Persia.

Aurignacian Stone Age culture revealed in the caves of Aurignac, France. Rock paintings and engravings, flints, tools, and Venus figurines made of stone and ivory have been found.

Aurora *See* Eos.

Auschwitz (Polish: Oswiecim) Town in Poland where the Nazis built their largest concentration camp. A. was actually a complex of factories and work and killing facilities. As many as two million people – most of them Jews – were killed there.

Ausculum City in southern Italy. The Romans were defeated there by King Pyrrhus of Epirus in 279 BC. The latter suffered such heavy losses, however, that the victory gained him little, giving rise to the term "pyrrhic victory."

Ausgleich The 1867 agreement which made the Hapsburg Empire into a "Dual Monarchy": an Austrian Empire and a Hungarian Kingdom, ruled by one monarch.

Austerlitz Town in southern Moravia (now Czechoslovakia) where Napo-

Aurangzeb

leon won a great victory (1805) over Alexander I of Russia and Francis I of Austria. The battle is also called the "Battle of the Three Emperors."

Austrasia Merovingian kingdom between the Meuse and Rhine Rivers. It came into being when the Frankish Empire was divided after the death of Lothar I in 561. At the end of the 7th century, Austrasia gained hegemony over Neustria. In 751, it was integrated into the Carolingian realm.

Austrian Succession, War of the War in Europe that broke out in 1740 after the death of Holy Roman Emperor Charles VI. Prussia, Bavaria, Saxony, France, and Spain refused to recognize Charles's daughter, Maria Theresa of Austria, as his successor, which was provided for by the Pragmatic Sanction. After a lengthy struggle in which Britain and Russia supported Austria, the Treaty of Aachen (Aix-la-Chapelle) was signed (1748), recognizing Maria Theresa's right of succession. In the course of the struggle, Austria ceded Silesia to Prussia.

Austro-Hungarian Empire Union between the two countries dating back to 1526, when the Hapsburg Ferdinand of Austria was chosen king of Hungary. Austria was dominant until 1867, when both countries were given equal status in the "Dual Monarchy." In 1918 the A. collapsed. *See* Ausgleich.

Auto-da-fé (Latin: *auctus fidei*, "seizure because of faith") Name of the juridical pronouncement, and later also of the executions, of the Spanish and Portuguese Inquisitions, practiced for the last time in 1781.

Avaris (now Tell el-Dabaa) City in Egypt, in the Nile River delta. The capital of the Hyksos, it was founded c.1700 BC.

Avars Mongol nomadic tribe from Turkestan. The A. came to the valley of the Danube River in the middle of the 6th century. They dominated the Hungarian plain until defeated by Charlemagne at the end of the 8th century.

Averroes (1126-1198) Important Islamic philosopher and follower of the teachings of Aristotle. His ideas

Averroes

had great influence on the Jewish philosophers in Spain and, through them, on Christian scholasticism.

Avicenna (980-1037) Persian medical doctor and philosopher. His *Canon of Medicine* remained in use in the Islamic and Western world for hundreds of years.

Avignon City in the Provence region of France. It was the papal residence between 1309 and 1378, during the so-called Babylonian Exile of the Papacy, and the residence of several antipopes during 1378-1408. It was incorporated into France after a plebiscite in 1791.

Avila City in central Spain. During the 11th and 12th centuries, A. was a citadel of the kings of Castille against the Moors. The Spanish mystic Saint Theresa lived there in the 16th century.

Avitus, Eparchus (d.456) Emperor of the Western Roman Empire, 455-456. He was proclaimed emperor by the Visigoths. A. unsuccessfully fought the Vandals. He was deposed by Ricimer and became Bishop of Placentia but died soon afterward.

Ayatollahs Spiritual leaders of the Shiite Muslims. They have great influence over both religion and politics. *See* also Khomeini.

Aymara Indian tribe in South America. They ruled over the whole of Peru in the 9th and 10th centuries from their religious center of Tiahuanaco on Lake Titicaca. Later they frequently fought wars with the expansionist Incas.

Aztecs Indian people who developed a highly advanced civilization in Mexico. The A. came to Central Mexico in

the 14th century from the northwest. They founded what became their capital Tenochtitlan (present-day Mexico City) in 1325. The A. constructed pyramid-shaped temples on which they sacrificed thousands of war captives to the gods. They employed a hieroglyphic mode of writing and had a very accurate calendar. The Aztec Empire of vassal states

Avicenna

extended virtually from coast to coast in central and southern Mexico. The Spanish conquistador Cortès conquered their realm for the Spanish crown in the early 1520s, in part by enlisting the aid of many of the vassal states who resented the Aztecs' haughty behavior and demands for tribute. The Spanish brutally destroyed much of the Aztecs' culture.

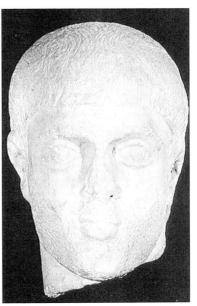

Eparchus Avitus

35

The Aztecs

The Aztecs were an American Indian people who settled in the valley of Mexico around 1300 AD. They built a sophisticated and powerful civilization, which flourished until Hernando Cortès conquered it for Spain in the 1520s.

1

3

1. Hernando Cortès and his Mayan mistress and interpreter Marina. *See* Cortès.
2. An Aztec warrior from the time of the Spanish conquest. *See* Aztecs, Incas, Mayas.
3. The Aztecs sacrificed still-beating human hearts to their gods.
4. Montezuma II receives Hernando Cortès, whom he for a time may have believed to be a god. That may have been one reason why Montezuma did not initially resist the Spanish when they invaded Mexico.

2

4

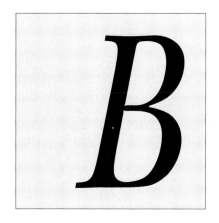

Ba'ath Party Political party, founded by Michele Aflaq and Salah al-Din Bitar in Damascus in 1941, which strives to unite all Arabs in a socialist confederation. Based in Syria, the party has been banned in most other Arab countries. It has, however, gained power in Syria and in Iraq, although relations between the two regimes have not always been good.

Baal Canaanite god of fertility later adopted by numerous peoples in the ancient world.

Baal

Baalbek City in Lebanon. It was known as Heliopolis (City of the Sun) in the Hellenistic period. Augustus made it a Roman colony called Julia Augusta Felix. In the 2nd and 3d centuries it was the center of the cult of Jupiter-Heliopolitanus. B. has impressive Roman ruins.

Babeuf, François Noel (1760-1797) Radical political leader during the French Revolution. B. advocated a form of communism under which all would own land and share in the economy's output. He was arrested for plotting to overthrow the government and executed in 1797.

Babi Yar Ravine near Kiev, Ukraine. There, during the German invasion of the Soviet Union during World War II, the Nazis murdered thousands of Jews and others in 1941-1943.

Babington, Anthony (1561-1586) English Catholic nobleman. In 1586 he became involved in a conspiracy against Queen Elizabeth I. The plot was discovered and B. was executed. A letter from Mary Stuart found in his possession brought about her execution as well.

Babur (1483-1530) First Mogul emperor of India. From his capital Kabul, he invaded India, defeating the sultan of Delhi at Panipat (1526). He conquered most of northern India. B. was also a fine poet.

Babylon Ancient Mesopotamian city on the Euphrates River. The name means "Gateway of God." Hammurabi (18th century BC) made it the capital of Babylonia. After being destroyed by the Assyrians (c.689 BC), it was rebuilt during the New Babylonian, or Chaldean dynasty (7th-6th centuries BC). Nebuchadnezzar (d.562 BC) greatly added to its beauty. The hanging gardens were one of the Seven Wonders of the World. Also famous was the city wall with its Ishtar Gate. In 539 BC the city was captured by Cyrus of Persia. Alexander the Great wanted to make it the capital of his empire but died before he could do so.

Babylonia Ancient empire in Mesopotamia. In the third millennium before Christ, the realms of Sumer and Akkad flourished there. Under the first Babylonian dynasty (see Hammurabi), B. became the most powerful state in Mesopotamia. It was conquered first by the Hittites (18th century BC) and, shortly thereafter, by the Kassites, who managed to hold it until c.1180 BC. B. became a part of the Assyrian Empire in the 9th century BC. Nabopolassar established the New Babylonian, or Chaldean, Empire (late 7th century BC). His son was the great Nebuchadnezzar. During the latter's reign, the Babylonian Captivity of the Hebrews took place. In 539 BC, B. was conquered by Cyrus of Persia.

Babur

Babylonian Captivity (597-536 BC) Period during which thousands of Hebrews were deported from Israel by Nebuchadnezzar and forced to live in Babylon, where they remained until permitted to return home by Cyrus of Persia.

Babylonian Captivity of the Papacy Period (1309-1378) during which the popes resided in Avignon. In 1378 Pope Gregory XI returned to Rome.

Bach, Johann Sebastian (1685-1750) German musician, one of the greatest composers in Western music. Bach was born into a musical family in

Johann Sebastian Bach

Eisenach. During his lifetime, he was famed mainly as an organist and teacher. He worked principally in Weimar, Cothen, and Leipzig, where in 1723 he became cantor. Bach wrote works of the greatest genius in nearly all the forms and styles, both sacred and secular, of the Baroque period: passions, masses, cantatas, organ and keyboard works of all kinds, orchestral works, concertos, and suites and sonatas for various ensembles and solo instruments. His music has had an enormous influence on subsequent composers.

Bacon, Roger (c.1220-1292) English philosopher. Influenced by the writings of Islamic scholars, he proved to be an innovative thinker in the field of natural sciences. He was first Westerner to describe the making of gunpowder (1242).

Bacon, Francis (1561-1626) English statesman and philosopher. B. became lord-chancellor under James I. After his dismissal on charges of corruption, he dedicated himself to science. Among his better known works is the posthumously published *Novo Atlantis*, in which he discusses the ideal society.

Roger Bacon

Bactria Region in central Asia where present-day Turkmenistan, Afghanistan, Uzbekistan, and Tajikistan meet. It formerly was part first of the empire of Alexander the Great and then of the Seleucid Empire. Circa 250 BC, B. was briefly independent and became a center for Hellenistic culture.

Baden-Powell, Sir Robert (1857-1941) British general. He led the defense of Mafeking during the Boer War (1899-1902). In 1908 he founded the Boy Scouts.

Badoglio, Pietro (1871-1956) Italian field marshal. He led the Italian campaign in Ethiopia in 1936. B. was

Pietro Badoglio

involved in the overthrow of Mussolini (1943) and was subsequently appointed premier. He served until June 4, 1944.

Badr Town in Saudi Arabia. In c.624 followers of Muhammad won a victory there over a force from Mecca.

Baghdad Capital of Iraq, founded in 762 by Al-Mansur. It was the residence of the Abbasids. The city was destroyed by the Mongols in 1258 and by Tamerlane in 1401. In 1638 it became part of the Ottoman Empire, and the Turks held the city until 1917. It has been the capital of Iraq since 1920.

Baghdad Pact A defensive alliance concluded between Turkey, Iraq, Iran, Pakistan, and Britain in 1955. In 1957 the U.S. also joined the alliance. After Iraq's withdrawal in 1959, the alliance's name was changed to the Central Treaty Organization. It was dissolved in 1979 after the Iranian Revolution.

Bahadur Shah I (1643-1712) Mogul emperor of India, 1707-12. He succeeded Aurangzeb.

Bahadur Shah II (1775-1862) The last Mogul emperor of India, he reigned from 1837 under the superintendence of the British East India Company. After the Indian Mutiny of 1857, he was dethroned and exiled.

Bahawalpur City on the Indus River in Pakistan. It was founded in 1748 by Bahawal Khan I.

Bahram The name of five Sassanian kings. Bahram V reigned from 420-435 and was a model sovereign.

Bahrites Name of the first Mameluke dynasty. From 1254-1382 they ruled over Egypt, Syria, and a portion of Arabia. The Bahrites waged war against the Mongols and routed the crusaders from Syria.

Baihars I (1223-1277) Mameluke general who battled successfully against the Mongols at Nablus and thereafter was installed as sultan.

Bailly, Jean-Sylvian (1736-1793) French astronomer and politician. After the storming of the Bastille (1789), he was proclaimed the first mayor of Paris. Because of his support for the monarchy, however, he was guillotined during the Reign of Terror.

Bajezid I (c.1360-1403) Ottoman Empire sultan, 1389-1402. B. defeated the army of Sigismund of Hungary near Nikopol (1396) and conquered part of the Balkans. In the Battle of Ankara in 1402, he was defeated by Tamerlane and taken prisoner. He died while in captivity.

Bajezid II (c.1447-1513) Ottoman Empire sultan, 1481-1512. The successor of Muhammad II, B. had no success in his wars against the Mamelukes, and was succeeded by his son Selim I in 1512.

Bahadur Shah I

Sir Robert Baden-Powell

Baji Rao I (1698-1740) Peshwa of the Maratha Empire in India. 1720-1740. He fought successfully against the Mongols.

Baji Rao II (1775-1853) Last peshwa of the Maratha Empire. Although he acceded to British authority (1802), he was nonetheless removed by the British in 1818.

Bajuvars Germanic tribe that entered southern Germany along with part of the Marcomans in the 6th century. In 788 their realm was added to the Frankish Empire.

Bakongo Native people of West Africa who inhabit the lower Congo region. Dom Henrique, a son of the native Bakongo king, Affonso I, became the first bishop in central Africa.

Bakunin, Mikhail (1814-1876) Russian anarchist. B. studied philosophy in Moscow and Berlin. He fought in Dresden during the revolution of 1848-1849 but was eventually imprisoned for his activities. In 1861 he escaped from Siberia and became active in Europe. His anarchism brought him into conflict with Karl Marx, who had him expelled from the socialist First International in 1872.

Mikhail Bakunin

Balaklava Battleground of the Crimean War, southeast of Sevastopol in the Crimea. There, in October 1854, the Russian general Liprandi attacked British positions in vain. The battle served as the inspiration for Tennyson's "Charge of the Light Brigade."

Balbo, Italo (1896-1940) Italian fascist and aviator. He was a rival of Mussolini. B. was killed when his plane was accidentally shot down over Libya.

Balboa, Vasco Nunez de (1475-1519) Spanish conquistador. In 1513 he became the first European to see the Pacific Ocean, which he called the South Sea. After a rival accused him of treason, he was beheaded.

Balduinus (d.1190) Archbishop of Canterbury. He accompanied Richard the Lionhearted during the Third Crusade (1189) and was slain in Syria.

Baldwin I (Baldwin of Boulogne) (d.1118) Brother of Godfrid of Bouillon, he participated in the First Crusade. In 1100 he was crowned King of Jerusalem as successor to his brother.

Baldwin I (1171-1205) First Latin emperor of Constantinople, 1204-1205. As count of Flanders (Baldwin IX) he played a part in the Fourth Crusade. With the conquest of Constantinople in 1204, the Crusaders chose him emperor. The next year he was captured by the Bulgarians and died in captivity.

Baldwin II (Baldwin of Courtenay) (1217-1273) The last emperor of Constantinople, 1228-1261. In 1261 his realm was conquered by the Byzantine Emperor Michael VIII.

Baldwin IX of Flanders *See* Baldwin I of Constantinople.

Baldwin, Stanley (1867-1947) British political leader and prime minister. A Conservative, B. was first elected to Parliament in 1908. He was three times prime minister: 1923-1924, 1924-1929, and 1935-1937. He arranged the abdication of Edward VIII in 1936.

Balewa, Sir Abubakar Tafawa (1912-1966) Nigerian political leader. He became the first federal prime minister of Nigeria in 1957. B. led his country to independence in 1960 but was later murdered.

Balfour, Arthur James (1848-1930) British political leader and prime minister (1902-1905). A Conservative, B. first entered Parliament in 1874. He opposed Irish Home Rule. B. was prime minister 1902-1905. As

Vasco Nunez de Balbao

foreign secretary, he issued the 1927 Balfour Declaration that promised British support for a Jewish homeland in Palestine.

Baliol, John (1249-1315) King of Scotland, 1291-1296. B.'s involvement with Philip the Fair of France led to the invasion of Scotland by his perennial adversary, Edward I of England, and forced him to abdicate.

Balkan Entente (1934) Accord concluded between Yugoslavia, Greece, Romania, and Turkey meant to ensure their territorial integrity against Bulgarian aggression.

Balkan League (1912) A series of agreements concluded between Bulgaria, Greece, Montenegro, and Serbia meant to oppose Turkey. Actual war with Turkey broke out the same year.

Stanley Baldwin

Balkan Wars Two wars fought over the European portion of the Ottoman empire. In the first Balkan War, 1912-1913, members of the Balkan League – Bulgaria, Greece, Montenegro, and Serbia – forced Turkey to cede all of its European territories except for the Constantinople area. In the Second Balkan War, 1913, Greece, Serbia, and Romania clashed with Bulgaria over the former Turkish possessions. Under the terms of the Third Treaty of Bucharest (1913), Bulgaria was compelled to relinquish almost all the Turkish territory it had earlier gained.

Balzac, Honoré de (1799-1850) French writer. Balzac started writing after abandoning a career as a lawyer. His huge cycle of novels *The Human Comedy* minutely describes French society during the first half of the 19th century. Among them are *Eugénie Grandet* (1833), *Lost Illusions* (1837), and *Cousin Bette* (1847). Balzac, a realist, also wrote fine short stories.

Honoré de Balzac

Bambra States Two Sudanese states situated in present day Mali. They controlled the gold mines in the region and conducted trade with European charter companies on the west coast of Africa (17th century). Eventually the states crumbled at the hands Islamic invaders and around 1818 were absorbed into the Fulani Empire.

Bandung Conference 1955 meeting of 29 independent, nonaligned Asian and African states under the chairmanship of India's Nehru and China's Chou En-Lai in the West Java, Indonesia, city of Bandung. The con-

ference condemned racial discrimination, colonialism, and nuclear war, and called for economic and cultural cooperation and general disarmament.

Banér, Johan Swedish field marshal under Gustav Adolfus. He was supreme commander of the Swedish forces in Germany (1638). The following year, he was victorious at the Siege of Chenmintz.

Bandurian Culture Prehistoric culture the name of which is derived from its distinctive earthenware. In the years 4500-5000 BC, they disseminated from the Danube region throughout the entirety of Europe. They were skilled farmers and cattlemen and lived in triagonal dwellings of approximately 131 feet in length.

Banér, Johan (1596-1641) Swedish general. During the Thirty Years War, he was the commander of the Swedish armies in Germany. In 1639 he won the Battle of Chemnitz against the Saxons.

Bank of the United States At the recommendation of Secretary of the Treasury Hamilton, Congress created the B. (1791), a private corporation, to handle the U.S. government's financial business, despite doubts by some of its constitutionality. The B.'s charter expired in 1811. Congress created the Second B. in 1816. President Jackson, accusing the B. of favoring the rich, prevented its renewal (1836).

Bannockburn River in Scotland. It was there that in 1314 an army of English knights under Edward II was defeated by the Scots under Robert Bruce.

Banting, Sir Frederick Grant (1891-1941) Canadian physician. Together with Charles H. Best, he discovered insulin in 1941.

Bantu languages Languages spoken by 70 million Africans south of the Equator. The B. languages are a subgroup of Niger-Congo branch of the Niger-Kordofanian language family. In South Africa the word is also used as a derogatory term for blacks.

Bar Kokba, Simon Leader of the last Jewish insurrection against the

Romans (132-135). He was ultimately defeated by the Roman general Julius Severus. In 1952 and 1960, letters from his military archives were discovered in a cave in the Judean desert.

Baratieri, Oreste (1841-1901) Italian general. In 1896 he suffered a crushing defeat at Adua in the Ethiopian War. As a result, the Treaty of Addis-Ababa established the independence of Ethiopia.

Barbarossa Code name for the German invasion of the Soviet Union in World War II. The invasion began on June 22, 1941.

Barbarossa (Italian: "Red Beard") Kahyr ad-Din (d.1546) Turkish pirate. He raided the Mediterranean and from 1533-1544 sailed for Suleyman I ("the Magnificent"). B. defeated expeditions sent against him by the Hapsburg Charles V and Francis I of France.

Barbarossa, Frederick *See* Frederick I.

Frederick Barbarosa

Barbary Pirates Marauders from the coast of North Africa. The B. raided throughout the Mediterranean from the 17th through the 19th centuries. The capture of Algiers by the French in 1830 ended their power.

Barber, Samuel (1910-1981) American composer. B. wrote in a conservative style for his period. His *Adagio* for strings, from his *String Quartet* (1936), attained phenomenal popularity. Other works include *Dover Beach* (1931), violin, cello, and piano concertos, orchestral works, and the operas *Vanessa* (1956) and *Antony and Cleopatra* (1966).

Barclay de Tolly, Mikhail (1761-1818) Russian field marshal. He defeated the French under Napoleon at Bautzen and Leipzig in 1813. After the invasion of France in 1813, he was made a prince under the name Mikhail Bogdanovich.

Bardi Prominent banking family of Florence from the 12th through the 14th centuries. Support of the English King Edward III in the Hundred Years War with France and aid to Florence in its clash with Lucca led to the family's bankruptcy (1345).

Bardo, Treaty of (1881) Agreement between France and the bey of Tunis that established France's protectorate over Tunesia.

Barebone's Parliament (Parliament of Godly Men) Convened by Oliver Cromwell after the dissolution of the Rump Parliament, it sat from July 4 until December 12, 1653, and was composed of defout Puritans and Presbyterians, among them the preacher and merchant Praise-God Barebone.

Barents, William (c.1550-1597) Dutch navigator. He undertook three voyages searching for a northeast passage from Europe to Asia. On the homeward leg of his last voyage, during which he discovered Spitzbergen, he died after being forced to winter on Novaya Zemyla.

Barère de Vieuzac, Bertrand (1755-1841) French revolutionary leader. He was a leader in the movement to execute Louis XVI. In 1815 he was

banished as a murderer of the king, but 15 years later he returned.

Bari, Siege of (1071) Bari, a city in southern Italy, was the last Byzantine stronghold on the Italian mainland. It was conquered by the Normans after a siege of three years.

Barmakids Persian clerical family. They exercised considerable influence among the early Abbasid caliphs (8th century) by serving them as scribes and advisers.

Barnard, Christiaan (1922) South African surgeon. He performed (1967) the first successful human heart transplant at Groote Schuur Hospital in Cape Town.

Barnave, Antoine (1761-1793) French political leader and member of the National Assembly between 1789 and 1791. He remained loyal to the royal family and was therefore executed.

Barnet, Battle of In this battle (1471) in the War of the Roses, an army loyal to Henry VI was defeated by Edward IV. Barnet is now part of greater London.

Baron Title of Germanic origin that originally meant simply "man" and in the Middle Ages came to mean "tenant." In more modern times it came to a title of nobility not necessarily based on land tenure.

Barry, Jeanne Bécu, Countess of (1743-1793) Mistress of King Louis

Jeanne Bécu, Countess of Barry

XV of France. A dressmaker, she was married to Guillaume de Barry. B. was executed during the French Revolution.

Great Battles

The art of war is as old as mankind itself. Only in the 20th century, however, has war involved the possibility of total destruction. In earlier centuries, armies, the wars they fought, and the destruction they caused were more modest, although still terrible enough.

1

2

3

1. Henry V of England wins a great victory against the French near Agincourt in 1415 during the Hundred Years War.
See Agincourt, Battle of; Henry V; Hundred Years War.
2. The Battle of Hastings (1066) depicted on the famous Bayeux Tapestry. In this scene King Harald of England removes an arrow from his eye.
See Harald III; Hastings; William the Conqueror.
3. The Battle of Roncevaux (778) in which Charlemagne's troops were attacked from behind by the Basques.
See Charlemagne; Roland.
4. The Battle of the Milvian Bridge (AD 312), where the Roman emperor Constantine the Great defeated Maxentius. After his victory Constantine converted to Christianity.
See Constantine I, the Great; Maxentius; Milvian Bridge.
5. The Battle of Waterloo (1815), where Napoleon was finally defeated.
See Napoleon I; Waterloo, Battle of.

5

4

Barth, Karl (1886-1968) Swiss Protestant theologian. His thinking about the relationship between God and man was influenced by the horrors of World War I. B. was a staunch opponent of Nazism.

Bartholomew's Day, Saint, Massacre of The August 1572 massacre of French Huguenots that began in Paris on the night of August 23-24 and spread into the rest of the country. It was precipitated by the marriage of the Protestant Henry of Navarre to the Catholic Margaret of Valois, sister of King Charles IX of France. Approximately 20,000 Huguenots died, including Gaspard de Coligny, who had been an adviser to King Charles IX but was resented by Charles's mother, Catherine de Medici. The massacre prompted a resumption of civil war in France.

Bartók, Bela (1881-1945) Hungarian composer. He was greatly influenced by Magyar folk music, which he and Zoltan Kodaly did pioneering work in collecting. B. is one of the most significant composers of the 20th century. He wrote much piano music, six string quartets, concertos for violin and for piano, orchestral music, and other works.

Basil II Bulgaroctonus ("Basil the Bulgar Slayer") (957-1025) Byzantine emperor, 976-1025. He annexed Bulgaria and extended the empire to the Caucusus.

Basil the Great (c.329-379) Bishop of Caesarea (Cappadocia) and one of the great church fathers. He standardized church liturgy in the Eastern Roman Empire.

Basil the Great

Basques People of northwestern Spain and the Franco-Spanish border regions in the foothills of the Pyrenees. The origin of the Basques is unknown. Their language, Basque, is distinct from Indo-European languages. *See* ETA.

Bastarnae Germanic tribe that settled around the Danube Delta. They were subdued by the Romans in 29 BC and became their confederates.

Bela Bartók

Batavian Revolution The founding (1795) of the Batavian Republic in the Netherlands during the French Revolution by the French army under Pichegru supported by Dutch republicans. Former state institutions were abolished and Stadtholder William V fled to England.

Batavian Republic The Dutch state between 1795 and 1806. In 1795 the Netherlands were captured by the French led by Pichegru. Stadtholder

William V was driven out, and Dutch republicans proclaimed the Batavian Republic. In 1806 the republic ended when Napoleon Bonaparte transformed it into the kingdom of Holland governed by his brother Louis Napoleon.

Batavians Germanic tribe from the Betuwe (Netherlands). They were allies of the Romans against the Teutons. Under Julius Civilis, they unsuccessfully revolted in 68-70 along with other Germanic and Gallic tribes against the Romans.

Baudelaire, Charles (1821-1867) French symbolist poet. The only volume of his poetry published during his lifetime was *Les fleurs du mal* (*The Flowers of Evil*) (1857). B. believed beauty and corruption were inevitably linked. He was also a brilliant critic.

Bavaria Region in the south of Germany. It was the Roman province of Raetia in the 1st-5th centuries AD. It was conquered by Charlemagne and subsequently went through many political changes. In 1805 it became a kingdom, and after World War I, a republic. It now is a state within Germany.

Bavarian Succession War (1778-1779) Waged between Frederick the Great of Prussia and Emperor Joseph II of Austria over the issue of who would succeed Count Maximilian III as elector of Bavaria. At the Peace of Teschen, Austria recognized the succession of Charles of Zweibrücken.

Bay of Pigs Bay in southern Cuba. There, in 1961, Cuban exiles landed with the support of the U.S. and attempted to overthrow the regime of Fidel Castro. The invasion was a complete failure and was a great embarrassment to the American government.

Beaker People (ca. 2200-1600 BC) Early European culture of the late Stone and early Bronze Ages. The name derives from the characteristic bell-shaped beakers that were found in graves from the period. The civilization, based on agriculture and trade, probably spread across Europe from Spain.

Becquerel, Henri (1852-1908) French physicist. He discovered the radioactive properties of uranium (1896).

Beecham, Sir Thomas (1879-1961) British conductor. B. had an enormous repertory. Among his specialties were Handel, Mozart, Berlioz, and Sibelius. He also championed the music of Frederick Delius. B. was a colorful personality who became an idol of the public in his later years.

Saint Bede

Bede, Saint (c.672-735) English ecclesiastic. Often called the Venerable Bede, he was the greatest scholar of his time. He wrote on theology, history, and science.

Bedeau, M.A (1804-1863) French general in Algeria. He became minister of war after the Revolution of 1848, but gas later exiled following a coup (1851).

Beethoven, Ludwig van (1770-1827) German composer. One of the greatest composers in Western music, Beethoven is usually considered the last composer of the Classical period, although some of his works foreshadow Romanticism in certain respects. He wrote his greatest music after 1800, despite becoming increasingly deaf. B. wrote 9 symphonies, 16 string quartets, 32 piano sonatas, five piano concertos, a violin concerto, the opera *Fidelio,* and other works. B.'s music is the cornerstone of the classical repertory today.

Begin, Menachem (1913-1992) Israeli political leader. Starting in 1943, he led the terrorist organization

Menachem Begin

Irgun in opposition to British rule in Palestine. A member of the conservative Likud Party in Israel, he became Israel's prime minister in 1977 and negotiated a peace accord with President Sadat of Egypt (see Camp David). During his second administration, Israel invaded Lebanon. B. retired from politics in 1983.

Behistun Cliff in western Persia (Iran), on which Darius I had an inscription carved in three languages in cuneiform script: Persian, Assyrian, and Susian. This inscription formed the key for the deciphering of cuneiform script.

Behring, Emil Adolf von (1854-1917) German physician. He applied serum therapy in combating diphtheria and received the first Nobel Prize for Medicine (1901).

Belalcazar, Sebastian (1479-1551)

Ludwig van Beethoven

Charles Baudelaire

Spanish conquistador. He sailed with Columbus, served with Pizarro in Peru, and explored Ecuador and Colombia.

Belgian Revolution (1830) Revolt of the southern provinces of the United Kingdom of the Netherlands that gave rise to the modern nations of Belgium and the Netherlands. On October 4, 1830, a provisional Belgian government declared independence. This independence was recognized by William I of the Netherlands in 1831.

Belgica Roman province between the North Sea and the Rhine, Seine, and Saone Rivers. It was organized in 16 BC by the Roman Emperor Augustus. At the end of the 1st century AD, Germania Superior and Germania Inferior were separated from Belgica. The part that remained was split into Belgica Prima (with Trier as its capital) and Belgica Secunda (with Rheims as its capital) under Diocletian.

Belgrade, Treaty of (1739) Made peace between the Ottoman Empire on the one hand and Russia and Austria on the other.

Belgrano, Manuel (1770-1820) Argentinean revolutionary. He was a principal figure in the struggle for independence against Spain and a member of the junta that proclaimed independence (1810).

Belisarius (c505-565) Byzantine general. Serving under Emperor Justinian, he destroyed the kingdom of the Vandals in North Africa (534), conquered Rome and Italy (536), fought the Persians (541-542), and drove the Bulgarians from Constantinople (559).

Bell, Lawrence (1894-1956) American aviation scientist. He invented the X-1, the first plane to break the sound barrier.

Bell, Alexander Graham (1847-1922) American scientist and inventor. B. began his career as a teacher of the deaf. Building upon the work of others, B. invented the telephone (1876), worked on the phonograph record, and did notable work on deafness.

Belle-Isle, Charles, Duke of (1684-1761) French political leader and

general. He fought in the Spanish, the Polish and the Austrian Succession Wars. From 1758 until his death he was the French Minister of War.

Bellovaci Belgian tribe that took part in the great unsuccessful Gallic revolt of 52 BC against Julius Caesar.

Belshaazar (6th century BC) King of Babylonia. According to the Bible, he was the son Nebuchadnezzar and the last independent King of Babylonia. In 539 BC he was defeated by Cyrus of Persia. *See also* Mene mene tekel.

Belzec Place in Poland where the Nazis built a concentration camp in 1942. It is estimated that over 500,000 people were killed there.

Ben-Gurion, David (1886-1973) Israeli political leader and prime minister. Born in Poland, he came to Palestine in 1906. He was one of the leaders of the Israeli war for independence and of the Mapai (Labor) Party and the Histadrut organization. B. became the first prime minister of

David Ben-Gurion

independent Israel (1948-1953) and served as prime minister several additional times.

Benares *See* Varanasi.

Benckendorff, Alexander, Count of (1783-1844) Russian general and head of the secret police under Nicholas I.

Benedek, Ludwig von (1804-1881) Austrian general. He was defeated at Königgrätz (1866) by the Prussians.

Benedict, Saint (Benedict of Nursia) (c.480-547) Italian monk. He founded the Benedictine Order at a monastery in Monte Cassino and was responsible for the Rule of St. Benedict, the most important rule in Western monasticism.

Saint Benedict

Benevento, Battle of *See* Manfred.

Benjamin *See* Israel, Tribes of.

Bennington, Battle of (1777) Battle in southwestern Vermont during the American Revolution. The Americans routed a British force of 800.

Benten Japanese god of literature, arts, and femininity.

Berbers People native to North Africa. They are Sunni Muslims but their native languages differ from Arabic. Their skin color varies between pale yellow and dark brown.

Bergen-Belsen Nazi concentration-camp in northern Germany, near Hamburg. More than 35,000 people were killed there, among them Anne

The Berlin Wall

After World War II, the victorious Allied powers occupied Germany. With the development of the Cold War, the Soviet zone of occupation became East Germany and the American, British, and French zones became West Germany. Berlin also was divided in the same way. In 1961 the Soviets and East Germans erected a wall to physically separate East and West Berlin and prevent East Germans from fleeing to the West. The Berlin Wall became a symbol of the Cold War. When the Cold War ended in 1989, the citizens of Berlin tore down the Wall, and the reunification of Germany followed.

1

2

3

4

1. The Berlin Wall during the Cold War.
2. The Brandenburg Gate, just across the Wall in East Berlin. Before the Wall was built, it marked the border between West and East Berlin.
3. Berliners hacking away at the Wall in November 1989.
4. Berliners celebrate the tearing down of the Wall.
5. The October 3, 1990, ceremony marking the official reunification of the two Germanies.

5

Frank. The camp was liberated on April 15, 1945.

Beria, Lavrenti Pavlovich (1899-1953) Soviet Communist leader. Stalin made him head of the secret police in 1938. B. was notorious for his brutality. Several months after Stalin died, Beria's rivals in the party had him arrested and executed.

Bering, Vitus (1680-1741) Danish explorer. He discovered the Bering Strait while on a voyage for Peter the Great in 1728.

Berlichingen, Götz von (1480-1562) German knight. He traveled around Europe taking part in various battles. In one he lost his right arm and wore an iron substitute. Sometimes an opponent of Holy Roman Emperor Charles V, he fought for him against the Turks and the French. His exploits are the subject of a play by Goethe.

Berlin, Irving (1888-1990) American songwriter. B was born in Siberia and came to the U.S. as a child. He was self-taught. He first became famous for "Alexander's Ragtime Band" (1916). Other great successes include "Oh, How I Hate to Get Up in the Morning" (1918), "God Bless America" (1938), "Blue Skies" (1926), and "White Christmas" (1942). B. wrote many successful musicals.

Berlin, Blockade of (March 1948-May 1949) Disputes over Germany and Berlin between the Soviet Union and the Western occupying powers —the U.S., Britain, and France — led to the Soviet blockade of West Berlin, which was surrounded by the Soviet-controlled zone of Germany. An airlift led by the U.S. saved the West Berliners fbom starvation.

Berlin, Colonial Conference of (1884-1885) Meeting of European nations and the United States to discuss the European colonies in Africa. Various territorial adjustments were made.

Berlin Congress (1878) Meeting of Britain, Germany, France, Austria-Hungary, Italy, and Russia to discuss relations with the Ottoman Empire, in particular the Treaty of San Stefano, which Russia had forced on Turkey earlier in the year.

Berlin Revolt (June 1953) A protest

Lavrenti Pavlovich Beria

against Communist rule in East Germany. It began when construction workers in East Berlin demonstrated against increased production quotas. Soviet troops had to be used to put down the resulting unrest.

Berlin Wall A barrier between East and West Berlin built by East Germany at the instigation of the Soviet Union in August 1961. Its purpose was to end the stream of refugees from East to West Germany. When the policies of Soviet leader Gorbachev led to reforms throughout Eastern Europe, the wall was torn down in November 1989, and the reunification of Germany shortly followed.

Berlioz, Hector (1803-1869) French composer. B. was greatly inspired by

Hector Berlioz

the literary works of Virgil, Shakespcarc, and Goethe. He wrote almost entirely for the orchestra and for the voice. He was a brilliant and innovative orchestrator and is sometimes called the father of the modern orchestra. His guide to instrumentation is still important today. Among his greatest works are the *Fantastic Symphony, Requiem, Romeo and Juliet, Damnation of Faust, The Infant Christ*, and the opera *The Trojans*. Berlioz was also a brilliant writer. His *Memoirs* and *Evenings with the Orchestra* are still read today.

Berlusconi, Silvio (1930-) Italian media business man and political leader. He founded a new political party, *Forza Italia*, and in 1994 became head of a coalition-government with other right-wing groups. He had to resign the same year, however, because of his attempts to monopolize the Italian state-television and internal divisions within the coalition.

Bernadette, Saint (1844-1879) French peasant girl. In 1858 she claimed the Virgin Mary appeared to her in a cave near her home at Lourdes. She later entered a convent. B. was canonized in 1933. Lourdes has become one of the most important places of pilgrimage in the world.

Bernadotte, Folke (1895-1948) Swedish count and diplomat. He helped evacuate prisoners from Nazi camps late in World War II and conducted negotiations in 1945 with the Nazi leader Himmler about peace between Germany and the Allies. During an inspection-trip to Palestine for the United Nations, he was assassinated by Jewish terrorists.

Bernadotte, Jean-Baptiste *see* Charles XIV.

Bernard I (d.818) King of Italy (810-818). A grandson of Charlemagne, he revolted against his father, Louis the Pious, in 817, and died of injuries after he had surrendered.

Bernardus of Clairvaux (1090-1153) French abbot, mystic and church-father. He founded the abbey of Clairvaux in 1115 and had great influence on the Cistercian Order. B. favored the

Silvio Berlusconi

restoration of religious fervor and ecclesiastical discipline. He also advocated the Second Crusade (1147-1149). In 1174 he was made a saint.

Bernardus of Clairvaux

Bernini, Gian Lorenzo (1598-1680) Italian sculptor and architect. He did much work on St. Peter's in Rome, including designing the colonnade, the bell-tower, and the tabernacle over the papal altar.

Bernstorff, Johann Heinrich (1862-1939) German diplomat. He was ambassador to the U.S. between 1908 and 1917. During World War I he argued unsuccessfully against the German adoption of unlimited submarine warfare.

Berry, Charles Ferdinand, Count of (1778-1820) Son of the Count of Artois, who later became Charles X of France. In 1816 he married Mary Carolina of Naples. He was killed in 1820.

Berry, John, Count of (1340-1416) Son of John II of France. He played a major part in French government after the death of Charles V in 1380.

Berry, Mary Carolina, Countess of (1798-1870) Wife of Charles Ferdinand, Count of Berry. Her husband was killed in 1820, shortly before the birth of their son, Henry of Bordeaux. She went into exile after the overthrow of King Charles X (1830). In 1832 she organized an unsuccessful revolt in

Gian Lorenzo Bernini

the Vendée against the government (1832) on behalf of her son's claim to the throne.

Berthier, Alexandre (1753-1815) French general. He fought in the

Bes

American Revolution and under Napoleon. After Napoleon's exile to Elba (1814), he entered service with the Bourbons. Napoleon's return greatly conflicted him, and he committed suicide or was killed in June 1815.

Bertrand, Henry Gratien, Count (1773-1884) French supporter of Napoleon. He went with Napoleon into exile on Elba and St. Helena and wrote a history of him.

Berwick, James, Duke of (1670-1734) English aristocrat. He was a follower of James II, whom he backed in the Battle of the Boyne (1690). Later he went into the service of Louis XIV, and in 1702 he was naturalized as a French citizen. A few years later he was appointed marshal of the French-Spanish armies in Spain.

Bes Egyptian deity of fertility, often depicted as a gnome.

Bessières, Jean-Baptiste (1768-1813) French general. He fought with Napoleon in Italy (Marengo) and led the defense against the British invasion of Zeeland (1809).

Bessus (d.c.329 BC) Ruler of Bactria. He assassinated Darius III and was executed by Alexander the Great.

Bethmann-Hollweg, Theobald von (1856-1921) German political leader. Chancellor 1909-1917, he opposed World War I but once it started called the treaty guaranteeing Belgian neutrality, which Germany had violated, "a scrap of paper." He opposed unrestricted submarine warfare. Hindenburg and Ludendorff made him resign.

Theobald von Bethmann-Hollweg

Betrade Wife of Pepin III and the mother of Charlemagne, whom she greatly influenced.

Bevan, Aneurin (1897-1960) British political leader. He was a member of the Labour Party and as minister of health (1945-1951) was responsible for the introduction of national health insurance in Britain (1951).

Bey A title of respect among Turkish people. Originally it meant the leader of a tribe.

Beza, Theodorus (1519-1605) French scholar and theologian. He was a close follower of Calvin.

Bhutto, Benazir (1953-) Pakistani political leader. The daughter of Prime Minister Zulfikar ali Bhutto, she was Pakistan's first woman prime minister (1988-1990). She was chosen again in 1993, but deposed in

Benazir Bhutto

late 1996. She was exiled from 1984 to 1986.

Biafra Region of Nigeria. The Ibos are the major ethnic group. In 1967, the Ibos, feeling they were oppressed within Nigeria, declared their independence, led by the East Nigerian military governor, Chukumeka Odumegwu Ojukwu. A civil war followed. After three years and millions of deaths, Biafra capitulated.

Biarritz, Meeting in (1865) Meeting of Emperor Napoleon III of France and Chancellor Bismarck of Prussia. Napoleon promised France would remain neutral in a war between Prussia and Austria.

Bibracte Capital city of the Celtic Aedui people, central France. It was captured by Julius Caesar in 58 BC. In 12 BC the Aedui were forced to leave the city and live in the surrounding plains. There Augustodunum (modern Autun) developed.

Bidault, Georges (1899-1983) French political leader. He fought in the French Resistance during World War II. After the war, he served as premier and foreign minister. B. was an opponent of De Gaulle's Algerian policy, and he cooperated with the OAS, who wanted to keep Algeria under French domination. He was exiled (1962) and lived in Brazil, until returning to France in 1968.

Beer Cellar Putsch Failed attempt by Adolf Hitler and other extreme right Germans to overthrow the Bavarian government in 1923. Hitler spent some time in jail as a result, and there he wrote *Mein Kampf.*

Bierut, Boleslaw (1892-1956) Polish

Communist. Under his leadership, Poland became a Soviet-style state in 1947.

Bierstadt, Albert (1830-1902) American painter. Born in Germany, B. became an outstanding painter of American landscapes. His vast canvases of Western mountain scenes are particularly striking.

Bill of Rights The first ten amendments to the U.S. Constitution. They were ratified in 1791. The B. contain important limitations on the power of the federal government — and by later interpretation, the state governments — and protect individual rights and liberties, such as freedom of the speech, press, assembly, and religion.

Billaut-Varenne, Jean Nicholas (1756-1819) French revolutionary leader. A cleric and lawyer, B. brought about the fall of Robespierre but was himself deported to Guyana in 1795.

Bismarck, Otto Edward Leopold, Count of (1815-1898) Prussian political leader. He was first appointed chancellor, or premier, by William I of Prussia (1862). B. became known as the "Iron Chancellor." He maneuvered Prussia into successful wars with Denmark (1864), Austria (1866), and France (1870-1871). More than any other single person, B. was responsible for the unification of Germany (1871). Though a conservative, he also sponsored some reform legislation, such as old age insurance and maximum working hours laws. William II disliked B. and dismissed him (1890).

Otto Edward Leopold, Count of Bismarck

Bissing, Moritz Ferdinand, Freiherr von (1844-1917) German general. He was military governor of occupied Belgium during World War I.

Bixio, Gerolamo (1821-1873) Italian revolutionary. He participated in the Italian War of Independence (1848-1849). He was also one of the leaders of Garibaldi's Sicilian expedition (1860).

Björkö, Treaty of (1905) A defensive alliance between Germany and Russia. Emperor Wilhelm II of Germany and Czar Nicholas II of Russia signed it while visitng each other's yachts, but the treaty was denounced by the latter the same year.

Black Hand 1. A criminal society, linked to the Mafia, that operated in Sicily and the U.S. in the late 19th and early 20th centuries. 2. A Serbian secret society in the pre-World War I years that advocated pan-Slavism and engaged in terrorist acts. It was responsible for the assassination (1914) of Austrian Archduke Franz Ferdinand that led to the outbreak of World War I.

Black Muslims (Nation of Islam) A militant religious-political movement of black people in the U.S. Founded in 1930, it was led for many years by Elijah Muhammad. The group initially advocated strict separation of the races and a separate black state within the United States. One of their most prominent leaders in the 1950s and 1960s was Malcolm X. In the 1990s Louis Farrakhan became their leading spokesman.

Black Panthers Radical black party in the U.S. It was founded (1966) by Bobby Seale and Huey Newton. The Panthers had frequent violent clashes with the police, in which dozens of people died. During the seventies, the party became less radical.

Black Power The slogan and vaguely defined ideology of radical black activists in the U.S. developed in the 1960s. The aim was the improvement of the condition of black people in the country. At times, however, advocates became associated with violence, which was counterproductive.

Black September 1. The term for the Jordanian Army's campaign to oust Palestinian guerillas from Amman, the Jordanian capital, in September 1970. It led to the withdrawal of the Palestine Liberation Organziation from Jordan. 2. The name of the Palestinian terrorist group which, among other things, was responsible for murdering many Israeli athletes at the Munich Olympic Games in 1972.

Black Shirts Term used to refer to the followers of Benito Mussolini. They were organized in paramilitary groups that terrorized opposing leftist parties and politicians. Mussolini disbanded the B. in 1925.

Black Thursday (October 24, 1929) The day on which the New York Stock Exchange began a sharp decline. The decline ended years of rising stock prices and heralded the Great Depression. Stock prices did not regain their earlier levels for many years.

Bladensburg Maryland village, near Washington D.C.. In 1814, during the War of 1812, British forces routed an American army there and proceeded to burn Washington.

Blair, Francis Preston (1791-1876) American political leader. B. was a close friend of Andrew Jackson and a member of his "Kitchen Cabinet." Opposed to the extension of slavery, he became one of the founders of the Republican Party and a supporter of Abraham Lincoln.

Blake, Robert (1599-1657) English admiral. Under Cromwell, he successfully fought the Dutch and Spanish fleets and the pirates in the Mediterranean.

Blériot, Louis (1872-1936) French avistion pioneer. He was the first to fly over the English Channel in an airplane that he had designed himself (July 25, 1909).

Blitzkrieg Term for the sudden attacks of overwhelming force waged by the German armed forces in the early years of World War II. The Germans used concentrated tank attacks and air bombardments, tactics that were new at the time.

Robert Blake

Blood-field, Battle of *See* Roger of Antioch.

Bloody Sunday
1. (November 13, 1887) British police violently struck down a demonstration for the release from jail of an Irish member of Parliament.
2. (January 9, 1905) Russian soldiers in St. Petersburg fired on a peaceful demonstration. The protesters wanted to offer a petition to the Czar asking for an eight-hour work day, a legislative assembly, and the release of political prisoners.
3. (January 30, 1972) British soldiers in Londonderry, Northern Ireland, killed 13 Roman Catholic protesters.

Blücher, Gebhard Leberecht von (1742-1819) Prussian field-marshal. His timely arrival at the Battle of Waterloo (1815) was decisive in the defeat of Napoleon.

Blut und Boden ("Blood and Soil") Nazi slogan, expressing the supposed link between race and earth. It was taken from the book *Befreiung*, written by A. Winning (1926).

Boccaccio, Giovanni (1313-1375) Italian writer and humanist. He is best-known for the *Decameron*, a collection of 100 sometimes erotic stories, that form a sketch of the morals in 14th-century Italy.

Boer Wars Wars of the South African Boers against Great Britain in 1880-1881 and 1899-1902. The first war broke out when the Republic of Transvaal refused to be incorporated with British Natal. The second war was about the independence of the republics of Transvaal and Orange Free State. In 1902 the Treaty of Unification was signed, which resulted in the foundation of the Union of South Africa in 1910.

Bogdanov, Alexander Alexandrovich (1873-1928) Russian doctor, sociologist, and economist. An early Bolshevik, he nevertheless disagreed philosophically with Lenin.

Boghazkoy Former city in Turkey that was the capital of the Hittites. Around 1200 BC it was sacked by the Phoenicians.

Bogumils Bulgarian religious sect. In the 10th-15th centuries, they spread

Giovanni Boccaccio

throughout the Balkans. The B. held beliefs similar to Manichaeism and opposed ecclesiastical organization.

Bohemund IV (1237-1275) King of Antioch, 1252-1268. In 1268 his kingdom was conquered by the Mameluke sultan Baibars.

Bohemund I (1050-1111) One of the leaders of the First Crusade, who captured Antioch in 1098 and became king of this state. He also participated in the siege of Jerusalem.

Bohr, Niels (1885-1962) Danish

Niels Bohr

physicist. He was a pioneer in atomic physics and did important work on quantum theory and atomic structure. He received the Nobel Prize for Physics in 1922.

Boii Celtic tribe. They settled in the northern Italy at the end of the 5th century BC. In 191 BC they were subdued by the Romans.

Boisdeffe, Raoul le Mouton de (1839-1919) French general. He was forced to resign in 1898 because of his part in the Dreyfus affair.

Bokassa, Jean Bédel (1921-) President of the Central African Republic, 1966-1976, and Emperor of the Central African Empire 1976-1979. He had served in the French army before becoming the Central African Repubic's chief commander (1963). He became president in a coup (1966) and in 1976 proclaimed himself emperor. He was deposed in 1979 after being accused of butchering about 100 schoolchildren and suspected of eating his opponents. B. fled to France but returned in 1986 and was imprisoned. He was released in 1993.

Jean Bédel Bokassa

Bokchoris (8th century BC) Egyptian king, c.718-712 BC. According to the legend of Manetho, he was burned alive by an Ethiopian king. Later

Greek sources refer to him as a wise and righteous lawyer.

Boleyn, Anne (?1507-1536) Second wife of King Henry VIII of England and mother of Queen Elizabeth I. Her husband had her decapitated.

Bolívar, Simón (1783-1830) South American general and political leader. Born in Caracas, he was called "the Liberator" for his prominence in the independence wars against Spain starting in 1810. From 1813-1821 his armies liberated Venezuela, Colombia, Ecuador, Peru, and Bolivia. He served in various high political offices but died out of power and unpopular.

Simón Bolívar

Bolsheviks ("members of the Majority") The faction of the Russian Social Democratic Labor Party led by Lenin. Lenin split the B. from the parent party in 1903. They were opposed by the Mensheviks, led by Martov. The B. became the Communist Party after the 1917 revolution.

Bomilcar (d.306 BC) Carthaginian general. He led the forces in the war (310-307 BC) against Agathocles of Syracuse. His attempt at a coup d'état in Carthage failed and he was executed.

Bonaparte (Buonaparte), **Carolina** (1782-1839) Youngest sister of Napoleon I. She married Joachim Murat in 1800 and was Queen of Naples between 1808 and 1815.

Bonaparte, Eugène Napoleon (1856-1879) Only child of Napoleon III and Empress Eugénie and pretender after his father's death (1870). He died

fighting in the British army against the Zulus in South Africa in 1879.

Bonaparte (Buonaparte), **Jerôme**, (1784-1860) Younger brother of Napoleon I. He was king of Westphalia between 1807 and 1813.

Bonaparte, (Buonaparte), **Joseph** (1768-1844) Oldest brother of Napoleon I. He was king of Naples between 1806 and 1808 and king of Spain between 1808 and 1813. In 1815 he moved to the United States.

Bonaparte (Buonaparte), **Laetitia** (1750-1836) Mother of Napoleon I. She fled to Rome after Napoleon's final defeat in 1815.

Bonaparte (Buonaparte), **Louis** (1778-1846) Brother of Napoleon I. He married (1802) the latter's step-daughter, Hortense de Beauharnais. He was king of Holland between 1806 and 1810 and fled to Italy after Napoleon fell from power.

Bonaparte, Louis Napoleon *See* Napoleon III.

Bonaparte (Buonaparte), **Lucien** (1775-1840) Brother of Napoleon I. He played an active role in the coup d'état of 18-19 Brumaire 1799 but later on quarrelled with his brother.

Bonaparte (Buonaparte), **Napoleon** *See* Napoleon I.

Bonaparte, Napoleon Francis Charles Joseph (1811-1832) Son of Napoleon I and Empress Mary-Louise. The "Eagle's child" was called both king of Rome and duke of Reichstadt. After his father fell from power, he was raised at the Austrian court.

Bonaparte, Pierre Napoleon (1815-1881) French politician. The son of Lucien Bonaparte, he killed the journalist Victor Noir in a quarrel (1870) but was acquitted. The latter's funeral escalated into a demonstration against Na»oleon III.

Bonapartists 1. Supporters of Napoleon I during his lifetime. 2. Party that aimed at the restoration to power of the House of Bonaparte.

Bonaventura, Saint (Johannes Fidenza) (1217-1274) Medieval scholastic. He is considered the most

Joseph Bonaparte

important medieval theologian after Thomas Aquinas.

Bonchamps, Charles, Marquis de (1760-1793) French soldier. He fought in the American Revolution. During the French Revolution he led the revolt in the Vendée in 1793. He was killed during the decisive battle there.

Bonhoeffer, Dietrich (1906-1945) German Protestant theologian and opponent of the Nazis. He was arrested in 1943 and hanged two years later for his connections with the participants in the 1944 assassination attempt on Hitler.

Boniface, Saint (c.675-754) Anglo-Saxon clergyman. Originally called Winfrith, he was a missionary among the Frisians from 716 onwards. In c.722 he was sent as a missionary to Germany by Pope Gregory II, who also gave him the name Boniface. He founded many monasteries, including the one at Fulda. He became Archbishop of Mainz in 745. In 754 he was killed by Frisian pagans.

Boniface II (6th century) Pope, 520-532. Backed by the king of the Goths, he became the first German pope.

Boniface VIII (c.1235-1303) Pope, 1294-1303. Born Benedetto Gaetani, he became pope after the abdication of St. Celestine V. He repeatedly clashed with Philip IV of France over the issue of the proper authority of pope and monarch, and he issued several bulls against Philip. The king attempted unsuccessfully to depose him.

Boniface of Montferrat (c.1150-1207) Leader of the Fourth Crusade in 1201. He later died in battle against the Bulgars.

Saint Boniface

Bono, Emilio de (1866-1944) Italian general. For a short time he was the commander in Ethiopia until he was replaced by Badoglio. In 1944 B. was found guilty of conspiring with Mussolini. He was executed together with Mussolini's son-in-law, Count Ciano.

Bor (1895-1966) Pseudonym of Tadeusz Komorowski, the supreme commander of the Polish resistance forces during World War II. B. led the 1944 Warsaw Uprising. After the war he fled from Poland when the communist regime took over.

Borden, Lizzie American woman. She was accused of murdering her father and stepmother with an axe in Fall River, Massachusetts, on August 4, 1892. B. was acquitted, and the crime was never solved. The case became part of American folklore.

Borghese Italian family. Originally from Siena, they settled in Rome in the middle of the 16th century. Camillo Borghese (1552-1621) became Pope Paul V in 1605 and made his family into one of the richest in Italy. In 1803 his namesake married Marie-Pauline, a sister of Napoleon I.

Borgia Spanish noble family. They settled in Italy in the middle of the 15th century. Alfonso Borgia became Bishop of Valencia and ruled as Pope Calixtus III between 1455 and 1458. His cousin Rodrigo became Pope Alexander VI in 1492.

Borgia, Cesare (1475-1507) Italian aristocrat. Son of Rodrigo Borgia (Pope Alexander VI), he became a notable patron of the arts and sciences as well as a clever and unscrupulous political leader. After a career as a clergyman, he conquered Romagna with the help of the French (after 1498) and also ruled Umbria. He may have been the model for Machiavelli's *The Prince*.

Lucrezia Borgia

Borgia, Lucrezia (1480-1519) Italian aristocrat. Daughter of Rodrigo Borgia (Pope Alexander VI), and sister of Cesare Borgia, she was married off by her father several times for political reasons. She is rumored to have poisoned people and engaged in various vices including incest, although the stories have not been proved.

Cesare Borgia

Boris III (1894-1943) King of Bulgaria, 1918-1943.In 1918 he succeeded to the throne after the abdication of his father, Ferdinand I. He became dictator in 1935 and allied with the Axis Powers in World War II. A few days after a meeting with Hitler in which he refused to participate in the invasion of the Soviet Union, however, he died under suspicious circumstances.

Bormann, Martin (1900-1945?) Nazi leader. As head of Hitler's Party Chancery, he accumulated great power. B. was with Hitler in his bunker nearly to the end of World War II. He then disappeared, and it is presumed he died trying to escape from Berlin. At the Nuremberg Trials he was sentenced (1946) to death in absentia.

Borobudur Magnificent Buddhist temple in central Java, Indonesia. It was built between the 8th and the 10th centuries and restored by the Dutch in 1907-1911.

Borodin, Alexander (1833-1887) Russian composer. A professional chemist, B. had little musical training. He was one of the group of Russian composers known as "the Five." B. wrote several symphonies and other orchestral pieces, chamber music and the opera *Prince Igor.*

Alexander Borodin

Borodino Place on the Moskva River, near Moscow, Russia. After the battle of Borodino in September 1812, Napoleon entered Moscow. Tolstoy's *War and Peace* contains an account of the battle.

Borsippa Ancient city near Babylon in Mesopotamia. It attained its greatest prosperity during the rule of Nebuchadnezzar II (605-562 BC). The city was ruined by Xerxes I of Persia.

Bosch, Hieronymus (c.1450-1516) Dutch painter. An artist of fantastic imagination, B. created a world of his own, in which the torments of hell and the pleasures of life play a central role. Some of his works are thought to be allegories, although their precise meaning is unknown. Among B.'s best-known works are *The Temptation of St. Anthony, The Mocking of Christ,* and *The Garden of Earthly Delights.* Philip II of Spain was a great admirer of his work.

Bose, Subhas Chandra (1897-1945) Indian nationalist. Together with Nehru, he founded the Independence League (1928). During World War II he supported the Japanese side.

Bosnia-Herzegovina Country in the Balkan region of Europe. B. and H. were both was ruled by the Turks for over four centuries. The Congress of Berlin (1878) placed the region under Austrian administration. At the end of World War I, it became part of Yugoslavia. After the death of Tito in 1980, Yugoslavia began to fall apart under the stress of ethnic conflict. In 1991 B. and several other constituent republics of Yugoslavia declared their independence. B, however, with a population consisting of Croatians, Serbs, and Muslims, fell victim to a vicious civil war, aggravated by aggression from neighboring Serbia. In 1995-1996, a fragile settlement was worked out by the international community led by NATO.

Boston Tea Party (1773) Protest by citizens of Boston, Massachusetts, against British restrictions on North American trade. Dressed up as Indians, a group of Bostonians threw boxes of tea of the English East India Company into Boston harbor. The actions was one of the incidents that culminated in the American Revolution (1775-1783).

Botassis, Payotis (1784-1824) During the Greek War for Independence, he supported the siege of Missolongi with a fleet in 1823.

Hieronymus Bosch

Botha, Louis (1862-1919) South African general. He fought in the Second Boer War and became commander-general of the Transvaal forces in 1900. After the foundation of the South African Union in 1910, he became Prime Minister and served until his death.

Louis Botha

Botha, Pieter Willem (1916-) South African political leader. He was initially a supporter of the apartheid policy that aimed at keeping whites and blacks separate in many areas of life. B. became prime minister (1978) and later president (1984) of South Africa and took steps to moderate the apartheid policy. After it became clear that apartheid was isolating South Africa internationally, B. was succeeded in 1989 by De Klerk.

Botticelli, Sandro (1445-1510) Italian Renaissance painter. Born Alessandro di Mariano Filipepi, he was a master of delicate depictions of women and angels. He also painted many portraits for the Medici family. Among his best works are *The Birth of Venus*, *Spring*, and *Portrait of a Young Man*.

Botzaris, Markos (1788-1823) Fought in the Greek Independence War against the Turks and defended Missilonghi against far superior forces (1822-1823). After he had killed the Turkish pasha with his own hands, he himself was killed.

Boucicaut, Jean le Maingre (c.1366-1421) French knight. He fought for the King Charles VI of France at Westrozebeke in 1382 and defended Constantinople against the Ottomans in 1399. He was captured by the English at the Battle of Agincourt in 1415.

Boudicca (d. AD 60) Queen of the Iceni, a Celtic tribe in Brittany. In 60 she led a major but unsuccessful revolt against the Romans.

Boule In ancient Athens, the town council. In most of the Greek city-states a council of nobles served to help the king. In Athens, the lawmaker and reformer Solon had founded a b. of 400 members, a number that was extended to 500 by Cleisthenes. The members of the b. were elected for one year. Daily affairs were taken care of by 50 of its members, called the prytany.

Bourbon French royal house. Originally from Central France, they were pobably related to the Carolingians. In 1598 Henry of Bourbon, who already was King of Navarre, became king of France. He ruled as Henry IV, and the House of Bourbon remained on the French throne until 1848, inter-

rupted only by the period of the French Revolution and Napoleon between 1792 and 1814. Louis Philippe, from the related House of Orleans, ruled between 1830 and 1848. The Bourbons also were kings of Naples and Sicily (1738-1830), dukes of Parma (1731-1738, 1748-1802, and 1847-1860), and kings of Spain (1700-1931). From 1801 till 1807 Louis of Bourbon-Parma and his son Charles II Louis were also kings of Etruria.

Bourbon, Charles of (1490-1527) French aristocrat. In 1515 he commanded the armies of Francis I of France against Holy Roman Emperor Charles V. Later, however, he quarrelled with Francis and went over to Charles's side. Fighting against the French, he died while attacking Rome.

Bourbon, Louis Marie of (1777-1823) Prince of Spain and cousin of King Charles III. He was also a cardinal and the archbishop of Toledo. In 1820 he became the leader of a revolutinary party during the reign of Ferdinand VII.

Bourbons, Family treaty of (1761) Agreement made in Paris in which the Bourbon rulers of France, Spain, Naples and Parma guaranteed each other's territories.

Bourguiba, Habib (1903) Tunisian political leader. In 1934 he was one of the founders of the Neo-Destour party that fought for independence from France. B. was often imprisoned by the French. In 1957 he became the first president of independent Tunisia. In 1987, however, he was deposed.

Habib Bourguiba

Bouvines Village near Lille, northern France. There, in 1214, the French King Philip II Augustus beat the armies of Holy Roman Emperor Otto

IV, King John Lackland of England, and Count Ferrand of Flanders and Hainault. The battle was significant in establishing the power of the French monarchy.

Boxer Rebellion (1899-1900) Revolution in China, partly organized by court circles and aimed at reducing the influence of foreigners in China. The name stems from a secret Chinese society, the "Righteous Fists," that was anti-foreigner. At the height of the rebellion, the Boxers occupied Beijing for eight weeks. A force of British, French, German, Russian, American, and Japanese troops put down the uprising.

Boyacá, Battle of Important battle in the South American Wars of Independence fought in 1819 near Bogotá, Colombia. South American revolutionaries defeated a Spanish army. The Spanish lost Colombia and Venezuela as a result.

Boyars Nobles in Russia during the 10th-17th centuries. Their power originally stemmed from their military strength, but they became great landholders and advisers to the rulers. Eventually the czars curtailed their power, and Peter the Great (early 18th century) abolished the rank and title of boyar.

Boyer, Jean-Pierre (1776-1850) President of Haiti, 1818-1843. He united Haiti in 1822 but became unpopular after introducing compulsory labor. That and other factors led to his overthrow in 1843. He fled to Jamaica.

Boyne River in eastern Ireland. In 1690 James II of England, a Roman Catholic, was defeated there by his Protestant son-in-law, William III.

Bozeman Trail *See* Red Cloud.

Brabant A province in Belgium and the Netherlands. It consists of a portion of the former duchy of B., which is now divided between Belgium and the Netherlands.

Brabant Revolt 1830 rebellion in the Southern Netherlands that led to the creation of independent Belgium.

Braddock, Edward (1695-1755) British general. He fought in the Austrian

Charles of Bourbon

Succession War and in 1754 he became commander-in-chief of the British forces in North America. He died in a battle in the French and Indian War.

Edward Braddock

Omar Nelson Bradley

Bradley, Omar Nelson (1893-1981) American general. He served in World War I and, prominently, in Europe during World War II. He was the first chairman of the joint chiefs of staff, 1949-1953.

Braga, Téofilo (1843-1924) Portuguese political leader and writer. He was active in the Portuguese Revolution in 1910 and became the first

president of Portugal, 1910-1911, and again was president in 1915. B. also wrote poetry.

Braganza Portuguese royal house. The Braganzas ruled Portugal between 1640 and 1853 and Brazil from 1822 to 1889.

Brahe, Tycho (1546-1601) Danish astronomer. He was one of the most precise observers in a time without telescopes. His careful observations enabled the astronomer Kepler to formulate the laws of the motion of the planets.

Brahms, Johannes (1833-1897) German composer. In his music B. combined Romantic sensibility with the rigor of Classical forms. B. wrote four symphonies, four concertos, much piano, chamber, and vocal music, and the highly popular *Hungarian Dances*. He was also a music scholar and, in his earlier years, a great pianist.

Braille, Louis (1809-1852) French teacher and inventor of the Braille system of printing and writing for the blind. B. himself became blind when he was three years old. In addition to his work for the blind, he was an organist.

Bramante, Donato (1444-1514) Italian Renaissance architect and painter. He prepared the main plans for the construction of St. Peter's in Rome.

Brandeis, Louis Dembitz (1856-1941) American lawyer and U.S. Supreme Court Justice, 1916-1939. As a lawyer B. insisted that social and economic realities had to be considered in evaluating the constitutionality of legislation. He was a close adviser of Woodrow Wilson, who appointed him to the Supreme Court. He served there until 1939. B. was also a Zionist and helped found the American Jewish Congress in 1916.

Brandt, Willy 1913-1992) German political leader. Born Herbert Ernst Karl Frahm, B. was a Social Democrat. He fled to Norway during the Nazi period. B. returned to Germany in 1947 and in 1957 was elected mayor of West Berlin. In 1969 he was chosen chancellor of West Germany. Two years later he was awarded the Nobel Peace Prize because of his efforts to

Tycho Brahe

normalize relations with Eastern Europe. He resigned in 1974, when his advisor Guillaume was exposed as an East German spy.

Brandywine, Battle of 1777 battle near Philadelphia in the American Revolution. The British under Howe defeated the Americans under Washington and then occupied Philadelphia.

Brant, Sebastian (?1458-1521) German humanist and professor of law. His 1494 satire *Das Narrenschiff* (*The Ship of Fools*) deals with 112 fools, each representing a common folly. It inspired the novel *Ship of Fools* by the 20th century American writer, Katherine Anne Porter.

Willy Brandt

Braque, George (1882-1963) French painter. Earlier a Fauvist and a follower of Cézanne, he and Picasso are considered the founders of Cubism. B. worked in what is called "analytical" cubism.

Brasidas (d.422 BC) Spartan general. He defeated the Athenians several times in the Peloponnesian War. He died during the defense of Amphipolis against the Athenian army.

Brauchitsch, Walther von (1881-1948) German general. He distinguished himself as commanding officer during the Battle of Verdun in World War I. In 1938 he was appointed commander-in-chief of the German army and won great victories in France in 1940 during World War II. But disagreements with Hitler led to his being fired in 1941.

Braun, Wernher von (1912-1977) German and later American rocket scientist. He led the German rocket research center at Peenemünde (1932-1945), where the V1 and V2 were developed. After the war he went into service of the U.S.. As head of NASA, he helped to bring about the successful moon landing in 1969.

Braun, Eva (1912-1945) Wife of Adolf Hitler. She met him in the mid-1930s through her job as assistant to his photographer. They were married on April 29, 1945, and committed suicide on the very next day.

Brecht, Bertholt (1898-1956) German playwright. He left Germany after the Nazi takeover in 1933 because of his left-wing sympathies. After the end of World War II, he returned to live in East Germany.

George Braque

Well-known works are *The Threepenny Opera* (1928), *Mother Courage* (1941), and *The Caucasian Chalk Circle* (1955). B. and Kurt Weil collaborated in several musical theater works.

Breda, Peace of (1667) Ended the Second English-Dutch War.

Breitscheid, Rudolf (1874-1944) German political leader. Leader of the Social Democrats in the Reichstag since 1928, he fled to France after Hitler came to power in 1933. In 1941 he was extradited to Germany by the Vichy government and imprisoned in Buchenwald, where he was killed in 1944.

Brennan, William Joseph (1906-) U.S. Supreme Court Justice, 1956-1990. B. was named to the Court by President Eisenhower. He became one of the great liberal justices, particularly interested in civil liberties.

Brennus (4th century BC) Legendary commander of the Gauls, who supposedly captured Rome in c.390 BC.

Brest-Litovsk, Peace of (March 1918) Treaty between Germany and the new government of Russia headed by Lenin that ended World War I on the eastern front. In it Russia conceded

vast territories to Germany. Russia annulled the treaty after the armistice of November 11, 1918.

Brétigny, Treaty of (1360) Agreement made at Bretigny, a village near Chartres, France, by Edward III of England and John the Good of France, who was an English prisoner-of-war. The treaty marked a lull in the Hundred Years War. John ceded to Edward various territories in France.

Bretton Woods Conference (1944) International conference held at Bretton Woods, New Hampshire. The conference established an international monetary system and created the International Monetary Fund and the World-Bank. The agreements of Bretton Woods were signed by 44 countries.

Brezhnev, Leonid Ilyich (1906-1982) Soviet political leader. B. joined the Communist Party in 1931 and benefitted from the opportunities created by Stalin's purges. He became first secretary of the party following Khrustchev's ouster in 1964 and soon after became the top leader in the Soviet Union. B. maintained a policy of détente with the West. At home his regime clamped down on dissent and became increasingly corrupt.

Leonid Ilyich Brezhnev

Bertholt Brecht

The British Empire

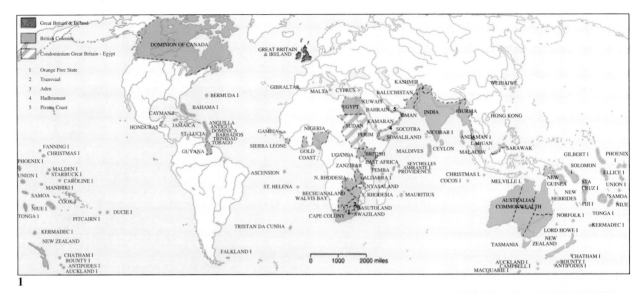

1

England acquired its first colonies in the 16th century. By 1800 the British Empire was the greatest in the world, despite the loss in 1783 of the 13 North American colonies that had rebelled in 1776 and formed the United States. Britain maintained its great empire well into the 20th century, when many of the colonies became independent.

3

4

2

1. The British Empire at the height of its power in the 19th century. *See* Victoria.
2. A portrait of Henry VIII, the great 16th-century king who founded the Church of England. *See* Henry VIII.
3. An English nobleman from the time of Elizabeth I, a very glorious era for England. *See* Elizabeth I.
4. David Livingstone, the British missionary and explorer in Africa, who claimed many regions for the British crown. *See* Livingstone, David.
5. The great battle between the Spanish Armada and the English navy in 1588, during which the Spanish were thoroughly defeated. *See* Armada; Philip II.

5

58

Brezhnev Doctrine (1968) Foreign policy enunciated by Leonid Brezhnev stating that the Soviet Union would intervene in neighboring countries if Communist rule were threatened. The B. was cited in justification of Soviet intervention in Czechoslovakia in 1968 and Afghanistan in 1979.

Brhadratha The last monarch of the Indian Mauryan dynasty. He was killed by one of his own generals in 185 BC.

Briand, Aristide (1862-1932) French political leader, who was a member of many governments since 1905, from 1909 onwards also as president. He

Aristide Briand

strove for a reconciliation with Germany after World War I, a goal that was fulfilled with the Treaty of Locarno (1925). In 1926 he and his German colleague Stresemann were awarded with the Nobel Peace Prize.

Brienne, John of (1148-1237) King of Jerusalem, 1210-1237. He participated in the Fifth Crusade and was temporarily emperor of Constantinople in 1231.

Brigantes Celtic tribe in middle England. They were not subdued by the Romans until the second century AD.

Bright, John (1811-1889) British political leader. He was one of the founders of the Anti-Corn-Law League. B. was a pacifist and opposed British involvement in the Crimean War (1853-1856). He served in Gladstone's cabinets but opposed Home Rule for Ireland.

Brinkmanship Self-proclaimed foreign policy tactic of U.S. Secretary of State John Foster Dulles (1953-1959). Dulles claimed by going to the brink of nuclear war, the U.S. could obtain concessions from the Communist world.

Brinno Chief of the Canninefates, who together with Julius Civilis led the great revolt in 69 BC against the Romans.

Brion, Philippus Ludovicus (1782-1821) Dutch-South American soldier and political leader. He fought against the British in Holland (1799) and on the Caribbean island of Curaçao during the Napoleonic Wars. Afterwards he fought with Simón Bolívar to free South America from Spain.

Brisson, Eugène-Henri (1835-1912) French political leader. As premier, he strived for the disclosure of the Panama Canal and for the reconsideration of the Dreyfus affair.

Brissot de Warville, Jacques-Pierre (1754-1793) French revolutionary leader. He was a journalist and strong opponent of slavery. He was a Girondist during the French Revolution and favored spreading the revolution throughout Europe. Differences with the Jacobins led to his execution in 1793.

Britain, Battle of (June 1940-April 1941) In World War II, the battle in the skies over Britain between the German and British air forces. The Germans were terror bombing British cities and seeking air superiority preparatory to an invasion of Britain. The

John Bright

RAF – the Royal Air Force – inflicted such heavy losses on the Germans that the bombing campaign was called off and the invasion never took place.

Britannia Roman name for Britain, which became a province of the Roman Empire in the 1st century AD.

Britannicus, Claudius Tiberius (d.55 AD) Roman nobleman. He was the son of Emperor Claudius and Messalina. After Claudius married Agrippina, her son Nero became the heir to the throne. B. was poisoned, probably by Nero, after Nero became emperor.

Brockdorff-Rantzau, Ulrich, Count of (1869-1928) German political leader. He resigned as minister of foreign affairs in 1919 because he disagreed with the conditions for peace that Germany had accepted to end World War I.

Charlotte Brontë

Brontë, Charlotte (1816-1855), **Emily** (1818-1848), and **Anne** (1820-1849) British writers. They were the daughters of Patrick Brontë, a clergyman. Their mother died in 1821. All three wrote poetry and novels under pseudonyms. Charlotte is best-known for *Jane Eyre* (1847), Emily for *Wuthering Heights* (1847), and Anne for *Agnes Grey* (1847).

Bronze Age Period that followed the Neolithic. In Europe it lasted from c.2000 to c.1000 BC. During this time metal was first used for tools and weapons.

Brothers of the Sword German military and religious order, also known as the Livonian Brothers of the Sword. It was founded in 1202 by Bishop Albert of Livonia to conquer and convert the pagans in the Baltic region of Europe.

Brougham, Henry Peter, Baron of Vaux (1778-1868) British political leader. He championed many liberal causes, such as the abolition of the slave trade and education reform. B. entered Parliament as a Whig in 1810 and was lord chancellor in the cabinet led by Grey that pushed through the Reform Bill of 1832.

Brown, John (1800-1859) American abolitionist. B. was fanatical in his hatred of slavery, believing he was carrying out the will of God. He murdered proslavery men in Kansas in 1855. In 1859 he raided a federal arsenal at Harpers' Ferry, Virginia, hoping to spark and arm a general slave uprising. He was caught and executed shortly after.

Bruegel

Heinrich Brüning

Bruce, Robert (1274-1329) King of Scotland, 1306-1329. He defeated the English at the Battle of Bannockburn (1314). He was recognized as the Scottish king by the pope in 1323 and in 1328 by the English.

Bruegel (also Breugel) Family of Dutch painters. The most important was Pieter Bruegel the Elder (c.1525-1569), who is called "the Farmers' Bruegel" because of his paintings of lively scenes of farm life, although he also painted other subjects including fantastic allegorical scenes. His sons were Pieter (1564-1638), who copied many of his father's works, and Jan (1568-1625), who painted landscapes and flowers.

Brueys, François-Paul (1753-1798) French admiral. He led Napoleon's fleet to Egypt. He died during the naval battle with the British near Abukir in 1798.

Brumaire (Month of Mists) Month on the French Republican calendar. On Brumaire 18-19, in the year VIII (November 18-19, 1799), Napoleon Bonaparte's coup d'état ended the regime of the Directory.

Brune, Guillaume (1763-1815) French general. During the Wars of the French Revolution, he fought near the Rhine and in Italy. In 1799 he was commander-in-chief of the French and Batavian troops that battled the British and the Russians in northern Holland. He was assassinated in Avignon in 1815.

Brunhild 1. In Germanic mythology, a great female warrior. She is Brunn-hilde in Richard Wagner's music dramas *The Ring of the Nibelungs*. 2.(c.534-613) Wife of Sigebert of Austrasia. After his death in 575, she defended the realm against Neustria, but after long years of bloody rule she was captured and killed by Clotaire II.

Brüning, Heinrich (1885-1970) German political leader. He was the leader of the Catholic Center Party and became chancellor in 1930. Two years later he was dismissed by President Hindenburg and replaced by Franz von Papen. He fled after Hitler had come to power in 1933. After World War II, B. taught in the U.S.. He returned to Germany in 1951.

Bruno, Giordano (1548-1600) Italian philosopher. He believed that all perceptions were relative to the observer's position in time and space. His unconventional ideas led to his being charged with heresy, and he was executed by burning.

Bruteres German tribe living on the rivers Ems and Lippe. They took part in the great revolt against the Romans in 69-70 AD.

Brutus, Lucius Junius Roman hero. He expelled the last Roman king, Tarquinius Superbus, in 509 BC. The latter's son, however, took revenge and killed him a year later.

Brutus, Marcus Junius (85-42 BC) Roman leader. He was one of the assassins of Julius Caesar in 44 BC; Ceasar had favored him, although B. had sided with Pompey, Caesar's rival. After Caesar's death, B. and Cassius opposed Octavian and Antony. After his defeat at Philippi in Macedonia, he committed suicide.

Marcus Junius Brutus

1

In all times and cultures, people have paid special attention to their dead. Funeral monuments are therefore found all over the world. Some may look very different from others, but their purpose is always the same: to remember the deceased members of the community. This was considered important thousands of years ago, and it still is today.

2

1. On the sarcophagus of the ancient Egyptian pharaoh Ramses II, the goddess Isis spreads her wings to protect the deceased pharaoh's mummy.
2. The mausoleum of Lenin in Red Square in Moscow.
3. Rock-graves in India, dating from the 4th to 8th century AD. Mummies of ancestors were placed in the chambers carved out of the cliff.
4. The tombstone of the ancient Greek warrior Aristion (6th century BC).
5. The cemetery of the soldiers killed at Verdun, France, in World War I.

4

3

5

Brutus Albinus, Decimus Junius (d.43 BC) Roman general. He served under Caesar in Gaul but joined in the conspiracy to assassinate Caesar. After Caesar's death, Antony had him killed.

Bucephalus The favorite horse of Alexander the Great. He died in 326 BC, and Alexander founded the city Bucephala in present-day Pakistan in his honor.

George Villiers Buckingham

Bucentaur Ceremonial vessel on which the Doge of Venice each year sailed on Ascension Day to consecrate the city's marriage to the sea.

Bucharest, Peace of *See* Serbian-Bulgarian War.

Buchenwald Nazi concentration-camp near Weimar. More than 50,000 people died there. It was liberated in 1945 by the British and the Americans.

Buchanan, James (1791-1868), 15th president of the U.S., 1857-1861. Born in Pennsylvania, B. had a long political career as a Democrat. He was secre-tary of state (1845-1849) under President Polk. As president, B. was domi-nated by the Southern, pro-slavery wing of his party, and the crisis between North and South gravely worsened during his administration. He thought secession was wrong but believed he had no power to do any-thing about it. The Civil War began shortly after his term ended.

Buckingham, George Villiers, Duke of (1592-1628) English aristocrat. A favorite of James I and Charles I, he antagonized Parliament by his favorit-ism in granting monopolies. He spon-sored Charles's unpopular marriage (1624) to Henrietta Maria of France. After a foreign policy failure, Charles dismissed Parliament (1626) to pre-vent B.'s impeachment. He was killed by a deranged naval officer.

Buckingham, George Villiers, 2nd Duke of (1628-1687) English aristo-crat. Son of the first duke, he was a royalist during the English Civil War and a close adviser of Charles II and member of his CABAL. Dismissed for corruption in 1674, he joined the anti-Catholic enemies of the Duke of York, who later became James II.

Buckingham, Henry Stafford, Duke of (c.1454-1483) English aristocrat. After the death (1483) of Edward IV, B. supported a rebellion on behalf of the claim of Henry, Earl of Richmond, to the throne. Richmond's rebellion failed, and B. was executed by Richard III.

Buddhism One the world's major reli-gions. It was founded in India during the 6th-5th centuries BC by Siddhar-tha Gautama (c.563-483 BC), known as the Buddha ("the Enlightened One"), who was of noble Indian birth. The Buddha taught that living means suffering, a process that is repeated over and over again through reincar-nation. The person who manages to free himself of longing for and attach-ment to life will find peace and happi-ness; he will attain Nirvana. Buddh-ism spread throughout Asia but is no longer strong in India. There are two main branches: the Theravada, or Hinayana, in Southeast Asia; and the Mahayana, in China, Japan, and Korea.

Buena Vista, Battle of Battle in the Mexican War, February 1847. U.S. General Zachary Taylor defeated the Mexicans under Santa Anna. The battle gave Taylor control of northern Mexico.

Bull, John A fictitious short, stocky man who is a symbol for Britain.

Bull, Ole (1810-1880) Norwegian violinist who toured Europe and the U.S..

Bull Run A stream in northeast Virgi-nia and the site of two Confederate victories in the American Civil War. The first, on July 21, 1861, was the first major battle of the war. Confederates under Johnston and Beauregard drove back Union forces under McDowell. In the second, on August 29-30, 1862, Lee defeated Pope.

Buller, Sir Redvers Henry (1839-1908) British general. He served in the Zulu War and the First Boer War and was commander-in-chief of the Brit-ish forces in the Second Boer War.

Sir Redvers Henry Buller

Bullinger, Heinrich (1504-1575) Swiss Protestant theologian. He suc-ceeded Zwingli and together with Calvin managed to unite the Protes-tants in Switzerland.

Bülow, Friedrich Wilhelm, Freiherr von (1755-1816) Prussian general. In 1813 he led the defense of Berlin against the French under Napoleon and liberated the Netherlands. B. played a crucial part in the Battle of Waterloo (1815).

Bülow, Hans Guido, Freiherr von (1830-1894) German musician. A pianist and conductor, B. studied with

The Byzantine Empire

The Eastern Roman Empire became the Byzantine Empire. Byzantium was the name of the old city on the site of the empire's capital, Constantinople. The Byzantine Empire lasted until 1453, when it was conquered by the Turks. The Byzantines developed their own version of Christianity.

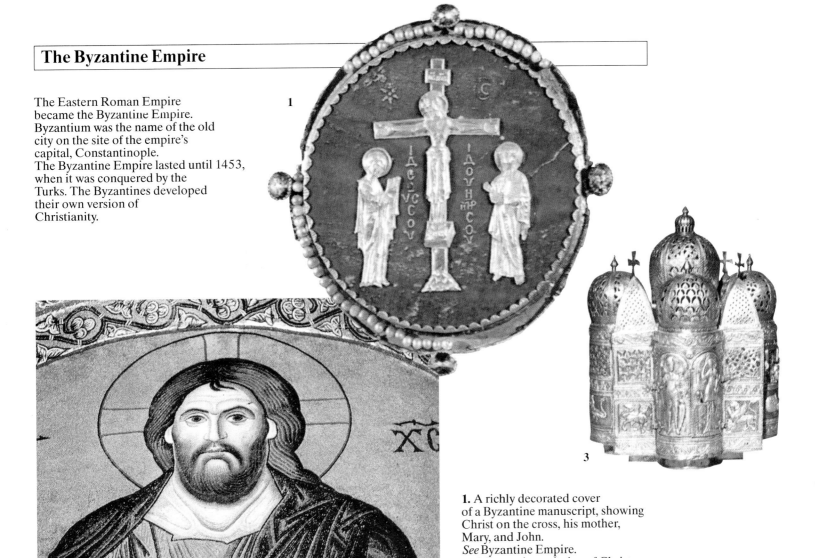

1. A richly decorated cover of a Byzantine manuscript, showing Christ on the cross, his mother, Mary, and John.
See Byzantine Empire.
2. A Byzantine painting of Christus Pantokrator (Greek: the ruler over everything).
3. A Byzantine reliquary in the shape of a church.
4. Emperor Michael II (9th century) and the patriarch Nicephorus, on a miniature from the chronicle of Skykitzes.

The Byzantine Empire

5. Emperor Basil II Bulgaroctonus ("Basil the Bulgar Slayer"), who ruled from 976 to 1025, on a battlefield. This miniature is from an 11th-century imperial psalter.
See Basil II Bulgaroctonus.
6. A Byzantine church in Greece, dedicated to St. Luke.
7. Byzantine coins struck in the 8th and 9th centuries, showing Emperor Justinian II and Christ.
8. A Byzantine church, carved out of a rock. This church was dedicated to St. Barbara, and was built in Göreme, Cappadocia, in present-day Turkey.

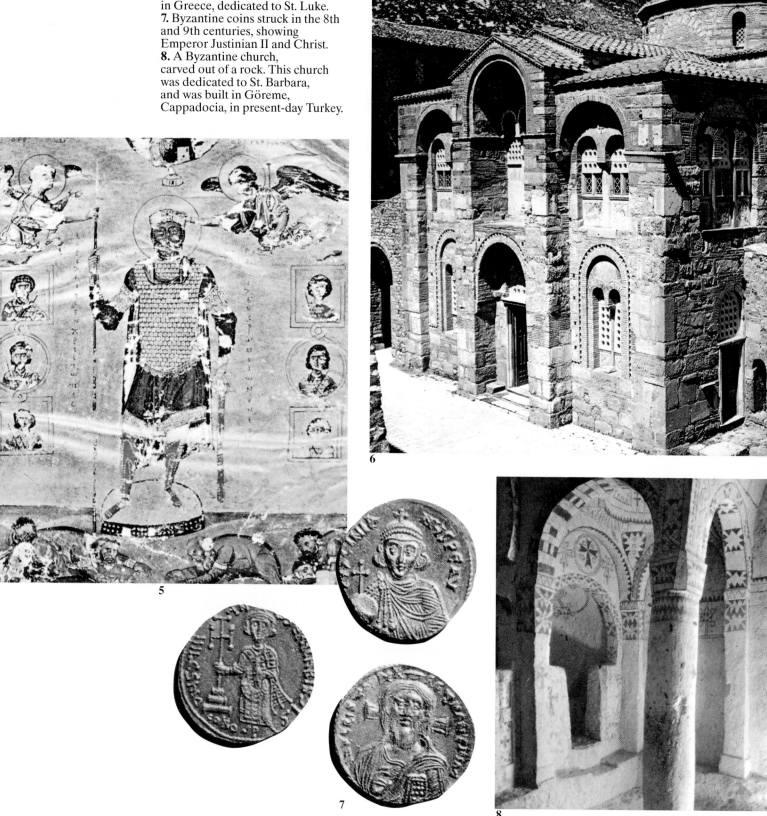

5

6

7

8

Liszt and was the first husband of his daughter Cosima. He was closely associated with both Wagner and Brahms. B. prepared many careful editions of the great works of the piano literature.

Bülow, Karl von (1846-1921) German general. He fought in the Franco-Prussian War of 1870-1871 and led the 1914 German invasion of Belgium in World War I. He was defeated at the First Battle of the Marne (September 1914).

George Herbert Walker Bush

Bunker Hill Name of the first major battle of the American Revolution, fought near Boston in June 1775. The battle actually took place on Breed's Hill. The British drove off the Americans but suffered unexpectedly heavy casualties.

Bunyan, Paul Mythical American lumberjack, the hero of many folk tales. He was of huge size and strength and owned Babe the Blue Ox.

Burgoyne, John (1722-1792) British general. He lost the fateful Battle of Saratoga in New York State in the American Revolution. B.'s surrender to American General Gates in October 1777 persuaded France to sign a treaty of alliance with the U.S.. The French aid was critical to the eventual American victory in the war.

Burgundy Historic region in France, centered around the junction of the Rhone and Saone Rivers. The region was conquered by the Romans under Caesar and divided into several provinces. In the 5th century AD, it was invaded by a Germanic tribe and then by the Burgundii from Savoy, who founded a kingdom. The kingdom was conquered in 543 by the Franks. The

area then underwent many political changes. The duchy of Burgundy was created in 877. In the 14th and 15th centuries, Burgundy was a major power in Europe. Louis XI of France made it a part of his realm in 1477.

Burgundy, Anton of 1. (1384-1415) Duke of Burgundy. The son of Philip the Bold, he died in the Battle of Agincourt. 2. (1421-1504) "The Great," a bastard-son of Philip the Good. He led the army in his father's wars and those of Charles the Bold. In 1477 he was captured by the French near Nancy, and afterwards he was in the service of King Louis XI of France.

Burr, Aaron (1756-1836) American political leader and adventurer. B. was talented but untrustworthy. He served in the American Revolution and then went into politics. He successfully built up the Democratic-Republican Party in New York and was chosen the party's vice-presidential candidate in 1800. The accidental tie electoral vote almost made him president instead of Thomas Jefferson. While vice president in 1804, B. killed Alexander Hamilton in a duel. He then engaged in mysterious conspiracies in the American west and was accused of treason but acquitted.

Burschenschaft The extremely nationalistic German student fraternities of the 19th century.

Bush, George Herbert Walker (1924-) 41st president of the U.S., 1989-1993. B. served in World War II and entered politics as a Republican. He was elected to the House of Representatives in 1960. In 1973 he became head of the CIA, and between 1981 and 1989 he was vice-president under Ronald Reagan. As president, B. waged the Persian Gulf War against Iraq. A weak economy contributed to his defeat in 1992 by Bill Clinton.

Buxtehude, Dietrich (1637-1707) Swedish composer and organist. In 1668 B. became the organist at Lubeck, where musicians from all over Europe, including the young J.S. Bach, came to hear him play. B.'s compositions greatly influenced Bach.

Byblos Ancient Phoenician city. It was northeast of present-day Beirut in Lebanon. B. had close commercial connections with Egypt as early as the

third millennium BC and remained an important port for thousands of years. It traded in papyruses. The Greeks called books made of papyrus "byblion" after the city, and from that term derives the word "Bible."

Byron, George Gordon Noel (1788-1824) British poet. Born with a club foot, he inherited a baronetcy in 1798. B. wrote satiric and romantic poetry. Among his best-known works are *Childe Harold* (1812), *Manfred* (1817), and *Don Juan* (1819-1824). He became notorious for his relationships with women, including an incestuous affair with his half-sister, Mrs Augusta Leigh. B.'s handsome appearance and colorful life made him a legend of romanticism. He left Britain in 1816 and became interested in the cause of Greek independence. He died in Greece.

George Gordon Noel Byron

Byzantium Greek colony, founded on the Bosporus in the 7th century BC. By the 3d century AD it had degenerated, and Constantine the Great founded (330) a new city in the very same place. He called it Constantinople (now Istanbul) and made it his capital.

Byzantine Empire The Eastern Roman Empire, named after the old city on the site of its capital, Byzantium. The B. began when Emperor Theodosius I divided the Roman Empire between his sons Honorius and Arcadius (395). It came to an end when the Turks captured Constantinople (the former Byzantium) in 1453.

The Caliphs of Córdoba

The Spanish city of Córdoba became the center of a powerful Islamic emirate in the 8th century. Under the Umayyed ruler Abdr el-Rahman III, Córdoba became a caliphate in 929. The city was a wealthy cultural center, tolerant of Christians and Jews. With the start of the Christian Reconquista in the 11th century, Córdoba declined. *See* Córdoba.

1

3

2

1. King Alfonsus I of Spain, who began the Reconquista. *See* Reconquista.
2. The interior of the great mosque in Córdoba, built in the time of the caliphs.
3. A dinar struck during the rule of Caliph Hisjam II.
4. Christian horsemen and infantry fighting during the Reconquista.
5. A decorated ivory vessel used for holding scented water. It was made during the reign of Caliph al-Hakam II, 961-976.
6. Map of the caliphate of Córdoba.

4

5

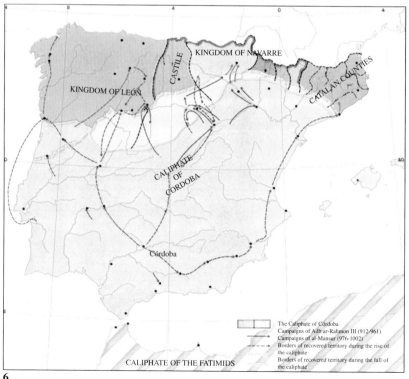

KINGDOM OF NAVARRE

CASTILE

KINGDOM OF LEÓN

CATALAN COUNTIES

CALIPHATE OF CÓRDOBA

Córdoba

CALIPHATE OF THE FATIMIDS

The Caliphate of Córdoba
Campaigns of Adb ar-Rahmon III (912-961)
Campaigns of al-Mansur (976-1002)
Borders of recovered territory during the rise of the caliphate
Borders of recovered territory during the fall of the caliphate

6

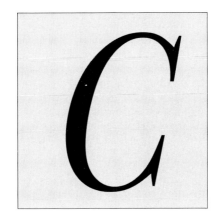

CABAL Initials of the advisers to Charles II of England between 1667 and 1673 (e.g., B=Buckingham). The modern word *cabal* meaning "a conspiratorial group" comes from that period.

Cabeza de Vaca, Alvarez Nuñez (1490-1551) Spanish conquistador. He explored Florida, Texas, and South America.

Cabot, John (c.1450-1499) Explorer for England. Born Giovanni Caboto in Italy, he sailed westward from England in 1497 seeking to reach Asia and discovered the coast of what is now Canada. He sailed to America again in 1498. What happened to him then is not known.

Cabot, Sebastian (c.1476-1557) Explorer for England and Spain. He was the son of John Cabot. C. made voyages of discovery to North and South American under the Spanish and English flags. Later (1553) he became the head of a company that wished to trade with China.

Cabral, Pedro Alvares (c.1467-1520) Portuguese navigator. C. accidentally discovered Brazil (1500) when a storm blew him off course during a voyage to India.

Cadorna, Count Luigi (1850-1928) Italian general. He was the Italian commander during World War I. He was defeated by the Germans and Austrians at Caporetto in 1917.

Caelius One of the seven hills of ancient Rome.

Caesar, Gaius Julius (100-44 BC) Roman statesman and general. In 60 BC, he formed the first triumvirate (three-man joint rule) with Pompey and Crassus. He became consul in the following year. From 58-50 BC, C. conquered Gaul and invaded Britain.

In 49 BC C. initiated the Second Civil War (49-45 BC) and defeated his rival Pompey at Pharsqlus. In 47 BC he conquered Egypt where he established his mistress Cleopatra on the throne. Two years later Caesar was appointed dictator for life. He was assassinated on March 15, 44 BC — "the Ides of March" — by Brutus, Cassius, and others.

Caesarion (47-30 BC) The son of Cleopatra and, probably, Caesar. His formal name was Ptolemy Caesar. He was murdered at the age of seventeen on the orders of Octavian.

Cagoulards A French secret committee of revolutionary action, an extreme right-wing underground organization. The C. were active principally from 1932-1940. They were opposed to the Third Republic and communism and collaborated with the Germans and the Vichy Government in World War II. The name is derived from the French *cagoule* ("hair shirt").

Cahier de doléances At the end of the Ancien Régime in France, the "Letters of Credence" of delegates to the States General that contained the wishes of the voters that elected them.

Cairo Conference (November 1943) Meeting between Roosevelt, Churchill and Chiang Kai-shek to discuss further military steps against Japan in World War II. A second C. took place between Churchill and Roosevelt (December 1943) in an attempt to persuade Turkey to join the Allies.

Calhoun, John Caldwell (1782-1850) American political leader. C. started his career as a strong nationalist. He was one of the "War Hawks," eager for war with Britain at the time of the War of 1812. Later, however, he became an ardent proponent of states' rights. He wrote South Carolina's "Exposition and Protest" in 1830, claiming a state's right to nullify federal laws, and developed a theory justifying slavery. C. held many offices, including secretary of war in Monroe's cabinet (1817-1825), vice president (1829-1832), and, for many years, senator from South Carolina.

Caligula (12-41 AD) 3rd Roman emperor, 37-41 AD. Born Gaius Caesar Germanicus, C. was the son of

Gaius Julius Caesar

Agrippina Major and Germanicus. He was an unpredictable tyrant and was murdered by the Praetorian Guard. "Caligula" means "little boot."

Caligula

Caliph Title of the successors to Muhammad as political and religious leaders of Islam.

Calixtines Moderate Hussites in Bohemia and Moravia. They became part of the Protestant movement with the publication of their *Confessio Bohemica* (1575).

Calixtus I (c.160-222) Pope, 217-222. He extended the granting of absolution to previously unforgivable sinners such as murderers and apostates.

Calixtus II (d.1124) Pope, 1119-1124. Born Guido di Borgogne, he pressured Holy Roman Emperor Henry II to agree to the Concordat of Worms (1122), which ended the investiture struggle by giving the Church the freedom to chose its leaders.

Calixtus III (1378-1458) Pope, 1455-1458. Born Alfonso di Borgia, C. undertook a successful crusade against the Turks. He played a substantial role in the growing power of the Borgias.

Callias (5th century BC) Athenian statesman. C. fought in the Battle of Marathon (490 BC) and was Athens' envoy to Persia. He concluded a treaty (c.449 BC) with Artaxerxes I (Peace of Callias) in which each party agreed to respect the other's area of influence.

Callisthenes (c.360-327 BC) Greek historian. A nephew of Aristotle, C. accompanied Alexander the Great on his expedition to the east but grew critical of him and was accused of conspiracy and executed.

Callistratus (d.c.360 BC) Greek orator and statesman. His speech defending himself against impeachment in 366 BC is said to have inspired Demosthenes.

Calpurnia (d. after 44 BC) Roman matron. She was Caesar's fourth and last wife.

Calvin, John (1509-1564) French Protestant theologian. C. had a Roman Catholic upbringing. While a student in Paris, he came under the influence of humanism and Lutheranism. In 1533 he underwent what he termed a "sudden conversion" and became a Protestant. The next year he began work on *The Institutes of the Christian Religion* (completed 1536), in which he discussed all the aspects of Protestant thought. He rejected papal authority, accepted justification by faith, and set forth the doctrine of predestination. After moving from one city to another several times owing to conflicts, he settled in Geneva in 1541, where he devoted himself to refining his thought and establishing his church. Calvinism became a tremendously influential religion in Western civilization.

Calvo Sotelo, José (1893-1936) Spanish conservative politician. His assassination in 1936 was the immediate cause of the outbreak of the Spanish Civil War.

Cambon, Pierre-Joseph (1756-1820) French statesman and financier. During the French Revolution, C. managed France's finances from 1791-1795. When the Bourbons came back after Napoleon's fall, he was exiled.

Cambon, Pierre-Paul (1843-1924) French diplomat. He helped create the Entente Cordiale with Britain. (1904).

Cambrai, League of (1508) Agreement among Maximilian I of the Holy Roman Empire, King Louis XII of France, King Ferdinand of Aragon, Pope Julius II, and several Italian city states to limit the territorial expansion of Venice.

Cambyses I (6th century BC) King of Ansham in Persia. He was succeeded by his son Cyrus the Great in c.558BC.

Cambyses II (d.521 BC) King of Persia, 529-522 BC. The son of Cyrus the Great, C. conquered Egypt in 525 BC. He may have committed suicide when confronted by a rebellion at home.

Camillus, Marcus Furius (d.365 BC) Roman hero. In 396 BC he conquered the city of Veii (Etruria) and in c.390 BC drove the Gauls out of Rome.

John Calvin

Camisards Protestants peasants from the Cévennes region of France. In 1702 they rebelled unsuccessfully against Louis XIV after Louis had revoked the Edict of Nantes guaranteeing religious freedom. The name refers to the shirts they wore.

Camm, Sir Sydney (1893-1966) British aviation engineer. He designed the Hurricane fighter plane, used in the Battle of Britain, and the Harrier bomber.

Camorra Italian secret society, possibly founded in the 16th century, active in Naples. It was crushed by Mussolini.

Camp David Accords Set of 1978 agreements concluded between Egyptian President Sadat and Israeli Prime Minister Begin with the help of U.S. President Carter at the president's Maryland retreat, Camp David. They included a peace treaty and an Israeli commitment to withdraw from the Sinai and to grant administrative autonomy for the West Bank and the Gaza Strip occupied by Israel. The peace treaty and the withdrawal from Sinai were achieved, as was Palestinian self-determination in Gaza and Jericho (*see* Arafat, Yasser). Begin and Sadat were awarded the Nobel Peace Prize in 1978.

Campo Formio, Peace of *See* Lunéville, Peace of.

Canaan Biblical name for the area west of the Jordan River.

Candic War (1644-1669) Conflict between Turkey and Venice for control of the eastern end of the Mediterranean Sea. The C. was fought around Crete, where the Venetian city of Candia was surrendered to the Turks.

Cannae Ancient village in southern Italy. It was the site of the destruction of a Roman army by Hannibal's Carthaginians in 216 BC.

Canninefates Germanic tribe occupying the Dutch coastal region in the 1st century AD. Together with the Batavi, the C. rose against the Romans in 69 AD. *See* Brinno.

Canute Name of several kings of Denmark, including Canute II the Great (995-1035). From 1016 onward, C.

ruled England and, after the death of his half brother Harald in 1018, Denmark. He managed to regain power over Norway in 1030.

Canute

Capetians French dynasty that succeeded the Merovingians and Carolingians. The C. ruled France from 987 to 1328. The succeeding House of Valois was a branch of the C.

Capitol Fortress on the Capitoline Hill in Rome where the chief temples of Jupiter, Minerva, and Juno stood. The Romans retreated there in 390 BC, after the Gauls had taken most of Rome.

Capitoline One of the seven hills upon which ancient Rome was built.

Caporetto Village in Northern Italy. In World War I, German and Austrian troops inflicted a severe defeat on the Italian army there in October 1917.

Capuchins Roman Catholic order of Franciscan friars. The C. were founded in Italy (1525-1528). They were active in preaching and missionary work and helped the Church regain ground in areas in Europe lost to the Protestants.

Caracalla (188-217). Roman emperor, 211-217. His real name was Marcus Aurelius Antoninus; he was called "Caracalla" because of the Gallic shirt of that name that he often wore. C. murdered many rivals for power. To increase his tax base, he granted Roman citizenship to all freeborn persons in the empire. The Baths of Caracalla were built while he was emperor. He was murdered by Macrinus, his successor, during a campaign against the Parthians.

Carausius, Marcus Aurelius (d.293 AD) Gallic (Belgian) general. He fought against the Germanic tribes in the service of Rome. He proclaimed himself ruler in Britain in c.287 and was assassinated several years later.

Carbonari Members of the Carboneria, an early 19th century movement that advocated political freedom and Italian independence. A similar organization also existed in Spain.

Carlists Supporters of Don Carlos (1788-1855) and his successors as pretenders to the Spanish throne under the Salic Law. Ferdinand VII had abrogated the Salic Law to secure the succession for his daughter Isabella II (1833-1868). The Carlists made several attempts to put their candidates on the throne. Their revolts of 1833, 1840, 1849, 1872, and 1876 all failed.

Carloman II (d.771). Son of Pepin the Short and the younger brother of Charlemagne. After Pepin's death, C. ruled the southern part of his kingdom. When C. died, Charlemagne seized his realm.

Carlson, Chester Floyd (1906-1968) American inventor of the Xerox machine (1938).

Carmina burana Collection of about 275 German and Latin students' poems and songs written in the 13th century. They were found in the monastery of Benediktbeuern. In 1936 German composer Carl Orff made a popular choral work from them.

Carnutes Gallic tribe living in the Seine-Loire region. In 57 BC they were subdued by the Romans, though they rebelled five years later.

Caracalla

Carol I (1839-1914) King of Romania, 1881-1914. Born Karl von Hohenzollern-Sigmaringen, he was a Prussian officer. He was chosen prince of Romania in 1866 and began the modernization of the country. After the 1878 Congress of Berlin made Romania independent, he became king.

Carol II (1893-1953) King of Romania, 1927-1940. The son of Ferdinand I, C. first renounced (1925) the right of succession in favor of his own son Michael, but then had himself proclaimed king in 1927. He was at odds with the Fascist Iron Guard, whose leader, Ion Antonescu, forced him to abdicate in 1940. He died in Portugal.

Carolingians Frankish royal family founded in the 7th century by Pepin of Landen. It is named after Charlemagne.

Carpetbaggers Derogatory term used in the American South after the Civil War to refer to Northerners who came to the South during the Reconstruction period to get rich.

Carrera, José Miguel (1785-1821) Chilean revolutionary. In 1812 he became the first president of Chile, but was forced from office by General Bernardo O'Higgins. In 1814 he fomented a civil war that enabled Spain to regain control of Chile. He was murdered in Argentina to prevent him from reentering Chile.

Carrera, Raphael (1814-1865) Guatemalan leader. A mestizo, he gained power in 1840 and was Guatemala's leading political figure until his death. he was a conservative and restored the influence of the Church.

Carter, Jimmy (James Earl) (1924-) 39th president of the U.S., 1977-1981. Before becoming president, C. was

Jimmy Carter

governor of Georgia (1970-1974). As president, he negotiated the Panama Canal treaty and facilitated the Egyptian-Israeli Camp David Accords. His inability to free the hostages taken by Iran at the American Embassy in Teheran and economic problems contributed to his 1980 defeat by Ronald Reagan.

Carthage Ancient city in North Africa near the present Tunis. It was founded by Phoenician colonists in 814 BC. C. was destroyed in the Third Punic War with Rome 149-146 BC. It was rebuilt and romanized by Augustus. In the 5th

and 6th centuries AD it was the capital of the Vandals. Belisarius captured it for the Byzantine Empire in 533. The Saracens largely destroyed it c.700.

Carthusians Order of monks founded in 1084 at La Grande Chartreuse in France by Bruno of Cologne. The C. form a very austere order, in which life is devoted to seclusion, prayer, and penance. There are also a small number of Carthusian nuns.

Casanova, Giovanni Giacomo (1725-1798) Italian adventurer and writer. He became a celebrity for escaping from the prison of Venice (1756), but is best-known for his *Memoirs* (1826-1838), in which he describes his many travels in Europe and his romantic adventures.

Cassander (c.358-297 BC) King of Macedonia, 318-297 BC. The son of Antipater, one of the Diadochi, he fought his father's successor, Polyperchon, and defended Macedonia against Antigonus I. C. was the murderer of the mother, wife, and young son of Alexander the Great.

Cassatt, Mary (1845-1926) American painter. Born in Pennsylvania, she went to Europe in 1866 and lived in Paris for the rest of her life. Her work was strongly influenced by the French impressionists and by Japanese prints.

Cassius, Gaius Cassius Longinus (d.42 BC) Roman politician and general. After the battle of Pharsala (48 BC), C. left Pompey's camp and joined Caesar. He and Brutus, however, plotted and carried out the assassination of Caesar in 44 BC.

Cassivellaunus (1st century BC) King of the Britons. He led the Britons' resistance against Caesar's Roman invasion in 54 BC.

Castiglione Village in northern Italy. Napoleon's army defeated the Austrians nearby in 1796.

Castle Hill Rising (1804) Prison riot near Sydney, Australia, which caused great fear. The ringleaders were executed.

Castra Vetera Large fortress of the Roman legions near Xanten on the Rhine River. During the major revolt

of 69 AD it fell into the hands of Julius Civilus, who destroyed it.

Castra A Roman military camp that was usually big enough to house one legion. Often these camps later became important cities.

Giovanni Giacomo Casanova

Castro, Fidel (c.1927) Cuban political leader. A lawyer and Communist sympathizer, C. led the movement to oust Cuban dictator Batista that began in the early 1950s. Batista finally fled in January 1959. C. and the Cuban Communist Party have ruled Cuba since then, and Cuba and the U.S. have been at odds. With the collapse of the Soviet Union in 1991, Cuba has been isolated internationally.

Fidel Castro

Catacombs Underground caverns and tunnels. In the Roman period the catacombs of Rome were used by the Christians as burial places for their dead. They also served as a refuge in times of persecution.

Catalaunian Fields Area near Troyes, France, where a great battle took place

Medieval Castles

2

Among the fascinating legacies of the Middle Ages are the many medieval castles scattered throughout Europe and parts of North Africa. These impressive buildings formerly belonged to kings, knights, and nobles and often housed many people.
A few examples are shown here.

The Medieval Castle
KEEP
Trapdoor
Battlements
Machicolate
Sleeping rooms
GATEWAY
Great hall
Gallery
Defence wall
Portcullis
Waiting room and chapel
COURT YARD
Escape gate
Store room
Draw bridge
Dungeon
Well
Moat

1

3

4

5

1. Medieval castles were often located on strategically favorable locations. They served not only defense purposes, but were also used as housing. This is a cross-section of a medieval castle.
2. The castle of Falaise in France, which dates from the 11th century. William the Conqueror was born there. *See* William the Conqueror.
3. A page from the celebrated 15th-century book of hours *Les très riches heures de Duc de Berry*, showing a castle of the period in its full splendor.
4. This is the castle at Pontferrada, built for the Knights Templar. *See also* Knights Templar.
5. The castle of Eltz is strategically situated on a bend of the Eltz River in Germany. It once belonged to a family of river pirates.

in 451 BC in which the Romans led by Aetius defeated the Huns led by Attila.

Catalina, Lucius Sergius (Cataline) (c.108-63 BC) Roman politician, who conspired to overthrow the Roman Republic in 63 BC. The conspiracy was discovered by Cicero and the rebel army crushed. Catalina was killed.

Cateau-Cambrésis, Peace of 1559 between France, England, and Spain. It ended the Italian Wars between France and Spain by acknowledging Spanish hegemony in Italy.

Catesby, Robert (1573-1605) English Catholic aristocrat. He organized a conspiracy against James I of England (1605). He was executed; *see* Gunpowder Plot.

Catharine of Aragon (1485-1536) Queen of England, 1509-1533. The daughter of Ferdinand of Aragon and

Catharine of Aragon

Isabella of Castille, in 1501 she married Arthur, the oldest son of Henry VII of England. After he died in 1502, she married his brother, who became Henry VIII. C. gave birth to Henry's daughter Mary Tudor in 1516. In 1527 Henry fell in love with Anne Boleyn. His desire to annul the marriage with C. contributed eventually to England's break with the Roman Catholic Church. After the break with Rome, the marriage was annulled.

Cathars Medieval religious movement in Europe. They believed in a dualistic universe, with God and

Satan in conflict. The C. were persecuted and largely wiped out by the 15th century.

Cathay Medieval name for China, derived from the name of the Khitai, a nomadic Manchurian people.

Cather, Willa (1876-1947) American writer. Born in Virginia, she grew up in Nebraska. C. is considered one of the greatest American novelists. She wrote of pioneer life in *O Pioneers!* (1913) and *My Antonia* (1918), the growth of an artist in *The Song of the Lark* (1915), and colonial New Mexico in *Death Comes for the Archbishop* (1927), thought by many to be her best work.

Catherine I (1684-1727) Czarina of Russia, 1725-1727. A peasant, she became the mistress of Peter the Great, who married her in 1712 after divorcing his first wife. He made her joint ruler, and she retained power after his death in 1725.

Catherine II, the Great (1729-1796) Czarina of Russia, 1762-1796. A German princess, she married the heir to the throne, Peter, in 1744. He became czar in 1762 but was soon murdered. C. took power in the same year. She encouraged the arts and corresponded with French Enlightenment figures such as Diderot and Voltaire. C. began her rule as a reformer but became more conservative and strengthened the powers of both the central government and the nobility. C. also increased Russia's stature internationally.

Catherine de Medici (1519-1589) Queen of France, 1547-1559. The daughter of Lorenzo II, Duke of Urbino, she married the future Henry II of France in 1533 and was regent for their second son, Charles IX. C. was a fierce opponent of the Huguenots and helped instigate the Massacre of St. Bartholomew's Day in 1572.

Catherine Howard (d.1542) Queen of England, 1540-1542. Henry VIII married her, his fifth wife, after his divorce from Anne of Cleves. She was beheaded on suspicion of adultery.

Catherine Parr (1512-1548) Queen of England, 1543. Twice widowed, she became the sixth and last wife of Henry VIII in 1543 and was regent in

1544. She married again in 1547 but died in childbirth.

Catherine of Siena, Saint (1347-1380) Italian mystic. She had visions since childhood and devoted herself to caring for the poor and sick. C. was also a skilled diplomat. She helped bring an end to the Babylonian Captivity of the Papacy (1376).

Cato, the Elder, Marcus Porcius (234-149 BC) Roman political leader and writer. A conservative, he was devoted to the old Roman ways. C. warned continuously about the growing might of Carthage.

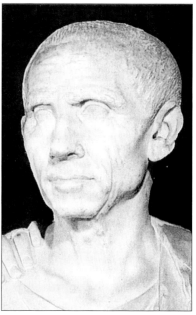

Marcus Porcius Cato

Catherina de Medici

Cato the Younger, Marcus Porcius (95-46 BC) Roman political leader. The grandson of Cato the Elder and like him a conservative, he was an opponent of Caesar and a supporter of Pompey. C. committed suicide after losing the battle of Thapsus to Caesar in North Africa.

Cato Street Conspiracy An 1819 conspiracy organized by the English eccentric radical Arthur Thistlewood (1774-1820) to assassinate the entire British cabinet. The plot was uncovered and the conspirators arrested at their Cato Street arsenal and later executed.

Catulus, Caius Lutatius Roman consul. He brought the First Punic War with Carthage to an end by annihilating the Carthaginian fleet at the Aegates Islands in 241 BC.

Catulus, Quintus Lutatius (d.87 BC) Roman consul. Together with Marius, beat the Germanic Cimbri near Vercelli in 101 BC. During the Social War he was an ally of Sulla but either committed suicide or was killed in 87 BC.

Catullus, Caius Valerius (c.84-54 BC) Roman lyric poet. About 100 of his poems are extant. Best known are the love poems addressed to Lesbia.

Caudillo Spanish for "army chief." The word is used for various South American revolutionary leaders. In Spain, General Francisco Franco also used it.

Cavaliers Name of the supporters of Charles I during the English Civil War (1642-1649). The Tories later emerged from this party. See Roundheads.

Caxton, William (c.1422-1491) English printer. While serving as consul-general in Bruges in 1474, Caxton had his book *Recuyell of the Historyes of Troye* printed, the first book printed in English. When he returned to England, C. continued to print books, about 100 in all.

Ceausescu, Nicolae (1918-1989) Romanian political leader. Of peasant birth, he joined the Communist Party in the 1930s. C. became party leader and president of Romania in 1965. His rule was marked by economic disruption, repression, and the glorifica-

Nicolae Ceausescu

tion of his own personality. Following the 1989 revolution, he was arrested and executed.

Celsius, Anders (1701-1744) Swedish astronomer. In 1742 he invented the Celsius, or centigrade, thermometer, which divides the difference between the freezing and boiling points of water into 100 degrees.

Celtic Iberians Celtic peoples who began settling in Spain in the 4th century BC, merging with the Iberians. Between 195-133 BC they waged war against the Romans, but were suppressed.

Celts Indo-germanic tribes inhabiting the area of the Danube and Rhine Rivers in the second millennium BC. They moved into France, northern Italy, and the British isles, among other territories, and brought with them an iron culture. In the east and north, the C. were displaced by Scythians and Germanic tribes. In France, they were conquered in c.50 BC by Caesar. The Celtic civilization survived only in Ireland. Much of their folklore was absorbed into other cultures.

Censors The highest magistrates in the Roman Republic. They enumerated the population, which gave them the power to levy taxes and assign military service. They also controlled public works and filled vacancies in the Senate.

Central Intelligence Agency (CIA) The main intelligence-gathering agency of the U.S. government. It was created by the 1947 National Security Act. The director of the CIA is appointed by the president and confirmed by the Senate.

Central Powers Term used to refer to Germany, Austria-Hungary, Turkey, and Bulgaria in World War I.

Centumviri Law courts in ancient Rome.

Centurion (hundredman) Officer in the Roman army who led 100 soldiers. Each Roman legion had 60 centurions.

Ceres See Demeter.

Cervantes Saavedra, Miguel de (1547-1616) Spanish writer. He led a very adventurous life as a soldier, a slave to Barbary pirates, and a businessman. His best-known work today is *Don Quixote* (1605), in which an impover-

Miguel de Cervantes Saavedra

ished eccentric roams as a knight errant through the Spanish countryside having all manner of adventures. One of the greatest works in Western literature, it can be interpreted as a satire on illusions, as a discussion of idealism and realism, and in other ways. C. also wrote plays, stories, and poetry.

Chabrier, Alexis Emmanuel (1841-1894) French composer. He wrote piano pieces, colorful orchestral works including *Espana* (1883), and operas.

Chaco War (1929-1935) War between Paraguay and Bolivia over the dispute Gran Chaco region in central South America. More than 100,000 lives were lost in the fighting. A treaty in 1938 finally gave Paraguay most of the territory and Bolivia an outlet to the sea.

Chaeronea Ancient city in Boeotia. Greece. In 338 BC the Thebans and the Athenians were defeated there by Philip II of Macedonia. There also Mithradates VI of Pontus was defeated by the Roman under Sulla in 86 BC.

Chalchiuhtlicue Aztec goddess of the waters.

Chaldeans Semitic people who settled after 1000 BC in southern Babylonia and in 625 BC assumed power under Nabopolassar. Under Nebuchadnezzar II their empire achieved great power and wealth. The empire was conquered by Cyrus the Great in 538 BC.

Chalybes People living south of the Black Sea, who c.1500 BC invented the tempering of iron.

Chalid ibn al-Walid (d.642) Arabian general. He was one of the most faithful allies of the prophet Muhammad. In 636 he defeated an army of the Byzantine Emperor Heraclius near the Jarmuk River, and he also conquered Palestine.

Chalturin, Stepan (1856-1882) Russian revolutionary who assassinated Tsar Alexander II in 1881.

Jean-François Champollion

Chamberlain, Austen Sir (1863-1937) British political leader. A Conservative, he held many cabinet positions and became Conservative leader in 1921. For his part in achieving the Locarno Pact (1925), he was awarded the Nobel Peace Prize. His half-brother was Neville Chamberlain.

Chamberlain, Neville (1869-1940) British political leader. At the age of 50, he entered Parliament as a Conservative. C. was chancellor of the exchequer and minister of health before becoming prime minister in 1937. Until 1939 he believed in appeasement and concluded the Munich Agreement with Hitler in 1938. He resigned in May 1940 and was succeeded by Churchill.

Chambers, Whittaker (1901-1961) American Communist and writer. He joined the Communist Party in 1925 and spied for the Soviet Union. C. broke with the party in 1939, and after World War II named others before a congressional committees as Communists and spies, notably Alger Hiss, who denied the charges. After leaving the party, Chambers moved to the right politically and worked as a journalist.

Champa Vietnamese kingdom of the Cham people (2nd-17th centuries). It frequently warred with the Chinese and the Khmers. It was conquered by the Kingdom of Annam in the 17th century.

Champa Empire *See* Le Thanh Tong.

Champlain, Samuel de (1567-1635) French explorer. He first sailed to America in 1603 and explored the St. Lawrence River. In 1608 he founded Quebec in what became Canada.

Champollion, Jean-François (1790-1832) French Egyptologist. He founded the science of Egyptology. With the aid of the Rosetta Stone and the study of Coptic, C. was able to begin deciphering Egyptian hicroglyphics in 1821.

Chancellorsville Town in Virginia. During the the American Civil War, the Confederates under Lee defeated

Neville Chamberlain

a Union army under Hooker there in May 1863. The great Confederate general Stonewall Jackson was killed in the battle, however.

Samuel de Champlain

Chandragupta (d.c.298) Indian emperor. He founded the Mauryan dynasty empire and defeated Seleucus I in c.305 BC. One tradition says he abdicated, became a monk, and fasted to death.

Changamira Dombo I *See* Rozwi.

Chaplin, Charlie (Sir Charles Spencer Chaplin) (1889-1977) British actor, filmmaker, and composer. Born in London, he lived for a time in an orphanage. C. came to the U.S. at the age of 17. He soon became a silent film star, portraying a wistful tramp. His greatest films are *City Lights* (1928), *Modern Times* (1936), *The Great Dictator* (1940), and *Limelight* (1952). C. was knighted in 1975.

Chapultepec Hill near Mexico City. There, General Winfield Scott won the decisive American victory in the war between Mexico and the U.S. (1846-1847).

Charette de la Contrie, François-Athanase (1763-1796) Leader of the royalist revolutionaries in the Vendée during the French Revolution. He was captured and executed.

Charlemagne (Charles the Great or Charles I) (c.742-814) Emperor of the

The Celts

The Celts were a group of peoples speaking Indo-European languages who spread throughout Europe after 2000 BC. They developed the most important Iron Age culture of Europe and were very skilled craftsmen, especially in metalwork.
Their artwork is characterized by intricate, interweaving geometric patterns. Although the Celts were also skilled fighters, they were pushed out of what is now Germany by Germanic tribes in c.400 BC.
See Celts.

1

2

4

3

1. A page from the *Book of Kells*, an Irish 8th-century illustrated manuscript of the Gospels in Latin. *The Book of Kells* is considered the finest extant Celtic illustrated book.
2. Two pieces of Celtic beak pottery.
3. An early medieval Celtic cross from Ireland.
4. Celtic jewelry, dating from the 5th century BC.
In the foreground, a golden torque that was worn around the neck.

West, 800-814, and king of the Franks, 768-814. The son of Pepin III, C. reorganized the Frankish kingdom following the death of his brother Carloman in 771 and extended it, and Christianity, eastward to the Elbe and Danube Rivers. He was crowned emperor by Pope Leo III in 800. Unable to read himself, C. nevertheless respected learning and kept a circle of scholars at his court in Aachen.

Charles the Great or Charles I

Charles I (1600-1649) King of England, 1625-1649. One of the Stuart kings, C. was the son of James I. He repeatedly came into conflict with Parliament. The conflict led to the English Civil War, 1641-1649, which began when C. attempted to imprison the leaders of the parliamentary opposition. In 1646 the Scottish army captured C. and handed him over to parliamentary leaders. He escaped but was recaptured in 1648. Parlia-

ment tried and convicted him of treason. C. was beheaded in 1649.

Charles I (1887-1922) Emperor of Austria, 1916-1918, and, as Charles III, king of Hungary, 1916-1918. The son of Archduke Otto of Hapsburg, C. succeeded his uncle Franz Joseph as the last emperor of Austria and king of Hungary. He tried in vain to secure a separate peace treaty with Allies in World War I. C. was forced to abdicate in 1918.

Charles I King of Spain. *See* Charles V, Holy Roman emperor

Charles II the Bald (823-877) Emperor of the West, 875-877, and king of the Franks, 843-877. The son of Louis the Pious, he acquired the western part of the Frankish empire through the Verdun Treaty of Partition (843). In 870 with the Treaty of Meersen, he added a part of the central kingdom, Lorraine, which he shared with his half brother Louis the German.

Charles II (1630-1685) King of England, 1660-1685. The son of Charles I, he fled to the continent in 1646. After his father's execution, he was crowned king of Scotland (1651). The same year he entered England but was defeated by Oliver Cromwell at Worcester (1651) and again fled to the continent. In 1660, however, he was accepted back in England as king and reigned in what is termed the Restoration. He wished to pursue a more tolerant policy toward religious differences than Parliament would permit. C. was personally popular. He died a Roman Catholic. He had many mistresses but no legitimate children. He was succeeded by his brother James.

Charles II (1661-1700) King of Spain, 1665-1700. Son and successor of Philip IV, C. was the last of the Spanish Hapsburgs. He was crippled and mentally retarded. Real power was exercised by his mother, Mariana of Austria. During C.'s reign, Spain declined. He died without heir and wanted Philip of Anjou to succeed him as Philip V. This led to the War of the Spanish Succession.

Charles III the Fat (839-888) Emperor of the West, 881-887, king of the East Franks, 882-887, and king of the

West Franks, 884-887. The son of Louis the German, he was a weak ruler. He briefly reunited Charlemagne's empire but was deposed in 887.

Charles III (1716-1788) King of Spain. 1759-1788, and of Naples and Sicily, 1735-1759. The son of Philip V, he succeeded his half brother Ferdinand VI on the Spanish throne and then gave up the throne of Naples and Sicily. (between 1734-1759). C. was an enlightened monarch. He limited the power of the Church and the Inquisition and banned the Jesuits from Spain (1767).

Charles IV (1316-1378) Holy Roman emperor, 1355-1378, German king, 1355-1378, and king of Bohemia, 1346-1378. The son of John of Luxembourg, he founded the University of Prague (1348). C. issued the Golden Bull in 1356, which determined the process for choosing the Holy Roman emperor.

Charles V, the Wise (1338-1380) King of France, 1364-1380. Following the battle of Maupertuis (1356) during which his father, John II the Good, was captured by the English, C. became regent. During this period he was confronted with a peasant revolt (*see* Jacquerie). After C. became king, he regained almost all the territory France had lost to England.

Charles V (1500-1558) Holy Roman emperor, 1519-1558, and Charles I, king of Spain, 1516-1556. The Son of

Charles V

Philip the Handsome and Joanna the Mad, he ruled over the Netherlands and Burgundy from 1515. In 1516 C. succeeded his grandfather Ferdinand of Aragon in Spain, and in 1519 his grandfather Maximilian of Austria as Holy Roman emperor. C. tried in vain to restore royal power in Germany and to repress the Reformation. Under his rule Spain became an important colonial power. He fought many wars with François I of France. In 1556 he retired to the monastery at Yuste. The kingship of Spain and its possessions was transferred to his son Philip II in 1555-1556; the Holy Roman Empire was formally transferred too. In Germany he was formally succeeded by his brother, Ferdinand I in 1558.

Charles VI (1685-1740) Holy Roman emperor, 1711-1740, king of Bohemia, 1711-1740, and, as Charles III, king of Hungary 1712-1740. He successfully waged war against the Ottoman Empire (1716-1718) but lost the Polish War of Succession (1733-1738).

Charles VII (1403-1461) King of France, 1422-1461. He was the son and successor of the mentally ill Charles VI. During C.'s reign, the Hundred Years War ended and the English were largely driven out of France. (See Joan of Arc).

Charles IX (1550-1574) King of France, 1560-1574. The second son of Henry II and Catherine de Medici, C. succeeded his brother, Francis II. His reign was strongly influenced by his mother and by the Huguenot leader Coligny. His mother persuaded him to authorize the St. Bartholomew's Day massacre in which Coligny and thousands of other Huguenots were killed.

Charles X (1622-1660) King of Sweden, 1654-1660. He became king when Queen Christina abdicated and fought wars that, after his death, resulted in Sweden gaining lands from Denmark in agreements made by his son and successor Charles XI (1655-1697).

Charles XII (1682-1718) King of Sweden 1697-1718. The son and successor of Charles XI, he was a brilliant general and is regarded in Sweden as a great hero. Despite many amazing

feats, however, he left Sweden weaker than it had been when he became king.

Charles XIV (1763-1844) King of Sweden and Norway, (1818-1844). Born Jean-Baptiste Bernadotte, he was a French general who served under Napoleon. Napoleon was influential in having him made crown prince of Sweden (1810). Nevertheless in 1813 C. joined the coalition against Napoleon and in 1814 conquered Norway for Sweden. He succeeded to the Swedish throne in 1818.

Charles Albert (1798-1849) King of Sardinia, 1831-1849. He succeeded Charles Felix. He granted a constitution in 1848. Having lost battles to Austria at Custozza (1848) and Novara (1849), C. abdicated in favor of his son, Victor Emmanuel II, and went into exile in Portugal.

Charles Edward Stuart *See* Stuart, Charles Edward.

Charles Martel (c.688-741) Illegitimate son of the Frankish king Pepin II. He governed the Frankish kingdom from 719, although he never formally became king. At Tours in 732, he defeated the Moors under Abd el-Rahman who were advancing from Spain. C. was the grandfather of Charlemagne.

Charles the Bold (1433-1477) Duke of Burgundy, 1467-1477. The son and successor of Philip the Good, he was the last reigning duke of Burgundy. He opposed the increasing power of King Louis XI of France. For a time he was allied with England. Attempting to link his separate possessions, he went to war with the Swiss in 1474 but was killed in battle at Nancy three years later. He was succeeded by his daughter Maria of Burgundy, who, however, lost her power through war and marriage.

Charlotte of Bourbon (1546-1582) Daughter of Duke Louis of Bourbon, who fled from France in 1572 and converted to Protestantism. She married William of Orange in 1575 and died in Antwerp in 1582.

Charta 77 Human rights and dissident movement in Czechoslovakia, set up in 1977 when 241 prominent Czechs signed a manifesto calling for the civil rights and freedoms guaranteed in the

1975 Helsinki Final Act to be respected. The Communist Czechoslovakian government attempted to suppress C. by force. When the Communist regime fell in 1989, the leader of C., Vaclav Havel, became president of Czechoslovakia.

Charles VII

Charte Institutionelle Constitution promulgated by Louis XVIII of France in 1814 when he took power after Napoleon had been exiled to Elba.

Chattanooga City in Tennessee. During the American Civil War, General

China's Early Dynasties

China's civilization is one of the oldest
in the world. Its history goes back more than 4000
years, when the people of China already were
writing, producing
silk, and playing
dominoes.

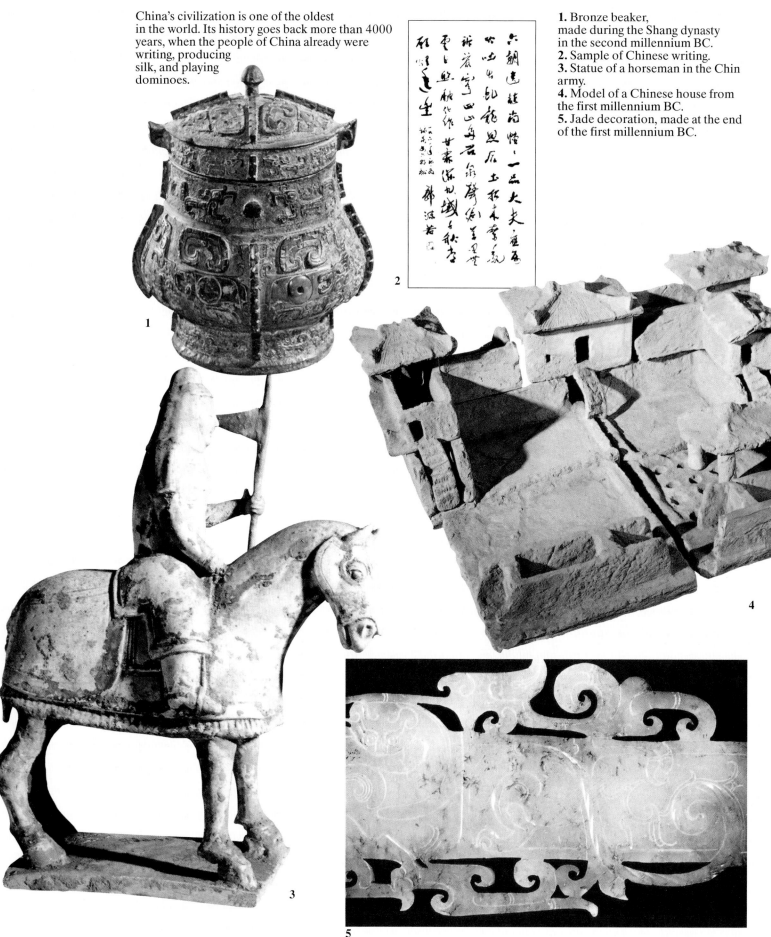

1. Bronze beaker,
made during the Shang dynasty
in the second millennium BC.
2. Sample of Chinese writing.
3. Statue of a horseman in the Chin
army.
4. Model of a Chinese house from
the first millennium BC.
5. Jade decoration, made at the end
of the first millennium BC.

Grant won an important victory for the North there in November 1863.

Chatti Germanic tribe that lived in the Fulda and Eder area of modern Germany. Frequently in revolt (for example, AD 162 and 213), the C. were never really subjugated by the Romans.

Chaucer, Geoffrey (c.1343-1400) English poet. One of the greatest medieval writers, C. was born in London and served as a soldier and diplomat. His early works were influenced by French and Italian models. His greatest work is the unfinished *Canterbury Tales* (1387-1400), short stories in Middle English verse that give a good picture of 14th century English society.

Geoffrey Chaucer

Cheka The secret police founded in Communist Russia (later renamed the Soviet Union) in 1918 during the civil war. The name is the Russian acronym for All-Russian Extraordinary Commission for the Suppression of Counterrevolution and Sabotage. The Soviet secret police underwent numerous name changes in succeeding years, among them GPU, OGPU, NKVD, and KGB. It ran the huge network of prison and labor camps in the country.

Cheops (27th century BC) King of Egypt. The founder of the 4th dynasty, C. built near Gizeh the largest pyramid.

Chephren (26th century BC) 4th dynasty Egyptian king. He was a son of Cheops and had his pyramid built in Gizeh near that of his father. His face may be represented on the Sphinx.

Chernobyl City in the former Soviet Union where a nuclear reactor exploded on April 26, 1986, releasing a massive radioactive cloud that contaminated part of Europe.

Cherokee *See* Five Civilized Tribes.

Cheyenne Native American tribe. Formerly farmers in present-day Minnesota, they moved westward in the 17th century. When they acquired horses in the 18th century, they became buffalo hunters. The C. were less hostile to whites than some other tribes, but an unprovoked massacre at Sand Creek in Colorado (1864) led to a war that ended with their surrender in 1877. *See* Custer.

Chiang Kai-shek (1887-1975) Chinese military leader and political leader. C. participated in Sun Yat-sen's revolution against the Manchus in 1911. He became the leader of the Quomintang (Nationalist Party) after Sun's death in 1925. C. fought against Japan in World War II but lost the civil war to the Communists in the late 1940s. He and the Nationalist government fled to Taiwan in 1949.

Chiang Kai-shek

Chicherin, Georgi Vasiliyevich (1872-1936) Soviet Russian diplomat. C. succeeded Trotsky as Foreign Commissar in 1918. He negotiated the Treaty of Rapallo with Germany in 1922 and was succeeded by Litvinov in 1930.

Chickamauga, Battle of A battle of the American Civil War (September 1863) in which a Union army under Rosecrans was defeated by Confederates under by Bragg.

Chickasaw *See* Five Civilized Tribes.

Childebert I (d.558) Merovingian king. The son of Clovis I, whose kingdom he and his three brothers inherited (511). He fought wars against the Visigoths.

Childebert II (570-595) King of Austrasia, 575-595, and King Burgundy (593-595). The son of Sigebert and Brunhild, his mother actually governed for him.

Childebert III (c.683-711) King of Austrasia. The son of Theodoric, his kingdom was actually governed by the mayor of the palace, Pepin II.

Childeric I (c.436-481) Merovingian king. Little is known of him except that he was an ally of Rome against the Visigoths and the father of Clovis.

Childeric III (d.755) The last Merovingian king, he was deposed by Pepin III in 751 and became a monk.

Children's Crusade Disastrous crusade in 1212 from Marseille to the Holy Land by French and Germans. The word *puer* ("child") for the participants in the crusade refers actually to the social status of the participants and has given rise to the misapprehension that the C. was carried out by children. Some sources say the participants were sold into slavery. *See* Crusades.

Chilperic I (d.584) King of Neustria, 561-584. A Merovingian, he fought his brother Sigebert and later Sigebert's widow Brunhild for Neustria. He was assassinated, probably by Brunhild.

Chimu Ancient Peruvian civilization on the Pacific coast. The capital was Chan Chan. It was conquered by the Inca under Topa Inca Yupanqui in c.1460.

Chin or Tsin Chinese dynasty that ruled from AD 265 to 420.

Chi'ng or Manchu Chinese dynasty that ruled from 1644 to 1912. The

Childebert III

Manchu were a Mongolian people who invaded China and captured Beijing in 1644. They ruled until overthrown by Sun-Yat-sen's republican movement.

Church State State within Italy controlled by the Vatican from the Middle Ages until 1970.

CIA *See* Central Intelligence Agency.

Chlodwig *See* Clovis.

Chlotar I (d.561) Merovingian king and youngest son of Clovis I, whose kingdom was partitioned among C. and his brothers (511). He subsequently conquered Thuringia, Burgundy, and Provence. In 558 he ruled for a short time over the entire kingdom of the Franks.

Chmielnicki, Bogdan (1595-1657) Hetman (leader) of Ukraine. He joined the Cossacks and led a revolt against the Poles in 1648. For protection against Poland, he led Ukraine into a protectorate under Russia in 1654. C. became notorious for killing tens of thousands of Jews in eastern Poland.

Choctaw *See* the Five Civilized Tribes.

Frederick Francis Chopin

Chopin, Frederick Francis (1810-1849) Polish pianist and composer. Chopin lived mainly in France. He is one of the greatest composers for the piano and wrote little for other instruments. Virtually every pianist plays C.'s waltzes, nocturnes, ballads, preludes, polonaises, sonatas, and other pieces.

Chorsabad Site in Iraq that was the capital city of the Assyrian King Sargon II.

Chou En-lai (Zhou En-lai) (1898-1976) Chinese political leader. Born into a Mandarin family, Chou was imprisoned for his radical activities as a young man. He was a founder of the Chinese Communist Party c.1922. He took part in the Communists' Long March in 1934-1935. When the Communists came to power in China in 1949, C. became premier (1949-1976) and foreign minister (1949-1958). It is believed he was largely responsible for China's willingness to improve ties with the West in the 1970s.

Chrétien de Troyes (d.1180) French poet. He wrote the first notable treatments of the King Arthur legends. C.'s works such as *Lancelot* and the unfinished *Conte du Graal* greatly influenced the chivalric poets Hartmann of Aue and Wolfram of Esschenbach.

Christian IV (1577-1648) King of Denmark, 1588-1648. He took part in the Thirty Years' War on the Protestant side from 1625-1629 but was defeated. He also had little success in his war with Sweden of 1643-1645, in which Denmark lost provinces in Norway.

Christian X (1870-1947) King of Denmark, 1912-1947. He granted a new constitution in 1915 that gave women the vote. During World War II C. was the symbol of resistance to the Germans in occupied Denmark. The Germans placed him under house arrest.

Christian of Anhalt (1568-1630) Prince of Anhalt, 1603-1630. He led the Protestant Union during the Thirty Years War but was badly defeated at the Battle of the White Mountain, near Prague, in 1620.

Christiansen, Friedrich Christian (1879-1972) German military leader. C. was the commander of the German troops in the Netherlands from 1940-1945. He was convicted of war crimes in 1948 but was pardoned in 1951.

Christophe, Henri (1767-1820) Haitian revolutionary leader. A former

Chou En-lai

slave, he participated in the revolution that freed Haiti in the early 1800s. C. proclaimed himself king in 1811. Having ruled as an absolute despot, he committed suicide during a popular revolt.

Chuans Smugglers and farmers in the Normandy and Brittany regions of France. Named after their emblem (*chuan* means "night owl"), the C. opposed the French Revolution and were associated with the royalist insurrection in the Vendée. In the 19th century, the C. were supporters of the Bourbons.

Churchill, Sir Winston Leonard Spencer (1874-1965) British soldier, political leader, and writer. After mili-

Sir Winston Leonard Spencer Churchill

tary training at Sandhurst, C. became a war correspondent in Africa during the Boer War. He entered politics in 1900 and occupied increasingly important posts. Differences of opinion caused him to join the Conservative, the Liberal and again the Conservative party. He served as prime minister during World War II, from 1940 to 1945, when he rallied the British people to resist the Nazis, and again from 1951 to 1955. C. wrote distinguished works of history, including *The Second World War* (1948-1953) and *a History of the English-Speaking Peoples* (1956-1958).

Ciano, Count Galeazzo (1903-1944) Italian diplomat. In 1930 he married Mussolini's daughter Edda, and served as foreign minister from 1936 to 1943. After breaking with Mussolini in 1943, the Germans arrested him and he was convicted of high treason and executed.

Christianity's Rise in the West

The first Christians in the early Roman Empire were a persecuted minority. The conversion of Emperor Constantine I in 312, however, initiated the success of Christianity in Europe.

1. A fresco of a praying Christian, dating from the 3rd century AD.
2. Emperor Constantine I, who had himself baptized and ended the persecution of Christians in the Roman Empire. *See* Constantine I, the Great.
3. The evangelist Mark, who wrote one of the New Testament Gospels some 100 years after Christ's death.
4. The spread of Christianity in the Roman Empire.

5. Catacomb in Rome. Originally these were collective Christian graves, but in times of persecution they functioned as churches.

6. Mural from one of the catacombs in Rome depicting Christians commemorating the Last Supper.

7. An illustration from a 10th-century manuscript showing the baptism of Christ.

8. A central concept in Christianity is the belief in heaven or hell after death. Here, an angel and the devil weigh a person's soul.

5

6

7

8

Cicero, Marcus Tullius (106-43 BC) Roman political leader and philosopher. Appointed consul in 63 BC, C. exposed and thwarted the conspiracy of Catalina. The speeches he gave in the Senate on the conspiracy are studied by Latin students today. He supported Pompey during the civil war. Though pardoned by Pompey's opponent Caesar, who won the civil war, C. was the enemy of Caesar's follower. After Caesar's assassination, Marc Antony had C. arrested and executed. In addition to many notable speeches, C. wrote interesting letters and works of Stoic philosophy.

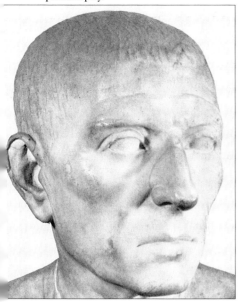

Marcus Tullius Cicero

Cid Campeador (Rodrigo Diaz de Vivar) (c.1043-1099). Spanish heroic soldier. He fought against and with the Moors and ruled Valencia from 1094 till his death. C. is the subject of the Spanish epic, *The Song of the Cid.*

Cimbri Germanic tribe from Jutland. At the end of the 1st century BC, they moved south. In 105 BC they defeated the Romans at Arausio (Orange). The Roman military commander Marius smashed the C., however, at Vercelli (101 BC).

Cimmerians Indo-European nomadic people from Southern Russia. The C. invaded Anatolia c.750 BC and destroyed the Phrygian Empire. In 637 or 626 BC the C. were driven out of Anatolia by the Lydian prince Alyattes.

Cimon (d.449 BC) Athenian political leader. The son of Miltiades, he and Aristides led the Athenians against the Persians. Later he was the head of the pro-Spartan party in Athens. C. was exiled but recalled in 451 BC to make peace with Sparta. He died while attacking Citium in Cyprus.

Cincinnatus, Lucius Quintus (5th century BC) Roman hero. According to legend, C. repeatedly left his farm to save Rome during crises. After the crises were over, he returned to his farm.

Cincinnatus, Society of the American patriotic organization. It was formed in 1783 by officer veterans of the American Revolution. George Washington was its first president. During the 1790s it was attacked by some as being too aristoctatical.

Cinq-Mars, Henri, Marquis of (1620-1642) Protégé of King Louis XIII of France and officer in his bodyguard. Together with Gaston of Orléans, the king's brother, C. conspired against Cardinal Richelieu. He was arrested and executed in Lyons.

Circassians A nomadic and warlike people in the northern Caucasus. They became Muslims in the 17th century and fought the Russians throughout the nineteenth.

Cistercians Monastic order founded in 1098 in Citeaux (Cistercium), France. The C. wanted to revive the ideals of the Benedictines. Their white habits led to their being called the White Monks. St. Bernard of Clairvaux was a notable Cistercian.

Citizen King Term sometimes used to refer to King Louis Phillipe of France.

Civilian Conservation Corps (CCC) Agency established in 1933 during U.S. President Franklin D. Roosevelt's New Deal. The CCC employed young men in conservation and road building. It was ended in 1942.

Civilis, Julius (AD first century) Batavian chief. C. led a great revolt against the Romans in 69-70 AD, which was ultimately put down by the general Cerialis.

Civil War, English *See* English Civil War.

Civil War, U.S. *See* American Civil War.

Clarendon Constitutions Sixteen articles of law promulgated in January 1164 by Henry II of England. They defined the relationship between the Church and the monarchy.

Clark, George Rogers (1752-1818) American general. Born in Virginia and the older brother of William Clark, C. led expeditions during the American Revolution against British strongholds in the Northwest. He heroically led a force through flooded lands to recapture the outpost of Vincennes in 1779.

Clark, William (1770 1838) American explorer. A Virginia-born army officer and the younger brother of George Rogers Clark, C. and Meriwether Lewis led the great expedition (1802-1806) that President Jefferson sent to explore the Missouri and Columbia Rivers. Later he fought in the War of 1812 and was superintendent of Indian affairs. *See* Lewis and Clark Expedition.

Classicism Movement in literature and the visual arts inspired by classical antiquity. C. originated in France in the second half of the 17th century and spread to influence art and literature throughout Europe. It is characterized by harmony, clarity, order, and austerity of composition. Well-known representatives of C. are the sculptors Girardon and Croisevoix, the architects Perault and Van Campen, the painter Poussin, and the writers Molière and Racine.

Claudius I (Tiberius Claudius Drusus Nero Germanicus) (10 BC-54 AD)

Claudius I

Roman emperor, AD 41-54. C. was proclaimed successor to Caligula by the Praetorian Guard. He made Britain a Roman province. During his reign public administration was reorganized, giving the provinces more power and reducing that of the Senate, with which he had a troubled relationship. His third wife was Messalina, whom he executed. His fourth wife was Agrippina Minor, whose son Nero he adopted as his successor and who may have had him poisoned.

Clausewitz, Karl von (1780-1831) Prussian general and military strategist. After serving in the Napoleonic Wars, in 1818 C. became the director of the War College in Berlin. His posthumous work *On War* is still studied today. C. stressed that war is the continuation of diplomacy by other means and originated the concept of "total war."

Clay, Henry (1777-1852) American political leader. Born in Virginia, C. represented Kentucky in both the U.S. House of Representatives, where was at times Speaker, and the Senate for many years. At the time of the War of 1812, he was a War Hawk. C. was secretary of state under John Quincy Adams (1825-1829). A fervent nationalist, he became one of the leaders of the Whig Party. C. lost races for the presidency in 1832, 1836, and 1844. He was influential in the passage of the Compromises of 1820 and 1850 and the resolution of the 1832 nullification crisis.

Clay, Lucius (1897-1978) American general. C. directed the American operation to supply Berlin during the Soviet-imposed blockade of 1948-1949.

Clayton-Bulwer Treaty (1850) Agreement between the U.S. and Britain concerning either the construction of a railroad or the digging of a canal across Central America. The C. provided that neither nation would exclusively control such a route. See Hay-Paunceforte Treaty.

Clemenceau, Georges (1841-1929) French journalist and political leader. He was called "the tiger" because of his pugnacious honesty. C. defended Alfred Dreyfus and was twice premier, in 1906-1909 and in 1917-1920. In the negotiations over the Versailles

Treaty at the end of World War I, he pushed for tough measures against Germany.

Clement V (1264-1314) Pope, 1305-1314. Born Bertrand de Got, he succeeded Benedict XI. C. was crowned pope in France and spent the rest of his life there, beginning the so-called Babylonian Captivity of the Papacy in Avignon in 1309.

Clement VII (1478-1534) Pope, 1523-1524. Born Giulio de Medici, he succeeded Adrian VI. C. became the enemy of Holy Roman Emperor Charles V, who sacked Rome in 1527 and held the pope prisoner for a time. He refused Henry VIII of England permission to divorce his wife, which led to England's break with the Roman Catholic Church in 1534. C. was a great patron of Renaissance artists such as Raphael and Michelangelo.

Clement XIV (1705-1774) Pope, 1769-1774. Born Giovanni Ganganelli, C. succeeded Clement XIII. The Jesuits were disbanded (1773) during his pontificate.

Cleon (d.422 BC) Athenian political leader. An opponent of Pericles, C. was called a demagogue by the writers Thucydides and Aristophanes. He was killed during the Peloponnesian War at the battle of Amphipolis.

Georges Clemenceau

Clement V

Cleopatra (69-30 BC) Queen of Egypt, 51-30 BC. The daughter of Ptolemy XI, C. was married at age 17 to her younger brother Ptolemy XII. After he drowned accidentally, she married another brother, Ptolemy XIII. When the Roman Julius Caesar came to Egypt (48 BC), he helped her secure power. She became his mistress (and may have had a son by him) and returned to Rome with him. After Caesar's death (44 BC), she became the mistress of Marc Antony, whom she married in 36 BC and supported in his struggle with Octavian. She and Antony lost the Battle of Actium to Octavian in 31 BC. After Antony committed suicide, she tried to win over Octavian but failed and killed herself.

Cleisthenes (c.570-508 BC) Athenian political leader. He completed the democratization of Athens about 509 BC.

Cleveland, Grover (1837-1908) 22nd and 24th president of the U.S., 1885-1889 and 1893-1897. C. was born in New Jersey but started his career in New York. A Democrat, he was mayor of Buffalo and governor of New York before becoming president. C. supported civil service reform and a lower tariff in his first term. He was narrowly defeated for reelection by Benjamin Harrison in 1888. Running for a third time, C. defeated Harrison in 1892,

The Cold War

The years after World War II were marked by growing tensions between the two superpowers, the Soviet Union and the United States. The two never went to war with each other, although the United States did fight wars with the Soviet allies North Korea and North Vietnam. But the two powers competed for influence all over the world. The competition involved ideology, economics, and military and political strength. It ended only in the late 1980s.

1

2

4

1. Airplanes flying supplies from the United States and their allied countries to Berlin during the blockade of the city's access routes by the U.S.S.R.
2. U.S. General Douglas MacArthur, who wanted to conquer North Korea during the Korean War (1950-1953). See Korean War.
3. Leonid Brezhnev, leader of the Soviet Union from the mid 1960s until his death in 1982.
4. A famous refugee from the Soviet Union to the West: the dancer Rudolf Nureyev.

3

5. Soviet troops suppressing the Hungarian Revolution in 1956.

6. During the 1980s hundreds of thousands of demonstrators marched against the deployment of nuclear missiles in their countries in various European capital cities

7. U.S. Secretary of State Henry Kissinger initiated the first Strategic Arms Limitation Talks (SALT) between the United States and the Soviet Union in 1972.

8. U.S. President Ronald Reagan and Soviet leader Mikhail Gorbachev signing a disarmament treaty in 1987.

5

6

7

8

becoming the only president to serve nonconsecutive terms. The sharp economic downturn of 1893 shadowed his second term. He was unable to secure the Democratic nomination again in 1896.

Clinton, Bill (William Jefferson) (1946-) 42nd president of the U.S., 1993-. C.'s father, William Blythe, died before he was born, and his stepfather, Roger Clinton, adopted him. A Democrat, C. served as Arkansas' attorney general and governor before defeating Ross Perot and incumbent president George Bush in the 1992 presidential election. Plagued by accusations of personal and financial scandal and failing in his attempt to reform America's health care system, he took credit for improving the nation's economy, reducing the deficit, and helping to solve problems in Haiti, Bosnia, and the Middle East. He was reelected in 1996.

Clovis I (466-511) King of the Franks, 481-511. Also known as Chlodwig, C. was the founder of the Merovingian dynasty. C. ended the Roman domination of Gaul in 486, after which he continued to extend his kingdom. C. chose Rheims and later Paris as his seat. In 493 C. married the Catholic Burgundian princess Clotilda and was converted to Christianity.

Jean-Baptiste Colbert

Cochin China (Nam Ky) The southern part of present-day Vietnam. Following the French colonization of Vietnam (1859-1867), C. became part of the colony of Indochina. After the French were defeated by the Viet Minh in 1954, it became part of South Vietnam. When the North Vietnamese defeated the South Vietnamese and the Americans in 1975, C. was became part of the reunited Vietnam.

Cochise (c.1815-1874) Apache chief. Enraged by the unjust imprisonment of his tribe, C. waged war against the U.S. from 1861 until 1872, when he surrendered.

Code Napoleon The French code of law, a revision of Roman law, instituted by Napoleon in 1804.

Cod War Crisis A dispute between Iceland and Great Britain in the 1970s over fishing rights in the waters around Iceland.

Codrington, Edward Sir (1770-1851) British admiral. While commander of a French-British-Russian fleet, C. defeated the Turks at Navarino in 1827.

Cohort Roman military unit. A Roman legion consisted of 10 cohorts.

Colbert, Jean-Baptiste (1619-1683) French finance minister. Following the fall of Fouquet in 1665, Louis XIV appointed him to overhaul France's finances. He was a proponent of mercantilism, hoping to make France economically self-sufficient, and patronized the arts. His task was made increasingly difficult by the aggressive foreign policy espoused by Louis XIV.

Cold War Period of conflict between the U.S. and its allies (the West) and the Soviet Union and other Communist states (the East). It began in the years following World War II and ended in the 1980s. The U.S. and the Soviet Union never actually went to war with each other, but there were several crises (over Berlin in 1948-1949 and 1961 and Cuba in 1962, for example) when war came very close. The U.S. did fight wars against Soviet allies in Korea (1950-1953) and Vietnam (1965-1975), and there were numerous other places where one side or the other employed military force in some way. Basically the war may be interpreted as the attempt of the West to contain the spread of Communist power and maintain the balance of power status quo. The West was largely successful in Europe, where the Truman Doctrine (1947) and the North Atlantic Treaty Organization (NATO) (1949) prevented Communist gains. In Asia, however, the West's attempt to maintain a non-Communist South Vietnam was a total failure. Nevertheless, the collapse of Communist regimes in Eastern Europe and the Soviet Union during 1989-1991, though due mainly to internal factors, is by some seen as a victory for the West.

Coloman the Booklover (c.1070-1116) King of Hungary, 1095-1116. C. is known for his law forbidding the trial of witches. He conquered Croatia in 1102.

Coligny, Count Gaspard de (1519-1572) French Huguenot leader. He was an adviser to King Charles XIX but was an enemy of Charles's mother, Catherine de Medici. He was murdered in the 1572 St. Bartholomew's Day massacre.

Count Gaspard de Coligny

Collins, Michael (1890-1922) Irish nationalist. He participated in the 1916 Easter Rebellion. In 1922 C. succeeded Arthur Griffith as president of the Irish Free State but was murdered by extremists after 10 days in office.

Collodi, Carlo (1826-1890) Italian writer. Born Carlo Lorenzini, he wrote the children's classic *Pinocchio* (1880).

The first half of the 20th century was a time of unrest in China. A revolution deposed the last emperor in 1912, and conflict between war lords followed.
Political instability was compounded when the Japanese invaded in the 1930s. Civil war between Nationalists and Communists was won by the Communists in 1949.

1

2

4

3

1. P'u-i (Hsuan T'ung), the last emperor of China, came to the throne when he was only a toddler. He was forced to abdicate in 1912. *See* P'u-i.

2. In 1911, a revolution took place in China, and a republic was proclaimed. Sun Yat-sen was elected president, but he served only a few months.
See Sun Yat-sen.

3. Mao Zedong during the Long March, in which he led 90,000 people on a 6,000-mile-trip from Kiangsi province to Yenan in Shensi. *See* Mao Zedong; Long March.

4. Mao's great opponent was Chiang Kai-shek, who for a time was supported by the United States.

Colosseum Large amphitheater in Rome. Construction began in 70 AD, and about two-thirds of it has been preserved. It held 50,000 spectators and was used for gladiatorial contests and performances.

Colt, Samuel (1814-1862) American inventor. He patented a revolver in 1835-1836 and also invented an underwater battery and telegraph cable.

Christopher Columbus

Columbus, Christopher (1451-1506) Explorer. Born in Genoa, C. became a skilled sailor during voyages north and south of Europe. He became convinced that one could reach the trading ports of Asia by sailing westward and persuaded the Spanish court to finance an expedition to prove it. After departing from Spain on August 3, 1492, he reached land in the New World – a small island in the Bahamas – on October 12, 1492. He made three more voyages to the Americas, discovering many islands and the coasts of Central and South America. Apparently, however, C. always believed that the lands he reached were in Asia.

Comanche Native American tribe of the southwest Plains regions. Skilled fighters and riders, they were greatly feared by white settlers.

Combarelles, Les Grotto Caves in southern France, where in 1901 approximately 300 Ice Age paintings were discovered.

Comédie Française French national theater company, located in Paris. It was established by Louis XIV in 1680.

Comenius, John Amos (1592-1670) Moravian clergymen and educator. His great work is the *Didactica Magna* (1628-1632). He advocated relating education to everyday life, teaching in the vernacular, and educating women.

Commando Term used during the Boer War (1899-1902) for small, mobile Boer units. Now it is used generally to refer for elite forces.

Commodus (Lucius Aelius Aurelius Commodus) (AD 161-192) Roman emperor, 180-192. The son and successor of Marcus Aurelius, C. differed from his father in being cruel, extravagant, and boastful. He wished to rename Rome after himself. His advisers had him assassinated.

Commodus

Commune of Paris The name of radical movements that governed Paris for short periods during the French Revolution and the Franco-Prussian War. Most often it refers to the government of March to May 1871, at the end of the Franco-Prussian War. The C. was opposed to the moderate Thiers government and its willingness to make peace with the victorious Prussians. Loyal government troops crushed the C. and executed thousands.

Communism A system of social organization in which property, especially the means of production, is held in common; also the ideology advocating such a system. In the history of political thought, C. and socialism are very closely related. The 19th-century German philosophers Karl Marx and Friedrich Engels advocated C. in *The Communist Manifesto, Das Kapital,* and

John Amos Comenius

other works. In practice C. is associated with the dictatorial and repressive regimes established in Russia (later the Soviet Union) by the 1917 Bolshevik Revolution, in Eastern Europe after World War II, and in China by the Communist Revolution of the late 1940s. In these regimes, all power was held by a Communist Party—and often a small clique within that party—and the stated ideals of democracy, equality, and economic prosperity were largely betrayed. The collapse of the East European and Soviet regimes in 1989-1991 has seriously discredited C.

Comnenus Byzantine ruling family. They reigned in Constantinople from 1081 to 1185. A branch of the family ruled the Trebizond Empire along the southern shore of the Black Sea from 1204 to 1461, whcn it was conquered by the Turks.

Compiègne French city on the Oise River. The November 11, 1918 Armistice ending World War I was signed there, and in World War II Hitler forced the French to capitulate on the same spot on June 22, 1940.

Comuneros, Revolt of (1520-1521) Uprising led by Juan de Padilla of

Communism in Russia

In the first decades of this century, Russia underwent revolution. In 1917, the old regime of the czars came to an end, and the Communist Party took power and created the Soviet Union. The Communists were socialists who put into place a radical, undemocratic system. After World War II, the East led by the Soviet Union and the West led by the United States became opponents in the Cold War, which did not end until Gorbachev's Perestroika in the 1980s.

1. Karl Marx (1818-1883), the German journalist and thinker who formulated the philosophy and ideology of communism in *The Communist Manifesto* and *Das Kapital. See* Marx, Engels.
2. Lenin (1870-1924). He led the Bolsheviks, the early name of the Communists, to power in the Revolution of 1917 and was the first ruler of the Soviet Union. *See* Lenin, Russian Revolution.
3. Russian poster from the 1930s intending to promote industrialization. *See* communism.
4. Stalin (1879-1953). After Lenin's death, Stalin made the Soviet Union into one of the leading nations of the world, but was responsible for untold suffering and the deaths of millions of people.
5. Under the leadership of Soviet President Mikhail Gorbachev, with his policy of Perestroika, relations between East and West improved, and the Cold War ended.

Toledo of several cities in Castille in Spain against King Charles V. The rebels were decisively defeated at Villalar by troops loyal to the government.

Concentration camp A prison not part of the regular penal system, established for special categories of prisoners. In Cuba in the 19th century, Spain set up C. for prisoners of war. During the Boer War (1899-1902) the British used them to hold Boer families. During World War II the Germans and Japanese created notorious C. for political opponents, prisoners of war, and, in the German case, categories of people they considered inferior, such as Jews and Gypsies. The death rate among prisoners was extremely high due to overwork, starvation, disease, and general brutality. Among the German camps were extermination camps, such as a facility at Auschwitz, where killing was the main purpose. The labor camps in the Soviet Union, where millions also died, can be considered C. as well.

Conclave of Cardinals Meeting of the Roman Catholic cardinals at the Vatican in order to choose a new pope. The cardinals meet in secret and avoid contact with the outer world during this meeting.

Concordat An agreement between the pope and the political authority of a country establishing their respective spheres of authority. For example, the Concordat of 1801 between Napoleon and Pope Pius VII set up guidelines for the reestablishment of Roman Catholicism in France. The term is sometimes also used for agreements between political authorities.

Condé The family name of a branch of the French House of Bourbon.
It was founded by **Louis I** (1530-1569), who was a leader the Huguenots (French Protestants). **Louis II** (1621-1686) is called the Great Condé. He was an outstanding general and for a time 1653-1658) led a revolt of the nobles, the Fronde, against Mazarin and the French court. Pardoned, he later fought for Louis XIV, defeating William of Orange at Seneff in 1674.

Condottieri Mercenary soldiers in Europe during the late Middle Ages and the Renaissance. They raised and led bands of soldiers for whatever authority would hire them.

Confederate States of America Also called "The Confederacy." The name for the new nation that the 11 Southern states of the U.S. attempted to form after they seceded from the Union in 1861. The states were Virginia, North Carolina, South Carolina, Tennessee, Alabama, Georgia, Florida, Mississippi, Arkansas, Louisiana, and Texas. In the American Civil War (which *see*), the Confederacy was defeated in 1865, and within a few years all 11 states were admitted back into the Union.

Confederation, Articles of *See* Articles of Confederation.

Confederation of the Rhine League of German states set up by Napoleon in 1806 after he defeated Austria at Austerlitz (1805).

Confucius (c. 551-479 BC) Chinese philosopher. The teachings of C., collected by his students in the *Analects,* form an ethical system for organizing society that has become a virtual religion in China. Little is known about C. himself. He may have been a civil servant. Apparently concerned about the disorder and corruption he saw around him, he developed his rules for the proper conduct of individuals in their private and public capacities. Although Confucianism does not deal with the supernatural, by the 1st century AD, shrines and sacrifices were being devoted to C.

Conquistadors Spanish military leaders. The word is particularly associated with the Spanish explorers and conquerors of the 16th century, such as Cortés and Pizarro, who conquered Mexico and Peru, respectively.

Conrad von Hoetzendorf, Count Franz (1852-1925) Austrian general. At the start of World War I, he was the chief of staff of the Austro-Hungarian army and later commanded the Tirol front.

Conrad III (c.1093-1152) German king, 1138-1152. He was the first of the Hohenstaufen dynasty. St. Bernard of Clairvaux persuaded C. to join Louis VII of France in the Second Crusade (1147-1149). He was never crowned by the pope and thus was never Holy Roman emperor.

Confucius

Conrad, Joseph (1857-1924) British writer. Born Josef Teodor Konrad Walecz Korzeniowski in Poland, he was sailor as a young man and did not start writing until nearly 40. All his work is in English, his second language. His best-known novels are *Lord Jim* (1900), *Heart of Darkness* (1902), *Nostromo* (1904), and *The Secret Agent* (1907). C.'s subject matter often deals with the clash of modern civilization with more primitive societies. His highly-regarded work is rich in atmosphere, character, and symbolism.

Conrad of Marburg (c.1180-1233) German clergymen. C. was the first papal inquisitor in Germany. He encouraged Holy roman Emperor Frederick II to start the Sixth Crusade. C. was despised for his ruthlessness and was eventually assassinated.

Joseph Conrad

Constans I (c.323-350) Roman emperor, 337-350. The youngest son of Constantine the Great, he and his two brothers, Constantine II and Constantius II, divided the empire on their father's death in 337. C. received Italy, Africa, Pannonia, and Dacia. He was murdered during a coup.

Constantine I the Great

Constantine I, the Great (288?-337) Roman emperor, 324-337. The son of Constantius I and St. Helena, he was proclaimed emperor in 306 by the army in Britain, where he was serving. He did not become sole ruler until 324, however. In 312 C. had become the first emperor to adopt Christianity. His 313 Edict of Milan confirmed an earlier edict making Christianity lawful. He convened the Council of Nicaea in 325 to deal with the Arian heresy. C. rebuilt Byzantium as Constantinople and made it the capital of the empire in 330.

Constantine II (316-340) Roman emperor, 337-340. Oldest son of Constantine the Great, he received Britain, Gaul, and Spain on his father's death in 337. Attempting to win Italy from his brother, Constans I, he was defeated and killed in battle at Aquileia.

Constantine XI (1404-1453) Byzantine emperor (1449-1453). The last Byzantine emperor, C. died fighting in 1453 when Constantinople was captured by the Turks.

Constantinople Former name for Istanbul, city in Turkey situated on the Bosporus. C. was founded on the site of the former Byzantium by Constantine the Great in 330 as the new capital of the Roman Empire. After the division of the empire in 395, it continued as the capital of the Eastern Roman, or Byzantine Empire, until its conquest by the Turks in 1453. The Turks renamed the city Istanbul, and it served as the capital of the Ottoman Empire until 1923.

Constantius I (Constantius Chlorus) (d.306) Roman emperor, 305-306. A general, he and Galerius became emperors when Diocletian and Maximilian abdicated in 305. C. was the father of Constantine the Great. He died in Britain.

Constantius II (317-361) Roman emperor, 337-361. A son of Constantine the Great, he received Asia Minor, Syria, and Egypt on his father's death in 337. Following the murder of his brother Constans I in 350, he gained control of the entire empire. C. was an Arian and disagreed with St. Athanasius.

Constitution of the U.S. The document that sets forth the basic framework, powers, and procedures of the U.S. government. It was written at a convention in Philadelphia in 1787 and went into effect in 1789. The C. replaced the Articles of Confederation. It provides for its own amendment and so far (1996) has been amended 27 times. The first 10 amendments, known as the Bill of Rights, were ratified in 1791.

Consul 1. In the ancient Roman Republic, the highest elected official. Consuls served for one year. 2. In France from 1799-1804, the name of the three highest authorities; Napoleon was the First Consul.

Contadora Group 1983 arrangement whereby Mexico, Venezuela, Panama, and Colombia act together to mediate conflicts in Central America.

Continental Congress Name for several American national governmental bodies just before, during, and after the American Revolution. In 1774 representatives from the American colonies met in the First C. to coordinate their responses to Great Britain. The Second C. organized the Continental Army in 1775 and proclaimed American independence in 1776. The Congress that governed under the Articles of Confederation (1777-1789) is also sometimes called the C.

James Cook

Continental System The attempt by Napoleon to blockade Britain and bar its trade from the European continent. He proclaimed it in the Berlin Decree (1806). The attempt failed.

Contras Nicaraguan guerilla fighters, backed, supplied, and financed by the U.S. who fought against the leftist Sandinista regime in the 1980s. Many though not all of the C. were former backers of the ousted dictator Somoza. Following the electoral defeat of the Sandinistas in 1990, the C. halted their struggle.

Cook, James (1728-1779) British explorer. He made many explorations in the Pacific and conclusively disproved the reports of a southern continent. C. also learned how to prevent scurvy. He was killed in Hawaii.

Cooper James Fenimore (1789-1851) American novelist. C. was the first significant American writer to make use of American subject matter. His most

James Fenimore Cooper

important books are the series of *Leatherstocking Tales*, which include *The Last of the Mohicans* (1826) and *The Deerslayer* (1841). They deal with the frontier and relations between settlers and Native Americans.

Copán Former Mayan city in modern Honduras, the site of impressive ruins of pyramids and other temples.

Copernicus, Nicolaus (1473-1543) Polish astronomer. Born Mikotaj Kopernik, C. formulated the heliocentric theory, according to which the planets

Nicolaus Copernicus

move about the sun and the Earth revolves on its own axis. The theory was developed in his book *De Revolutionibus Orbium Coelestium*, written about 1530 but not published till more than 10 years later.

Copland, Aaron (1900-1990) American composer. He was born in Brooklyn and studied in France with Nadia Boulanger in the 1920s. C. is probably the most popular American composer of concert music. In his best-known-works—among them the ballets *Billy the Kid* (1938), *Rodeo* (1942), and *Appalachian Spring* (1944) — he created a kind of outdoor, wide-open-spaces sound that has come to seem characteristically American.

Copperhead During the American Civil War, a derogatory term for citizens of the North who supported the South.

Copts Egyptian Christians, descendants of the Egyptians who did not convert Islam many centuries ago. They form only 10 to 15 percent of the Egyptian population. The Coptic Church is headed by the patriarch of

Alexandria. The Coptic language, the ancient Egyptian language, is now extinct.

Corday, Charlotte (1768-1793) French assassin. A supporter of the Girondists during the French Revolution, when they fell from power C. took vengeance by stabbing Jean Paul Marat, their opponent, to death in his bath (1793). C. was guillotined.

Córdoba, Emirate of Independent emirate (756-1031) in Spain, ruled by the Umayyed dynasty. Under Abdr el-Rahman III, it became a caliphate in 929. C. included most of Muslim Spain and was a wealthy cultural center tolerant of Christians and Jews.

Cordon Sanitaire Term for the new, small countries created in eastern Europe by the Treaty of Versailles (1919). It was hoped that these countries—especially Poland and Czechoslovakia—would serve as a buffer between the Soviet Union and the rest of Europe.

Coral Sea, Battle of the May 1942 World War II naval battle in which the U.S. prevented Japan from invading Port Moresby on New Guinea. It was the first major naval action decided by aircraft.

Corfu question (1923) Conflict between Italy and Greece after the assassination of an Italian general and four members of his staff who were trying to determine the Greek-Albanian border. Italy bombarded and occupied Corfu.

Corinth Greek city in the northeastern Peloponnesus. It was founded in the 9th-8th centuries BC at the foot of Acrocorinthus hill. In ancient Greece a busy port, it was often a rival of Athens and ally of Sparta (though *see below*, Corinthian War). There was an important early Christian community in C., to which Paul wrote two epistles. The city has often been damaged by earthquakes.

Corinthian war (395-386 BC) War between Sparta and a coalition of Athens, Thebes, Corinth, and Argos. The coalition's intention was to end Sparta's hegemony. This was eventually achieved but it took another war to do so.

Corneille, Pierre (1606-1684) French dramatist. He and Racine are considered the greatest writers in French of classical tragedies. His work characteristically features by strong leading characters who struggle with conflicts between passion and duty. Among his best works are *Le Cid* (1637), *Horace* (1640), and *Polyeucte* (1643).

Pierre Corneille

Cornelia (2nd century BC) Roman matron. Daughter of the general Scipio Africanus the Elder, she was the mother of the Gracchus brothers. C. was considered the ideal Roman matron.

Coronado, Francisco Vasquez de (c.1510-1554) Spanish conquistador. Starting out from Mexico (1540), he explored what is now the American Southwest, searching for the mythical golden Seven Cities of Cibola.

Correggio (1494-1534) Italian painter. Born Antonio Allegri, he was named after his birthplace. C. is one of the major artists of the Renaissance and a forerunner of the early Baroque style. He painted mythological, allegorical, and religious paintings marked by grace and light. Examples are *Io*, in Vienna, and *The Assumption of the Virgin*, in Parma.

Corregidor Philippine island in Manila Bay. During World War II U.S. forces made a determined though futile stand there in the spring of 1942 against advancing Japanese forces.

Cortés, Hernán (1485-1547) Spanish conquistador. In 1519 he invaded Mexico with a small force, and within a few years had conquered and destroyed the Aztec Empire. He bene-

Hernán Cortés

fitted from superior weapons and animals, the aid of rebellious vassal cities of the Aztecs, and the diseases the Europeans unknowingly brought with them that devastated the Mexicans. C. made several expeditions into Central America. *See* Montezuma.

Corupedium, Battle of *See* Lysimachos.

Coster, Laurens Janszoon (c.1370-1440) Dutch printer. He also invented moveable type, which reduced the cost of printing, making it available to a wider public. Gutenberg in Germany made the same discovery.

Coubertin, Baron Pierre de (1863-1937) Frenchman who was instrumental in reviving the modern Olym-

pic Games, first held in Athens in 1896.

Council, Ecumenical In Christianity, a meeting of church authorities, also called "general council," that officially speaks for the Church. A C. may deal with questions of doctrine or internal Church discipline. *See* Trent, Vatican.

Counter Reformation Roman Catholic movement largely in response to the Protestant Reformation (16th-17th century), although certain reforms of the C. were being discussed even before the Reformation. The principal institutional forum of the C. was the Council of Trent (1545-1563).

Cranach, Lucas the Elder (1572-1553) German painter and graphic artist. He is best-known for his portraits, which include many of Martin Luther, whom C. met when he settled in Wittenberg (1505).

Cranmer, Thomas (1489-1556) English clergymen. He was an adviser of Henry VIII, who made him archbishop of Canterbury. C. advised Henry concerning his divorce from Catharine of Aragon and the establishment of the Anglican Church. He compiled the first editions of the Book of Common Prayer. C. was burned at the stake under the Catholic queen, Mary Tudor.

Crassus, Marcus Licinius (115-53 BC) Roman political leader. Together with Pompey and Caesar, C. was a member of the First Triumvirate. He was killed at the Battle of Carrhae.

Crazy Horse (?1842-1877) Sioux chief. One of the greatest Sioux leaders and a bitter opponent of the whites, he participated in the 1877 victory at the Little Big Horn. Near starvation, he was forced to surrender later that year and was arrested. He was killed while trying to escape.

Crècy Village, northern France. It was the site of a notable 1346 battle in the Hundred Years War. Edward III of England defeated Philip VI of France,

Lucas Cranach the Elder

Famous Criminals

Famous thieves and murderers, pirates, or spies have always kindled the popular imagination. Some were legendary; others were very real. Many have even become national heroes despite the fact that, in some cases, they committed terrible deeds.

1. Al Capone, a notorious gang leader in Chicago in the 1920s.
2. The actor Errol Flynn portraying Robin Hood, the legendary medieval English hero, who supposedly stole from the rich and gave to the poor.
3. Engraving depicting Jack the Ripper, who killed London prostitutes in the 1890s, but was never captured.
4. The famous pirate Captain Kidd supervising the burial of his treasure on a tropical island.
5. The Cold War spy Kim Philby, who defected to the U.S.S.R.

The Crusades

At the Council of Clermont in 1095, Pope Urban II urged Christians to go to the Holy Land and liberate the Holy Sepulcher from the Muslims. The series of expeditions and wars known as the Crusades followed. In the end the Holy Land remained in Muslim hands, but the Crusades had a profound impact on history.

1

2

3

4

5

1. The Christian cross Crusaders wore on their chest. *See* Crusades.
2. Godfrey of Bouillon prepares for his voyage to the Holy Land. *See* Crusades; Godfrey of Bouillon.
3. A stone statue of a knight saying goodbye to his wife as he leaves for the Holy Land. *See* Crusades.
4. The Krak des Chevaliers, one of the Crusaders' strongholds in the Holy Land. *See* Crusades.
5. The Crusaders' siege of Constantinople in 1204, depicted in a manuscript from the 15th century. *See* Constantinople; Crusades.
6. The routes of the Crusades.

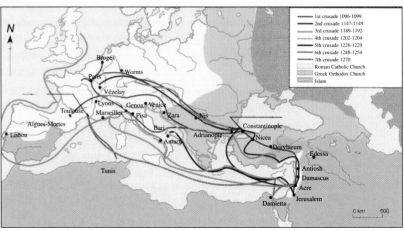

6

thanks largely to his army's use of the longbow, which had a greater range than the French crossbow.

Creek Indians *See* Five Civilized Tribes.

Crèpy, Treaty of (1544) Agreement between Francis I of France and Charles V of the Holy Roman Empire. Charles abandoned his claim to Burgundy, and Francis gave up his claims to Naples, Flanders, and Artois.

Crimean War (1853-1856) War between Russia on one side and Britain, France, Turkey, and Sardinia on the other. The war concerned the rivalry between Russian and Turkey in the Balkans and Russia's desire for a sea route to the Mediterranean. It was precipitated by a dispute between Russia and France over guarding the Christian places in Palestine. Most of the fighting took place in the Crimea, a Russian peninsula in the Black Sea. A treaty signed in Paris (1856) ended the war. One result of it was the weakening of Russia's position in the Balkans. The sufferings of the wounded in the war gave impetus to the founding of the Red Cross. *See* Florence Nightingale.

Crispi, Francesco (1819-1901) Italian political leader. C. took part in Garibaldi's Sicily campaign, which led to the creation of an independent Italy in 1861. He was Italian premier 1887-1891 and again 1893-1896. He vigorously pursued Italy's colonial interests in East Africa. His political career ended following the Italian defeat by the Ethiopians at Adowa (1896).

Croesus (d.547 BC) King of Lydia, 560-c.547 BC. Famous for his great wealth, C. was defeated by Cyrus the Great of Persia.

Cro-Magnon Man Humans who lived c.35,000 years ago. The name comes from the place where their remains were first found (1868), the cave of Cro-Magnon in the Dordogne region of France. C. were of the same species as modern man and came after Neanderthal Man. They made tools out of bone, ivory, and flint. The caves they inhabited contain colorful paintings of animals and hunting scenes.

Cromwell, Oliver (1599-1658) Lord protector of England. C. was a leader

Oliver Cromwell

of the parliamentary opposition to Charles I and led Parliament's forces in the civil war. He supported Charles's execution (1649) and led the Commonwealth that was established after it until his death.

Cromwell, Richard (1626-1712) Lord protector of England. The third son of Oliver Cromwell, he followed his father as the ruler of the Commonwealth. Not as gifted a leader as his father, he was forced from office in 1659.

Cromwell, Thomas (1485-1540) English statesman. C. was first an aide to Cardinal Wolsey and then became a close adviser of Henry VIII in his conflict with the Pope. When Henry's marriage to Anne of Cleves, which was negotiated by C., failed, however, Henry turned against him, charged him with treason, and had him executed.

Cronkite, Walter (1916-) American reporter and news broadcaster. Born in Missouri, he began his career as a reporter for *The Houston Press.* Later he worked for the United Press wire service before joining CBS. C. covered the Nuremberg Trials after World War II. For many years he was the "anchor" on the CBS evening news television show. At one time a poll reported he was the most trusted man in America.

Croy, William of, Lord of Chièvres (1458-1521) An adviser to Philip I of Spain and his son Charles V of the

Holy Roman Empire. His greed caused the Comuneros revolt in Spain (1520).

Crusades Expeditions in the 11th to 13th centuries by Western Europeans attempting to gain control of the Holy Land from Muslims. They failed in that goal but by bringing the civilization of the West into contact with other cultures and societies, the C. had an enormous historical impact. The C. also significantly affected relations between political authorities and the Church in Europe and between Western Europe and the Byzantine Empire. There were nine numbered C. and a so-called Children's C. The dates of the C. were: First, 1095-1099; Second, 1147-1149; Third, 1189-1192; Fourth, 1202-1204; Children's C., 1202; Fifth, 1217-1221; Sixth, 1228-1229; Seventh, 1248-1254; Eighth, 1270; Ninth 1271-1272.

Cuban Missile Crisis Conflict between the U.S. and the Soviet Union over missiles in Cuba (1962). It was the most serious crisis of the Cold War. Fidel Castro had made Cuba an ally of the Soviet Union. Wishing to deter a feared American invasion of Cuba, counter the U.S. superiority in the nuclear arms race, and alter the world balance of power, Soviet Premier Khrushchev surreptitiously placed nuclear missiles capable of reaching the U.S. in Cuba. When the missiles were discovered, U.S. President Kennedy insisted (October 1962) they be removed, blockaded Cuba, and threatened full retaliation on the Soviet Union if any of the missiles were fired. After tense negotiations, Khrushchev agreed to remove the missiles.

Cubism Movement in the visual arts, especially painting. It developed in Paris in the early 1900s; Picasso and Braque were its leading proponents. C. is based on the idea that every natural form can be reduced to a few fundamental shapes, such as the cube and cylinder.

Culloden, Battle of Highlanders under Charles Edward Stuart, fighting to place his father, James Stuart, on the English throne, were defeated on C. moor in Scotland in April 1746 by a British army under the Duke of Cumberland. The battle ended the Jacobite Uprising of 1745.

Cultural Revolution (1966-1969) Vast movement in China organized by Mao Zedong. His goal was to advance China's revolution by restoring vitality to the Chinese Communist Party, strengthening its control of the country, and speeding the development of China's economy. The C. brought chaos and suffering to millions. Thousands of innocent people were killed, arrested, or sent to reeducation camps by fanatical followers of

![Marie, Pierre and Irene Curie]

Marie, Pierre and Irene Curie

Mao known as the Red Guards. The economy was damaged by foolish schemes for rapid development. After Mao's death (1976), other leaders, the so-called Gang of Four, were held responsible for the C.

Cumae Ancient city, near modern Naples, Italy. Founded in the 8th century BC, it was the oldest Greek colony in Italy. It was destroyed in 1207.

Cunaxa Ancient town in Babylon, near the Euphrates River in present-day Iraq. Artaxerxes of Persia defeat-

ed a Greek mercenary army led by his brother Cyrus the Younger there in 401 BC. *See* Xenophon.

Cupid *See* Eros.

Curie, Irène *See* Irene Joliot-Curie.

Curie, Marie (1867-1934) French-Polish scientist. Born in Poland, she became famous as Madame Curie. C. worked with her husband, Pierre Curie (1859-1906), on radioactivity. In 1898 they discovered radium and polonium. They shared the 1903 Noble Prize for Physics with Antoine Henri Becquerel. Marie received the 1911 Nobel Prize for Chemistry.

Curie, Pierre *See* Marie Curie.

Curzon Line Border between Russia and Poland proposed by a commission headed by the British statesman Lord Curzon of Kedleston (1859-1925) in 1919 and established in 1920.

Cush Ancient (11th to 4th centuries BC) kingdom in Nubia (present-day Sudan) on the Nile River. The wealth of the kingdom derived from the export of gold and ivory. Its capital was Meroë, south of present-day Khartoum. C. was overrun by the Ethiopians in the 4th century.

Custer, George Armstrong (1839-1876) American general. He fought for the Union in the Civil War and later led many campaigns against the Indians. He was killed at the Battle of Little Big Horn.

Cyarxes (d.585 BC) King of Media. His troops conquered Ninevah, the Assyrian capital, in 612 BC.

Cybele Goddess of ancient Asia Minor, worshipped as the mother of the gods. Both the Greeks and Romans had cults devoted to her.

Cyprus Island in the Mediterranean Sea. As early as c.1400 BC, Greek colonies were founded there. In the centuries that followed it belonged successively to the Persian, the Roman, and the Byzantine Empires. In 1193 it became French, and in 1489 it was acquired by Venice. C. was captured by the Turks in 1570, who lost it to Britain in 1878. After much agitation, complicated by competing claims and

demands by Greece and Turkey, Britain granted C. its independence in 1960. Since then tensions have remained high between the Turkish and Greek populations on the island.

Cyrano de Bergerac, Savinien (1619-1655) French writer. After a short military career, C. took up writing. He wrote satiric fantasies about trips to the moon and the sun. C. suffered because of his appearance—his large nose has become famous owing to the play *Cyrano de Bergerac* (1897) by Rostand—which frequently led him into duels.

Cyrenaica Coastal region in east Libya. It was successively ruled by Greeks, Romans, Byzantines, Arabs, and Ottoman Turks. From 1912 to World War II it was an Italian colony.

Cyrus II, the Great (d.529 BC) King of Persia, Founder of the Achaemenid dynasty, C. defeated the Medes c.555 BC and built a great empire. He extended his power over Lydia in 546 BC and Ionia and Babylon in 539 BC, and Syria and Palestine, where he enabled the Jews to return to power, also came under his sphere of influence. He was killed in a battle against the Scythians.

Cyrus II, the Younger (d.401 BC) Persian prince. He was the son of Darius II and intrigued against his brother Artaxerxes II, Darius's heir. He gathered a huge army to fight Artaxerxes but was defeated and killed at Cunaxa. The story is told in Xenophon's *Anabasis.*

Cyrus II, the Younger

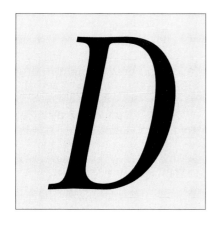

Dachau City in Bavaria, Germany. It was the site of a Nazi concentration camp in World War II. Some 35,000 people died here.

Dacia The Roman name for the region north of the Danube River, approximating modern Romania. It was conquered by Emperor Trajan in 106 AD and became a Roman province for more than a century. The Romans were driven out by the invading Goths.

Dadaism Nihilistic artistic and intellectual movement. Based on the nonsense word "dada," it was originated in Switzerland in 1916 by the Romanian poet Tristan Zara. D. protested against conventional values in art, which it sought to replace with the unpredictable, absurd, and childlike. Other Dada artists included Marcel Duchamp and Jean Arp. Though short-lived, D. was a forerunner of Surrealism.

Daedalus Greek mythological character who built the Minotaur's labyrinth in Crete and made wings of wax and feathers. His son Icarus flew too close to the sun and drowned when his wings melted. D. was traditionally regarded as the inventor of the potter's wheel.

Dagobert I (c.612-c.639) king of the Franks. He was the last of the Merovingian kings to rule personally. After his father, Clotaire II, died in 629, he ruled Aquitaine, Austrasia, and Neustria but was forced to give Austrasia to his son Sigebert III in 634.

Dagobert II (c.650-679) King of Austrasia. The son of Sigebert III and grandson of Dagobert I, he was crowned king in 676 but was murdered shortly afterwards.

Dagon Semitic god of rain and fertility.

Daguerre, Louis-Jacques (1787-1851) French painter and inventor. He invented c. 1830 the daguerreotype, the first photographic process.

Dahshur Village in Egypt, south of Cairo. It is the site of the Bent Pyramid of Pharaoh Snefru, so-called because of the steep angle of its slope.

Daimler, Gottlieb (1834-1900) German engineer. He devised important improvements (1880s) in the internal combustion engine, making the automobile industry possible.

Gottlieb Daimler

Daimyo Powerful Japanese landholders. Their estates were acquired starting in the 8th century. They were vassals of the shogun in the Tokugawa period (1603-1867). When the Meiji regime, starting in 1868, put an end to the feudal system, the D. were obliged to relinquish their land to the emperor and give up their privileges.

Daladier, Edouard (1884-1970) French political leader. A Socialist, D. became premier in 1938. He supported Neville Chamberlain's appeasement policy and signed the Munich Agreement with Hitler. Arrested by the Vichy government during World War II, he was active in French politics until 1958.

Dalai Lama The spiritual leader of Tibetan Buddhism. He is believed to be the reincarnation of the ancestor of the Tibetan people. The first D. was proclaimed in 1641. Following the 1959 Tibetan revolt against Chinese rule, the D. has become a symbol of

Louis-Jacques Daguerre

Tibetan independence. In that year, the D. went into exile to India and has since led efforts to bring about the nonviolent liberation of his people. He was awarded the Nobel Peace Prize in 1989.

Dali, Salvador (1904-1989) Spanish painter. D. was the most celebrated exponent of Surrealism. Utilizing his own intensely personal style, D.'s paintings, such as *Persistence of Memory* (1931) and *Burning Giraffe* (1935), are characterized by bizarre dream symbolism. D. came to the U.S. in 1940.

Dalai Lama

Salvador Dali

John Dalton

Dalmatia Region along the Adriatic coast, now part of Croatia.

Dalton, John (1766-1844) British scientist. He developed the atomic theory of matter. D. also formulated Dalton's Law, concerning the pressures of mixes of gases.

Damascus Affair (1840) Unrest precipitated by the disappearance from Damascus of the monk Tomaso. He was rumored to have been murdered by Jews so they could use his blood for ritual purposes. Many Jews were arrested and tortured, and riots broke out in many parts of the Middle East.

Damocles (4th century BC) Character in Greek mythology. Supposedly he was a courtier of Dionysius I, tyrant of Syracuse. To demonstrate his own power and show that nothing is certain, Dionysius had a sword suspended over D.'s head from the ceiling by a single horsehair. Hence the phrase "the sword of Damocles" to indicate the imminent threat of disaster.

D-Day Code name, abbreviated from "Decision Day," for the date of Allied invasion of Normandy, France, in World War II. The invasion began on June 6, 1944.

Dan *See* Israel, Tribes of.

Danaeans One of the names used in Homer for the Greeks.

Da Nang Vietnamese port city. Its French name was Tourane. During the Vietnam War, it was a major American base.

Dan Fodio, Usuman (1754-1817) Fulani emir of Sokoto, now a city in Nigeria. He led a jihad against the king of Gobir.

Dandolo, Enrico (d 1205) Doge of Venice. Elected Doge of Venice in 1192, D. was responsible for the rise of Venice to power in the Mediterranean.

Danegeld A tax introduced in the 9th century by the Anglo-Saxon kings to raise money to buy off Danish invaders. Later it became a tax to pay for military expenses.

Danelaw Initially the law that governed the area of England ruled by the Danes after 886. It then became the term for that area. Many Danish customs and procedures survived well beyond the Norman conquest of the 11th century.

Daniel 1. 6th century BC Jewish official at the court of King Nebuchadnezzar of Babylon. 2. Book of the Old Testament about Daniel. Scholars believe the book was written c.165 BC.

D'Annunzio, Gabriele (1863-1938) Italian writer and nationalist. His writing—poetry, novels, plays—is rich in imagination and imagery. D. lost an eye in combat in World War I and wrote *Notturno,* an account of recovering partially from blindness. In 1919, when it appeared that Fiume was not to be given to Italy under the Treaty of Versailles, D. and his supporters occupied the city for two years. Pro-Fascist, he was an early supporter of Mussolini.

Dante Alighieri (1265-1321) Italian poet. One of the world's greatest writers, he is celebrated for his masterpiece *The Divine Comedy.* D. was born into the Guelph nobility and was deeply involved in Florentine politics until banished in 1302. *The Divine Comedy,* in three parts, is the story of a poet's trip through Hell, Purgatory, and Heaven. It deals with religion, philosophy, human nature, and the Italian society of the author's day. It had a profound influence on the development of the Italian language and subsequent Western literature.

Danton, Georges-Jacques (1759-1794) French revolutionary leader. A lawyer, he was a founder of the Cordeliers. He advocated the abolition of the monarchy (1792) and the spread of the revolution throughout Europe. D. was a prominent figure in the new republican government but he opposed Robespierre's Reign of Terror and was put on trial in 1794. He was convicted of conspiracy to overthrow the government and was guillotined.

Georges-Jacques Danton

Dante Alighieri

Danzig Question Issue in European politics in the 1930s. Danzig, now the Polish city of Gdansk, had been part of Germany when the Treaty of Versailles (1919) made it a free city that served Poland as a port. German leader Adolf Hitler demanded that the city be returned to Germany, and the issue was one of his pretexts for the German invasion of Poland that started World War II in Europe (1939).

Dardanelles Question The D. is the strait that connects the Aegean Sea and the Mediterranean with the Sea of Marmara and ultimately the Black Sea. The right of passage through it has been the source of conflict throughout European and Turkish history. Russia long sought the right so that it would have year-round access to the world's seas.

Dardani Ancient people who lived northwest of Macedonia. Between c. 300 BC and 200 AD they were frequently at war with Macedonia and Rome.

Dare, Virginia (b.1587) The first white child of English parents born in America. Her parents were Ananias and Elizabeth Dare. They were part of Sir Walter Raleigh's Roanoke colony on the coast of North Carolina, which disappeared c. 1590.

Darius I, the Great (550-486 BC) King of Persia, 521-486 BC. He vastly expanded the Persian Empire. His administrative measures included standardization of the coinage and the institution of a courier service. D.'s attempts to conquer Greece ended, however, when the Athenians defeated his army at Marathon (490 BC). He permitted the rebuilding of the temple at Jerusalem in 515 BC.

Darius II (d.404 BC) King of Persia, 423-404 BC. The son of Artaxerxes I and a mistress, he was sometimes known as Darius the Bastard. D. formed an alliance against Athens with Sparta.

Darius III (Darius Codommanus) (d.330 BC) King of Persia, 336-330 BC. He was defeated twice by Alexander the Great, at Issus (333 BC) and Gaugamela (331 BC). After Gaugamela, he was murdered by the satrap Bessus while fleeing eastward to Bac-

tria. His reign marked the end of the Persian Empire.

Darlan, François (1881-1942) French admiral. He was at first minister of the navy and then vice-premier and foreign minister in the Vichy government. D. concluded an armistice with the Allies in Algiers in 1942. He was killed by a pro-Gaullist assassin.

Darnand, Joseph (1897-1945) French fascist. In World War II, D. served with the Waffen SS and was appointed head of the French police in 1944. He was executed after the war.

Darnley, Henry Stewart (1545-1567) Great-grandson of Henry VII of England and second husband of Mary, Queen of Scots. He married Mary in 1565; their son became James I of England. The marriage was unhappy. D. was murdered in February 1567, possibly with Mary's connivance.

Dartmouth College Case (1819) U.S. Supreme Court case. The case concerned the New Hampshire legislature's attempt to amend the charter of Dartmouth College. In his decision Chief Justice Marshall ruled that the legislature had violated the sanctity of contract guaranteed by the Constitution. The decision made it more difficult in later years for public authorities to regulate private corporations.

Darwin, Charles Robert (1809-1882) British naturalist. D. soundly established the theory of evolution through natural selection, now know as Dar-

Charles Robert Darwin

winism. In 1831 he began a five-year trip on the ship *Beagle* to South America and the Pacific, and during that voyage he began work on the theory. D.'s view of the gradual evolution of species was set forth in *On the Origin of Species* (1859) and elaborated in *The Descent of Man* (1871). D.'s work's has had an incalculably profound effect on humanity's view of life in the universe.

Dathan Old Testament figure who with his brother Abiram rejected the leadership of Moses. As punishment "the earth opened her mouth and swallowed them up..." (Numbers 16).

Dauphin Title of the heir apparent to the French crown. The last D. was Henri de Chambord (d. 1883).

David (d. 972 BC) Ancient Hebrew king. He was the successor of Saul. D. was the second of the Israelite kings

David

who made Jerusalem his capital, and he greatly enlarged his dominions. He is the subject of many of the most famous stories in the Bible and considered the author of many of the Psalms. D. was succeeded by Solomon.

David I (1084-1153) King of Scotland, 1124-1153. By granting land to Anglo-Norman families, D. built up Scotland's aristocracy. He also stimulated the development of cities.

David II (David Bruce) (1324-1371) King of Scotland, 1329-1371. He succeeded his father, Robert I. D. was captured during an invasion of England in 1346 and held prisoner until 1357, when he promised to pay a huge ransom. The rest of his reign was spent trying to raise the money.

Da Vinci, Leonardo *See* Vinci, Leonardo da.

Davis, Angela Yvonne (1944-) American communist. A black activist and Black Panthers supporter, she was arrested on suspicion of complicity in the escape attempt of the four so-called Soledad Brothers from Soledad Prison in California (1970). Four persons were killed in the attempt. A world-wide campaign was waged to demand her release, and in 1972 she was acquitted of all charges.

Davis, Jefferson (1808-1889) President of the Confederate States of America, 1861-1865. Born in Kentucky, D. grew up in Mississippi and served in the Mexican War, as a U.S. senator, and as secretary of war in the Pierce administration. After the Confederacy lost the Civil War, he was captured by Union troops and imprisoned for two years (1865-1867).

Dawes Plan (1924) Arrangement for the payment of Germany's reparations for World War I. It was worked out by an international commission chaired by the American banker Charles C. Dawes, who at the time was director of the U.S. Bureau of the Budget. The D. also provided for the 1925 withdrawal of the Belgian and French troops who had been occupying the Ruhr region of Germany. The Young Plan of 1929 again rearranged Germany's reparation payments.

Dayan, Moshe (1915-1981) Israeli soldier and political leader. He lost an eye fighting in the British army during World War II. D. led the defense of the Jewish quarter of Jerusalem in the Israeli-Arab War of 1948. He was Israel's chief of staff (1953-1958) and a minister in various governments. As defense minister he successfully directed Israel's military in the Six-Day War of 1967 but was criticized for Israel's performance in the 1973 Yom Kippur War.

Daylight Saving Time Setting clocks ahead by an hour in the spring so that there are more usable hours of daylight. In the fall clocks are set back to standard time. During World War I many European countries adopted a procedure of this kind, and the U.S. did so as well in 1918-1919. The U.S. enacted D. again in World War II and has maintained it in some form since then.

Dayton, Preliminary Agreement *See* Paris Accord (1995).

Dead Sea scrolls Documents and scroll fragments found in caves near Qumran on the shores of the Dead Sea in Israel. They were written or copied in the period from the 1st century BC to the 1st century AD. The D. contain passages from many books of the Old Testament and other materials relating perhaps to the Essenes, a Jewish sect that lived in the area. The first scrolls were found by shepherds in 1947. Since then archaeologists have made additional discoveries. The D. shed light on life in Israel in Old Testament times.

Deák, Ferenc (1803-1876) Hungarian political leader. He promoted the 1867 Ausgleich (Compromise) by which the Austro-Hungarian Empire (Dual Monarchy) came into being. *See* Ausgleich.

Dean, James Byron (1931-1955) American movie actor. In his few films — *East of Eden* (1955), *Rebel Without a Cause* (1955) and *Giant* (1956)—D. personified nonconformist American youth. He became a cult figure after his death in an automobile accident.

James Byron Dean

Debussy, Claude Achille (1862-1918) French composer. D. is the foremost Impressionist composer. Many of his works make use of the whole-tone scale to create delicate, sensuous, and highly evocative effects. D. wrote many works for the piano, chamber music, the opera *Pelleas and Melisande* (1892-1902), songs, and orchestral masterpieces including *Prélude à l'après-midi d'un faune* (1894), *Images* (1899), and *La Mer* (1905).

Decembrists Members of a secret revolutionary group in Russia who rebelled in 1825. The D. were mainly aristocratic officers who wished to introduce constitutionalism and other liberal Western reforms into Russia. The rebellion took place at the start of the reign of Czar Nicholas I. The rebellion was easily put down. Some D. were executed, and others exiled to Siberia. It had a lasting effect on Russian society. The government became more oppressive while many educated Russians considered the D. heroes.

Decius (Caius Messius Quintus Decius Traianus) (c.201-251) Roman emperor, 249-251. D. was a general proclaimed emperor in 249 by the legions in Moesia and Pannonia (southeast Europe). The systematic persecution of Christians began in his reign. D. was killed in battle with the Goths in Moesia.

Declaration of Independence Document proclaiming the independence of the U.S. from Great Britain. It was written largely by Thomas Jefferson at the request of the Second Continental Congress in late spring and early summer 1776. In beautiful language the D. states general principles about human rights—including the memorable phrases "all men are created equal" and entitled to "life, liberty, and the pursuit of happiness"—and goes to indict the British king and Parliament for violating them. July 4, 1776, the date usually cited as the "birthday" of the U.S., was the day the Continental Congress approved the D.

Declaration of the Rights of Man and of the Citizen Important document of the French Revolution. It was proclaimed by the Constituent Assembly on August 26, 1789, and made the preamble to the 1791 Constitution. The D. declares the individual's right to freedom, property, security, and to resist oppression. Its authors were influenced by the American Declaration of Independence.

Decretum horribile (frightful ordinance) John Calvin's label for the concept of predestination: God has determined from eternity whom He will save and whom He will damn.

Defoe, Daniel (1660-1731) English writer. He was the son of an English butcher and for a time was a merchant. After D. went bankrupt in 1692, he turned to writing. At the age of 59 he

Daniel Defoe

wrote the work that was to bring him lasting fame, *The Life and Strange Surprising Adventures of Robinson Crusoe* (1719). Based partly on the experiences of the castaway Alexander Selkirk, it is often considered the first English novel. Crusoe endures terrible hardships but preserves his humanity. D. also wrote the novel *Moll Flanders* (1722), about a prostitute.

De Gaulle, Charles (1890-1970) French general and statesman. He fought in World War I and became an advocate of mechanizing the French army. When France was quickly defeated by Germany in World War II, D. became the leader of the Free French. He was briefly president at the end of the war. In 1958 D. returned to power to solve the Algerian crisis and founded the Fifth Republic. He reas-

serted France's stature as a strong, independent power. D. remained president until 1969, when he resigned.

Deir el Bahri Valley on the west bank of the Nile near Karnak in Egypt. It is the site of renowned terraced mortuary temple of Queen Hatshepsut. Near the temple are secret burial chambers, which held royal mummies of the 18th-20th dynasties.

Deir el Medina Village on the west bank of the Nile near Karnak in Egypt. There the workmen and artisans who constructed the royal tombs in the Valley of the Kings lived. They left behind many "ostraca," shards on which they jotted down all sorts of notes not only on the construction of the tombs but on their daily lives as well.

Deists Term usually applied to thinkers of the 17th and 18th centuries who denied the claims of orthodox Christianity. Instead they claimed the evidence of Nature was sufficient to reveal the existence of God. Voltaire, Jefferson, and Franklin are often considered D.

de Kooning, Willem (1904-) American painter. Born in Holland, D. came to the U.S. in 1926. He and Jackson Pollack are considered the outstanding American abstract expressionists. His works include the *Black Paintings* (1946-1948) and *The Woman* series (1950s-1960s).

Delacroix, Eugène (1798-1863) French painter. D. may have been the illegitimate child of the great diplomat Talleyand. He is the outstanding French romantic painter. *The Death of Sardanapalus* (1826) and *The Women of Algiers* (1834) are just two of the many works that reveal his skill with color and love of the exotic.

Delatores (informers) In ancient Rome, informers who reported crimes to the authorities. During the Roman Empire, informing was a lucrative profession because informers were rewarded. If the offender was executed, they received a share of his confiscated estate.

Delhi Sultanate (1192-1398) The first Muslim empire in India. It was founded by the Afghan Muhammad

of Ghor when he captured Delhi in 1192. The D. ended with Tamerlane's capture of the city in 1398.

Delian League Two alliances of Greek city-states established under the leadership of Athens. The first (478-404 BC) was directed against Persia. The Peloponnesian War ended it. The second (378-338 BC) ended when the league was crushed by Philip II of Macedonia at Chaeronea.

Delilah Character in the Old Testament. The beautiful D. is an agent of the Philistines, the enemies of Israel. Samson, the great judge of Israel loves her. She revealed to the Philistines the fact that Samson's power lay in his long hair, so that after they had shorn him he was easily overcome. Blinded and chained in the Philistine temple, he regained his strength and pulled the temple down.

Delius, Frederick (1862-1934) British composer. D. was a highly individual composer, sometimes described as an "English impressionist." His music is very original harmonically, somewhat diffuse structurally, and reveals his deep feeling for nature. He spent several years while a young man on an orange plantation in Florida, and several of his compositions reflect that experience. For most of his life, however, D. lived in France. His best works are vocal and orchestral. Among them are *Sea Drift* (1903), *A Mass of Life* (1904-1905), the opera *A Village Romeo and Juliet* (1907), and numerous small pieces that give impressions of nature.

Delos Greek island in the Aegean Sea. In Greek mythology, the island was sacred to Apollo. D. was a great commercial and political center in the ancient world.

Delphi Place in Greece near Phocis. In antiquity it was the site of a temple to Apollo and the most important Greek oracle. The great and famous came to D. to have the future predicted by a priestess called the Pythia. The prestige of the oracle decline during the Hellenistic period. D. was plundered by the Roman general Sulla, among others. Nero is said to have carried off 500 of its statues.

Demagogue In 4th century BC Athens, leaders who appealed to the prejudices of the people. The modern word means very much the same thing.

Demeter (Roman name: Ceres) The Greek goddess of agriculture and grain.

Demetrius I (c.337-283 BC) King of Macedonia, 294-285 BC. The son of Antigonus I, he was a skilled general who murdered his rivals to obtain the Macedonian throne. He was driven from Macedonia in 285 BC by Lysimachus and Pyrrhus.

Democratic Party One of the two major political parties in the U.S., the other being the Republican. Today's D. traces its origins back to the party organized by Thomas Jefferson and James Madison in the 1790s in opposition to the Federalists. Confusingly, that party was first known as the Republican or Democratic-Republican Party.

Democritus (c.460-370 BC) Greek philosopher who believed that all material was composed of indivisible particles, which he called atoms. In this respect his ideas are considered to be the forerunner of modern physics.

Demos In ancient Greece a village or district which was not a "polis," or city state. The word was also used refer to the ordinary people (those whom the Romans called "plebeians") and is thus the source of our word "democracy" (government by the people).

Demosthenes (384-322 BC) Outstanding Greek orator, known principally for his Philippics, speeches in which he tried to warn the Greeks against Philip of Macedonia.

Denarius The most commonly used ancient Roman coin. During the Roman Empire, the face of the emperor was shown on the coin.

Deng Xiaoping (1904-) Chinese political leader. He joined the Chinese Communist Party in 1924 and became a member of its Central Committee in 1945 and general secretary in 1956. He lost his positions during the Cultural Revolution but regained power in 1977. In the 1980s D. was the most powerful person in China and layed the foundations for China's economic revival. In 1989, though partly retired, he supported the military's suppression of the prodemocracy movement.

Denis, Saint (d.258) The first bishop of Paris and the patron saint of France.

Denktash, Rauf (1924-) Turkish-Cypriot political leader. In 1975 D. proclaimed himself president of a new Turkish-Cypriot state on Cyprus. Only Turkey, however, recognized (1983) the independence declaration.

Dentatus, Manius Curius (d.270 BC) Roman general. Famous for his honesty, D. defeated Pyrrhus of Epirus (275) and conquered the Samnites (290).

Depression, Great (c.1929-1939) Worldwide economic downturn, symbolized though not caused by the crash of prices on New York's Stock Exchange in October 1929. In the U.S. the D. helped bring to power (1933) President Franklin D. Roosevelt and his New Deal. In Europe and Asia, it engendered unrest that facilitated the rise of fascist movements such as Hitler's Nazis in Germany and was an underlying cause of World War II.

Descartes, René (1596-1650) French philosopher, mathematician, and scientist. D. made outstanding contributions to geometry (the Cartesian coordinates), algebra, optics, psychology, physiology, and philosophy. His statement *Cogito ergo sum*—"I think, therefore I am"—has been called the foundation of modern philosophy.

Deshima Artificial island off the Japanese port of Nagasaki. Between c. 1640 and 1850 the Dutch operated a trading post on the island, established

Deng Xiaoping

by the Dutch East India Company at a time when the Dutch were the only foreigners permitted to trade with Japan.

Saint Denis

Desiderius of Lombardy See Lombards.

De Soto, Hernando (c.1500-1542) Spanish conquistador. He fought Pizarro against the Incas in Peru. D. headed an expedition that sailed from Spain to Florida in 1538. He traveled through what is now the Southeast U.S., looking unsuccessfully for gold and silver and fighting many battles with the region's inhabitants. In the course of his wanderings, D. reached the Mississippi River in 1541, near which he died the next year.

Demosthenes

Dessalines, Jean-Jacques (c.1758-1806) Emperor of Haiti, 1804-1806. A former black slave, D. was a colleague of Toussaint L'Ouverture. He defeated the French on Haiti in 1803. The next year he crowned himself emperor. His megalomania and cruelty led to his murder in 1806.

Devadatta (6th century BC) A disciple of Buddha, he nevertheless made several attempts on the former's life. A sect established by D. failed to acquire a significant following.

Devil's Island Island in the Caribbean Sea off French Guiana. France ran a penal colony there, mainly for political prisoners, from 1852-1951. It was notorious for its harsh conditions. Alfred Dreyfus was imprisoned on D. *See* Dreyfus Affair.

Devlin, Bernadette (1947-) Northern Irish activist for equal rights for Roman Catholics. She was elected to the British House of Commons in 1969 and in the same year received a short prison sentence.

Devolution, War of (1667-1668) Conflict between France and Spain over the Spanish Netherlands. The war ended quickly when England, Sweden, and the Netherlands concluded the Triple Alliance (1688) to preserve the balance of power. In the Peace of Aix-la-Chapelle, France had to return territory to Spain but was able to retain a number of cities in the Netherlands.

Dewey, John (1859-1952) American educator and philosopher. D. gave much thought to the role of education in a democracy and was a leader of the progressive education movement. He developed the philosophy of instrumentalism, maintaining that as problems change, society must develop new tools for dealing with them.

Diadochi (Greek for "successors") The Macedonian generals who, following the death of Alexander the Great (323 BC), were engaged in warfare until 280 BC over the division of his empire. In 280 three large kingdoms were finally established: Egypt, ruled by the Ptolemies; Syria, ruled by the Seleucids; and Macedonia, ruled by the Antigonids.

Diaghilev, Sergei Pavlovich (1872-1929) Russian ballet impresario. D. founded the Ballet Russes (c.1910) in Paris, which created a sensation in the worlds of dance, music, and art. The company's productions greatly influenced future work in each of those fields. The company made use, among others, of the artists Picasso, Chagall, and Derain, the composers Ravel, Stravinsky, and Prokofiev, and the dancers and choreographers Nijinsky, Pavlova, Fokine, Massine, and Balanchine.

Diana *See* Artemis.

Dias, Bartholomeu (c.1450-1500) Portuguese navigator. In 1488 he became the first European to sail around the southernmost tip of Africa, which he called the Cape of Storms (later it was named the Cape of Good Hope). He was also on the 1500 voyage of Cabral that discovered Brazil.

Diaspora (Greek for "dispersion") Dispersion of the Jews outside Palestine. After the destruction of the Temple in Jerusalem (586 BC) by the Babylonians, Jews began to settle elsewhere in the Middle East. In Roman times the Jews spread across France and Spain. Later, persecution drove them to other places in Europe. Today the word D. is also used to refer to Jews who do not live in Israel.

Diaz, Armando (1861-1928) Italian general. In World War I, D. became the commander-in-chief of the Italian army in 1917 and led the decisive 1918 offensive against the Austrians at Vittorio Veneto that led to their unconditional surrender.

Diaz, José de la Cruz, Porfirio (1830-1915) Mexican political leader. D. was president of Mexico for most of the years from 1876 to 1911. He was an authoritarian ruler who brought in foreign capital to develop the economy but cared little for social justice or political freedom. A revolution led by Francisco Madero drove him from office in 1911, and he died in exile.

Dickens, Charles (1812-1870) British writer. D. is one of the best-loved novelists of all time. His family was poor, and all his life D. showed great sympathy for children and the poor, while attacking social injustice and callous privilege. His work is also full of sentiment, humor, and unforget-

Diana

table characters. In general D. wrote about the lives of ordinary people in the Britain of his time. Among D.'s

Charles Dickens

105

many novels, his own favorite was the partly autobiographical *David Copperfield* (1850). Others include *The Posthumous Papers of the Pickwick Club* (1836-1837), *Oliver Twist* (1838), *Bleak House* (1850), *A Tale of Two Cities* (1859), and *Great Expectations* (1861). The short novel *A Christmas Carol* (1843) quickly became a classic. D. also wrote stories and interesting reports of his travels in Italy and America.

Dictator During the Roman republic, a magistrate appointed in times of emergency and given special powers. The word has come to mean a ruler who governs by his own whim, ignoring any legal constraints or institutional framework.

Dictatorship of the Proletariat Term in Marxism, appearing in Marx's and Engels's *Communist Manifesto* of 1848. Supposedly the working class, or proletariat, will, when it gains power in the transition to a classless society, exercise dictatorial authority that will benefit all humanity.

Denis Diderot

Diderot, Denis (1713-1784) French writer and philosopher. One of the most influential *philosophes* of the Age of Enlightenment, D. was the editor of the epochal *Encyclopédie* (begun 1745).

Didius Julianus (Marcus Didius Salvius Julianus) (c. AD 135-193) Roman emperor, 193. He was consul when Emperor Pertinax died. The Praetorian Guard took bids from aspirants to be emperor, and D. bid the highest. He was murdered two months later by a rival, Septimus

Severus, who succeeded him.

Didriksen, Babe (Margaret) (1913-1956) American athlete. Considered the greatest American woman athlete, she won prizes in track, field, and golf.

Dienbienphu French military base in northwest Vietnam. In May 1954, after a long siege, Viet Minh forces under General Giap captured the base. The battle brought about the end of French rule in Indochina.

Dieppe Coastal town in Normandy, France. In World War II Canadian commandos made a costly and unsuccessful raid in August 1942 on German defenses there.

Diet A term for an assembly or council, often applied to such bodies in Europe.

DiMaggio, Joe (Joseph Paul) (1914-) American baseball star. D. played for the New York Yankees from 1936-1951 and was an outstanding outfielder and batter. He holds the record for hitting safely in consecutive games: 56, in 1941. D. was briefly married to the actress Marilyn Monroe.

Dingane (d.1843) Zulu king who was defeated by the Boers in 1838.

Diocletian, Caius Aurelius Valerius Diocletianus (AD 245-313) Roman emperor, 284-305. D. was the son of an emancipated slave. He strengthened the empire's frontiers and divided it for administrative purposes. D. persecuted Christians and unsuccessfully tried to regulate prices and wages (301).

Diogenes (c.412-323 BC) Greek philosopher. D. renounced all contact with society and civilization and attempted to live as simply as possible. When asked by Alexander the Great what he wished for, he replied that he wished Alexander to move aside because he was blocking out the sun. He is famous for walking around with a lantern, saying he was looking "for an honest man."

Dionysius I (c.430-367 BC) Tyrant of Syracuse. He repeatedly fought with the Carthaginians and aligned with Sparta against Athens. D. was a great patron of the arts and wrote tragic dramas. *See* Damocles.

Dionysius II (4th century BC) Tyrant of Syracuse. The son of Dionysius I, he succeeded his father in 367 BC as tyrant of Syracuse but was forced to step down in 357 BC, returned to power 346-344 BC, and was expelled again in 344 BC. For a time he was advised by the philosopher Plato.

Directory Name of the executive council that governed France from 1795 to 1799. A coup by Napoleon Bonaparte in 1799 (*see* Brumaire) brought the D.'s rule to an end.

Discordia *See* Eris.

Disney, Walter Elias (1901-1966) American filmmaker and producer. D. started working on animated car-

Walter Elias Disney

toons in Los Angeles in 1923. He created the great cartoon characters Mickey Mouse, Goofy, and Donald Duck. *Snow White and the Seven Dwarfs* (1937) was the first of his full-length cartoon movies. Later he made successful nature films and movies using live actors, such as *Davy Crockett* (1955) and *Mary Poppins* (1964). He opened the Disneyland amusement park in 1955.

Disraeli, Benjamin (1804-1881) British political leader and writer. D.'s family was Jewish, but he was baptized in 1817. He wrote novels and entered Parliament as a Tory in 1837 after having been defeated four times. He held

Dining through the Ages

1

Throughout history and among all human cultures, dining has meant more than merely eating. Whether the meal be humble or grand, dining is often a significant social event and can have great importance in human affairs. Weddings, funerals, the forming of business or political alliances –these inescapable human activities often involve dining.

2

3

4

1. The Bible offers many examples of significant events occurring at meals. One is the wedding dinner at Cana, when Jesus changed water into wine.
2. A festive banquet in Frankfurt celebrating the 1765 coronation of Joseph II as Holy Roman emperor. *See* Joseph II.
3. A banquet depicted on a 14th-century miniature.
4. A fresco from the Roman city of Herculaneum showing a private dinner. In Roman times people usually dined while reclining. *See* Herculaneum.

high office in several cabinets and was the architect of the Reform Bill (1867). He first became prime minister in 1868 and served again from 1874 to 1880. In addition to sponsoring domestic reforms, he energetically expanded the British empire and made Queen Victoria empress of India in 1877. D. was made earl of Beaconsfield in 1876.

Benjamin Disraeli

Divine Right The idea that monarchs derive their power and right to rule from God. *See* Absolutism.

Dix, Dorothea Lynde (1802-1887) American reformer. D. did important work in improving the treatment of the mentally ill. During the Civil War she was in charge of the Union's program to recruit, train, and place women nurses.

Djabarti, Abd ar-Rahman (1753-1825) Arab historian. He wrote a history of Egypt since the 17th century and included the invasion of Egypt by Napoleon (1798).

Djenné Town in south Mali Founded by the Songhai in the 8th century, it became a great commercial and Mus-

lim cultural center in the 13th, rivaling Timbuktu. It was conquered by Mali c.1471 and colonized by France in the late 19th century.

Djoser (27th century BC) 3rd dynasty king of Egypt. He is known principally for his burial monument at Saqqarah, where he built the first pyramid in Egyptian history.

Doenitz, Karl (1891-1980) German admiral. D. was the commander of German submarines in World War II and was made chief of the navy in 1943. Just before Hitler died in 1945, he named D. his successor. D. arranged for Germany's unconditional surrender. The Nuremberg Trials sentenced him to 20 years' imprisonment.

Dole, Bob (Robert) (1923-) U.S. senator from Kansas. Dole fought in World War II and was badly wounded. A Republican, he served in the House of Representatives (1961-1969) and has been in the Senate since 1969. He was Gerald Ford's vice-presidential running mate in 1976. He ran for president in 1996.

Dollfuss, Engelbert (1892-1934) Austrian political leader. He became chancellor in 1932 and governed in an increasingly authoritarian manner. He resisted Nazi demands for Austria's merger with Germany, however, and was murdered by the Nazis during a failed coup. *See* Anschluss.

Dolmen A prehistoric burial site consisting of large standing stones capped by huge horizontal slabs. They are found in Ireland, Brittany, Spain, and other places in Europe.

Dombrowski, Jaroslav (1838-1871) Polish revolutionary. He took part in the Polish revolt against Russia (1863) and fled to France, where he joined the Paris Commune. He died fighting on the barricades there.

Domesday Book Record of a survey of land ownership in England (1085-1086) ordered by William the Conqueror for tax purposes. The D. thus serves as a marvelous historical source.

Dominic, Saint (?1170-1221) Castilian clergymen. Born Domingo de Guzmán, he did missionary work

among the Albigenses in southern France. D. founded (1216) the Dominican religious order, dedicated to preaching and study.

Domitian (Titus Flavius Domitianus) (AD 51-96) Roman emperor, 81-96. He was the son of Vespasian and brother and successor of the childless Titus. A despotic ruler, he was murdered at his wife's instigation in 96, thus bringing to an end the Flavian dynasty.

Donatello (Donato di Niccolò di Betto Bardi) (c.1386-1466) Italian sculptor. An innovative Renaissance artist, D. developed new techniques for depicting perspective and depth and studied ancient sculpture closely. D. worked mainly in marble and

Donatello

bronze. An example is the bronze equestrian statue of the condottiere Gattamelata (1447-1453).

Don Carlos (1545-1568) Eldest son and heir of Philip II of Spain. C. was mentally deranged. He was imprisoned by his father and died shortly afterwards.

Don Carlos (1788-1855) Second son of Charles IV of Spain. C. and his brother Ferdinand were forced by Napoleon in 1808 to renounce their claims to the throne. He returned in 1814, and following the death of Ferdinand VII in 1833, considered himself to be the legal successor. His claim led to the Carlist War. Defeated (1839), C. fled to France and abandoned his claim in favor of his son.

Don Carlos (1818-1861) Grandson of Charles IV of Spain. He led the Carlists after his father renounced his claim. His 1860 coup attempt failed.

Don Carlos

Dong Son culture Bronze Age culture in Southeast Asia (c.700-200 BC), named after the site in Vietnam where it was found. Nomads spread it as they traveled westward across Eurasia.

Dorea, Andrea (c.1467-1560) Italian admiral and political leader. He began as a condottiere, fighting first for Francis I of France and then for Charles V of Spain and the Holy Roman Empire. D. ruled Genoa for many years. He captured Tunis from Barbarossa for Charles V (1535).

Dorians Ancient Greek people. The migrated into Greece from the northwest 1100 and 950 BC and reached Crete, the Ionic Islands, and Asia Minor. They made important contributions to Greek culture, and the Doric order of architecture is named after them.

Dostoyevsky, Feodor Mikhailovich (1821-1881) Russian novelist. One of the world's greatest writers, he is renowned for his magnificent insight into the varieties of human character and for his discussion of the most profound issues of human existence. Many of his plots involve murder and

guilt, perhaps partly because his father was killed by his own serfs. D.'s life was troubled. A radical in his youth, he was arrested and spent four years in Siberia. He suffered from epilepsy and for a time was a compulsive gambler. His greatest novels are *Crime and Punishment* (1866), *The Idiot* (1868), *The Possessed* (1871-1872), and *The Brothers Karamazov* (1879-1880).

Douglas, William Orville (1898-1980) U.S. Supreme Court Justice, 1939-1975. D. was appointed by Franklin Roosevelt. He was a liberal on the court, greatly concerned with civil liberties and free speech. Earlier in his career, he had taught law and served on the newly created Securities and Exchange Commission (1936-1939).

Douglass, Frederick (c.1817-1895) American black leader. D. escaped from slavery in 1838. He went to the North and became a speaker for an abolitionist group in Massachusetts. D. published the *Narrative* of his life (1845, later revised) and edited a newspaper for many years. After the Civil War, he held a number a government posts, including ambassador to Haiti (1889-1891).

Dowding, Hugh (1882-1970) British air force commander. Appointed air chief marshal in 1937, during World War II he was instrumental in Britain's victory over the Germans in the Battle of Britain.

Dowland, John (1562-1626) English composer. D. was a lutanist and composed many works for that instrument, alone, in ensembles, and with voice.

Doyle, Sir Arthur Conan (1859-1930) British author. Although he wrote many other works, including plays and historical novels, D. is best-known for his Sherlock Holmes detective stories, the first of which, *A Study in Scarlet*, was published in 1887. D. became a spiritualist in his later years.

Drachma Ancient Greek silver coin, made up of six obols. One hundred drachmas were worth one mina, and sixty minas were worth one Attic talent.

Draco (7th century BC) Athenian lawgiver. He codified Athens's laws in

c.621 BC. By modern standards the penalties were extremely harsh. The term "draconian" is still used to indicate repressive legal measures.

Feodor Mikhailovich Dostoyevsky

Drake, Sir Francis (?1540-1596) English explorer and admiral. D. was the first Englishman to sail around the world (1577-1580) and explored the western coast of North America. He fought to break the Spanish domination of the New World. During a voyage in 1585-1586 he plundered Spanish possessions including Santo Domingo and Cartagena. His attack in 1587 on the Spanish harbor of Cádiz caused the sailing of the Armada to be delayed a year, and he played a major role in the defeat of the Armada in 1588.

Sir Francis Drake

Dravidians Peoples living in central and southern India and northern Sri Lanka. They may have been driven from North India by the Aryans. The Dravidian languages are not related to any other language family.

Dreadnought The first of a new class of British battleships, launched in 1906. The D. was faster and more heavily armed than any previous battleship. Its launching spurred an arms race with Germany. *See* Fisher.

Drebbel, Cornelis Janz (1572-1634) Dutch inventor. He made the first navigable submarine and invented the thermostat.

Dred Scott Case U.S. Supreme Court case. Dred Scott was a Missouri slave who sued for his freedom on the grounds that his master had taken him to live for a time in Illinois and the Wisconsin Territory, places where slavery was illegal. Chief Justice Roger Taney's 1857 opinion for the Court denied his suit. Taney said blacks were not citizens and thus could not sue. Moreover he ruled the Missouri Compromise, which banned slavery in certain areas, was unconstitutional. The decision infuriated antislavery sentiment in the U.S. and increased the tensions between North and South.

Dreyfus Affair Political scandal in France at the end of the 19th century. It centered around the Jewish army captain Alfred Dreyfus (1859-1935). D. was unjustly convicted (1894) of spying for Germany and given a life sentence on Devil's Island. When it was shown that he had been convicted on forged evidence and was the victim of antisemitism, army authorities attempted to cover up the injustice. Eventually this failed, thanks largely to the writer Emile Zola, who published an open letter *"J'accuse"* ("I accuse"). The affair became a major scandal and divided French politics for many years. Dreyfus was pardoned in 1899 and acquitted in 1906. *See* Esterhazy.

Druids Celtic wise men and priests. Most of what is known about them comes from Roman writers and Irish sagas.

Druj ("People of the Lie") Evil doers in the Zoroastrian religion.

Druses Members of a religious sect named after its founder, Ad-Darazi. The D. live in Lebanon, Syria, Jordan, and Israel. Their religion is a variant of Islam and they speak Arabic. The D. believe the Caliph al-Hakim (996-1021) to be the last incarnation of God.

Dubcek, Alexander (1921-1992) Czechoslovakian political leader. A Communist, D. became the party's first secretary in 1968. He was instrumental in the liberalization of the Communist regime (Prague Spring) in 1968. This effort was crushed when the Soviet Union and other Warsaw Pact nations invaded Czechoslovakia in August 1968. The next year D. was forced to resign.

Alexander Dubcek

The Dutch Golden Age

The 16th and 17th centuries
were an age of both great turbulence
and great cultural achievement
in the Netherlands. Wars were waged
against Spain and England,
and bitter religious controversy
took place.
During the same years,
however, extensive foreign trade
made the Netherlands a rich
country and the great masterpieces of
Dutch painting were produced.
The period is now regarded as the
Golden Age of Dutch history.

2

1

3

1. William of Orange (1533-1584), prince of the Netherlands.
See Orange, House of.
2. Spanish troops capture Maastricht (1673), one of the major cities
in the southern Netherlands.
3. On August 8, 1588, a combined Dutch and English fleet defeated the
supposedly invincible Spanish Armada near Dover. *See* Armada.
4. Hugo Grotius (1583-1645), a great political philosopher and one
of the founders of international law. *See* Grotius, Hugo.

4

5

6

5. The signing of the Peace
of Westphalia in 1648. One of its
many provisions recognized
that the Netherlands was Protestant.
See Westphalia, Peace of.
6. Michiel Adriaanszoon de Ruyter,
one of the great admirals in
Dutch history. *See* Ruyter, Michiel
Adriaanszoon de.
7. One of the key events in the
second English-Dutch War was the
destruction of the British fleet
near Chatham in 1667.
See English-Dutch Wars.

7

Dutch and Flemish Painters of the Golden Age

1

2

3

4

5

1. Rembrandt (1606-1669), *The Night Watch.*
2. Rembrandt, *Self portrait.*
3. Vermeer (1632-1675), *The Art of Painting.*
4. Van Gogh (1853-1890), *Sunflowers.*
5. Van Gogh, *Self Portrait.*

Dutch and Flemish Painters of the Golden Age

6. Pieter Bruegel the Elder
(1530-1569),
The Wedding Dance.
7. Pieter Bruegel the Elder,
Self Portrait.
8. Rubens (1577-1640),
The Garden of Love.
9. Rubens, *Self Portrait.*
10. Hals (1580-1666),
Self Portrait.

Du Bois, William Edward Burghardt (1868-1963) American civil rights leader and writer. An economist and historian, D. was an early advocate of full social and political equality for American blacks. In 1909 he helped set up the National Association for the Advancement of Colored People and edited its magazine, *Crisis,* for many years. He joined the Communist Party in 1961 and moved to Ghana in 1962, where he died.

Duce The Italian word for "leader." It was the title assumed by the Italian fascist dictator Benito Mussolini.

Dukakis, Michael Stanley (1933-) American political leader. Governor of Massachusetts (1975-1979, 1983-1991), he was the unsuccessful Democratic candidate for president in 1988 against George Bush.

Duke (Latin *dux:* leader) The hereditary title of the highest-ranking nobility in several European countries. In the early Middle Ages, a D. was a military leader. Later some acquired civil authority, such as the Duke of Burgundy. The region ruled by these dukes is called a "duchy."

Dulles, Alan Welsh (1893-1969) American public official. A lawyer and the brother of John Foster Dulles, D. led the American intelligence. effort in Europe during World War II. He became the director of the Central Intelligence Agency in 1953 and remained in that post until 1961.

Dulles, John Foster (1888-1959) American lawyer and diplomat. D. was involved in the negotiations that resulted in the Treaty of Versailles (1919), the United Nations (1945), and the Japanese Peace Treaty (1945). He served as secretary of state in the Eisenhower administration from 1953-1959, during which time he ardently fought the Cold War against the Soviet Union.

Duma The Russian word for a legislative body. The first D. in Russian history met in 1906 as a concession by Czar Nicholas II after the Revolution of 1905.

Dumbarton Oaks Conference (1944) Conference held near Washington, D.C., between China, the Soviet Union, Britain, and the United States, at which the basis for the United Nations was laid.

Dunant, Henri (1828-1910) Swiss banker and philanthropist who founded the Red Cross in 1864. He was awarded the Nobel Peace Prize in 1901.

Dürer, Albrecht (1471-1528) German painter and engraver. The outstanding German artist of his time, D. was influenced by his European travels; he incorporated in his work features of the art of the Italian Renaissance and the Low Countries. He painted a large number of self portraits and religious pieces, such as *Adam and Eve* (1507). Probably his best work is his copper engravings and woodcuts, such as *Knight, Death, and the Devil* (1513).

Dust Bowl Region in the southwest Great Plains of the United States that was afflicted with severe dust and sand storms in the 1930s. The storms caused thousands of people to leave the area. Many headed for California and the Pacific Northwest, where they were employed as migrant workers to pick fruit. John Steinbeck wrote about these people in *The Grapes of Wrath* (1939).

Dutch East India Company. A private company formed in 1602 and granted a monopoly by the Dutch government on all Dutch trade from the Cape of Good Hope east to the tip of South America. Its headquarters were in Batavia. The D. founded a colony (1652) in South Africa that the British acquired in 1814. The D. was dissolved in 1798 because it was corrupt and insolvent.

Antonín Dvorák

Duvalier, François (1907-1971) Haitian dictator, 1957-1971. A physician, he was elected president, with army backing, in 1957. After being reelected in 1961, he announced that he was president for life. He ruled by terror, using the security police known as the Tonton Macoute. D. was called "Papa Doc." After his death in 1971, his son Jean-Claude (b.1951), "Baby Doc," succeeded him but was deposed in 1986 and fled to France.

Albrecht Dürer

Dvorák, Antonín (1841-1904) Bohemian composer. D. composed successful music in many forms: symphonic, chamber, concerto, oratorio, and opera. At its best his music is characterized by great melodic appeal, lively rhythms, and piquant harmonies. For several years in the 1890s, he taught at the National Conservatory in New York City. Among his most popular works are the *Slavonic Dances* (1878 and 1886), the last of his nine symphonies ("From the New World," 1893), the Cello Concerto (1895), and the opera *Rusalka* (1901).

The Eastern Roman Empire

Emperor Diocletian
(284-305 AD) divided
the Roman Empire into Western and
Eastern parts for more efficient
administration and defense. After the
death of Emperor Theodosius (395),
the division became permanent.
The capital of the Eastern Empire was
Constantinople (Byzantium).
After the fall of the Western Roman
Empire in the 5th century AD,
the Eastern Empire continued to exist
as the Byzantine Empire.
Constantinople became a great city
with as many as one million
inhabitants.

2

1

1. This mosaic from the church
of San Vitale in Ravenna, Italy, shows
the Empress Theodora I and her
attendants. *See* Justinian; Ravenna;
Theodora I.
2. The interior of the San
Apollinare church in Classe
(Ravenna). It was built in the middle
of the 6th century. *See* Ravenna.
3. The historian Flavius Cassiodorus
(6th century) in his library.
He wanted to save as much of Roman
culture as possible and arranged
for the copying of many manuscripts.
4. A 6th-century decorated
ivory throne of an Eastern Roman
bishop.
5. St. John Chrysostom
(Greek: the golden-mouthed) became
the patriarch of Constantinople
in 358. He was very critical of the
immorality of the imperial
court and was banished.

4

3

5

Eckhart

Ea Mesopotamian water god, considered humanity's great benefactor.

Eanes, Antonió (1935) President of Portugal from 1976-1986. While an army officer, he put down a left-wing revolt in 1975.

Earhart, Amelia (1897-1937) American aviator. The first woman to fly solo across the Atlantic Ocean (1932), she disappeared during an attempted around-the-world flight in 1937.

Amelia Earhart

Eastern Roman Empire Emperor Diocletian (AD 284-305) had divided the Roman Empire for more efficient administration and defense. After the death of Theodosius (395) the division into Western and Eastern Empires became permanent. The capital of the Eastern Empire was Constantinople (Byzantium). The E. became the Byzantine Empire and lasted until 1453, when it was conquered by the Turks.

Eastern Schism Rift between the Churches of Rome and Constantinople, which began in the 5th century. The definitive break occurred when Pope Leo IX excommunicated the patriarch of Constantinople in 1054.

Easter Rebellion (1916) Uprising in Ireland against British rule on Easter Sunday. It was organized by the Irish Republican Brotherhood. After a week of fighting, the rebels surrendered and 15 of their leaders were executed.

Eastman, George (1854-1932) American inventor and industrialist. E. was a pioneer in the popularization of photography. He invented roll film, the Kodak camera (1888), color film (1928), and other innovations. He founded the Eastman Kodak Company (1892). Later he became a philanthropist, founding, among other projects, the Eastman School of Music.

Ebert, Friedrich (1871-1925) German political leader. A socialist, E. supported Germany's participation in World War I. When the monarchy collapsed at the end of the war, he became the first president of the Weimar Republic (1919-1925).

Ebla Ancient Syrian city. In 1975 a practically intact palace archive of c.20,000 clay tablets, dating back to the 25th century BC, was discovered here.

Eburons Celtic tribe living in ancient Belgium. Their king Ambiorix revolted against the Romans in 54 BC. In retaliation Julius Caesar virtually exterminated the tribe.

Ecbatana Greek name for the capital of Media, located on the site of the present-day Iranian city Hamadan. E. became the residence of the Persian Achaemenid and of the Parthian kings.

Ecevit, Bülent (1925-) Turkish political leader. He became the prime minister of a coalition government in January 1974 and was responsible for the Turkish invasion of Cyprus in the same year. He was prime minister again in 1978-1979 but was imprisoned in the 1980s on charges of sedition.

Eckhart (1260-1327) German mystic. A Dominican, E. preached to the common people and wrote tracts in German, not Latin. He tried to com-

Friedrich Ebert

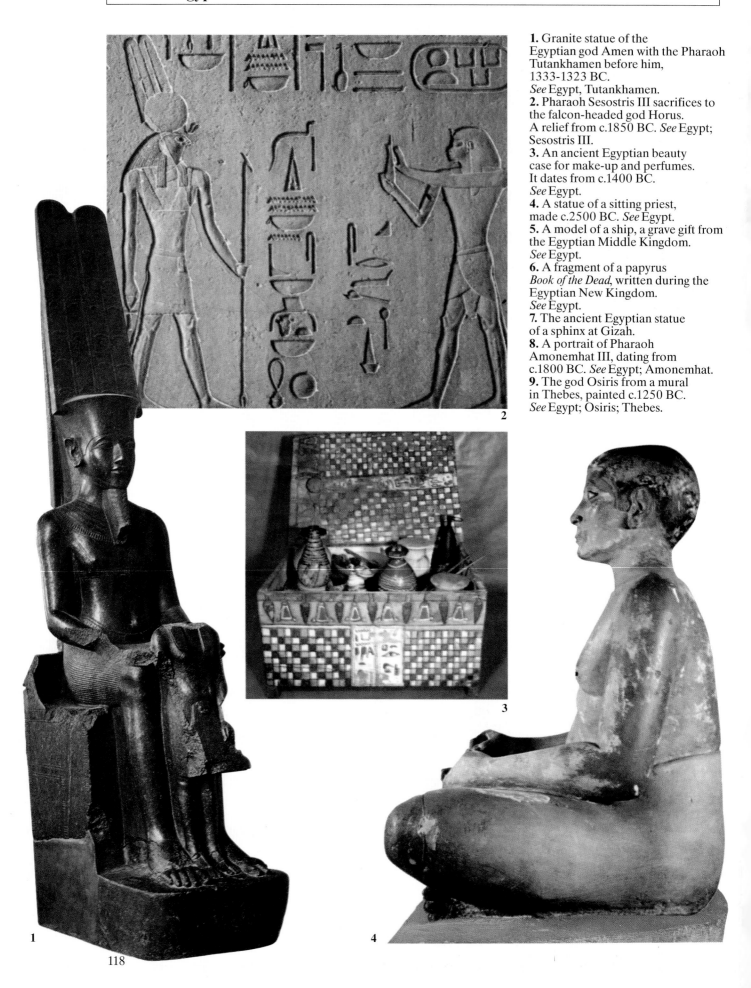

1. Granite statue of the Egyptian god Amen with the Pharaoh Tutankhamen before him, 1333-1323 BC.
See Egypt, Tutankhamen.
2. Pharaoh Sesostris III sacrifices to the falcon-headed god Horus. A relief from c.1850 BC. *See* Egypt; Sesostris III.
3. An ancient Egyptian beauty case for make-up and perfumes. It dates from c.1400 BC. *See* Egypt.
4. A statue of a sitting priest, made c.2500 BC. *See* Egypt.
5. A model of a ship, a grave gift from the Egyptian Middle Kingdom. *See* Egypt.
6. A fragment of a papyrus *Book of the Dead*, written during the Egyptian New Kingdom. *See* Egypt.
7. The ancient Egyptian statue of a sphinx at Gizah.
8. A portrait of Pharaoh Amonemhat III, dating from c.1800 BC. *See* Egypt; Amonemhat.
9. The god Osiris from a mural in Thebes, painted c.1250 BC. *See* Egypt; Osiris; Thebes.

5

6

7

8

9

municate his sense of God's closeness. In 1329 Pope John XXII condemned many of his ideas as heresies.

Edda The name of two works of literature written in Old Icelandic. One is a late 13th century collection of ancient Norse songs about heroes and gods, probably written in Iceland or Norway in c.800-1200. The other is a prose guide to Icelandic poetry, written by the Icelandic historian and poet Snorri Sturluson (1178-1241).

Eddy, Mary Baker (1821-1910) American founder of the Christian Science religion. She was born in New Hampshire and was often in poor health. Recovering from an illness in 1866, she conceived of the doctrine that she expounded in her 1875 book *Science and Health.* Christian Science maintains that illness and sin can be overcome by mental effort based on the precepts and life of Jesus. Believers reject medical science in fighting illness.

Sir Robert Anthony Eden

Eden, Sir Robert Anthony (1897-1977) British diplomat and political leader. He became a Conservative member of Parliament in 1923.

120

Named foreign minister in 1935, E. resigned in 1938 in disagreement with Neville Chamberlain's appeasement policy. He returned to serve in the cabinet as foreign minister under Churchill (1940-1945 and 1951-1955). E. became prime minister in 1955 but resigned in 1957 after the Suez crisis. He was named earl of Avon in 1961 and published his memoirs.

Edessa Ancient Mesopotamian city, on the site of Urfa, Turkey. It was the capital of the kingdom of Osroene c. 137 BC. Later a Roman city, Shapur I of Persia defeated Emperor Valerian there and captured him (260 AD). It fell to the Arabs (639) and the Crusaders (1097). Baldwin I ruled E., but the Muslims recaptured it in 1144.

Edict of Milan (313) Decree of Constantine the Great that reaffirmed the legality of Christianity as a religion in the Roman Empire.

Edict of Nantes (1598) Decree of Henry IV of France that permitted Protestants freedom of religion. In 1685 it was revoked by Louis XIV.

Edison, Thomas Alva (1847-1931) American inventor. Despite having only a few months of formal education and suffering from deafness, E. was a phenomenally fertile inventor of practical devices. Among them were the automatic telegraph receiver and transmitter, the phonograph, the incandescent light bulb, an electrical distribution system, the storage battery, and the synchronization of moving pictures and sound. In all he was granted more than 1,300 patents.

Edo Old name for Tokyo, Japan.

Edom Region in the Middle East from the Dead Sea to the Gulf of Aqaba. According to the Bible it was given to Esau and his descendents, the Edomites, who were enemies of the Jews.

Edward I (1239-1307) King of England, 1272-1307. The son of Henry III, he was on the Ninth Crusade when his father died. He annexed Wales (1284) and repeatedly attempted to subjugate Scotland. E. greatly improved England's legal structure and summoned the Model Parliament (1295) because he needed money.

Edward III (1312-1377) King of England, 1327-1377. The Hundred Years War in France (begun 1337) dominated his reign. E. won the Battle of Crécy (1346). While he was king, the Commons became a distinct entity within Parliament. His mistress Alice Perrers was increasingly influential toward the end of E.'s reign and supported E.'s son John of Gaunt (one of seven) against John's older brother, Edward the Black Prince.

Edward IV (1442-1483) King of England, 1461-1470, 1471-1483. The son of Richard, duke of York, he led the Yorkists in the War of the Roses after his father died in 1460. He deposed Henry VI in 1461 but was briefly driven from the throne by Richard, earl of Warwick, in 1471. E. killed Warwick at the Battle of Barnet later that year.

Edward VI (1537-1553) King of England, 1547-1553. The only son of Henry VIII, his mother was Jane Seymour. E., a Protestant, became king at age 9 and died of tuberculosis at 15. During his reign the government was dominated first by Edward Seymour, duke of Somerset, and then by John Dudley, duke of Northumberland.

Edward VII (1841-1910) King of Britain, 1901-1910. E. was the eldest son of Queen Victoria. He married Alexandra, the daughter of King Christian IX of Denmark, in 1863. E. was an

Thomas Alva Edison

active figure in society and had many mistresses. He was succeeded by George V.

Edward VIII (1894-1972) King of Britain, 1936. E. became the first English king to give up his throne voluntarily when he abdicated on December 11, 1936. The issue was his determination to marry Wallis Warfield Simpson, an American woman who was divorcing her husband. E. was given the title duke of Windsor. His brother succeeded him as George VI. E. and Mrs. Simpson were married in 1937.

Edward the Black Prince (1330-1376). Eldest son of King Edward III of England. He was active in the Hundred Years War and wore black armor, which apparently led to his name. E. captured John II of France at Poitiers in 1356. Toward the end of Edward III's reign, E. and his younger brother John of Gaunt were rivals for power.

Efialtes Ancient Greek traitor who aided the Persians at Thermopylai (480 BC) so that they could attack the Spartans under Leonidas from the back.

Efraim *see* Israel, Tribes of.

Egmont, Lamoral, Count of (1522-1568) Flemish general. Serving Philip II of Spain, E. gained decisive victories over the French at Saint-Quentin (1557) and Grevelingen (1558) and became governor of Brabant and Artois. He quarreled with the Duke of Alba over the Spanish persecution of Protestants and was beheaded, which led to a rebellion against Spanish rule. Goethe wrote a drama about him, for which Beethoven later wrote music.

Egypt, ancient Historic civilization situated in and around the valley (Upper Egypt) and delta of the Nile River (Lower Egypt). The legendary King Menes (c.3000 BC) supposedly united Upper and Lower Egypt and founded the Old Kingdom or Empire, which lasted until about 2250 BC. The Middle Kingdom ran from 2000 to 1786 BC, and the New Kingdom from 1570 to 332 BC. In 332 BC Egypt was conquered by Alexander the Great and governed by Greeks until 30 BC, when it became Roman.

Ehrlich, Paul (1854-1915) German pathologist and chemist. In 1907 E.

discovered salvarsan for the treatment of syphilis. Later he devised neosalvarsan, a less toxic preparation. In 1908 he shared the Nobel prize for Physiology and Medicine with Elie Metchnikoff.

Eichmann, Adolf (1906-1962) German Nazi civil servant. E. had responsibilities at the highest level for the transportation, imprisonment and execution of Jews as part of the Nazi's "Final Solution of the Jewish Question." After the German defeat in 1945, he was arrested but escaped to Argentina. Israeli agents kidnapped him in 1960 and brought him to Israel, where he was tried and hanged for his crimes.

Adolf Eichmann

Eiffel, Alexandre Gustave (1832-1923) French engineer. He designed the Eiffel Tower (1887-1889), constructed in Paris for the 1889 Exposition.

Einstein, Albert (1879-1955) German-American physicist. E. is among the greatest scientists of all time. He was born in Ulm, Germany. While working at the Swiss patent office in Bern, E. did work on the photoelectric effect and Brownian movement, and developed (c.1905) the epochal spacial theory of relativity that related mass to energy. Later he formulated the general theory of relativity (c.1915). In 1921 E. received the Nobel Prize for physics. After the Nazis came to power in Germany (1933), he emigrated to the U.S. and worked at the Institute for Advanced Studies in Princeton, New Jersey. His

Albert Einstein

goal, unmet, was a unified field theory. E. became a U.S. citizen in 1940. Although he helped start the American work on the atomic bomb, he was a pacifist and advocate of disarmament.

Eisenhower, Dwight David (1890-1969) 34th president of the U.S., 1953-1961. E. was born in Texas and grew up in Kansas. He graduated from West Point (1915) and became a successful army staff officer. In World

Dwight David Eisenhower

War II, E. commanded the invasion of North Africa (1942) and the Normandy invasion of France (1944). After the war he was the commander in chief of NATO and briefly the president of Columbia University. A Republican, he was elecded president by landslides in 1952 and 1956. E. was an enormously popular president, and his two terms were periods of general peace and prosperity, though problems were accumulating that future presidents would have to solve.

Kurt Eisner (left)

Eisner, Kurt (1867-1919) German socialist. He led the uprising that overthrew the Bavarian monarchy at the end of World War I and became Bavaria's premier. He was assassinated in 1919.

Elagabalus or **Heliogabalus** (Marcus Aurelius Antoninus) (205-222) Roman emperor, 218-222. Born Valerius Avitus Bassianus, he was priest of the sun god Elagabalus in Syria. The army there made him emperor. E. made his cult the state religion. His reign shocked even jaded Romans by its excesses. He and his mother were murdered by the Praetorian Guard. He was succeeded by Alexander Severus.

Elamites People of antiquity. The E. founded (4th millennium BC) in what is now western Iran the kingdom of Elam, a union of states with Susa as its capital. Their writing (Elamitic) was a simplified version of cuneiform script. In 640 BC their empire was brought down by the Assyrian Assurbanipal.

Elba Italian island in the Mediterranean Sea, six miles east of Tuscany. Napoleon was exiled there in 1814.

Elcano, Juan Sebastián de (c.1476-1526) Basque navigator. After Magellan's death in the Philippines, E. became the leader of his expedition (1521-1522) which was the first to circumnavigate the earth.

El Dorado (Spanish: "the golden man") Legendary country of gold in South America and elsewhere in the New World. E. was the destination of many Spanish expeditions but was never found. The legend may have had its origin in the custom of an ancient chief who was covered with gold and then ritually washed in a mountain lake in present-day Colombia.

Eleanor of Aquitaine (1122-1204) Queen of France, 1137-1152, and of England, 1154-1204. Her marriages had great significance for European politics. The daughter of William X, duke of Aquitaine, she married Louis VII of France in 1137. The marriage was annulled in 1152. She then married Henry, duke of Normandy, who became Henry II of England in 1154. Two of their children became English kings, Richard I and John. The lands Henry acquired by marrying E. led to centuries of conflict with France. Their marriage deteriorated, however, and E. set up her own court in Poitiers (1170), which became a center of culture.

Eleazar Name of several Jewish characters in the Bible. One of them was a leader of the Masada uprising of the Zealots (AD 66-73).

Electoral College The group of people that formally elects the president and vice president of the U.S. When Americans go to the polls to vote for president, they are actually voting for the members of the E. According to the Constitution, each state's legislature chooses a number of electors equal to the total of that state's representatives and senators in Congress. The electors then vote for president and vice president. The Constitution intended that the electors would be respected, wise men who would make disinterested choices. Over time, as the American political process has become more democratic, the reality has turned out to be far different. In most presidential elections, the voting of the E. is a mere formality. Usually the electors simply ratify the choices made in the popular election in each state. But since electors are not always required to do so, the possibility of the popular will being flouted remains. Because of the E. mechanism, three presidents have been elected who did not win the most popular votes: Quincy Adams in 1824, Hayes in 1876, and Harrison in 1888. A peculiarity of the original E. procedure, remedied by the Twelfth Amendment (1804), nearly cost Jefferson the election of 1800.

Electors The princes who elected the rulers of the Holy Roman Empire. (The ruler was usually crowned as emperor; if not, he was merely a king.) At first the E. simply ratified what was a hereditary succession. After 1125, however, they began actually choosing the new ruler. Because there were disputes as to who was entitled to be an elector, Emperor Charles IV issued the Golden Bull (its seal was golden) in 1356. It provided for seven E.: the archbishops of Mainz, Cologne, and Trier, the count palatine of the Rhine,

Eleanor of Aquitane

the king of Bohemia, the duke of Saxony, and the margrave of Brandenburg. In 1623 the count lost his vote, and it was given to the prince of Bavaria, but the count was made an eighth elector in 1648. In 1692 a ninth elector was created in the elector of Hanover. Napoleon changed the electors in 1803 and abolished the Holy Roman Empire altogether in 1806.

Elefantine Island in the Nile River in Egypt near Aswan. It is the site of an ancient temple to the ram god Chnum. Aramese papyri and ostraca that give information about a Jewish garrison in ancient Egypt have been found there.

Eleusis Ancient Greek city, northwest of Athens. It was the site of the worship of the Eleusinian mysteries, a temple to Demeter, and the Eleusinian games. Little is known about the secret mysteries, which may have originated from agricultural rites. The cult was maintained down through Hellenistic and Roman times.

Elgar, Sir Edward William (1857-1934) British composer. A brilliant orchestrator, E.'s music is often used to represent the pomp of the Victorian and Edwardian eras and the British Empire. In fact, however, E. often suffered from insecurity and doubt. He wrote little after the death of his wife, Caroline, in 1919. He most popular works are the *Enigma Variations* (1899) and the *Pomp and Circumstance* marches (1901-1903). He also wrote two symphonies, a concerto each for violin and cello, oratorios, chamber music, and other works.

Elgin, Thomas Bruce, Earl (1766-1841) British diplomat. While serving in Constantinople (1799-1803), he had a large collection of magnificent ancient Greek sculptures, including a frieze from the Parthenon in Athens, shipped to London. These have become known as the Elgin Marbles.

Elijah or **Elias** (9th century BC) Prophet of the Old Testament. He fought idolatry, specifically the worship of Baal, and prophesied the coming of the Messiah.

Eliot, Thomas Stearns (1888-1965) American-British writer. E. was born in St. Louis but became a British citizen in 1927. A teacher, bank clerk, and editor, E. began publishing poetry in 1917. His complex, allusive, and symbolic poetry deals with the emptiness of modern life, the anxieties of the individual, and the means of human salvation. His greatest works are perhaps *The Waste Land* (1922), *Ash Wednesday* (1930), and the *Four Quarters* (1935-1942). He was also an important playwright (*Murder in the Cathedral*, about the murder of Thomas à Becket of Canterbury, 1935) and critic. In 1948 he received the Nobel Prize for literature.

Elizabeth (1837-1898) Empress of Austria, 1854-1898, and Queen of Hungary, 1867-1898. A Bavarian princess, she married Emperor Franz Joseph I of Austria in 1854. E.'s personal life was tragic. Her son killed himself in 1859, and she was assassinated in Geneva by an Italian anarchist.

Elizabeth I (1533-1603) Queen of England, 1558-1603. The daughter of Henry VIII and Anne Boleyn, E. succeeded her half-sister Mary I as queen. She was a Protestant, and religious questions plagued England throughout her reign. Nevertheless it was one of the greatest periods in English history. England defeated the Spanish Armada (1588) and became a major European power. Shakespeare, Spenser, Dowland, Bacon, and other greats were active in the arts and sciences. E. never married and was succeeded by the son of Mary Queen of Scots, James VI of Scotland, who became James I of England.

Elizabeth II (1926-) Queen of Britain, 1952-. E. succeeded her father, George VI. She married Philip Mountbatten, the duke of Edinburgh, in 1947.

Ellington, Duke (Edward Kennedy) (1899-1974) American musician. E. was an outstanding jazz bandleader and composer. Born in Washington, D.C., where his father had been a White House butler, he studied piano as a boy and later formed a band that played at parties. He moved to New York in 1923 and opened at the famous Cotton Club in Harlem in 1927 with a band under his own name. By the 1930s his compositions, recordings, and broadcasts had made him world famous. E. tried with some success to bridge the worlds between jazz and concert music; he wrote lengthy suites such as *Black, Beige, and Brown* (1943) for concert performance.

Ellison, Ralph (1914-1994) American writer. E., a black, wrote *The Invisible Man* (1952), a classic of 20th-century American literature. Partly autobiographical, it concerns the struggle of a young black man to find his place in the world. He also published essays and was working on a second novel at the time of his death.

Elizabeth I

Ellora Village in Maharashtra, India. It is the site of an elaborate complex of Hindu, Buddhist, and Jain rock and cave temples (5th-13th century).

Emancipation Act British law (1828) that restored full civil rights to Roman Catholics.

Emancipation Proclamation (1863) Executive order issued by President Abraham Lincoln during the American Civil War. The E. theoretically freed the slaves in the areas controlled by the Confederate States of America. Lincoln issued the E. using his war powers.

Embargo Act of 1807 Law passed by the U.S. Congress that forbade Ameri-

The Enlightenment

The late 17th century and most of the 18th century was a time of great optimism—man seemed to know more than ever and to be able to solve the problems and mysteries of the world. Tradition and prejudice were rejected in favor of an unshakable belief in reason and progress.

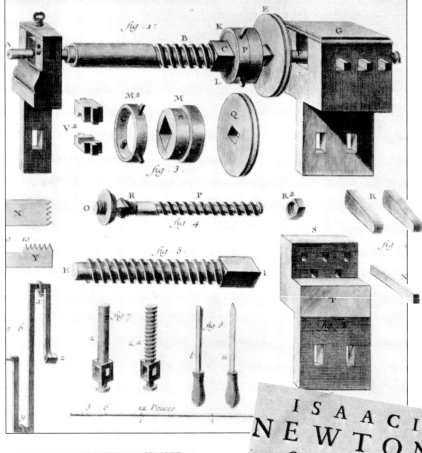

1. An illustration from the great *Encyclopédie* (encyclopedia), compiled and written by Diderot and his philosopher colleagues, 1751-1772. *See* Enlightenment; Diderot.
2. The English philosopher Thomas Hobbes, who developed political theories supporting royal absolutism.
3. A letter from political philosopher John Locke to Isaac Newton, discussing a philosophical problem. *See* Newton.
4. The first page of the Latin edition of one of Newton's works. Latin is still used as the standard scientific language. *See* Newton.
5. A geography lesson. Education was very much encouraged for everybody during the Enlightenment. *See* Enlightenment.
6. One of the first manned balloon flights in 1783, shown in a late 18th-century picture. *See* Enlightenment.

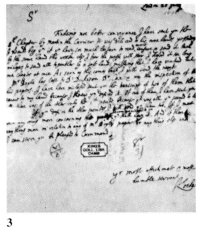

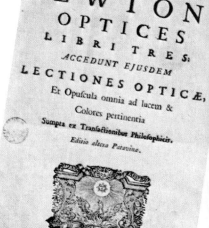

ISAACI NEWTON OPTICES LIBRI TRES. ACCEDUNT EJUSDEM LECTIONES OPTICÆ, Et Opuscula omnia ad lucem & Colores pertinentia Sumpta ex Transactionibus Philosophicis. Editio altera Patavina.

PATAVII, Typis Seminarii. MDCCLXXIII. Apud Joannem Manfrè.

5

6

can ships from carrying goods to other countries. Requested by President Jefferson, the E. was an attempt to pressure Britain and France, by cutting off their trade with America, to remove restrictions on American shipping that each had imposed to hurt the other during the Napoleonic Wars. The law caused such hardship at home, however, that it was repealed early in 1809.

Emerson, Ralph Waldo (1803-1882) American philosopher and writer. E. was a leading Transcendentalist thinker and is one of the outstanding figures in American thought and culture. He was a Unitarian minister and wrote essays and poetry. E. stressed the uniqueness of the American experience. Among his most significant writings, originally delivered as lectures are the essays "The American Scholar" (1837) and "Self-Reliance" (1841).

Emigrant Aid Company (1854) American organization that helped antislavery people emigrate from the Eastern states to the Kansas territory in the mid-1850s.

Emin Pasha (1840-1892) German explorer. Born Eduard Schnitzer, he served with General Gordon in the Sudan and became (1878) the British governor of Equatoria, in the southern Egyptian Sudan. The 1885 Mahdist uprising left him cut off for a while. He was murdered by Arab slave traders while exploring the Lake Tanganyika region.

Empire State Building Office building in Manhattan, New York City. Built in 1930-1931, it has 102 stories and for many years was the tallest building in the world.

Ems Dispatch Telegram sent from the German resort town of Bad Ems by King William of Prussia to his chancellor, Otto von Bismarck on July 13, 1870. It concerned the question of the succession to the Spanish throne. Bismarck, who wanted war with France, edited the telegram in a way certain to anger the French and made it public. France declared war six days later, and the Franco-Prussian War, which France lost, resulted.

Encyclical Letter from the pope to the Church as a whole discussing a matter

of importance. Each E. is named after the first words it contains. An example is Pope John XXIII's *Pacem in terris* (1963).

Emin Pasha

Engels, Friedrich (1820-1895) German socialist. His father was a prosperous textile manufacturer, and as a young man he worked in the business near Manchester, England. E. wrote *The Condition of the Working Class in England in 1844* (1845). He and Karl Marx were life-long collaborators. They met in 1844 and wrote the 1848 *Communist Manifesto*. E. often provided the funds for Marx's work, and edited his writings after his death

(1883). E. was one of the founders of the First And Second Socialist Internationals.

Friedrich Engels

English-Burman wars Three wars (1824-1826, 1852, 1885) fought between Britain and Burma. They ended with Britain gaining complete control over Burma.

English Civil War (1642-1648). War between Charles I of England and his internal opposition, the parliamentarians. Charles was defeated, captured, and executed (1649). The parliamentarians established in place of the monarch a republic known as the Commonwealth. The conflict concerned the respecitve powers of the crown and Parliament. The king claimed a divine right to rule independently of any authority, which Parliament would not accept. The struggle was complicated by religious issues, leading some historians to call it "The Puritan Revolution," as Puritans predominated in the parliamentary forces in opposition to the "high Anglican" nature of the king's forces.

English-Dutch Wars Six wars—1652-1654, 1665-1667, 1672-1764, 1780-1784, 1795-1802, and 1803-1813—fought mainly at sea between Holland and Britain. They largely concerned overseas trade, although the rivalry of the two nations also got caught up in the worldwide struggles between Britain and France.

Enlightenment (German *Aufklärung*) The primary intellectual movement of the 18th-century in Europe. E. figures were known in France as *philosophes.* Among them were Rousseau, Diderot, Condorcet, and Voltaire. Jefferson and Franklin may be considered their counterparts in America; Moses Mendelssohn, Lessing, and Herder in Germany. Influenced by the great scientific thinkers and philosophers of the previous century—such as Newton, Locke, and Descartes—the people of the E. believed that truth was discoverable through reason and that rationalism would produce progress. They tended to be deists in religion and opposed intolerance and state regulation of society. Rulers such as Frederick the Great of Prussia and Catherine the Great of Russia corresponded with and patronized E. thinkers and consequently are sometimes called "enlightened despots."

Enlil The god in ancient Mesopotamian religion responsible for order in the universe, who could also bring great natural disasters upon humanity.

Enragés (French: "crazy people") During the French Revolution working class people who rioted in early 1793 in protest against high prices and food shortages.

Entartete Kunst (German: "decadent art") Term used by the Nazis for art and music that displeased them. It might have been too "modern" for their tastes or created by peoples such as Jews, whom they considered racially inferior.

Entebbe City in Uganda, on Lake Victoria. In July 1976 an Israeli commando raid there freed about 100 hostages who were being held by Palestinian terrorists.

Entente Cordiale (1904) "Friendly understanding" between France and Britain, expanded to include Russia in 1907 and also known as the "Triple Entente." These three nations were allied when war—World War I—broke out with Germany and Austria-Hungary in 1914.

Entente, Little (1920-1922) "Friendly understanding" among Czechoslovakia, Yugoslavia, and Romania against Hungary and Bulgaria. The rise of German power in the 1930s made it irrelevant.

Enuma Elish Babylonian Creation story about the god Marduk, who had to conquer the primal monster Tiamat to become the chief god. After his victory over Tiamat, Marduk reorganized heaven and earth, and man was created.

Enver Pasha (1881-1922) Turkish general and political leader. He was one of the leaders of the Young Turks who forced Sultan Abd al-Hamid II to accept a constitution in 1908. He effectively became dictator in 1913 and brought Turkey into World War I as one of the Central Powers. When the war ended badly for Turkey, he fled to Berlin.

EOKA (National Organization of Cypriot Fighters) Independence movement of Greek Cypriots, formed in the 1950s to oppose British rule on Cyprus. Cyprus became independent in 1960. The E. helped overthrow the government of Archbishop Makarios in 1974.

Epaminondas (c.418-362 BC) Greek (Theban) general. He defeated the Spartans at Leuctra (371 BC), which

Enver Pasha

made Thebes supreme in Greece. E. also won the Battle of Mantinea against the Spartans (362 BC), but he died in the fighting.

Ephesus Greek city in Asia Minor, south of Izmir in modern Turkey. A great port, it was near the magnificent temple to Artemis that was one of the Seven Wonders of the World. The city became a Christian center; Paul wrote an epistle to its Christian community. The Goths sacked E. 262 AD.

Epicurus (341-270 BC) Greek philosopher. Starting in 306 BC, E. taught in a garden in Athens. His philosophy was that pleasure was the highest good and that justice, serenity and intellectual joys were the greatest pleasures. The word "epicurean" distorts this teaching by referring to a search for sensual pleasure.

Epidaurus Ancient Greek city, in the Peloponnesus. It was the site of the temple of Asclepius (built 4th century BC) and an amphitheater (3rd century BC) with renowned acoustics.

Epimenides (6th century BC) Cretan prophet. According to legend, E. was summoned to Athens during a plague to carry out cleansing rituals. He is supposed to have slept for 57 years.

Epirus Region of ancient Greece, present-day northwestern Greece and southern Albania. It was a powerful kingdom under Pyrrhus (3rd century BC). Allied with Macedonia against the Romans, it was conquered by the latter in 167 BC.

Epona Celtic goddess of the horse.

Erasmus, Desiderius (1469-1536) Dutch humanist. One of the key figures in the European intellectual life of his time, E. was ordained as a Catholic priest and remained loyal to the Church. He edited the classics and the Church fathers, prepared a Latin edition of the New Testament, and wrote many original works (among them *Manual of the Christian Knight,* 1503, and *The Praise of Folly,* 1509) as well as noteworthy letters. E. was a voice for tolerance and moderation in a time of bitter religious conflict.

Eratosthenes (c.276-195 BC) Greek scholar. Born in Cyrene (in present-

Epicurus

day Libya), E. directed the great library in Alexandria. Active in many fields including literature and philosophy, he was a notable astronomer. E. calculated the circumference of the earth and the sizes of the sun and moon and their distances from the earth.

Erechtheum Temple on the Athens Acropolis. A magnificent Ionic structure, the E. was built c.421-405 BC and contained shrines to Athena, Poseidon, and the mythical Athenian king Erectheus.

Desiderius Erasmus

Ereshkigal Mesopotamian goddess of the underworld.

Erfurt, Union of Alliance of 17 German states, established in 1850 by Frederick William V of Prussia as a step toward a united Germany.

Eric IX (d.1160) King of Sweden, 1150-1160. Known as Eric the Saint, he led a Christian crusade to Finland. E. is the patron saint of Sweden.

Eric the Red (10th century) Norse chief and discoverer of Greenland. Banished from Iceland for manslaughter, E. sailed west (c.982) and reached Greenland. A few years later, he colonized it with about 500 people.

Erikson, Erik Homburger (1902-1994) German-American psychoanalyst. E. was born in Frankfurt of Danish parents and studied with Anna Freud. He came to the U.S. in 1933. He did much work in developmental psychology and introduced the term "identity crisis." E. wrote studies of Luther (1958) and Gandhi (1969).

Eris (Roman: Discordia) Greek goddess of dissension.

Eritrea Country in Africa, along the Red Sea between Sudan and Djibouti. An Italian colony since 1889, E. came under British administration during World War II. It was made part of Ethiopia in 1952, but an independence movement became active in the 1960s. After a revolution in Ethiopia in 1991, E. achieved independence in 1993.

Eros (Roman: Cupid) Greek god of love, usually regarded as the child of Aphrodite and Ares.

Esarhaddon (7th century BC) King of Assyria, 681-668 BC). Son of Sancherib, E. conquered Egypt in a campaign in c.670 BC. He died while putting down an Egyptian revolt and was succeeded by Assurbanipal.

Esau Character in the Old Testament, also known as Edom. He was the son of Isaac and Rebecca and the first-born twin brother of Jacob. By a ruse of Jacob's, E. lost his inheritance as the first-born. *See* Edom.

Eschatology (Greek *Eschatos,* "last") Theology or mythology concerning

Eric the Red

the end of the world, the fate of man after death, or the return of Christ.

Escorial, El Monastery and palace of King Philip II of Spain, near Madrid. An architectural masterpiece, the E. was built 1563-1584. It contains a great art collection. Most of the Spanish kings are buried there.

Eshmun Phoenician healing goddess.

Essenes A Jewish religious sect that lived along the shores of the Dead Sea c.2nd century BC. They apparently held property in common and were devoted to purity and cleanliness. The Dead Sea Scrolls tell something about them.

Robert Devereux, Earl of Essex

Essex, Robert Devereux, Earl of (1567-1601) English courtier. He was for a time a favorite of Queen Elizabeth I, who gave him several important commands and appointed him lord lieutenant of Ireland. After disobeying her, however, and intriguing against her supporters, he was arrested and executed.

Esterházy Noble Hungarian family. Nikolaus Joseph, Fürst Esterházy von Galantha, 1714-1790, employed the composer Joseph Haydn as his music director for many years at the family estate at Eisenstadt, now in western Hungary.

Esterhazy, Ferdinand Walsin (1847-1923) French officer. E. committed the treason of which Alfred Dreyfus was accused. He fled to Britain in 1898. *See* Dreyfus Affair.

ETA (Euzkadi Ta Azkatasuna) Separatist movement in the Basque Provinces in northern Spain, which fights for Basque autonomy. Agitation has continued even after 1980, when Spain granted the Basque Provinces limited self-rule.

Etruscans Ancient people who inhabited Etruria, modern Tuscany and Umbria, in Italy. They may have come from Asia Minor. Their language, which is still not perfectly understood, apparently contains both Indo-European and non-Indo-European features. The culture of the E. developed in the 8th century BC and declined in the 5th-4th centuries BC. Their power was at its peak c.500 BC. Rome was greatly influenced by the E. and eventually conquered them. By 88 BC the E. had disappeared as an independent people.

Euboea or **Evvoia** Greek island in the Aegean Sea of the coast of Attic. Its main cities are Khalkis and Eretria. The name E. (Gr. *eu*=good, *bous*=cow) is indicative of the island's suitability for cattle-breeding.

Euclid (c.300 BC) Greek mathematician. A teacher in Alexandria, E.'s 13-volumed book *Elements* laid the foundation for geometry from his own time to the present. His deductive method is still taught.

Eugene III (d.1153) Pope, 1145-1153. Born Bernardo dei Paganelli di Montemagno. A Cistercian, he was driven from Rome in 1146 by the reform movement of Arnold of Brescia. E. helped organize the Second Crusade (1147-1149).

Ferdinand Walsin Esterhazy

Euripides (c.484-406 BC) Greek tragic poet. E., Aeschylus, and Sophocles are considered the greatest tragedians. E. wrote more than 90 plays, though only 19 have survived. Although he deals with many of the same great mythological subjects—such as Medea, Electra, and the Tro-

Euclid

Europe in the Early Middle Ages

After the power of the Roman Empire had slowly crumbled, kingdoms of Germanic tribes and other "barbarians" took over in the early Middle Ages (AD 500-1000), heralding a new chapter in the history of Europe.

1. Portrait of a Visigoth king, a miniature from an early medieval manuscript.
2. Frankish soldiers on a military expedition, a picture from a 9th-century manuscript. *See* Franks; Carolingians.
3. Gold coin, struck in the 7th century. It bears a portrait of the Merovingian king, Dagobert I. *See* Merovingians; Dagobert I.
4. This 7th-century basilica, dedicated to John the Baptist, is one of the oldest Christian churches of Europe.
5. Lombard belt-buckle, made in the 6th century. *See* Lombards.

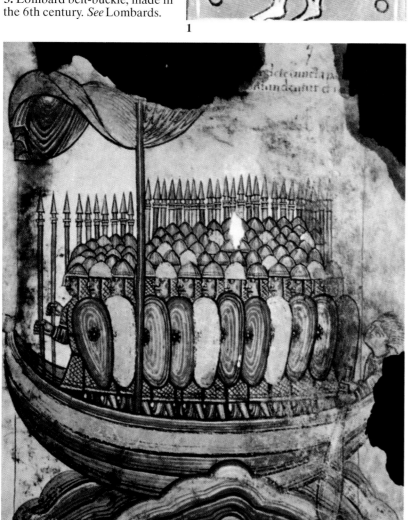

129

European Community

jan War, E.'s work is skeptical and more realistic than that of the other great tragedians.

European Community (EC) International entity formed in 1967 by joining together the European Economic Community, the European Coal and Steel Community, and the European Atomic Energy Community. The aim is the political and economic integration of Europe. The daily management of the EC is handled by the European Commission. The European Parliament has been the representative body since 1979. Final authority is exercised by the European Council, composed of the leaders of the member nations. In 1985 the members decided to create a common European market, which began to take effect in 1992.

Eurybiades (5th century BC) Spartan admiral. He led the Greek armada against the Persians near Artemisium and Salamis in 480 BC.

Eurypontids Dynasty of kings in ancient Sparta. *See* Agesilaos I and Agiedes.

Eusebius of Caesarea (c.263-339) Bishop of Caesarea, c.314-339. F. wrote the invaluable Church histories, *Chronicle* and *Ecclesiastical History.*

Eusebius of Nicomedia (d.342) Bishop of Nicomedia, 330-339, and patriarch of Constantinople, 339-342. E. was a supporter of the Arian heresy and an influential adviser of Emperor Constantius II.

Evans, Sir Arthur John (1851-1941) British archaeologist. He did excavations in Crete, 1898-1935, and discovered the palace of Minos and the culture he called Minoan.

Existentialism Schools of thought in philosophy that deals with the relation of the individual to the universe and to God. The 19th-century Danish thinker Soren Kierkegaard is often considered the originator of E. Others in the 20th century include Martin Heidegger, Karl Jaspers, and Jean Paul Sartre. Many existentialists see humanity's freedom as a source of dread and despair.

Expressionism Movement, mainly early 20th century, in the arts and lit-

Eusebius of Nicomedia

Euripides

erature in which reality is distorted as the artist or writer strives to convey an inner vision.

Eyck, Hubert Van (c.1370-1426) and **Jan Van** (1390-1441) Flemish painters and brothers. They painted works of extraordinary realism and fine detail. Jan perfected the technique of painting in oils. The brothers painted the altarpiece in Ghent's Church of Saint Bavon, one of the masterpieces of Flemish art.

Eylau Former name for Bagrationovsk, town in Russia, formerly in East Prussia. It was the site of an indecisive battle in February 1807 between Napoleon's army and Russian-Prussian forces.

Ezekiel or **Ezechiel** (6th century BC) Jewish prophet and priest during the Babylonian Captivity, after whom one of the books of the Old Testament is named.

Ezra Character in the Old Testament book of Ezra. He is described as a priest and scribe whom the Persian king Artaxerxes charged with restoring Jewish law in Jerusalem.

Ezzalino da Romano (1194-1259) Italian Ghibelline general. He fought in northern Italy on behalf of Holy Roman Emperor Frederick II against the pope and the Guelphs. Pope Innocent IV excommunicated him in 1254. In his *Inferno* Dante places E. in Hell for his cruelty.

Fabergé Firm of Russian goldsmiths and jewellers in St. Petersburg before the Russian Revolution. It was founded by Gustave F. in 1842. The firm made exquisite jewelry and luxury items, such as the famous Easter "eggs" the czar gave the czarina as presents. After the revolution, the firm moved to Paris.

Fabian Society (founded 1883-1884) Group of British socialist intellectuals who believed socialism could be achieved gradually through political reform rather than class struggle and violent revolution. among them were George Bernard Shaw and Sidney Webb. The F. strongly influenced the Labour Party. The name comes from the Roman general Fabian.

Fabius, Quintus Maximus Verrucosus (d.203 BC) Roman consul and general. He tried to defeat the Carthaginian invader Hannibal by harassing him and wearing him down, avoiding open battle. These so-called "Fabian" tactics gave him the name "the Delayer."

Fabricius, Johannes (1587-1615) Dutch astronomer. He discovered sunspots in 1610-1611.

Fahd ibn Abdul Aziz (1922-) King of Saudi Arabia, 1982-. The son of King Ibn Saud, F. was interior minister 1962-1975. He became king in 1982 when his half-brother, King Khalid, died.

Faidherbe, Louis Léon-César (1818-1889). French colonial official and general. He was governor of Senegal (1854-1861, 1863-1865) and increased the colony's size by defeating Haji Omar (1857-1859). In the Franco-Prussian War, he was defeated by the Germans near Saint Quentin in January 1871.

Fairbanks, Douglas (1883-1939) American movie star. Born in Denver, F. was one of the most celebrated silent film performers. He was married to another film star, Mary Pickford.

Fairfax of Cameron, Thomas Fairfax, 3d Baron (1612-1671) English general. In the English Civil War, F. commanded the parliamentarians' New Model Army at the Battle of Naseby (1645), where he defeated Charles I. He opposed the execution of the king in 1649.

Thomas Fairfax

Faisal I (1885-1933) King of Syria, 1920, and of Iraq, 1921-1933. He was the third son of Hussein ibn Ali, the sheriff of Mecca. F. fought with the Turkish Army until 1916, when he joined T. E. Lawrence against the Turks. In 1920 a Syrian congress proclaimed him king but the French forced him to abdicate. The British made him king of Iraq.

Falange Spanish fascist political party. It was founded in 1933 by José Primo de Rivera, the son of the former Spanish dictator Miguel Primo de Rivero. After Francisco Franco gained power, the F. was merged with the Carlist militia and became the only official party of the nation. After Franco's death in 1975, it was dissolved.

Falasha People in northwest Ethiopia who practice a form of Judaism. Supposedly they are descended from Solomon and the queen of Sheba. In the 1980s they were persecuted by the Menghistu regime, and many were transported to Israel by a secret airlift through Sudan (Operation Moses, 1984).

Falkenhausen, Alexander Ernst Alfred Hermann von (1878-1966) German general. In 1940 F. was appointed governor of Belgium and the north of France. He was involved in the attempt on Hitler's life in 1944 and was arrested but survived his internment in Buchenwald.

Falkenhayn, Erich von (1861-1922) German general. He was minister of war 1906-1915 and also made chief of the general staff at the start of World War I (1914). In 1915 F. defeated the Russians near Gorlice but was responsible for the disaster at Verdun in France (1916).

Erich von Falkenhayn

Falkland War 1982 war between Argentina and Britain over the Falkland Islands in the south Atlantic Ocean. The Falklands have been ruled by Britain since 1832, although Argentina also claims them. In 1982 Argentina invaded and seized the islands, but Britain quickly retook them.

Fanon, Frantz Omar (1925-1961) French West Indian psychiatrist and writer. F. was born in Martinique and educated in France. He became a leader of the Algerian National Front in the 1950s. F. wrote about the struggle of black and Third World peoples to liberate themselves.

Wretched of the Earth (1961) is his most influential book.

Farabi, Abu Nasr Muhammad al- (878-950) Arab philosopher. F. studied in Baghdad and taught in Aleppo. He was greatly influenced by Aristotle and in fact is sometimes called the "second master," Aristotle being the first. F. was also a great music theorist. In the West he is called Alfarabius.

Far East Term for the part of the world that commonly includes China, Mongolia, Taiwan, Hong Kong and Macao, the Koreas, Japan, the Ryukyu islands, and sometimes eastern Siberia.

Farinacci, Roberto (1892-1945) Italian fascist. After World War I, F. became a supporter of Mussolini and edited the daily newspaper *Regime Fascista*. He was executed by partisans at the end of World War II.

Farouk I (1920-1965) King of Egypt, 1936-1952. He succeeded his father, Fouad I. F. was corrupt and a playboy. In 1952 he abdicated after a coup led by Gamal Abdal Nasser.

Fars A province in modern Iran, it is roughly the same region as the ancient Pars, where the Persian Empire rose.

Fasces A bundle of rods and an axe, the Roman symbol of authority that was carried by the 12 lictors, or guards, in processions. The word gave rise to the term *fascism*.

Fascism Ideology that glorifies power, war, and the nation, and, frequently, a supposedly superior race. It dismisses the value of democracy and individual rights. Benito Mussolini founded a fascist party in Italy in the early 1920s. Other significant fascist movements were Hitler's Nazis in Germany and Franco's Falange in Spain.

Fashoda Incident 1898 dispute between France and Britain. Fashoda (now Kodok) is a village on the Nile River in southern Sudan. Both the British under Kitchener and the French under Marchand sought to claim it for their respective countries. Eventually the French withdrew, and France abandoned its claim.

Fatehpour Sikri City in Uttar Pradesh, northern India. It was founded in 1569 by Akbar as his royal seat and contains masterpieces of Mogul architecture.

Fates (Roman: Parcae; German: Norns) In Greek mythology the three goddesses who governed humans' lives.

Fatima (c.606-632) Daughter of Muhammad. She was the wife of Ali, the fourth caliph, and supposedly the ancestor of the Fatimids.

Fatimids Islamic dynasty that reigned from 909 until 1171. The F. established a caliphate on the basis of their claim of descent from Muhammad's daughter Fatima. Starting from Tunis, their power expanded to Egypt (969), where they made Cairo their capital, and to Syria, Palestine, and Arabia. They started to decline in the 11th century, and the caliphate was ended by Saladin in 1171.

Faulkner, William (1897-1962) American writer. Born in Mississippi, F. was one of the greatest American

William Faulkner

novelists. Many of his books are set in a fictional Mississippi county and deal with post-Civil War Southern society, but his themes transcend their particular locale. In 1949 he was awarded the Nobel Prize for literature. Among his works are the novels *The Sound and the Fury* (1929), *Light in August* (1932), *Absalom, Absalom!* (1936), and *Requiem for a Nun* (1951).

Fauré, Gabriel (1845-1924) French composer. F. studied with Saint-Saëns

Gabriel Fauré

and was head of the Paris Conservatory for many years. He wrote much piano and chamber music, songs, a requiem, and the opera *Penelope* (1913). His music is restrained and subtle and often of great beauty.

Faust (16th century) German doctor and scholar. According to legend, F. sold his soul to the Devil in exchange for youth, knowledge, and power. The story has been widely treated in literature and music, most notably in the dramatic poems by Goethe.

Fauvism Movement in early 20th century painting. *Fauve* is French for "wild beast," and the term was applied by hostile critics to painters such as Matisse, Roualt, Derain, and Vlaminck, who employed strong colors and distorted shapes.

February revolution Two notable revolutions. 1. The revolution that overthrew King Louis Philippe of France in 1848. It inspired revolutions in many other European countries. 2. The first phase of the 1917 Russian Revolution, which overthrew Czar Nicholas II and established the Provisional Government headed by Kerensky.

Fedayeen Palestinian fighters who conducted many attacks against Israel after its creation in 1948. Later they joined the Palestine Liberation Organization.

Federalist Papers Series of essays written by Alexander Hamilton, John Jay, and James Madison in support of the ratification of the 1787 U.S. Constitu-

Views on Fashion

In all societies throughout history, people have wanted to look good.
For many, this means following the latest fashion.

1

2

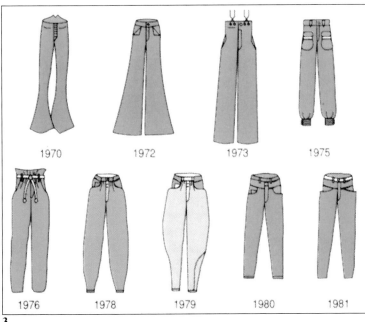

3

4

1. The latest fashions being presented at a Paris fashion show in 1996.
2. The French Queen Marie Antoinette, wife of King Louis XIV, wearing a fashionable wig.
3. From the 1960s on, jeans have been the most popular item of clothing in western countries.
During this period, jeans have been produced in various styles.
4. A Member of the Peul tribe in Niger, Africa, applying his make-up of various colors.
5. Detail of a poster from the 1920s, advertising gentlemen's clothing.

5

6

7

9

8

6. The 1994 Miss
World competition.
7. Japanese woman wearing the
traditional kimono.
8. Chinese imperial summer dress
from the 18th century.
9. A Hell's Angel in characteristic full
dress, with tattoos, leather jacket,
and other standard regalia.
10. An advertisement for a crinoline
dress, c.1853.

10

tion. They are still studied today for their brilliant insight into government.

Federalist Party American political party. Originally the term referred to supporters of the ratification of the 1787 Constitution. Once the Constitution went into effect (1789), differences over foreign and domestic policies led to the formation of two loose parties: the Federalists, led by Hamilton and John Adams, who generally favored a strong federal government and were partial to Britain; and the Republicans, or Democratic-Republicans, led by Jefferson and Madison, who feared a strong federal government would be harmful to liberty and were partial to France. The Federalists disappeared in the years after the War of 1812.

Feng Tao (881-954) Chinese administrator. In 932 he ordered the teachings of Confucius to be printed and so initiated their wide dissemination.

Fenians Secret movement organized (c.1858) in Ireland and the U.S. to agitate for Irish independence from Britain. The name is derived from the Celtic *fianna,* "band of warriors." The British made many efforts to suppress the movement but never totally succeeded. After World War I, many members of the F. joined a new group, Sinn Fein.

Ferdinand I (1503-1564) Holy Roman emperor, 1558-1564, and king of Bohemia and Hungary, 1526-1564. He formally succeeded his brother, Charles V, as emperor in 1558 but had effectively been ruling since 1556. He negotiated the Peace of Augsburg in 1555.

Ferdinand II (1578-1637) Holy Roman emperor, 1619-1637, king of Bohemia, 1617-1637, and of Hungary, 1618-1637. The grandson of Ferdinand I, his militant Catholicism provoked the Bohemian nobles to start the Thirty Years War in 1618.

Ferdinand III (1608-1657) Holy Roman emperor, 1637-1657, king of Hungary, 1626-1657, and of Bohemia, 1627-1657. The son and successor of Ferdinand II, In 1648 he concluded the Treaty of Westphalia, ending the Thirty Years War.

Ferdinand I, the Just (1379-1416)

King of Aragon, 1412-1416. F. claimed the vacant throne in 1412 and secured it in 1413.

Ferdinand II, the Catholic (1452-1516) King of Aragon, 1479-1516, and king (as Ferdinand V) of Castille and Léon, 1474-1504. He married Isabella I of Castille in 1469. When the couple drove the Moors from Granada in 1492, all of Spain was united under one monarchy. They also expelled the Jews in 1492, started the Inquisition, and financed Columbus's epochal voyage westward.

Ferdinand III (1199-1252). King of Castille (1217-1252) and Léon (1230-1252). Also called Saint Ferdinand, he drove the Moors from all of Spain except Granada.

Ferrari, Enzo (1898-1988) Italian racing driver and car designer. F. began his career as a racing driver for Alfa Romeo. In 1929 he founded his own Scuderia Ferrari. The first Ferrari car was produced in 1947.

Feudalism The system of organizing society and distributing power prevalent in Europe from roughly 850 to 1500 and persisting much longer in some areas. At its core were complex arrangements of responsibilities and obligations between persons of different ranks. For example, a lord might grant a vassal land. The vassal farmed the land but would owe the lord military service, payments of goods or money, and other services. The lord, in turn, was expected to protect the vassal, his family, and his land, and to see that justice was done him. All members of society, from the mightiest kings to the poorest peasants, had duties and obligations.

Enzo Ferrari

Feuillants Political group during the French Revolution. The F. favored a constitutional monarchy. They were driven from power by the Girondists in March 1792.

Fianna Fáil Irish political party. It was

Ferdinand II, the Catholic

Forebodings of the First World War

The second half of the 19th century was characterized by growing tensions among the five great European powers: France, Russia, Austria, Britain, and Germany. Competition for colonies in Africa and Asia was one aspect of the rivalry among the great powers. Alliances changed and shifted, and eventually, in August 1914, World War I broke out.
See Bismarck; Entente Cordiale; Three Emperors' League; William II.

1

2

1. When Britain tried to incorporate South Africa into its empire, the Boers—European settlers of Dutch descent—resisted violently. In the end Britain had to give up its efforts, and the Union of South Africa became independent. *See* Boer Wars.
2. At the end of the 19th century, France and Russia became allies. Here a French naval unit visits a Russian city.
3. This 1874 Spanish cartoon shows the five European powers playing a game of billiards with the world.
4. The French defend a fortress near the Niger River in Africa. Overseas colonies were valued by the European powers for their prestige and presumed economic value.
5. Negotiations between French soldiers and the leaders of several North African tribes. Britain had to accept French dominance in Morocco.

3

4

5

founded in 1926 by advocates of a total separation from Britain.

Fibonacci, Leonardo Pisano (c.1175-1245) Italian mathematician. He introduced the use of Arabic numbers in a 1202 book.

Fields, W.C. (1880-1946) American comic actor. Born Claude William Dukenfield, first worked as a juggler. He is renowned for his film roles, starting in the 1920s, in which he played lovable, sometimes drunken, n'er-do-wells.

Fierabras Epic poem in Old French from c.1170. It consists of two legends: the campaign of Charlemagne in Spain; and the transfer of relics to Saint Denis near Paris, after the Saracen giant Fierabras had been subjugated and christianized.

Fifth Column Term for secret sympathizers of a foreign cause who work behind the lines to subvert the opponents of their cause. It was first applied to supporters of Franco in Madrid during the Spanish Civil War, when four columns of Franco's men were marching on the city.

Fillmore, Millard (1800-1874) 13th president of the U.S., 1850-1853. Born in New York, F. was a prominent Whig and served several terms in the House of Representatives. In 1848 the Whigs nominated him to run for vice president with General Zachary Taylor. He became president when Taylor died in July 1850. F. supported and signed the Compromise of 1850. The Whigs failed to nominate him in 1852, and he ran for president as a Know-Nothing in 1856, hoping to bring about a compromise between North and South on the slavery question.

Final Solution The German Nazi euphemism for their plan to exterminate most of the Jews in the regions they controlled. The Nazis had always spoken of the "Jewish problem" or "question," and this plan was their "final solution" of it. The decision for the mass murder was made by Hitler, most probably sometime in early 1941. A meeting of Nazi officials—the Wannsee Conference—was held in early 1942 to discuss its implementation. The F. resulted in the murder, mainly by shooting and gassing, of about six million European Jews, many in camps built expressly for killing.

Firdausi (c.940-1020) Persian poet. Born Abul Kasim Mansur, he wrote the epic poem *Shah Namah* (*Book of Kings*), which tells the history of Persia from the earliest times to the arrival of the Arabs, and is dedicated to Mahmud of Ghazni. It is the first great work of Persian literature.

First World War See World War I.

Fischer controversy Discussion among German historians about World War I and the thesis of the historian Fritz Fischer (*Germany's Aims in the First World War,* 1967). Fischer claimed that Germany had deliberately provoked the war in order to become a great world power.

Fisher, John Arbuthnot, Baron (1841-1920) British Admiral. In his capacity as First Sea Lord, F. commissioned in 1905 the HMS *Dreadnought,* the largest battleship of its time.

Five Civilized Tribes Collective name given by whites to the Cherokee, Chickasaw, Choctaw, Creek, and Seminole tribes of Native Americans, who lived in the southeast U.S. in the early 1800s. The name came about because the F. lived in settled communities, in some cases with schools, legislatures, and other supposedly civilized institutions. Despite this starting c.1830, most were forced to move west—many to the Indian Territory that is now Oklahoma—because whites wanted their lands. Thousands died during the forced removals, known as the "Trail of Tears."

Fitzgerald, F. Scott (1896-1940) American writer. F. was one of the great American writers of the 1920s. His subjects were typically bored, spoiled, upper-middle-class white Americans very much like himself. His four completed novels are *This Side of Paradise* (1920), *The Beautiful and the Damned* (1922), *The Great Gatsby* (1925), and *Tender Is the Night* (1934). F. married Zelda Sayre in 1920, and they became a famous society couple.

Flagellants Groups of Christians who publicly beat themselves while calling on the populace to repent. The movement first appeared in the 13th cen-

W.C. Fields

Flaminius

tury in Perugia and reappeared in Europe at times of great stress, like the period of the Black Death (mid 1300s). The practice was condemned by the Church at the Council of Constance (1417). Flagellants have also appeared in the Americas.

Flaminius, Caius (died 217 BC) Roman general and statesman. While consul he lost the Battle of Lake Trasimeno against Hannibal and was killed in action.

Flaubert, Gustave (1821-1889) French novelist. F. was a master of the realistic novel. He strove for complete objectivity and perfection of detail. His greatest work is *Madame Bovary* (1856), the story of an unhappy young married woman. Other major works include *Salammbo* (1862), *A Sentimental Education* (1869), and *The Temptation of St. Anthony* (1874).

Fleming, Sir Alexander (1881-1955) British bacteriologist. In 1928 he discovered penicillin. In 1945 he shared the Nobel Prize in physiology and medicine with Ernst B. Chain and Sir Howard W. Florey.

Ian Lancaster Fleming

Fleming, Ian Lancaster (1908-1964) British writer. During World War II F. served with the British Naval Intelligence Service. After the war he became rich and famous for his stories about the dashing British secret agent James Bond.

138

Ferdinand Foch

Foch, Ferdinand (1851-1929) French general. He was active in World War I. Made commander-in-chief of the Allied forces in April 1918, he devised the strategy that defeated the Germans.

Foedo Japanese god of wisdom.

Fokker, Anthony Herman Gerard (1890-1939) Dutch-American aircraft builder. Born in Java, he worked in Germany before World War I and invented a mechanism for preventing machine gun bullets from hitting the propeller blades. He came to the U.S. in 1922.

Fontenoy Village in southwest Belgium. There in 1745 Count Maurice de Saxe led the French to victory over the Dutch, British, and Austrians in the Austrian War of Succession.

Ford, Gerald Rudolph, Jr. (1913-) 38th president of the United States, 1974-1977. A Michigan Republican, F. was elected to the House of Representatives in 1949 and served there until President Nixon appointed him to replace Vice President Spiro Agnew, who resigned in 1973. When Nixon himself was forced to resign the next year, F. became president. He was the only president unelected to either top office. F. was narrowly defeated by Jimmy Carter in the 1976 election.

Ford, Henry (1863-1947) American industrialist. In 1903 he founded the Ford Motor Company in Detroit. He initiated the assembly-line mass production of automobiles in 1908, which made the "Model T" Ford car affordable to millions of Americans.

Henry Ford

Foreign Legion French mercenary army, composed mainly of foreigners. It was begun by King Louis Philip in 1831 to serve in Algeria. It has fought all over the world and in World Wars I and II. The F. fought at Dienbienphu (1954) and in the Persian Gulf War (1991).

Formosa The Portuguese name for the island of Taiwan. When the Portuguese first reached Taiwan in 1590, they called it *Ilha Formosa,* "beautiful island." In 1949 Chiang Kai-shek and his followers withdrew to the island after being driven out of mainland China by the Communists.

Fort Sumter A U.S. fort in the harbor of Charleston, South Carolina. In April 1861 forces of the Confederate States of America fired on the fort, starting the American Civil War.

The Forty Martyrs of England and Wales Roman Catholics who were martyred between 1535-1679. In 1970 the 40 were beatified by Pope Paul VI.

The Forty Martyrs of Sebaste Roman soldiers who were executed by the governor of Sebaste (now Sivas, Turkey) for their Christian beliefs under Emperor Licinius (308-325).

Forum The central area in Roman cities that was the center of political, socio-economic, and religious life. The grandest F. was that in Rome itself.

Foucault, Jean Bernard Léon (1819-1868) French physicist. He did work on the speed of light and invented the gyroscope. To prove that the earth revolves around its axis, F. carried out his famous pendulum experiment in the Panthéon in Paris (1851).

Founding Fathers Term for the men considered to be the architects of the American republic, c.1775-1800. They include Benjamin Franklin, George Washington, John Adams, Thomas Jefferson, James Madison, Alexander Hamilton, and others.

Fourteen Points Plan for a just end to World War I and a peaceful future, presented by U.S. President Wilson in January 1918. Highlights of the F. included open diplomacy, freedom of the seas, worldwide lowering of tariffs,

disarmament, regard for the interests of the populations in colonies, self-determination in eastern Europe, and creation of an international organization to keep the peace. Wilson tried to have its principles written into the Treaty of Versailles in 1919 but had only limited success.

Fox, George (1624-1691) English religious leader. Trained as a shoemaker, he had a mystical experience in 1646 that led to his founding the Society of Friends, or Quakers, c.1670.

Francía, José Gaspar de (1766-1840) Dictator of Paraguay, 1814-1840. He participated in the 1811 revolution against Spain and declared himself dictator three years later. He isolated the country from the rest of the world.

Francis of Assisi, Saint (?1182-1226) Italian priest. Born Giovanni di Bernardone, he was the son of a wealthy merchant. After serving as a soldier, F. had a conversion in his early 20s. He

Saint Francis of Assisi

became devout and lived in poverty. After a 1206 pilgrimage to Rome, he began preaching his message of humility, charity, and devotion to others. F. founded the Franciscan order in 1209 but gave up its leadership in 1221. In 1224 he received the stigmata.

Francis I (1708-1765) Holy Roman Emperor, 1745-1765. F. inherited the duchy of Lorraine from his father but ceded it to Stanislaus of Poland to end the Polish Succession War in 1735. In exchange he became duke of Tuscany. F. married Maria-Theresa of Austria in 1736. She and Chancellor Kaunitz were the actual rulers during his reign.

Francis II (1768-1835) Holy Roman emperor, 1792-1806, emperor of Austria 1804-1835, and king of Hungary and Bohemia, 1792-1835. He was the last Holy Roman emperor. After Napoleon defeated the Austrians at Austerlitz (1805), he dissolved the empire. F. became Emperor Francis I of Austria.

Francis I, emperor of Austria *See* Francis II, Holy Roman emperor.

Francis I (1494-1547) King of France, 1515-1547. F. succeeded his cousin Louis XII. He was a fierce opponent of Holy Roman Emperor Charles V, against whom he waged many wars. Great artists and writers such as Leonardo da Vinci, Benvenuto Cellini, and François Rabelais were patronized by his court, and he built beautiful chateaux.

Francis II (1544-1560) King of France, 1559-1560. The son of Henry II and Catherine de Medici, he married Mary Queen of Scots in 1558.

Franciscans Roman Catholic religious orders that follow the rule of St. Francis of Assisi. St. Francis founded the first order in 1209.

Francis Ferdinand *See* Franz Ferdinand.

Francis Joseph *See* Franz Joseph.

Francis Xavier, Saint (1506-1542) Spanish Jesuit missionary. Born to noble parents in Navarre, he met Ignatius of Loyola in Paris and was one of the original Jesuits. After some years in Venice and Rome, F. went to in India (1841) and also to the Moluccas and Japan. An enormously successful missionary, he is buried in Goa.

Franco, Francisco (1892-1975) Spanish general and dictator. F. became a general at age 32 after serving in Spanish Morocco. He assumed leadership of the military rebellion that began the Spanish Civil War in 1936 and was head, *Caudillo,* of the right-wing government that took power as a result of the war (1939). He made his fascist party, the Falange, the official party of Spain. Despite having received aid from Germany and Italy, F. kept Spain neutral in World War II. In 1969 he decreed that after his death Juan Carlos of the House of Bourbon would

Francisco Franco

succeed him and be king. Soon after this happened in 1975, Spain became a democracy.

Franco-Prussian War (1870-1871) Conflict between France and Prussia. It brought on the end of the Second French Empire and the unification of Germany. The immediate cause was a dispute over the succession to the Spanish throne. Prussian Chancellor Bismarck used the dispute to force France into war (July 1870) and unite the German states behind Prussia. (*See* Ems Dispatch.) French Emperor Louis Napoleon was defeated at Sedan and surrendered (September). Shortly thereafter, all the German states agreed to form a German empire with the Prussian king as emperor. In Paris, however, the Third French Republic was proclaimed and attempted to continue the war. Paris was besieged for four months before giving up. In the Treaty of Frankfurt (May 1871), France ceded Alsace and part of Lorraine to Germany and agreed to pay a huge indemnity.

Frank, Hans (1900-1946) German Nazi official. In 1939 F. became governor-general of the part of Poland that had been annexed by Germany. In 1946 he was executed as a war criminal.

Frankfurt, Treaty of *See* Franco-Prussian War.

Benjamin Franklin

Franklin, Benjamin (1706-1790) American founding father and inventor. F. was born in Boston and moved to Philadelphia as a teenager, already a skilled printer. In 1732 he began writing and publishing the enormously popular *Poor Richard's Almanac*, a collection of wise sayings. F. started the first lending library in America as well organizations that became the American Philosophical Society and the University of Pennsylvania. He invented a better stove and bifocals and did experiments with electricity. He improved the American colonial postal service. F spent many years in Europe representing first the colonies and then the U.S. He was the first U.S. minister to France and helped negotiate the Treaty of Paris (1783) in which Britain recognized American independence. F. participated in the writing of the Declaration of Independence (1776) and the U.S. Constitution (1787).

Franks Germanic tribes. Their leader Clovis I defeated the Romans in 486 AD and founded the Frankish kingdom. *See* Carolingians, Charlemagne, Clovis I, and Merovingians.

Franz Ferdinand (1863-1914) Archduke of Austria and nephew and heir apparent of Franz Joseph. He and his wife were assassinated by a Serbian nationalist while visiting Sarajevo on June 28, 1914, which precipitated World War I.

Franz Joseph (1830-1916) Emperor of Austria 1848 to 1916, king of Hungary, 1867 to 1916. F. ruled as an absolute monarch until 1867, when pressure from Hungary made him the constitutional ruler of the Dual Monarchy (*see* Ausgleich). He lost Lombardy (1859), Venice, and his influence in Germany (1866). His reign was troubled by nationalist agitation that helped bring on World War I. F.'s private life was tragic: his brother Maximilian was executed in Mexico (1867), his son Rudolph committed suicide (1889), and both his wife Elizabeth (1898) and nephew and heir Franz Ferdinand (1914) were assassinated.

Frederick I, Barbarossa ("Red Beard") (1123-1190) Holy Roman emperor, 1155-1190, and king of Germany, 1152-1190. F. feuded with Popes Adrian IV and Alexander III. He drowned in Cilicia (Turkey) while on the Third Crusade. Legend has him asleep in the mountains of eastern Germany, waiting for the time to restore German greatness.

Frederick IV (1671-1730) King of Denmark and Norway, 1699-1730. He waged several wars with Sweden, losing south Sweden but gaining Schleping.

Frederick II, the Great (1712-1786) King of Prussia, 1740-1786. The son and successor of Frederick William I, F. was an amoral strategist, a brilliant general, and a cultivated enlightened despot who played the flute and composed. He was succeeded by Frederick William II.

Frederick II, the Great

Frederick V (1596-1632) King of Bohemia, 1619-1620. A Protestant, F. was defeated at the Battle of the White Mountain (1620) in the Thirty Years War. The Hanoverian kings of Britain were descended from him.

Frederick William I (1688-1740), King of Prussia, 1713-1740. He built up the Prussian army, preparing the way for his son and heir, whom he despised but who became Frederick the Great.

Frederick William IV (1795-1861) King of Prussia, 1840-1861. The son of Frederick William III, he put down revolutionary agitation in 1848. Desirous of uniting Germany, he nevertheless rejected the imperial crown offered by the Frankfurt Parliament on the belief that an elected assembly could not grant a monarch power.

Famous French Painters

1

1. Chagall (1887-1985), The Blue Cock.
2. Renoir (1841-1919), Moulin de la Galette.
3. Matisse (1869-1954), Dance.

2

3

Famous French Painters

4. Manet (1832-1883), The Fife Player.
5. Monet (1840-1926), Water Lilies.
6. Degas (1834-1917), The Dancer.

4

5

6

Frederick William, the Great Elector (1620-1688) Elector of Brandenburg, 1640-1688. He consolidated the scattered Hohenzollern lands and built up the Prussian state.

Free French During World War II, followers of General de Gaulle who after the fall of France in 1940 continued to fight against the Germans from a base in Britain.

French, John Denton Pinkstone, Earl of Ypres (1852-1925) British general. He led the British forces in France and Belgium at the start of World War I.

French Revolution Upheaval that began in France in 1789. The immediate cause was the French government's need for money, which led King Louis XVI to convene (May 1789) the Estates-General, an assembly of commoners, clergy, and nobles that had last met in 1614. The commoners—the Third Estate—and some other delegates called for sweeping political, economic, and social reforms and eventually wrested power away from the king. The revolutionaries abolished feudalism and issued the Declaration of the Rights of Man (August 1789), abolished the monarchy (September 1792), and executed the king (January 1793). In the Wars of the French Revolution (begun April 1792), France tried to export its revolutionary ideas to the rest of Europe. Within France, various revolutionary factions gained and lost power (e.g., Girondists, Cordeliers, Jacobins), and thousands lost their lives during Robespierre's Reign of Terror (1793-1794). The corrupt Directory ruled from 1795 to 1799, when Napoleon Bonaparte's 18 Brumaire coup replaced it. Napoleon then conducted more wars throughout Europe, in the process spreading liberal and nationalist ideas, and made himself emperor in 1804. He was finally defeated in 1815, and Louis XVIII, brother of Louis XVI, became king as a constitutional monarch. Issues raised by the F. continued to divide France for the rest of the 19th century and influenced developments all over the world.

Freud, Sigmund (1856-1939) Austrian psychiatrist. One of the key thinkers of the modern world, F. is the founder of psychoanalysis. He attempted to find the key to people's

Sigmund Freud

problems in conflicts that they repress in their unconscious minds. F.'s work, done in Vienna, emphasized the importance of the Oedipus complex and infantile sexuality.

Freya Nordic goddess of love, marriage, fertility, and death.

Frick, Wilhelm (1877-1946) German Nazi official. He served as minister of the interior in Hitler's regime and was executed after being convicted at Nuremburg of crimes against humanity.

Wilhelm Frick

Friedan, Betty (1921-) American feminist. One of the most widely known feminist spokeswomen, F. wrote *The Feminine Mystique* (1963), a critique of the traditional roles assigned to women in modern society. In 1966 she was a founder of the National Organization for Women.

Frobisher, Sir Martin (1535-1594) English explorer. Searching for the Northwest Passage, F. made three voyages to the Arctic in the 1570s. He fought against the Spanish with Drake in 1585 in the West Indies and again in 1588 in the battle against the Spanish Armada.

Friedrich Wilhelm Auguste Froebel

Froebel, Friedrich Wilhelm Auguste (1782-1852) German educator. In 1837 F. started the first kindergarten.

The French Revolution

The upheaval that began in France in 1789 raised issues that continued to divide France for many decades and influenced developments all over the world, even into the 20th century. The immediate cause of the Revolution was the French government's need for money, which led King Louis XVI to convene the Estates-General, an assembly of commoners, clergy, and nobles that had last met in 1614. Sweeping reforms followed, and eventually the monarchy was abolished and the king executed. In the French Revolution, France tried to export its revolutionary ideas to the rest of Europe. Within France,

1

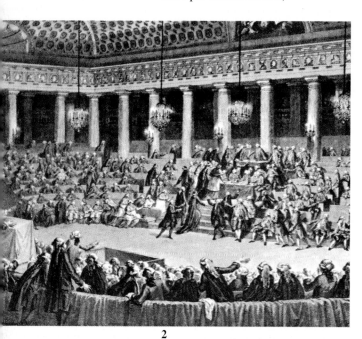

2

4

turbulence continued as various political factions rose and fell, and thousands lost their lives during the Reign of Terror.

1. A painting that depicts the storming of the Bastille, a Paris prison, on July 14, 1789, in the early days of the French Revolution.
2. The Estates-General meeting in August 1789. During the meeting the nobility and clergy agreed to give up some of their privileges. *See* French Revolution.
3. Marie Antoinette, the French queen, led a very frivolous life and was despised by many of the French people. *See* Marie Antoinette.
4. A map of Paris, on which the most important sites of the Revolution are indicated.
5. On February 31, 1793, the French beheaded their king, Louis XVI. *See* Louis XVI; Robespierre.

3

5

Fronde (French for a type of catapult) Several uprisings in France during the period 1648-1653, when Anna of Austria, advised by Mazarin, was regent for the young Louis XIV. The unrest had various causes: attempts to limit the monarch's power, ambitions of discontented aristocrats, and grievances of the overtaxed populace.

Frontline States Term for the African nations Angola, Botswana, Mozambique, Tanzania, Zambia, and Zimbabwe, which opposed South Africa's apartheid policy in the 1980s and early 1990s.

Frunze, Mikhail Vasilyevich (1885-1925) Russian general. In the civil war that followed the Bolshevik revolution, F. led the Red armies that defeated Kolchak and Wrangel.

Fuchs, Klaus (1911-1988) German-British nuclear physicist and Soviet spy. As a student in Germany, F. joined the Communist Party. When the Nazis came to power in Germany, he fled to Britain. He worked on the development of the American atom bomb and simultaneously conveyed information about it to the Soviet Union. He was arrested in 1950. After his release in 1959, he went to East Germany.

Fugger German merchant and banking family, highly influential in the 15th and 16th centuries. The weaver Hans F. lived in Augsburg after 1367 and started the family's accumulation of wealth. His descendants were merchants and bankers. Jacob Fugger II, "Jacob the Rich," built a fortune in the metal business. He made loans to the Hapsburgs, who in turn made the Fuggers nobles and gave them special privileges. The family patronized the arts were philanthropists.

Fugitive Slave Laws Legislation passed by the U.S. Congress in 1793 and 1850 to aid slaveholders recover slaves who had escaped. The 1850 law, in particular, was bitterly opposed by antislavery Americans. The agitation over it contributed to the split between North and South that resulted in the Civil War.

Fukuzawa, Yukishi (1835-1901) Japanese samurai and reformer. In 1860 he traveled through Europe and the U.S. and wrote a book about what he saw. Influenced by western ideas, he advocated democracy. Later he supported the Meji restoration and wanted Japan to be wealthy country with a strong, aggressive army.

Jacob Fugger II (right)

Fulton, Robert (1765-1815) American engineer and inventor. After studying painting in London with Benjamin West, F. returned to the U.S. and built the *Clermont* (1807), the first commercially successful steamboat.

Fürstenbund League of the rulers of Prussia, Saxony and Hanover, formed in 1785 against the Austrian emperor Joseph II.

Furtwängler, Wilhelm (1886-1954) German conductor. F. led the Berlin Philharmonic for many years. He was a renowned conductor in a subjective style of German repertory, although he also gave attention to contemporary music.

Klaus Fuchs

145

Gad *See* Israel, Tribes of.

Gagarin, Yuri Alexseyevich (1934-1968) Russian astronaut. He was the first person to orbit the earth.

Yuri Alexseyevich Gagarin

Gaikward dynasty Family of rulers in Baroda (now Gujarat state, India), founded by Damaji I (1740). The last G., Baji Rao III, died in 1939.

Gaiserik (c.390-477) King of the Vandals, 428-477. He led (429) his people from Spain to North Africa and in 455 sacked Rome.

Gaja Mada (d.1364) Leader of the Madjapahit kingdom and a national hero in Indonesia.

Galatia Ancient region in Asia Minor, now central Turkey. It was settled by the Gauls, a Celtic people who came from the west, in the 3rd century BC. The Romans conquered it in 189 BC.

Galba (Servius Sulpicius Galba) (3 BC-69 AD) Roman emperor, 68-69 AD. G. was an official in Gaul and Spain when, in a rebellion against Nero, soldiers proclaimed him emperor. Nero committed suicide. A few

months later, G. was killed in a rebellion led by Otho. *See* Otho.

Galen (c.130-200) Physician. Born in Pergamum, G. was renowned for his studies in medicine and physiology. He was the doctor of Emperor Marcus Aurelius.

Galerius (Caius Galerius Valerius Maximianus) (d.310) Roman emperor, 305-310. He was the son-in-law of and successor to Diocletian as emperor in the East. Having earlier supported the persecution of Christians, in 309 he issued a decree granting them toleration.

Galicia 1. Region in southeast Poland and western Ukraine. In modern times it has changed hands frequently between Poland, Austria, the Soviet Union, and Ukraine. 2. Region in northwest Spain. In the 6th century BC it was settled by Celtic tribes, and in 137 BC the Romans conquered it. The Germanic Suevi had a kingdom in G. in the 5th-6th centuries AD. They were followed by the Moors, who were driven out by the king of Asturias c.800.

Galilee Northern Israel. Nazareth, the place where Jesus lived, lies in G.

Galileo (Galileo Galilei) (1564-1642) Italian physicist and astronomer. He worked in Pisa, Padua and Florence. G. made fundamental contributions to physics and astronomy. He discovered the laws of falling bodies and, with the aid of a telescope he built himself, the mountains on the moon and the satellites of Jupiter. G. supported the Copernican theory of the solar system and was persecuted by the Inquisition for it.

Galileo

Gallas, Matthias (1584-1647) Holy Roman general. He succeeded Wallenstein as imperial commander in the Thirty Years War, and he won the battle of Nördingen (1634), defeating the Swedish and Bernhard of Saxe-Weimar.

Gallatin, Albert (1761-1849) American statesman. Swiss born, G. came to the U.S. in 1780 and lived in Pennsylvania. He became a leader of the Jeffersonian Republicans and was secretary of the treasury under Jefferson and Madison (1801-1813). He served on the delegation that negotiated the Treaty of Ghent ending the War of 1812 (1814) and was minister to France (1816-1823) and Britain (1826-1827).

Gallé, Emile (1846-1904) French designer of glass and ceramics. G. was renowned for his Art Nouveau creations in glass (Jugendstil). He founded the so-called Ecole de Nancy, which was the leading producer of glass art objects until 1914.

Galle, Johann Gottfried (1812-1910) German astronomer. In 1846 he discovered Neptune.

Gallic Wars (58-51 BC) Campaigns conducted in Gaul by Julius Caesar. They resulted in Roman control of virtually all of modern France. Caesar's own *Commentaries on the Gallic Wars* are the best historical source on them.

Gallienus (Publius Licinius Valerianus Egnatius) (218-268) Roman emperor, 253-268. He was first co-ruler with his father Valerian (253-260) and then sole ruler. G. tolerated the Christians. He was murdered in Milan by soldiers.

Gallifet, Gaston Alexandre Auguste, Marquis de (1830-1909) French general. In 1871 G. crushed the rebellion of the Paris Commune.

Gallipoli city and peninsula in western Turkey, at the eastern end of the Dardanelles. During World War I the Allies attempted to capture the peninsula in 1915. The attempt was poorly coordinated and ended in costly failure.

Gallup, George Horace (1901-1984) American public opinion analyst.

Born in Iowa, G. first worked for an advertising agency. He founded the Gallup Poll (1935), which conducts surveys of public opinion on various issues and events.

Gallus Irish monk and pupil of Colombanus. In 612 G. built a hermitage that became the monastery of St. Gallen in 720.

Galvani, Luigi (1737-1798) Italian physician and naturalist. He did research on electricity in animals. Galvanic current and other terms in electricity are named after him.

Gama, Vasco da (1460-1524) Portuguese explorer. In 1498 he became the first European to sail to India. During a second expedition (1502) he founded colonies in East Africa. He died in India, where he was sent as viceroy.

Vasco da Gama

Gambetta, Léon (1838-1882) French political leader. During the Franco-Prussian War, he proclaimed the Third Republic in September 1870. When Paris was surrounded by Prussian troops, G. escaped in a hot-air balloon. He returned with an army in an attempt to relieve the city but failed. He served in several important positions in the Third Republic.

Gambrinus Legendary Flemish king who invented the brewing of beer.

Gambling, Matrices Stave (1872-1958) French general. He commanded the Allied forces in France at the start of World War II. The Vichy government arrested him, and he was imprisoned until 1945.

Gamla Site of ancient town in the Golan Heights, Syria, east of Lake Tiberias (Galilee). Flavius Josephus describes a battle there between the Jews and 25,000 Romans commanded by Vespasian during the Jewish revolt (66-70 AD) that resulted in the town being completely demolished.

Gandhi, Indira (1971-1984) Indian political leader. The daughter of Jawaharlal Nehru, she was prime minister (1966-1977 and 1980-1984). G. increased governmental involvement in the economy and led India to victory over Pakistan in the 1971 war. She was assassinated by one of her own Sikh bodyguards. Her son Rajiv succeeded her as prime minister (1984-1991). He was assassinated in 1991 by Tamil separatists.

Gandhi, Mohandas Karamchand (1869-1948) Indian nationalist leader. G. was educated in India and Britain and became a lawyer. While living in South Africa, he became devoted to Hindu acetic ideals and civil disobedience as a means of reforming unjust laws. After returning to India (1915), he became the leader of the nationalist resistance to British rule, always stressing the importance of nonviolence. He was known as Mahatma, or "Great Soul." Shortly after India

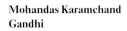

Mohandas Karamchand Gandhi

became independent, G. was assassinated by a Hindu extremist.

Gang of Four Pejorative name for four prominent Chinese leaders blamed by the Chinese government for the Cultural Revolution (which *see*) and accused of planning a coup after the deaths (1976) of Mao Zedong and Chou (Zhou) En-lai. The four are Jiang Qing, Mao's widow, Wang Hongwen, Yao Wenyuan, and Zhang Chunqiao. All were arrested and imprisoned in 1981.

Garbo, Greta (1905-1990) Swedish-American film star. Born Greta Louise Gustafson, she won a beauty contest at 16 and made her first film in Sweden in 1924. G. had a classic, refined beauty. The Hollywood film *Anna Christie* (1930) made her an international star. She made 13 more films before retiring in 1941 and lived as a recluse for the rest of her life.

Garfield, James Abram (1831-1881) 20th president of the U.S., 1881. Born in Ohio, G. served in the Civil War. A Republican, he was elected to the Ohio Senate and the U.S. House of Representatives before running for president in 1880. In July 1881 he was shot by Charles Guiteau, a crazed office seeker. G. died 79 days later.

Garibaldi, Giuseppe (1807-1882) Italian revolutionary and Risorgimento (which *see*) leader. Born in Nice, G. first fought with independence movements in South America. In 1848 he returned to Europe and fought in several campaigns to free areas of Italy from the Austrians and the French. In 1860 he led the Red Shirts in a successful attempt to conquer the kingdom of the Two Sicilies for Victor Emmanuel of Sardinia. This led to the unification of nearly all Italy. G. engaged in further, mainly unsuccessful, campaigns but remained a great Italian hero.

Garrison, William Lloyd (1805-1879) American abolitionist. G. called the U.S. Constitution a "covenant with death" because it legitimated slavery. He published the abolitionist newspaper the *Liberator* from 1831 until

Giuseppe Garibaldi

1865, when the Thirteenth Amendment, prohibiting slavery, went into effect.

Garuda Creature in Hindu mythology, half bird, half man, mount of the god Vishnu and opponent of the Nanga demons.

Garvey, Marcus (1887-1940) American black nationalist leader. Born in Jamaica, G. in 1914 founded the Universal Negro Improvement Association "to promote the spirit of race pride." He came to the U.S. in 1916 and urged blacks to form their own state in Africa. In 1927 he was charged with mail fraud and imprisoned. Later he was extradited to Jamaica.

Gaspee, Burning of the (1772) Act of defiance by Rhode Island colonists protesting British trade regulations. The British revenue cutter *Gaspee* was burned in Narragansett Bay.

Gatling, Richard Jordan (1818-1903) American inventor. He invented (1862) the Gatling gun, precursor of the machine gun.

Gaudí, Antoni (1852-1926) Spanish architect. Working mainly in Barcelona, he introduced new shapes, materials, and colors into architecture. His most important work is the Church of the Holy Family (1882-1930).

Antoní Gaudí

Gaugamela Site in Asia Minor where Alexander the Great defeated the Persians under Darius III in 331 BC.

Gauguin, Paul (1848-1903) French painter and woodcut artist. One of the founders of modern art, G. gave up his career as a stockbroker and left his family to become a full-time painter at age 35. He lived for years in the South Pacific. He used flat planes and strong colors to depict primitive and symbolic subjects.

Gaul Ancient name for the region between the Alps, the Pyrenees, the Atlantic, and the Rhine. Gaul was inhabited by Celtic tribes in the 4th and 3rd centuries BC. About 130 BC the southern part of G. became a Roman province, and the rest was conquered between 58 and 51 BC by Caesar. Roman rule was strong for hundreds of years until the 5th and 6th centuries AD, when G. was overrun by various Germanic tribes. *See* Vercingetorix, Franks.

Gauss, Carl Friedrich (1777-1855) German mathematician, physicist, and astronomer. He did highly important work in number theory, geometry, and topology and invented (1833) the electric telegraph.

Gaza Strip Region on the Mediterranean coast between Egypt and Israel. It is the site of large camps of Palestinian refugees. When Palestine was partitioned in 1948, it was intended to be part of the new Palestinian state, but Egypt took it over in the War of Israeli Independence. Israel won it in 1956, handed it back to Egypt, and captured it again in 1967. In May 1994 Israel granted the Palestinians limited self-rule.

GDR The German Democratic Republic, or East Germany. It was created by the Soviet Union in 1949 out of its zone of occupation in Germany following World War II. Berlin was the capital. The GDR was a member of the Warsaw Pact. Political oppression caused many East Germans to flee to the West, an exodus that was brought to a halt by the construction of the Berlin Wall in 1961. The GDR ceased to exist after the reunification of East and West Germany in 1991.

Geb The Egyptian god of the Earth and the third (legendary) pharaoh of Egypt.

Gelo (c.540-478 BC) Tyrant of Syracuse, 485-478 BC. In 480 BC, near Himera, he defeated the Carthaginians who had invaded Sicily.

Paul Gauguin

Gempei War (1180-1185) War between the Japanese clans Taira and Minamoto. The latter won and founded the Kamakura Shogunate that dominated Japan until 1219.

Geneva, Convention of (1864) International agreement reached in Geneva concerning the protection of and care for war victims, the treatment of prisoners-of-war, and the protection of civilians in time of war. *See* Hague Peace Conferences.

Genghis Khan (1167-1227) Mongol leader. Born Temujin ("the smith"), he was one of history's greatest conquerors. His empire stretched from Korea to the Black Sea. Its capital was Karakorum.

Genghis Khan

Genocide The intentional destruction, in whole or in part, of an ethnic, racial, or religious group. The word is attributed to the scholar Raphael Lemkin, who used it in his 1944 book *Axis Rule in Occupied Europe*. The concept was made a crime in international law by a 1949 United Nations convention.

Gentlemen's Agreement (1907) Agreement between Japan and the U.S. that provided for an end to Japanese immigration into California in exchange for an end to discrimination against those Japanese already there.

George, Saint (4th century) Legendary knight who supposedly died while being tortured. In many stories he slays a dragon threatening to devour a princess. G. is the patron saint of England.

George Gershwin

George I (1660-1727), King of Britain, 1714-1727. The elector of Hanover (Germany), G. succeeded Queen Anne, as provided for in the Act of Settlement, becoming the first British monarch from the House of Hanover. He could not speak English and spent most of his time in Hanover.

George III (1738-1820) King of Britain, 1760-1820. The grandson and successor of George II, G. tried to reassert the powers of the crown. His policies contributed to the disaffection of the American colonies, which resulted in the American Revolution (1775-1783) and the creation of the U.S. G. suffered nervous breakdowns and became permanently insane in 1810. He may have suffered from porphyria disease.

German Confederation (1815-1866) Loose organization of German states created by the Congress of Vienna to replace the defunct Holy Roman Empire. It consisted of 35 monarchies and 4 cities. For many years it was dominated by Austria. After the Austro-Prussian War, it was dissolved.

Germanic Peoples Collective name for tribes who lived along the shores of the Baltic before migrating into other areas of Europe c.4th century BC. In the 1st century BC, they first came into contact with the Romans. The G. had a profound impact on European history. *See* separate entries on the various tribes.

Geronimo (1829-1909) Apache chief. Leading small bands, G. repeatedly escaped from U.S. reservations and raided white settlements in Arizona and Mexico (1871-1886). After

his final surrender, he eventually settled in Oklahoma, where he converted to Christianity and became a farmer. He appeared at the 1903 St. Louis World's Fair and the 1905 inauguration of President Theodore Roosevelt.

Gershwin, George (1898-1937) American composer. G. composed many successful songs, often to lyrics by his brother Ira, and musical comedies. He wrote the opera *Porgy and Bess* (1935), which deals with an American black community, and attempts to blend jazz and symphonic music, such as *Rhapsody in Blue* (1923), the piano concerto in F (1925), and *An American in Paris* (1928).

Gestapo German secret police under the Nazi regime (1933-1935). It began as the Prussian state police under Hermann Goering. Henrich Himmler took it over in 1936 and merged it with the SS, originally Hitler's elite guard, and the SD, the security service. These agencies had virtually unlimited power throughout Germany and Nazi-controlled Europe.

Getae Ancient people, called Dacians by the Romans. They lived in what is now roughly Romania. Trajan conquered them for Rome in the early 2nd century AD.

Gettysburg Address Speech delivered by President Abraham Lincoln on November 19, 1863, at the dedication of a cemetery for the soldiers killed at the Battle of Gettysburg in the American Civil War. In fewer than 300 words, Lincoln movingly explained the meaning of the war and set new ideals for American democracy.

Gettysburg, Battle of (July 1-3, 1863) The largest battle of the American Civil War. While invading the North, the Confederates led by Robert E. Lee encountered the Union Army of the Potomac led by George C. Meade at the small southern Pennsylvania town of G. After three days of fierce fighting, Lee, having lost about one-third of his 75,000 men, retreated. The battle is considered one of the turning points of the war.

Ghana empire Ancient African kingdom, north of present-day Ghana. It was founded c. 6th century AD and prospered between the 7th and the

11th centuries, when it traded gold and slaves with the Arabs. The G. started to decline when the Almoravids from North Africa invaded (1076). By 1400 it had disappeared.

Ghassanides An Arab Christian dynasty that ruled in southern Syria, Jordan, and other areas in the 5th and 6th centuries and was a vassal state of the Byzantine Empire. It was conquered by the Arabs in the 7th century.

Ghent, Treaty of (1814) Agreement between the U.S. and Britain that ended the War of 1812.

Ghetto A section of a city that is the only or major place where a particular minority race or ethnic group lives, either by law or societal custom. The word comes from a island of Venice where Jews were permitted to live in 1516. The first ghettos for Jews had been set up in Spain and Portugal in the 14th century. During the Nazi Holocaust of the Jews, the Nazis established new ghettos where Jews were assembled before they were carried off to the concentration camps.

Ghibellines and Guelfs Rival factions in Germany and Italy during the late Middle Ages. The Ghibellines were supporters of the Holy Roman emperor; the Guelphs supported the pope. The names were also used to refer to the Hohenstaufens (Ghibellines) and Welfs (Guelphs), opposing German princely houses.

André Gide

Gide, André (1869-1951) French dramatist and novelist. In works such as

The Immoralist (1902), *Strait Is the Gate* (1909), and *The Counterfeiters* (1926), he wrote about people exploring their own personalities even at the expense of flouting society's norms. In 1947 he was awarded the Nobel Prize for Literature.

Gideon One of the Israelite judges who vehemently opposed the Baal cult. He refused to become king of Israel because he said God was its king.

Gilbert, William (1544-1603) English scientist. He did work on magnetism and electricity and coined the latter word.

Gilgamesh Epic Babylonian epic poem from c.2000 BC. Found among the ruins of Ninevah, it is the oldest surviving epic and deals with G., king of Erech (Uruk). When his friend Enkidu dies, G. seeks a plant that will give eternal life. The G. contains a story of a great flood that is remarkably similar to that in the Bible.

Gillespie, Dizzy (John Birks) (1917-1993) American jazz musician. Born in South Carolina, G. began to play the trumpet as a teenager. He developed "bebop" jazz in the 1940s and led his own bands.

Gillette, King Camp (1855-1932) American inventor and businessman. He invented the safety razor c.1895.

Giotto (Giotto di Bondone) (c.1266-1337) Italian painter. Chiefly known for his frescoes, G. broke with Byzantine formulas and created powerful and realistic depictions of human figures and space, profoundly influencing subsequent European painting. His 38 frescoes in the chapel at Padua (1303-1306) are masterpieces.

Girondists Political faction in the French revolution. Their original leaders came from the Gironde district. They favored war with Europe's monarchies but opposed executing the king. *See* Jacobins.

Giscard d'Estaing, Valéry (1926-) French political leader. He was a minister under De Gaulle and Pompidou and was elected president in 1974 as an Independent Republican, a conservative Gaullist group. In 1981 he was defeated by the socialist Mitterand.

Gladiators (swordsmen) In ancient Rome a class of professional fighters (usually slaves and prisoners) who fought each other or wild animals as a popular entertainment.

Gladstone, William Ewart (1809-1898) British political leader. G. began his political career as a Tory but became a Liberal (1840s) after the Tories split over the Corn Laws. A man of great moral fervor, he was prime minister four times: 1868-1874, 1880-1885, 1886, and 1892-1894. G. opposed Disraeli's aggressive imperial polices, favored domestic reform and social welfare legislation, and proposed home rule for Ireland.

Glasnost ("openness") A word used by Soviet leader Gorbachev (1985-1991) to indicate his desire for new ideas to revitalize the Soviet Union and improve its foreign relations.

Globe Theatre London theater, first built in 1598. Many of Shakespeare's plays were first performed there.

Glorious Revolution The events in England of 1688-1689 that resulted in the accession to power of William III and Mary II after the flight of Mary's father, James II. The new monarchs accepted the Declaration of Rights and the Bill of Rights, by which Parliament barred a Catholic from the throne and set limits to the power of the crown.

Valéry Giscard d'Estaing

William Ewart Gladstone

Gluck, Christoph Willibald Ritter von (1714-1787) German composer. G. is noted for his many operas, which were innovative in their dramatic and emotional power. Among the most highly regarded are *Orpheus and Euridice* (1762), *Alceste* (1767), *Iphigenia in Aulis* (1774), and *Iphigenia in Tauris* (1779).

Goa Former Portuguese colony on India's west coast. In 1510 Alfonso de Albuquerque seized it for Portugal from the sultan of Bijapur. The Portuguese capital of G. was Old Goa. In 1962 India annexed Goa and made Panjim the capital.

Gobineau, Joseph-Arthur, count of (1816-1882) French diplomat and author. A racist and antisemite, his book *The Inequality of Human Races* (1853-1855) was highly influential.

Godfried of Bouillon (c.1058-1100) Duke of Lorraine, c.1082-1100. He went on the First Crusade (1095-1099) and after the capture of Jerusalem was chosen its ruler with the title "Defender of the Holy Sepulcher."

Godiva, Lady (c.1040-1080) Wife of Leofric, earl of Mercia. Her husband founded the monastery of Coventry. According to legend, her husband agreed to lower the people's taxes if she rode through the town naked on a white horse.

Godoy, Manuel de (1767-1851) Spanish statesman. G. became the lover of Queen Maria Luisa of Spain and was made King Charles IV's chief minister

Gods and Goddesses of the Ancient World

The ancient Greeks and Romans worshipped many gods, who often resembled ordinary human beings in both appearance and behavior. The Greeks and Romans left a very rich mythology in which the deeds of their gods are described.

1. Zeus, supreme god of the ancient Greeks, marries his sister Hera, the queen of the heavens and goddess of power and wealth. The Romans worshipped him as Jupiter. *See* Zeus, Jupiter.

2. The Apollo of Piombino, a statue from the 5th century BC. Apollo was worshipped by both Greeks and Romans as the god of music and poetry. *See* Apollo.

3. Dionysus, son of Zeus and god of fertility, wine, and theater, is offered a deer by two ladies in this scene from Greek pottery of the 6th century BC. *See* Dionysus.

4. The so-called "Venus of Arles." Venus, txe Greek Aphrodite, was the Roman goddess of love and beauty. *See* Venus, Aphrodite.

5. The Parthenon on the Acropolis in Athens, where Athena Parthenos, daughter of Zeus and goddess of wisdom and industry, was worshipped. *See* Athena, Diana.

1

2

3

4

5

151

in 1792. His corruption and pro-Napoleon policies made him unpopular and the French had to rescue him from an angry mob in 1808.

Godunov, Boris (c.1551-1605) Czar of Russia, 1598-1605. A favorite of Ivan IV, he was regent for Ivan's son Feodor. After Feodor's death, he was chosen czar, although there were stories he had had the heir Dmitri murdered. G. made the Russian church independent of Constantinople and continued the weakening of the boyars. A "false" Dmitri invaded Russia in 1604 and secured the throne after G.'s death.

Goebbels, Paul Joseph (1897-1945) German Nazi minister of information, 1933-1945. G. had been a journalist and novelist when he joined the Nazi Party in the early 1920s. Because of his skill as a propagandist—G. developed the technique of the "Big Lie"—and intellectual leanings, Hitler gave him power over all Germany's communication media and cultural activities. On May 1, 1945, he and his wife murdered their six children and committed suicide in Hitler's bunker in Berlin.

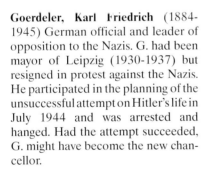

Paul Joseph Goebbels

Goerdeler, Karl Friedrich (1884-1945) German official and leader of opposition to the Nazis. G. had been mayor of Leipzig (1930-1937) but resigned in protest against the Nazis. He participated in the planning of the unsuccessful attempt on Hitler's life in July 1944 and was arrested and hanged. Had the attempt succeeded, G. might have become the new chancellor.

Goering, Hermann (1893-1946) German Nazi leader. In World War I, G. was an ace pilot. Soon after the war, he joined the new Nazi Party and took part in Hitler's failed 1923 coup in Munich. G. served in the Reichstag and was elected its president in 1932. After the Nazis came to power, G. was for many years second only to Hitler. He initially headed the Gestapo and built up the German air force (*Luftwaffe*), planning the terror bombing of such targets as Guernica, Warsaw, Rotterdam, London, and Coventry. After being sentenced to hang at Nuremberg, he committed suicide by poison.

Hermann Goering

Goethe, Johann Wolfgang (1749-1832) German writer and scientist. G. was a wide-ranging genius and possibly Germany's greatest writer. Born in Frankfurt, his first poems were published in 1769. In addition to poetry, he wrote plays, novels, and autobiography. His *The Sorrows of Young Werther* (1774) strongly influenced an entire generation. G.'s greatest work may be the two-part dramatic poem *Faust* (1808 and posthumous). Many of his works inspired or were set to music. G. did research in biology, color theory, and acoustics.

Golan Heights Plateau in southwest Syria, east of the Jordan River. The site of Arab attacks on Israel for many years, the region was occupied by Israel in 1967 and annexed in 1981. Its status has been a major obstacle to peace between Israel and Syria.

Gold Coast Coastal area in west Africa, now part of Ghana. Portugal established a colony there in 1482 that traded in slaves and gold. The British, French, and Dutch also established trade centers in the region. In 1874 the British organized the area as the G. A nationalist movement developed after World War II, and in 1957 the G. became part of the independent nation of Ghana.

Golden Bull A "bull" was an edict. Edicts of the Byzantine and Holy Roman emperors often had golden seals. The term usually refers to the edict issued by Holy Roman Emperor Charles IV in 1356 that specified regulations governing the election of the Holy Roman emperor. *See* Electors.

Golden Fleece 1. In Greek mythology, the fleece of a winged ram that per-

Johann Wolfgang Goethe

formed miraculous good deeds. The ram was sacrificed and became the constellation Aries while the fleece was guarded by a dragon in a forest. Jason and the Argonauts searched for it. 2. Secular order of knights, established in 1430 by Duke Philip the Fair of Burgundy at the time of his marriage to Isabella of Portugal.

Golden Horde Mongol Empire from c.1250 to 1400. Founded by Genghis Khan's grandson Batu Khan, it consisted of most of modern Russia. In the early 14th century, Islam became its official religion. Tamerlane conquered it in 1395.

Gold Rushes Rapid flow of people, hoping to get rich quickly, to areas where gold has been found. The most famous occurred in 1848 when gold was discovered in California. About 80,000 people from all over the world came to California hoping to make their fortunes. Other notable G. occurred in South Africa (1884) and the Alaskan and Canadian Klondike (1897-1898).

Gombos, Julius (1886-1936) Hungarian political leader. G. became premier in 1932 and followed a fascist agenda. To counter German influence, however, he pursued closer ties with Austria and Italy.

Gómez, Juan Vicente (1857-1935) Venezuelan dictator, 1908-1935. A poorly educated mestizo, he became president in 1908 and continued to rule until his death, whether in or out of formal office. He enriched himself and ruled brutally but greatly advanced the economic development of the country. Unmarried, he had scores of illegitimate children.

Gomulka, Wladyslaw (1905-1982) Polish political leader. G. became a Communist in 1927 and the general secretary of the Polish party in 1943. He was imprisoned 1951-1954 for alleged sympathy with Titoism but became head of the government in 1956 as anti-Soviet feeling mounted in Poland. Despite Soviet pressure he managed to liberalize Polish society to some degree. Protests over food price increases forced him to resign in 1970.

Gondwana Empire Empire (14th-18th centuries) in central India that was governed by the Gond dynasty and managed to coexist with the Mogul Empire. It was conquered by the British, 1818-1853.

Goodman, Benny (Benjamin David Goodman) (1909-1986) American musician. Born in Chicago, G. was an outstanding jazz clarinetist and bandleader. He formed his first jazz orchestra in 1934 in New York. He was so successful that he became known as the "King of Swing." G. also played classical clarinet, and Bartók, Copland, and Bernstein wrote music for him.

Goodyear, Charles (1800-1860) American inventor. Born in Connecticut, he invented the vulcanization rubber (1844) but died in poverty.

Gorbachev, Mikhail Sergeyevich (1931-) Soviet political leader and last president of the U.S.S.R. (1988-1991). G. joined the Communist Party in 1952 and succeeded Vitaly Chernenko as general secretary in 1985. In foreign policy he improved relations with the U.S. and was largely responsible for ending the Cold War, as Soviet domination of Eastern Europe ended and Germany was permitted to reunify. He was awarded the Nobel Peace Prize in 1990. At home he attempted to reinvigorate Soviet society and in particular revive the country's stagnant economy. His general program was called *glasnost* ("openness") and *perestroika* ("restructuring"). An unintended consequence was the emergence of long-suppressed nationalist movements that caused the breakup of the

Mikhail Sergeyevich Gorbachev

Soviet Union in 1991. With little authority left, he resigned in December of that year. G. became the head of the International Green Cross, a new environmental organization, in 1993.

Gordian Three Roman emperors. **Gordian I (Marcus Antonius Gordianus Africanus)** (d.238) at the age of 81 was made coemperor with his son **Gordian II** (192-238) in 283 by opponents of the usurper Maximin. Attacked in Carthage by supporters of Maximin, he committed suicide after learning that his son had died in battle. His grandson **Gordian III** (c.223-244) became emperor in 242. After defeating the Persians, he was murdered by Philip (Philip the Arabian), the next emperor.

Gordon, Charles George (1833-1885) British general. G. served in China and helped suppress the Taiping Rebellion, which led to his being called "Chinese Gordon." In Africa he was governor of Equatoria (South Sudan) and the Sudan in the 1870s. He returned to Africa to battle Muhammad Ahmad (*see* Mahdi) and was besieged at Khartoum for 10 months. Only days before relief forces arrived, he was killed.

Goryo In the traditional Shinto religion of Japan, the evil spirits of the dead.

Gotarzes III (d.AD 51) King of Parthia, 38-51. He murdered two of his brothers to attain the throne and was eventually murdered himself.

Gothic The dominant trend in European architecture and art from the

12th through the 15th centuries. The G. style may be said to have been born in 1144 with the consecration of the abbey church of Saint-Denis. G. architecture may be distinguished from its Romanesque predecessor by it lightness and vivacity. The use of the flying buttress and pointed arch enabled tall windows to be set into the walls. Notable G. cathedrals include those in Cologne, Strasbourg, Rheims, Chartres, and Amiens. While in the G. era architects sought to create a heavenly environment, the direction in sculpture and painting was toward a more courtly style and a secular ideal. An example is the *Virgin of Paris,* a sculpture in Notre-Dame Cathedral, with her swaying pose and voluminous drapery.

Goths Germanic tribe, probably originating in southern Sweden. In the 2nd century AD the G. migrated, passing through the Baltic eastern seaboard areas, to the Black Sea. There they split up into Ostrogoths and Visigoths. Invasions by the Huns beginning in the late 4th century drove the G. westward. They settled in Italy, Spain, and other areas.

Goto, Shojiro (1838-1897) Japanese political leader. He was one of the architects of the Meiji restoration and an advocate of adopting western technology.

Gourgaud, Gaspard (1783-1852) French soldier. He fought under Napoleon and saved his life at Brienne (1814). He accompanied Napoleon into exile on St. Helena and after his death (1821) returned to active duty.

Gowon, Yakubu (1934-) Nigerian head of state, 1966 to 1975. He led the war against Biafra (1969-1970) and was deposed in a coup in 1975.

Goya y Lucientes, Francisco José de (1746-1828) Spanish painter and graphic artist. He became a favorite painter of the Spanish court, yet many of his works are satiric or are brutally frank depictions of corruption and evil. In 1793 he suffered a serious illness that left him deaf. Among his celebrated works are the *Maja Nude* and *Maja Clothed* and the series of etchings *Disasters of War.*

Francisco José de Goya y Lucientes

GPU One of the names of the secret police of the Soviet Union. *See* Cheka.

Gracchi Two Roman brothers and reformers: **Tiberius Sempronius Gracchus** (d.133 BC) and **Caius Sempronius Gracchus** (d.121 BC). Both served as tribunes of the people (Tiberius, 133 BC; Caius, 123-122 BC) and attempted to remedy the inequitable distribution of land and wealth in the Roman Republic. Each was killed during riots provoked by his proposals.

Grand Alliance, War of the (1688-1697) Conflict between a coalition of European powers, the Grand Alliance, also known as the League of Augsburg, and France under Louis XIV over France's attempt to expand at the expense of the Holy Roman Empire. It was ended by the Treaty of Ryswick.

Grand Armée Great army formed by Napoleon. Originally intended to invade Britain, it invaded Russia in 1812 and was virtually destroyed in the winter retreat from Moscow.

Grand Army of the Republic (GAR) Organization of American Civil War veterans, formed in 1886. It had close ties to the Republican Party. The last GAR meeting was held in 1949, and the last member died in 1956.

Grand Duke In the Russian royal family, the title of the czar's brothers.

Grand Vizier Formerly, a high-ranking official in various Muslim countries, in particular the Ottoman Empire.

Grant, Ulysses Simpson (1822-1885) American general and 18th president of the U.S., 1869-1877. Born in Ohio, G. graduated from West Point and served in the Mexican War. After failing in civilian pursuits, he rejoined the army at the start of the Civil War and won several notable victories in the west, including the capture of Vicksburg (1863). Lincoln then brought him east where he took overall command of the Union armies and personally led the Army of the Potomac against Lee. Lee surrendered to him at Appomattox on April 9, 1865. He served briefly as secretary of war under Andrew Johnson and was nominated by the Republicans for president in 1868. His presidency was

Ulysses Simpson Grant

not distinguished, being plagued by financial scandals involving several of his high appointees. His *Memoirs* (1885-1886) are notable.

Gratian (359-383) Roman emperor in the West, 375-383. G. directly governed Britain, Gaul, and Spain and was guardian for his brother, Valentinian II, in Italy, Illyricum, and Africa. He was a zealous Christian. G. was murdered by the soldiers of Maximus near Paris.

Graziani, Rodolfo (1882-1955) Italian general and colonial administrator. G. was governor of Italian Somaliland and viceroy of Ethiopia. In World War II he was defeated by the British in Libya (1940-1941). In 1945 he was tried for treason for collaborating with the Germans and convicted but was quickly released, after which he became active in neofascist politics.

Great Leap Forward (1958-1960). The failed attempt of Mao Zedong to transform China in a short time from an agrarian country into an industrial one. As a result an estimated 200,000 people died of starvation.

Great Mogul or Mughal Title of the rulers of the Muslim Mogul Empire in India, 1526-1857. *See* Akbar.

Great Northern Expedition (1733-1742) An expedition sponsored by the Russian government and planned and commanded by the Danish explorer Vitus Jonassen Bering to explore the Siberian Arctic.

Great Society (1964) General term for the policies of the administration of U.S. President Lyndon B. Johnson after the election of 1964 that

El Greco

Rodolfo Graziani

attempted to fight poverty and discrimination and improve American cities and education.

Great Trek (1835-1836) The migration of 10,000 Boer farmers in southern Africa who, in order to be free of British rule, left the Cape Colony and traveled north to found Natal, Transvaal, and the Orange Free State.

Great Wall Fortification approximately 1500 miles long in northern China running from Kansu province to Hopeh province. It was built in 1368-1644 during the Ming dynasty to defend China from attack by northern nomads, although portions of it date back to the 3rd century BC. It had little effect in deterring invasions.

Greco, El (c.1541-1614) Greek-Spanish painter. Born Domenicos Theotocopoulos on Crete, G. studied with Titian in Venice and by 1577 was working in Toledo, Spain. He received commissions from the Spanish court and nobility. Although underappreciated in his own time, he is now ranked among the greatest visionary artists. Notable paintings include *Burial of the Count Orgaz*, *St. Jerome*, and *View of Toledo*.

Greece Country in southeastern Europe at the end of the Balkan Peninsula. In ancient times, G. was the center of a culture that has had an incalculable influence on subsequent Western civilization. In politics, philosophy, mathematics, architecture, sculpture, poetry, drama, religion, and other fields, the Greeks made great contributions. Developed societies in

The Greeks

Ancient Greece was the center of a culture that has had an incalculable influence on subsequent Western civilization. In politics, philosophy, mathematics, architecture, sculpture, poetry, drama, religion, and other fields, the Greeks made great contributions. Ancient Greece was not a single country; rather it consisted of numerous city-states that frequently were at war with one another. Among them were Athens, Corinth, Sparta, and Thebes. Athens, which had its "Golden Age" under Pericles in the mid-5th century B.C., was especially rich in culture.

1

2

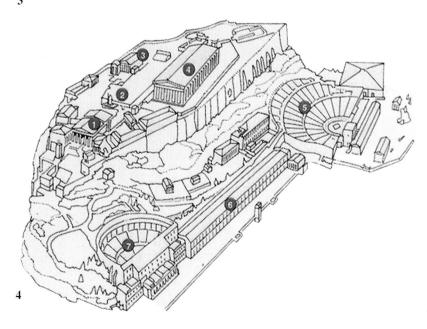

3

5
1. A Greek vase from the 5th century B.C., depicting the conquest of Troy. *See* Homer; Trojan War.
2. A so-called Athenian owl, the currency used in Athens in the 6th century B.C. *See* Athens.
3. The entrance to the Acropolis in Athens. *See* Acropolis.
4. A map of the Athenian Acropolis:
1. Propylaea (entrance gates);
2. Bronze statue of the goddess Athena;
3. Erechtheum (temple);
4. Parthenon, temple dedicated to the goddess Athena; *5.* Theater of Dionysus; *6.* Stoa of Eumenes II;
7. Odeon of Herodes Atticus.
5. A Greek funerary monument from the 5th century B.C.

4

6. A mosaic from the 2nd century BC, depicting the god
Dionysus riding a panther.
7. A bust of Thucydides (c.459-399 BC), the most famous historian
of ancient Greece.
8. The ancient Greek theater in Epidaurus.
9. An early, 8th century BC, example of Attic geometric decoration.
10. The Charioteer of Delphi, a bronze statue
from c.470 BC that was donated as a gift to the temple of
Apollo at Delphi.

G. are known to have existed as early as 2800 BC. Ancient G. was not a single country; rather it consisted of numerous city-states that frequently were at war with one another. Among them were Athens, Corinth, Sparta, and Thebes. (*See* separate articles.) Athens, which had its "Golden Age" under Pericles in the mid-5th century BC, was especially rich in culture. The period ended with a series of struggles for hegemony between Athens, Sparta, and Thebes. In about 339 BC, G. was united by Philip II of Macedonia. His son, Alexander the Great, spread G. culture throughout Asia Minor and as far east as India. By 146 BC, however, G. had become a Roman province. With the fall of the Byzantine Empire in 1453, G. was ruled by the Turks. It did not regain its independence until 1829, following the Greek War of Independence.

Greek Orthodox Church One of the eastern Orthodox Christian Churches, all of which reject the authority of the pope in Rome. There are others in Russia, the Balkans, and Turkey.

Greek-Persian Wars (492-449 BC) Series of wars between the Greek city-states and the Persian Empire. The Persians suffered notable defeats at Marathon (490 BC) and Salamis (480 BC). (*See* separate articles.). The wars ended with the Peace of Callias (449 BC). *See* Callias.

Greenpeace Environmental organization, founded in the U.S. in 1970. G.'s original aim was to prevent the extinction of whales. It has broadened its activities, however, to environmental problems in general, and it draws world-wide attention to them through dramatic actions, such as sailing ships into areas where nuclear tests are about to take place.

Gregory I, Saint (c.540-604) Pope, 590-604. The successor of Pelagius II, he established the authority of the papacy, encouraged monasticism, and insisted on clerical celibacy. He ordered a codification of the official music of the Church, and Gregorian chant is named after him.

Gregory VII, Saint (c.1020-1085) Pope, 1073-1085. Born Hildebrand, he succeeded Alexander II. Attempting to purge the Church of corruption, he fought lay investiture, and this brought him into conflict with King Henry IV of Germany, whom he excommunicated (1076). A later quarrel with Henry led to G. being driven from Rome (1084), and he died in exile.

Gregory IX (c.1143-1241) Pope, 1227-1241. Born Ugolino di Segni or Anagni, he succeeded Honorius III. G. created the papal inquisition. He quarrelled repeatedly with Holy Roman Emperor Frederick II. He died as Frederick was preparing to attack Rome.

Gregory of Tours, Saint (538-594) Frankish historian. The bishop of Tours, he wrote a monumental history of the Franks and other works. He was closely involved in the conflict surrounding Chilperic I's succession.

Grenada, invasion of (1983) U.S. action to restore stability on the Caribbean island of Grenada following the assassination of its leader, Maurice Bishop, by more radical elements within his New Jewel Movement.

Grieg, Edvard (1843-1907) Norwegian composer. G. studied in Germany but became greatly attracted to Norwegian folk music, which strongly influenced all his best work. His piano works, piano concerto in A minor (1869) songs, and music for Ibsen's *Peer Gynt* (1876) are well-known.

Griffith, Arthur (1872-1922) Irish political leader. An Irish nationalist, he founded Sinn Fein (1905) and was imprisoned by the British several times. He took part in the negotiation of the Irish Free State treaty (1921).

Grimaldi Genoese family that became

Saint Gregory I

the ruling house of the principality of Monaco in the 13th century. The male line died out in 1731, but the French family that succeeded it adopted the Grimaldi name. Since 1949 Monaco's ruler has been Rainier III.

Grimm Family of two German philologists, **Jakob** (1785-1863) and **Wilhelm** (1786-1859). They are best-known for their work in collecting German folk tales, which they first published (1812-1815) as *Grimm's Fairy Tales.*

Jakob and Wilhelm Grimm

Gromyko, Andrey Andreyevich (1909-1989) Soviet diplomat. G. joined the Communist Party in 1931 became a diplomat in 1939. During World War II he was ambassador to the U.S. He became foreign minister in 1957 and served until 1985, when Premier Gorbachev gave him the largely ceremonial job of president, which he held until 1988.

Groote, Gerard or Geert (1340-1384) Dutch Roman Catholic reformer. A scholar in Cologne, he started itinerant preaching c.1375 and founded the Brothers of the Common Life, or Modern Devotion, a communal monastic group. He is thought by some to be the author of *The Imitation of Christ.*

Grotefend, Georg Friedrich (1775-1853) German archaeologist and philologist. G. was the first to decipher a Persian cuneiform inscription.

Grotius, Hugo (1583-1645) Dutch jurist. G. became a lawyer at the age of 15. Political conflict forced him to flee to Paris in 1621, where he did the work that made him the father of international law. His principal book is *Concerning the Law of War and Peace* (1625), which maintains that nations, like individuals, are subject to natural law.

Hugo Grotius

Grouchy, Emmanuel, marquis de (1766-1847) French general. A supporter of Napoleon, his late arrival at Waterloo may have cost Napoleon the battle (1815).

Guadeloupe Hidalgo, Treaty of (1848) It ended the war between the U.S. and Mexico.

Guanche Inhabitants of the Canary Islands who were virtually annihilated when the Spanish settled on the islands (15th century).

Guarneri Distinguished family of violinmakers in Cremona, Italy. The first was Andrea G., who worked in the late 1600s. His grandnephew Giuseppe (c.1647-1745) is considered the most outstanding G. and second only to Stradivari as a great violinmaker.

Guderian, Heinz (1888-1954) German general. G. was a strong advocate of tank warfare and introduced its principles in the German army during the Weimar Republic. Under Hitler he had great influence in formulating the *blitzkrieg* tactic and led successful tank attacks on the western and eastern fronts in World War II.

Guelphs *See* Ghibellines.

Guernica (Guernica y Luno) Town in northern Spain. Many civilians were killed when it was bombed by the Germans during the Spanish Civil War (1937). Picasso made a painting of the scene that has made the name a symbol of the madness of modern warfare and the evil of fascism.

Guevara, Ernesto "Che" (1928-1967) Argentinian-Cuban revolutionary. Born in Argentina and a physician, G. met Fidel Castro in 1954. He became Castro's second-in-command in the Cuban Revolution and Cuba's minister of industry (1960-1965) He left to participate in revolutionary activity elsewhere in Latin America and was captured and executed in Bolivia.

Guido of Arezzo (c.990-1050) Italian monk. He made valuable contributions to music theory and notation, including improving the staff and devising an early form of solfège.

Guillotine A machine for beheading people by means of a falling blade, invented by the French physician Joseph Guillotin (1738-1814) as a more humane means of execution. It was widely used in the French Revolution.

Guise Ducal family of France. **François de Lorraine, duke of Guise** (1519-1563) commanded the French army under François I and Henry II and persecuted the Huguenots. **Henri de Lorraine, duke of Guise** (1550-1588), the son of François, helped organize the Saint Bartholomew's Day Massacre (1572) and formed (1576) the Catholic League against the Huguenots.

Gujrat Town in Pakistan, where the British decisively defeated (1849) the Sikhs, enabling them to annex the Punjab.

Gulag Term for the network of prisons and labor camps in the Soviet Union run by the secret police. It attained its largest extent during the rule of Stalin. The G. is extensively discussed in the works of Solzhenitsyn.

Gulf War (1991) Conflict between Iraq and the United Nations (UN) led

Ernesto "Che" Guevara

Guido of Arezzo

Gulf War

Johann Gutenberg

ing successes in Germany, he was killed in action in the battle of Lützen.

Gutenberg, Johann (c.1397-1468) German printer. Working in Mainz, he is believed to have been the first in Europe to print with movable type.

Guzmán Blanco, Antonio (1828-1899) President of Venezuela. First elected in 1870, G. dominated the country until 1888, even when not formally in office. He reorganized the economy and improved the educational system. A revolution ended his power in 1888.

Gwyn, Nell (1650-1687) English actress who became the mistress of king Charles II (1669) and bore him two children.

Gyges King of Lydia, c.687-657 BC. G. was an ally of the Egyptian king Psammetichus I in his war against the Assyrians. He was killed when the Cimmerians attacked the town of Sardes.

by the U.S. It was caused by Iraq's invasion of Kuwait (1990). The UN demanded that Iraq withdraw. When it did not, a large-scale air offensive started in early 1991 and was followed by a successful ground offensive. On March 2 a cease-fire was declared and Iraq withdrew.

Gunpowder Plot (1605) Conspiracy of English Catholics to kill King James I and blow up Parliament on its opening day, November 5. The conspiracy was revealed and the plotters killed or arrested. One of them was Guy Fawkes, and November 5 is celebrated as a holiday, Guy Fawkes Day.

Gupta dynasty Indian dynasty that ruled c.320-550 AD. Known as the Golden Age in Indian history, the period was characterized by great economic prosperity and flourishing arts and sciences. The dynasty was founded by Chandragupta I. It reached its peak under Chandragupta II (c.400), when it ruled much of modern-day India. The G. declined with invasions by the White Huns.

Gurkhas An ethnic group of Nepal. G. have served in the British and Indian armies.

Gustavus I (1496-1560) King of Sweden, 1523-1560. G. started the Vasa dynasty and established Lutheranism in the country (1527). He freed Sweden from Danish oppression and liberated its economy from control by Hanse towns.

Gustavus II (Gustavus Adolphus) (1594-1632) King of Sweden, 1611-1632. G. fought in the Thirty Years War on the Protestant side and against the Holy Roman Empire. After gain-

Gustavus I

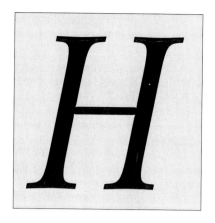

H

Haakon I (Haakon the Good) (c.920-961) King of Norway, c.935-961. Raised as a Christian in England, he tried unsuccessfully to Christianize Norway.

Haakon VII (1872-1957) King of Norway, 1905-1957. The second son of King Frederick VIII of Denmark, he was elected king of Norway by the Storting on the separation (1905) of Norway and Sweden. H. headed the Norwegian government in exile in World War II. He was succeeded by his son, Olav V.

Haakon VII

Habeas Corpus (Latin for "you have the body") Writ designed to release people from unlawful imprisonment. It was formalized in a law enacted in 1679 in England. H. was one of the fundamental rights incorporated into the U.S. Constitution.

Haddad, Saad (1937-1984) Lebanese Christian militia leader. During the civil war in Lebanon in the 1970s, he established his own area of power in the south of the country with the help of the Free Lebanese Army. In 1978 he supported the Israeli occupation of southern Lebanon.

Hadrian (76-138) Emperor of Rome, 117-138. The successor of Trajan, he expanded his empire and protected its frontiers by building fortified walls, including Hadrian's Wall in England. Under his rule the Bar-Kokba uprising broke out in Judea and was ruthlessly crushed.

Haeckel, Ernst (1834-1919) German biologist and philosopher. He formulated the laws of biogenetics in the *General Morphology of Organisms* (1868). His interpretations of Darwinism were popular during his lifetime but are given little credence today.

Hafsied Berbers who ruled in North Africa from the 13th to the 16th century. Their dynasty ended in 1574 with the capture of their capital, Tunis, by the Turks.

Haganah (defense) Illegal Jewish military organization in British Palestine. Established in 1920 to protect Jewish settlements against Arab attacks, the H. formed the core of the Israeli army in 1948.

Hague Peace Conferences Two international peace conferences held in The Hague. Their purpose was to attempt to create internationally recognized conventions of war. The first H. was held in 1899 on the initiative of Czar Nicholas II of Russia and the second in 1907 on the initiative of President Theodore Roosevelt of the United States. The first H. established a permanent court of arbitration and established precedents txat were later part of the League of Nations and the United Nations. Many of the war conventions, however (for example, a prohibition on the use of aerial bombardment and submarine warfare) were later ignored.

Hahn, Otto (1879-1968) German physicist and chemist. He made important contributions in the understanding of radioactivity and its uses in chemistry. For his work in splitting the uranium atom (1939) he received the Nobel Prize in Chemistry in 1944.

Haig, Douglas Haig, 1st Earl (1861-1928) English field marshal. He fought in the Boer War and was commander in chief of the British forces in World War I. Because of the hostility of the British prime minister, Lloyd

Hadrian

George, H. was usually under French command, during which time the Allies suffered some of their greatest casualties.

Haile Selassie (1891-1975) Emperor of Ethiopia, 1930-1974. In the period 1936-1941, he lived in exile during the Italian occupation of Ethiopia. H. instituted a number of reforms, including the suppression of slavery and the creation of a national assembly. He was a strong supporter of pan-Africanism and of international cooperation. In 1974 the army staged a coup and H. was deposed. He died one year later.

Haithabu Important Viking trading city in South Jutland (8th-10th century). It had close ties with Dorestad.

Hajj Pilgrimage to Mecca that every Muslim is required to make at least once in his life.

Halder, Franz von (1884-1972) German general. As chief of staff of the German army during World War II, he helped plan the invasions of Western Europe (1940) and Russia (1941).

Halifax, George Savile, 1st marquess of (1633-1695) English statesman. He played a major role in the restoration of the Stuarts (1660). A close adviser to Charles II, he opposed efforts to deny the crown to James II but then turned against James because of this pro-Catholic policies. H. was a leader of the Whigs who formally asked William III to accept the crown in 1689 after James was overthrown. He wrote a famous pamphlet, *The Character of a Trimmer*, which describes the virtues of the middle course in politics.

Halifax, Edward Frederick Lindley Wood, 1st Earl of (1881-1959) British statesman. A leading Conservative, he was viceroy of India (1926-1931). As Neville Chamberlain's foreign secretary, H. supported the appeasement of Nazi Germany at Munich in 1938. He resigned in 1940 and during World War II served as the British ambassador to the United States.

Halley, Edmund (1656-1742) English astronomer. He discovered (1682) the comet named after him and calculated the trajectories of numerous comets, planets, and distant stars.

Edmund Halley

Hallstatt Town in Austria. During the 19th century, archaeologists discovered remains from a culture (750-400 BC) that came to be known as the Hallstatt epoch of the Iron Age.

Hals, Frans (c.1580-1666) Dutch portrait painter. He spent most of his life in Haarlem, where in his early years he painted pictures of everyday life. In his later years he painted individual and group portraits that are brilliant in their frankness and economy of means. The work of H. demonstrates great mastery. Among his later masterpieces are *The Governors of the Almshouse* and *Lady Regents of the Almshouse.*

Hamilcar Carthaginian general. He was killed in the battle of Himera (480 BC), which was fought in Sicily against the Greeks.

Hamilcar Barca (d.c.229 BC) Carthaginian general. A brilliant general, he fought in the First Punic War against the Romans and conquered part of Spain after 237 BC. H. was the father of Hannibal and Hasdrubal.

Hamilton, Alexander (1755-1804) American statesman. A leading Federalist, he was one of the authors of the U.S. Constitution and an advocate for a strong national government. As Washington's first secretary of the treasury, H. pressed for the creation of a national bank and for a strong national economy based on manufactures, free trade, and sound money. The Federalists were defeated in the election of 1800, and H. played a role in helping Jefferson become president, which infuriated Aaron Burr. In 1804 the feud culminated in a duel in Weehawken Heights, New Jersey, in which H. was fatally wounded.

Hamite Peoples of North and East Africa. They are believed to be the original settlers of North Africa and may have come from Arabia or points further east in a long series of migrations. The Egyptians, Ethiopians, and Somalis, are counted among the Eastern H.

Hammadids Berber dynasty who ruled in the period 1014-1152 in North Africa. Their rule followed that of the Zirids, who separated from the Fatamids in the 10th century.

Hammarskjöld, Dag (1905-1961) Swedish statesman and economist. He was secretary general of the United Nations (1953-1961) in its formative years and attempted to make it a viable instrument for world peace. H. died in a plane crash in Northern Rhodesia (Zambia) in 1961. He posthumously

Frans Hals

received the Nobel Peace Prize in 1961.

Hammurabi (18th century BC) King of Babylonia. He reunited the kingdom of Sumer and Akkad and reorganized the Babylonian kingdom. H. had the laws of his empire written in cuneiform on a diorite block, which in now kept in the Louvre. The Code of H. is one of the great ancient codifications of law.

Handel, George Frederick (1685-1759) German-English composer. He is considered one of the great masters of baroque music. Of German

Dag Hammarskjöld

George Frederick Handel

descent, he was employed by the elector of Hanover, who became King George I of England. H. eventually settled in England and produced his numerous operas, including *Rinaldo* (1711), *Julius Caesar* (1724), *Atalanta* (1736), and *Serses* (1738). After the failure of his last opera in London (1741), H. turned to oratorios. Undoubtedly his most famous work, *Messiah*, was performed in Dublin in 1742. H. composed a total of 32 oratorios plus numerous concertos, solo cantatas, harpsichord suites, and ceremonial anthems for royal occasions. He is buried in Westminster Abbey.

Hannibal (247-183 BC) Leader of Carthage in the Second Punic War. The son of Hamilcar Barca, he advanced into Italy from Spain in 218 BC. In 216 BC, he defeated the Romans at Cannae, but after that lost the initiative to the Romans. He was recalled to Carthage in 203 BC to defend the city against Scipio but lost the battle of Zama in 202 and fled in 195 to Syria. H. committed suicide to avoid falling into Roman hands.

Hanno (5th century BC) Carthaginian seafarer. He made a sea voyage along the west coast of Africa (c.500 BC), exploring almost as far south as the equator.

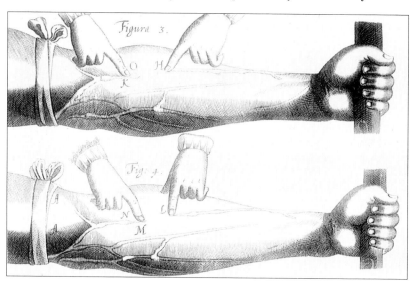

Hannibal

Hanriot, Franéois (1759-1794) French revolutionary. He led a coup in Paris (1793) against the Girondists and was guillotined along with Robespierre.

Hanse Medieval guilds of merchants. They existed to protect trade. The most important guilds were the German H. and the Flemish H. of London.

Hapsburg German princely family named after the Castle of H. in the Swiss canton of Aargau. The dynasty was founded by Guntram the Rich (10th century). Rudolf I became the first H. to be German king, or Holy Roman Emperor (13th century). In the 16th and the beginning of the 17th centuries the family dominated all of Europe. The Spanish branch, however, died out in 1700, followed by the Austrian in 1780. The house of Hapsburg-Lorraine ruled until 1918 in Austria-Hungary, when they were deposed in the aftermath of Austria-Hungary's defeat in World War I.

Harald III (1015-1066) King of Norway from 1046-1066. He died in battle in England at Stamford Bridge during a failed Norse invasion of northern England.

Harappa Ancient city in India. Together with Mohenjo-daro, H. was a center of the Indus Valley civilization, which flourished from the 3rd to the 2nd millennium BC.

Harding, Warren G. (1865-1923), 29th president of the U.S., 1921-1923. He began his career as a newspaper publisher before entering politics in Ohio. H. was elected to the U.S. Senate in 1914 and emerged as a compromise candidate for the Republican presidential nomination in 1920, winning an overwhelming victory against the Democrat's James Cox. H. called for a return to "normalcy," but his administration became enmeshed in the Teapot Dome Scandal. H. died in San Francisco in August 1923 and was succeeded by Calvin Coolidge.

Harmodius (d.c.514 BC) Athenian rebel. He and Aristogiton were the leaders of a conspiracy against the Athenian tyrants Hippias and Hipparchus.

Harold (c.1022-1066) King of England, 1066. The successor of Edward the Confessor, he died (1066) at the Battle of Hastings during the invasion by William the Conqueror.

Harrison, Benjamin (1833-1901), 23rd president of the U.S., 1889-1893. A grandson of President William Henry Harrison, he served as a general in the Civil war and was elected to the U.S. Senate from Indiana in 1881. Nominated by the

Republicans for president in 1888, H. lost the popular vote to incumbent president Grover Cleveland but won in the Electoral College. As president he supported the McKinley Tariff and the Sherman Anti-Trust Act. H. faced Cleveland again in the 1892 election and was defeated.

Harrison, William Henry (1773-1841) 9th president of the U.S., 1841. He was governor of the Indiana Territory (1800-1812) and became famous as an Indian fighter who defeated Tecumseh's forces at the battle of Tippecanoe (1811). After serving in the War of 1812, H. was elected to the U.S. House of Representatives (1816-1819) and the U.S. Senate (1825-1828) from Ohio. Nominated by the Whig Party for president in 1836, he lost to Martin Van Buren but was renominated in 1840 and won. He died 30 days after taking office, becoming the first U.S. president to die in office.

Harun ar-Rashid (764-809) 5th Abbasid caliph 786-809. His empire extended from SW Asia into North Africa, but at the time of his death, Africa had become all but independent. H. was a great patron of the arts and letters, and during his reign, Baghdad was at its peak. He is a central figure in many of the stories in the *Thousand and One Nights*.

Harvey, William (1578-1657) English physician. Through his early work in comparative anatomy and in the study of the function of the heart, he is considered one of the founders of modern medicine.

Experiments by William Harvey

Hasdrubal (d.221 BC) Carthaginian general. He was the son-in-law and successor of Hamilcar Barca as leader of the Carthaginian troops in Spain. H. was murdered and succeeded by Hannibal.

Hasdrubal (d.207 BC) Carthaginian general. He was the brother of Hannibal. As commander of the Carthaginian troops after Hannibal left for Italy in 218 BC, H. waged war in Spain for years. He eventually followed Hannibal to Italy, where he died in the battle on the Metaurus. His defeat was a decisive moment in the war because it denied Hannibal crucial Carthaginian aid.

Hashemite Royal house that ruled over Arabia between 1908-1925, over Iraq between 1921-1958, and over Jordan since 1921. The latest of the reigning H. is Hussein II, who has been king of Jordan since 1953.

Hasidim (Hebrew for "the pious") Term used by rabbis to describe Jews who are particularly strict in their observance of religious tenets. It has been applied to particular Jews in three different periods: a sect (300-175 BC) opposed to the hellenizing policies of Antiochus IV of Syria and which was partly responsible for the Maccabean revolt; mystical and egalitarian groups in Germany during the 12th and 13th centuries; and a movement founded in the 18th century in Poland by Baal-Shem-Tov.

Hastings Town in the southern England. It was the site of the invasion (1066) by William the Conqueror and the defeat of King Harold.

Hatshepsut (d.1468 BC) Queen of ancient Egypt, c.1486-1468 BC (18th Dynasty). H. was a daughter of King Thutmose I and regent for Thutmose III. Egypt was at peace during most of her reign.

Hattin Site in Palestine of the defeat of the crusaders by Saladin in 1147.

Hattusilis (Khattushilish) Name of several Hittite kings, including Hattusilis III, who reigned from 1275-1250 BC. He fought an inconclusive war against Ramses II of Egypt.

Hauser, Kaspar (c.1812-1833) Mysterious German foundling. He appeared in Nuremberg in 1828 and claimed to have spent his early life in a dark prison. A British historian, the earl of Stanhope, took an interest in H. and assumed responsibility for his education. In 1833 H. died of a knife wound. It was unclear if he was a suicide or was murdered. At the time, some people believed he was a the son of a duke.

Haussa Predominantly Islamic people of Africa. They played a prominent role before the European colonization of West Africa and reemerged after decolonization, for example in Nigeria.

Haussmann, Georges Eugène, Baron (1809-1891) French city planner. He

Baron Georges Eugène Haussmann

redesigned the streets and plazas of Paris during the time of Napoleon III, giving the city its present appearance. The Boulevard H. bears his name.

Havel, Vaclav (1936-) President of Czechoslovakia, 1989-1992, and of the Czech Republic from 1993. A playwright, he wrote absurdist stage pieces that frequently attacked totalitarianism. As a dissident, he was one of the founders of Charter 77 and was occasionally imprisoned by the communist regime. After the collapse of communism in Czechoslovakia, he became (1989) that country's president. H. resigned as president (1992) to protest the breakup of Czechoslovakia, but he was elected (1993) president of the newly created Czech Republic shortly thereafter.

Hay-Paunceforte treaties Agreements signed in 1899 and 1901 by U.S. Secretary of State John Hay and Lord Paunceforte, British ambassador to the U.S. The second treaty was a revision of the 1899 agreement, which had been drastically amended by the U.S. Congress to the dissatisfaction of the British. Both treaties granted the U.S. the right to build an Isthmian canal in Central America and to assume responsibility for its security.

Hayes, Rutherford Birchard (1822-1893), 19th president of the U.S., 1877-1881. He served in the Civil War and was elected (1868) governor of Ohio. Nominated as the Republican presidential candidate in 1876, he lost the popular vote to Democrat Samuel Tilden. Tilden also led 184-165 in the Electoral College, but 20 votes remained in doubt because of fraud and violence in three southern states and because of questions about an Oregon elector's eligibility. Congress created an electoral commission to examine the question, and it awarded all 20 votes to H., who was thereby elected by a vote of 185-184. During his term, all Federal troops were withdrawn from the South, a part of the compromise that got him elected. H. retired after one term.

Haymarket Square riot Violent incident that occurred in Chicago's Haymarket Square on May 4, 1886. During a peaceful labor rally, someone threw a bomb that killed seven policeman. Four anarchists were later hanged and three were sent to prison. Several years later, the three were par-

Vaclav Havel

doned by Governor John P. Altgeld of Illinois because of his belief that they had not received a fair trial.

Hearst, William Randolph (1863-1951) American newspaper magnate. He acquired the *San Francisco Examiner* from his father and by the 1930s owned some 28 newspapers throughout the U.S. He filled his papers with sensational stories and lowered their prices to make them available to a mass market. The H. papers coverage of the Cuban revolt against Spain helped inflame pro-war public opinion (1898). H. built a huge castle, San Simeon, in California and filled it with priceless treasures. He was one of the most influential figures in the history of American journalism.

Hébert, Jacques René (1757-1794) French journalist and revolutionary. A leader of the Enragés and founder of the newspaper *Le Père Duchesne* (1790), he posed a threat to Robespierre, who had him executed in 1794.

Hebrews Members of one of a groups of northern Semitic peoples, including the Israelites.

Hecate In Greek mythology, Greek goddess of the spirits and sorcery.

Heemskerck, Jacob van (1567-1607) Dutch seafarer. He took part in an expedition to the East Indies in 1596 and was stranded at Nova Zembla. H. died in a sea battle off Gibraltar.

Hegira Flight of Muhammad from Mecca to Medina in 622. The Muslim era is dated from the first day of the lunar year in which the H. took place.

Heian period (794-1185) Period of Japanese history, named after the capital city Heian. In 794 the shogun's residence was moved from Nara to Heian (the present-day Kyoto), to limit the influence of the Buddhist priests.

Martin Heidegger

Heidegger, Martin (1899-1985) German philosopher. He is often considered an existentialist, although hew strongly objected to this title. His major work, *Sein und Zeit* (*Being and Time*, 1927), influenced Sartre and Protestant theologians like Tillich and Bultmann. H. supported Hitler but later became disillusioned with the dictator.

Heidelberg Catechism Profession of faith of the German Reformed (Calvinist) church, written in 1562 by Ursin and Olevian.

Heiligerlee Village in the the Netherlands. The troops of Adolf and Louis van Nassau defeated a Spanish army near H. in 1568.

Heine, Heinrich (1797-1856) German romantic poet. He is considered on of the greatest German lyric poets. Feelings of love, poignancy, and grief were depicted with clarity in H.'s many poems. A Jew, he left Germany embittered by its anti-Semitism and spent the remainder of his life in Paris, where he supported revolutionary ideals.

Heisenberg, Werner (1901-1976) German nuclear physicist. One of the founders of the quantum theory, he created the uncertainty principle as it applied to subatomic particles. H. received the Nobel Prize in Physics in 1932.

Helena, Saint (c.248-328) Mother of Constantine I. According to tradition, she found a relic of the true cross in Jerusalem.

Heliand (Old Saxon for "savior") Long poetic work of the life of Christ told in alliterative verse.

Heliogabalus *See* Elagabalus.

Heliopolis (Greek for "city of the sun") City in ancient Egypt. A center for the worship of the Egyptian sun god Ra, it was a flourishing city in the ancient empire. Under Ramses III the temple of H. was one of the most prominent in the empire after those of Thebes and Memphis.

Heliopolis Greek name for the city of Baalbek, Syria.

Helios In Greek mythology, the sun god.

Hellas Greek name for ancient Greece.

Hellenism Culture and ideals of ancient Greece as seen in classical times. The term is usually applied to writers, artists, and thinkers who were inspired by what they believed were the ideals of ancient Greece in the time of Pericles.

Heinrich Heine

Helmholtz, Hermann von (1821-1894) German scientist. A physicist, biologist, and physician, he formulated the law of conservation of energy (1847).

Hermann von Helmholtz

Helsinki Accords Declaration of intent signed (1975) by the Soviet Union, European countries, the U.S., and Canada at the Conference on European Security and Cooperation. The accords covered common goals in human rights, weapons reduction, and the environment.

Helvetii In the Roman period, the original inhabitants of the western part of the present Switzerland. The name is still used on Swiss postage stamps.

Hemingway, Ernest (1898-1961) American writer. One of the most important American novelists, H. achieved fame as a spokesman for the "lost generation" with his *The Sun Also Rises* (1926). Other major works include *A Farewell to Arms* (1929), *For Whom the Bell Tolls* (1940), both of which have war-time themes, and *The Old Man and the Sea* (1952). H. was an ambulance driver in World War I and covered the Spanish Civil War as a journalist. He won the 1954 Nobel Prize in Literature. Plagued with ill health and the effects of his hard-living lifestyle, he committed suicide in 1961.

Ernest Hemingway

Henges Prehistoric monuments (2500-1800 BC) found in Great Britain and Ireland. They are oval or circular walls surrounding a ditch and often have two entrances. There are about 50 of varying sizes throughout the British Isles.

Henrietta Anna (1644-1670) Daughter of Charles I of England and Henrietta Maria. She married Philip of Orleans, the brother of Louis XIV of France, in 1661 and was known as "Madame." H. negotiated (1670) the Treaty of Dover with her brother, King Charles II.

Henrietta Maria (1609-1669) Queen consort of King Charles I of England.

The daughter of Henry IV of France, she married Charles in 1625. Her Roman Catholicism made her an object of suspicion and contributed to Charles's difficulties during the English Civil War. H. fled to France in 1644, five years before her husband's execution and returned to England with the Restoration. She moved back to France, however, in 1665 and remained there until her death.

Henry II (973-1024) Holy Roman Emperor, 1014-1024, and German king, 1002-1024. The last of the Saxon line, he waged war with the Poles, the Lombards, and his own vassals.

Henry IV (1050-1106) Holy Roman Emperor, 1084-1105, and German king, 1056-1105. He was the central figure in the long struggle between the Holy Roman Empire and the papacy. H. came into conflict with Pope Gregory VII and was deposed in 1105 by his son Henry V.

Henry V (1081-1125) Holy Roman Emperor, 1111-1125, and German king, 1105-1125. He deposed his father, Henry IV, and sought reconciliation with the pope. During his reign, he concluded the Concordat of Worms (1122).

Henry VI (1165-1197) Holy Roman Emperor, 1191-1197, and German king, 1190-1197. The son of Frederick Barbarossa, he inherited Naples and Sicily and brought a large part of Italy under his control. H. died at Messina while preparing to go on a Crusade.

Henry II (1133-1189) King of England, 1154-1189. The founder of the Plantagenet dynasty, he conquered the English throne in 1154, claiming it through his mother, Matilda, queen of England. H. strengthened the central authority and waged countless wars with France. He came into conflict with his former chancellor, Thomas à Becket, after H. appointed him archbishop of Canterbury. H. is considered one of England's greatest kings.

Henry IV (1367-1413) King of England, 1399-1413. Called Henry Bolingbroke, he was the founder of the Lancastrian dynasty. H. deposed Richard II in England in 1399, and was ratified as king by Parliament. He faced constant rebellions during his

Henry II

reign, which saw the kingdom's finances fall into ruin.

Henry V (1387-1422) King of England, 1413-1422. He restored order in England and crossed to France in 1415, where he defeated the French army at Agincourt. After concluding the Treaty of Troyes (1420) he married Catherine, the daughter of Charles VI of France.

Henry VII (1457-1509) King of England, 1485-1509. He deposed Richard III in 1485, thus ending of the Wars of the Roses. His marriage to Elizabeth of York united the houses of Lancaster and York and created the Tudor dynasty. A strong ruler, H. was highly popular even though he used ruthless methods to suppress opposition from the nobles. His diplomatic skills kept the kingdom at peace throughout his reign.

Henry VIII (1491-1547) King of England, 1509-1547. The son and successor of Henry VII, he led England out of the Roman Catholic Church and helped the country become a significant European power. By making himself head of the English church when the pope refused to dissolve his marriage to Catherine of Aragon, H. aligned England with the Reformation and gave the country its religious character to this day. A harsh autocrat, H. frequently had people executed, including two of his five wives; however, during his reign, Parliament increased in importance.

Henry the Navigator

Henry VIII

Henry III (1551-1589) King of France, 1574-1589. He became king of Poland in 1573 and succeeded his brother Charles IX one year later as king of France. With his mother, Catherine de' Medici, he instigated the Saint Bartholomew's Day Massacre (1572) of the Huguenots. The last male member of the house of Valois, H. left France torn by civil war. He was assassinated during a siege of Paris.

Henry IV (1533-1610) King of France, 1589-1610. He also reigned as Henry III of Navarre from 1572-1610. Originally Huguenot, he converted to Catholicism to reinforce his claim to the French throne (1593). In 1588, H. signed the Edict of Nantes, which established some political and religious rights for the Huguenots. H. restored order to the kingdom and was highly popular. He was assassinated by a fanatic at the height of his powers.

Henry the Navigator (1394-1460) Portuguese prince. he was the son of King John I. H. established a base in Sagres, in southwest Portugal, from which numerous explorations of the west coast of Africa were made. He also founded a school of geography and navigation at the base. H.'s patronage of exploration laid the groundwork for the Portuguese colonial empire and for the country's rise as a international power in the 1500s.

Hephaestus In Greek mythology, the god of fire and metalwork. The Roman counterpart was Vulcan.

Hera In Greek mythology, the queen of the Olympian gods. She was wife and sister of Zeus and the protector of marriage, childbirth, and the family. The Roman counterpart was Vulcan.

Heraclitus (c.540-480 BC) Greek philosopher. He believed that fire was the basic element and that all other elements were a variation of it. According to H., there was no permanence in life, only change. He also believed that everything carried within it its opposite.

Heraclius (c.575-641) Byzantine emperor, 610-641. He succeeded Fokas and defeated the Persians (627), but later lost Mesopotamia, Syria, and Egypt to the Arabs.

Herculaneum Ancient Roman city in Italy. At the foot of Mt. Vesuvius, H. and Pompeii were buried during volcanic eruption of Vesuvius in 79 AD. Subsequent excavations (begun in the 1700s) have unearthed a sumptuous villa, a basilica, and a theater.

Hermandad (Spanish for "brotherhood") Leagues or federations of town in late medieval Spain, mainly in Castile. They were formed to protect roads and municipalities from bandits and lawless nobles. The H. acquired judicial powers over time. They were suppressed by the crown in the 15th century.

Heraclitus

Hermes In Greek mythology, the messenger of the gods and the conductor of souls to Hades. The son of Zeus and Maia, H. was also the god of herds, roads, travelers, merchants, and trade. The Roman counterpart was Mercury.

Hermits People who live solitary, ascetic lives. Hermits appear in almost all cultures. In ancient Christian times, hermits commonly lived in the desert.

Hermocrates (d.c.408 BC) Syracusan politician. In the war started by H. between Syracuse and Athens (415-413 BC), he succeeded in defending Syracuse, but his fleet was later defeated by Alcibiades at Cyzicus, to which H. was later exiled.

Herod the Great (73-4 BC) King of ancient Judea. He was appointed by the Romans in 37 BC. With Roman help, H. maintained control of his kingdom and had countless works of construction carried out, especially in Jerusalem. He made great efforts to mollify the Jews by publicly observing the Law and reestablishing the Sanhedrin. In his later years he apparently went mad and had many associates and relatives executed. It was H. who, at the time of Jesus's birth, ordered the massacre of the Innocents described in the book of Matthew.

Herod Antipas (21 BC-AD 39) Tetrarch of Galilee from 4 BC. He was the king who had John the Baptist beheaded and who later played a role in the trial of Jesus. He died in Lyons in Gaul.

Hermes

Herod Agrippa II (27 BC-39 AD) King of Judea and Samaria. He supported the Romans in 70 AD in the conquest of Jerusalem.

Herodotus (c.484-425 BC) Greek historian. He produced detailed accounts of his experiences in the course of his many travels throughout the ancient world. Western historical writing beings with H., who has been called the Father of History.

Herrenvolk German term favored by the Nazis and meaning, roughly, "master race."

Herschel, William (1738-1822) English astronomer. Born Friedrich Wilhelm Herschel in Germany, he trained as a musician before moving to England in 1757. H. discovered the planet Uranus (1781) and several new moons of Saturn, and he described the characteristic motion of the solar system in 1783. His sister, Caroline Herschel, was also a noted astronomer who discovered numerous comets and nebulla.

Hertz, Heinrich (1857-1894) German physicist. He was the first person to artificially produce electromagnetic waves. Through his work, H. is the founder of radio technology. The unit of frequency called the hertz is named in his honor.

Herzl, Theodor (1860-1904) Founder of the Zionist movement. He was a newspaperman working in Paris when he published his influential pamphlet *Der Judenstaat* (The Jewish State, 1896). H. believed that Jews would never be accepted in Europe and that the only solution was the creation of a Jewish national state. He founded the Zionist World Congress, which met first in 1897. In 1949, H.'s body was moved from Vienna for reburial in Israel.

Hesiod (c.8th century BC) Greek didactic poet. Probably a contemporary of Homer, he wrote *Works and Days*, which dispenses all kinds of advice, in poetic form, about agricultural life.

Hess, Rudolf (1894-1987) Nazi leader. Once considered a successor to Hitler, H. flew secretly to Scotland in 1941 to negotiate peace with Britain. He was sentenced to life imprison-

Herodotus

ment at the Nuremberg trials. When he died in 1987, he was the last of the major war criminals still imprisoned.

Hesse, Hermann (1877-1962) German author. H. was a pacifist and fled during World War I to Switzerland. His novels, which are heavily symbolic and psychoanalytic, deal with loneliness and estrangement from the world. Among his most well-known works are *Steppenwolf* (1927) and *Narziss und Goldmund* (1930). H. was awarded the Nobel Prize for Literature in 1946.

Hesiod

Heuss, Theodor (1884-1963) President of the Federal Republic of Germany, 1949-1959. A prominent anti-Nazi, he was the founder of the Free Democratic Party (FDP) after World War II.

Heutsz, Johannes B. van (1851-1924) Dutch general and colonial ruler. He was governor general of the Dutch East Indies from 1904-1909.

Heydrich, Reinhard (1904-1942) Nazi SS leader. He was protector of occupied Bohemia and Moravia, where he earned a reputation for extreme brutality. H. was deeply involved in planning the extermination of the Jews. He was assassinated by Czech partisans in 1942. Within days, the male population of the village of Lidice was murdered in retaliation.

Heyerdahl, Thor (1914-) Norwegian anthropologist. H. became famous for his voyage (1947) from Peru to Polynesia on the *Kon-Tiki*, a raft made of balsa wood. He embarked on a journey from Morocco to Barbados in 1970 on the *Ra*, a boat made of papyrus. In this voyage he hoped to prove that ancient Mediterranean civilizations could have sailed in reed boats to America.

Thor Heyerdahl

Heyn, Pieter (1577-1629) Dutch admiral. He conquered the Spanish silver fleet off Cuba in 1628 while in the service of the West India Company. H. died in the fight against privateers.

Hezekiah (8th-7th centuries BC) King of Judah. He withstood two invasions by the Assyrian king Sennacherib. During his reign, the country prospered.

Hiawatha (c.1550) Legendary Onondonga chief. He is often credited with being the founder of the Iroquois Federation, a coalition of several North American tribes. H. is the subject of a poem by Longfellow.

Hidalgo y Costilla, Miguel (1753-1811) Mexican revolutionary and priest. He started an armed uprising against the Spanish in 1810 and raised an Indian army of some 80,000 men. After initial military victories, his forces were routed, and he was captured and executed.

Hiero I (d.466 BC) Tyrant of Syracuse (Sicily), 478-466 BC.
He succeeded his brother Gelo as dictator of Syracuse in 478 BC and defeated an Etruscan fleet at Cumae in 474 BC.

Hiero II (d.c.215 BC) Tyrant of Syracuse (Sicily), c.270-215 BC. He originally supported the Carthaginians, but became an ally of Rome from 263 BC, during the Punic Wars. H. was known as a just ruler and a patron of the arts.

Hieroglyphics Ancient form of writing used by peoples in Egypt, Crete, Asia Minor, and Central America. H. employed pictographs. Egyptian H. are completely understood, but those of other cultures are not as well deciphered.

Hieronymus, Sophronius Eusebius (St. Jerome) (c. 347-420) Roman name of St. Jerome. He was a Father of the Church and a scholar. His translations of the Bible are the basis of the Vulgate.

Hieronymus of Prague (c.1356-1416) Bohemian religious reformer. A defender of Huss, he was burned at the stake in 1416.

Hildebrand, Lay of Fragment of a German epic poem composed around 800 in Low and Old High German. The H. deal with the life of the armorer Hildebrand.

Hilferding, Rudolph (1877-1941) German socialist and theoretician. His ideas influenced the thinking of Lenin. H. fled in 1933 at the time of Hitler's seizure of power, but he fell into Nazi hands in 1940 and died in prison in Paris.

Hill, Sir Rowland (1795-1879) British educator and postal reformer. He invented a system of prepaid penny postage that was adopted throughout Britain in 1839.

Hillary, Sir Edmund (1919-) New Zealand explorer. He was the first man to reach the summit (May 29, 1953) of Mount Everest, the highest mountain in the world.

Himmler, Heinrich (1900-1945) Nazi leader. The founder of the SS, he was responsible for the establishment and operation of the network of concentration and extermination camps throughout Europe. In 1943 he became minister of the interior. As World War II ended, H. attempted to negotiate with the Allies in an effort to save himself. He was captured by the British in May 1945 and committed suicide while in custody.

Hindemith, Paul (1895-1963) German-American composer. A major figure in 20th-century music, he combined the traditional and experimental into a uniquely modern style. His early works are often atonal, while his later compositions are tonal and neoclassical. Among his best-known works are the opera *Mathis der Maler* (1938).

Sophronius Eusebius Hieronymus

Hindenburg, Paul von (1847-1934) German general and statesman. He fought in the Franco-Prussian War (1870-1871) and was retired at the start of World War I. Returning to duty, he achieved a great victory over a larger Russian army at Tannenburg. A revered figure within Germany, H. was elected president in 1925 and was ree-

Hinduism and Buddhism

Starting in the 6th century BC, the teachings of Buddha (born an Indian prince) and his followers developed into one of the world's major religions. Buddhism spread throughout Asia. After the 3rd century BC, however, it lost followers in India, where it had begun, to the older Hinduism.

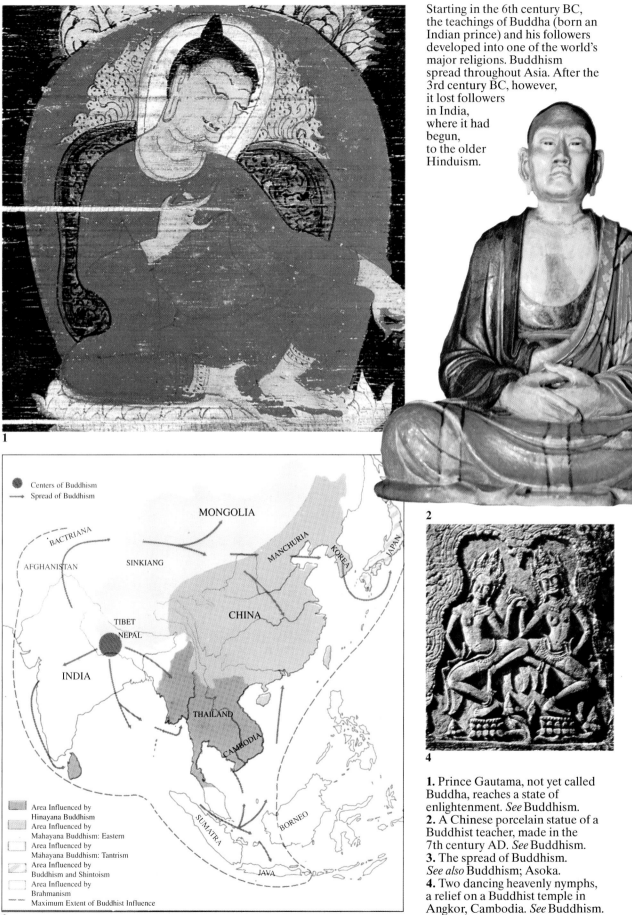

1

2

4

Map legend:
Centers of Buddhism
Spread of Buddhism

MONGOLIA

BACTRIANA

AFGHANISTAN

SINKIANG

MANCHURIA

KOREA

JAPAN

TIBET
NEPAL

CHINA

INDIA

THAILAND

CAMBODIA

SUMATRA

BORNEO

JAVA

Area Influenced by
Hinayana Buddhism
Area Influenced by
Mahayana Buddhism: Eastern
Area Influenced by
Mahayana Buddhism: Tantrism
Area Influenced by
Buddhism and Shintoism
Area Influenced by
Brahmanism
Maximum Extent of Buddhist Influence

3

1. Prince Gautama, not yet called Buddha, reaches a state of enlightenment. *See* Buddhism.
2. A Chinese porcelain statue of a Buddhist teacher, made in the 7th century AD. *See* Buddhism.
3. The spread of Buddhism. *See also* Buddhism; Asoka.
4. Two dancing heavenly nymphs, a relief on a Buddhist temple in Angkor, Cambodia. *See* Buddhism.

5

6

8

7

5. A stone statue of Buddha, who resicts the temptations of the evil god Mara. *See* Buddhism.
6. A Hindu goddess in one of the yoga positions. This sculpture was made in the 10th century.
See Hinduism; Krishna.
7. Krishna, one of the shapes of the supreme Hindu god Vishnu, meets the nymph Radha. *See* Hinduism; Krishna; Vishnu.
8. Kali, also called Durga, the wife of the great Hindu god Shiva. In some forms of Hinduism, she is venerated as a mother goddess. *See* Hinduism.
9. Two Hindu dancers, in a 17th-century painting. *See* Hinduism.

9

lected in 1932. In 1933, he appointed Adolf Hitler as chancellor.

Paul von Hindenburg

Hinduism Primary religion of the peoples of India. H. has no founder but developed over a 4,000-year period. It has no ecclesiastical system and is divided into numerous sects. Two common strains that run through all H. are a caste system and a belief in the Veda as the most sacred scripture. H. is s synthesis of religion brought to India by the Aryans c.1500 BC and indigenous beliefs.

Hipparchus (d.514 BC) Athenian political figure. The son of Pisistratus, he ruled Athens with his brother, Hippias. H. was killed by Aristogiton and Harmodius.

Hipper, Franz von (1863-1932) German admiral. He became head of the German fleet near the end of World War I.

Hippias (d.490 BC) Tyrant of Athens, 527-510 BC. The son of and Pisistratus, he ruled with his brother Hipparchus. His rule became harsher over the years, and in 510 BC he was overthrown and exiled to Persia. H. took part in the battle of Marathon (490 BC) on the side of the Persians.

Hippocrates (c.460-370 BC) Greek physician. He is considered the father of medicine. He believed that medicine should be oriented toward the patient, and in the course of his life, he made careful observations and notations of diseases and symptoms. The so-called Hippocratic oath, which cannot be directly credited to him despite the name, does, however, represent his ideals.

Hirohito (1901-1989) Emperor of Japan, 1926-1989. He played a decisive role in convincing the Japanese military to accept surrender in World War II (1945) rather than fight to the death. After the war, he was allowed to remain as emperor but was forced to renounce (1946) his divinity. A revered figure among his people, H. was also a respected marine biologist. He was succeeded by his son, Akihito.

Hiroshima City in Japan. During World War II, the U.S. dropped the first atomic bomb used in warfare on H. (August 6, 1945), destroying the city and killing some 100,000 people.

Hirtius, Aulus (c.90-43 BC) Roman general and author. He served under Caesar in Gaul and became consul in 43 BC. He died in the Battle of Mutina against Marc Anthony. H. was probably the author of the eighth book of Caesar's *Gallic Wars*.

Histiaeus (d.c.494 BC) Tyrant of Miletus under Darius I. He took part in the Scythian campaign of Darius in 513 BC, whose life he saved by holding a bridge over the Danube. He later played what the Persians considered to be a suspect role in the Ionic Uprising. H. was later executed by the Persians.

Hirohito

Hitler Adolf (1889-1945) German dictator, the founder and leader of National Socialism (Nazism). He was born in Austria and served in the Bavarian army in World War I. In 1921 he became leader of the National Socialist German Workers' (Nazi) Party. After an unsuccessful putsch in 1923 against the Bavarian government, H. was briefly imprisoned and he wrote *Mein Kampf*. His party grad-

Hippocrates

Adolf Hitler

ually increased its share of the vote through the 1920s, and in 1933 he was appointed chancellor of Germany. He soon eliminated all internal opposition and turned the government into a dictatorship. In 1939, H. invaded Poland, triggering World War II. After spectacular victories that included the defeat and occupation of France (1940) and the near-defeat of Russia (1941), the military tide turned against Germany. In 1945, H. committed suicide in his bunker in Berlin as the Russians entered the city. The mass destruction caused by the war he started, as well as his genocide of more than 6 million European Jews, makes H.'s legacy one of the greatest tyrannies in human history.

Hitopadesha (Sanskrit for "wholesome instruction") Old Indian book of fables, probably compiled between the 9th-14th centuries by Narayana.

Hittites People of Asia-Minor who flourished between c.2000-1000 BC. The H. were formidable warriors and were almost always at war with Syria, Mesopotamia, and Egypt. The H. were among the first peoples to smelt iron.

Ho Chi Minh (1892-1969) Vietnamese communist revolutionary and nationalist leader. He lived in the U.S. during World War I, then moved to France, where he was a founder of the French communist party. H. returned to Vietnam during World War II to fight the Japanese. After the war he led the Vietnamese independence movement against the French. He became president of North Vietnam in 1954 and continued leading the struggle for a unified Vietnam, now against the South Vietnamese and the Americans. After the fall of South Vietnam (1975) the city of Saigon was named after H.

Hoare-Laval pact Accord (1935) between the foreign ministers of Britain (Sir Samuel Hoare) and France (Pierre Laval) in which large parts of Ethiopia would be surrendered to Italian control. The agreement provoked outrage in Britain and led to H.'s resignation.

Hoche, Lazare (1768-1797) French general. He suppressed the uprising in the Vendée in 1796.

Hofer, Andreas (1767-1810) Tyrolean patriot. He led an uprising against the Bavarians and the French in 1809 but was betrayed and executed in Mantua.

Andreas Hofer

Hohenlohe, Philip (1550-1606) General in the Netherlands from 1575. After the assassination of William of Orange, he became the commander of the Dutch army against Spain. H. was married to William's eldest daughter

Hohenstaufen German princely family that ruled Germany between 1138-1208 and 1212-1254. Their name is derived from the castle at Staufen, which was built in 1077.

Hohenzollern German princely family. They ruled in Brandenburg (1415-1918), then in Prussia (1525-1918), and then in all of Germany (1871-1918). The H. family divided into a Frankish and a Swabian branch. The former branch included the last German emperor, William II, and the latter branch included the last kings of Rumania, Michael and Carol II.

Hojo Japanese family who ruled from 1199-1333 during the Kamakura Shogunate.

Hojo, Masako (1157-1225) Wife of Minamoto Yorimoto, the first shogun of Japan. She retained power after his death.

Hojo, Tokimun (1251-1284) Regent of the shogun, under whom two Mongol invasions (1247 and 1281) were repulsed.

Holbein, Hans (the elder) (c.1465-1524) German painter. He painted altar pieces, did portraits, and designed stained glass. His works show both Flemish and Italian influences.

Holbein, Hans (the younger) (c.1497-1543) German painter, the son of Hans Holbein the elder. A religious and portrait painter, he was one of the outstanding artists of the northern Renaissance. His superb portraits were done in both Basel and England.

Holland House Family of counts who governed Holland between c. 889-1299 and occasionally Zealand and West Friesland.

Holocaust Name given to the period of persecution and murder of European Jews by the Nazis (1933-1945). During the Holocaust, some 6 millions Jews perished across Europe.

Holy Alliance *See* Alliance.

Holy Land Name used to refer to

Palestine as the center of the world's major religions. The region of ancient Palestine is the "holy land" for Jews, Christians, and Muslims.

Holy League (1511) Alliance formed by Pope Julius II to drive France out of Italy. The main members were Venice, the Swiss cantons, Ferdinand of Aragon, Henry VIII of England, and Holy Roman Emperor Maximilian I.

Home Rule Political slogan adopted by Irish nationalists in the 19th century to describe their objective of self-government and freedom from British rule.

Homer Greek poet. Two great epic poems, the *Iliad* and the *Odyssey,* are attributed to H. They constitute two of the greatest works of Western literature and the basis for all epic poetry. The *Iliad* describes the siege of Troy by the Greeks. The *Odyssey* describes the adventures of the clever Odysseus, who wandered for years after the capture of Troy before finally arriving in the kingdom of Ithaca. Little is known about H., although scholars tend to agree that each work is the product of one poet. It is assumed that H. lived at the end of the 9th century BC.

Honorius (384-423) Roman emperor of the West, 395-423. He was the son of Theodosius I. His general Stilicho, was powerful in the early years of H.'s reign, putting down a Visigoth invasion. H., however, had him murdered (408). At the end of his reign he was forced to accept joint rule with Constantine. Under H., Ravenna was the capital of the empire from 402.

Honorius

Honorius I (d.638) Pope, 625-638. He was declared a heretic by the Third Council of Constantinople because of his apparent support of the Monotheletist heresy.

Honorius III (d.1227) Pope, 1216-1227. Born Cencio Savelli, he pressed for a resumption of the Crusades. In 1220, H. crowned Frederick II of Hohenstaufen as Holy Roman Emperor.

Hood, Robin In old English folklore, a 12th-century hero who robbed the rich and helped the poor. The character of H. represented many of the ideals of yeoman and was the subject of numerous ballads.

Hoorn, Philip de Montmorency, Count of (c.1518-1568) Dutch nobleman. Together with William of Orange and count Egmont, he fought after 1561 to gain greater influence for the the Dutch nobility the government of the Netherlands. H. was arrested by the duke of Alva at the end of 1567 and was beheaded in 1568. His execution sparked great outrage and led to the open revolt of the Dutch against the Spanish.

Hoover, John Edgar (1895-1972) American public official. He was head of the Federal Bureau of Investigation (FBI) from 1924-1972. H. was a staunch anti-communist and a crime fighter, but after his death, his reputation was clouded by the discovery of numerous illegalities that he engaged in as FBI director, including harassment of groups he considered "subversive," illegal wiretapping, and the blackmail of public officials to retain his position in government. Because of the abuses of his administration, Congress limited the term of the FBI director to 10 years.

Hoover, Herbert C. (1874-1964) 31st president of the U.S., 1929-1933. Born into a poor family in Iowa, H. attended Stanford University and received a degree in mining. He made a considerable fortune in private business before serving as food relief administrator during World War I. His efforts to prevent starvation and his considerable organizational abilities led to his appointment as secretary of commerce in 1921. H. was elected president on the Republican ticket in 1928. His ill-fated administration,

however, was plagued from the outset by the Great Depression. H. was unable to halt the slide or to gain the confidence of the nation as a leader, and he was defeated for reelection in 1932 by Franklin D. Roosevelt. In his later years, he served on a number of government commissions for President Harry S. Truman.

Hopkins, Harry Lloyd (1890-1946) American public official. As a domestic adviser to President Franklin D.

Robin Hood

Herbert C. Hoover

Roosevelt, he administered many welfare and relief programs. During World War II, his responsibilities shifted largely to foreign affairs, where he served as a special emissary to Churchill and Stalin and as administrator (1941) of Lend Lease.

Horatio (Quintus Horatius Flaccus) (65-8 BC) Roman poet. His work consisted of letters, the poetry text *Ars Poetica,* and many odes and lyrical poems about friendship, wine, and love.

Horemheb (14th century BC) King of ancient Egypt, c.1342-1303 BC, founder of the 19th Dynasty. Originally a general under a number of kings, he restored prosperity to Egypt and rebuilt many buildings that had fallen into disarray.

Horthy, Miklós (1868-1957) Hungarian admiral, regent of Hungary. He became national leader in 1920, at which time he barred the attempt of the Hapsburg Emperor Charles I to regain his throne in Hungary. H. led Hungary in the years between World Wars I and II. Although he allied Hungary with Germany in World War II, H. protested the German invasion of his country in 1944. He was arrested by the Germans and imprisoned until he was freed by the Allies. H. spent his final years in exile in Portugal.

Houtman, Cornelis de (c.1540-1599) Dutch mariner. He led the first Dutch expedition to the East Indies between 1595-1597. He was murdered during his second expedition.

Howard, Charles (1536-1624) English admiral. He commanded the English fleet against the Spanish Armada in 1588.

Hoxha, Enver (1908-1985) Albanian communist politician. He became leader of Albania in 1945 and led his country into a period of extreme isolation from the outside world. Alienated from the Soviet Union, H. allied Albania with Communist China. After his death, H. was succeeded by Ramiz Alia, who sought to improve relations with the West.

Huayna Capac *See* Incas.

Hubert, Saint (d.727) Roman Catholic saint, the patron saint of hunters. According to tradition, he saw a deer with a radiant cross in its antlers during a hunting party. He later became a priest and bishop of Maastricht.

Hudson, Henry (c.1565-1611) English navigator. Working for both the English and the Dutch, he undertook several voyages to find the North Passage to China. While employed by the Dutch he sailed up the Hudson River, which bears his name. He continued his attempts to find a passage to Asia, sailing into Hudson Bay in 1610. The following year his crew, beset by hardship, mutinied and set Hudson, his son, and seven others adrift in a boat without food or water. They were never seen again.

Hugh Capet (c.938-996) King of France, 987-996. he was the founder of the Capetian dynasty.

Hugo, Victor (1802-1885) French writer. A revered poet, dramatist, and novelist of his day, H. was a leading exponent of 19th-century French romanticism. His *Notre Dame de Paris* (1831) and *Les Misérables* (1862) are well known.

Huguenots French Protestants, followers of John Calvin. They were brutally repressed until the Edict of Nantes (1598) gave them some degree of religious freedom. The Edict, however, was revoked by Louis XIV (1685), whereupon most H. fled the country.

Hulagu Khan (c.1217-1265) Mongol conqueror. The grandson of Genghis Khan, he conquered Baghdad (1258) and reached Damascus. He was turned back in Egypt by the Mamelukes (1260).

Hull, Cordell (1871-1955) American statesman. He served in the U.S. House of Representatives and Senate before being appointed secretary of state (1933) by President Franklin D. Roosevelt. H. worked for better relations between the U.S. and Latin American and was a founder of the UN. He resigned in 1944 and was awarded the Nobel Peace Prize in 1945.

Humayun (c.1508-1556) Mughal emperor of India, 1530-1556. The son of Babur, he lived a dissolute life and was deposed in 1540, after which the Suri dynasty briefly ruled. In 1555, one year before his death, H. came to the throne again. He was succeeded by his son Akbar.

Victor Hugo

The Hundred Years' War

The Hundred Years' War (1337-1453) was in fact a series of battles between England and France, with long periods of relative peace between the battles. The conflict started when Edward III of England claimed the French throne. At first the English were successful, but France regained the initiative, partly as a result of an alliance with Flanders. As a result of the war, England ceased to be a continental power and relied increasingly on naval strength, and France, because of the decimation of its nobility, became more of a centralized monarchy.

1

2

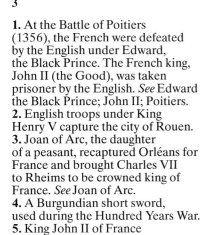

3

4

5

1. At the Battle of Poitiers (1356), the French were defeated by the English under Edward, the Black Prince. The French king, John II (the Good), was taken prisoner by the English. *See* Edward the Black Prince; John II; Poitiers.
2. English troops under King Henry V capture the city of Rouen.
3. Joan of Arc, the daughter of a peasant, recaptured Orléans for France and brought Charles VII to Rheims to be crowned king of France. *See* Joan of Arc.
4. A Burgundian short sword, used during the Hundred Years War.
5. King John II of France and the knights of the Golden Fleece, his bravest and most faithful followers.

Christiaan Huygens

Hundred Days Period after the return of Napoleon from Elba. The hundred days are counted from March 20, 1815, when Napoleon returned to Paris, until June 28, 1815, when Louis XVIII was restored as king after Napoleon's defeat at Waterloo.

Hundred Years' War (1337-1453) Series of wars between England and France about domination in Western Europe. The trigger was the claim to the French throne by Edward III of England. In the beginning the English were successful, but France regained the initiative, partly as a result of an alliance with Flanders. The war inflicted untold misery on Europe. As a result of the H., England ceased to be a continental power and relied increasingly on sea power, and France, because of the decimation of the nobility, became more of a centralized monarchy.

Huns Nomadic people who originated in central Asia and appeared in Europe in the 4th century AD. They were organized militarily and occupied the lands that are now Russia, Poland, eastern Germany, and other parts of central Europe. Their greatest leader was Attila. The H. were defeated in 451 in France, and they invaded Italy the same year, but their empire collapsed after the death of Attila (453).

Hurrians Persian people who settled in Anatolia c.2000 BC and who established the Mittani kingdom (c.1600-1350 BC). The H. were ultimately conquered by the Hittites.

Huss, John (c.1372-1415) Czech nationalist cleric. He denounced the abuses of the church, denied papal infallibility, and preached that the state should supervise the state. Many of his ideas anticipated the Reformation. H. was made rector of the University of Prague (1409) and was excommunicated in 1411. He journeyed to the Council of Constance (1414) to defend himself, but was arrested and was burned at the stake as a heretic. H. is a Czech national hero.

Hussein, Ibn Ali (c.1854-1931) Arab sherif of Mecca. In World War I, he supported the British, who promised him independence. When they failed to honor their promise, H. captured Mecca and Jedda and he was recognized as king of the Hejaz. He was expelled, however, by Ibn Saud (1924), and spent the next years in exile in Cyprus.

Hussite Wars (1419-1436) Wars between the Hussites (followers of Huss) and the German emperor and the pope. The pope encouraged the Bohemian crusade to subdue the Hussites. The Holy Roman Emperor Sigismund succeeded in 1436 in defeating the internally divided Hussites.

Huygens, Christiaan (1629-1695) Dutch mathematician and physicist. The son of Constantine Huygens, he was the first to develop the wave theory of light. H. also invented the pendulum clock and improved the microscope and telescope.

Huygens, Constantine (1596-1687) Dutch poet, composer, and diplomat. He was secretary to Frederick Henry and William III, and left a wide correspondence with contemporary scholars and humanists.

Hyder Ali (1722-1782) Muslim ruler in India. He was the ruler of Mysore from 1761 and defeated the British in 1769. H. was defeated, however, at Madras in 1781 and his kingdom became part of the British Empire.

Hyksos Semitic nomads, who ruled in Syria and Palestine in the 18th-17th centuries BC and occupied a part of Egypt. Their capital city there was Avaris (now Tell el-Daba). After 1550 BC, they were expelled by the Egyptians.

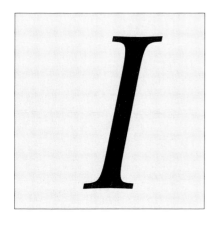

Ibárruri Gómez, Isidora Dolores (1895-1989) Spanish revolutionary. Called *La Pasionaria* ("the Passionate One"), I. was an active Republican (Loyalist) during the Spanish Civil War (1936-1939). Following Franco's victory, she fled to Moscow, where she lived until 1977, when the Spanish Communist Party was legalized.

Isidora Dolores Ibárruri Gómez

Iberians The ancient inhabitants of Spain, a non-Indo-European people that migrated to Spain from North Africa in the Neolithic and Bronze Ages and settled in eastern Spain and the Ebrus Valley.

Ibn Batuta (c.1304-1378) Muslim traveler. Born in Tangier, I. made extensive travels throughout Spain, Africa, the Middle East, and Asia. His journals are the best source for the geography and culture of the places he visited.

Ibn Khaldun, Abd ar-Rahman (1332-1406) Arab historian. The greatest Arab historian, he was born in Tunis but lived most of his life in Cairo as a teacher. He negotiated the Egyptian

surrender of Damascus to Tamerlane (1400). His masterpiece is the *Kitab-al-Ibar* (*Universal History*), mainly about the Muslims, Arabs, and Berbers, which offers a science and philosophy of history.

Ibn Saud, Abdul Aziz Two kings of Saudi Arabia 1. (c.1888-1953) I. founded modern Saudi Arabia and

Abdul Aziz Ibn Saud

ruled until his death in 1953. The leader of the orthodox Wahabis (which *see*), he defeated Ibn Ali Hussein in 1924-1925 and declared himself king of Hijaz and Najd. From Riyadh he conquered the greater part of the Arabian peninsula and in 1932 named it Saudi Arabia. Under his rule the development of the country as a great oil producer began. 2. (1902-1969) Son of the above, he succeeded his father as king in 1953 but was deposed by his brother Faisal (1964).

Ibrahim I (1615-1648) Sultan of Turkey, 1640-1648. I. succeeded his brother, Murad IV. He began a war with Venice over Crete (1645-1664). When the war went badly, the Janissaries and the clergy revolted, murdered I., and put the six-year old Muhammad IV on the throne in 1648.

Ibrahim Pasha (1789-1848) Egyptian general. The son of Muhammad Ali, he took Mecca and Medina from the Wahabis (1816-1818). When Egypt went to war with Turkey, he conquered Syria (1832-1833) but was forced to abandon it by the British and Austrians (1838). He ruled Egypt in 1848 when his father became insane.

Ibsen, Henrik (1828-1906) Norwegian playwright and poet. In his most characteristic work, I., who greatly influenced subsequent drama, portrayed individuals rebelling against societal conventions. Among

his best-known works today are *Peer Gynt* (1867), *A Doll's House* (1879), *Ghosts* (1881), *Hedda Gabler* (1890), and *The Master Builder* (1892).

Icarians Utopian communities founded in the mid 1800s in Texas, Illinois, and Iowa by the Frenchman Etienne Cabet (1788-1856) and his followers. They were based on the communal ownership of property. The last was disbanded in 1898.

I-Ching (Book of Changes) Ancient Chinese book of fortune-telling and one of the classics of Chinese literature. Parts are believed to date from the 7th century BC.

Iconoclasm In religion, opposition to the use and worship of images. In the Byzantine Empire there was a prolonged controversy over the matter (726-843). The Council of Nicaea rejected iconoclasm. Many of the early Protestants were iconoclastic.

Iconoclastic Fury Destruction of religious statues and images, especially during the beginning of the Reformation.

Idris al-Sanusi, (Sayyid Mehmet) (1890-1983) King of Libya, 1950-1969. I. resisted Italian colonial authority and fled to Egypt in 1922. After the British and Americans invaded North Africa in World War II (1942), he returned and became king when Libyan independence was reestablished. He was deposed in a 1969 coup.

Henrik Ibsen

Idrisids Two Muslim families. 1. Shiite dynasty of Morocco (788-974), named after Idris I (d.793), a descendant of Caliph Ali. 2. Rulers of Arabia who lost their power when the kingdom of Saudi Arabia was created in 1934.

Idun In Old Norse mythology, the goddess who possessed apples that bestowed eternal youth upon the gods. Apples are a symbol of fertility, and I. can therefore be regarded as a goddess of fertility.

IG Farben (Interessen-Gemeinschaft Farbenindustrie) German industrial cartel that includes Bayer and BASF. During World War II it produced many products for the German war effort. It also manufactured Zyklon-B, the gas used in the death camps' gas chambers for human extermination.

Ignatius of Antioch, Saint (d.c.107) Bishop of Antioch and early Christian martyr. On his way to Rome to be put to death, he wrote epistles to Christian communities in Rome and Asia Minor that give important information about early Christianity. He stressed the significance of the virgin birth and was the first to use the word "Catholic."

Ignatius of Constantinople, Saint (c.800-877) Patriarch of Constantinople. The son of Emperor Michael I, he was castrated and imprisoned by Leo V, who had deposed Michael. Empress Theodora made him patriarch (846 or 847). He opposed iconclasm.

Ignatius of Loyola, Saint (1491-1556) Spanish clergyman, founder of the Jesuits. A nobleman, I. was wounded in battle (1521) and had a religious conversion. He became a priest in 1537 and founded a new order, the Jesuits, in 1540. Its main purposes were missionary work and education. Over several years I. wrote the *Spiritual Exercises* that aim at union with God.

Ikhnaton *See* Akhenaton.

Il-Khan Mongolian dynasty. It was founded by Hulagu Khan, a grandson of Genghis Khan, after his defeat by the Mamelukes at Ayn Jalut in Syria in 1260 and his conversion to Islam. The dynasty ruled all of Persia and lasted until 1335.

Ilescu, Ion (1930-) Romanian political leader. He led the opposition National Salvation Front after the revolution against Ceaucescu (1989) and in 1990 became president of Romania.

Iliad Great ancient Greek epic. *See* Homer.

Illyrians Eastern European Indo-Germanic people. Around 1000 B.C. the I. spread through the Balkans and intermarried with the Slavs. Between 35-33 BC the southern Illyrians were conquered by the Romans under Augustus and later the rest of the lands of the Illyrians were added to the Roman Empire as the province of Illyricum.

Imam A religious leader in Islam. Among Sunni Muslims an I. is the person who leads the prayers in a mosque. The term is also used for a caliph or deputy of God. Shiites believe that only a descendant of Ali, the son-in-law of Muhammad, can be such an imam. They recognize twelve imams, the last of whom died in 873 and who is expected to return as the Mahdi.

Saint Ignatius of Loyola

Imhotep (Greek Imouthes) Legendary Egyptian thinker who lived in the time of King Zoser (c.2700 BC). I. He was later deified and worshipped as a god of healing. The Greeks accorded him a status equal to that of Asclepius.

Imperialism The extension of the power of one nation over another. I. is especially associated with the rise of great empires, such as the Roman,

Ion Ilescu

Aztec, and British, and with the attempts of European nations in the 19th century to acquire colonies in Africa and Asia.

Impressionism Movement in the arts, especially in painting, and largely French. Impressionists aimed to depict the fleeting impact of nature, especially light. They often used brush strokes of pure, unmixed color. The leading artists of I. included Edouard Manet, Claude Monet, and Pierre Auguste Renoir. The movement is often considered to have begun with an exhibition in Paris in 1874. In music, impressionist composers like Claude Debussy and Maurice Ravel reacted against the overt emotionalism of Wagner and stressed atmosphere, often exotic, and mood.

Incas Inhabitants of a powerful and sophisticated civilization in South America and centered in present-day

Incas

The Industrial Revolution

The *Industrial Revolution* is the term applied to the broad socioeconomic changes that accompanied the change from an agricultural to an industrial society. It began in Britain around 1750, then gradually spread to most of Europe and North America, and more slowly, to elsewhere in the world. Inventions that played an important role in the Industrial Revolution included the spinning jenny (invented 1764), the steam engine (1776), the power loom (1787), and the steam locomotive (1825).

1

2

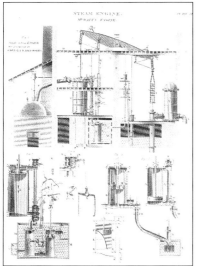
3

4

5

1. A spinning jenny, used for making thread, from 1780.
2. The interior of an 19th century factory with child laborers.
3. Luddites, early industrial workers in Britain who smashed machines as a protest against industrialization, which they feared would lower wages and take away their jobs.
4. The British industrial town of Sheffield in 1879, when the early factories were still located inside the city walls.
5. Watt's steam engine. Print from 1820.
6. Caricature from c.1828 denouncing the water pollution of the River Thames in London. The same water that was distributed for domestic purposes was used

6

to dispose of the waste of households, hospitals, abbatoirs and factories. This resulted in regular epidemics of cholera.

Peru. Its capital was Cuzco. The Incas were master road builders and architects. Their society was tightly controlled by the government, which, however, assumed responsibility for its subjects' welfare. The word "Inca" refers to the ruler as well as the civilization. At its peak in the early 16th century, the Inca Empire reached from northern Ecuador south to Chile. The society seems to have begun to take shape c.1200. The rulers Pachacuti (1438-1471), Tupac Yupanqui (1471-1493), and Huayna Capac (1493-1525) expanded it. A civil war over Huayana Capac's succession had just ended when the Spanish under Franciso Pizarro arrived in 1532. Through luck, deceit, superior weapons, and the effects of disease, the Spanish quickly destroyed the Inca Empire.

Inchon Port city in western South Korea. During the Korean War, U.S. troops under MacArthur made an audacious amphibious landing there in September 1950 that changed the course of the war.

Index librorum prohibitorum (List of Forbidden Books) First compiled by the Roman Catholic Church in 1559, the I. contains books considered by the church to threaten the faith or to be morally offensive.

India Before 1947 I. was understood to refer to the Indian subcontinent, then British India, and including the present India, Pakistan, and Bangladesh. The king of Great Britain was simultaneously emperor of I. In 1947 India and Pakistan became independent. In 1971 East Pakistan seceded and became Bangladesh. (*See* Mujibur Rahman.) Burma is sometimes also included in British India. It became independent in 1948.

Indian Affairs, Bureau of Administrative agency of the U.S. government. It was created in 1824 as part of the War Department and in 1849 was transferred to the Interior Department. For many years it administered the reservations where many Native Americans, or Indians, were forced to live. Today it also provides a wide range of services to Native Americans.

Indians Collective term for Native American peoples. The name I. is the result of an error. When Columbus discovered America, he believed he had landed near India and called the natives I. The I. in North America suffered grievously as white settlers relentlessly moved westward and drove them off their lands. (*See* Custer, Sitting Bull, Wounded Knee.) Warfare and diseases have drastically reduced their numbers. Much of the current population—c.800,000 in the U.S. and 250,000 in Canada—lives on reservations allocated by the U.S. and Canadian governments. In Central and South America (*see* Aztecs, Cortés, Incas, Mayas, Montezuma) many I. intermarried with the Spanish and Portuguese colonists. Some tribes still inhabit the Amazon basin; these are threatened by deforestation.

Indian wars Collective name for the wars between Native Americans and whites in North America, especially the U.S. They ended in the late 19th century with the complete defeat of the Native Americans. The massacre of Sioux at Wounded Knee, South Dakota, in 1890 is often considered the last "battle" of the I.

Indochina Former name for the area of Southeast Asia that is now the countries of Cambodia, Laos, and Vietnam. It was colonized by France in the 19th century. All three nations became independent in 1954, although Vietnam was divided between North and South until 1975.

Indochina Wars Two wars in Indochina fought after World War II. In the first (1946-1954), France, fighting the Communist-led nationalist Vietminh, was forced to grant independence to Cambodia, Laos, and Vietnam. In the second (c.1959-1975), Communist North Vietnam defeated pro-Western South Vietnam and its backer, the U.S., and reunited the country.

Indo-Europeans or Indo-Germans Collective name for a large group of European and Asiatic peoples who speak related languages. There are great differences among the current forms of these languages: Dutch and Russian, for example, are both Indo-European. The connection between these languages was demonstrated in the 18th century by William Jones.

Indo-Pakistani Wars Three wars between India and Pakistan. When British India was partitioned into India and Pakistan in 1947, the rulers of the princely states could decide which country they wanted to join. The Hindu ruler of Kashmir chose India, but his predominantly Muslim subjects wanted to be part of Pakistan. This led to the first war (1948-1949), which failed to resolve the problem. The second war (1965-1966) also largely concerned Kashmir. A cease-fire was brokered by the Soviet Union. The third war (1971) was sparked by civil war in Pakistan, where East Pakistan was demanding autonomy. India supported East Pakistan. Pakistan was defeated, and East Pakistan became the independent country of Bangladesh. *See* Mujibur Rahman.

Indus Culture (Harappan Culture) Prehistoric civilization (4th-2nd centuries BC), revealed at archaeological sites on the Indus and Harappa Rivers in what is now Pakistan. The finding of unburied, mutilated human skeletons suggests that the culture came to a very abrupt end (c.1700 BC), probably as the result of an Aryan invasion.

Industrial Revolution The term for the broad socioeconomic changes that accompanied the change from an agricultural to an industrial society. The I. first took place in Britain starting c.1750 and then gradually spread to most of Europe and North America and, more slowly, to elsewhere in the world. Four inventions that played an important role in the I. were the spinning jenny (1764), the steam engine (1776), the power loom (1787), and the steam locomotive (1825).

Inisfallen Annals of Irish history from the time of the Creation until 1326. Written partly in Irish and partly in Latin, they were probably started in the 10th century.

Inkatha Freedom Party Zulu organization South Africa founded by Mangosuthu Gatsha Buthulezi in 1975. The I. opposed apartheid but maintained a bloody rivalry with the African National Congress. In the elections of 1994, despite initially boycotting them, I. became the third largest party in South Africa.

Inkerman Suburb of Sebastopol, the Crimea, Russia. During the Crimean War, the Russian army was badly defeated by the French and British there (1854).

Technological Geniuses: Famous Inventors

The ideas of the great inventors have changed the world dramatically. Innovations like photography, radio, and the telephone have revolutionized human life. This page shows a few of the world's great inventors. See the separate entries on each person.

1. Alexander Graham Bell, inventor of the telephone.
2. Louis Braille, who devised a system of writing and printing for the blind.
3. Guglielmo Marconi, a pioneer in the development of radio.
4. The Montgolfier brothers, Joseph Michel and Jacques Etienne, and their first hot-air balloon.

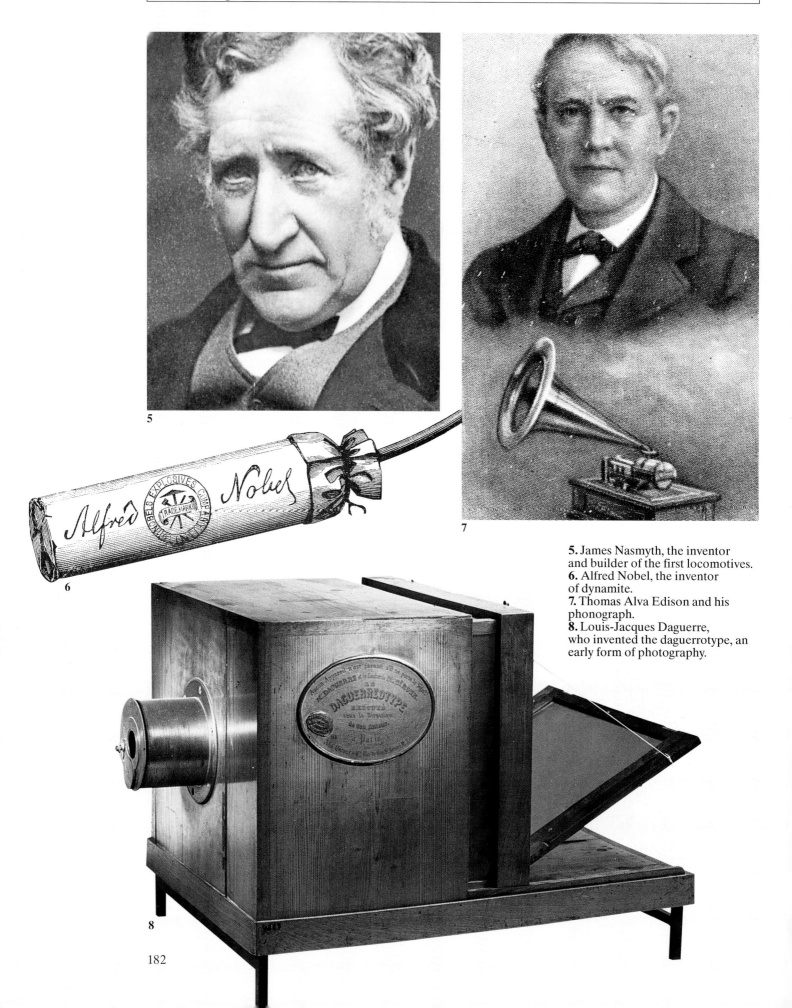

5. James Nasmyth, the inventor and builder of the first locomotives.
6. Alfred Nobel, the inventor of dynamite.
7. Thomas Alva Edison and his phonograph.
8. Louis-Jacques Daguerre, who invented the daguerrotype, an early form of photography.

Innocent III 1. (1160/61-1216) Pope, 1198-1216. Born Lotario di Segna, he succeeded Celestine III. I. believed that monarchs should be subordinate to the pope, and he intervened in political affairs throughout Europe. He sponsored the disastrous Fourth Crusade (1202-1204) and convened the Fourth Lateran Council (1215). 2. An antipope, Lando de Sezze, who reigned 1179-1180. He was later imprisoned.

Innocent III

Innocent VIII (1432-1492) Pope, 1484-1492. Born Giovanni Battista Cibo, he succeeded Sixtus IV. He made peace with the Turks in 1490.

Innocent VIII

Innocent X

Innocent X (1574-1655) Pope, 1644-1655. Born Giambattista Pamfili, he succeeded Urban VIII. I. condemned the dogmas of Jansen and the veneration of Confucius.

Inönü, Ismet (1884-1973) Turkish general and political leader. He won an important victory over the Greeks in 1921. He succeeded Kemal Atatürk as president of Turkey in 1938 and served until 1950. Under the 1960 constitution he was premier from 1961 to 1965.

Inquisition A court established by Pope Gregory IX in 1233 to suppress heresy. Trials were held in secret, and torture was common. A guilty verdict sometimes resulted in a sentence of burning at the stake. The I. was not formally abolished until 1965. In 1478 Spain established its own I., run by the Spanish monarch, which existed until 1834.

INRI The first letters of the Latin inscription on the cross of Jesus: Iesus Nazarenus, Rex Iudaeorum (Jesus of Nazareth, King of the Jews).

Insubres A Celtic people who in Roman times lived north of the Po River. Their capital was Mediolanum (Milan). When the Carthaginian Hannibal invaded Italy in 218 BC, they joined him. They were subjugated by the Romans in 196 BC.

Intef I King of Egypt (c.2130-2120 BC) I. was the first king of the 11th dynasty. At his accession, Egypt con-

sisted of a number of small states. The most important of these was Heracleopolis, and its leader regarded himself as the king of all Egypt. I., who was the ruler of Thebes, rebelled against him.

Intef III King of Egypt (c.2070-2065 BC) I. made peace with Heracleopolis. One of his administrators, Amenemhet, later became the first king of the 12th dynasty.

International The name of several socialist and communist organizations. The First I. was founded in London in 1864 by Marx and others. It was disbanded in 1876 following a conflict with the anarchist Bakunin. The Second I. was founded in Brussels in 1889. It lasted until the outbreak of World War I (1914), when the support of the various socialist parties for their countries' war efforts caused its collapse. The Third I. was created in Moscow in 1919 by the Bolsheviks (Communists) to sponsor world revolution. It was disbanded in 1943. The Fourth I. was founded in 1936 by Trotsky, who had been exiled from the Soviet Union.

Internationale A workers' anthem, composed by the Belgian worker Pierre de Geyter in 1888. The words were written by Eugène Pottier after the suppression of the Paris Commune in 1871. It was the national anthem of the Soviet Union for many years.

International Brigades Units of foreign volunteers who fought on the Republican (Loyalist) side in the Spanish Civil War. Communists were active in organizing the I. There were about 37,000 volunteers from dozens of countries, many of them intellectuals such as George Orwell and Simone Weil.

INTERPOL (International Criminal Police Organization) An international police information center. It was founded in Vienna in 1923. Since 1946 Paris has been the headquarters. The I. collects and supplies information to help catch criminals; it does not apprehend them itself. More than 125 countries are affiliated.

Inti The Inca sun god.

Intifada An uprising of Palestinians against Israeli rule in the Gaza Strip

Ismet Inönü

Irene

and the West Bank of the Jordan River that began in December 1987.

Intolerable Acts A series of laws enacted by the British Parliament in 1774 that curtailed the freedom of the American colonists. They were in part a response to the Boston Tea Party. The I. spurred the colonists to set up the First Continental Congress.

Investiture Struggle Conflict between popes and monarchs, particularly the German emperors, over the power to appoint bishops and abbots who would be invested with ecclesiastical and temporal power. It began in 1075 when Pope Gregory VII forbade lay investiture, the selection of clerics by monarchs. The I. was largely settled at the Concordat of Worms (1122). *See* Canossa; Gregory VII; Henry IV, Holy Roman emperor.

Ionian Rebellion A revolt against the Persians in the Ionian cities of Asia Minor. It broke out in 499 BC and was led by the town of Miletus. In 494 BC the Greek fleet, to which Athens and others had contributed, was defeated at Lade, and the Persians achieved hegemony temporarily. Miletus was devastated. *See* Histiaeus.

Ionians Ancient Greeks who established colonies before 1000 BC on the island of Euboea, on islands in the Aegean Sea, and in the coastal areas of Asia Minor. They may have been driven from mainland Greece by the Dorians.

Ipsus City in Phrygia, Asia Minor, where in 301 BC Antigonus I was defeated by the other Diadochi. Antigonus was killed.

Iqbal, Sir Muhammad (1873-1938) Indian Muslim poet and political leader. He was a prolific poet and essayist and was elected (1930) president of the Muslim League. I. is considered the father of Pakistan.

IRA (Irish Republican Army) Organization favoring the unification of Ireland as an independent country under Irish Catholic rule. It was founded after the 1916 Easter Rebellion by Michael Collins. Starting in the 1970s, the "Provisional Wing" of the I. mounted a terror campaign in its attempt to bring about the unification of Northern Ireland with the Irish Republic.

Irala, Domingo Martínez de (1486-1557) Spanish conquistador. He was the first ruler in the Americas elected by colonists and governed what is now Paraguay from 1539 until his death.

Iran-Contra Scandal U.S. political and constitutional scandal during the administration of President Reagan. It was revealed in 1986 that the administration secretly had been delivering weapons to Iran in exchange for the release of American hostages in Lebanon. The money earned was channelled to the Contra rebels in Nicaragua. Both actions were illegal.

Iranian Revolution (1979) Revolution that ended the reign of the shah of Iran and established the Islamic Republic of Iran. The revolution was led by Ayatollah Ruhollah Khomeini, who wielded ultimate authority in Iran until his death in 1989.

Iran-Iraq War (1980-1988) Conflict sparked by the long-standing dispute between the two nations over control of the Shatt al-Arab, the waterway between the Iraqi port of Basra and the open sea. Shortly after the 1979 Iran Revolution, Iraq invaded Iran and seized the land around the waterway, but Iran recaptured it in 1982. The war continued until 1988, when the United Nations arranged a cease-fire. No final settlement has been made. Iraq used chemical weapons, and casualties on both sides were enormous—an estimated 1.5 million were killed.

Irenaeus, Saint (d.c. 200) Father of the Church. Born in Asia Minor, I. became bishop of Lyon. His theological writings were often cited by others, although only two have survived into modern times.

Irene (c.752-803) Byzantine empress, 797-802. When her husband Leo IV died (780), she became regent for their son, Constantine VI. She opposed iconoclasm. After she was made joint ruler with Constantine, he was deposed, and I. had him blinded. The absence of an emperor enabled Charlemagne to be crowned emperor in Rome. A palace revolution brought an end to I.'s rule, and she was exiled to Lesbos.

Irgun Zvai Leumi (Military National Organization) Jewish terrorist organization in Palestine set up (1931) by members of the right-wing radical wing of the Haganah to fight British rule. Menachim Begin became its head in 1943. It was disbanded in 1949.

Irish Civil War Two conflicts in Ireland: 1. (1922-1923) Between the government of the Irish Free State and the IRA, which opposed the partition of Ireland and any connection with Britain. Hostilities ceased in April 1923. 2. (1968-1994) Between Catholics and Protestants in Northern Ireland, particularly Belfast. Britain sent troops to restore order and they got caught up in the violence. A cease-fire was arranged in 1994, and negotiations began.

The Investiture Controversy

By the end of the 11th century, it had become common practice for the Holy Roman emperor appoint and invest new bishops, which gave him great influence over the Church. Pope Gregory VII, as part of his program of Church reform, insisted on determining Church appointments. A bitter struggle between Emperor Henry IV and the pope resulted.

1

2

3

1. Holy Roman Emperor Henry IV asks for advice about his struggle with Pope Gregory VII.
See Grugory VII; Henry IV.
2. An 11th-century sculpture of a bishop, who is making the gesture of a blessing.
3. A 12th-century fresco depicting Pope Silvester being led through the streets of Rome by Constantine the Great.
4. The crown of the powerful Holy Roman emperors.

4

Islam

1

2

Islam—the Arabic word for "peace with God"—began c.AD 610, when the Arabian merchant Muhammad had a vision in which the archangel Gabriel spoke to him. Muhammad became the prophet of Islam, one of the world's major religions.

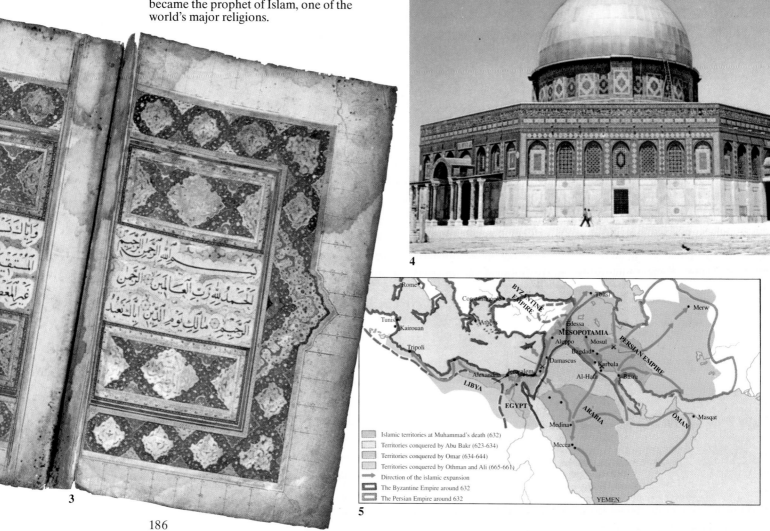

3

4

5

Islamic territories at Muhammad's death (632)
Territories conquered by Abu Bakr (623-634)
Territories conquered by Omar (634-644)
Territories conquered by Othman and Ali (665-661)
Direction of the islamic expansion
The Byzantine Empire around 632
The Persian Empire around 632

6

8

7

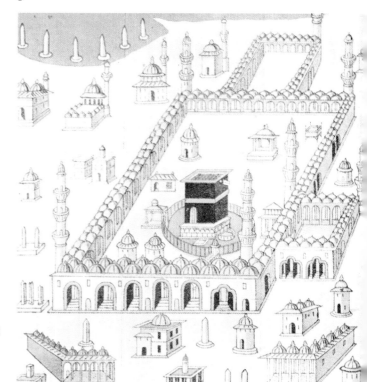

1. The archangel Gabriel appears to Muhammad. *See* Islam; Muhammad.
2. Reliquary with a tooth of the prophet Muhammad. *See* Islam; Muhammad.
3. Two pages from a richly decorated Koran, the holy book of Islam,
made in the 16th century. *See* Koran; Muhammad.
4. The Dome of the Rock in Jerusalem, the most famous Islamic mosque.
See Islam.
5. The spread of Islam under Muhammad's successors, the caliphs.
See Islam; caliph.
6. Holy War (Jihad) was one of the main principles of early Islam. Here, Arabs
are defeated by Greeks. *See* Jihad; Arabs; Islam.
7. Muhammad strips the Kaaba, the most sacred Islamic sanctuary,
of all holy statues, leaving only the Black Stone. *See* Muhammad; Kaaba.
8. Ali's followers swear an oath of fidelity, while Muhammad's two-pointed
sword is shown. *See also* Ali; Caliphs; Muhammad
9. Arabic miniature depicting the city of Mecca. The Kaaba is the most striking
building.
10. Muhammad and his son-in-law and successor, Ali.
See Muhammad; Islam; caliphs; Ali.
11. Two of Muhammad's swords. *See* Muhammad; Jihad.

9

10

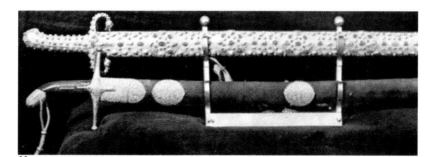

11

Isabella I, the Catholic

Irish Famine (1845-1849) When the Irish potato harvest was severely reduced by blight, a famine resulted. The loss of the staple crop caused the death of approximately one million Irish people. More than 1.5 million immigrated to the U.S.

Irish Republican Army *See* IRA.

Irmingard (8th century) Daughter of Diederik, the king of the Lombards. I. was the first wife of Charlemagne, but he renounced her in 771.

Iron Age Period in the development of civilization when iron was first widely used. Its dates vary according to region. In Asia, Egypt, and Europe, it followed the Bronze Age. In southern and central Europe, the I. began between 900-800 BC, and in northern Europe around 450 BC. Iron was known in Egypt as early as 1500 BC. In the Americas the I. did not begin until the arrival of the Europeans, after 1500 AD.

Iron Curtain Term originated by Winston Churchill in 1946 to refer to the sphere of influence hostile to the West created by the Soviet Union in Eastern Europe following World War II. It soon was applied to the Cold War division of Europe into two hostile blocs, West and East.

Iron Guard Romanian nationalist and antisemitic terrorist organization established in 1924. King Carol tried unsuccessfully to suppress it. The I. helped Ion Antonescu come to power in 1940, but then he too clamped down on it. It disappeared after World War II.

Iroquois Federation *See* Hiawatha.

Irra The Babylonian god of plague, death, and war.

Irving, Washington (1783-1859) American writer. Born in New York City, I. is best-known for picturesque stories such as *Rip Van Winkle* and *The Legend of Sleepy Hollow* (1819-1820) that offer tales of colonial New York in the days when it was ruled by the Dutch.

Isa The Arabic name for Jesus. In the Koran I. appears as a prophet, and miracles are attributed to him. Muslims do not believe, however, that he is the son of God who died on the cross.

Isabella I, the Catholic (1451-1504), Queen of Castille and Léon, 1474-1504. The daughter of John of Castille, she married Ferdinand of Aragon in 1469. After I. succeeded to the throne of Castille, she and Ferdinand in effect became the first rulers of united Spain. I. supported the Inquisition and the removal from Spain of the Jews and Moors who would not convert to Christianity. She also financed the voyages of Columbus to the New World.

Isabella II (1830-1904) Queen of Spain, 1833-1868. She was the daughter and successor of Ferdinand VII. Her uncle, Don Carlos, disputed her right to succeed, leading to the Carlist Wars. I. was deposed in 1868 and went to France. She renounced the throne two years later in favor of her son Alfonso XII. *See* Carlist Wars, Don Carlos.

Isabella of Bavaria (1371-1435) Queen of France, 1385-1435. I. married Charles VI of France in 1385 and served as regent for him during his periods of mental unbalance. She helped arrange the Treaty of Troyes (1420), which disinherited her son, the future Charles VII, in favor of Henry V of England.

Ishtar (Astarte) The principal goddess of the ancient Mesopotamians. She was the goddess of both fertility and war.

Isocrates

Isidore of Seville, Saint (c.560-636) Spanish clergyman and scholar. I. was bishop of Seville. A prolific writer, he compiled the *Etymologies* that aimed to preserve all the knowledge of his time. He also wrote a history of the Goths, Vandals, and Suevi.

Isis Egyptian nature goddess, daughter of the sky goddess Nut and the earth god Geb. I. was the sister and wife of Osiris and mother of Horus. Worship of her became widespread in the ancient world and was a major religion in the Roman Empire.

Isis

Iskander The name for Alexander the Great in the Middle East. The Egyptian port of Alexandria is known as Al-Iskandariya in Arabic.

Islam (Arabic: submission to or at peace with God) One of the world's major religions, I. was founded by the Arabian merchant Muhammed c.610 after receiving a vision. It is monotheistic, and its sacred book is the Koran. I. is the religion of millions of people in Asia, the Middle East, and Africa. Followers are called Muslims.

Ismail Pasha (1830-1895) Ruler of Egypt, 1863-1879. The son of Ibrahim Pasha and successor of his uncle, Said Pasha, I. mismanaged Egypt's finances and put the country seriously in debt. He was deposed by the Turks in favor of his son Tewfik Pasha.

Isocrates (436-338 BC) Greek orator. A pupil of Socrates and one of the

Israel: the Formation of a New State

The Zionist movement was founded in the 19th century. Its goal was a national homeland for the Jewish people. Many Zionists wanted the homeland to be in Palestine, where Jews lived in Biblical times. The Nazi murderous attempt to eradicate the Jews of Europe gave impetus to the establishment of a Jewish state in Palestine. In 1948, the new nation of Israel was proclaimed, but it was opposed by the Arabs who had been living in Palestine for centuries. Conflict between Israelis and Arabs has continued to the present.

2

1

3

4

5

1. Theodore Herzl, the founder of Zionism. *See* Herzl, Theodore.
2. The proclamation of the State of Israel in 1948. *See* Israel.
3. An Israeli kibbutz.
4. Israeli Prime Minister Menachim Begin and Egyptian President Anwar Sadat sign the Camp David Accords in 1978. *See* Camp David Accords.
5. Members of the Palestine Liberation Organization, an organization of Palestinian Arabs who for many years fought Israel but in 1993 officially recognized its right to exist. *See* Arafat, Yasser; Palestine Liberation Organization.

Sophists, I. urged the Greeks to unite against Persia. He is said to have committed suicide after Philip II of Macedonia defeated the Greeks at Chaeronea.

Isolationism Long-standing sentiment in U.S. thought regarding foreign affairs. The founding fathers, notably Washington and Jefferson, advised Americans to stay out of the affairs and quarrels of other nations, although they themselves found this practically impossible. The Monroe Doctrine (1823) reinforced the notion that the U.S. could remain apart from world politics. Isolationist feeling contributed to the reluctance of the U.S. to enter World Wars I and II. *See* Monroe, James.

Isonzo, Battles on the (1915-1917) In World War I the Isonzo River in Italy and present-day Slovenia was the most important part of the Italian-Austrian front. Many battles were fought there, including Caporetto, where the Italians were badly defeated in late 1917.

Israel The name I. is roughly synonymous with the Jewish people. As a political entity, I. was the name of the nation of the Jews in the north of Palestine after the Hebrew kingdom separated into two parts in 945 BC; the southern kingdom was Judah. Present-day I. became an independent republic in 1948. Under United Nations auspices, the British mandate of Palestine was to be partitioned into Jewish and Arab states. Neither Jews nor Arabs, however, accepted the partition, and the Israeli War for Independence resulted. I. succeeded in establishing itself, although several more wars—including full-scale ones in 1956, 1967, and 1973—were fought between it and its Arab neighbors. Egypt was the first Arab nation to make peace with I. (1978, in the Camp David Accords.) Israeli-Arab and Israeli-Palestinian relations remain poor.

Israel, Tribes of According to the Bible, the people of Israel were the chosen people of God. There were 13 Hebrew tribes: 10 are named after sons of Jacob: Reuben, Simeon, Judah, Zebulun, Issachar, Dan, Gad, Asher, Naphtali, and Benjamin; and 2 after the sons of Jacob's son Joseph: Ephraim and Manasseh. The 13th

tribe is Levi. When the Hebrew kingdom under Rehoboam split, the tribes of Judah, Benjamin, and a part of Levi formed the southern kingdom of Judah, while the others formed Israel. The latter were deported to Assyria in 721 and are called the 10 "lost" tribes.

Issachar. *See* Israel, Tribes of

Issus Ancient city on the coast of Cilicia in modern Turkey. It was there that Alexander the Great defeated the Persians under Darius III in 333 BC.

Itagaki, Seishiro (1885-1948) Japanese general. During World War II, I. committed many crimes against Allied prisoners. For these he was executed in 1948 as a war criminal.

Itala Name of the first translation of the Bible into Latin (195).

Italia Initially the Greek name for the southern tip of what is now Calabria (6th century BC) and then for southern Italy, or Magna Graecia (4th century BC). It was only in the 3rd century BC that the entire Italian peninsula as far north as the Alps became known as I.

Italian Wars (1494-1559) Wars between the European powers over possession of the various small independent Italian states.

Ito, Hirobumi (1841-1909) Japanese political leader. I. traveled several times overseas to study the West and was a member of the Iwakura Mission (1871). He became the first prime minister of Japan (1885) and served several terms. As Japanese ambassador in St. Petersburg, I. attempted to prevent the Russian-Japanese war. He was assassinated in Korea in 1909.

Itúrbide, Agustín de (1783-1824) Mexican revolutionary and emperor, 1822-1823. Initially a royalist general, he switched sides and helped Mexico win independence from Spain (1821). I. became dictator and was proclaimed emperor by his army. He was overthrown in 1823 and exiled; when he attempted to return, he was captured and executed.

Ivan III, the Great (1440-1505) Grand Duke of Moscow, 1462-1505. I. consolidated various Russian territories and freed Muscovy from its control by the Golden Horde (1480). He is con-

sidered the founder of the Russian state.

Ivan IV, the Terrible (1530-1584) Grand Duke of Moscow, 1533-1584, and first czar of Russia, 1547-1584. I. succeeded in limiting the power of the boyars and proclaimed himself czar ("caesar" or "emperor"). He began Russia's expansion to the east, although he lost territory in the west to

Ivan IV, the Terrible

Poland. In his later years he became increasingly cruel and tyrannical. In a fit of anger, he killed (1581) his son and heir, Ivan. I. was succeeded by Boris Godunov.

Ivory Coast Nation in West Africa, on the Gulf of Guinea. Formerly a French colony, it became independent in 1960. Historically the region was a great trading center for ivory and slaves. Portugal established the first European posts in the 16th century; the French colony was established in the late 19th century.

Iwakura Mission Japanese delegation headed by Prince Tomomi Iwakura that traveled to Europe and the United States (1871). It brought back information on Western technology and institutions that helped Japan modernize quickly.

Izvestia (Russian: "news") A Russian daily newspaper. During the time of the Soviet Union, it was the official paper of the Soviet government. I. was founded in 1917.

The Italian Renaissance

At the end of the Middle Ages, the rich cities of Italy witnessed an extraordinary flourishing of culture we call the Renaissance. One of its major aspects was a renewed interest in ancient Greek and Roman learning. The art and literature of the Renaissance are among the glories of Western civilization.

1

2

3

1. Illustrations from Dante's *Divina Commedia* (Divine Comedy) in a 14th-century manuscript. *See* Dante Alighieri; Renaissance.

2. Giovanni Boccaccio (1313-1375), writer of the *Decameron*, one of the great works of the Renaissance. *See* Boccaccio; Renaissance.

3. Lorenzo de Medici (1449-1492) ruled Florence and encouraged the arts and sciences. *See* Medici; Renaissance.

4. Francesco Petrarca (1304-1374), a great Italian poet and humanist. *See* Renaissance; Petrarca.

5. Some Italian cities were very wealthy from trade and banking during the Renaissance. This picture from the 14th century shows Italian bankers. *See* Renaissance.

4

5

Artists of the Italian Renaissance

The Italian Renaissance was
a period of tremendous achievement
in science, literature, and the arts.
Wealthy merchants and rulers
patronized outstanding artists and
commissioned many masterpieces.
A few very famous examples
of great Italian Renaissance painting
are shown here.

1

3

4

1. Leonardo da Vinci, *The Last Supper.*
2. Leonardo da Vinci, *The Mona Lisa.*
3. Botticelli, *The Birth of Venus.*

5

6

2

4. Michelangelo, *The Sistine Chapel* in the Vatican.
5. Titian, *The Bacchanal.*
6. Raphael, *The Madonna of Granduca* and *The School of Athens.*

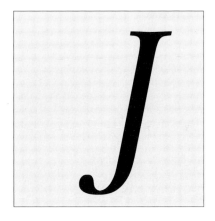

Jacratra (Jacarta) Capital of a Javanese empire that was destroyed in 1619 by Jan Pieterszoon Coen. Afterwards he founded Batavia, now called Djakarta, on the same spot.

Jackson, Andrew (1767-1845) American general and 7th president of the U.S., 1929-1837. J. was born in North Carolina and later moved to Tennessee. He fought as a boy in the American Revolution. He successfully fought the Creek Indians and won a great victory (1815) at New Orleans against the British in the War of 1812. He also served as a judge and a U.S. senator. After running for president unsuccessfully in 1824, he was elected as a Democrat in 1828 and 1832. J., a fiery, strong-willed personality, came to represent the common man in American politics. As president he vigorously exercised the powers of the office, crushed the Second Bank of the U.S., and forced South Carolina to back down in the nullification crisis.

Jackson, Helen Hunt (1830-1885), American writer. Born in Massachusetts, J. wrote *A Century of Dishonor* (1881) about the plight of the Native Americans and *Ramona* (1884), a novel about them.

Jackson, Stonewall (Thomas Jonathan) (1824-1863) Confederate general. J. was born in Virginia and graduated from West Point. J. was one of the ablest commanders in the American Civil War. He was called "Stonewall" because at the First Battle of Bull Run his brigade stood firm against a fierce Union attack. J. was accidentally killed by his own men during the Battle of Chancellorsville.

Jacobins Political faction during the French Revolution. The J. were named after the place where they met, the monastery of St. Jacques in Paris. They became quite radical and oppo-

sed the more moderate Girondists. After the defeat of the Girondists (June 1793), the J. led by Robespierre and Saint-Just instituted the Reign of Terror. After Robespierre himself fell from power, the J. lost influence.

Jacobites Christians in the Middle East and India. Their spiritual head is the Syrian Orthodox patriarch of Antioch. They are Monophysites. Their church was founded in the 6th century by Jacob Baradaeus (c.490-578), who united the Monophysites after they had been dispersed by persecutions.

Andrew Jackson

Jacobites Supporters of the Catholic pretenders to the English throne from the House of Stuart, after King James II (who ruled between 1685 and 1688) had been deposed by Parliament. The J. were strong in Scotland in Ireland.

Jacquerie (1358) French peasant revolt. Starting north of Paris, oppressed and impoverished peasants led by Guillaume Karle attacked castles and committed other violent acts. They were put down by Charles II of Navarre, and thousands were killed.

Jadwiga (1373/74-1399) Queen of Poland, 1384-1399. The daughter of Louis I of Hungary and Poland, she married Jagiello, grand duke of Lithuania (1386). In Poland she is regarded as a saint.

Jagger, Mick (1943-) British rock musician. J. is a songwriter and the leader of the Rolling Stones.

Mick Jagger

Jagiello (1354-1434) Grand Duke of Lithuania, 1377-1434, and, as Ladislaus II, King of Poland, 1386-1434. He founded the J. dynasty, which ruled Poland from 1386-1572, Bohemia from 1471-1526, and Hungary from 1490-1526.

Jahn, Johann Friedrich Ludwig Christoph (1778-1852) German nationalist. J. taught high school in Berlin. During the Napoleonic period, he organized a gymnastic association as a means of uniting Germans of all classes in the struggle against the French. He was later imprisoned for his political activities (1819-1825) and was a delegate to the Frankfurt Parliament of 1848. Jahn invented the horizontal bar and the parallel bars.

Jainism Religion of India. It was founded in the 6th century BC by Vardhamana, who is also called Mahavira (great hero) or Jina (victor). Jains value animal life and asceticism. They believe in the need to escape the cycle of rebirth.

Jaja of Opobo (1821-1891) Nigerian merchant. A former slave, he became a successful merchant and founded (1869) the state of Opobo (Nigeria). Because he restricted their business, British merchants had him arrested and deported to the West Indies (1887).

Jalalabad City in eastern Afghanistan. The Mogul emperor Akbar built the city c.1570. It was the site of battles between Afghan rebels and Soviet forces during the Soviet occupation of Afghanistan (1979-1989).

James I (1566-1625) King of England, 1603-1625, and as James VI, king of Scotland, 1567-1625. The son of Mary Queen of Scots, J. succeeded Elizabeth I on the English throne. He believed in the divine right of kings and had close contacts with Spain, although he was a Protestant. These policies resulted in frequent conflicts with Parliament.

James II (1633-1701) King of England, 1685-1688. The second son of Charles I and brother of Charles II, whom he succeeded, J. was sympathetic to Catholicism and probably became a Catholic in 1688. He was deposed in the Glorious Revolution (which *see*) because of conflicts with Parliament over religion and the powers of the crown. He attempted to regain the throne but was defeated at the Battle of the Boyne (1690).

James I (1394-1437) King of Scotland, 1406-1437. The son and successor of Robert III, J. was captured by the English while a prince (1406) and remained in prison in England until his ransom was paid in 1423. He was finally crowned in 1424.

James V (1512-1542) King of Scotland, 1513-1542. The son and successor of James IV, James warred with Henry VIII of England. He was badly defeated at Solway Moss (1542).

Mary Queen of Scots was his daughter.

James VI, king of Scotland. *See* James I, king of England.

James, Henry (1843-1916) American writer. Born in New York City, J. lived most of his adult life in Europe. He wrote many novels and short stories in which the motives and feelings of his characters—usually people of the upper classes—are subjected to intense psychological analyses. Among them are *Daisy Miller* (1879), *Washington Square* (1881), *The Wings of the Dove* (1902), *The Ambassadors* (1903), and *The Golden Bowl* (1904). He was the brother of William James.

James, William (1842-1910) American philosopher and psychologist. Born in New York City, J. taught for many years at Harvard. He started the country's fist psychological laboratory and wrote *Principles of Psychology* (1890). J. developed the philosophy of pragmatism and explored religion in *Varieties of Religious Experience* (1902).

James I

Jameson, Sir Leander Starr (1853-1917) British colonial administrator. In the service of Cecil Rhodes, he led the unsuccessful Jameson Raid (1895) into the Boer colony of Transvaal in an attempt to support a rebellion by British settlers. Later J. became

Japan's Early History

Historians have had a difficult time unraveling the early history of Japan, since reliable records date back only to c.400 AD. Archaeologists, however, have done a lot of work on early Japanese cultures, so that we now know that Japan has a history more than 7,000-years old.

1

2

3

1. The great Buddhist temple of Todai-ji in Nara, built in the 8th century by the emperor Shomu.
2. A granite sculpture from the island of Sado that depicts Jizo-sama, the god who protects children in traditional Japanese religion.
3. A drawing of an eye operation, made in the 12th century.
4. A painting on silk of Fudo-myo-o, one of the kings of heaven, dating from the 12th century.
5. A statue of Buddha dating from the 8th century.

4

5

the premier of the Cape Colony (1904-1908) and participated in the creation of the Union of South Africa (1908-1909).

Sir Leander Starr Jameson

Janiculum One of the seven hills on which Rome was built.

Janissaries A corps of elite troops in the Ottoman Empire. Founded by Sultan Murad I (c.1375), the J. at first were prisoners of war and Christians forced to convert to Islam. They acquired great power in the empire, and membership became hereditary. After a rebellion in 1826, Sultan Mahmud II destroyed the J. by having them all murdered.

Jansenism Religious movement begun within the Catholic Church in the 17th century and named after the Dutch theologian Cornelis Jansen (1585-1638). Its goal is to bring people to greater holiness. J. believes in predestination. At times the Catholic Church has condemned Jansenist doctrines.

Jansky, Karl (1905-1950) American radio astronomer. Born in Oklahoma,

J. discovered cosmic radiation in 1931.

Japanese Red Army Radical left-wing movement, part of the student-movement Zengakoeren. It has carried out numerous terrorist acts.

Jarl Old Norse name for members of the Scandinavian nobility. The English word *earl* is derived from it.

Jarnac, Battle of (1569) French Catholics led by the duke of Anjou (later Henry III) defeated the Protestants and killed Louis of Condé. Jarnac is a town in the Cognac region of France.

Jaruzelski, Wojciech (1923-) Polish general and political leader. A general since 1956 and Communist, J. became Polish leader in 1981 during the crisis involving the Solidarity union. He declared martial law, outlawed Solidarity, and arrested its leader, Lech Walesa. The situation eased during the next several years, and in 1989 J. resigned his Communist party posts. He left the government in 1990, as Walesa and other reformers came to power.

Jason Hero in Greek mythology. J. led the Argonauts to Colchis to find the Golden Fleece. He married and later betrayed Medea.

Jay, John (1745-1829) American political leader, diplomat, and Supreme Court justice. J. was from New York. He was one of the delegates who negotiated the Treaty of Paris (1783) ending the American Revolution, and an author, with Madison and Hamilton, of the *Federalist Papers* in favor of ratifying the American Constitution (1787-1788). J. was the first chief justice of the Supreme Court (1789-1795). He negotiated the Jay Treaty (1794) with Britain and served as governor of New York (1795-1801).

Jay Treaty (1794) Agreement between the U.S. and Britain concerning shipping rights, British forts in the Old Northwest that should have been abandoned after the 1783 Treaty of Paris, and American debts to British creditors dating from before the American Revolution. John Jay was the American negotiator. The treaty was very unpopular in the U.S.

Jazz Style of music developed in the

U.S. in the late 19th and early 20th centuries. J. is America's most significant contribution to music. It developed from various strands in black culture—spirituals, hymns, work songs—and was strongly influenced by blues and ragtime. J. originated in New Orleans and other Mississippi ports and spread to the rest of the country, and eventually all over the world.

Jeanne d'Arc *See* Joan of Arc.

Wojciech Jaruzelski

Jefferson, Thomas (1743-1826) 3rd president of the U.S., 1801-1809. One of the main founding fathers, J. did much to establish America's democratic ideology. He was born in Virginia. He wrote the Declaration of Independence (1776) and was active as a legislator in Virginia (1770s) and the national Congress (1780s). J. served as

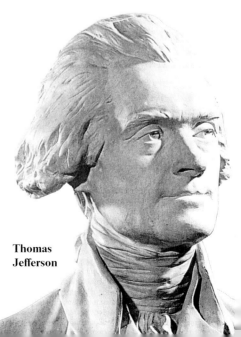

Thomas Jefferson

governor of Virginia (1779-1781), minister to France (1784-1789), the first secretary of state (1790-1793), and the second vice president (1797-1801) before being elected president. To oppose the Federalists, he and James Madison founded (1790s) the political party that later became the Democrats. During his two terms as president, J. acquired the Louisiana Territory (1803), sponsored the Lewis and Clark Expedition (1804-1806), and proposed the unsuccessful Embargo (1807-1809) to protect American neutral rights. J. was a man of many interests and talents: among other activities, he designed his own home, Monticello; invented an improved plow and other devices; wrote *Notes on Virginia* (1782); and at the end of his life created the University of Virginia.

Jellicoe, John Rusworth, Earl (1859-1935) British admiral. He led the British fleet in World War I and fought the inconclusive Battle of Jutland (1916). J. was dismissed as first sea lord (1917) by Lloyd George for opposing the use of convoys to protect shipping from submarine attack.

Jemappes, Battle of (1792) In this battle in the Wars of the French Revolution, fought near the Belgian town of Jemappes, the French led by Dumouriez defeated the Austrians under Bender.

Jena, Battle of (1806) Napoleon decisively defeated the Prussians led by Hohenlohe at Jena, a city in southeastern Germany.

Jenatsch, Georg (1596-1639) Swiss Protestant leader. During the Thirty Years' War, he went over to the Catholic side (1637) in the battles for the Valtelline Pass. He was assassinated in 1639.

Jenkins' Ear, War of (1739-1741) Conflict between Britain and Spain about overseas trading rights. The British sea captain Robert Jenkins claimed that the Spanish had cut off his ear in 1731, and he displayed the ear in the House of Commons. The war became part of the larger Austrian Succession War.

Jenner, Edward (1749-1823) British physician. He developed a vaccine against smallpox in 1796.

Jericho Ancient city, now the town of Ariha, west of the Jordan River. The site may have been inhabited as early as 8000 BC. The Amorites built a city there in the third millennium BC, and the Canaanites (Hebrews) lived there around 1900 BC. After the fall of Jerusalem (70 AD), it declined. Now part of the Israeli-occupied West Bank, it is under Palestinian self-rule.

Jesuits The largest religious order of the Catholic Church. It was founded by Saint Ignatius and approved of by Pope Paul III in 1540. The J. are ruled by its general and subject to the will of the pope. *See* Ignatius of Loyala, Saint.

Jesus (Jesus Christ) (c.6 BC-30 AD) Religious prophet; according to Christianity, the Son of God. He was born in Bethlehem, the son of Mary and the carpenter Joseph, raised as a Jew, and lived in Nazareth for thirty years. He then began to preach in Galilee. His message was one of justice, compassion and charity for the poor, and opposition to the corrupt people of power. Some of his followers regarded him as the long-awaited Messiah and believed he worked miracles. The Jewish and Roman authorities charged him with subversion and blasphemy, tried him, and had him crucified (put to death by nailing to a cross). He was buried and three days later is said to have resurrected (rose from the Dead and ascended to Heaven). His story is related in the four Gospels of the New Testament and is the basis of all the Christian faiths. A Jesus of Nazareth is mentioned in several Roman sources.

Edward Jenner

Jewish Agency (1929) Zionist organization formed to stimulate and assist Jewish settlement in Palestine.

Jews Adherents of the Jewish religion and their descendants. Initially the J. were the members of the tribe of Judah in Palestine, but after the Babylonian Exile (586-536 BC), all Hebrews were called by that name. After the destruction of Jerusalem by the Romans in AD 70, the Jews scattered all over the world. (*See* Disapora.) They have been persecuted throughout history. In the 19th century, the Zionist movement developed, seeking a national home for the Jewish people where they would be safe from persecution. In the 20th century, the Nazis attempted to exterminate all the Jews in the areas they controlled (*see* Final Solution) and succeeded in killing millions. Partly as a result of the horrors the J. suffered under the Nazis, Zionists succeeded in establishing (1948) the country of Israel as a Jewish state.

Jihad Arabic word for "holy war." Muslims use it to refer to a just struggle against unbelievers, and it was the rallying cry that accompanied the great expansion of Islam across North Africa and into Spain after the time of Muhammad.

Jim Crow laws Legislation passed in the Southern states of the U.S. in the late 19th century that effectively segregated blacks and made them second-class citizens by, for example, denying them equal access to public services. Most of these laws remained in force until the 1950s and 1960s, when the civil rights movement and federal legislation and court decisions forced their repeal or invalidated them.

Jinnah, Muhammad Ali (1876-1948) Indian Muslim leader and founder of Pakistan. J. was born in Karachi and was educated in Britain as a lawyer. At first an advocate of Hindu-Muslim unity, after 1934 he struggled for the creation of a separate Muslim state out of British India. Shortly before his death, he was elected president of the constituent assembly of the newly created Muslim Pakistan.

Joan of Arc (Jeanne d'Arc) (1412-1431) French national heroine. While a peasant girl in her native village of

Jews in History

In the second millennium BC, a people from Canaan—roughly modern Israel and Palestine—led by Abraham came to Egypt. These people were the Jews. They were persecuted and driven out of Egypt, and eventually returned to Canaan. The Jews venerated their one god, Yahweh, and had a collection of holy writings known as the Torah.

1

3

5

2

4

6

1. Moses and his brother Aaron led the Jewish people out of Egypt and in their wanderings through the desert. *See* Moses; Tribes of Israel.
2. The head of Baal, a local god of Canaan, who was considered an evil idol by the Jewish people. *See* Baal.
3. A portrait of Saul, the first king of Israel, painted by Rembrandt.
4. A decorated ivory scroll containing the Ten Commandments.
5. A scroll of Torah, the holy scripture of the Jews.
6. The remains of Masada, a Jewish stronghold that was captured by the Romans in AD 70. Most of the inhabitants committed suicide rather than be enslaved by the Romans.

Joan of Arc

Domrémy, J. began to hear heavenly voices urging her to go to the aid of King Charles VII of France and expel the English from France in the Hundred Years War. Eventually she led a French army that took Orleans from the English (1429), and she accompanied Charles VII to Rheims for his coronation. In 1430 the Burgundians, allies of the English, captured J. She was tried for heresy and witchcraft and burned at the stake in Rouen (1431). In 1920 she was canonized.

Jodl, Alfred Gustav (1890-1946) German general. J. was chief of operations of the German army during World War II and signed its surrender in May 1945. He was hanged in Nuremberg as a war criminal after the war.

Alfred Gustav Jodl

Joffre, Joseph Jacques Césaire (1852-1931) French general. J. commanded the French army at the beginning of World War I and succeeded in holding back the Germans at the First Battle of the Marne (1914). After Verdun (1916) he was removed from active command.

John XII (c.937-964) Pope, 955-964. Born Octavian, J. succeeded Agapetus II and was elected pope when he was only 18. He crowned Otto I the first Holy Roman emperor (962) but later quarrelled with him and was deposed by him. According to legend, he died while having sex.

John XXII (d.1334) Pope, 1316-1334. Born Jacques Duèse in France, J. succeeded Clement V. He ruled from Avignon and was an opponent of the Franciscan ideal of poverty. He reorganized the Church's finances and laws.

John XXIII (d.1419) Antipope, 1410-1415. Born Baldassarre Cossa, J. was a cardinal and was chosen to succeed Alexander V by the Council of Pisa. At this time the papacy was undergoing the Great Schism, and there were two others claiming to be pope: Gregory XII and Benedict XIII. The Council of Constance deposed J. in 1415. After being imprisoned in Germany for three years by Pope Martin V, he returned to Italy as bishop of Tusculum.

John XXIII (1881-1963) Pope, 1958-1963. Born Angelo Guiseppe Roncalli, He succeeded Pius XII. A greatly beloved pope, J. worked actively for social causes such as aid to underdeveloped countries and adequate wages for workers. He convened the Second Vatican Council in 1962 to make the Church more relevant to the modern world. J. issued two important encyclicals: *Mater et Magistra* (1961) and *Pacem in terris* (1963).

John (1167-1216) King of England, 1199-1216. The youngest son of Henry II and Eleanor of Aquitaine, J. was called John Lackland because he at one time was left out of his father's inheritance plans. He succeeded his brother, Richard the Lionhearted, whom he had plotted against. He may have murdered his other brother, Arthur, in 1203. A quarrel with the Pope resulted in his excommunication from

Joseph Jacques Césaire Joffre

1209-1213. The incessant need of J. and his predecessors for money to wage wars in France led to a revolt of the English barons, and in 1215 he was compelled to accept the Magna Carta. A milestone in English constitutional

John (1167-1216)

history, it put limits on the power of the crown. J. died while fighting the barons.

John II, the Good (1319-1364) King of France, 1350-1364. J. succeeded his father, Philip VI. He was defeated and captured by the English at the Battle of Poitiers (1356). He was ransomed in 1362 and returned to

John II, the Good

France, but when a hostage held by the English escaped, J. went back to England where he died.

John II (John Casimir) (1609-1672), King of Poland, 1648-1668. The son of Sigismund III, J. was elected to succeed his brother, Ladislaus IV. The years of his reign are known as the Deluge. Poland was at war with the Cossacks, Russia, Sweden, and Transylvania. J. abdicated in 1668 and became an abbot in France.

John III (John Sobieski) (1624-1696) King of Poland, 1674-1696. A victorious general, J. was elected to succeed King Michael. Allied with Holy Roman Emperor Leopold I, he lifted the Turkish siege of Vienna (1683).

Poland effectively lost its independence after J.'s death when the elector of Saxony was elected king.

John Birch Society Extreme right-wing anticommunist organization in the U.S. It was founded in 1958 by Robert Welch, a wealthy candy manufacturer. John Birch was a U.S. intelligence officer who had been killed in China by Communists in 1945. The J. accused prominent Americans such as President Eisenhower and Chief Justice Earl Warren of serving Communist purposes. It faded away in the 1970s.

John Henry Legendary American black. Folktales and songs tell of J.'s immense strength. Using a huge hammer, he is said to have outperformed a steam drill but died from the effort.

John of Austria (1547-1578) Spanish military leader. The illegitimate son of Holy Roman Emperor Charles V, he commanded the fleet of the Holy League that defeated the Turks at Lepanto (1571). Philip II of Spain sent him to the Netherlands (1576) to crush a rebellion.

John Paul II (1920-) Pope, 1978-. Born Karol Joseph Woytyla in Poland, J. is the first non-Italian pope since 1523. He succeeded Paul VI. He supported the Solidarity movement in Poland and other humanitarian causes but was very conservative in

John of Austria

matters of Church doctrine. J. survived an assassination attempted in May 1981.

John Paul II

Andrew Johnson

Johnson, Andrew (1808-1875) 17th president of the U.S. Born in North Carolina, J. moved to Tennessee in 1826. He entered politics as a Democrat and became governor (1853-1857) and U.S. Senator (1857-1862). When Tennessee seceded in 1861, J. remained loyal to the Union. The Republicans nominated him for vice president in 1864, and he succeeded to the presidency when Lincoln was assassinated. J. clashed repeatedly with the Radical Republicans in Congress, and in 1868 they impeached him. He avoided conviction by one vote. Tennessee returned him to the Senate in 1875, but he died after serving only a few months

Johnson, Lyndon Baines (1908-1973) 36th president of the U.S., 1963-1969. Born in Texas, J. was a teacher before entering politics as a Democrat. A follower of Franklin Roosevelt, he served in the U.S. House of Representatives (1937-1949) and the U.S. Senate (1949-1961). J. quickly became an extremely powerful senator and was majority leader (1955-1961). He was elected vice president (1961) and succeeded to the presidency after the assassination of John F. Kennedy (1963). In 1964 he was elected president in his own right by an enormous landslide. As president J. achieved a great deal in civil rights, education, health care, and other domestic reform issues, but all that was overshadowed by his escalation of the Vietnam War, which proved to be a disaster. J. chose not to run again in 1968.

Johnston, Joseph Eggleston (1807-1891) American Confederate general. A Virginian, J. graduated from West Point (1829) and served in the Mexican War. He fought in several major Civil War battles and surrendered the last significant Confederate army to Union General Sherman in April 1865 in North Carolina.

John the Baptist, Saint (1st century AD) Jewish prophet. The son of Zacharias and Elizabeth, after living in the desert he began preaching repentance and baptizing followers in the Jordan River. He baptized Jesus, whom he recognized as the Messiah. Having offended Herodias, the wife of King Herod, he was decapitated at the request of Salome, her daughter.

John the Fearless (1371-1419) duke of Burgundy, 1404-1419. The son of Philip the Bold, he had Louis of Orleans assassinated (1407) and sided with the English when Henry V invaded France. He seized Paris (1418) and was assassinated the next year.

Joliot-Curie, Irène (1897-1956) French scientist. The daughter of Pierre and Marie Curie, J. and her husband Frèderic Joliot-Curie won the Nobel Prize in chemistry in 1935 for their work on the artificial production of radioactivity. They later did work on atomic fission but were removed from high-ranking positions because of their Communist sympathies.

Jones, John Paul (1747-1792) American naval hero. J. was born in Scotland and joined the American navy at the start of the American Revolution (1775). While commanding the *Bonhomme Richard* against the British *Serapis* (1779), he replied when asked whether he wanted to surrender, "I have not yet begun to fight," and went on to win the battle.

Joplin, Scott (1868-1917) American composer. J. was born on the Texas-Arkansas border, the son of a former slave father. Largely self-taught, he became an accomplished pianist and composer. J. was one of the creators and finest composers of ragtime music, which he thought worthy of rank with the greatest classics. His "Maple Leaf Rag" (1899) became a tremendous hit. Not long after the failure of his opera *Tremonisha* (1915), he died of syphilis.

Jordanes (6th century) Priest and historian. Born in the Danube region, J. lived in Ravenna. He wrote c.551 the *History of the Goths*, an abridgement of an earlier work, which is a main source for the history of the Ostrogoths.

Joseph I (1678-1711) Holy Roman emperor, 1705-1711, king of Hungary, 1687-1711, and of Bohemia, 1705-1711. J. was the son and successor of Leopold I. He unsuccessfully supported the claim of his brother, who succeeded him as Charles VI, to the Spanish throne in the Spanish Succession War and put down a rebellion in Hungary.

John the Fearless

Joseph II (1741-1790) Holy Roman emperor, 1765-1790, king of Bohemia and Hungary, 1780-1790. The son of Francis I, whom he succeeded, and Maria Theresa, he ruled jointly with his mother until her death in 1780. J. attempted far-reaching reforms, including the abolition of serfdom, a more humane penal code, and religious toleration. Much of his work was undone, however, by his successor, his brother Leopold II, and the reaction that followed the French Revolution. J. was a patron of Mozart.

Joseph, Chief (c.1835-1904) Native American leader. C. was the chief of the Nez Percés, a peaceful tribe living in Oregon. When they were forced to abandon their traditional lands, he led them on a 1,500-mile journey to Canada. With his people starving and cold, he surrendered to the U.S. Army only a few miles from the Canadian border (1877) and made a moving speech. J. ended his life on a reservation in Washington. He visited Washington, D.C., in 1903.

Joseph of Arimathea, Saint (1st century AD) An acquaintance of Jesus, he may have been a member of the Sanhedrin that condemned him. He asked Pilatus for Jesus's body and gave it a proper burial.

Josephinism The political practice, named after Holy Roman emperor Joseph II, of the state intervening in church affairs.

Josephus Flavius (c.37-100) Jewish soldier and historian. J. was governor of Galilee and led a small army during the Jewish rebellion against Roman rule. He surrendered to, and became a friend of, Vespasian, who later became emperor. J. wrote several books on Jewish history, including *The Jewish War* on the rebellion.

Joubert, Barthélemy Catherine (1769-1799) French general. In 1798-1799 he commanded the French troops in the Batavian Republic. He also occupied Piemonte in Italy but died in battle against the Russians.

Joubert, Petrus Jacobus (1831-1900) Boer general and political leader. One of the leaders of the Traansval (1880-1883), he defeated the British twice in 1881.

Joumblatt, Kamal (1917-1977) Leader of the Lebanese Druses. His militia (Fahr ad-Din army) fought in the Lebanese Civil War on the side of the left-wing Islamic forces. He was assassinated in 1977.

Joumblatt, Walid (1949-) Leader of the Lebanese Druses. The son of Kamal Joumblatt, he has led the Druse militia since 1983.

Jovian (Flavius Claudius Jovianus) (c.331-364) Roman emperor, 363-364. J. succeeded Julian the Apostate. He negotiated peace with Persia and made Christianity again the Roman religion.

Joyce, James Augustine Aloysius (1882-1941) Irish writer. J. is one of the greatest and most influential 20th-century writers. Born in Dublin, he lived most of his life on the European continent. His work is highly innovative in form and technique. J.'s first major works were *The Dubliners* (1912), a collection of short stories,

James Augustine Aloysius Joyce

and *A Portrait of the Artist As a Young Man* (1916). Probably his greatest book is *Ulysses* (1922), a landmark in modern literature. Based in certain fundamental respects on Homer's *Odyssey*, it depicts one day in the life of a Dublin salesman. J. also wrote *Finnegan's Wake* (1939), in which his linguistic manipulations are at their most extreme.

Juan Carlos *See* Franco.

Juarez, Benito (1806-1872) Mexican political leader. Of Indian descent, J. is Mexico's great national hero. A lawyer, he led the revolution that overthrew Santa Anna (1855). In the new government he enacted reforms of the army and the Church. He led the liberals in the successful War of Reform (1858-1861) and was president (1861-1864) until the French installed Maximilian as emperor (1864). When Maximilian was deposed, he returned to the presidency (1867) and was reelected in 1871.

Juba I (c.85-46 BC) King of Numidia. An ally of the Roman Pompey, he defeated two Roman legions in the

Battle of Utica (49 BC) but was beaten by Julius Caesar (46 BC), after which he killed himself.

Juba II (c.50 BC-24 BC) King of Numidia and Mauretania and a scholar. The son of Juba I, after Caesar defeated his father (46 BC), J. was taken to Rome and raised there. In 29 BC Octavian appointed him king. He married Cleopatra Selene, the daughter of Anthony and Cleopatra. He also wrote works of history and geography.

Judaea or Judea Ancient Greek and Roman name for southern Palestine. In 6 AD it became a Roman province, governed by a procurator (one of whom was Pilatus, who decided Jesus's fate c.30 AD). The name also denotes the Israeli-occupied West Bank of the Jordan River, where settlements have been made by certain Israeli Jews who claim the area was given by God to the Jews.

Judah *See* Israel, Tribes of.

Judas of Galilee (d.6 AD) Jewish revolutionary. A Zealot, J. led a rebellion against the Romans in Palestine in 6 AD at the time of the taxation census. He lost three sons in the fighting and was himself killed.

Judas Maccabeus (d.160 BC) Jewish revolutionary leader J. led a successful rebellion against the King Antioch IV of Syria. In 165 BC he occupied Jerusalem and rededicated the Temple there, but he was defeated and killed by an expedition led by Bacchides. *See* Maccabees.

Benito Juarez

Jugendstil or Art Nouveau A movement in the visual arts that began in London c.1880. "Jugendstil" was the German term for the movement and was derived from a Munich magazine called *Die Jugend*. J. artists were most successful in jewelry, book design, and furniture. They used swirling plant and animal motifs, often dreamlike or erotic in nature. Representatives of the movement in Britain included the graphic artists Beardsley and Mackmurdo; on the continent the architects Van de Velde, Guimard, and Gaudi and the painter Klimt; in the U.S. the architect Sullivan and the designer Tiffany. The movement ended with World War I.

Jugurtha (c.160-104 BC) King of Numidia, 118-104 BC. J. fought several wars with Rome. Caius Marius captured him (106 BC) and brought him to Rome, where he was imprisoned and killed.

Julia (c.76-54 BC) Daughter of Julius Caesar. She married Pompey, who, after her death, became her father's opponent.

Julia the Elder (c.39 BC-14 AD) Daughter of the Roman emperor Augustus. She was first married to her cousin Marcus Claudius Marcellus, then to Marcus Vipsanius Agrippa, and then to Tiberius, who later became emperor. In 2 AD Augustus exiled her because of her promiscuity.

Julia the Younger (c.19 BC-28 AD) Daughter of Julia the Elder and Agrippa. The wife of Julius Aemilius Paulus, she, like her mother, was banished by Augustus because of her immoral way of life.

Julian the Apostate (Flavius Claudius Julianus) (c.331-363) Roman emperor, 361-363. J. was a nephew of Constantine the Great and the successor of Constantius II. He was proclaimed emperor by the army in 361. J. attempted to restore paganism, which is why he is called "the Apostate." He died in a battle against the Persians.

Julius III (1487-1555) Pope, 1550-1555. Born Giovanni Maria del Monte, J. called the Council of Trent, which began the work of the Catholic Counter Reformation. He was the patron of Michelangelo and Palestrina.

July Revolution (1830) Revolution in France in response to King Charles X's July Ordinances, which attempted to restore some of the features of the *ancien régime*. Charles was deposed, and the duke of Orleans became king as Louis Philippe.

June Days (1848) Workers' revolt in Paris protesting the betrayal of the promises made to them in the February 1948 revolution. For four days—June 23-26—there was fighting in the streets until the workers were brutally crushed by troops under General Cavaignac.

Jung, Karl Gustav (1875-1961) Swiss psychiatrist. J. ranks with Freud and Adler as the most significant psychiatric thinkers. Although he was initially a follower of Freud, J. developed his own theories of the importance of archetypes and the collective unconscious, the anima/animus, synchronicity, and individuation. His major works include *Psychology of the Unconscious* (1916) and *Psychological Types* (1921).

Junkers Great Prussian landowners, descendents of medieval knights, who formerly lived east of the Elbe River. The term is derived from the German for "young lords." The J. were the ruling elite, first of Prussia and then of the German Empire established in 1871. They remained powerful until the creation of East Germany after World War II.

Juno *See* Hera.

Jupiter *See* Zeus.

Justa Gratia Honora (5th century AD) Sister of the Western Roman emperor Valentinian. She is said to have asked Attila, king of the Huns, to marry her, but he demanded half the empire as a dowry, which was refused. He then invaded Gaul (450) and Italy (451).

Justin I (c.420-527) Byzantine emperor, 518-527. J. succeeded Anastasius. His nephew Justinian, who followed him as emperor, did most of the governing for him.

Justin II (d.478) Byzantine emperor, 565-578. J. succeeded Justinian I. He persecuted the Monophysites. Sometimes insane, he made the general

Tiberius his son (574), and Tiberius succeeded him.

Justinian I (483-565) Byzantine emperor, 527-565. J. was the nephew and successor of Justin I. His wife was Empress Theodora. He codified Roman law, and his generals Belisarius and Narses conquered large parts of North Africa from the Vandals (533-548) and Italy from the Ostrogoths (535-554). He fought less successfully against the Persians and the Slavs. Justinian was a great builder. Among his projects was the Hagia Sophia church in Constantinople.

Karl Gustav Jung

Jutland, Battle of (1916) World War I naval battle off Jutland, a peninsula of Denmark. The British fleet led by Jellicoe battled the Germans under Scheer. The smaller German force inflicted heavy casualties on the British. The British blockade of Germany, however, was not broken.

Juvenal (Decimus Junius Juvenalis) (c.AD 55-127) Roman poet. J. wrote 16 satires in poetry that deal with Roman society during the empire. He was very critical of Emperor Domitian.

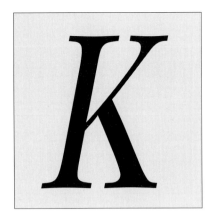

Kaaba The holiest sacred place in Islam. The K. is a small cube-shaped building in the Great Mosque in Mecca, Saudi Arabia. It houses the Black Stone, Islam's most sacred object, which Adam supposedly received when he was driven from paradise. Millions of people make pilgrimages to the K. every year.

Kab ibn Zuhayr (7th century) Arab poet. K. converted to Islam c.630. Earlier he had had a serious conflict with Muhammad. Muhammad forgave him and, as a symbol of his forgiveness, threw a cloak (burda) over him. K. subsequently wrote his famous burda poem, which inspired many to produce their own versions.

Kabarega (c.1850-1923) Last independent monarch (from 1869) of the Bunyoro kingdom (Uganda). He fought successfully against the Egyptians (1870) but his kingdom was absorbed by Buganda (1880s) and later annexed by the British. K. was exiled in 1899.

Kabbala or Cabala Jewish mystical system for interpreting the Bible, supposedly based on a tradition beginning with Abraham.

Kabyles Berbers in Northern Algeria. They bitterly resisted both the Arab conquerors of the 8th century and the French in the 19th.

Kádár, János (1912-1989) Hungarian communist leader. K. was the party's first secretary when the Hungarian Revolution (1956) began. He initially supported the rebels but then joined with the Soviets in crushing the uprising and executing its leaders. He was prime minister 1956-1958 and again 1961-1965. He pushed economic reforms that made Hungary a relatively prosperous Eastern Bloc country but also supported the Soviet invasion of Czechoslovakia (1968).

204

Kaffir Wars (1779-1878) Nine wars between the white Boer settlers in southern Africa and the Bantu-speaking Xhosa natives. The Boers wanted and eventually won the Xhosa grasslands. "Kaffir" was the name the Boers used for the Xhosa and later became a pejorative term for all black Africans.

Kafka, Franz (1883-1924) German-Czech writer. K was born into a German-speaking Jewish family in Prague. He became a lawyer and worked as a government bureaucrat. He was a master at describing the plight of modern man, isolated and anxious, caught up in a senseless bureaucratic world run by forces he cannot understand. Well-known works include *The Metamorphosis* (1916), *The Trial* (1925) and *The Castle* (1926).

Kahane, Meir (1932-1990) American-Israeli right-wing leader. K was a rabbi and in America started the Jewish Defense League, a group willing to use violence. In Israel he founded the extreme right-wing Kach movement. It advocated the expulsion of the Arab inhabitants from the areas occupied by Israel. K. was elected to the Knesset, the Israeli parliament, in 1984. He was assassinated in New York.

János Kádár

Franz Kafka

Kahlemberg, Battle of (1683) Battle in which a European coalition led by King John II of Poland defeated the Turks under Kara Mustafa and lifted the siege of Vienna.

Kaiserchronik (c.1150) A chronicle written in Middle German of the emperors from Caesar to Conrad III (d.1152). It is the oldest historical text in German.

Kalakh or Calah Assyrian city, also known as Nimrud, south of modern Mosul, Iraq. King Ashurnasirpal II made it his capital (c.880 BC). The site is rich in archaeological finds.

Kali (Hindi: the black one) Hindu goddess, also known as Durga and as Parvati the consort of Shiva. She is associated with death and destruction but is also known as the Divine Mother. K. was the patron of the Thugs.

Kállay, Miklós (1887-1967) Hungarian political leader. K. was prime minister of Hungary 1942-1944. He tried to protect the Jews from the Nazis. Following their occupation of Hungary (March 1944), the Germans imprisoned him at Mauthausen and Dachau.

Kalmar, War of (1611-1613). War in which Denmark defeated Sweden for possession of the Norwegian coast. Kalmar is a city in southeastern Sweden.

Kalmar, Union of (1397) Arrangement by which Denmark, Sweden, and Norway agreed to have a single monarch. King Eric was the first monarch under the agreement. It broke down when Gustavus I became king of Sweden (1523).

Kalmucks Mongol nomads who settled on the Volga River in the 17th century. After World War II, Stalin forced many K. to move to Siberia, accusing them of having collaborated with the Germans. They were permitted to return in 1958.

Kaltenbrunner, Ernst (1903-1946) Nazi official. An Austrian, K. succeeded (1943) Heydrich as head of the Reich Security Main Office, one of the foremost instruments of terror of the Nazis. He was executed (1946) for war crimes and crimes against humanity.

Kamakura Period (1185-1333) Period of Japanese history named after the city of Kamakura, which the Minamoto clan made the capital. Following his victory over the Taira clan, Yoritomo, the Minamoto leader, became shogun (1192). Power was taken over by the Hojo family in 1205. The K. period ended in 1333. In 1338 the Hojo general Ashikaga Takauji established his own shogunate, and the Ashikaga, or Muromachi, Period began.

Kamehameha I, the Great (c.1758-1819) King of Hawaii, 1790-1819. The founder of the Kamehameha dynasty, K. united all the Hawaiian islands under his rule.

Lev Borisovich Kamenev

Kamenev, Lev Borisovich (1883-1936) Russian revolutionary and Soviet leader. After Lenin's death, (1924), K. formed a triumvirate with Stalin and Zinoviev to rule, excluding Trotsky, his brother-in-law. Stalin soon drove both K. and Zinoviev from high office. At the start of the great purges, Stalin in 1934 had K. arrested, falsely accusing him of conspiring to kill Kirov. He was executed two years later.

Kamerlingh Onnes, Heike (1853-1926) Dutch physicist. K. discovered superconductivity at low temperatures in 1911. He received the Nobel Prize for physics in 1913.

Kamikaze (Japanese: divine wind) In 1274 and 1281, Mongol fleets attempting to invade Japan were destroyed by typhoons. That inspired the name K. for the suicide planes and ships that Japan, near the end of World War II, sent crashing into Allied ships in a desperate attempt to stave off defeat.

Kammu (737-806) Emperor of Japan, 781-806. K. moved the capital from Nara to Heian (Kyoto) to escape the influence of the Buddhist priests.

Kamperduin, Battle of (1797) In this battle near the Dutch village of Kamp, the British decisively defeated the Dutch. The battle marked the end of the Netherlands as a great maritime power.

Kanaris (Canaris), Constantine (c.1790-1877) Greek revolutionary and political leader. K. commanded the Greek fleet in the Greek War of Independence. After independence he served several times as minister of the navy and as premier. He led the 1862 revolution that replace King Otto with King George I.

Kandinsky, Vasili (1866-1944) Russian painter. K. is considered the founder of abstract painting. Influenced by Gauguin, the neoimpressionists, and the Fauves, he developed his ideas of nonrepresentational painting c.1910. For a time he worked with the Blue Rider group in Munich.

Kanem-Borno Former African kingdom in the region of Lake Chad. It was founded c.800 by the Sefawa people, who later converted to Islam. In the late 19th century, Britain, France, and Germany divided it up.

K'ang Shi (1654-1722) Second emperor of the Chinese Ch'ing (Manchu) dynasty in China. He ruled between 1661-1722, during which time the country thrived. In 1683 he added Taiwan to the empire.

Vasili Kandinsky

Kaniska (AD 1st century) King of Gandhara (now northwest Pakistan). K. was the most powerful ruler of the Kushan dynasty and a great champion of Buddhism. His capital was Peshawar.

Kant, Immanuel (1724-1804) German philosopher. K. was one of the greatest philosophers. He did important work in metaphysics, ethics, and aesthetics. His formulation "Act as if the maxim from which you act were to become through your will a universal law" is widely known even among nonphilosophers. K.'s major writings include *Critique of Pure Reason* (1781), *Critique of Practical Reason* (1788), and *Critique of Judgment* (1790).

Kapp Putsch (1920) Attempt by the right-wing German politician Wolfgang Kapp (1858-1922) to seize power in Berlin and restore the monarchy. He got control of the government for a few days but a general strike ended his power. K. died while being tried for treason.

Kappel Wars Religious wars waged in 1529 and 1531 between Catholic and Protestant cantons in Switzerland. At the Battle of Kappel (1531), the Protestant army was defeated and their leader Ulrich Zwingli killed. The Swiss cantons remained divided in religion.

Kara Mustafa (1634-1683) Turkish grand vizier, 1676-1683. K. served under Sultan Muhammad IV. He was defeated at the siege of Vienna (1683) by a European coalition under John III of Poland, and his retreat was disastrous. He was ordered to commit suicide by the sultan.

Karageorge or Black George (1752-1817) Serbian freedom fighter. Born George Petrovic, K. led a Serbian popular uprising against the Turks in 1804. He entered Belgrade in 1807 and was named hereditary leader of the Serbs. He was forced to flee to 1813 to Austria and to Russia in 1814. He returned after an uprising led by the rival revolutionary Milos Obrenovic, who may have had him assassinated.

Karamanlis, Constantine (1907-) Greek political leader. K. was prime minister for most of the period 1955-1963. During the period of military

Immanuel Kant

rule, (1967-1974), he was in exile. He returned to be prime minister again (1974). K. also served as president 1980-1985 and 1990-.

Karkemish (Jerablus) Ancient city on the Euphrates River in modern Iraq. In 605 BC the Egyptian king Necho II was defeated there by Nebuchadnezzar II of Babylon.

Karlowitz, Treaty of (1699) Agreement that ended the war between Turkey and the coalition of Austria, Poland, Venice, and Russia. It marked the beginning of the decline of the Ottoman Empire. Karlowitz, or Sremski Karlovci, is a town in northern Serbia.

Karlstad, Convention of (1905) Agreement that ended the union of Sweden and Norway. Karlstad is a city in southern Sweden.

Karnak Village, central Egypt. Near Luxor, it is the site of the ancient capital of Thebes and contains elaborate ruins including a temple complex dedicated to the Theban triad of Amon (the head of the Egyptian pantheon), Mut, and Chons.

Kasavubu, Joseph (?1910-1969) Zairan political leader. K. became (1960) the first president of the Republic of the Congo, now Zaire. With the aid of General Mobutu, he defeated Patrice Lumumba in a power struggle (1961) but was himself deposed by Mobutu four years later.

Kasimir (Casimir) Name of four kings of Poland, including Kasimir III, the Great who ruled 1333-1370. He founded the first Polish university. He lost territory in the west to the German knights but expanded Poland in the east.

Kassites Ancient people who lived on the western Iranian plateau. The K. invaded the Babylonian Empire c.1800 BC, captured Babylon in 1531 BC., and ruled Babylon until c.1150 BC from their capital Dur Kurigalzu. They were driven out by the Elamites.

Katanga Uprising Katanga is the former name for Shaba, a province in Zaire, formerly the Republic of the Congo. It is an area rich in mineral resources. Shortly after the Congo became independent (1960), Moise Tshombe, with support from Belgium, the former colonial power, led a rebellion against it. After much confusion, the rebellion was put down in 1963 with United Nations help. It flared up again in 1978 and was again suppressed, this time with French and Belgian help.

Katyn Village in Belarus, formerly the Soviet Union. During World War II, the Germans discovered a mass grave there in 1943 containing the bodies of more than 4,000 Polish officers. After denying responsibility for their murder for many years, the Soviet Union in 1990 finally admitted the men had been killed on the orders of Stalin after the Soviet Union had invaded Poland in 1939.

Joseph Kasavubu

Kenneth David Kaunda

Kaunda, Kenneth David (1924-) Zambian political leader. K. was born in what was then Northern Rhodesia and became active in the nationalist movement. H was chosen Zambia's first president in 1964. In 1972 he started one-party rule, which lasted until 1990. In the 1991 elections he was defeated.

Keaton, Buster (Joseph Francis) (1895-1966) American movie star. K. did his best work as silent film comedy performer. His most successful films were *Sherlock, Jr.* (1921), *The Boat* (1921), *The Navigator* (1924), and *The General* (1927).

Keiki (d.1913) Japanese leader. Born Hitosubashi Yoshinobu, he became shogun in 1866. The last shogun, K. played an important role in opening Japan up to foreigners. He resigned in 1867.

Keitel, Wilhelm (1882-1946) German general. Under Hitler he was chief of staff of the armed forces and always carried out Hitler's wishes. K. was tried at Nuremberg and hanged.

Kellogg, Frank Billings (1856-1937) American political leader and diplomat. K., a Republican from Minnesota was a lawyer, U.S. senator (1917-1923) and ambassador to Britain (1923-1925). While secretary of state (1925-1929) in the Coolidge administration, he negotiated the Kellogg-Briand Pact. He received the Nobel Peace Prize in 1930. *See* Kellogg-Briand Pact.

Kellogg-Briand Pact 1928 international agreement worked out by U.S. Secretary of State Kellogg and French Foreign Minister Briand in which 15 nations promised to settle disputes peacefully. The agreement had little effect.

Kemal Pasha, Mustafa (Atatürk, Kemal) 1881-1938) Turkish political leader. K. founded modern Turkey. The name Atatürk means "Father of the Turks." K. was one of the Young Turk reformers who aimed to liberalize the Ottoman Empire. He was an outstanding military leader. At the end of World War I, he set up in Ankara a government in opposition to the sultan. After the last sultan, Muhammad VI, fled in 1922, he became the president of the Turkish Republic and brought about the rapid modernization of the country.

Kennan, George F. (1904-) American diplomat and historian. K. served in numerous diplomatic posts, including ambassador to the Soviet Union (1952) and Yugoslavia (1961-1963). He is considered the author of the containment policy that the U.S. adopted toward the Soviet Union after World War II. K also wrote several distinguished books of diplomatic history and memoirs.

Kennedy, John Fitzgerald (1917-1963) 35th president of the U.S., 1961-1963. K. was the second son of Joseph P. Kennedy and Rose Fitzgerald Kennedy. He served heroically in the Pacific during World War II and was elected as a Democrat to the House of Representatives after the war (1946). After two terms in the House, he was elected to the Senate (1952, 1958). In 1960 K. became the first Catholic to be elected president, defeating Richard Nixon in a very close race. He faced foreign policy crises in Cuba (Bay of Pigs, 1961, and Missile Crisis, 1962), Berlin (Berlin Wall, 1961), and Southeast Asia, where he deepened the American involvement in Vietnam. K. negotiated a Nuclear Test Ban Treaty (1963) and started the Peace Corps. He increased the government's commitment to civil rights and proposed Medicare and other reforms that were enacted after his November 1963 assassination in Dallas.

Kennedy, Joseph Patrick. (1888-1969) American businessman and public official. The son of Irish immigrants, K. became very wealthy in the 1920s from various business activities. President Franklin Roosevelt appointed him head of the Securities and Exchange Commission (1934-1935) and ambassador to Britain (1937-1940). Fearing another world war, he supported the appeasement of Hitler. He and his wife Rose Fitzgerald had a large family. Of their four sons, Joseph, Jr., died in World War II; John became president of the U.S., and Robert and Edward became U.S. senators. Both John and Robert were assassinated during his lifetime.

Kennedy, Robert Francis (1925-1968) American political leader. The third son of Joseph P. Kennedy and Rose Fitzgerald Kennedy, K. became a lawyer. His brother President John F. Kennedy appointed him attorney general (1961-1964). He served as U.S. senator from New York (1964-1968) and was assassinated while running for president.

Kenneth I (d.858) The founder of Scotland, he united the thrones of the Dalriads and the Picts.

Kent, Kingdom of Kingdom in England founded by the Jutlanders (5th century). *See* Aethelbert.

Kenyatta, Jomo (c.1894-1978) Kenyan political leader. K. was one of the first African nationalists. In 1946 in London he founded with Kwame Nkhrumah the Pan-African Federation. After returning to Kenya he was sentenced in 1953 to 7 years hard labor by the British for his ties to the Mau Mau, who committed terrorist acts. From 1964 till his death, K. was the first president of the independent republic of Kenya.

Kepler, Johannes (1571-1630) German astronomer. Influenced by Copernicus, K. made use of Tycho Brahe's observations and calculations and for the first time accurately stated the movements of the planets around the sun.

Kerensky, Aleksandr Feodorovich (1881-1970) Russian revolutionary. A lawyer, K. was a moderate socialist. After the February revolution, he became first minister of justice, then war minister, and then prime minister in the Provisional Government. When the Bolsheviks overthrew the Provisional Government in October, he fled to Paris. In 1940 K. came to the U.S.

Kerouac, Jack (1922-1969) American writer. K. is the most highly-regarded author of the Beat Generation. He is known mainly for *On the Road* (1957), an autobiographical book, that tells of its characters restless and aimless search for new experience.

Kersten, Felix (1898-1960) German-Baltic masseur. K. was the personal physician of the Nazi leader SS chief Heinrich Himmler between 1939-1945. Through his influence over Himmler, he achieved the release of hundreds of Jews and other prisoners.

Kesselring, Albert (1885-1960) German general. He led the air war against Poland (1939) and in the west (1940). In 1943 he became supreme commander in Italy and in 1944, after the invasion of Normandy, of the western front. After the war he was convicted of war crimes and imprisoned until 1952.

Keynes, John Maynard (1883-1946) British economist. K. was one of the most influential economists of the first half of the 20th century. He showed that capitalist economies are not always self-regulating and that under certain circumstances government spending is needed to stimulate demand. His principal work was *The General Theory of Employment, Interest, and Money* (1935-1936).

KGB *See* Cheka.

John Maynard Keynes

Aleksandr Feodorovich Kerensky (left)

Khaddafi, Moamar al (1942-) Libyan political leader. His name may also be written as Muammar al-Qaddafi. While serving in the army, K. led a coup that deposed King Idris in 1969, and he has been the dictator fo Libya since then. He has pursued fundamentalist Islamic and extreme nationalist Arab policies. His support of international terrorism has considerably isolated Libya from the rest of the world. In retaliation for K.'s support of terrorism, the U.S. in 1986 bombed his headquarters.

Khazars Turkish people who emerged in the 2nd century in the Transcaucasus and established a kingdom around the Black Sea (8th-10th centuries). They were defeated by the duke of Kiev in 965.

Khedive Official title of the viceroy of Egypt between 1867 and 1914.

Khmer The principal ethnic group in Cambodia. The K. are one of the oldest peoples in Southeast Asia. They flourished during the Angkor Empire (889-1434). *See* Khmer Rouge.

Khmer Rouge Cambodian Communists. In 1975 they succeeded, with help from North Vietnam, in overthrowing the pro-Western regime of Lon Nol. Led by Pol Pot, the K. then began an attempt to reshape Cambodia that resulted in the deaths of as many as 1.5 million people. Disputes with Viet-

nam led to a Vietnamese invasion (1978-1979) that drove the K. from power. They continued to maintain an army, however, and fighting between them and other Cambodian factions has continued off and on since then.

Khomeini, Ruhollah (?1900-1989) Iranian spiritual leader and head of state. An ayatollah revered by Iran's Shiite Muslims, K. was exiled in 1964 because of his opposition to the regime of the shah. From exile he led the revolution that deposed the shah, and he returned to Iran to establish an Islamic republic, which he headed (1979). His anti-American attitudes inspired the the occupation of the American embassy and the taking of American hostages (1979-1981).

Ayatollah Ruhollah Khomeini

Khosrau I (d.579) King of Persia, 531-579. K. was the greatest Sassanid king. He succeeded his father, Kavadh I. K. fought successfully against the Byzantine Emperor Justinian and extended Persian rule over Arabia, where Muhammad was born during his reign.

Khosrau II (d.628) King of Persia, 590-628. The last great king of the Sassanid dynasty, K. succeeded his father, Hormizd. Byzantine Emperor Maurice helped him regain his throne after losing it to the usurper Bahram. Later K. warred against Maurice's murderer, Phocas, but was defeated by the Emperor Heraclius in 623 and 628. He was murdered by his own son, Kauadh II Shinya.

Khrushchev, Nikita Sergeyevich (1894-1971) Soviet political leader. K. came from a peasant family and rose to power under Stalin. After Stalin's death (1953) he became first secretary of the Communist Party and by 1955 was the most powerful leader. He served as premier from 1958-1964. K. gave the "secret speech" to the 20th Party Congress (1956) on Stalin's crimes and relaxed Stalin's tyranny to some degree but brutally crushed the Hungarian Revolution (1956). He repeatedly provoked international crises over Berlin and secretly put missiles into Cuba, which led to the Cuban Missile Crisis with the U.S. (1962), but he later agreed to the Nuclear Test Ban Treaty (1963).

Kiel, Treaty of (1814) Agreement between Denmark and Sweden in which Denmark ceded Norway to Sweden.

Kierkegaard, Søren (1813-1855) Danish philosopher and theologian. Much of his work dealt with individual subjectivity. K. is considered a major influence on existentialism.

Kiesinger, Kurt Georg (1904-1988) German political leader. K. served as leader of the Christian Democratic Party and chancellor of West Germany (1966-1969), despite having earlier been a member of the Nazi Party and having worked in the foreign ministry in the Hitler regime.

Kim Il Sung (1912-1994) North Korean dictator. K. joined the Communist Party in 1931. When North

Kim Il Sung

Korea was created in 1948, he became its dominant figure and remained so for the rest of his life. His attempt to unify Korea under his rule led to the Korean War (1950-1953). During his regime, he was glorified and the country largely cut off from most of the rest of the world.

King, Ernest Joseph (1878-1956) American admiral. K. was the com-

Søren Kierkegaard

mander-in-chief of the U.S. navy during World War II.

King, Martin Luther (1929-1968) American civil rights leader. Born in Atlanta, K. became a Baptist minister and gained national recognition when he led the campaign to integrate the Birmingham, Alabama, bus system (1956). Advocating a strategy of non-violent passive resistance highly influenced by Gandhi, K. became the

Martin Luther King

most prominent civil rights leader in America. He delivered a stirring speech during the 1963 March on Washington. He received the Nobel Peace Prize in 1964. K. was assassinated in 1968 in Memphis, Tennessee.

King Philip's War (1675-1676) Conflict between the New England colonists and Native Americans of the region. King Philip (Indian name: Metacom) was the chief of the Wampanoag Indians. The basic cause of the war was the colonists' desire for the Indians' land. It ended with the Indians' defeat. Philip was killed, and his head displayed on a pole. The war was very costly to both sides.

Kinsey, Alfred Charles (1894-1956) American sex researcher. K. began his career as a professor of entomology at Indiana University. When helping to organize a course on marriage, he realized how little information was available and founded the Institute for Sex Research (1942). He interviewed thousands of people and published two books: *Sexual Behavior in the*

Human Male (1948) *and Sexual Behavior in the Human Female* (1953).

Kipling, Rudyard (1865-1936) British writer. K. lived in India until he was six, was then sent to school in Britain, and returned to India in 1882. There he wrote his famous *Jungle* books for children (1894-1895), among others. His stories and poems did much to create the image of the noble Englishman doing the great work of empire building. He received the Nobel Prize for Literature in 1907.

Kircher, Athanasius (1601-1680) German Jesuit, archaeologist, and scientist. K. was one of the first to believe that disease was caused by microorganisms. He worked unsuccessfully to decipher Egyptian hieroglyphics.

Kirchhof, Gustav Robert (1824-1887) German physicist. Working with Robert Bunsen, K. made advances in spectrum analysis and also did important work in electricity and thermodynamics.

Kirov, Sergei Mironovich (1886-1934) Soviet political leader. K. became leader of the Communist Party in Leningrad in 1926 and a popular figure. He was assassinated in 1934. Stalin used the event as the pretext for a massive purge of the party. Some experts believe that Stalin himself was behind the murder.

Kish Ancient Mesopotamian city on the Euphrates River, near the modern city of Hillah, Iraq. It was where, according to a Sumerian royal geneology, the first dynasty after the Flood was established.

Kissinger, Henry Alfred (1923-) American political scientist and presidential adviser. K. was born in Germany and came to the U.S. in 1938. He taught at Harvard University. In the Nixon and Ford administrations he was national security adviser (1969-1971) and secretary of state (1971-1976). K. played a key role in improving U.S. relations with China and in the negotiations with North Vietnam on ending the Vietnam War, for which he received the Nobel Peace Prize in 1973.

Kitab al-Aghani (Arabic: Book of Songs) A collection of poems compiled by Abu al-Faraj al-Isfahani (d.967). It contains poems set to music from the earliest period of Arabic literature down to the 9th century. The music can no longer be read, but the collection contains valuable information about the poets and composers. The collection was made on the orders of Caliph Harun ar-Rashid.

Kita Ikki (1888-1937) Japanese nationalist. K. was in favor of a militarily strong Japan in which the emperor had absolute power. He advocated driving the Western powers out of the Far East. He was executed for complicity in the attempt (February 1936) by military officers to establish a military dictatorship.

Kitchener, Horatio Herbert (1850-1916) British general and political leader. K. led the British army that recaptured the Sudan between 1896-1898 from supporters of the Mahdi. He also fought in the Boer War and in India. K. became minister of war at the start of World War I. He drowned while on his way to talks in Russia when his ship hit a German mine.

Horatio Herbert Kitchener

Kittikachorn, Thanom (1911-) Thai general and political leader. K. became minister of defense in 1957 following a coup and served as prime minister for many years. His government ended after bloody riots in 1973, and he retired to a monastery.

Kléber, Jean-Baptiste (1753-1800) French general. K. accompanied Napoleon to Egypt (1798) and remained there as commander of the French army. In 1800 he defeated a Turkish army at Heliopolis and conquered Cairo. He was assassinated in Egypt.

Paul Klee

Klee, Paul (1879-1940) Swiss artist. K. created thousands of works that use color and imagery in highly imaginative ways. Among them are *The Twittering Machine* (1922) *and Fish Magic* (1925).

Kleist, Heinrich von (1777-1811) German writer. One of the greatest German Romantic writers, K. wrote comedies, tragedies, and stories. He committed suicide in 1811.

Klerk, Frederik Willem de (1936) South African political leader. A member of the National Party, K. succeeded P.W. Botha as party chairman and as president (1989). Under him South Africa abandoned apartheid, released political prisoners including the African National Congress leaders Sisulu and Mandela, and held free elections for the first time. In 1993 he and Mandela received the Nobel Peace Prize. *See* African National Congress; Mandela.

Klinger, Friedrich Maximilian van (1782-1831) German writer. His 1776 play *Wirrwarr; oder, Sturm und Drang* (*Confusion; or Storm and Stress*) gave its name to an epoch in literature.

Klitos (d.327) Macedonian general. A friend of Alexander the Great, K. was murdered by Alexander in a drunken brawl.

Klotz, Sebastian (1697-1767) German violinmaker. Born into a German violin-making family, K.'s instruments are considered to be the best German violins ever made.

Knights Hospitalers (Knights of St. John and of Jerusalem) Order of knights founded in the 11th century to protect Christian pilgrims to the Holy Land and care for those who fell ill. The K. took part in some of the major campaigns of the Crusaders. The order was first based in Jerusalem. When Jerusalem fell to the Muslims in 1187, the order moved first to Margat, then to Acre, Cyprus, Rhodes, and eventually to Malta. In 1530 Emperor Charles V made the K. the rulers of Malta. The present Knights of Malta are a charitable organization.

Knossos Ancient city in Crete that was the center of the Minoan culture (c.2800-1200 BC). In 1900 the British archaeologist Evans discovered there a large palace consisting of many corridors, rooms, and staircases around a courtyard. It had been destroyed c.1400 BC by causes unknown and was probably the residence of the legendary king Minos.

Know-Nothings American political movement. The K. originated in the 1840s as a secret movement opposed to immigration. Leaders replied to questions about the movement by saying "I know nothing." For a time they were allied with the Whig Party. In the 1850s they tried to become a national political organization called the American Party, but they split over the slavery issue. The K. supported Millard Fillmore for president in 1856.

Knox, Henry (1750-1806) American general and political leader. K. was born in Boston. He was a close aide of George Washington during the American Revolution, and Washington made him the first secretary of war under the Constitution (1789-1794).

Knox, John (c.1514-1572) Scottish religious leader. A follower of Calvin, K. introduced Presbyterianism into Scotland c.1560. He debated theology with Mary Queen of Scots. K. wrote the *History of the Reformation in Scotland* (1564).

Koch, Robert (1843-1910) German physician and scientist. K. discovered the bacteria that cause anthrax in sheep (1876) and the tuberculosis bacillus (1882). He succeeded in isolating the cause of cholera (1883). He also did work on sleeping sickness, malaria, bubonic plague, and other diseases. K. received the Nobel Prize for Physiology and Medicine in 1905.

Köchel, Ludwig von (1800-1877) German musicologist. K. compiled and published (1862) a catalogue of Mozart's works. Revised several times since, it is still used today.

Helmut Kohl

Kohl, Helmut (1930-) German political leader. A Christian Democrat, K. became chancellor of West Germany in 1982. With the reunification of Germany in 1990, he became the leader of the new united country.

Henry Knox

Koine The Greek language of the eastern Mediterranean in the Hellenistic and Roman periods.

Kokinshu A collection of 1100 Japanese poems, the earliest extant Japanese poetry. It was compiled on the orders of Emperor Daigo (897-930).

Kokoschka, Oskar (1886-1980) Austrian expressionist painter. K was a pupil of Klimt in Vienna. He exhibited in 1912 with the Blue Rider group in Munich. His works show a great deal of psychological tension. Among them are a portrait of Nijinsky and landscapes of Jerusalem and Prague.

Oskar Kokoschka

Kolchak, Alexandr Vasilyevich (1874-1920) Russian admiral. K. served in the Russo-Japanese War and World War I. After the 1917 revolution, K. led an anti-Bolshevik government based in Omsk, Siberia. His 1919 military campaign against the Bolsheviks failed, however, and he was captured and shot.

Koldewey, Robert (1855-1925) German archaeologist. K. worked on excavations on Lesbos and in Ashur. He is most well-known for his work in Babylon.

Kolkhoz An agrarian cooperative in the Soviet Union, created as part of the collectivization program (1929). Inhabitants of a K. possessed only a dwelling, a vegetable garden, and some animals. The government told them what to grow and how much, and determined what they would be paid for it.

Kolokotronis, Theodorus (1770-1843) Greek freedom fighter. K. was a successful general in the Greek War of Independence. Political disputes in Greece led to his conviction as a traitor (1834). Sentenced to death, he was pardoned by King Otto I.

Kömer, Theodor (1873-1957) Austrian general and political leader. statesman. K. fought in World War I. He was an opponent of the Nazis and the Anschluss. He became president of Austria in 1951.

Konarak Hindu temple, Orissa state, India. It is dedicated to the sun god Surya. Made of red sandstone, it is known as the Black Pagoda and was built c.1240.

Kondylis, Georgios (1879-1936) Greek general and political leader. K. served in the Balkan Wars and World War I. He served briefly as prime minister in 1926 and again in 1935 after coups. He was nicknamed "the Greek Cromwell" because of his persistent striving to increase his own power.

Königgrätz, Battle of (1866) A decisive battle in which the Prussians defeated the Austrians during the Austro-Prussian War. It was fought at a village in Bohemia now known as Sadová.

Konungs Skuggsja (King's Mirror) An Old Norse story from c.1250. It contains a dialogue between a father and his son and was probably written at the court of Hakon Hakonson.

Konyev, Ivan Stepanovich (1897-1973) Soviet general. K. fought in the Russian Civil War and World War II. In 1946 he became supreme commander of the Soviet armed forces and in 1955 of the armies of the Warsaw Pact.

Koprulu, Ahmed (1635-1676) Grand vizier of the Ottoman Empire, 1661-1676. The son of Mehmed Koprulu, he suffered defeats in Hungary (1664) and at the hands of John III of Poland

but conquered Crete and made peace with Venice (1669).

Koprulu, Mehmed (1575/1578-1661) Grand vizier of the Ottoman Empire, 1656-1661. K. reinvigorated the empire by conquering Transylvania, reorganizing the fleet, improving the finances, and restoring internal order.

Koran or Quran The holy book of Islam. It contains the revelations God gave to Muhammad.

Korean War (1950-1953) After World War II, Korea became divided into two zones: the Communist North and the pro-Western South. The 38th parallel separated the two. In June 1950 North Korea, supported by China and the Soviet Union, invaded the South. United Nations forces, led by the U.S., came to the aid of the South. After they pushed the Northern forces back across the 38th parallel and in late 1950 advanced toward the Yalu River, which separates Korea from China, Chinese troops entered the war. After much bitter fighting, a cease-fire was established in June 1953 that left Korea divided as it had been before the war.

Kornilov, Lavr Georgyevich (1870-1918) Russian general. K. was appointed as supreme commander by the Provisional Government in 1917 but organized a right-wing coup against it. He was arrested, escaped, and formed an army in southern Russia. He was killed while fighting against the Bolsheviks.

Korolyev, Sergei Pavlovich (1907-1966) Soviet scientist. He directed the Soviet space program and was responsible for the launching of the Sputnik in 1957, among other achievements.

Kossuth, Louis (1802-1894) Hungarian revolutionary. A lawyer, K. was one of the leaders of the revolution against Austria in 1848 and became the president of an independent Hungary in 1849. When Russian troops intervened, K. was forced to flee. He visited the U.S. and lived in Britain and Italy, where he died.

Kosygin, Alexei Nikolayevich (1904-1980) Soviet political leader. K. joined the Communist Party in 1927. He became deputy prime minister in

1956 and in 1960 a member of the Presidium. In 1964 he replaced N. Khrushchev as premier and shared power with L. Brezhnev. Later he was overshadowed by Brezhnev.

Krak-des-chevaliers A stronghold of the Crusaders, near the modern Jordanian town of Al Karak. It was built in the 12th century and captured by Saladin in 1188.

Kreisler, Fritz (1875-1962) Austrian-American violinist. K. was born in Vienna and won a gold medal at the Vienna conservatory when he was 10. He settled permanently in the U.S. in 1940. A greatly loved violinist, he also composed many short works for the instrument. Elgar wrote his violin concerto for him.

Krishna (Sanskrit: black) Hindu deity, the eighth avatar of Vishnu. He appears in much of Hindu literature.

Kristallnacht (German: night of broken glass) The night of November 9-10, 1938, during which Nazi-inspired gangs beat up Jews, burned synagogues, and wrecked Jewish shops and property throughout Germany and Austria.

Kritias (c.460-403 BC) Athenian political leader and writer. K. was a relative of Plato, who mentions him in several of his dialogues, and wrote poetry and dramas. He was one of the 30 Tyrants Sparta forced on Athens. He was killed in battle against Thrasybulus.

Kronstadt Uprising (1921) Anti-Soviet revolt of sailors at the Kronstadt naval base near St. Petersburg. The sailors had earlier supported the Bolsheviks but now demanded economic reforms and democratic rights. The Red Army stormed Kronstadt and captured the base. Subsequently hundreds of sailors were executed.

Kruger, Paul (1825-1904) South African general and political leader. As a boy K. moved north in the Great Trek. He fought in the Kaffir Wars and took part in the negotiations with Britain that established an independent Traansval (1881). K. was several times president of the Traansval. After the Boer Wars, he went into exile, and he died in Switzerland. *See* Kaffir Wars; Boer Wars.

Paul Kruger

Kruger telegram Message sent (1895) by Kaiser William II of Germany to President Kruger of the Traansval congratulating him on successfully resisting the Jameson Raid. It was a deliberate insult to Britain. *See* Jameson.

Krupp German family of industrialists. Beginning c.1810, the family owned steel plants, armaments factories, and financial institutions. It cooperated with the Nazis. After World War II, Alfried Krupp von Bohlen und Halbach (1907-1967) was tried as a war criminal and sentenced to prison for 12 years but served only 3.

Kuang Chu (1871-1908) Emperor of China, 1875-1908. In 1898 K. attempted to modernize China by decree. His plans were opposed by the dowager empress, Tse-si, who had him declared mad and imprisoned. K. died under suspicious circumstances.

Kublai Khan (1215-1294) Mongol emperor. K. was the grandson of Genghis Khan and succeeded his brother Mangu. He founded the Yüan Chinese dynasty. K. ended the reign of the Sung dynasty (1279). K. ruled all China and Mongolia. Marco Polo described the glories of his realm.

Ku Klux Klan American secret societies. The first K. was established in the South after the Civil War. Its members were ex-Confederates who believed in white supremacy and wanted to block measures to improve the conditions of the free blacks. The K. members dressed themselves in white sheets and often resorted to terror attacks on blacks and on whites who attempted to help them. A second K. was founded in 1915 in Georgia by William J. Simmons. In addition to being antiblack, it was anti-Catholic and antisemitic. It gained members in the North as well as the South, and for many was more a social organization than anything else. It declined in the late 1920s when some its leaders were found to be corrupt. The rise of the civil rights movement in the 1960 led to a resurgence of the K. as an antiblack movement.

Kulak (Russian: fist) Derogatory Soviet Communist term for wealthy peasants. It was used especially to refer to peasants who became prosperous, or relatively so, as a result of Lenin's New Economic Policy in the 1920s. During Stalin's collectivization drive that started in the late 1920s, these peasants were brutally persecuted, and millions died.

Kulturkampf (German: conflict of cultures) (c.1871-1887) Conflict between the German government under Bismarck and the Roman Catholic Church. At issue were church-state relations and the doctrine of papal infallibility, proclaimed by Pope Pius IX, as it applied to those relations. In 1887 Bismarck and Pope Leo XIII resolved the conflict.

Kun, Béla (1886-?1939) Hungarian revolutionary. K. organized the Communist Party in Hungary in 1918 and established a Communist-led government in 1919. Romania intervened

Béla Kun

and drove him from power. K. fled to Vienna and later to the Soviet Union. He was arrested during Stalin's purges in the 1930s, and it is thought that he died in Siberia.

Kuomintang (Chinese: National People's Party) Chinese political party, founded in 1912. Sun Yat-sen was an early leader, and its original program called for democracy and socialism. Chiang Kai-shek became the leader in the 1920s. At one time the K. was allied with the Communists, but civil war between the two began in 1927. The K. established a government that was recognized diplomatically by most of the world's nations in 1928. After Japan was defeated in World War II, the conflict with the Communists worsened, and in 1949 the Communists drove the K. forces off mainland China to Taiwan.

Kurds Ethnic group related to the Iranians who live in parts of Turkey, Syria, Iran, Iraq, and Armenia. Mainly Sunni Muslims, the K. have resisted control by others but have not been independent since the 7th century. Before the 20th century, they were ruled by Arabs, Seljuk Turks, Mongols, and, for hundreds of years, by the Ottoman Turks. Kurdish nationalist movements have existed in Turkey, Iran, and Iraq but have always been suppressed.

Kurozumikyo Japanese nationalistic and religious movement, named after Munetada Kurozumi. An important part of its daily ritual is inhaling the sun's power.

Kursk, Battle of (July 1943) World War II battle between Germany and the Soviet Union, fought near the Soviet city of Kursk. It was the largest single battle of the war, involving millions of men and thousands of planes and tanks. The Soviets turned back the German offensive, and Germany was never again able to mount a major offensive on the eastern front.

Kutuzov, Mikhail Ilarionovich (1745-1813) Russian general. K. fought against the Poles, the Turks and the French. When Napoleon invaded Russia in 1812, K. was his great opponent. Although driven back at the Battle of Borodino (1812), K.'s patient strategy eventually forced Napoleon to retreat from Russia.

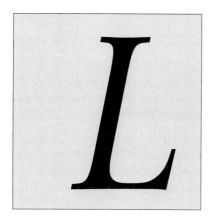

Labarnas I (17th century BC) King of the Hittite Empire, c.1680-1650. L. founded the Old Hittite Empire (c.1700-1500). Starting from his capital at Kusara in Anatolia, he expanded the empire westward to the Mediterranean coast.

Labienus, Titus (c.100-45 BC) Roman general. L. was a colleague of Caesar in Gaul. In 49 BC he defected to Pompey. He died in the battle of Munda.

Lacandon Central American Mayan people. Living in several jungle villages, they maintained their ancient culture well into the 20th century until the arrival of modern tourism.

François
d'Aix Lachaise

Lachaise, François d'Aix (1624-1709) French Jesuit. He was the confessor of Louis XIV. His country estate, formerly outside of Paris, is now the site of the famous Père Lachaise cemetery, established in 1804.

Lachmides (3rd-6th centuries) Arabic dynasty. Their capital was Hira. The L. were vassals of the Sassanids and waged incessant war against Byzantium.

Lactantius, Lucius Caelius Firmianus (c.240-320) Christian philosopher. Born in Africa, L. became (317) the tutor of Crispus, the son of Constantine the Great. A well-known work by L. is *On the Deaths of the Persecutors*, which describes the terrible ends of the lives of the Roman emperors who persecuted the Christians.

Ladies' Peace (Treaty of Cambrai) (1529) An agreement concluded between Holy Roman Emperor Charles V and Francis I of France at Cambrai. Francis renounced his claims to Flanders, Artois, and territories in Italy. The negotiations leading to the agreement were conducted by Margaret of Austria and Louise of Savoy, mother of Francis I.

Ladysmith Town in Natal, South Africa. During the Second Boer War, the British base there was unsuccessfully besieged by the Boers, 1899-1900.

Lafargue, Paul (1842-1911) French socialist. He was one of the founders of a Marxist party in France. A son-in-law of Karl Marx, he and his wife committed suicide together because they did not believe in a useless old age.

Lafayette, Marie Joseph, Marquis de (1757-1834) French general and political leader. In 1777 L. came to America to fight with the Continental Army against the British in the American Revolution. He quickly became a favorite of George Washington, and he played a key part in the American victory at Yorktown (1781). L. also played an important role in the French Revolution, particularly in its early stages. Between 1792-1797, he was imprisoned by the Austrians. He lived in retirement during the Napoleonic years and made a triumphant return visit to America in 1824-1825. L. was a moderate in the 1830 Revolution and was instrumental in making Louis Philippe king.

Lafitte, Jean (?1780-?1825) Pirate. Probably born in France, L. came to New Orleans in the early 1800s and led a group of pirates and smugglers.

He took part in the battle of New Orleans (1815) on the American side, after which President Madison pardoned him for his piracy. He later founded Galveston, Texas.

La Follette, Robert Marion 1855-1925 American political leader. L. served as a U.S. senator from Wisconsin 1906-1925, after having been the state governor for five years. L. favored an active role for government in regulating business and protecting citizens from the injustices of industrial society. Initially a Republican, he became a leading Progressive and was the Progressive candidate for president in 1924. He opposed American entry into World War I and the League of Nations.

Lafontaine, Jean de (1621-1695) French writer. He is celebrated for his more than 200 "fables" that use stories of animals, mainly taken from Aesop, to illustrate aspects of human behavior.

Lagash Ancient Sumerian city, southern Mesopotamia. L. was inhabited as early as 4000 BC and flourished c.2400-2050 BC. It contained the striking sculptures of Gudea. L. was conquered by Sargon of Akkad.

Lagerlöf, Selma (1858-1940) Swedish author. She became famous for her first novel *Gösta Berling* (1891). Much of L.'s work deals with peasant life in her native Värmland region of Sweden or is based on traditional folk legends. She wrote the classic children's stories

Selma Lagerlöf

The Wonderful Adventures of Nils (1906). L. was the first woman to win the Nobel Prize for Literature (1909).

Lahmu and Lahamu In ancient Mesopotamian mythology, twin gods who were the first born out of the primeval chaos.

Laissez-faire (French: let things alone) Principle of political economy that expresses the view that government should regulate economic affairs as little as possible. It was originated in France in the 18th century by the physiocrats, who were reacting against mercantilism. *See* Mercantilism.

Lakis An ancient stronghold in southwest Judaea. It was destroyed in 701 BC by the Assyrian king Sennacherib, as described on 21 shards (ostraca) that were found at the site.

Lalibela (13th century) King of Ethiopia. In the village of Roha, later the capital Lalibela, he founded eleven churches. Later he was canonized by the Ethiopian church.

Lamarck, Jean-Baptiste (1744-1829) French naturalist. L. did much work on invertebrate biology. A precursor of Darwin, he developed a theory of evolution based on the idea of acquired characteristics.

Jean-Baptiste Lamarck

Lamian War Lamia is a city in central Greece, founded in the 5th century BC. The war was a conflict between Greek cities, led by Athens, and Macedonia after the death of Alexander the Great (323 BC). The Macedonian general Antipater was besieged in Lamia but managed to escape and then defeated the Greeks at Crannon (322 BC).

Lamoricière, Christophe de (1806-1865) French general. L. fought in the French conquest of Algeria and captured Abd al-Kader in 1847. During the June 1848 uprising in Paris, he was the garrison commander there. His opposition to Louis Napoleon led to his being exiled in 1851.

Landsteiner, Karl (1868-1943) Austrian-American physician and bacteriologist. L. was born in Vienna and came to the U.S. in 1922. He discovered the human blood types. In 1930 he received the Nobel Prize for Physiology and Medicine.

Lannes, Jean (1769-1809) French general. A favorite of Napoleon, he fought in almost every major battle of the Napoleonic Wars. He died in the Battle of Essling in 1809.

Lan Tian (14th-18th centuries) Kingdom in Laos founded by Fa Ngoun. In 1707 it split into the kingdoms of Luang Prabang and Vientiane.

Lanuvium Ancient city in modern Albania. The Romans conquered it in 338 BC. L. was the birthplace of the emperors Antonius Pius and Commodus.

Lanza, Giovanni (1810-1882) Italian nationalist and political leader. L. was the prime minister of Italy 1869-1873. During his term Rome was annexed to Italy.

Lanzmann, Claude (1925-). French journalist and filmmaker. L. was part of Jean-Paul Sartre's circle. He is best known for his documentary *Shoah* (1985), which gives a penetrating portrait of the Holocaust by means of interviews with people involved as victims, perpetrators, or bystanders.

Lao-tze (6th century BC) Chinese philosopher. A legendary figure, L. is considered the founder of Taoism.

Lappo movement (1929-1932) Fascist movement in Finland, named after the village of Lappo, where an anticommunist uprising took place. General Wallenius of the L. attempted a coup d'état in 1930 that failed, as did another coup attempt in 1932.

Lares Roman guardian spirits of the farm and the household. Offerings were made to them at meals and on special occasions.

La Rochejaquelein, Henri Du Vergier, count of (1772-1794) Leader of the Vendée uprising during the French Revolution, he was killed in battle.

Larsa Ancient city in southern Babylon, modern Iraq. It was the seat of the Larsa dynasty (fourteen rulers) that played a major role in Mesopotamia for 250 years. L. controlled all south Mesopotamia c.2000 BC. In 1763 BC Hammurabi conquered the city.

La Salle, Robert Cavalier, Sieur de (1643-1687) French explorer. L. explored the Great Lakes region. He was the first European to descend the entire length of the Mississippi River (1682). He led an expedition from France to the mouth of the Mississippi (1684) but landed instead in what is now Texas. Attempting to travel by land to the river, he was murdered by his men.

Las Casas, Bartolomé de (1474-1566) Spanish missionary and historian. L. first came to the New World in 1502. He was active in Hispaniola, Peru, Mexico, and Guatemala. A priest, he became greatly interested in the condition of the native inhabitants and was instrumental in the passage of the so-called New Laws in Spain that were designed to improve their treatment by Spanish colonists. He wrote the invaluable *History of the Indies.*

Lascaux Cave in southwest France, in the Dordogne, that contains wall paintings by Cro-Magnon man. The cave was discovered in 1940. It was closed to the public in 1961 to preserve the paintings, which were deteriorating from the presence of many tourists. A cave with simulated paintings was created nearby.

Lat, Al Goddess worshipped in north Arabian goddess before the time of Muhammad. She was worshipped together with Manate (Fate) and Uzza (the Strong).

La Tène Culture Late Iron Age Celtic culture named after an archeological site on Lake Neuchâtel, Switzerland. Artifacts were found there that date from c.475-450 BC.

Robert Cavalier La Salle

Lateran Council, First (1123) Called by Pope Calixtus II, it was the ninth ecumenical council of the Roman Catholic Church. The council confirmed the Concordat of Worms and ended the Investiture Controversy.

Lateran Council, Fourth (1215) Called by Pope Innocent III, it was the twelfth ecumenical council of the Roman Catholic Church. The council defined a new statement of faith including transubstantiation, established annual confession and Easter communion as requirements for all Catholics, and called for a new crusade, the fifth.

Lateran Treaty (1929) Concordat between the Roman Catholic Church and Italy. It settled issues in the relations between the Vatican and Italy. Vatican City was recognized as a sovereign state. Roman Catholicism became the Italian state religion, and children at public schools were to receive a Catholic education.

Latifundia The great landed estates in ancient Rome. When Rome declined, the L. became the local centers of power and culture.

Latimer, Hugh (c.1485-1555) English clergymen and Protestant martyr. Henry VIII made L. a bishop after he defended Henry's divorce from

Hugh Latimer

Katharine of Aragon, though L. later resigned because Henry would not move as far in the Protestant direction as he wanted. L. was Anne Boleyn's chaplain and one of the leaders of the English Reformation. After the accession of the Catholic Mary Tudor, he was burned at the stake.

Latin Alliance A coalition of 30 Italian villages, led by Alba Longa, for mutual support and defense against Rome. It ended when Rome became dominant in the region 338 BC.

Latin Empire of Constantinople (1204-1261) A crusader state set up in the Balkans and Greek islands by leaders of the Fourth Crusade. The first emperor, Baldwin I, was Baldwin IX of Flanders. The empire ended when Constantinople was captured by Emperor Michael VIII of Nicaea.

Latium Region, in central Italy. In ancient times L. was inhabited by several Italian tribes. Rome conquered it in the 3rd century BC.

Arthur Stanley Jefferson Laurel

Laurel, Arthur Stanley Jefferson (1890-1965) British-American comedy film star. Born in England, L. toured America as Charlie Chaplin's understudy in 1910 and 1912. He made his first film in 1914 but became famous from his comedy movie collaborations with Oliver Hardy, starting in 1927. L. was the thin, shy, bumbling character; Hardy the fat, extroverted, domineering one. L. was the creative genius behind their films.

Laurens, Henry (1724-1792) American Revolutionary War leader. A South Carolina merchant, L. served in the Continental Congress and in the delegation that negotiated the Treaty of Paris (1783). From 1780-1782 he was imprisoned by the British; he was exchanged for General Cornwallis.

Lausanne Pact (1932) An international agreement, never ratified, concerning Germany's World War I reparations.

Lausanne, Peace of (1912) The agreement that ended the Tripolitan War between Italy and Turkey.

Lausanne, Treaty of (1922-1923) Agreement that superseded the Treaty of Sèvres concerning Turkey's relations with its neighbors. It was made necessary by the coming to power of the new nationalist government in Turkey headed by Atatürk. *See* Kemal, Mustafa.

Lautaro (d.1557) Chief of the Araucanian Indians (Chile). L. led a revolt against the Spanish that nearly succeeded in driving them out of southern Chile.

Laval, Pierre (1883-1945) French political leader. L. began his career as a Socialist but gradually moved to the

Pierre Laval

right. He served in the Vichy government and was frankly pro-German. In April 1942 he became virtual dictator. When the Allies invaded France in 1944, he retreated to Germany. After the war he was arrested, convicted of treason, and executed.

Lavalette, Jean P. de (1494-1568) Grand Master of the Knights of Malta, 1557-1568. L. had defended Malta against the Turks in 1566.

Lavalleja, Juan Antonio (1788-1858) Uruguayan freedom fighter and political leader. L. was leader of the "33 Immortals," the men who fought against Brazil in 1825 for an independent Uruguay. The competition between him and Fructuoso Rivera for the leadership of Uruguay led to a long civil war (1843-1851) and the growth of political factions—the Blancos ("Whites," initially led by L.) and the Colorados ("Reds," led by Rivera) that remain to this day.

Lavoisier, Antoine Laurent (1743-1794) French scientist. L. is considered the founder of modern chemistry. He explained combustion and the role of oxygen in animal and plant respiration. He also pioneered the modern classification of the chemical elements. L. was executed during the French Revolution's Reign of Terror.

Antoine Laurent Lavoisier

Lawrence, Thomas Edward (1888-1935) British soldier and writer. Known as "Lawrence of Arabia," L. was in the British army in Egypt when

Thomas Edward Lawrence

World War I started. In 1916 he joined with the Arabs in their fight against Turkish rule. At the Paris Peace Conference, he sought unsuccessfully for independence for the Arabs. Later he served in the British tank corps and air force. He wrote *Seven Pillars of Wisdom* (1926) about his work with the Arabs.

Layamon (c.1200) English chronicler and poet. A priest, L. wrote a verse chronicle about the history of Britain that is one of the sources of the legend of King Arthur.

League of Augsburg *See* Augsburg.

League of Cambrai *See* Cambrai.

League of Cognac (1526) Coalition of Pope Adrian VI, Milan, Venice, Florence, and France against Spain.

League of Roman Catholic German Rulers (1609) Coalition formed as a counterbalance to the Protestant Union. It was headed by Duke Maximilian I of Bavaria.

Leakey, Louis (1903-1972) British paleoanthropologist. In 1959 he discovered a 2.5 million-year-old hominid skull in the Olduvai Gorge in Tanzania. The discovery meant that humans developed much earlier than had previously been thought.

Leakey, Richard (1944-) British paleoanthropologist. The son of Louis

Leakey, he made discoveries in the 1970s in east Africa that offered further evidence of the great age of *homo sapiens.*

Lebanese Civil War A conflict that began in the 1970s among the various ethnic and religious groups of the Lebanese population. One split was between the Christian and Muslim populations. Since World War II Lebanese Christians had been dominant in the country's power structure. Muslims now challenged that dominance. There was also conflict between non-Christian groups, however. The Druses fought with left-wing Muslims. The situation was further complicated by the on-going war between Palestinians and Israelis. Palestinian terrorists staged attacks on Israel from Lebanon, which led to devastating Israeli retaliatory strikes and invasions. Syria supported some of the more extreme Palestinian factions. A tenuous settlement among many of the Lebanese groups was reached in the early 1990s, although the conflict between Israelis and Palestinians based in Lebanon continued.

Lebensraum (German: living space) Term referring to the view of some late 19th-century German thinkers that Germany needed to acquire additional territory to support and feed its population. Adolf Hitler took up this position and frequently cited it as the justification for Germany's expansion in eastern Europe.

Lebrun, Albert (1871-1950) French political leader. L. was the last president of the Third Republic (1932-1940). The Vichy government ended his authority, and in 1943 he was imprisoned by the Germans.

Lechfeld Plain near Augsburg, Germany, where King Otto I defeated the Magyars in 955.

Leclerc Jacques Philippe (1902-1947) French general. Fighting for the Free French in World War II, he commanded a heroic march in Africa of more than 1500 miles from Lake Chad to Tripoli (1942-1943). In 1944 he led the first Allied troops into Paris.

Albert Lebrun

Le Corbusier (1887-1965) Swiss-French architect. Born Charles Edouard Jeanneret, L. was one of the most celebrated architects of this century. L. used elementary geometric forms and wished to integrate exterior and interior space. In his "modular" architecture, he tried to relate human and mathematical proportions. Among his most well-known buildings are an apartment complex in Marseilles (1952) and the government offices in Chandigarh, India (1951-1964).

Ledru-Rollin, Alexandre Auguste (1807-1874) French political leader. A radical, L. was prominent in the 1848 revolution. He unsuccessfully opposed Louis Napoleon in the election that year. When his 1849 coup against Louis Napoleon failed, he fled to England. He returned to France after the fall of the Second Empire and was again active in politics.

Le Duc Tho (1911-1990) Vietnamese diplomat. L. was one of the founders of the Communist Party in Indochina (1930). In 1971 and 1972 he conducted secret negotiations with U.S. Secretary of State Henry Kissinger on ending the Vietnam War. In 1973 he was awarded but refused the Nobel Peace Prize.

Le dynasty Dynasty that ruled the kingdom of Vietnam 1428-1788. It was founded by Le Loi, who freed the country from the Chinese. An uprising by the brothers Tay Soy ended the dynasty.

Robert Edward Lee

Lee, Robert Edward (1807-1870) American Confederate general. One of the greatest generals in American history, L. was also universally respected for his character and humanity. Born in Virginia, L. graduated second in his class at West Point (1829). He served with great distinction in the Mexican War and captured John Brown at Harper's Ferry (1859). When the Civil War began, he declined an offer to command the Union forces and reluctantly supported Virginia's secession. At first L. was military adviser to Confederate President Jefferson Davis. In 1862 he was given command of the South's main army, the Army of Northern Virginia. Despite inferiority in men and equipment, for almost three years L. repeatedly defeated the Union armies sent against him. His attempts to invade the North, however, failed at Antietam (September 1862) and Gettysburg (1863). By April 1865 L.

could no longer defend against the overwhelming forces Union General Grant brought against him, and he surrendered at Appomattox. Near the end of his life, he served as president of Washington College (now Washington and Lee University).

Antony van Leeuwenhoek

Leeuwenhoek, Antony van (1632-1723) Dutch scientist and microscope maker. With his microscopes L. made the first thorough studies of microorganisms.

Legate In ancient Rome, an official responsible to the Senate, frequently sent to a province. Under Caesar, a L. was often a captain of a legion.

Leges barbarorum (Latin: barbarian laws) Laws of the Germanic tribes that, after the tribes' migration into the Roman Empire, were written down between the 5th and the 9th centuries.

Legion A unit of the Roman army. An L. typically consisted of 5,000 men, divided into 10 cohorts.

Legitimist After 1830 the term for a supporter of the Bourbon family's claim to the French throne.

Lehár, Franz (1870-1948) Hungarian composer. L. is best-known for his operettas. His most successful work is *The Merry Widow* (1905).

Leibniz or **Leibnitz, Gottfried Wilhelm, Baron von** (1646-1716) German diplomat, mathematician, and philosopher. L. served various German princes as a diplomat and adviser. He discovered the calculus at the same time as did Newton and published his findings (1684) three years before Newton did. His rationalist philosophy had a great influence on Kant and the German enlightenment.

Leicester, Robert Dudley, Earl of (?1532-1588) English courtier. L. was a favorite of Elizabeth I and for a time had hopes of becoming her husband. During the time of the Spanish Armada (1588), she appointed him commander of the army.

Robert Dudley

Leif Ericson (c.1000) Norse discoverer of America. The son of Eric the Red, L. was born in Iceland and

Leif Ericson

grew up in Greenland. According to Norse sagas, he made a settlement called Vinland somewhere on the North American coast.

Leipzig, Battle of (1813) Battle, also called the Battle of the Nations, near the German city of Leipzig in which Napoleon was decisively defeated by an Austrian, Prussian, and Russian army.

Lend-Lease Act (1941) American law designed to aid Britain and China in World War II, enacted while the U.S. was still officially neutral. It gave the president the power to sell or lease vital war equipment; payment could be in kind or in property and could be deferred until the end of the war. After Germany invaded Russia, Lend-Lease aid was also given to that country and later to other Allied countries.

Lenin, Vladimir Ilyich (1870-1924) Russian revolutionary and political leader. Born Vladimir Ilyich Ulianov, L. became one of the greatest theorists of Marxism and was the founder of the Communist Party. He organized the

Vladimir Ilyich Lenin

October Revolution (1917) and became the first leader of Communist Russia (later the Soviet Union).

Leningrad, Siege of (1941-1944) During World War II the city of Leningrad (now St. Petersburg) was besieged by the German army from late 1941 to early 1944. The population endured terrible hardship-nearly one million people died—before the siege was ended.

Lennon, John (1940-1980) British rock musician, member of the Beatles. L. and Paul McCartney were the leaders of the Beatles. He and his wife, Yoko Ono, became active in various

John Lennon

political causes after the Beatles ceased performing as a group. He was murdered in New York City by John Hinckley.

Lens City, northern France. The last major battle of the Thirty Years War took place there in 1648. The Spanish were defeated by the French under de Condé.

Leo I, Saint, the Great (d.461) Pope, 440-461. L. succeeded Saint Sixtus III. A doctor of the church, he defined the nature of Christ and fought against Manichaeism. He negotiated with Attila the Hun (452) and persuaded him not to invade Rome.

Leo X (1475-1521) Pope, 1513-1521. Born Giovanni de Medici and the son of Lorenzo de Medici, L. succeeded Julius II. He was a great patron of the arts but was not successful as leader of the Church. The indulgences sold to pay for his elaborate building program in Rome were one of the abuses Luther protested against and were a contributing cause of the Protestant Reformation.

Leo XIII (1810-1903) Pope, 1878-1903. Born Vincenzo Gioacchino Pecci, L. succeeded Pius IX. He is considered the first modern pope, as he tried to make the Church a vital participant in the modern world. He ended the *Kulturkampf* with Bismarck

and wanted the Church to be a force for social progress.

Leo I (c.400-474) Byzantine emperor, 457-474. L. was chosen emperor when the line of Theodosius died out. He suffered a great naval defeat against the Vandals under Gaiserik (468)

Leonardo da Vinci *See* Vinci, Leonardo da.

Leonardo Pisa *See* Fibonacci, Leonardo Pisano.

Leonidas (died 480 BC) King of Sparta. L. led the small army of Spar-

Leo X

Leo XIII

tans and Thespians that defended to the death the pass of Thermopylae against the Persians in 480 BC.

Leonov, Alexei Archpovich (1934-) Russian cosmonaut. L. took the first space walk, outside the Voschod-2 spaceship, on March 18, 1965.

Leopold I (1640-1705) Holy Roman emperor, 1658-1705, king of Bohemia, 1656-1705, and king of Hungary, 1655-1705. L. was the second son and successor of Ferdinand III. He spent much of his time defending the empire against the Ottoman Turks and the French. L.'s claim to the Spanish throne formed the reason for the War of the Spanish Succession (1701).

Leopold II (1747-1792) Holy Roman emperor and king of Bohemia and Hungary, 1790-1792. L. was the son of Maria Theresa and the sister of Marie Antoinette. He succeeded his brother Joseph II as emperor and reversed most of his reforms. He was largely responsible for the Declaration of Pillnitz (1791), which led to the Wars of the French Revolution.

Leopold I (1790-1865) King of Belgium, 1831-1865. L. was the son of Francis Frederick, the duke of Saxe-Coburg. His first wife, Princess Charlotte, was the daughter of the future George IV of Britain. She died in 1817. When Belgium became independent in 1831, L. was chosen king. The next year he married Louise Marie, the daughter of Louis Philippe of France. Britain's Queen Victoria was his niece, and her husband, Prince Albert, was his nephew. Carlotta, briefly empress of Mexico, was his daughter.

Leopold II (1835-1909) King of Belgium, 1865-1909. The son of Leopold I, whom he succeeded, L. was very interested in colonizing Africa. The Congo Free State (now Zaire) became his personal possession in 1885, and he exploited it brutally to build his personal fortune. In 1908 he was forced to turn it over to the Belgian government. L. was succeeded by his son, Albert I.

Leopold III (1901-1983) King of Belgium, 1934-1951. The son of Albert I, whom he succeeded, L. tried to be neutral in World War II and mediate a settlement of the conflict, but Ger-

many invaded Belgium in 1940. He surrendered and was taken prisoner by the Germans. After the war some Belgians accused him of having collaborated with the Germans, and he was forced to abdicate in favor of his son Baudoin in 1951.

Lepanto, Battle of (1571) Naval battle between the Holy League and the Turks, fought off Lepanto, Greece. The Turkish fleet was destroyed, and the battle prevented the Turks from gaining control of the Mediterranean.

Lepidus, Marcus Aemilius (d.13/12 BC) Roman official and follower of Caesar. After Caesar's murder, L. formed a triumvirate with Mark Anthony and Octavian in 43 BC and was given control of Africa. Later Octavian deprived him of most of his power.

Lepsius, Karl Richard (1810-1884) German Egyptologist. L. traveled to Egypt and the Sudan (1843-1845) and wrote an important 12-volume work on the archaeology of the region (1849-1859).

Lerma, Francisco Gómez de Sandoval y Royas (1553-1625) Spanish statesman. A favorite of Philip III, L. made peace with England (1604) and the Netherlands (1609) and expelled the Moriscos from Spain (1609-1614).

Lescure, Louis, marquis de (1766-1793) L. was one of the leaders of the Vendée uprising during the French Revolution.

Lesseps, Ferdinand Marie, Vicomte de (1805-1894) French diplomat and engineer. While serving as a diplomat in Egypt (1854), L. developed the idea of the Suez Canal. He supervised the canal's construction (1859-1869). He then formed a company to build a canal in Panama, but the project was abandoned amid accusations of financial scandal.

Le Thanh Tong (d.1497) King of Vietnam, 1460-1497. L. organized the kingdom after the example of the Chinese bureaucracy. He defeated the Tiampa kingdom in 1471.

L'état, c'est moi (French: I am the state) Saying attributed to Louis XIV of France; he supposedly uttered it during a meeting of the Parliament of

Paris in 1655. It summarizes the absolute monarchy, based on the idea of the divine right of kings, that Louis's reign exemplified.

Lettre de Cachet During the Ancien Régime in France, the L. was a royal writ, signed by the king or an undersecretary, as a result of which a person could be imprisoned or exiled without trial.

Leuctra Ancient Greek town in Boeotia, near Thebes. The Spartans were defeated there by the Theban general Epaminondas in 371 BC.

Leuthen Village near Breslau (modern Wroclaw in Poland) where Frederick the Great of Prussia defeated the Austrians in 1757 during the Seven Years War.

Levi See Israel, Tribes of.

Levi, Primo (1919-1987) Italian chemist and writer. A Jew, L. was seized by the Italian Fascists in 1943 and sent to Auschwitz. He wrote several books, including *Survival in Auschwitz* (1958) and *The Reawakening* (1961), about his experiences. He died by suicide.

Lévi-Strauss, Claude (1908) French anthropologist. Based on his research into the myths of primitive peoples, L. founded structural anthropology.

Lewis and Clark Expedition (1803-1806) U.S. expedition that explored the regions of the Missouri and Columbia Rivers. It was conceived and planned by President Thomas Jefferson and led by Meriwether Lewis and William Clark. As instructed by Jefferson, the expedition brought back a huge body of information on the flora, fauna, and Indian populations of the lands of the Louisiana Purchase and what later became the far Northwest of the U.S.

Lewis, Meriwether American explorer. L., a Virginian, and William Clark led the great expedition (1803-1806) that President Jefferson sent to explore the region of the Missouri and Columbia Rivers. See Lewis and Clark Expedition.

Lexington and Concord Towns in Massachusetts, near Boston, where the first shots of the American Revolution were exchanged between British soldiers and American rebels April 19, 1775.

Ley, Robert (1890-1945) German Nazi official. L. was responsible for the employment of millions of foreign workers in German industry during World War II. He committed suicide during the Nuremberg Trials.

Leyden, Lucas van (1494-1533?) Dutch painter and engraver. L. was the first significant Dutch painter of daily life. He created hundreds of etchings, engravings, and paintings. One of his best known paintings is *The Last Judgment* (c.1526)

Leyte Gulf, Battle (October 1944) World War II naval battle between Japan and the U.S. Fought off Leyte island in the Philippines, it was the greatest sea battle in history. In it the U.S. destroyed the Japanese navy as a significant factor in the war.

Liaquat Ali Khan (1895-1951) Pakistani political leader After having been educated in Britain as a lawyer, L. became a leader of the Muslim League and a main follower of Muhammad Ali Jinnah. He was chosen the first prime minister of independent Pakistan in 1947 but was assassinated four years later.

Libavius, Andreas (c.1540-1616) German chemist. He wrote the first chemistry textbook, *Alchymia* (1606)

Liberalism Political philosophy concerned with maximizing individual freedom. Classical liberalism, which developed in England in the late 17th century (especially in the work of John Locke) and was refined there and in the U.S. during the next 150 years, stressed the need for individuals to be free from government interference. In the late nineteenth century, however, the development of industrial society persuaded thinkers such as T.H. Green that to protect individual freedom and maximize individual opportunity, government should take a more positive role. Thus contemporary liberals are supporters of the welfare state.

Liberté, Egalité, Fraternité (French: Liberty, Equality, Fraternity) Motto of the French Revolution. It was formulated by the Cordeliers in June 1793.

Life Before Man

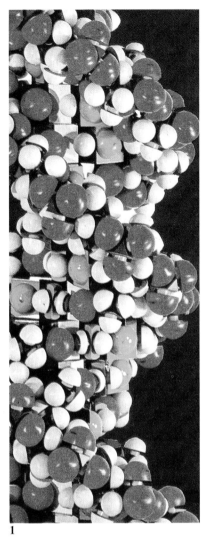

1

2

3

Life existed on earth for millions of years before the first humans evolved. For instance, from 225 to 65 million years ago, dinosaurs roamed the earth. Only with great difficulty have scientists been able to form an idea of what the world of the dinosaurs was like, and the disappearance of the dinosaurs is still an unsolved question. Much of our knowledge comes from fossils, which give us an idea of time long before the coming of man.

4

1. Structure model of a DNA molecule. DNA forms the basis for all life on earth.
2. A fossilized tree from a prehistoric forest near Glasgow, Great Britain.
3. A fossilized bird that was found in Germany
4. Reconstruction of a Tyrannosaurus Rex, the most fearsome dinosaur, standing on its hind legs.

Libya Country in northern Africa. The name Libya appears on the so-called Israel Stele of the Egyptian king Merneptah (c.1215 BC). There L. is described as the enemy neighbor west of Egypt. The Greeks viewed all of North Africa except for Egypt as L. The country was conquered by the Ottoman Turks in the 16th century and remained mainly under Turkish rule until 1911, when it was conquered by Italy. After World War II it became independent. *See* Idris al-Sanusi.

Licinius, Valerius Licinianus (d.325) Roman emperor, 308-325. L. became coemperor with Galerius. After Galerius's death, L. and Constantine I defeated Maximin, and L. became the emperor in the east. He quarrelled with Constantine, however. After losing to him at Adrianople (324), L. was imprisoned and executed.

Lictors In ancient Rome, the officials who accompanied the magistrates in public appearances and carried the *fasces* (bundles of axes) that were the symbol of Roman authority.

Lidice Village in the Czech Republic. In June 1942 the Germans destroyed it, killing all the men and deporting the women and children, in retaliation for the assassination in Prague of the SS leader Reinhard Heydrich.

Lidj Jasu (1895-1935) Emperor of Ethiopia, 1913-1916. L. succeeded his grandfather Menelik. In 1916, shortly after his conversion to Islam, L. was deposed in favor of a daughter of Menelik.

Lie, Trygve (1896-1968) Norwegian political leader and diplomat. During World War II, L. he was minister of foreign affairs in the Norwegian government in exile in Britain. He served as the first secretary-general of the United Nations 1946-1953.

Liebknecht, Karl (1871-1919) German political leader. A radical socialist, L. opposed World War I. During the war he and Rosa Luxemburg founded the Spartacists, who later became the German Communist Party. L. was imprisoned for his anti-war position. He led an uprising against the moderate socialist government that was formed at the end of the war and was killed while being arrested.

Liegnitz City, now Legnica in southwest Poland. It was the scene of two battles: 1. In 1241 a German-Polish army was defeated by the Mongols; 2. In 1760 Frederick the Great of Prussia defeated the Austrians in the Seven Years War.

Lifan Yuan A bureau of the Chinese government that was created in the 17th century under the Manchu dynasty. It handled contacts with foreigners and issued trade permits, among other things. It was discontinued in 1906.

Ligny Village in central Belgium. In June 1815 Napoleon defeated the Prussians under Blücher there, shortly before the Battle of Waterloo.

Ligurian Republic In 1797 Napoleon Bonaparte transformed the Republic of Genoa into the L. In 1805 it was annexed by France.

Ligurians Ancient people who lived along the Mediterranean coast between the Rhone and Arno Rivers after being driven south by the Celts in the 4th century BC. They were conquered by the Romans in the 2nd century BC.

Li Hshuteng (d.1864) Chinese general. He was a leader of the Taiping Rebellion (1850-1864).

Lilienthal, Otto (1848-1896) German engineer and aeronautical pioneer. L. did work with gliders, in part based on his observations of birds. He died in the crash of a glider.

Lilith Jewish mythological female demon, possibly based on Assyrian myths. In one story she was Adam's first wife. She is a symbol of dangerous sexuality.

Liliuokalani (1838-1917) Queen of Hawaii, 1891-1893. L. became queen after the death of her brother, King Kalakaua. She was dethroned by a revolt led by American sugar growers. She renounced her claim to the throne in 1895 and spent most of her remaining years in the U.S.

Liman von Sanders, Otto (1855-1929) German general. In World War

Otto Lilienthal

Karl Liebknecht

I he commanded Turkish troops that defended the Dardanelles. *See* Gallipoli.

Limes The borders of the Roman Empire that were fortified with walls and fortresses. An example is Hadrian's Wall in Britain, built 122-128 AD.

Lin Biao (1907-?1971) Chinese general and political leader. L. became China's defense minister in 1959. He

Lin Biao

was considered Mao's heir apparent, but he supposedly died in a 1971 plane crash. After his death, it was reported that he had been planning a coup.

Lincoln, Abraham (1809-1865) 16th president of the U.S., 1861-1865. L. was one of the very greatest presidents. He was born in a log cabin in Kentucky; his family later moved to Indiana and Illinois. Largely self-educated, L. became a successful Illinois lawyer. He entered politics as a Whig and served one term in the U.S. House of Representatives (1847-1849). In the 1850s L. became one of the leaders of the new Republican Party, which opposed the expansion of slavery. He ran for the U.S. Senate against Stephen A. Douglas in 1858 and, although defeated, attracted national attention for his views. The Republicans nominated him for president in 1860. His election precipitated the secession of 11 Southern states, and the Civil War

followed. Lincoln led the North through the war, the most awful crisis the nation ever experienced. Reelected in 1864, he was assassinated in April 1865, just as the war was ending. Lincoln preserved the Union, ended slavery in the U.S., and redefined the nation's democratic creed. *See* American Civil War; Confederate States of America; Gettysburg Address.

Lindbergh, Charles Augustus (1902-1974) American aviator. In 1927 L. became the first person to fly alone across the Atlantic Ocean. He flew 33.5 hours from New York to Paris in the *Spirit of St. Louis.* L. became an enormously popular figure. His son was kidnapped and killed in 1932; a celebrated trial followed. In the years preceding America's entrance into World War II, L. was an isolationist.

Linear A and B Ancient languages. Linear A was a Minoan script used on Crete since the 19th century BC. It was superseded by an archaic form of Greek called Linear B, which has been found both at Knossos on Crete (from the 14th century BC) and in Mycenaean centers on the Greek mainland (13th century BC). Linear B is 500 years older than the language used by Homer. It was deciphered by Michael Ventris in 1952.

Lingones Celtic tribe that lived in the region of the Seine and Marne Rivers. Around 400 BC they migrated to the Po Plain (Italy). The Romans conquered them in 299 BC and granted them citizenship in 69 BC.

Linnaeus, Carolus (1707-1778) Swedish botanist. L. originated the

Abraham Lincoln

modern classification system for plants and animals.

Carolus Linnaeus

Lin Tse-chu (1785-1850) Chinese civil servant. L.'s actions to end the opium trade in Canton (1839) led to the first Opium War. *See* Opium Wars.

Lipit-Ishtar (20th century BC) King of Isin, a Mesopotamian city. His law code has been excavated; it gives information about matters such as leases, inheritance, and marriage.

Lisht, el- Ancient Egyptian city, on the western bank of the Nile River. Amenemhet I moved the capital there from Thebes c.2000 BC.

Li Shu (?280-208 BC) Chinese scholar, adviser to Emperor Shi Hwang-ti. L.'s advice led to the founding of the Ch'in dynasty (221 BC) and the unification of China.

Liszt, Franz (1811-1886) Hungarian composer and pianist. L. was one of the greatest piano virtuosos of all time and profoundly influenced the development of piano technique and composition. He toured all over Europe astounding audiences with his performances but after 1848 devoted most of his time to composition and teaching. He composed an enormous amount of music for piano, orchestra (L. pioneered the symphonic poem), and voices and also made hundreds of piano arrangements of other composers' works. As a conductor and publicist, he was also a great champion of the music of Berlioz and Wagner. His daughter Cosima became Wagner's second wife, after having been married earlier to Hans von Bülow.

Li Tchuchen (?1605-1654) Chinese rebel who seized Beijing, causing the last Ming emperor, Tchungcheng, to hang himself (1644). Shortly after, L. was driven off by Ming and Manchu armies.

Lit de Justice (French: sitting of the court) During the Ancien Régime in France, a special meeting of the Parliament of Paris held when the king personally came to order an ordinance to be registered.

Little Bighorn, Battle of the (1876) Battle on the bank of the Little Bighorn River in Montana between the U.S. army under General George A. Custer and Native Americans led by the Sioux chiefs Sitting Bull and Crazy Horse. The entire U.S. force was annihilated.

Litvinov, Maxim Maximovich (1876-1951) Soviet diplomat. L. was an early Bolshevik. In 1930 he became the Soviet foreign minister. Stalin replaced him with Molotov in 1939 because he wanted to negotiate a pact with Hitler, and L. was Jewish. From 1941-1943 L. was ambassador to the U.S.

Liu Yuan (d.310) Nomad who invaded China in 304 and had himself proclaimed king. His son succeeded him but had to give up the throne in 329.

Livia Drusilla (58 BC-29 AD) Roman matron. Her first husband was Tiberius Claudius Nero. In 38 BC at the insistence of Octavian, later the emperor Augustus, L. divorced Tiberius so she could marry Octavian. He adopted her son by her first marriage,

Tiberius, and Tiberius succeeded Augustus as emperor.

Livingstone, David (1813-1873) British missionary and explorer. In 1840 L. started work in South and Central Africa, where he discovered (1855) the Victoria Falls and other natural

David Livingstone

features. After not being heard from for some time, he was found (1871) by the American journalist Henry Stanley, who spoke the words "Dr. Livingstone, I presume."

Livingston, Robert R. (1746-1813) American lawyer and diplomat. A New Yorker, L. administered the presidential oath to George Washing-

Livia Drusilla

ton in 1789. He was the American minister to France at the time of the Louisiana Purchase (1803). Later he financed Robert Fulton's steamboat experiments.

Livonia (Livland) Region along the Baltic coast of Europe, including present-day Estonia and part of Latvia. It was inhabited by the Livs, a Finnic tribe, when it was conquered by the Teutonic Knights in the 13th century. Later Poland and then Sweden controlled it. In the Peace of Nystadt (1721), Sweden ceded it to Russia.

Livonian War (1558-1583) In 1558, Conflict between Russia on one side and the coalition of Poland, Latvia, and Sweden on the other. Russia was forced to give up its claims to Livonia.

Livy (Titus Livius) (64/59 BC-17 AD) Roman historian. In his *History* L. wrote the story of Rome since its founding in 754 BC. Of the 142 "books" of his work, only 35 have been preserved in their entirety. The contents of some of the others, however, is known from the works of other historians.

Lloyd George, David (1863-1945) British political leader. L. entered Parliament as a Liberal in 1890. He was

David Lloyd George

an anti-imperialist and radical. As chancellor of the exchequer in 1909, he proposed the budget containing social insurance that the House of Lords rejected, which led to the Parliament Act of 1911. In 1916 L.

became prime minister and remained in office until 1922. He was instrumental in bringing about a unified command of the Allied forces in World War I. L. negotiated the 1922 treaty that established the Irish Free State.

Loango, Kingdom of (Congo) Founded in 1485, L. flourished by trading in ivory and slaves but declined in the 18th century.

Lobengula (c.1836-1894) King of Matabeleland (now part of Zimbabwe), 1870-1894. L. succeeded his father. He ceded mineral rights to Cecil Rhodes in 1888. After leading a disastrous rebellion against the influx of British gold traders, he was killed while fleeing north.

Locarno Pact (1925) A series of treaties signed by Britain, France, Italy, Belgium, Czechoslovakia, Poland, and Germany. They guaranteed borders and provided for arbitration of disputes. France signed defense pacts against Germany with Poland and Czechoslovakia. Germany was allowed to join the League of Nations. Hitler denounced the Pact when Germany reoccupied the Rhineland in 1936.

Lodi City in Italy, southeast of Milan. In 1796 Napoleon defeated the Austrians there, courageously leading his troops over the contested Adda bridge.

Lodi Dynasty (1451-1526) Line of Afghan rulers who were the last of the Delhi sultans. The dynasty ended when the Mogul Babur defeated Ibrahim Shah Lodi at the Battle of Panipat in 1526.

Logothete (7th-14th centuries) In the Byzantine Empire, a highly placed civil servant and special emissary of the emperor.

Loki In Norse mythology, a god or giant who was evil incarnate.

Lollards (Dutch: mumblers) The followers of John Wyclif, the 14th-century English church reformer. Wyclif denounced priestly wealth and believed each person could interpret the Bible for himself.

Lombards Germanic tribe that was living along the Elbe River in the 1st century AD. In the 6th century the L. migrated to Italy and founded a kingdom in the Po Plain. Reaching its height in the 8th century, the kingdom led by Aistulf threatened Rome. Pope Stephen II enlisted the aid of the Franks. The Frankish king Pepin II defeated the L. and gave some of their lands to the papacy in the Donation of Pepin (756). Charlemagne defeated them again when led by Desiderius and became their king (774).

Lombardy League A coalition of North Italian cities. The L. fought against Holy Roman Emperor Frederick I Barbarossa and defeated him at Legnano in 1176. In 1177 Barbarossa concluded a temporary peace that became permanent with the Peace of Konstanz (1183).

Lombardy-Venetia Kingdom created by the Congress of Vienna (1815) and placed under Austrian rule. The population repeatedly rebelled against Austrian rule, and by the treaties of Zurich and Veneto it became part of the Italian kingdom of Piedmont (1859).

Lombroso, Cesare (1835-1909) Italian criminologist. In his book *Criminal Man* (1876) L. argued that there was a criminal type that could be recognized by certain physical characteristics (such as a low forehead) or behavior (such as capriciousness).

Loménie de Brienne, Étienne Charles de (1727-1794) French clergymen and financier. He succeeded Calonne as finance minister in 1787. His call for a land tax led to the summoning of the Estates-General. He resigned in 1788 and became a cardinal. Although he supported some of the early measures of the French Revolution, he was arrested and died in prison. *See* French Revolution.

Lon Nol (1913-1985) Cambodian political leader. Supported by the U.S., L. was president of Cambodia 1972-1975. He was driven out by Pol Pot and the Khmer Rouge in 1975.

London, Conference of (1830-1831) Meeting of the European powers that provided for the independence of Belgium from the Netherlands.

London, Maritime Conference of (1930) Meeting at which the U.S., France, Italy, Japan, and Great Britain agreed to certain limitations on naval construction and rules for submarine warfare.

Long, Huey Pierce (1893-1935) American political leader. L. was born into a family of poor Louisiana farmers. A salesman, he rose in politics and became governor in 1928. He enacted numerous reforms, including improved education and health services, and large public works projects; he also used corrupt methods and became virtual dictator of the state. L. was elected U.S. senator in 1931. At first a supporter of Roosevelt's New Deal, he broke with the president in 1934 and announced his own radical "Share-the-Wealth" program. Considered a possible 1936 presidential candidate, L. was assassinated in 1935.

Longinus Roman soldier who guarded the cross at Golgotha on which Jesus was crucified. He acknowledged that Jesus was the Son of God. By some accounts he was also the soldier who speared Jesus while He was on the cross.

Long Island, Battle of (1776) Engagement in the American Revolution in which the British under Howe drove the Americans under Washington off Long Island, New York. Washington retreated through Manhattan island and White Plains before camping in New Jersey.

Long March (1934-1935) Journey of c.6,000 miles made by the Chinese Communists led by Mao Zedung. When their base in Kiangsi province was encircled by Kuomintang troops, the c.90,000 Communists escaped and, after terrible hardships eventually reached remote Shensi province, where they established a new base at Yenan. On the way more than half their number died.

Long Parliament (1640-1660) The Parliament that was called in 1640 by King Charles I of England because he needed money. It remained officially in session until 1660, when the Restoration under Charles II began. While it sat, the English Civil War was fought and Charles I was executed. In 1648 the L. became the Rump Parliament when Cromwell purged the par-

Étienne Charles de Loménie de Brienne

liamentary cause's enemies. *See* English Civil War.

Longueville, Anne-Geneviève de Bourbon-Condé, duchess of (1619-1679) L. was the daughter of Henry II de Condé and sister of Louis II de Bourbon, prince de Condé, and of Armand de Bourbon, prince de Conti. Along with her lover, the duke of La Rochefoucauld, her husband, and her brothers, she was one of the leaders of the Fronde. After the failure of the revolt, she lived mainly in convents.

Longueville, Henri, duke of (1595-1663) L. participated in the conspiracy against Cardinal Richelieu in 1626 and was one of the leaders of the Fronde, together with his wife, Anne-Geneviève de Bourbon-Condé, her lover, and her brothers, the princes Condé and Conti. L. was arrested in 1650; after his release he ruled Normandy.

Henry, duke of Longueville

López, Francisco Solano (1827-1870) President of Paraguay, 1862-1870. L. succeeded his father, Carlos Antonio López, as president. Suspicious and cruel, he desired to become the Napoleon of South America, but the war he began (1865) with Brazil, Argentina, and Uruguay was disastrous for Paraguay. He was killed while in retreat.

Lord Dunmore's War (1774) War of British North American colonists against Shawnee Native Americans in Kentucky. It is named after the royal governor of Virginia, John Murray, lord of Dunmore. The Shawnee were defeated in the Battle of Point Pleasant.

Loris-Melikov, Mikhail Tarielovich (1825-1888) Russian general and minister. He fought in the Russo-Turkish War (1877-1878). As minister of the interior under Alexander II, L. proposed reforms in education and representation. Alexander approved them just prior to his assassination (1880); his successor, Alexander III, disapproved them and forced L. to resign.

Los Alamos Town in north central New Mexico. During World War II, it was the center of the work on the U.S. atomic bomb.

Lotf Ali Khan Zand (1769-1794) Shah of Persia, 1789-1794. L. was the last king of the Zand dynasty. He was defeated in the civil war of 1779-1794 and tortured to death.

Lothair I (795-855) Emperor of the West, 840-855. L. was the eldest son of Louis I, the Pious. In 817, Louis made him coemperor, but he twice rebelled against his father and also fought with his brothers Pepin and Louis the German and his half-brother Charles the Bald. The Treaty of Verdun (843) partitioned the empire among L. and his brothers Charles and Louis. On his death his three sons, Louis, Lothair, and Charles, divided his realm.

Lothair II (c.835-869) King of Lotharingia, 855-869. The second son of Lothair I, he inherited the region that later became Lorraine. On his death, his realm was divided among his uncles Charles the Bald and Louis the German.

Lothair (941-986) King of France, 954-986. The son of Louis IV, whom he succeeded. The early years of L.'s reign were dominated by Hugo the Great. L. and Holy Roman Emperor Otto II fought over Lotharingia (Lorraine). L. gave up his claim in 980 but after Otto's death died in a battle for it.

Louis I, the Pious (778-840) Emperor of the West, 813-840. A son of Charlemagne, L. was made king of Aquitaine in 781 and coemperor with his father in 813. H became sole emperor when Charlemagne died the next year. L. fought many conflicts with his sons—Lothair, Pepin, and Louis from his first marriage and Charles from his second marriage—over the division of his lands.

Louis II (c.822-875) Emperor of the West, 855-875. The son of Emperor Lothair I, L. was made king of Italy in 844 and coemperor in 850. He became sole emperor upon his father's death in 855. He successfully fought the Saracens in Italy.

Louis IV, the Bavarian (?1283-1347) Holy Roman emperor, 1328-1347, and German king, 1314-1347. L. expanded the holdings of his family, the House of Wittelsbach. He was involved in a long dispute with the papacy over the succession to the imperial throne. In 1322 L. defeated rival king Frederick the Fair at Mühldorf, but Pope John XXII refused to recognize him as emperor. Later Pope Clement VI had L. deposed (1846). L. died in a hunting accident.

Louis I (1786-1868) King of Bavaria, 1825-1848. The son and successor of Maximilian I, L. made his capital Munich into a center of the arts and sciences. He had an affair with Lola Montez that contributed to his unpopularity, and he abdicated in favor of his son Maximilian in 1848.

Louis II (1845-1886) King of Bavaria, 1864-1886. The son and successor of Maximilian II, L. was highly eccentric and eventually went insane. Greatly interested in the arts, he was a great patron of Richard Wagner. He drowned himself in a Bavarian lake.

Louis III (1845-1921) King of Bavaria, 1913-1918. The last Bavarian king, L. was the son of Leopold of Bavaria, who had been the regent for the insane Otto I. L. succeeded his father as regent in 1912 and the next year proclaimed himself king. The Bavarian Revolution of 1918 forced him to abdicate.

Louis I of France *See* Louis I, the Pious, Emperor of the West.

Louis V, the Lazy (967-987) King of France, 986-987. The son of King Lothair, L. was the last French Carolingian king of France. Childless, he was succeeded by Hugh Capet.

Louis VII, the Young (1120-1180) King of France, 1137-1180. The son and successor of Louis VI, the Fat, L. married Eleanor of Aquitaine before he became king. When he returned from the Second Crusade, he had the marriage annulled (1152) because he suspected her of being unfaithful. Eleanor subsequently married Henry II of England, and Henry and Louis fought many wars.

Louis IX, the Saint (1214-1270) King of France, 1226-1270. The son and successor of Louis VIII, L. was advised for many years by his mother, Blanch of Castille. L. dedicated himself to peace in the West and to fighting Islam. He settled territorial disputes with Henry III of England in the 1259 Treaty of Paris. L. went on the Seventh and Eighth Crusades. During the

Louis IX, the Saint

Seventh he was taken prisoner (1250) and ransomed. He died in Tunis shortly after the start of the Eighth.

Louis XI (1423-1483) King of France, 1461-1483. The son and successor of Charles VII, whom he frequently rebelled against, L. was constantly in conflict with his nobles and Charles the Bold of Burgundy. L. added important territories to France, including Anjou (1471) and Burgundy (1482).

Louis XII (1462-1515) King of France, 1498-1515. The son of Charles, duke of Orléans, L. succeeded Charles VIII and married his widow, Anna of Brittany. L. frequently warred in Italy because of his claims to Naples, Genoa, and Milan.

Louis XIII (1601-1643) King of France, 1610-1643. The son and successor of Henry IV, L. was at first dominated by his mother, Marie de

Medici, who excluded him from affairs of state. Later reconciled with her, he gave great power to her favorite Cardinal Richelieu and retained Richelieu even after she wished to dismiss him. L.'s reign was a period of great cultural and scientific achievement.

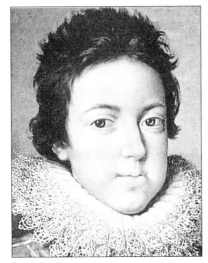

Louis XIII

Louis XIV, the Sun King (1638-1715) King of France, 1643-1715. The son and successor of Louis XIII, L.'s reign began with his mother, Anne of Austria as regent, but after the death of her adviser Mazarin in 1661 he ruled France himself. L.'s internal policy is well-summed up in the remark he supposedly made: "L'état, c'est moi" ("I am the state"). He vastly increased the power of the state and the monarchy, making the nobility dependent on him. He persecuted the Huguenots and in 1685 revoked the Edict of Nantes. L. conducted many wars to make France supreme in Europe. His reign was one of great splendor and glory—

Louis XII

Louis XIV, the Sun King

the magnificent Versailles palace was built for him—but laid the groundwork for the regime's financial troubles that led to the French Revolution.

Louis XV

Louis XV (1710-1774) King of France, 1715-1774. The great-grandson and successor of Louis XIV, L. was not a strong monarch. He was dominated first by his chief minister Fleury and then, after Fleury's death in 1743, by his mistresses (Mme. de Pompadour, Mme. du Barry). As a result of the Seven Years' War (1756-1763), France lost most of its overseas empire, and L. failed to solve the government's financial difficulties.

Louis XVI

Louis XVI (1754-1793) King of France, 1774-1792. The grandson and successor of Louis XV, L. had good intentions but could not master the difficult circumstances he faced. The regime's bankruptcy and the abuses of Ancien Régime created a revolutionary situation, but attempts at meaningful reform were opposed by powerful people at court, including L.'s wife, Marie Antoinette. During the Revolution, which began in 1789, L. was forced to accept a constitution (1791). In 1792 the monarchy was abolished, and L. and the queen put on trial. They were beheaded. They had two sons. The first died in 1789. The second, the so-called Louis XVII, was imprisoned with his parents and probably died in jail in 1795.

Louis XVIII (1755-1824) King of France, 1814-1824. The brother of Louis XVI, L. fled the country in 1791 during the French Revolution. After Napoleon's defeat in 1814, he

Louis XVIII

returned as king, though his rule was interrupted by Napoleon's return in 1815. L. granted a constitutional charter, but his reasonably moderate government became more repressive after the 1820 assassination of his nephew, the duke of Berry.

Louis I, the Great (1326-1382) King of Hungary, 1342-1382, and Poland, 1370-1382. The successor of his father, Charles I, in Hungary and his uncle, Casimir III, in Poland. Fighting against Venice and the Turks, L. conquered important territories in the Balkans. *See* Turin and Zara, Treaties of.

Louis II (1506-1526) King of Bohemia and Hungary, 1516-1526. The son and successor of Uladislaus II, L. was the last ruler of the Jagiello dynasty. In 1526 his outnumbered army was defeated by the Turks at Mohacs and L. fled and was drowned.

Louis, Joe (1914-1981) American boxer. The son of a black sharecropper, L. was born Joseph Louis Barrow in Alabama. He became world heavyweight champion in 1937 and retired unbeaten in 1949. In his entire career he was defeated only three times in 71 bouts.

Louise (1776-1810) Queen of Prussia. L. was a princess of Mecklenburg-Strelitz. The husband of Frederick William III of Prussia, she unsuccessfully pleaded with Napoleon at Tilsit for better terms for Prussia (1807).

Louise Reneé de Kéroualle, duchess of Portsmouth (1649-1734) Mistress of Charles II of England. French-born, L. became Charles's mistress in 1671 and influenced him in favor of France. She was made a duchess in 1673. She bore the king a son, Charles Lennox, duke of Richmond.

Louise of Savoy (1476-1531) Regent of France. The mother of Francis I of France, L. governed for him during the Italian Wars. Together with Margaret of Austria, she prepared the Ladies' Peace in 1529. *See* Ladies' Peace.

Louisiana Purchase (1803) Agreement by which the U.S. purchased for $15 million the territory between the Mississippi River and the Rocky Mountains from France. (The sum included $3.75 million to cover claims of American citizens against France.) The area included all or part of 15 present-day American states. President Thomas Jefferson was alarmed when he learned (1801) that Spain had transferred control of Louisiana, including the vital port of New Orleans, to France. He sent James Monroe to Paris to assist Minister Robert Livingston in negotiating the purchase of New Orleans with Napoleon. Napoleon offered all Louisiana. The precise boundaries of the L. were not determined for many years.

Louis Napoleon *See* Napoleon III.

Louis Napoleon

Louis of Baden (1655-1707) Margrave of Baden-Baden and Holy Roman Empire general. L. successfully fought the Turks near Vienna in 1683. He also participated in the War of the Grand Alliance and the Spanish Succession War.

Louis Philippe (1773-1850) King of the French, 1830-1848. The son of Philip of Orléans (Philippe Egalité), before becoming king L. was duke of Orléans. A deserter from the cause of the French Revolution (1793), in 1808-1809 he fought against Napo-

Louis Philippe

Louis XIV and His Time

The reign of Louis XIV of France, 1638-1715, is often considered the height of royal power in all its splendor and magnificence. The period of Louis's rule is sometimes referred to as "Le Grand Siècle," "the Great Age."

1

2

5

3

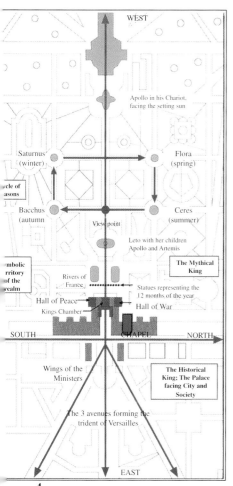

4

1. A portrait of Louis XIV, who was called "the Sun King." *See* Louis XIV.

2. A performance of a play by Racine, given in the gardens of the royal palace at Versailles. *See* Louis XIV; Racine, Jean.

3. A portrait of Madame de Maintenon, who for a time was Louis XIV's mistress and later became his wife. *See* Maintenon, Françoise d'Aubigné.

4. Louis XIV, his minister Colbert, and the members of the Royal Academy of Sciences. *See* Colbert, Jean-Baptiste.

5. Floorplan of the royal palace of Versailles, explaining how the layout reflects the position of the king as a symbolic ruler over time and space.

leon in Spain and returned to Paris in 1817. There he soon became the central figure of the liberal opposition against the Bourbons. In 1830 L. was proclaimed king during the July Revolution. A constitutional monarch, his last years in power were dominated by his conservative minister, Guizot. L. became unpopular both with the right-wing Bourbon supporters and Bonapartists and with the leftists. Demands for electoral reform led to his 1848 abdication in favor of his son, but a republic was proclaimed in the February Revolution.

Louis the German

Louis the Child (c.893-911) German king, 900-911. The son and successor of Arnulf, L. was the last German king of the Carolingian house.

Louis the German (c.804-876) Son of Louis the Pious, he became king of Bavaria in 817. He frequently rebelled against his father and allied with his half-brother Charles the Bald. Through the Treaty of Verdun (843), L. became king of the East Frankish kingdom.

Louis the Younger (c.830-882) German king, 876-882. The son of Louis the German, he divided his father's lands with his brothers Carloman and Charles the Fat. He defeated at Andernach in 876 the attempt of his uncle Charles II (Charles the Bald) to gain part of Lotharingia.

Louvois, François Michel le Tellier, marquis de (1639-1691) French minister. As minister of war under Louis XIV, L. introduced numerous new techniques and equipment that made the French army the best in Europe. He became notorious for the brutal manner in which he waged war. L. was also a ruthless persecutor of the Huguenots in France.

Lowe, Sir Hudson (1769-1844) British general. In 1815 he was appointed governor of the island of St. Helena, where Napoleon lived in exile until his death in 1821.

Lowry, Malcolm (1909-1957) British author. L.'s best-known work is the autobiographical novel *Under the Volcano* (1947), about the undoing of an alcoholic. L. penetratingly described the spiritual plight of 20th-century life.

Sir Hudson Lowe

Loyalists During the American Revolution, Americans who were loyal to Britain. L. were also called Tories.

Luba and Lunda (16th-19th centuries) African kingdoms in the Congo River basin. At the end of the 19th century, they were annexed to the Belgian Congo.

Lubbe, Marinus van der (1909-1934) Dutch Communist. In 1933 L. committed arson in government buildings in Berlin to protest Hitler's assumption of power. He was arrested for setting fire to the Reichstag building and executed. The Reichstag fire, which the Nazis blamed on a Communist plot, served as Hitler's pretext to outlaw left-wing parties, curtail civil liberties generally, and become a dictator.

Lübeck, Treaty of (1629) Agreement that ended Danish participation in the Thirty Years War the imperial forces under Wallenstein and Tilly defeated Christian IV. Lübeck is a German port city near the Baltic.

Lucius III (d.1185) Pope, 1181-1185. Born Ubaldo Allucingoli, L. succeeded Alexander III. He was an energetic opponent of heresies and laid the foundation for the Inquisition.

Lucretia (6th century BC) Legendary Roman matron. The wife of Lucius Tarquinius Collatinus, she committed suicide after having been raped by Sextus, the son of King Tarquinius Superbus, and having persuaded her husband to avenge her. The result was that the Tarquins were driven from Rome in 509 BC.

Marinus van der Lubbe

Lucretius (Titus Lucretius Carus) (1st century BC) Roman poet. Very little is known about L.'s life. His great work is the philosophical poem *The Nature of Things,* which, influenced by Democritus and Epicurus, argues than man need not fear death and that everything is made of atoms.

Lucullus (Lucius Licinius Lucullus Ponticus) (c.117-58/56 BC) Roman general. L. was a favorite of Sulla. He became consul in 74 BC and fought King Mithridates VI of Pontus. Unpopular in Rome and among his army, he retired from public life in 66 BC and lived in such a luxurious manner that the adjective *lucullan* has come to mean an overly lavish mode of life.

Luddites English workers who rioted in industrial cities 1811-1816. They destroyed machinery, which they held responsible for the increased unemployment and their low wages. The L. took their name from the mythical character Ned, or King, Ludd.

Ludendorff, Erich (1865-1937) German general. In World War I, L. began as Field Marshal Hindenburg's chief of staff. By the end of the war, he was virtually running the government. L. decided to ask the Allies for an armis-

Erich Ludendorff

tice in fall 1918. After the war he became active in extreme right-wing politics, taking part, for example, in Hitler's unsuccessful 1923 coup in Munich, and he promoted racist interpretations of history.

Lugalbanda The legendary king of the Mesopotamian city of Uruk. He was Gilgamesh's father. *See* Gilgamesh Epic.

Lugalzagezi (24th century BC) King of the Mesopotamian city of Umma, who ruled c.2375-2350 BC. He conquered the cities of Lagash, Kish, Ur, and Uruk and gained sway over all of Sumeria. Eventually he was defeated by Sargon of Akkad.

Lumpenproletariat A term in Marxism, referring to the lowest class of workers, those who are dislocated and alienated from their fellow workers. The L. also includes criminals and tramps.

Lumumba, Patrice (1925-1961) Congolese political leader. L. was the first premier of the newly independent Republic of the Congo (now Zaire) in 1960. In the midst of widespread unrest, he was driven from power by his rivals President Kasavubu and Colonel Mobutu and killed in Katanga province.

Lundy's Lane, Battle of (1814) Battle fought in southern Ontario, Canada, near Niagara Falls, during the War of 1812 between the U.S. and Britain. It was part of the unsuccessful American invasion of Canada.

Lunéville, Peace of (1801) Agreement between France and Austria that confirmed the Treaty of Campo Formio. With it France acquired hegemony in Europe. Lunéville is a town in northeast France.

Luristan bronzes Luristan is a region in western Iran. Beautiful and archaeologically significant bronzes were found there (1926). Probably made between 1500-500 BC by Scythians and other nomads, they include weapons and religious objects. Many have animal motifs.

Lusignan French noble house, powerful in the Middle Ages. The L. participated in many crusades. Guy de L. became king of Jerusalem in 1186 and was king of Cyprus 1192-1194. The house died out in 1475.

Lusitania 1. Roman province on the Iberian Peninsula, occupying portions of modern Spain and Portugal. The Lusitani were subdued by the Romans after a war in 147-139 BC. 2. A British ocean liner that was torpedoed and sunk during World War I by a German submarine without warning on May 7, 1915, with the loss of 1,198 lives, including 128 Americans. Although it was unarmed, the ship was also carrying munitions. The sinking caused a stern protest by the U.S., which was then neutral in the war. Eventually Germany apologized, but the incident contributed significantly to anti-German feeling in the U.S.

Patrice Lumumba

Luther, Martin (1483-1546) German clergymen and religious reformer. More than any other person, L. was responsible for the Protestant Reformation. He was born in Eisleben in Saxony and became an Augustinian monk, a priest, and a teacher at the University of Wittenberg. A devoted student of the Scriptures, L.'s convic-

Martin Luther

tions led him in 1517 to post 95 "theses" on the church door at Wittenberg, protesting various teachings and practices of the Roman Catholic Church. This is generally considered the start of the Reformation. In the following years, attempts at compromise between L. and Church authorities failed, and in 1521 he was excommunicated by the pope. L. translated the Bible into German and founded the Lutheran Church. In 1526 he married Katherina von Bora; they had six children.

Luthuli, Albert (1898-1967) South African freedom fighter. A Zulu chief, L. joined the African National Congress in 1946 and in 1952 became its chairman. He was an advocate of nonviolent resistance to apartheid. The government banished him to his village in 1960. Later that year he was awarded the Nobel Peace Prize, and the government was forced to allow him to go to Oslo to receive it.

Lützen Town in eastern Germany, near Leipzig. Two important battles were fought there: 1. In 1632 during the Thirty Years War, the Swedish under Gustavus II defeated the imperial forces under Wallenstein, but Gustavus was killed; 2. Napoleon defeated a Prussian-Russian army under Wittgenstein in 1813.

Lützow, Adolf Freiherr von (1782-1834) Prussian army officer. In 1813-1814 L. waged a guerilla war against the French with a small army of volunteers.

Luxembourg, François Henri de Montmorency-Bouteville, duke of (1628-1695) French general. With his cousin Condé, L. took part in the Fronde but was later restored to royal favor. He became one of Louis XIV's greatest generals and won victories in the Dutch War and the War of the Grand Alliance.

Rosa Luxemburg

Luxemburg, Rosa (1871-1919) Polish-German revolutionary. Born in Russian Poland, L. was active in revolutionary activities as a student. While in exile in Switzerland, she became a

Lycurgus

Marxist. She helped found the Polish Socialist Party, was active in the German Social Democratic Party, and, with Karl Liebknecht, formed the Spartacus League in Germany during World War I. L. predicted that Lenin's Bolshevik regime in Russia would turn into a dictatorship. After participating in an uprising in Berlin in 1919, she and Liebknecht were arrested and killed.

Luxor *See* Karnak.

Lyautey, Louis Hubert Gonzalve (1854-1934) French general and colonial administrator. L. took part in campaigns in Indochina, Madagascar, and Algeria. He spent many years governing French Morocco and in 1924 defeated the Berbers led by Abd el-Krim.

Lycia Ancient region in southwest Asia Minor, now southwestern Turkey. Homer mentions it. L. was held by the Persians and conquered in 334 BC by Alexander the Great. The Romans took it over in 189 BC. St. Paul visited the Lycian towns Patara and Myra.

Lycurgus 1. (?7th century BC) Legendary Spartan lawgiver. Herodotus and Plutarch wrote about him, but whether he actually existed is not known. Supposedly he was responsible for the character of Sparta's political and social system. 2. (c.390-324 BC) Athenian orator and public offi-

cial. A pupil of Isocrates, L. was an alley of Demosthenes in urging Athens to oppose Macedonia. He administered Athens's finances (338-326 BC) and helped preserve the works of Aeschylus, Sophocles, and Euripides.

Lydgate, John (c.1370-1450) English monk and poet. Highly prolific, L. wrote poetry influenced by Chaucer as well as religious and philosophical verse. He also translated works from Latin and French.

Lydia Ancient region in western Asia Minor, now northwest Turkey. It flourished under the Mermnade dynasty, founded by Gyges c.700 BC. Its wealthy capital was Sardis. Supposedly the Lydian kings were the first to use coined money. The last Lydian king was Croesus, who was defeated by the Persian Cyrus the Great c.546 BC. L. became a Roman province in 310 AD.

Lynch, Charles (1736-1796) American soldier and judge. During the American Revolution, L. dealt harshly with Tories in Virginia. It is sometimes said that the word *lynch*, meaning to execute or punish suspected criminals outside the legal process, is derived from his name.

Lysander (d.395 BC) Spartan admiral and political leader. L. repeatedly defeated the Athens toward the end of the Peloponnesian War. In Athens he imposed the rule of the Thirty Tyrants (404 BC).

Lysimachus (c.355-281 BC) General under Alexander the Great and one of the Diadochi. After Alexander the Great's death (333 BC), L. got control of Thrace and northwestern Asia Minor. Together with Cassander and Ptolemy, he fought against Antigonus. In 286 BC, L. drove Pyrrhus from Macedonia, but he was killed fighting Seleucus I in the Battle of Corupedium in Lydia (281 BC).

Lytton Committee (1932) Mission headed by British diplomat Lord Lytton and sent by the League of Nations to investigate the situation in Manchuria, where China charged Japan committed aggression. The committee recommended sanctions against Japan; in response, Japan left the League of Nations.

Ma Tuanlin (13th century) Chinese historian and author of a general encyclopedia that is of great value in the study of medieval China.

Mac Vietnamese family of ministers during the Le dynasty who established their own state in northern Vietnam between 1527-1592. They were bitterly opposed by the Trinh family.

MacArthur, Douglas (1880-1964) American general. During World War II he became (1942) commander of Allied forces in the southwestern Pacific. He accepted the surrender of Japan on September 2, 1945, aboard the battleship Missouri. After the war, M. was head of the U.S. occupation forces in Japan. He led the UN troops in the Korean War from 1950-1951, but was relieved of his command by President Truman for insubordination.

Douglas MacArthur

Macartney mission (1793) The first British diplomatic mission to China, led by Lord Macartney.

Macbeth (d.1057) King of Scotland, 1040-1057. He was overthrown and killed by Malcolm in 1057 at the battle of Lumphanan. Shakespeare's play is based on his life; *see* Shakespeare.

Maccabees A Jewish family that led the fight for freedom against the Seleucian rulers of Syria and brought about a restoration of Jewish political and religious life. In 165 BC, Judas Maccabeus reconquered Jerusalem. His brother, Simon, established the independence of Judaea in 142.

Macedonia (ancient Macedon) Region in southeastern Europe, in the Balkans. Its population (c.1000 BC) was made up largely of Illyrians, Thracians, and Greeks. The region was conquered by the Persians in the 5th century BC. Under Alexander the Great (d.323 BC), M. ruled Anatolia, Mesopotamia, Syria, Egypt, and Asia Minor. After Alexander's death, the region was divided among his successors. In 146 BC, M. became the first Roman province.

Macedonian War Refers to four wars: First Macedonian War (215-205 BC) Between Philip V of Macedonia and the Romans. Philip was able to negotiate favorable terms for himself in the Treaty of Phoenicia; Second Macedonian War (200-197/196 BC) Between the Romans and Philip V of Macedonia. It ended with the latter's defeat at Cynoscephalae; Third Macedonian War (171-168 BC) Between the Romans and Perseus of Macedonia (Philip V's son). He was defeated at Pydna; Fourth Macedonian War (149-148 BC) Between the Romans and Achaeanian League. It ended with the destruction of Corinth and the Roman conquest of Greece.

Macha Celtic goddess of war and great earth mother.

Machel, Samora Moises (1933-1986) President of Mozambique, 1975-1986. He joined Frelimo, the guerrilla movement, in 1963 and fought for the liberation of Mozambique from Portuguese colonial rule. M. became the first president of Mozambique in 1975. He was killed in a plane crash in 1986.

Machiavelli, Niccoló (1469-1527) Italian statesman and author, one of the major figures of the Renaissance. He is best known for his book, *Il Principe* (The Prince), in which he describes the means by which a prince may gain and maintain power. The adjective Machiavellian has come to mean amoral cunning and justification by power.

Niccoló Machiavelli

Machu Picchu Fortress city of the Inca empire. It is situated between two mountain peaks 2,000 feet above the Urubamba River in northwestern Peru. The Spaniards were never able to find the city, and it was discovered only in 1911 by the American explorer Hiram Bingham.

MacMahon, Marie Edmé Patrice de (1808-1893) French general and statesman, president of the French republic, 1873-1879. A commander during the Franco-Prussian War, he

Marie Edmé Patrice de MacMahon

233

took part in the battle that led to the defeat of France at Sedan. As president, he was unwilling to use his power to restore the monarchy and thus helped preserve the Third Republic.

Macrinus, Marcus Opellius (164-218) Roman emperor, 217-218. As prefect of the Praetorian Guard, he ordered the assassination of Emperor Caracalla in 217 and installed himself as emperor. M. was murdered by rebellious troops the following year.

Macro, Naevius Sertorius (d.AD 38) Prefect of the Praetorian Guard under Emperor Tiberius, who was his protector. He was forced to commit suicide by Emperor Gaius in 38.

Madison, Dolley (1768-1849) Wife of President James Madison. She presided over the White House with elegant style during her husband's presidency. During the War of 1812 she rescued the original Declaration of Independence and a Gilbert Stuart portrait of Washington from the White House shortly before the British burned the mansion.

James Madison

Madison, James (1751-1836) 4th president of the U.S., 1809-1817. In 1776 he was a member of the Virginia convention that wrote the state's constitution and declaration of rights. He served in the Continental Congress and was one of the leading architects of the U.S. Constitution. With Alexander Hamilton and John Jay, M. wrote

The Federalist, a collection of essays supporting the new Constitution. As a representative in Congress (1789-1797), he was a leader in the drive to add the Bill of Rights to the Constitution. M. served as secretary of state (1801-1809) under Thomas Jefferson. The War of 1812 was the chief event of his presidency.

Madjapahit Hindu empire that flourished on Java, Indonesia, between the 13th and 16th centuries. It was destroyed in the battle against Islam shortly before the arrival of the Dutch. Hinduism in Indonesia survived only on the island of Bali.

Madrid, Peace of (1526) Treaty signed during the Italian Wars. Under its terms, the Holy Roman Emperor Charles V forced the captured Francis I of France (*see* Pavia, Battle of) to relinquish his claims to Italian territory and to surrender Burgundy. After his release, Francis I renounced the treaty.

Maecenas, Gaius (d.8 BC) Roman statesman and patron of letters. He was a trusted adviser to Emperor Augustus, who used him for various political missions. M. was a friend and patron of Vergil, Horace, and Propertius.

Mafia Name given to a number of organized groups of Sicilian brigands during the 19th and 20th centuries. Today the name refers to organized crime groups in Italy and the United States involved in drug trafficking, gambling, and union racketeering.

Magellan, Ferdinand (c.1480-1521) Portuguese navigator. In 1519, M. sailed with five ships to find a passage to the South Seas via a western route. He reached the eastern coast of South America, then rounded the southern tip of the continent and proceeded westward across the Pacific. In 1521, M. reached the Philippines, where he was killed in a battle between natives. The survivors of the expedition returned to Spain in 1522, completing the first voyage around the world.

Magenta Town in northern Italy. It was the site of a battle on June 4, 1859, in which the French general MacMahon defeated the Austrian army.

Magersfontein Town in South Africa.

It was the site of a battle on December 11, 1899, during the South African War (Boer War). The British under Lord Methuen were defeated by the Boers under General Cronjé.

Maginot, André (1877-1932) French minister of war, 1929-1932. He directed the construction of a system of fortifications along the eastern border of France extending from Switzerland north to Belgium. Touted as impregnable, the Maginot Line was simply outflanked when the German army invaded France in 1940 during World War II.

Magna Carta Charter granted by King John of England in 1215 to his barons. It was issued by the king under pressure from his lords, and it mainly guar-

Gaius Maecenas

Ferdinand Magellan

André Maginot

anteed feudal rights. The Magna Carta also contains vague language about individual rights and is therefore seen as a major document of British constitutional history.

Magna Graecia Greek colonies of southern Italy. They were established c.800 BC and became thriving centers of Greek trade and culture. The colonies began to decline c.500 BC and were eventually absorbed into the Roman Empire.

Magnesia City in Lidya in Asia Minor, in present-day Turkey. King Antiochus III was defeated there by the Romans in 190 BC.

Magnetius, Flavius Magnus (d.AD 343) Roman general. He murdered Emperor Constans I in 350 and was then elected emperor by the western legions. In 351, M. lost the Battle of Mursa against Constantine II, brother of the murdered emperor. He later committed suicide.

Magnus I (1024-1047) King of Norway, 1035-1047, and of Denmark, 1042-1047. He captured Denmark from Canute the Great of Norway and England.

Magnus VI (1238-1280) King of Norway, 1263-1280. He introduced a new code of laws for the kingdom, including the foundations of municipal law. M. also created a royal council and new ranks of nobility.

Mago (d.203 BC) Youngest brother of Hannibal. He fought against the Romans in Italy and Spain but was defeated by them in northern Italy in 203. He died during the retreat to Carthage.

Magyars Nomadic people from the Urals region. They migrated westward through Rumania and settled in Hungary c.895. The term Magyar also refers to the Hungarian language.

Mahabharata Classic Sanskrit epic of India, probably composed between 200 BC and AD 200. An 18-book work, it is the longest single poem in world literature. A fable of dynastic struggle and civil war, M. is the foremost source about Indian civilization and Hindu ideals.

Mahan, Alfred Thayer (1840-1914) American naval officer and historian. His influential book, The Influence of Sea Power upon History, 1660-1783 (1890), argued that naval power was the key to power in international relations and modern warfare. Theodore Roosevelt and other proponents of a big navy and of U.S. imperialism were influenced by M.'s ideas.

Maharaja (Maharajah) Sanskrit term for "great king." M. is still used in India as the title for noble persons of high rank.

Mahdi Arabic term meaning "he who is divinely guided." In Sunni Islam, the Mahdi is the messiah who will appear at the end of time and establish universal Islam. The title mahdi was adopted by Muhammad Ahmad (1844-1885), the leader of an uprising and movement in the Sudan that was ultimately defeated in 1898 by Lord Kitchener.

Mahler, Gustav (1860-1911) Austrian composer and conductor. M. wrote nine symphonies and a fragment of a tenth. He is also known for his orchestral song cycles, including *Kindertotenlieder, Lieder eines fahrenden Gesellen,* and *Das Lied von der Erde.*

Mahmud II (1785-1839) Ottoman sultan, 1808-1839. Under his leadership the power of the Janissaries was broken. In 1829 M. was forced to recognize the independence of Greece.

Maimonides, Moses (1135-1204) Jewish philosopher and physician.

His greatest scholastic work, the Mishneh Torah, organizes the vast mass of Jewish oral law (the Mishna) into a reference work for laymen as well as rabbis. M. also attempted to reconcile Judaic teachings of the revelations and the philosophies of Aristotle and Plato.

Moses Maimonides

Gustav Mahler

Maintenon, Françoise d'Aubigné, Marquise de (1635-1719) Second wife of King Louis XIV of France. M. exerted great influence on the king and lifted the moral tone of the court. She devoted much of her attention to education and wrote a series of essays dealing with the subject.

Françoise d'Aubigné Maintenon

Major, John (1943-) Prime minister of Great Britain from 1990. After serving as foreign secretary and chancellor of the exchequer, he succeeded Margaret Thatcher as prime minister. M. negotiated with the Irish Republican Army for a settlement of conflict in Northern Ireland, and he struggled to hold the Conservative Party together on the issue of European union.

Majorian, Julius (d.461) Roman emperor of the West, 457-461. An able and honest ruler, M. was murdered by rebellious troops in 461 after failing to conquer the Vandals.

Majuba Mountain in Natal province, South Africa. At Majuba in 1881 a British force under Sir George Pommeroy Colley suffered a severe defeat at the hands of the Boers led by General P.J. Joubert.

Makarios III (Michael Christodolou Mouskos) (1913-1977) Cypriot archbishop and politician and the first president of Cyprus, 1960-1974. In 1950, M. became archbishop of Cyprus and the leader of the enosis movement, which called for union with Greece. He later advocated Cypriot independence and in 1960 became president of Cyprus. He was ousted during a Greek-sponsored coup in 1974.

Makonnen, Tafari *See* Haile Selassie.

Malan, Daniel François (1874-1959) South African theologian and politician, prime minister of South Africa, 1948-1954. A member of the Nationalist Party, M. initiated the racial separation laws known as apartheid.

Malcolm III (c.1031-1093) King of Scotland, 1057-1093, son of Duncan I. He defeated Macbeth in 1057 and regained his father's kingdom. After 1072, M. was forced to recognize William the Conqueror as his liege.

Malcolm X (1925-1965) Black militant leader in the U.S. Born Malcolm Little, he converted to Islam while in prison and adopted the name Malcolm X. He advocated black nationalism and separatism, but in 1963 broke with the more militant wing of the movement. M. was assassinated in 1965.

Malenkov, Georgi Maksimilianovich (1902-1988) Soviet communist leader. A close associate of Stalin, he became premier of the Soviet Union after Stalin's death in 1953. He was succeeded as party head by Khrushchev, who engineered M.'s replacement as premier by Bulganin in 1955. M. was ousted from the party in 1961.

Malesherbes, Chrétien Guillame de Lamoignon de (1721-1794) French statesman. During the reigns of Louis XV and Louis XVI, he held several ministerial posts. His responsibilities included ecclesiastical affairs and censorship. M. was appointed a defender Louis XVI at the king's trial. He was later arrested and guillotined.

Mali, Kingdom of Kingdom founded in the 12th century by the Malinka in what is currently Mali, West Africa. Its capital was Timbuktu. After converting to Islam, M. prospered under the rule of Mansa Musa in the 14th century. It became a center of Islamic culture and a major supplier of gold to the rest of the world. In 1591, M. was conquered by the Moroccans under Ahmad of the Sadi dynasty.

Malinovsky, Rodion Yakovlevich (1898-1967) Soviet marshal. He commanded an army at the battle of Stalingrad in 1943 during World War II. In 1957, M. became minister of defense and helped rebuild the Soviet army.

Malplaquet Village in northern France. It was the site of a battle on September 11, 1709, in which a joint British-Dutch-Austrian army led by the Duke of Marlborough defeated the French under Marshal Villars.

Malthus, Thomas Robert (1766-1834) English economist and pioneer in the study of population. M. argued that population growth would eventually outstrip production, and that

Thomas Robert Malthus

therefore the world would be plagued by famine, poverty, and war. His theories, which were controversial in his lifetime, influenced later classical economists.

Mamelukes (or Mamlukes) (Arabic term for slaves) A warrior caste for more than 700 years. They were dominant in Egypt and influential throughout the Middle East. The M.

formed the Egyptian cavalry that served the Turkish sultan early in the 13th century. They soon became extremely powerful and elected their leader Nurredin Ali as sultan of Egypt. The M. were defeated in 1517 by the Turks, who put an end to the Mameluke sultanate.

Mamertines Mercenaries who belonged to the Syracusan tyrant Agathocles (361-289 BC). They terrorized northern Sicily after his death.

Mamun, Al- (786-833) 7th Abassid caliph, 813-833. He was the son of Harun ar-Raschid. M. was interested in science and established a school to translate Greek works into Arabic.

Manasse *See* Israel, tribes of.

Manchu *See* Ch'ing.

Manchur, Abu Djafaral al- (Mansur, al-) (d.775) 2nd Abassid caliph, 754-775. He founded the city of Baghdad and reigned there from 762 until his death.

Mandela, Nelson Rolihlahla (1918-) President of South Africa since 1994. A leader of the African National Congress, M. was sentenced to life imprisonment in 1962 and became the symbol of black resistance to apartheid. He was freed in 1990 and worked with South Africa's white president, F. W. De Klerk, to bring an end to apartheid. They shared the Nobel Peace Prize in 1993. After the

Nelson Rolihlahla Mandela

1994 elections, which ended apartheid, M. became president of South Africa.

Mani

Mandingo Empire African Islamic empire that flourished in the 13th and 14th centuries in what is now Ghana. It was later incorporated into the Bambara kingdoms.

Manfred (c.1232-1266) King of Sicily, 1258-1266, the last of the Hohenstaufens to hold that throne. The illegitimate son of the Holy Roman Emperor Frederick II, M. clashed with the papacy, which sought to rid southern Italy of the Hohenstaufens. In 1258 he proclaimed himself king of Sicily. He died in the Battle of Benevento against Charles of Anjou, who had been invested by the pope as the ruler of Sicily.

Mani (c.216-276) Persian prophet. He founded a religion called Manichaeism, which taught the release of the spirit from matter through asceticism.

Manlius, Marcus M. Capitolinus (d.385 BC) Roman statesman. Legend says he saved Rome from an attack by Gauls in 389 BC after being awakened by geese cackling as the invaders entered the city.

Mann, Heinrich (1871-1950) German novelist. His works are dominated by themes of social criticism, especially the injustices of contemporary German society. *The Poor* (1917) and *The Chief* (1925) deal with the regeneration of society through democracy. His younger brother was the novelist Thomas Mann.

Mann, Thomas (1875-1955) German novelist and essayist. He is one of the outstanding figures of 20th-century

German literary history. M.'s works delve into inner human problems and their relationship to European cultural values. In his first novel, *Buddenbrooks* (1901), he describes the rise and fall of a rich merchant family. Other well-known works include *Death in Venice* (1912), *The Magic Mountain* (1924), the tetralogy *Joseph and His Brothers* (1934-1944), and *The Confessions of Felix Krull* (1954). M. won the 1929 Nobel Prize for Literature. His brother was the novelist Heinrich Mann.

Thomas Mann

Mannerheim, Carl Gustav Emil von, Baron (1867-1951) President of Finland, 1944-1946. A general, he was a commander during the Russo-Finnish War (1939-1940).

Manstein, Erich von (1887-1973) German general during World War II. M. clashed with Hitler about tactics in the Russian campaign and resigned. After the war, he was imprisoned for a number of years for war crimes.

Mansura City in northern Egypt, a port on the Nile River delta. An army of crusaders led by King Louis IX of

Manuscripts to Printed Books

Until the invention of movable type in the 15th century, which made the printing of books possible, a book was a great luxury. Books were written and copied by hand, often on parchment, which was expensive since it was made from the skins of many sheep. The development of a faster and more economical way to produce books was a revolutionary development that made printed materials available to a much wider audience.

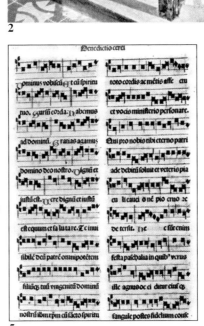

1. A page from the handwritten and richly decorated 15th-century *Les très riches heures de Duc de Berry.*
2. One of the earliest printing presses. It dates from the early 16th century.
3. A page from the so-called *Biblia pauperum*, an inexpensive printed and illustrated Bible intended for poor people.
4. A page from a book of writings by the ancient Roman philosopher and orator Cicero. This early printed book still looks very much like a manuscript. The owner has written his comments in the margin.
5. An early printed music book. It uses the medieval Gregorian method of music notation.

France suffered a crushing defeat there on February 8, 1250, at the hands of the Mamelukes.

Manteuffel, Edwin, Freiherr von (1809-1885) Prussian field marshal. He fought in Schleswig-Holstein during the Seven Weeks' War (1866) and in the Franco-Prussian War (1870-1871).

Manteuffel, Otto Theodor, Freiherr von (1805-1882) Prussian prime minister, 1850-1858, and cousin of Edwin von Manteuffel. He pursued generally reactionary policies in the wake of the revolutions of 1848.

Mantinea Ancient Greek city. During the Peloponnesian War a coalition led by Mancinea and Argos was defeated there (418 BC) by Sparta. It was also the scene of battle in 362 BC in which Epaminondas of Thebes defeated the Athenians and the Spartans.

Mao Zedong (1893-1976) Chinese communist leader, founder (1949) of the People's Republic of China. Under his rule, the country tried to

Mao Zedong

become a modern nation by means of five-year plans and government-ordered political campaigns. One of communism's most prominent theoreticians, M.'s ideas on revolutionary struggle were influential among Third World revolutionaries. *See* Gang of Four, Cultural Revolution, Great Leap Forward.

Maoism Chinese version of communism developed by Mao Zedong. As it evolved, M. diverged from the ortho-

dox Soviet model by stressing small, labor-intensive industries controlled by local peasants. Differing interpretations of Marxism and of communism's relationship with the West led to a breach between China and the Soviet Union after 1960.

Maoris Original inhabitants of New Zealand. They are believed to have migrated there from Polynesia. The Maori language is closely related to native language of the South Pacific, including Hawaiian. The Maoris fought against European encroachment during the 19th century but eventually made peace with the British in New Zealand.

Marat, Jean-Paul (1743-1793) French revolutionary. Leader of the Jacobins, he helped bring about the downfall of the Girondists after 1792. He was assassinated in his bath by the pro-Girondist Charlotte Corday on July 13, 1793.

Marathon Village on the east coast of Attica in Greece. An invading Persian army was defeated at Marathon in 490 BC by the Athenians under Miltiades.

Marc, Franz (1880-1916) German painter, a leading Expressionist. He mainly painted animals, especially horses, employing devices of distortion to express the animals' awareness of their own reality. He, Klee, and Kandinsky founded the Blauer Reiter (Blue Rider) group. He died in World War I at the battle of Verdun.

Marcel, Étienne (c.1316-1358) French bourgeois leader, provost of the merchants of Paris. Between 1355-1358, M. ruled Paris, but he was accused of treason because of his intrigues with the English and murdered by former supporters.

Marcellus, Marcus Claudius (c.268-208 BC) Roman general. M. was consul five times. In 214 he went to Sicily to prosecute the Second Punic War. He besieged and captured Syracusa in 212 and died in a skirmish with Hannibal's forces in 208.

Marcellus, Marcus Claudius (42-23 BC) Son of Octavia, the sister of Emperor Augustus. Through his marriage to Julia, the emperor's daughter, he was considered Augustus's heir until his death at 19.

Marcellus II (1501-1555) Pope, 1555. Born Marcello Cervini, he was considered a reformer, but he died on the 22nd day of his reign.

Jean-Paul Marat

Étienne Marcel

March Acts Acts adopted by the Hungarian Diet during the 1848 revolution that formed the legal foundation of the modern Hungarian nation. They were ratified by Emperor Ferdinand I.

March on Rome March of Italian fascists on Rome in October 1922. The march led to Mussolini's coming to power in Italy.

March Revolution Revolutionary movement in Germany and Austria-

Hungary that developed after the February revolution of 1848. It was short-lived and did not bring about any lasting changes; *see* Frankfurter Parliament, Kossuth.

Marchand, Louis, Count of (1791-1876) Napoleon's chamberlain. He accompanied Napoleon into exile on St. Helena in 1815.

Marcianus, Flavius (396-457) Roman emperor of the East, 450-457. He succeeded Theodosius II, whose sister, Pulcheria, he married in 450. His refusal to pay tribute to Attila precipitated the Hunnic invasion of the Roman Empire.

Marcius, Ancus According to legend the fourth King of Rome, 640-616 BC. M. warred with the Etruscans and founded Ostia.

Marco Polo (c.1254-1324) Venetian merchant and traveler in Asia. In 1271, he accompanied his father Noccoló and his uncle Maffeo to the court

Marco Polo

of the Kublai Khan, where they arrived in 1275. M. remained in China and entered the khan's diplomatic service. He returned to Venice in 1295. After Genoa conquered Venice, M. was captured and dictated an account of his travels to a fellow prisoner. During the Renaissance, Polo's writings

were almost the sole source of the West's information about the East.

Marcomanni Germanic tribe that fought against the Roman Empire during the 2nd century AD. They were repelled by Marcus Aurelius and Diocletian.

Marconi, Guglielmo (1874-1937) Italian physicist and inventor. He developed wireless telegraphy, sending long-wave signals for more than a mile for the first time in 1895. M. organized a company in 1897 to develop commercial applications of the telegraph. In 1901 the first wireless signals were transmitted across the Atlantic Ocean. M. won the Nobel Prize in Physics in 1909.

Marcos, Ferdinand Edralin (1917-1989) President of the Philippines, 1965-1989. M. was elected president in 1965 and was reelected in 1969. He declared martial law in 1972 and thereafter ruled as a dictator. When the leader of the opposition, Benigno Aquino, was assassinated after his return from exile in 1983, resistance to

Ferdinand Edralin Marcos

M. increased. He agreed to hold elections in 1986 and was challenged by Aquino's widow, Corazon, who won despite M.'s attempt to rig the outcome. When the army backed Aquino, M. fled to exile in Hawaii, where he died in 1989.

Marcus Aurelius (121-180) Roman emperor, 161-180. He was the adopted son of Antonius Pius and was married to Antonius Pius's daughter, Faustina. In addition to being a

Guglielmo Marconi

capable administrator, M. was interested in the arts and sciences. His *Meditations* is a moving expression of the Stoic philosophy. Much of his reign was spent repressing attacks by Parthians, Britons, and Germans.

Mardonius (d.479 BC) Persian general and son-in-law of Darius I. He commanded campaigns against Greece in 492 and 480 BC. M. was defeated and killed in a battle at Plataea by the Spartans.

Marengo Village in northern Italy. During the French Revolutionary Wars, the Austrians were defeated there on June 14, 1800, by Napoleon's armies and by an army led by General Desaix de Veygoux.

Margaret of Anjou (c.1430-1482) Queen consort of King Henry VI of England, The daughter of René of Anjou, she married Henry in 1445. M. fought for her son Edward's succession to the throne against Richard of York. The clash between the followers of York and the supporters of the king (Lancastrians) precipitated the War of the Roses. M. was captured at the Battle of Tewkesbury in 1471 and her son killed. In 1475, Louis XI of France bought her freedom, and she spent her final years in poverty in France.

Margaret of Bavaria (d.1356) Daughter of William I of Heinault (William III of Holland). She married Louis of Bavaria in 1324.

Margaret of Constantinople (1202-1280) Daughter of Emperor Bau-

Mapping the World

Ever since man began
to sail the seven seas, he has
attempted to make realistic images
of the world.
As geographic knowledge
increased over the centuries, map
making became more and more
sophisticated.

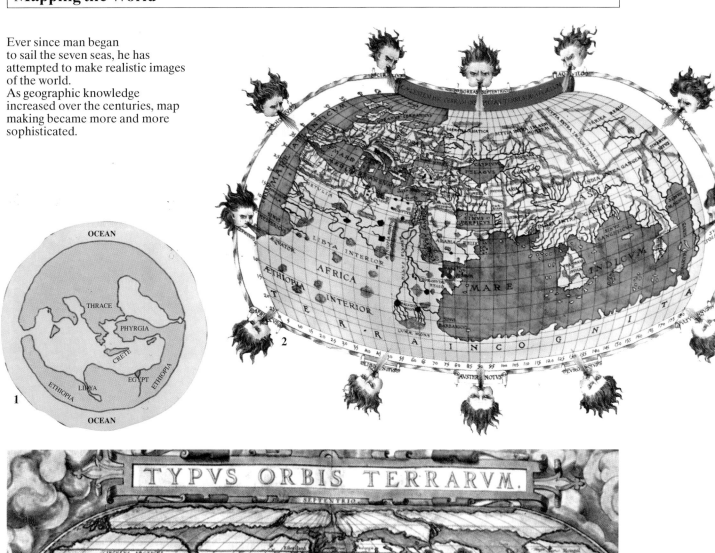

1. A map of the world as it was conceived in the time of Homer (c.900 BC). *See* Homer.
2. A map of the inhabited world as it was conceived by Ptolemy, a Greek geographer in the AD 2nd century. *See* Ptolemy.
3. A map of the world dating from the 17th century, drawn by the Flemish mapmaker Abraham Cortelius.

douin IX of Constantinople and the countess of Flanders and Heinault. Married first to Burchard of Avesnes and then William of Dampierre, she succeeded her sister Joan in 1244. The children of her marriage with Dampierre retained Flanders, while her Avesnes offspring received Heinault.

Margaret of Courtnay (d.1270) Countess of Namur. In 1237 she was forced to relinquish her duchy to her brother, Baudouin II, who became emperor of Constantinople in 1239. The duchy was sold to Guide of Dampierre in 1263.

Margaret of Navarre (Margareta of Angoulème) (1492-1549) Queen consort of Navarre. The sister of King Francis I of France, she married Henry d'Albret in 1525. He became king of Navarre in 1527. M. was an ardent supporter of religious liberty and a cultured woman whose court was frequented by literary figures of the day.

Margaret of Parma (1522-1586) Spanish regent of the Netherlands. The illegitimate daughter of Holy

Margaret of Parma

Roman Emperor Charles V, she was educated by Margaret of Austria and Ignatius Loyola and married Ottavio Farnese, duke of Parma, in 1538. In 1559, she became regent of the Netherlands, where she attempted to

keep the peace in the years preceding the Eighty Years' War. She resigned her position in 1567 with the arrival of duke of Alba, whose harsh measures she strongly opposed.

Margaret of Valois (1553-1615) Queen of France and Navarre. The daughter of King Henry II of France and Catherine de Medici, she married Henry of Navarre (later became King Henry IV of France) in 1572. The wedding was a prelude to the St. Bartholomew's Day Massacre. In 1599 she agreed to an annulment of her marriage, and she spent her remaining years at Usson, where she maintained a small court.

Margaret of York (1446-1503) Duchess of Burgundy. The daughter of Richard of York and the sister of kings Edward IV and Richard III of England, she married Charles the Bold, Duke of Burgundy, and played an important political role both in Burgundy and England.

Margaret Tudor (1489-1541) Queen consort of King James IV of Scotland. The daughter of Henry VII of England, she married James in 1502 and reigned briefly as regent after his death. She eventually was estranged from her son, James V.

Mari Ancient city of Mesopotamia (modern Syria). Located on the Euphrates River, it prospered from the 3rd to the first half of the 2nd millennium BC. Its site was unearthed by accident in the 1930s. In addition to the palace of Zimri-lim, an archive was discovered containing approximately 20,000 clay tablet texts in cuneiform script. The tablets contain information about palace administration and domestic policies of the times and also provide insights into military matters, irrigation, trade, and agriculture.

Maria Leszczynska (1703-1768) Queen of France, the wife of King Louis XV. The daughter of Stanislaus Leszczynski (Stanislaus I), king of Poland, she married Louis in 1725. She had 10 children, but she made no effort to rival the king's mistresses.

Maria Stuart *See* Mary II.

Maria Theresa (1717-1780) Austrian archduchess and queen of Bohemia

Maria Theresa

and Hungary, 1740-1780. She married Francis of Lorraine (later the Holy Roman Emperor Francis I) in 1736. The daughter of the Holy Roman Emperor Charles VI, she succeeded him in 1740. Her succession precipitated War of the Austrian Succession (1740-1748). When Francis I died in 1765, she governed her realms jointly with her son, Joseph II. Maria Theresa instituted agrarian reforms in her lands and revamped the royal administration. She had 16 children, some of whom became emperors and kings.

Marie Antoinette (1755-1793) Queen of France, the wife of King Louis XVI. The daughter of the Holy Roman Emperor Francis I and Maria Theresa, she married Louis in 1770. Her involvement in French foreign politics

Marie Antoinette

and her extravagance made her extremely unpopular. After the French Revolution, the royal family was imprisoned in the Temple (1792) and accused of treason. M. died on the guillotine on October 16, 1793.

Marie de Médici (1573-1642) Queen of France, the second wife of King Henry IV. The daughter of Francis I, grand duke of Tuscany, she married Henry in 1600. When he was assassinated, M. served as regent for her son, Louis XIII, until 1617. She was particularly ambitious and came into conflict with the nobility, her son, and Cardinal Richelieu. In 1631 she went into exile in the Netherlands and never returned to France.

Marie-Thérése (1638-1683) Queen of France, the wife of King Louis XIV. The daughter of King Philip IV of Spain, she married Louis in 1660 as part of an arrangement to seal the Treaty of the Pyrenees.

Marignano Town near Milan, Italy. It was the site of a decisive battle in 1515 between Francis I of France, supported by Venice, and a Swiss army supported by Pope Leo X and Milan. The Swiss forces were defeated and the French then claimed Lombardy and the city of Milan.

Marillac, Michel de (1563-1632) French statesman. He was minister of finance and keeper of the grand seal under Richelieu from 1624. M. supported Maria de Médici, he fell from power when she was exiled.

Marinids (13th-15th century) Berber dynasty that drove the Almohads from Morocco and founded their own empire.

Maritsa Site of battle in 1371 in present-day Bulgaria. The Ottoman Turks defeated a Serb army of 70,000 and were then able to invade Serbia and Macedonia.

Maritz, Gerhardus Martinus (1797-1838) South African Boer leader. He was one of the leaders of the Great Trek that left the Cape of Good Hope in 1836 to escape British domination. After the death of Retief, M. fought the Zulus in Natal.

Marius, Caius (c.157-86 BC) Roman statesman and general. He com-

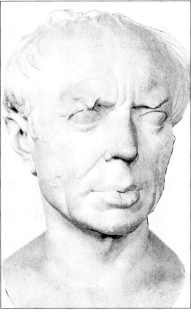
Caius Marius

manded an army in northern Africa against Jugurtha. After several victories, he moved to northern Italy, where he defeated the Cimbri and the Teutons at Aquae Sextiae and Vercellae. A plebeian, M. fought against his former consul, Sulla. In 88, M. was forced to flee, but he returned to massacre many of Sulla's followers, an event that led to the first civil war.

Marlborough, John Churchill, Duke of (1650-1722) English statesman and general. During the reign of Queen Anne (1702-1714), M. reached the peak of his political ascendancy, due in large measure to the influence of his wife, Sarah, over the queen. His military genius and gift for foreign diplomacy were revealed in the War of the Spanish Succession (1701-1714). The Churchills fell from grace in 1711 after quarreling with Anne. They went into exile abroad but returned after the acession of George I in 1714.

Marne, Battle of the Epic World War I battle in northern France. Between September 6-12, 1914, the advance of the German army was halted along the Marne River by the French and English.The final German offensive of 1918 was also halted on the Marne by American and English defenses.

Marobuduus of Marbod (d.37 BC) King of the Marcomanni. He entered into a peace treaty with the Romans, thereby coming into conflict with other Germanic tribes that had

formed a coalition under Arminius. M. fled to Rome in 19.

Maronites Christian community of Arabs. They are named after Maro, a Syrian hermit who lived some time in the 4th or 5th century AD. The sect originated in the 7th century and is one of the largest religious communities in Lebanon. Maronites recognize the pope in Rome as their spiritual leader.

Maroto, Rafael (1785-1847) Basque leader during the first Carlist War of 1834-1840.

Mars *See* Aries.

Marseillaise French national anthem. It was written by Claude Joseph Rouget de Lisle in 1792 as a march for the French army in the war against Austria.

Marshall, George Catlett (1880-1959) American general and statesman. He was chief of staff of the U.S. army during World War II. After the

George Catlett Marshall

war, he resigned from the army and served as secretary of state (1947-1949) under President Truman. He was the chief architect of the European Recovery Program (the Marshall Plan). M. also served as secretary of defense (1950-1951). He was awarded the Nobel Peace Price in 1953.

Marshall, John (1755-1835) 4th chief justice of the United States. A Federalist, he served in the House of Representatives and was secretary of state. President Adams appointed him chief justice in 1801. M.'s 34-year tenure on the Court had an immense impact on the American judicial system. He advocated a strong central

Karl Marx

government and gave the Court power to overrule states when conflicts arose. He also established judicial review and exercised it in the landmark case Marbury vs. Madison.

Marshall, Thurgood (1908-1993) U.S. Supreme Court justice, 1967-1991. A civil rights lawyer, M. was legal counsel for the National Association for the Advancement of Colored People (NAACP). He argued the landmark Brown vs. the Board of Education of Topeka (1954), which outlawed segregation in public schools, before the Supreme Court. The first black member of the Court, he was appointed associate justice by President Johnson in 1967.

Marston Moor Battlefield in Yorkshire, northern England. On July 2, 1644, Cromwell's armies defeated the royalist army led by Prince Rupert and the duke of Newcastle. Marston Moor was the first major victory of the par-liamentarians in the English Civil War.

Martin IV (c.1210/1220-1285) Pope, 1281-1285. A Frenchman named Simon de Brie, he was a supporter of the Angevin dynasty in southern Italy and Sicily. At the insistence of Charles of Anjou, his protector, M. excommunicated the Byzantine Emperor Michael VIII. This action ended the brief unification of the western and eastern churches reached at the Council of Lyons in 1274.

Martin V (1368-1431) Pope, 1417-1431. A Roman named Oddone Colonna, he was created a cardinal by Innocent VII. His election as pope by the Council of Constance ended the Great Schism.

Martínez de Campos, Arsenio (1831-1900) Spanish general. He played a leading role in the restoration of the Bourbon monarchy in Spain in 1874. Two years later he defeated the Carlists at Pena de Plata.

Martinits, Jaroslav Bolrita, Duke of (1582-1649) Bohemian nobleman. A member of Emperor Matthew's regency council, he and two other imperial counselors were thrown from a palace window in 1618 by members of the Bohemian Diet as a protest against the emperor. He was unhurt, but the so-called Defenestration of Prague precipitated the Thirty Years War.

Marty, André (1886-1956) French communist. In 1919, he led a mutiny aboard French warships that that had been sent to the Black Sea to oppose the Bolsheviks in Russia. He became a member of the French parliament in 1924 and organized the International Brigades. He was ousted from the party in 1953.

Marx, Karl (1818-1883) German social philosopher. The chief theorist of socialism and communism, M. received a PhD from the University of Jena in 1841 and became the editor of the Rheinische Zeitung. When the newspaper was repressed in 1843, M. moved to Paris, where he began his long association with Engels. They published the Communist Manifesto in 1847, which outlined their views about the triumph of the working class. M. settled in London in 1849. There he wrote his major work, *Das Kapital* (1867-1894), which established the theoretical foundations of Marxism and international socialism.

Mary I (1516-1558) Queen of England, 1553-1558. The daughter of King Henry VIII and Catherine of Aragón, she was raised as a Roman Catholic. Her marriage to Philip II of Spain allied England with Spain and created unrest in largely Protestant England. During her reign, Protestants were brutally persecuted, and she became known as "Bloody Mary."

Mary I

Mary II

Mary II (Maria Stuart) (1662-1694) Queen of England, 1689-1694. The daughter of King James II and Anne Hyde, she was raised as a Protestant despite her father's Catholicism. In 1677 she married William of Orange and moved to Holland. She returned to England after James II was overthrown in the Glorious Revolution of 1688 and was proclaimed joint sovereign with her husband, William III.

Mary of Burgundy (1457-1482) Wife of Maximilian of Austria. The only daughter of Charles the Bold, she succeeded her father as Duchess of Burgundy after his death in 1477. She married Maximilian of Austria in that same year. He routed the French armies that had invaded her Dutch territories.

Mary, Queen of Scots (Mary Stuart) (1542-1587) Queen of Scotland. She was the daughter of King James V and became queen at the age of 6 days. Mary, a Roman Catholic, was married to King Francis II of France from 1558-1560. When he died, she returned to Scotland. After several years of turmoil, she was forced to abdicate in favor of her son after the nobility and the Protestants turned against her. M. fled to England in 1568, but was imprisoned by Elizabeth I. M. laid claim to the English throne through her grandmother, Margaret Tudor. A threat to the English queen, she was suspected of plotting to kill Elizabeth and was executed in 1587. Her son, James I, succeeded Elizabeth as king of England in 1603.

Mary Stuart *See* Mary, Queen of Scots.

Mary Tudor *See* Mary I.

Masada Ancient mountaintop fortress in Israel, to the west of the Dead Sea. Built during the Jewish uprising against the Romans, M. was the last refuge of the Zealot Jews. After a two-year siege, the survivors committed mass suicide (73 AD) rather than surrender to the Romans.

Masaryk, Jan (1886-1948) Czechoslovak diplomat. The son of Thomas Masaryk, he served as minister to Great Britain (1925-1938) and as foreign minister in the Czechoslovak government-in-exile in London during World War II. He returned to his country after the war and retained the post of foreign minister. After the communist takeover (1948), M. either committed suicide or was murdered.

Masaryk, Thomas Garrigue (1850-1937) First president of Czechoslovakia. A professor of philosophy by training, he served in the Austrian parliament and the Bohemian diet in the 1890s. He founded the Czech Peoples Party in 1900 and fought for Czech and Slovak equality within the Austro-Hungarian Empire. He later advocated independence and headed a national council that was recognized by the Allies as the de facto government of the new Czechoslovak republic after World War I. M. served as president of Czechoslovakia until 1935. He was the father of Jan Masaryk.

Masséna, André, duke of Rivoli and Prince of Essling (1758-1817) French general under Napoleon. He served in the Italian campaigns and won the battle of Rivoli (1897).

Massinissa (c.238-148 BC) King of Numidia. M. first fought for the Carthaginians during Second Punic War in Spain, then went over to the Roman side. His struggle against the Carthaginians precipitated the Third Punic War in 150-149 BC. His empire was divided among his sons after his death; *see* Jugurtha.

Masulipatam, Treaty of (1768) Treaty that brought the Indian state of Hyderabad under English rule and led to a war that lasted until 1779.

Mata Hari (1876-1917) Dutch spy in German service during World War I. Born Margaretha Geertruida Zelle, she was a dancer and courtesan who betrayed secrets confided by Allied officers with whom she was on intimate terms. She was arrested and executed by the French at Chateau Vincennes.

Mata Hari

Mataram Empire on the island of Java, Indonesia. It prospered under the rule of Sultan Agung (1645) but in 1755 was divided into the kingdoms Surakarta and Yogyakarta.

Matilda (1102-1167) Queen of England. The daughter of King Henry I, she was married to the Holy Roman Emperor Henry V from 1114 until his death in 1125. M. succeeded her father as queen of England in 1135 but her claim was contested by various baronial factions. In 1148 she fled to Normandy, where she spent the remainder of her life. Her son, Henry II, was recognized as king in 1153.

Matteotti, Giacomo (1885-1924) Italian Socialist leader. He was the outstanding opponent of Mussolini's Fascists. His assassination by Fascists in 1924 removed the last remaining parliamentary obstacle to Mussolini's dictatorship.

Matthias of Austria (1557-1619) Holy Roman Emperor, 1612-1619. The son of Holy Roman Emperor Maximilian II, he succeeded Don Juan as governor-general of the Netherlands in 1577, but resigned after a few years. M.

Matthias of Austria

pursued a conciliatory religious policy after becoming Holy Roman Emperor, hoping to reconcile Catholics and Protestants within his realm. He was a poor administrator, however, and was unable to prevent the growing influence of his brother, Archduke Maximilian, who was pro-Catholic.

Mau Mau Secret terrorist organization in Kenya, consisting mainly of Kikuyu tribesmen. Its goal was to drive white settlers from Kenya. Founded in 1947, the movement began to take bloody reprisals against whites in 1952. It was eventually suppressed by British troops, who by 1956 had driven most of the Kikuyu into the mountains; see Kenyatta.

Mauchari Dynasty Northern Indian rulers in the 6th century AD. The lived autonomously for a time within the Gupta empire but were eventually conquered by the Guptas.

Maugham, William Somerset (1874-1965) English author. He is considered one of the greatest stylists in English literature. M. was trained as a physician but never practiced medicine. He served in the British Intelligence Service during World War I. M. had written eight novels before publishing his partly autobiographical masterpiece, *Of Human Bondage* (1915). Other noted works include *The Moon and Sixpence* (1919) and *The Razor's Edge* (1944). He is also famous for his short stories and essays.

Maurice, Duke of Saxony (1521-1553) German nobleman. He converted to Protestantism in 1539 but in 1546 entered into a secret treaty with the Holy Roman Emperor Charles V to support him in the Schmalkaldic Wars against the German Protestants. In return, M. received lands and the title of elector. M. later turned against Charles and forced him to accept the Treaty of Passau (1552), which freed the captured Protestant princes and guaranteed Lutherans the right to exercise their religion.

Maurice of Nassau (1567-1625) Prince of Orange. The son of William of Orange (William the Silent), M. became stadtholder of Holland and Zeeland in 1584 upon the assassination of his father, and general of the army a year later. Between 1590 and 1597 he defeated the Spanish armies in several battles. His military successes enabled the Netherlands to conclude a 12-year truce with the Spanish in 1609, thereby virtually establishing the independence of the seven United Provinces.

Mauromichalis, Peter (1765-1848) Greek freedom fighter. He fought in the rebellion against the Turks in 1821 and later opposed Capodistrias, who was assassinated by his son and his brother.

Maurras, Charles (1868-1952) French author, journalist, and politician. He was one of the leaders of the Action Française and a fervent supporter of Pétain of the Vichy government during World War II. In 1945 he

was sentenced to life imprisonment for collaboration with the Nazis.

Maurya Kingdom Kingdom in northern India and Afghanistan from c. 321-185 BC. The last Maurya king was deposed in 185; see Chandragupta.

Mausoleum Sepulchral monument in Asia Minor, erected c.352 BC by Artemisia, the widow of Mausolus of Halicarnassus, in his memory. In ancient times it was regarded as one of the seven wonders of the world.

Mausoleum, Hadrian's Circular structure in Rome, known also as Castel Sant'Angelo. A sepulchral monument built for Emperor Hadrian between 138-139, it contains his remains as well as those of his immediate successors.

Mauthausen Town in eastern Austria. It was the site after 1938 of a Nazi concentration camp.

Max, Prince of Baden (Maximilian of Baden) (1867-1929) German states-

Maurice of Nassau

man. The last chancellor of imperial Germany, he negotiated the armistice with the Allies. When the revolution broke out in Germany on November 9, 1918, M. forced Emperor William II to abdicate. Soon after he resigned himself and turned the government over to the Socialist Friedrich Ebert.

Maxamed, Cabdulle Xasam (1864-1920) Somali leader. Known as the "Mad Mullah," he fought a bitter guerrilla war against the English and the Italians in Somaliland.

Maximilian I (1459-1519)

Maxentius, Marcus Aurelius Valerius (d.312) Roman emperor. He was the son of Maximinus and co-emperor with Constantine I. Constantine later turned against him and defeated M. at the battle of the Milvian Bridge. M. drowned trying to escape.

Maximianus, Marcus Aurelius Valerius (d.310) Roman emperor who ruled jointly with Diocletian, 286-305. He and Diocletian abdicated in 305, after which he supported his son Maxentius in his struggle against Constantine I.

Maximilian I (1459-1519) Holy Roman Emperor and German king, 1493-1519. The son of Holy Roman Emperor Frederick III, M. married Mary of Burgundy in 1477. As emperor he desired to restore imperial leadership and inaugurate administrative reforms in his increasingly decentralized empire. In both domestic and foreign policy, however, he sacrificed German interests to the aggrandizement of Hapsburg posses-

sions. His son, Philip I (Philip the Handsome) ruled from 1493-1506.

Maximilian I (1573-1651) Duke of Bavaria, 1597-1651, and elector of Bavaria from 1623. An ardent supporter of the Catholic Reformation, M. was the leader of the Catholic League and played a significant role in the Thirty Years War.

Maximilian II (1527-1576) Holy Roman Emperor, 1564-1576. The son of Holy Roman Emperor Ferdinand I and Anne of Hungary, he was married to Mary, the daughter of Holy Roman Emperor Charles V. In 1562, M. became king of Bohemia and in 1563 king of Hungary. M. was unsuccessful in his war against the Turks and was forced to pay tribute to them.

Maximilian IV Joseph (1756-1825) King of Bavaria, 1806-1825, as Maximilian I. He received the royal title from Napoleon, with whom he was allied. He joined the coalition against Napoleon, however, during the French retreat from Russia. M. was devoted to Bavarian independence and abolished the last relics of feudalism in his kingdom.

Maximilian, Ferdinand Joseph (1832-1867) Archduke of Austria and emperor of Mexico, 1864-1867. The younger brother of Franz Joseph, Napoleon III persuaded M. to become emperor of Mexico in 1863. His power rested on occupying French troops, but when they were withdrawn, his support collapsed. Highly unpopular, he was captured by Juárez's forces and executed.

Ferdinand Joseph Maximilian

Maximinus, Caius Galerius Valerius (d.313) Roman emperor, 308-313. M. was an ally of Maxentius after 308 in his war against Constantine I but lost several important battles. He persecuted the Christians severely during his reign.

Maximinus, Caius Julius Verus (d.238) Roman emperor, 235-238. A Thracian and a general, he was proclaimed emperor by the legions in Germany in 235. He conducted several successful campaigns against the Germans. M. was assassinated by soldiers in Italy when trying to put down a rebellion.

Mayas Indian nation of Central America, centered in the Yucatán of Mexico and in parts of Guatemala and Honduras. The M. prospered between c.250-900 (Classic Period) and 900-1500 (Post-Classic Period) but declined as their civilization sank into civil war. They suffered also during the Spanish conquest of Mexico.

Mayenne, Charles de Lorraine, Duke of (1554-1611) French Catholic general in the Wars of Religion. He

Charles de Lorraine Mayenne

was the brother of Henri Guise and of Cardinal de Guise. M. was the leader of the League and opposed the King Henry IV. He made peace with the king in 1596.

Descendants of the ancient Mayas still live in Mexico and Central America. The ruins of the centers of their great civilization were only discovered in the 1930s, more than 1000 years after they were first built. The great Mayan cities were abandoned before the Spanish arrived in the 16th century.

3

4

1

5

1. The Mayas were great astronomers. This is one of their observatories, *El Caracol* in Chichen Itza. *See* Mayas.

2. A stone statue of a deity with a sacrificial plate on his stomach, a so-called "chac mool." *See* also Mayas.

3. The so-called "King of Kabab." *See* Mayas.

4. A Mayan statuette, from southeastern Mexico. *See* Mayas.

5. The great pyramid of Tikal. *See* Mayas.

Mayerling Village in eastern Austria. It is the site of a hunting lodge where Crown Prince Rudolf, the only son of Emperor Franz Joseph of Austria, and his mistress, Baroness Maria Vetsera, committed suicide in 1889.

Mayflower Ship that brought the Pilgrims from England to America in 1620.

Mazarin, Jules (1602-1661) French statesman and cardinal of the Roman Catholic Church. Born in Italy as Giulio Mazarini, he worked in the papal diplomatic corps before enter-

Jules Mazarin

ing the service of France. He became Louis XIII's chief minister, succeeding Cardinal Richelieu. M. brought about the end of the Thirty Years War in 1648, but continued the war against Spain until 1659. He suppressed an uprising of the Fronde, after which he ruled France without opposition.

Mazepa, Ivan Stepanovich (1640-1709) Cossack leader of the Ukraine. He maintained Ukrainian autonomy while keeping good relations with the Russian czar Peter I. When Peter's harsh demands on the Ukraine increased, however, M. allied with Sweden against Russia in the Northern War. M. and the Swedes were defeated by Peter at the Battle of Poltava in 1709, after which M. fled. He died a short time later in exile.

Mazyadid Arab dynasty that ruled central Iraq c.961-1150 from the capital city of Al-Hillah.

Mazzini, Giuseppe (1805-1872) Italian revolutionary. An outstanding figure of the Risorgimento, M. led sev-

eral uprisings of his Young Italy organization (founded in 1832) in Milan and Rome to oust the Austrians from dominance. He spent many years in exile but often returned secretly to Italy to foment rebellions. Throughout his life he advocated a unified, republican Italy, and remained staunchly opposed to monarchy.

McAuliffe, Anthony C. (1898-1975) American general during World War II. He defended Bastogne, Belgium, during the Battle of the Bulge in 1944. When presented with a German ultimatum to surrender, M. replied, "Nuts."

McCarthy, Joseph Raymond (1908-1957) American senator. He achieved national prominence in 1950 when he made unsubstantiated charges that Communists had infiltrated the State Department and the U.S. Army. Many innocent people, slandered by his Senate subcommittee, lost their jobs. His public support began to decline when the Army-McCarthy hearings were televised in 1954 and his bullying tactics were revealed. He was censured by the Senate in 1954.

McClellan, George Brinton (1826-1885) Union general during the American Civil War. A brilliant organizer, M. was overly cautious as a field general and was removed from command of Union forces by President Lincoln in 1862. He was reinstated briefly but was removed again after failing to pursue Confederate forces after the battle of Antietam (1862). M. was the Democratic presidential candidate against Lincoln in 1864 but lost decisively. He served a governor of New Jersey from 1878 to 1881.

McKinley, William (1843-1901) 25th president of the U.S., 1897-1901. He was born in Niles, Ohio, served in the Civil War, and was a Republican congressman from 1876 to 1890. As sponsor of the unpopular McKinley Tariff, he was defeated for reelection in 1890 but the following year was elected governor of Ohio. M. was elected president in 1896, defeating William Jennings Bryan. During his first term, the U.S. fought the Spanish-American War and gained a number of overseas territories in the Pacific and Caribbean. McKinley was reelected in 1900, but in 1901 was assassinated

while attending an exposition in Buffalo, New York. He was succeeded by Theodore Roosevelt.

Giuseppe Mazzini

Medes A nomadic people who lived in northwest Persia. They fought against Assyria during the 9th-6th century BC and extended their rule over Persia during the reign of Sargon I (d.705 BC). In 612 BC, they conquered the Assyrian capital of Nineveh. M. were incorporated into the Persian empire by Cyrus the Great in 550 BC.

Medici Prominent Florentine family who ruled the city from the 15th cen-

Medici

tury to 1737. Of obscure origin, they achieved immense wealth as merchants and bankers. The M. affiliated with the major royal houses of Europe through marriage and produced three popes, two queens of France, and numerous cardinals.

Medina City in Saudi Arabia. In Arabic it is called Medinat-an-Nabi (City of the Prophet). Muhammad spent his last years in Medina and used it as a base to from which to convert and conquer Arabia. M., the most important Islamic pilgrimage city after Mecca, contains the tomb of Muhammad and his daughter Fatima.

Philip Melanchthon

Medina-Sidonia, Alonzo Pérez de Guzmán, Duke of (1550-1615) Spanish nobleman. In 1588 Philip II made him leader of the Armada despite his lack of naval experience. Despite the defeat of the Armada, M. retained royal favor and held a number of high positions in later years.

Megaliths Communal tombs from the late Stone Age. M. were built with massive boulders, which were remnants of the Ice Age; see Dolmen.

Meiji Restoration Revolution in Japanese life and government that accompanied the accession of Emperor Meiji (Mutsuhito) to the throne in 1867. Replacing the moribund Tokugawa shogunate, the Meiji centralized the government in Tokyo and began to Westernize the country; see Mutsuhito.

Mein Kampf (German for "My Struggle") Autobiographical/political work written in 1925 by Adolph Hitler.

Meir, Golda (1898-1978) Prime minister of Israel, 1969-1974. Born in Kiev as Golda Mabovitz, she migrated with her family to the U.S. in 1906. She became a teacher in Wisconsin and joined the Zionist movement as a young woman. In 1921 M. and her husband migrated to Palestine, where she became involved in the labor movement. After Israeli independence in 1948, she became ambassador to the Soviet Union, minister of labor (1949-1956), and foreign minister (1956-1966). In 1969 M. became prime minister. She rallied the country during the 1973 Arab-Israeli War but resigned in 1974 after her government was accused of being unprepared for the conflict.

Melanchthon, Philip (1497-1560) German scholar and humanist. He was second only to Luther as a figure in the Lutheran Reformation. More conciliatory that Luther, M. often mediated between Lutheranism and those outside the movement. He was responsible for the Augsburg Confession.

Melas, Michael F., Baron von (1729-1806) Austrian general who fought in the Seven Years' War and became a general in the Austrian army in Italy in 1799. His troops were defeated by Napoleon at Marengo in June 1800.

Melchites Arabic-speaking Christian community in the Middle East. They follow a Byzantine rite but recognize the pope in Rome as their spiritual leader. The name Melchite is derived from the syriac word for "king" and was applied in the 18th century to Orthodox Eastern Christians who reunited with Rome.

Melville, Herman (1819-1891) American author. He is considered one of the greatest writers in American literature. As a young man, M. participated in several whaling expeditions. He married in 1847 and enjoyed some modest success as a writer. In 1851 he published his masterpiece, *Moby Dick*. Heavily symbolic, the book is at once a sea story, a critique of American society and racism, a philosophical inquiry into the nature of good and evil, and a repository of information about whaling. The public did not accept the work and much of his other later writings, and M. sank increasingly into debt and ill health. He supported himself with a low-paying job as a customs inspector in New York but died in poverty.

Memling, Hans (c.1430-1494) Flemish religious and portrait painter. He may have worked with Roger van der

Work by Hans Memling

Weyden in Brussels and later in Bruges, Belgium. M. is known in particular for his religious works that project an atmosphere of pleasing blandness and refinement.

Memphis Ancient city located 12 miles from Cairo, Egypt, at the apex of the Nile delta. It was reputedly founded around 3000 BC by Menes, the first king of a united Egypt. The pyramids of the Kings of the Old Kingdom were built at Sakkara, to the west of M. The god Ptah was the major deity worshiped in M.

Menchkov, Alexander Danilovich (1673-1729) Russian general and statesman. An adviser to Peter the Great. M. commanded an army that defeated Sweden at the battle of Poltava in 1709. In 1727, M. was banished to Siberia by Peter II.

Mencken, Henry Louis (1880-1956), American editor, author, and critic. He worked on a number of Baltimore newspapers and was editor of the magazine American Mercury, which he founded. M.'s pungent and iconoclastic wit was aimed at complacent attitudes, especially those of the middle class. In the field of philology, he compiled a monumental study, *The American Language* (1919).

Mendel, Gregor (1822-1884) Austrian monk and biologist. By crossbreeding peas he established that hereditary characteristics are determined by the combination of two hereditary units (genes), one from each of the parental reproductive cells. His findings, published in 1866, were ignored in his lifetime. Mendel's conclusions have become the basic tenets of genetics and have had enormous impact in plant and animal breeding.

Mendeleyev, Dmitri Ivanovich (1834-1907) Russian chemist. He is famous for the formulation of the periodic law (1869) and the invention of the periodic table, a classification of the elements.

Mendelssohn, Felix (1809-1847) German composer and conductor. He was a leading figure of 19th-century music. His first mature composition, the overture for *A Midsummer Night's Dream*, was composed at 17. Of his five symphonies, the Scottish (1830-1842), Italian (1833), and Reformation (1830-1832) are best known. M. also composed a violin concerto, songs, chamber music, choral music, and six organ sonatas. He conducted a performance of the St. Matthew Pas-

Felix Mendelssohn

sion in 1829 that helped stimulate a revival of interest in the music of J.S. Bach. M. was a founder of the conservatory at Leipzig (1842) and conducted the Gewandhaus concerts in that city.

Mendès-France, Pierre (1907-1982) French statesman. A socialist, he was prime minister between 1954 and 1955 and was instrumental in ending French involvement in the war in Indochina.

Mendoza, Bernardino de (1540-1604) Spanish diplomat and historian, and envoy of King Philip II in Paris. His autobiography includes a description of the struggle against Spain in the Low Countries.

Mene, Mene, Tekel, Upharsin In the Bible, the mysterious riddle written by a hand on the wall at Belshazzar's feast. The Aramaic words may be literally translated, "counted, counted, weighed, divided." Daniel interpreted the riddle to mean that the king's deeds had been weighed and found deficient, and that Babylon would fall in battle against the Medes and the Persians.

Bernardino de Mendoza

Menelik I Emperor of Ethiopia, 1270-1285. He is said to have been the son of King Solomon and the Queen of Sheba.

Menelik II (1844-1913) Emperor of Ethiopia, 1889-1913. He defeated an invading Italian army in a great victory at Aduwa in 1896. M. attempted to expand and modernize his kingdom. He moved the capital to Addis Ababa, ended the slave trade, and curbed the feudal nobility.

Menes King of ancient Egypt, c.3200 BC. The first Egyptian ruler for whom there are historical records, M. may have united the southern and northern kingdoms and founded the capital at Memphis. Recent scholarship identified M. as King Narmer.

Gerardus Mercator

Menhir Archaeological term meaning "long stone." It describes a kind of single, standing stone, square and tapered at the top, that is found in Western Europe. A large field of more than 1,000 Stone Age M. is found in Brittany, France.

Mennonites Sect of Protestant Christians. They originated in the 16th century as an offshoot of Anabaptists in Switzerland. Mennonite communities may still be found today in Canada and the United States.

Menshevism One of the two main branches of Russian socialism after 1903 (the other being Bolshevism, led by Lenin). M. (from mensheviki, or minority) believed that Russia could not pass from a peasant society to rule of the proletariat without an intermediate bourgeois regime. Mensheviks participated in the Kerensky government after the 1917 revolution and were suppressed in 1921.

Mentana Town near Rome. Garibaldi was defeated there in 1867 by papal and French troops during his unsuccessful attempt to capture Rome.

Mentuhotep *See* Middle Kingdom.

Mercantilism Economic system of major trading nations during the 16th 18th centuries. It was based on the premise that national wealth and power were best served by increasing exports and collecting precious metals in return. The major mercantile states—Holland, France, and England—tended to identify money (especially gold) with wealth and favored foreign trade over domestic trade.

Mercator, Gerardus (1512-1594) Flemish geographer and cartographer. He was the first to draw maps using the projection that carries his name. Mercator maps permit the straight-line navigation that is still used in marine maps.

Mercurius *See* Hermes, Wodan.

Mermnadae dynasty *See* Lydia.

Merovingians Frankish royal family. They were descended according to tradition from Merovech, chief of the Salian Franks. The M. ruled between c.476-751, when they were ousted by the Carolingians; *see* Pepin.

Mesopotamia Ancient region of the Middle East, located between the Euphrates and the Tigris rivers and including modern Iraq. Settlements in the northern part date as far back as 5000 BC, making M. one of the cradles of civilization. Over the millennia it changed hands many times between different empires and peoples; *see* Assyria; Babylon; Sumeria.

Messenic Wars Series of revolts in ancient Greece of the Messenians against Sparta. The first occurred c.700 BC and the last c.460 BC. All of the revolts failed to undo the dominance of Sparta over the lives of Messenians.

Messiah Hebrew word for "anointed." In Judaism, the Messiah would be sent by God to restore Israel and to rule righteously over all mankind.

Metaurus River in central Italy. In 207 BC, the Carthaginian general Hasdrubal was defeated there by the Romans under Claudius Nero. The defeat deterred Hannibal from further conquest in southern Italy.

Metaxas, Ioannis (1871-1941) Greek general and dictator. A prominent royalist, he became prime minister in 1936 and seized power in a army-backed coup d'état in August of that year. After the Italian invasion of Greece in 1940, M. successfully directed the resistance that drove the Italians into Albania. He died the following year.

Ioannis Metaxas

Methodism Protestant movement started in England by the teachings of John Wesley in the 1730s. Wesley believed in conducting one's life and religious study by "rule and method," hence the name Methodist. M. stressed personal piety and evangelistic preaching. After his death in 1741, the Methodists formally separated from the Church of England, in which their teachings had been barred.

Mexican War Armed conflict between the U.S. and Mexico (1846-1848). As a result of the war, Mexico gave up all claims to Texas and the U.S. acquired the lands known as the Mexican Cession. The acquisition of the new lands intensified the slavery controversy in the U.S., raising the question of whether the territories should be slave or free.

Michael Fyodorovich Romanov (1596-1645) Czar of Russia, 1613-1645. He was the founder of the Romanov dynasty. His election as czar followed successive appearances of false pretenders and ended the so-called Time of Troubles, a period of social and political chaos in Russia that began in the 16th century.

Michelangelo Buonarroti

Michelangelo Buonarroti (1475-1564) Italian painter, sculptor, and architect. M. was one of the driving forces of the Italian Renaissance. Most of his works of art can be found in his birthplace of Florence (for example, David and the Medici tombs) or in Rome (the Pietà and Moses). His painting on the ceiling of the Sistine Chapel is a profound masterpiece of style and spiritual content. During the last period of his life he worked as the chief architect of St. Peter's Basilica in Rome.

Midas Figure in Greek mythology, king of Phrygia. Dionysus granted him the power to turn everything to gold by touch, but when even his food turned to gold, M. begged to be relieved of the gift.

Middle Ages Period roughly between 395 (the collapse of the Roman Empire) and the 13th-15th century (depending on the time and place the Renaissance started). During the Middle Ages, Christianity increased in power and influence, assuming many responsibilities of the state. A feudal nobility also developed, cities and guilds were founded, specific cultures began to appear, and sovereign states were established. The term *Dark Ages* was used by humanists after 1500 to describe the Middle Ages. They tended to regard the Middle Ages as a period of ignorance and superstition, but now scholars regard it as a highly formative and creative millennium.

Middle Kingdom Period during which Egypt flourished (c.1940-1600 BC). Following a time of division, Mentuhotep II unified the country. The true Middle Kingdom began with Amonemhat I (12th dynasty). Another significant king of this period was Sesotris III, who secured the kingdom's borders. The 13th dynasty had some 70 kings over a period of 100 years, an indication of growing instability. The kingdom eventually collapsed and was ruled in the north by the invader Hykos during the Middle Period (c.1630-1523 BC).

Midhat Pasha (1822-1883) Turkish politician who modernized Bulgaria and Iraq. He deposed Sultan Abdul Aziz in 1876 and implemented the first Turkish constitution. In 1881, M. was condemned to death by Sultan Abdul Hamid II, but he was eventually exiled and then strangled by his guards in 1883.

Midway, Battle of Decisive U.S.-Japanese naval engagement during World War II. When the Japanese navy attempted to seize Midway Island in the Pacific in June 1942, they were challenged by an American force. The battle, fought mostly with aircraft, resulted in the loss of three Japanese aircraft carriers. After Midway, the Japanese went over to the defensive and never recovered their naval strength.

Mihailovich, Draza (1893-1946) Yugoslav general. He led the Serbian

chetnik forces in their struggle against the Nazi occupation in World War II and was appointed minister of war in the Yugoslav government in exile. An ardent royalist, he soon came to clash with Tito's partisans, who captured, tried, and executed him in 1946 for treason.

Mikado Former title of the emperor of Japan, which is used chiefly in English.

Miletus Greek colony on the coast of Asia Minor, near Sámos. In 499 BC, the Ionian Greeks revolted against Persian rule, and in 494 BC, Miletus was sacked.

Miltiades

Miltiades (d.489 BC) Athenian general. The son of Cimon, he took part in the Ionian revolt against the Persians in 499 BC, and in 490 BC defeated the Persians at Marathon with an army of Athenians.

Milvian Bridge Bridge across the Tiber River in Rome, built in 109 BC

The Mexican war of Independence

Much of the 19th century was a time of unrest in Mexico. First the Mexicans fought to free themselves from Spanish rule, and in part that struggle was a civil war, since for a while, conservative forces and the Church in Mexico were allied with the Spanish. Then Mexico fought and lost a war with the United States (1846-1848). A great reformer, Benito Juarez, became president in

1

2

1861, but in the 1860s France installed Maximilian, the brother of the Hapsburg emperor Franz Joseph, as emperor of Mexico. When Maximilian was deposed in 1867, Juarez returned to power. Later in the century, the dictator Porfirio Diaz ruled for many years.

3

4

1. American forces attack the Mexican fortress at Chapultepec in 1847. *See* Mexican War.
2. A portrait of Maximilian, emperor of Mexico from 1864 to 1867. *See* Juarez, Benito; Maximilian, Ferdinand Joseph.
3. French troops arrive in Mexico.
4. Maximilian and his generals are executed by the followers of Juarez.
5. Porfirio Diaz, president of Mexico from 1876 to 1911. *See* Diaz, José de la Cruz, Porfirio.

5

as part of the Flamian Way. Constantine I defeated Maxentius in 312 AD at the Milvian Bridge and while there saw the cross in the sky, leading to his conversion to Christianity.

Mine *See* Drachme.

Minerva *See* Athens.

Ming dynasty Dynasty of China that ruled between 1368 and 1644. Their capitals were Nanking and Peking. The Ming expelled the Mongols from all of China (1382). At its height, the Ming kingdom extended from Burma to Korea.

Minnesingers Medieval German poets, knights, and singers (13th and 14th centuries). Usually noblemen, they proclaimed their platonic love for ladies of the aristocracy in their songs of courtly love (Minne).

Minoan Civilization Ancient culture found on Crete and the surrounding islands between c.3000-1100 BC. It was named after the legendary King Minos by the archaeologist Sir Arthur Evans. The ports on eastern Crete and the round graves at Messara were built in the Early Minoan Era (c.3000-2200 BC). During the Middle Minoan Era (c.2200-1500 BC) extensive palace complexes were built at Knossos and Phaestus, and Minoan maritime power extended across the sea. In the Late Minoan Era (c.1500-1200 BC) the civilization was dis-

rupted, probably by earthquakes and volcanoes. The island was invaded by mainland Greeks c.1450, and the palaces were destroyed. Knossos was destroyed c.1375 by an unknown cause, and the civilization faded into poverty and obscurity sometime between 1200-1100 BC.

Minuit, Peter (c.1580-1641) Colonial official. He was appointed governor general of New Netherlands by the Dutch West India Company in 1625. M. bought Manhattan Island for about 60 guilders (approximately $24 at the time) from the Indians in 1626. He built Fort Amsterdam on the site, which later became New York City.

Miramón, Miguel (1832-1867) Mexican general. He was the leader of a conservative party that supported by the clergy. M. was president of Mexico for a brief period but fled from Juárez in 1860 and was later executed with Emperor Maximilian.

Miranda, Francisco de (1750-1816) Venezuelan revolutionary. M. joined the fight for the liberation of Spanish America in 1783 and also fought in the French Revolution. In 1811-1812, M. led the revolt against Spain in Venezuela, but he lost the support of Bolívar after surrendering Puerto Cabello to the Spanish. Angered by the capitulation, Bolívar and other patriots turned M. over to the Spanish, who deported him to Spain and kept him in a dungeon the rest of his life.

Missolonghi City in Greece, on the Gulf of Corinth. After 1821, M. was the Greek bulwark in the uprising against the Turks. Lord Byron died there of swamp fever in 1824. After being besieged twice, M. capitulated to the Turks on April 22, 1826.

Mitanni Ancient kingdom in northern Syria. It formed a buffer zone between Egypt and the Hittite empire c.1500-1360 BC. M. was annexed by Assyria in the 13th century BC.

Mithradates VI Eupator (Mithradates the Great) (c.131-63 BC) King of Pontus. He waged war against Rome and Bythnia and expelled the Romans from Asia Minor in 88 BC. It took three wars (the Mithradatic Wars) for the Romans to defeat him, after which he committed suicide. His kingdom then became a Roman province.

Mithradates VI Eupator

François Maurice Mitterand

Mitterand, François Maurice (1916-1996) President of France, 1981-1995. As Socialist, M. was cofounder of the U.D.S.R. (Union Démocratique et Socialiste de Résistance) in 1946. An outspoken opponent of De Gaulle, M. ran against him for president in 1965 and lost. He became chairman of the new Socialist Party in 1971, narrowly lost another bid for president in 1974, and was finally elected in 1981. He was reelected in 1987.

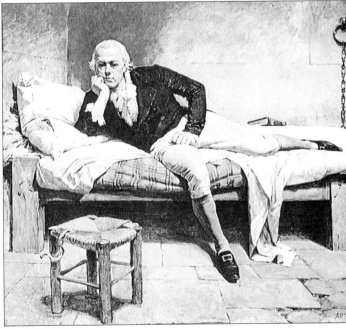
Francisco de Miranda

Model, Walther (1891-1945) German field marshal in World War II. He was commander the German forces on the western front in July 1944. When his army was surrounded by the Allied forces in the Ruhr in 1945, he committed suicide.

Great Moguls of India

The Mogul Empire in India was founded in the 16th century. The Moguls were Muslims. Although the word *Mogul* is derived from "Mongol," in fact the Moguls were mainly Turks. They ruled most of India until conquered by the British in the late 17th and early 18th centuries.

1

3

4

TIBET

NEPAL

BHUTAN

ASSAM

- Kabul
- Peshawar
- Lahore
- Multan
- Panipat
- Delhi
- Mathura
- Fatehpur Sikri
- Agra
- Benares
- Allahabad
- Patna
- Cambay
- Surat

Extension of the Mogul realm

Areas of the Great Mogul in 1556

Areas conquered till 1560

Annexations after 1560

Independent areas

5

2

1. Emperor Babur on his war-elephant during one of his campaigns. *See* **Babur.**
2. The harem quarter at the court of the Mogul emperor, from a 16th-century picture.
3. The Taj Mahal, a marble mausoleum built in the 17th century by the Emperor Shah Jahan in memory of his favorite wife. See Shah Jahan; Taj Mahal.
4. The expansion of the Mogul Empire in India during the 16th century.
5. A 16th-century miniature depicting women dancers and musicians at the Mogul court.

Mohács City in Hungary. Located on the Danube River, it was the site of a battle in which Louis II of Hungary was defeated by the Turks under Sulayman I in 1526. In 1687 the Turks were defeated at M. by an imperial army led by Charles V of Lorraine.

Molière, Jean Baptiste Poquelin (1622-1673) French playwright. His comedies mercilessly ridiculed hypocrisy and other human frailties, including religious hypocrisy (*Le Tartuffe*, 1664), antisocial behavior (*Le Misanthrope*, 1666), miserliness (*L'Avare*, 1668), and social pretentiousness (*Le Bourgeois Gentilhomme*, 1670). His troupe, under the patronage of Louis XIV, enjoyed continuous success, although M. always had to contend with critics who accused him of impiety.

Mollwitz City south of Breslau, Germany. There, in 1741, the Prussian army led by Frederick the Great defeated the Austrians under Neipperg during the First Silesian War.

Molotov, Vyacheslav Mikhailovich (1890-1986) Soviet political leader. A communist from 1906, he changed his name from Scriabin to M. (the hammer) to avoid arrest by imperial police. A hard line Stalinist, he served as foreign minister (1939-1949), during which time he negotiated the Molotov-Ribbentrop Pact. An opponent of Khrushchev, he was expelled from the Central Committee in 1957 and from the Communist Party sometime before 1964.

Molotov-Ribbentrop Pact (Hitler-Stalin Pact) Nonaggression treaty between the Soviet Union and Nazi Germany. Signed on August 23, 1939, by Soviet foreign minister Molotov and German foreign minister Ribbentrop, it freed Hitler to make war in the west. The treaty secretly partitioned Poland, which was invaded by the Nazis on September 1, 1939, precipitating World War II. The pact was broken by Hitler when he invaded the Soviet Union on June 22, 1941.

Moltke, Helmuth Johannes, Count von (1848-1916) German general. In 1906, M. succeeded Alfred von Schlieffen as chief of the German general staff. Immediately before the outbreak of the World War I, M. modified his predecessor's famous plan (*see* Schlieffen Plan). As a result, the Germans lost the first battle at the Marne and M. was immediately replaced as chief of staff. He was the nephew of Helmuth Karl von Moltke.

Helmuth Karl Moltke

Moltke, Helmuth Karl, Count von (1800-1891) Prussian field marshal. He became chief of the general staff of the Prussian army in 1858. M. worked tirelessly to make the Prussian army an efficient war machine. His organizational and tactical genius led to Prussian victories in the Danish War (1864), the Austro-Prussian War (1866), and the Franco-Prussian War (1870-1871). He was a presence in German politics as a member of the Reichstag from 1871 to 1891.

Monck, George, 1st Duke of Albemarle 1608-1670) English statesman, general, and admiral. Originally a

From the 4th century onwards, many Christians have felt the urge to abandon worldly matters and devote themselves completely to prayer. This urge led to the founding of monasteries, which in many cases became centers of religion, science, and power.

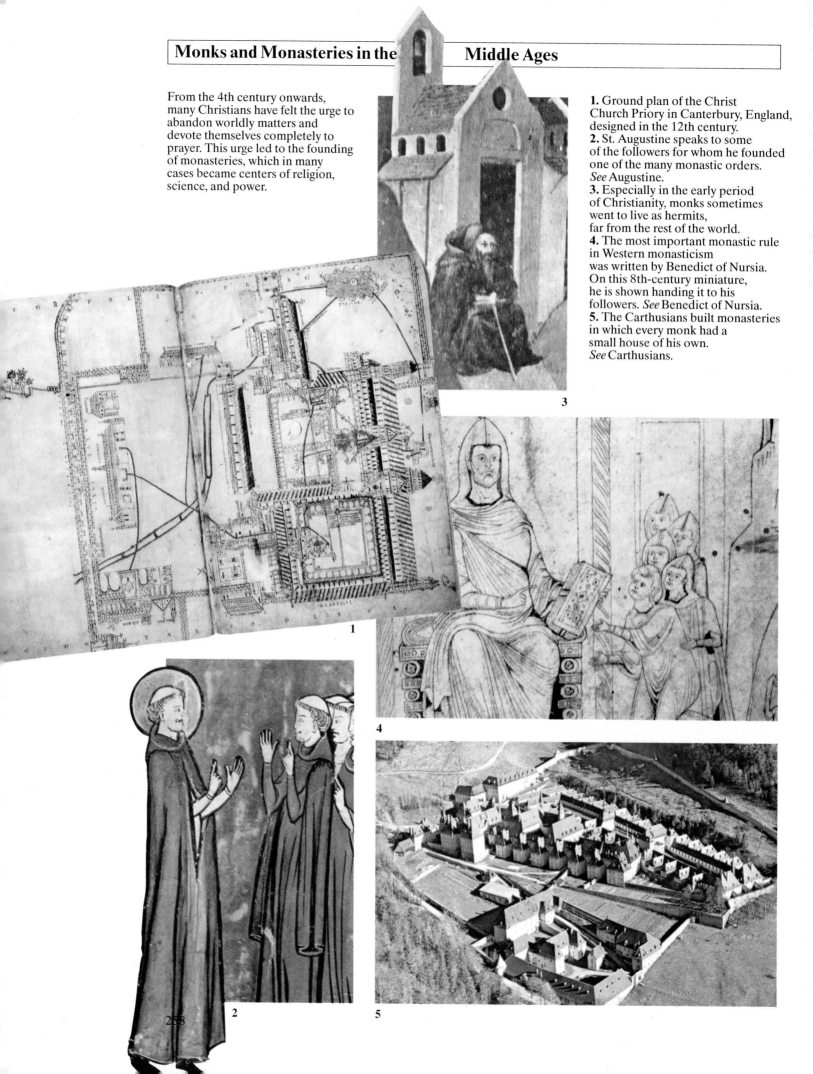

1. Ground plan of the Christ Church Priory in Canterbury, England, designed in the 12th century.
2. St. Augustine speaks to some of the followers for whom he founded one of the many monastic orders. *See* Augustine.
3. Especially in the early period of Christianity, monks sometimes went to live as hermits, far from the rest of the world.
4. The most important monastic rule in Western monasticism was written by Benedict of Nursia. On this 8th-century miniature, he is shown handing it to his followers. *See* Benedict of Nursia.
5. The Carthusians built monasteries in which every monk had a small house of his own. *See* Carthusians.

3

1

4

2

5

royalist, he joined Cromwell after the execution of Charles I. After Cromwell's death he invaded England, where he came into power and restored the Stuarts to the throne.

Mondriaan, Pieter Cornelis (1872-1944) Dutch painter. He started by painting naturalistic landscapes, progressed to expressionism, and ended by painting highly abstract works, mainly squares in the primary colors red, yellow, and blue. With Theo van Doesburg he founded the abstract art movement De Stijl (the Style).

Monet, Claude (1840-1926) French painter, the founder of Impressionism. One of his lifelong objectives was to portray the variations of light and atmosphere brought on by changes of hour and season. In hundreds of paintings he caught the flickering and fleeting effects of light by breaking it down into its color components much the way a prism does. He rejected the academic approach to landscape painting and allowed his vision to alter the real structures of his subjects. In doing so, he chose simple matter, making several series of studies of the same object over time. Among his most famous works are his large water-lily murals that were painted for the Musée de l'Orangerie in Paris.

Mongolians Equestrian people of east and southeast Asia. They conquered large parts of Europe in the Middle Ages (*see* Genghis Khan).

Monmouth, James Scott, Duke of (1649-1685) Pretender to the English throne. The illegitimate son of Charles II and his mistress, Lucy Walter, M. continually plotted against his father (*see* Shaftesbury) and later against James II. In 1685, shortly after James's accession to the throne, M. returned from exile and raised a small force in an effort to seize the crown. The nobles failed to rise in his favor. He was defeated at the battle at Sedgemoor and later beheaded for treason.

Monomotapa Kingdom in southern Africa. It flourished between the 12th and 16th centuries by trading gold with the Arabs and the Portuguese. M. was conquered by the Portuguese in the 17th century.

Monroe, James (1758-1831) 5th president of the U.S., 1817-1825. Born

James Monroe

in Virginia, M. was an aide to Washington, a member of the Continental Congress, a senator from Virginia, U.S. minister to France, Spain, and England, and governor of Virginia. He was Madison's secretary of state before being elected president in 1816. During M.'s presidency, the nation prospered economically and expanded westward. M. is remembered for the Monroe Doctrine (1823), which stated that the U.S. would not tolerate further colonization by Europeans in the Western Hemisphere.

Montagnards (Men of the Mountain) Nickname for the deputies of the extreme left in the National Convention during the French Revolution. They included the Jacobins, the Cordeliers, and the followers of Jacques Roux. They derived their name from the fact that their seats were the highest in the hall where the Convention met.

Montaigne, Michel Eyquem, Seigneur de (1533-1592) French essayist. He is considered one of the greatest masters of the essay as a literary form. The three volumes of his *Essais* reveal his judgments on a variety of subjects as well as a study of man and nature.

Montcalm, Louis Joseph de (1712-1759) French general who fought in the War of the Polish Succession and the War of the Austrian Succession. In 1756, M. became commander of the French troops in Canada during the French and Indian War. He defeated

the English at Ticonderoga on July 8, 1758, but he was killed in the defeat at Québec on the Plains of Abraham on September 13, 1759.

Monte Cassino Benedictine monastery south of Naples, Italy, founded by St. Benedict of Nursia c.529. During World War II German forces used the monastery, which is perched on a hill overlooking Cassino, as a fortress. Allied bombers destroyed most of the buildings trying to uproot the Germans. The monastery was rebuilt after the war.

Monteneros Small cavalry armies that served local lords in their struggle for the independence of Argentina (1816).

Montespan, Françoise, Marquise de (1641-1707) Mistress of King Louis XIV of France. A lady-in-waiting to Louis' wife, Queen Marie Thérèse, M. exerted a great deal of influence on the king and bore him seven children. In 1691 she retired to a convent.

Claudio Monteverdi

Monteverdi, Claudio (1567-1643) Italian composer. He is one of the great figures in the history of opera. His first opera, *Orfeo* (1607), was revolutionary in its dramatic power and expressive orchestral accompaniment. His succeeding works, culminating in the operas *Il ritorno di Ulisse in Patria* (1641) and *L'incoronazione di Poppea* (1642), showed marked development of characterization and emotional power. M. also wrote dramatic cantatas and secular madrigals.

Montezuma II (1480?-1520) Aztec emperor, c.1502-1520. The last Aztec ruler, M. received the Spanish conqueror Cortèz in 1519, but Cortèz took him hostage and attempted to govern through him. In 1520 the Aztecs rose against the Spanish, and M. was killed, although whether by the Spanish or the Aztecs is uncertain.

Montfort, Simon de (c.1160-1218) French knight who took part in the Fourth Crusade. M. later led the fight against the Albigenses from 1209. He died in 1218 during the siege of Toulouse, which he had received as a fief that same year.

Montfort, Simon de, Earl of Leicester (c.1208-1265) Son of Simon de Montfort. He acquired the earldom of Leicester and in 1238 married Eleonora, the sister of Henry III of England, with whom M. came into conflict. He defeated Henry III at Lewes in 1264 and ruled England as a virtual military dictator. He attempted to rally support at the Parliament of 1265, which included a cross-section of people from different segments of society, but he could not reach a legal settlement with the king, and the wars began again. At the Battle of Evesham (1265), M. had to concede the supremacy of Edward, who later became Edward I of England. M. was killed in battle.

Montgolfier, Joseph Michel (1740-1810) and **Jacques Étienne Montgolfier** (1745-1799) French inventors and brothers. Together they invented the first practical hot air balloon. They made their first flight in 1783.

Montgomery, Bernard Law, Viscount Montgomery of Alamein (1887-1976) British field marshal. M. became commander in chief of the British 8th Army in Africa in 1942 during World War II, driving General Rommel's Afrikakorps more than 2,000 miles from el-Alamein to Tunisia. He commanded British forces in Sicily and the Italian mainland in 1943 and in 1944 was made commander of all

Bernard Law Montgomery

Allied ground forces during the Normandy invasion. After the war, he headed British occupation forces in Germany and served (1946-1948) as chief of the imperial general staff.

Montmorency, Anne, Duke of (1493?-1567) Constable of France. His policy of pursuing peace with Holy Roman Emperor Charles V led to his falling out with King Francis I. Restored to favor under Henry II, he took Metz from the the Spanish in 1552. Although dismissed by Francis II, he was returned to office by Catherine de Medici and joined the Guises in the Wars of Religion. He died during the siege of St. Denis, near Paris.

Montmorency, Henri, Duke of (1595-1632) Admiral and marshal of France. The grandson of Anne, duke of Montmorency, he fought in the religious and foreign wars during the reign of Louis XIII. M. also fought against the Huguenots, but took part in a plot against Richelieu and was executed in 1632.

Montt Surname of three presidents of Chile. Manuel Montt (1809-1880) was president between 1851-1861. Jorge Montt (1846-1922), a distant relative, was president between 1891-1896. Pedro Montt (1848-1910), a son of Manuel Montt, was president between 1906-1910.

Moors Nomadic people of northern Africa, originally the inhabitants of Mauritania. Chiefly of Berber and Arab stock, they were converted to Islam in the 8th century and spread southwest into Africa and northwest into Spain. Moorish culture in southern Spain was centered in Cordoba, Seville, and Toledo. The M. were expelled or killed during the centuries of Christian reconquest, and were virtually exterminated in Spain during the Inquisition of the 16th century.

Moravian Empire Empire in central Europe (800s-900s) that included Moravia, Bohemia, Slovakia, Silesia, and parts of northern Hungary. The Greek monks Cyril (825-869) and Methodius (815-885) converted the population to Christianity in the 860s. The empire eventually collapsed under Magyar invasions during the 10th century.

More, Sir Thomas (Saint Thomas More) (1478-1535) English statesman, humanist, and Roman Catholic martyr and saint. His most important work is *Utopia* (1516), a picture of the ideal state founded entirely on reason. M. was a prominent figure in English government, becoming lord chancellor on the fall of Wolsey in 1529. He came into conflict with Henry VIII,

Sir Thomas More

however, who wanted to divorce Catherine of Aragón. M. then refused to recognize the Acts of Supremacy, which rejected the supremacy of pope and placed Henry at the head of the English church. M. was arrested for treason and beheaded in 1535. He was canonized in 1935 by Pope Pius XI.

Moreau, Jean Victor (1763-1813) French general during the French Revolutionary Wars. He commanded

Napoleon's forces in Germany after 1800 but gradually began to turn against the emperor. After a conflict concerning an alleged conspiracy against Napoleon, M. was exiled and settled in the U.S. He returned to Europe in 1813 to fight against Napoleon and was killed in the Battle of Dresden.

Moreno, Mariano (1778-1811) Argentine revolutionary. A champion of democracy, he participated in the uprising against the Spanish viceroy in Argentina. He became a member of a junta formed in 1810 in the wake of the revolution.

Jean Victor Moreau

Moriscos Moors who converted to Christianity after the Christian reconquest of Spain between the 15th and 17th centuries. Many secretly practiced Islam, and all were persecuted by the Inquisition. The M. arose in a rebellion between 1568 and 1571 that was put down by Philip II. In 1609, Philip III decreed their expulsion from Spain.

Mormonism (Church of Jesus Christ of Latter-Day Saints) Religion founded in America in the 1830s. Joseph Smith, the founder of M., claimed that the golden tablets containing the Book of Mormon, which recounts the early history of people in America starting in 600 BC, had been revealed to him at Palmyra, N.Y. Smith and his followers moved westward, and after having lived in a number of places, a group of Mormons under Brigham Young settled in what is now Utah.

Mornay, Philippe de, seigneur du Plessis-Marly (1549-1623) French Protestant leader and diplomat. He served under Coligny and the Henry of Navarre. Upon Henry's conversion to Catholicism, M. became leader of Huguenots. Louis XIII ousted him from positions of influence.

Morny, Charles Auguste, Duke of (1811-1865) French statesman. The illegitimate son of Hortense de Beauharnais, he was minister of the interior when he took part in organizing a coup d'etat (1851) that brought his half-brother, Napoleon III, to power.

Morocco Entente (Entente Cordiale) Secret treaty in which France and Spain partitioned Morocco and in which France agreed not to oppose British aims in Egypt in return for a free hand in Morocco. Because Germany had been excluded from the negotiations, Morocco became the focus of serious crises in 1905 and 1911.

Morosini, Francesco (1618-1694) Venetian statesman, doge of Venice, 1688-1694. He fought against the Turks in numerous wars and conquered the Peloponnesus in 1687. He became the doge of Venice in 1688 and fought his last war with the Turks in 1693.

Morse, Samuel Finley Breese (1791-1872) American inventor and artist. M. was one of the inventors of telegraphy and of a code (the Morse code) to transmit messages over wire. He demonstrated the practicality of the telegraph to Congress in 1844.

Mortimer, Roger de, 1st Earl of March (1287?-1330) English nobleman. He opposed King Edward II and was forced to flee to France in 1324. When Edward's queen, Isabella, came to France in 1325, she and M. became lovers. Together, they invaded England in 1326, forced Edward to abdicate, and had him murdered. Having secured the crown for the young Edward III, M. and Isabella virtually ruled England. In 1330 M. was seized by Edward III and executed as a traitor.

Moscow, grand duchy of State existing in central Russia from the late 14th to the mid-16th centuries, with the city of Moscow at its center. It gained gradual

Charles Auguste, Duke of Morny

ascendancy over other Russian principalities and over the Tatars of the Golden Horde. The grand duchy became the nucleus of the modern Russian state.

Samuel Finley Breese Morse

Moses (c.14th-13th century BC) Leader of the Israelites during their Exodus from Egypt, probably during the reign of Ramses II. He led his people to the edge Canaan and laid the foundations for a new state. The Bible is the source of information on

M.'s life, including his receiving of the Ten Commandments. M. is a central figure in Jewish religious tradition.

Moses

Mossadegh, Muhammad (c.1880-1967) Prime minister of Iran, 1951-1953. A nationalist, he fought Soviet and British interference in Iranian affairs. M. was highly popular, and the shah was forced to appoint him prime minister in 1951. M.'s oil nationalization plans and his refusal to negotiate with the British alienated him from the shah and the Iranian ruling class. In 1953, M.'s government was overthrown by the shah with secret help from the U.S. M. spent three years in prison and the rest of his life under house arrest.

Mountbatten, Louis, 1st Earl Mountbatten of Burma (1900-1979) British admiral and statesman. He was a great-grandson of Queen Victoria and uncle of Philip Mountbatten, duke of Edinburgh. In 1943, during World War II, M. was named head of South-

east Asia Command, where he commanded Allied operations against the Japanese in Burma. M. was the last British viceroy of India in 1947 and governor-general (1947-1948) of the dominion of India. He was killed in a terrorist bomb attack by the Irish Republican Army in 1979.

Mozarebs Christians of Muslim Spain. They continued practicing their faith during the Moorish occupation of Spain (718-1492) and had their own rulers, who were responsible to the Muslim emir or caliph. The Mozarebs were probably Arabic-speaking, and their culture was heavily influenced by Muslim civilization.

Mozart, Wolfgang Amadeus (1756-1791) Austrian composer. He is one of the greatest composers in the history of music. A prodigy who was taught by his father, Leopold, M. began composing before the age of five, and with his sister, played concerts for aristocrats of central Europe, Paris, and London. In 1771 he was appointed concertmaster to the archbishop of Salzburg, a position he held for six years before embarking on a concert tour in search of a better position. By 1782 he was living in Vienna and married to Constanze Weber, but a suitable position continued to elude him and he relied on teaching and concert

performances to support himself. In 1787, M. succeeded Gluck as the chamber musician and court composer to Joseph II, although at a salary lower than Gluck's. M. composed in virtually every genre, and his music combines emotional intensity with classical grace and technical perfection. The operas of his mature period include *Le Nozze di Figaro* (The Marriage of Figaro, 1786), *Don Giovanni* (1787), *Cosi fan tutte* (1790), and *Die Zauberflöte* (The Magic Flute, 1791). His 41 symphonies show a complete mastery of classical symphonic form and an intense personal emotion elevated to a universal plane. M. also composed concertos, sonatas, and chamber music. His last composition, a requiem, was not quite finished at the time of his death in 1791 at 35.

Mùawiyah (c.602-680) First Umayyad caliph, 661-680. He became caliph after Ali, nephew and son-in-law of Muhammad, was murdered. M. made Islam an autocracy and extended its territory in all directions, including to North Africa, finally leading to the downfall of the Byzantine Empire.

Mubarak, Muhammad Hosni Said (1928-) President of Egypt from 1981. M. was an officer in the air force and became chief-of-staff in 1969. In

Wolfgang Amadeus Mozart

Muhammad Ali

1975 he was appointed vice-president by Sadat. After Sadat's assassination in 1981, M. became president. He continued a policy of cautious democracy, economic liberalization, and peace with Israel. M.'s government faced a serious challenge from Islamic fundamentalists, who were increasingly repressed as their challenge increased.

Mudros, Armistice of (October 30, 1918) Pact that sealed the defeat of the Ottoman Turks in World War I, forcing them to yield vast territories, including Syria.

Mughal (Mogul) Muslim empire in India, 1526-1857. Founded by Babur, the Mughal empire implanted Persian culture in India and free of divisive battles for several centuries. The M. were eventually weakened by internal Hindu revolts, and their empire effectively ended when the British took control of India. Many administrative features of the M. were adopted by the British, but their most enduring impact was in art and architecture.

Muhammad (c.570-632) Prophet of Islam. A wealthy merchant, he felt chosen by God to be the Arab prophet of true religion. In the cave of Hira, near Mecca, he experienced a vision to preach. Throughout his life, he had revelations, which were written down and gathered in the Koran, the holy book of Islam. M. fled from Mecca in 622 (*see* Hegira) after the population opposed him. With the support of followers from Yathrib and Medina, M. conquered Mecca (*see* Badr) and entered the city in 630. At Medina he built his model theocratic state, and from there ruled his rapidly growing empire.

Muhammad II (Muhammad the Conqueror) (1429-1481) Ottoman sultan, 1451-1481. The son of Murad II, M. conquered Constantinople in 1453 and made it his capital, renaming it Istanbul. Because of his conquest of the Byzantine Empire and the Balkans, M. is regarded as the founder of the Ottoman Empire.

Muhammad V (1844-1918) Ottoman sultan, 1909-1918. He was proclaimed sultan by the Young Turk revolutionaries to replace his brother Abdul Hamaid II, but he did not have any actual power under the new constitution. During his reign, Turkey lost most of its remaining European possessions in the Balkan Wars (1912-1913). Turkey sided with the Central Powers in World War I. M. died shortly before the surrender.

Muhammad Ali (1769?-1849) Pasha of Egypt afer 1805. A common soldier at the start of his career, he rose to become pasha in Egypt. Although nominally under the Ottoman sultan, M. ruled Egypt with a free hand, modernizing the armed forces, building schools, and constructing public works. He exterminated the Mamelukes in 1811, conquered Sudan in 1820, and fought against the Turkish sultan with European support. The European powers, however, turned against him when he invaded Syria in 1839 and attacked the Ottoman sultan. In a compromise, M. withdrew in return for having the governorship of Egypt made hereditary in his line; *see* Ibrahim Pasha; Quadruple Alliance.

Muhammad Reza Pahlavi (1919-1980) Shah of Iran, 1941-1979. He succeeded his father, who was deposed by the British and Soviets for alleged collaboration with the Nazis. The shah attempted to Westernize the nation, developing its oil reserves and building it into a regional military power. His regime, however, was repressive, and in 1979 he was overthrown in an Islamic fundamentalist revolution. He died in exile the following year; *see* Khomeini.

Muhammad II

Mühlberg Town in eastern Germany. It was the site in 1547 of a battle in which the emperor Charles V defeated the Schmalkaldic League and captured the elector John Frederick I of Saxony.

Mukden (now Shen-yang) City in northeastern China. During the Russo-Japanese War of 1904-1905, it was an important military objective that fell to the Japanese on March 10, 1905. In 1931 it was the site of the so-called Mukden (Manchurian) Incident. An explosion on a railroad was used as a pretext by the Japanese to occupy all of Manchuria.

Mummius, Lucius (2nd century BC) Roman general and statesman. As consul, he fought against the Achaean League in 146, destroyed Corinth, and thereby ended Greek independence.

Joachim Murat

Münchhausen, Hieronymus Freiherr von (1720-1797) German officer. He was an inspired storyteller of ridiculous tales that were collected by Rudolf Raspe in 1785. They eventually became world famous.

Munda City in Spain near Córdoba. Caesar defeated the sons of Pompey at M. in 45 BC, thereby ending the second civil war.

Munich Pact (1938) Agreement between Chamberlain (Great Britain), Daladier (France), Mussolini (Italy) and Hitler (Germany) in which Hitler's claims on the Sudentenland region of Czechoslovakia were recognized. By appeasing Hitler, the British and French hoped to avoid war. The Munich Pact, however, failed to secure peace and has come to stand for appeasement.

Münster, Treaty of (1648) Part of the Peace of Westphalia (also known as the Peace of Osnabrück). It was a treaty between Spain and the Netherlands recognizing the independence of the Netherlands and ending the Thirty Years War.

Münster Empire (1534-1535) Theocratic community founded in 1534 by Anabaptists under Jan van Leyden in Münster, Germany. They believed in communal property and polygamy. During their time in power, general lawlessness prevailed throughout the city. The previous civil authority overthrew the Anabaptists in 1535 and then tortured and executed most of them.

Münzer, Thomas (c.1489-1525) German Protestant reformer. A radical, he led the peasants' revolt in Thuringia, which was condemned by Luther. When the peasants were defeated, M. was beheaded.

Murad II (1403-1451) Ottoman sultan, 1421-1451. The son and successor of Muhammad I, he waged war against the Venetians and later against the Poles and Hungarians, inflicting a crushing defeat on them at Varna in 1444. During his reign the arts and sciences flourished.

Murat, Joachim (1767-1815) French marshal and king of Naples, 1808-1815. A general who served under Napoleon, he married Napoleon's sister Caroline in 1808 and succeeded Joseph Bonaparte as king of Naples the same year. After Napoleon's fall he fled to Corsica. In an attempt to regain his throne in Naples, he was arrested and executed.

Muromachi Period (Ashikaga Period) Period of civil unrest in Japan between 1338-1573. It started when Ashikaga Takauji (1305-1358) founded a shogunate in Muromachi and rebelled against the emperor. The Ashikaga dynasty was eventually brought down by Oda Nobunaga.

Murray (Moray), James Stuart, 1st Earl of (1531?-1570) Scottish nobleman. An illegitimate son of James V of Scotland and a Protestant, he was at first an ally of his half-sister, Mary Queen of Scots. He turned against her after her marriage to Darnley in 1565 and plotted in the assassination of Rizzio in 1566. After her abdication (1567), he became the regent of the young James VI and worked tirelessly to perpetuate Mary's incarceration in England. M. was murdered in 1570 by a member of the Hamilton family.

Mursa, Battle of (351) Site of a bloody battle between the Roman emperor Constantine II and the usurper Magentius, who was defeated.

Murshilish I Hittite King, c.1620-1590 BC. He conquered Babylon and thereby ended the rule of the house of Hammurabi.

Murshilish II Hittite King, c.1346-1320 BC. He successfully opposed the Egyptians' attempt to recover their lost territory in Syria.

Murten Town in Switzerland. It is known mainly as the scene of the defeat (1476) of Charles the Bold of Burgundy by the Swiss.

Muslim Brotherhood Islamic organization founded in 1928 by Hasan al-Banah, an Egyptian. Its aim was to establish an Islamic state. In 1948, the M. was banned in Egypt and violently repressed after 1954. A faction of the M. was responsible for the murder of

Murad II

President Sadat of Egypt in 1981. During the 1980s the organization became influential throughout the Middle East and North Africa.

Mussert, Anton (1894-1946) Dutch Nazi. He was the leader of the National Socialist movement in the Netherlands and headed the puppet government after the German invasion in 1940. M. was executed in 1946.

Mussolini, Benito (1883-1945) Italian dictator and leader of the Fascist movement. He started his career as a Socialist journalist but soon came to espouse an authoritarian nationalism. After marching on Rome with his followers (1922), he was asked to form a government. Once in power, M. transformed the regime into a dictatorship. Driven by the desire to restore an Italian empire, M. allied himself with Hitler in the late 1930s. Entering World War II in 1940, M.'s military soon became bogged down in North Africa and Greece and was rescued

Benito Mussolini

from defeat by German intervention. By 1943, M., now completely under German domination, was dismissed by the Fascist grand council and arrested. Two months later he was rescued spectacularly by a group of German commandos and put in charge of a puppet regime in northern Italy. In the closing days of the war he was captured by Italian partisans and executed. His body was hung in a public square in Milan, where it was reviled.

Mussorgsky, Modest Petrovich (1839-1881) Russian composer. He was one

Modest Petrovich Mussorgsky

of the first Russian composers to promote a national style that made significant use of Russian folk songs and texts. His works include the operas *Boris Godonov* (1868-1872) and *Khovanshchina* (1886) and the piano suite *Pictures at an Exhibition* (1874). Much of his music was edited and revised after his death by Nicolai Rimsky-Korsakov and others, often to such an extent that the originals were misrepresented.

Mutina (Modena) Battle site in northern Italy. Marcus Antonius was defeated at M. in 43 BC by Octavius's army, commanded by Hirtius and Pansa.

Mutsuhito (reign name Meiji) (1852-1912) Emperor of Japan, 1867-1912. He succeeded the last Tukugawa shogun and turned Japan into a modern state. He was succeeded by his son Yoshihito.

My Lai Incident Massacre of 347 Vietnamese civilians by U.S. soldiers in 1968. The event aroused widespread controversy and contributed to the disillusion over the war in the United States.

Mycale Promontory, opposite the island of Samos in Asia Minor. The Persian fleet was destroyed there by the Greeks in 479 BC.

Mycenaean Culture Ancient Aegean civilization (c.2800-1100 BC), named after the city of Mycenae. Its sites were first unearthed by Heinrich Schliemann after 1876. The civilization is characterized by huge fortified palaces, the use of chariots, and a script known as Linear B. It was destroyed by the Dorians in c.1100 BC.

Mycerinus (Menkaure) Egyptian King who reigned during the Fourth Dynasty (26th century BC). Said to have been a just ruler, he built the smallest pyramid at Giza.

Mylae City on the northeastern coast of Sicily. There the Roman fleet commanded by Gaius Duilius defeated a Carthaginian fleet in 260 BC during the First Punic War.

Myriokephalum, Battle of (1176) Battle in which Manuel I Comnenus was defeated by the Turks from Anatolia.

Nabataeans Ancient people of the Middle East who from their capital of Petra (in present-day Jordan) controlled the caravan trade in northern Arabia. They later became allies of the Romans and in 106 AD were annexed by Trajan.

Nabis (d.192 BC) King of Sparta from 207. He systematically extended his power over the Peloponnesians but was defeated in 194 by Philopoemen. In 192, N. was assassinated by the Aetolian Greeks.

Nabo Popular Assyrian and Aramean god. He was the patron of writers and the god of vegetation.

Nabonassar King of Babylonia, 747-743 BC. As a vassal of the Assyrian king Tiglathpileser III, N. fought against the Arameans and the Chaldaeans.

Nabonidus The fifth and last king of the Chaldaean dynasty of Babylonia (New Babylonian Empire), 556-538 BC. He lost his kingdom to the Persians under Cyrus.

Nabopolassar King of Babylonia, 626-605 BC, and founder of the New Babylonian Empire. N. fought against the Assyrians until Babylonia became independent in c.620. He was succeeded by his son, Nebuchadnezzar, in 605 BC.

Nabor and Felix Two brothers from Africa who served in Maximian's army and who were beheaded in 304 because they refused to serve at Lodi. Their heads were found in Namen in 1959 and were brought to Milan.

Nadir Shah (1688-1747) Shah of Iran, 1736-1747. He was a powerful ruler who successfully fought against the Turks and the Mughal emperors in India, leading to his conquest of Delhi (1739). N. was assassinated by his own officers during a campaign against the Kurds.

Nadjibullah, Mohammed (1947-) President of Afghanistan, 1987-1992. He joined the Communist Party in 1965 and became a member of the politburo in 1979, following the Russian invasion of Afghanistan. In 1987 he became president. After the Russians left in 1989, N. remained in power but resigned in 1992.

Nag Hammadi Site in Egypt where thirteen Coptic books (4th century) were found in 1945. They provide an insight into the spiritual movements of the time (for example, Platonism) that were condemned by the church as being heretical.

Imre Nagy

Nagada Site north of Luxor, Egypt. It is famous for its prehistoric burial sites (c.4000-3000 BC). The dead were found buried on their sides with knees and arms raised in front of their faces. The bodies pointed to the west, where people of the time thought the underworld was located.

Nagano, Osami (1880-1947) Japanese admiral. He commanded Japanese fleet operations at Pearl Harbor during World War II. In 1946, he was arrested as a war criminal but died during his trial.

Nagasaki City on the island of Kyushu, Japan. Its port was the first to receive Western traders, first the Portuguese and Spanish, then the Dutch in 1567. On August 9, 1945, during World War II, N. was the target of the second American atomic bombing of Japan. About 75,000 people were killed or wounded. The city has since been completely rebuilt.

Naguib, Mohammed (1901-1984) Egyptian general and statesman. He served in the Egyptian army during the 1948 war against Israel. In 1952, he led a coup that overthrew King Farouk. N. declared an independent republic in 1953 with himself as president, but the following year he was ousted by Nasser.

Nagy, Imre (1895?-1958) Hungarian communist leader. He served in several government posts in postwar Hungary before becoming premier in 1953. A reformer, he became increasingly critical of Soviet influence in Hungarian affairs. Under pressure from Moscow, he was removed (1955) as premier and expelled from the party. After the 1956 Hungarian revolution, N. was recalled as premier of the new government. After the Soviets crushed the revolt, he was arrested and turned over the new Hungarian regime, which tried and executed him secretly in 1958. On June 16, 1989, as communism collapsed in Eastern Europe, N. was reburied in a state ceremony in Budapest.

Nahas Pasha, Mustafa al- (1876-1965) Egyptian statesman. He was leader of the Wafd Party (1927-1952) and was prime minister five times between 1928 and 1951. When King Farouk was overthrown in 1952, N. supported the new regime, but he was forced to disband the Wafd Party and was arrested in 1953. Released in 1954, he spent the rest of his life in retirement.

Najaf City in Iraq. Founded in 791 by Haruen ar-Rasjid, it is the most important center of the Shiite Muslims of Iraq.

Nakasone, Yasuhiro (1918-) Prime minister of Japan, 1982-1987. He served as secretary-general and leader

Yasuhiro Nakasone

of the Liberal Democratic Party. He resigned as prime minister in 1987 because of unpopular tax and defense policies.

Nakbe Site in Guatemala. It is the location of one of the oldest Mayan shrines (c.600-400 BC), which was discovered in 1930.

Nam Viet Ancient kingdom in northern Vietnam. A part of China from 207 BC, it was sinicized by the Han emperor Woe Ti in 111 BC. Between AD 939-954 it was briefly an independent kingdom that was later called Vietnam.

Nana Sahib (c.1821-1859) Leader during the Indian Mutiny (1857). After the outbreak of the mutiny at Kanpur, he and his men massacred the British garrison and colony. After the rebellion was suppressed, he fled to Nepal.

Nancy City in northeastern France, in Lorraine. It was near Nancy, in 1477, that the army of René II of Lorraine defeated the Burgundians under Charles the Bold, who died in the battle.

Nanda Dynasty Royal house of northern India that ruled Magadha between c.343-321 BC and directly preceded the Maurya Empire.

Nanking, Treaty of Pact that ended the Opium War (1842) between Great Britain and China. Under its terms, Hong Kong was surrendered to the British.

Nanna *See* Shamash.

Nansen, Fridtjof (1861-1930) Norwegian arctic explorer, statesman, and humanitarian. In 1893, he departed with the ship Fram in an attempt to reach the North Pole. Although he never reached the Pole, his expedition gave the world valuable new information about the Arctic Ocean. N. worked for the peaceful separation of Norway and Sweden and served the Norwegian ambassador to Great Britain (1906-1908). After World War I, N. helped famine-stricken Russia as well as the Armenians who had been driven out of Turkey. He was made

League of Nations high commissioner for refugees in 1921, and in 1922 won the Nobel Peace Prize.

Napata Ancient city of Nubia. Between c.750-590 BC, it was the capital of the Ethiopian Cushite Empire, which was situated in present-day Sudan.

Naphtali *See* Israel, Tribes of.

Napier, John (1550-1617) Scottish mathematician. He invented logarithms and published the first logarithmic tables.

Napoleon I (Napoleon Bonaparte) (1769-1821) Emperor of the French. N. first played a role in France after 1793, commanding the army of the interior and then conducting victorious campaigns in Italy. From 1798-1799, he led a campaign in Egypt. On 18 Brumaire (November 9-10, 1799) N. led a coup d'état that led to the fall of the Directory. From 1800, his armies triumphantly swept through Europe (Marengo, Austerlitz, Jena, Frideland, Wagram) and reorganized the political landscape of the continent. In 1804, N. installed himself as Emperor of the French. Under his rule, France became a highly centralized state. In addition, he reformed the law and the tax system. In 1812, N. invaded Russia, but despite significant successes, the campaign failed. He was defeated in 1813 in the Battle of the Nations at Leipzig and abdicated in 1814. After banishment to the

Title page of John Napier

Napoleon I (Bonaparte)

island of Elba, N. returned to France in 1815 (*see* Hundred Days). At Waterloo, he was finally defeated. N. was banished to St. Helena, in the South Atlantic, where he died in 1821.

Napoleon III (1808-1873) Emperor of the French, 1852-1870. Born Charles Louis Napoleon Bonaparte, he was the son of Louis Napoleon,

Fridtjof Nansen

brother of Napoleon I, and Hortense de Beauharnais. In 1836 and 1840, N. made two half-hearted attempts to carry out a coup d'état and was forced into brief exile in the U.S. after the second attempt. In 1848, following the revolutions that swept Europe, he was elected president of the Second Republic. In 1852 N. staged a plebiscite that created the Second Empire, with himself as Napoleon III. (The title "Napoleon II" had been carried by the son of Napoleon I, who died at the age of 21 in 1832.) N. exercised dictatorial powers in the early years of his reign. France prospered at home, and N.'s early foreign ventures were successful. By the 1860s, however, he suffered setbacks in his foreign policy in Italy, Mexico, and in Poland. Within Europe, Bismarck in Germany became his greatest opponent, and it was he who goaded N. into the disastrous Franco-Prussian War (1870-1871) in which France was defeated and N. taken prisoner at Sedan. He was released after the armistice and spent his final years in exile in England.

Naqsh-e-Rostam Burial site near the ruins of Persepolis, Iran. The graves of Darius I, Xerxes I, Artaxerxes I, and Xerxes II were found there.

Nara Period Period in Japanese history between 710-784. It was named after the city of Nara, which was the first imperial residence. Eight successive emperors ruled from Nara, and during this period, Buddhism flourished in Japan.

Naram-sin King of Akkad in Mesopotamia (c.2250 BC). He rebuilt the empire founded by his grandfather, Sargon I. The empire collapsed, however, soon after N.'s death.

Naranthihapate *See* Ngasaunggyan.

Narbonensis Roman province that comprised southeastern France. It was conquered quickly by the Romans following a campaign to liberate Massilia (Marseilles) from the Celts.

Narcissus (d.54 AD) Former slave who became secretary to the Roman emperor Claudius I. He had great influence on Claudius, revealing the intrigues of Messalina and expediting her death. His influence waned and after Claudius's death, and he committed suicide.

Naresuan (1555-1605) Thai national hero. As king, he liberated Thailand from its Burmese oppressors.

Narino, Antonio (1765-1823) Colombian revolutionary. He was one of the first to lead an uprising against the Spanish. Imprisoned from 1814 until 1820, he returned to help Bolivar and was briefly (1821) a vice president of Greater Colombia.

Narodniki Russian populists, an agrarian-socialist movement founded in the 1860s. They attempted to adapt socialist theory to Russian conditions. The N. were brutally repressed by the police, and a radical wing of the movement carried out the assassination of Czar Alexander II in 1881. In later years, the N. merged with the newly founded Social Revolutionary Party (1902).

Narragansett Early Native American people of North America. They lived in what is now the state of Rhode Island and in 1636 sold Roger Williams land on which to settle. The N. participated in King Philip's War against the colonists (1675). That conflict destroyed Indian power in southern New England. The surviving N. scattered northward to Canada and to the west.

Narses (c.480-574) Byzantine general under Emperor Justinian I, one of the eunuchs of the palace. He fought with Belisarius against the Ostrogoths in Italy and subjected the country (553-554) only after Belisarius had fallen from grace. He was subsequently appointed exarch of Italy, however his administration was unpopular, and he was dismissed in 567.

Narva City in Estonia, to the west of St. Petersburg, Russia. There, in 1700, King Charles XII of Sweden defeated the army of Peter the Great in the first great battle of the Northern War (1700-1721).

Narváez, Pánfilo de (c.1470-1528) Spanish conquistador. In the service of Velázquez, he led (1520) an unsuccessful expedition against Cortéz in Mexico. He died (1528) in Cabeza de Vaca's ill-fated mission in what is now Texas.

Narváez, Ramón Maria, Duke of Valencia (c.1800-1868) Spanish

general and statesman. He put down several Carlist uprisings. N. held the premiership, with only brief interruptions, from 1844 to 1851.

Naseby Site in England where, in June 1645, the largest battle of the English Civil War took place. King Charles I was finally defeated there by Cromwell.

Nashville, Battle of (1864) Decisive Union victory during the American Civil War. Confederate forces under J.B. Hood were defeated by a Union force commanded by G.H. Thomas.

Nasmyth, James (1808-1890) British engineer. He invented the steam hammer and built more than 100 steam locomotives.

James Nasmyth

Nasrad-Din (1831-1896) Shah of Persia, 1848-1896. He took the first steps toward westernizing Persia.

Nasrides Last Moorish royal house that ruled from its base in Granada in southern Spain.

Nasser, Gamal Abdal (1918-1970) President of Egypt, 1956-1970. An army officer, he instigated the coup d'état by Naguib (1952) that overthrew King Farouk. N. became prime minister in 1954 and president in

Napoleon

This French officer of Corsican birth became a living legend in the chaotic days after the French Revolution. A brilliant general, he became the leader of France in a 1799 coup and then conquered large parts of Europe. In 1804, Napoleon declared himself emperor of France. After years of glorious conquest, he was defeated and exiled to Elba in 1814. In 1815, Napoleon made a dramatic return, only to be defeated at Waterloo and exiled once again, this time to St. Helena, where he died in 1821.

1. Napoleon in battle. *See* Napoleon I; Waterloo.
2. Napoleon created a new law code for France, the Code of Napoleon, which remains the basis of French law today. *See* Code of Napoleon.
3. The map of Europe during the rule of Napoleon.
4. Napoleon attempted to conquer Russia, invading it with a huge army in 1812. After occupying Moscow, however, he was forced to retreat, and his army was virtually destroyed, in part because of the severe Russian winter.
5. A defeated and disillusioned Napoleon, just before his banishment to St. Helena in 1815. *See* St. Helena.

1956. His nationalization of the Suez Canal (1956) precipitated the short-lived, abortive Anglo-French invasion. After a war with Israel in 1956, Egypt joined with Syria to form the United Arab Republic (1958-1961), which N. headed. He provoked the disastrous 1967 war with Israel, which led to the Israeli occupation of the Sinai. N. resigned but was quickly "recalled" to power by massive demonstrations in his favor. The completion of the Aswan Dam in 1970 was the crowning achievement of his rule.

Gamal Abdal Nasser

Natchez Native American people of North America. Located in what is now in Mississippi, they were defeated and scattered in three wars with the French and the Choctaw Indians (1716, 1723 and 1729).

Nation, Carry (1846-1911) American temperance activist. She drew attention to her campaign against alcohol abuse by attacking saloons with her hatchet.

National Association for the Advancement of Colored People (NAACP) Civil rights organization in the U.S. Founded in 1908, the NAACP is the nation's oldest civil rights group. It was instrumental in the 1954 Supreme Court case that outlawed segregation.

National Organization for Women (NOW) Group formed in 1966 to promote equality for women in the U.S. Its founder was the feminist leader Betty Friedan. NOW seeks to advance its agenda through public relations, legislative lobbying, and litigation.

National Party South African political party, founded in 1914. Its leaders, and particularly Prime Minister Hendrik Verwoerd, advanced and implemented the policy of apartheid. The party did not renounce apartheid until the 1990s, when F.W. De Klerk was president.

National Urban League Voluntary community service agency founded in the U.S. in 1910. Its goal is to help end racial discrimination and to alleviate poverty through direct assistance.

National Socialism (Nazism) Doctrines and policies of the National Socialist German Workers' (Nazi) Party. Its leader, Adolf Hitler, ruled Germany from 1933 to 1945. Nazi racist ideology was primarily anti-Semitic. Vague and mystical, it was not a system of well-defined principles but a glorification of prejudice and of the leader (Führer). The party was founded in the Bavaria in the aftermath of World War I by Gottfried Feder. It was soon taken over, however, by Hitler, who made it an instrument of his quest for power.

NATO *See* North Atlantic Treaty Organization.

Natya-sastra Oldest theoretical manual on theater and dance in India, dating from between 350 and 150 BC.

Naukratis Ancient Greek trading colony in Egypt. Located in the western part of the Nile delta, it was founded by Miletus in the 7th century BC. Until the founding of Alexandria, N. was the center for the exchange of goods and culture between Greece and Egypt.

Naumann, Friedrich (1860-1919) German political leader. A founder of the German Democratic Party in 1918, N. was one of the authors of the Weimar constitution.

Nautilus Name of the first metal submarine, built by Fulton in 1800.

Nautilus First nuclear-powered submarine, launched by the U.S. in 1954. In the first journey of its kind, the N. reached the North Pole on August 3, 1958, by traveling under the polar ice.

Navana Area in northwest Spain. It was ruled from 1234 by French dynasties. In 1512, the Spanish part of N. was occupied by Ferdinand of Aragón.

Navarino City in Greece. It was the site of a sea battle in 1827 in which British, French, and Russian forces destroyed an Egyptian fleet commanded by Ibrahim Pasha during the Greek War of Independence.

Navas de Tolosa, Las Village in southern Spain. The Almohaden were defeated there in 1212 by an army from Castille, León, Aragón, Navarre, and Portugal.

Návplion Town in Greece. Located on the Gulf of Argolis, it was captured by the Greeks from the Turks in 1822 and was briefly (1830-1834) the first capital of independent Greece.

Naxos Ancient Greek colony in Sicily. Founded in 734 BC., N. was an ally of Athens against the Persians, but it was captured and destroyed in 403 BC by Dionysius I of Syracusa.

Nazarite In the Old Testament, a holy hermit who took a vow not to cut his hair and to abstain from wine.

Nazca culture Indian culture in the Nazca valley of southern Peru. It flourished in the first millennium AD. N. is well-known for its unique ceramics and textiles.

Nazism *See* National Socialism.

Neanderthal people Early form of humans (Homo sapiens). They lived

Neanderthal people

in the last glacial age between 100,000 and 40,000 years ago. Their remains were discovered in 1856 in Neanderthal, a valley in western Germany. Later, remains were also found in, among other places, Central and Southern Europe and South Africa. Neanderthal people used stones and fire and sometimes inhabited caves. The classic Neanderthal look is a large, thick skull with heavy brow ridges and a chinless jaw.

Near East Term meaning the Middle East.

Nearchus (d.312 BC) Macedonian general. A friend of Alexander the Great, he led the Macedonian fleet from the Indus to the Persian Gulf. In doing so he was the first to discover the sea route between the Indian subcontinent and the West.

Nebuchadnezzar II (c.630-562 BC) Second king of the New Babylonian Empire, c.605-562 BC. The son of

Nebuchadnezzar II

Nabopolassar, he defeated the Egyptian army under Pharaoh Necho II at Carchemish. N. expanded his sphere of influence into Syria and Palestine and in 597 besieged Jerusalem, sending the Judaean king Johoiakim and a group of supporters into exile. In 567, he recaptured the city and took all the remaining inhabitants with him to Babylonia (*see* Babylonian Exile). N. is known for his great building projects. Babylon, with its hanging gardens, was the greatest city of the ancient world.

Nechayev, Sergey Gennadiyevich (1847-1882) Russian revolutionary. He believed that deceit and murder were permissible in order to achieve a political goal. After the murder of one of his followers (1869), he was imprisoned in St. Petersburg.

Necho II Egyptian king of the 26th Dynasty. He reigned from 610-595 BC. N. lost the battle of Carchemish in 605 to Nebuchadnezzar II, thus ending his dreams of conquest. N. attempted to have a canal built from the Nile to the Red Sea. During his reign, Phoenician seafarers under his direction were said to have sailed around Africa.

Nectanebo I King of Egypt from 380-362 BC. Founder of the 30th Dynasty and a great builder, he saved Egypt from a Persian invasion in 373 BC.

Nederburgh, Sebastiaan Cornelis (1762-1811) Dutch conservative politician. His Charter of 1801 became the basis for Dutch colonial policy after the Dutch East India Company was taken over by the government.

Neerwinden Village in eastern Belgium. It was the site of several battles. On July 29, 1693, William III of England and Eugene of Savoy were defeated by the French during King William's War. In the French Revolutionary Wars, the Austrians defeated the French at N. on March 18, 1793.

Nefertiti (c.1372-1350 BC) Queen of ancient Egypt. She was the wife of King Achnaton (18th Dynasty). The limestone bust of Nefertiti in the Berlin Museum has given rise to the legend that she was one of the most beautiful women in the ancient world.

Negrin, Juan (1894-1956) Prime minister of Spain, 1937-1939. A Socialist, he served during the Spanish Civil War. With Franco's victory, he fled abroad, spending the remainder of his life in France and England.

Nehalennia Germanic mother goddess of prosperity. She was worshiped primarily in the Rhineland around 200 AD. In 1970, more than one hundred altars and images devoted to her worship were discovered in the Netherlands.

Nehawend City in central Iran. There,

Caliph Omar defeated the Sassanid peoples in the late 600s.

Nehru, Jawaharlal (1889-1964) Prime minister of India, 1947-1974. A prominent aide to Gandhi and a member of the Congress Party in British India, N. was imprisoned several times in his struggle for Indian independence. In 1947, he became India's first prime minister. N. was a major advocate of neutralism in foreign policy, although he was willing to tilt toward the West or toward the Soviet Union depending on his interpretation of Indian interests. He used force in Kashmir and to seize the Portuguese colony of Goa. His daughter, Indira Gandhi, became prime minister of India in 1966.

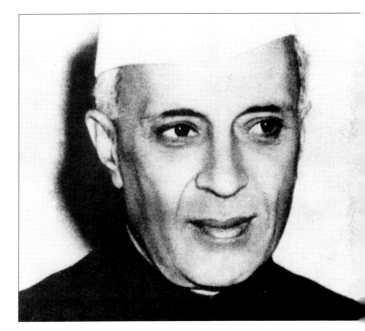

Jawaharlal Nehru

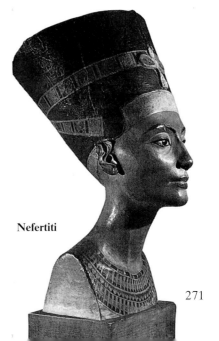

Nefertiti

271

Neipperg, Adam, Duke of (1775-1829) Austrian general and diplomat. In 1814, N. was appointed guard to Napoleon's wife, Marie Louise, whom he accompanied to Parma in 1821 and subsequently married after Napoleon's death.

Nekhbet Ancient Egyptian vulture god who protected Upper Egypt and the rulers of that kingdom. Its center of worship was at El-Kab.

Nelson, Horatio (1758-1805) British admiral. He played an important role in the war with France after 1793 and

Horatio Nelson

in 1797 defeated the Spanish fleet at Cape St. Vincent. He then went on to destroy the French expeditionary fleet at Aboukir Bay (1798), stranding Napoleon and the entire French army in Egypt. His most famous victory was against the French fleet at Trafalgar (1805). N. died during the battle.

Nemea City in ancient in Greece. It was the site of the Nemean games, which from 573 BC were one of the four Panhellenic festivals.

Nemea, Battle of (394 BC) Battle that took place during the Corinthian War, when the alliance of states under Athens were defeated by Sparta.

Nemesis Greek goddess. She was the personification of justified revenge.

Neo-Confucianism Official state philosophy during the Tokugawa period in Japan (1603-1867). N. stated that social order on earth was predetermined and approved by the heavenly powers.

Nepomucen, John (St. John of Nepomuk) (c.1350-1393) Patron saint of Bohemia. A monk, N. came into conflict with King Wenceslas IV of Bohemia when the king attempted to restrict the power of the church. Wenceslas had him thrown from a bridge into the Moldau River. N. was later canonized as a martyr of the church.

Nepos, Julius (d.480) Roman emperor of the West, 474-480. He was deposed by Orestes, who raised his own son to the throne in 475. N., however, continued to be recognized in the East and in Gaul as emperor of the West until his death in 480.

Neptune See Poseidon.

Nerchinsk, Treaty of (1689) Pact that ended the territorial war on the eastern border between Russia and China. It was the first treaty concluded between China and a European power.

Nero (Nero Claudius Caesar) (37-68 AD) Roman emperor, 54-68 AD. His mother had him adopted by Claudius, her third husband, and N. subsequently married Claudius's daughter Octavia. After the death of Claudius, N. became emperor and had his mother (59), wife (62), and many courtiers killed. The fire of Rome (64) was followed by persecution of the Christians, who were blamed by N. for the blaze. In 68 AD, N. committed suicide after being confronted with a revolt in the military. He was the last Roman emperor from the family of Julius Caesar.

Nerthus According to Tacitus, the German goddess of the earth (Terra Mater).

Ness, Eliot (1903-1957) American F.B.I. agent who, with a small group of colleagues (known as the Untouchables), fought organized crime and eventually managed to have Al Capone imprisoned.

Neto, Agostinho (1922-1979) Angolan poet and politician. In 1962, he became chairman of the Popular Movement for the Liberation of Angola (MPLA) and in 1975 president of Angola.

Neuilly, Treaty of (1919) Pact between Bulgaria and the Allies at the end of World War I. Bulgaria was required to cede some of its border areas to Greece, Yugoslavia, and Rumania, and to pay reparations.

Neustria Western part of the kingdom of the Franks from the 6th through the 8th centuries, under the Merovingians. Its principle towns were Soissons and Paris.

Neutrality Acts Series of laws passed by the U.S. Congress between 1935 and 1939 designed to keep the U.S. neutral in foreign affairs. The acts were replaced by the Lend-Lease Act in 1941.

Neva, Battle of (1240) Battle won by Novgorod against the Swedes, who had invaded northwestern Russia.

Neville's Cross, Battle of (1346) English victory over the Scots under David II. The Scottish king supported the French and wanted to force Edward III of England to give up his siege of Calais. After the battle, David was imprisoned until 1357.

New Deal Reform program of President Franklin D. Roosevelt to relieve the effects of the Great Depression and stimulate economic recovery. Enacted mainly between 1933 and 1939, its major legislative accomplishments included the National Recovery Act (NRA), the Agricultural Adjustment Act (AAA), the Civilian Conservation Corps (CCC), the

Nero

New Frontiers: The Early Days of Colonialism

In Europe, beginning in the middle of the 15th century, the desire for more profitable trade, the wish to spread the Christian faith, the thirst for new knowledge, and the yearning for adventure led to a great age of exploration and the founding of overseas colonies.
Spain and Portugal took the lead, but soon they were followed by other European powers in establishing great colonial empires.

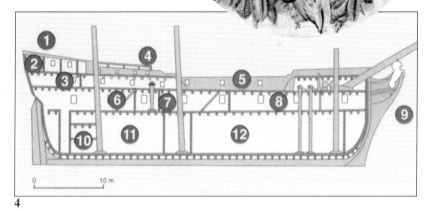

1. The coat of arms of the Dutch East India Company, the large colonial trading company founded in 1602.
2. A portrait of Vasco da Gama, the Portuguese explorer who was the first to sail from Europe to India. *See* Gama, Vasco da.
3. View of Calcutta, India, from 1788, showing palaces of rich western merchants and an English trading ship.

4. A cross-section of a ship equipped for voyages from Europe to the East Indies: *1.* Poop with henhouses; *2.* Captain's and officers' huts; *3.* Saloon, sheep pen and officers' and passengers' toilets; *4.* Canopy; *5.* Well deck with pigsties; *6.* Hand operated fan; *7.* Caboose; *8.* Main gun deck and crew's quarters; *9.* Galleon and crew's toilet; *10.* Powder magazine; *11.* Storage room for water and food; *12.* Cargo hold.
5. While looking for trade and new lands, the European explorers met many native peoples. This is a 16th-century drawing of a South American tribe.
6. Chinese porcelain carried by European East India Companies, 1777-1778.

Civil Works Administration (CWA), the Securities and Exchange Commission (SEC), and the Social Security Act.

New Empire Period in Egyptian history between c.1550-1075 BC. The empire was united under King Amasis I, who ousted the Hyksos. The city of Thebes and its god Amon were prominent. The N. was characterized by an aggressive foreign policy, with expansion into Asia under Tutmoses III and Amonhotep II. After Achnaton, more traditional kings came to power, including Ramses II, who fought the battle of Kadesh against the Hittites. Under the later kings royal power was restricted and the influential Amon priests were able to usurp the throne.

New Orleans, Battle of (1815) Battle in which U.S. troops under Andrew Jackson defeated the British during the War of 1812.

New Orleans, Battle of (1862) Naval engagement early in the American Civil War that led to the Union capture and occupation of New Orleans.

Newcomen, Thomas (1663-1729) British inventor. He invented (1711) the atmospheric steam engine, which was used to successfully pump water.

Sir Isaac Newton

Newton, Sir Isaac (1642-1727) English mathematician and physicist. He discovered the law of universal gravitation, began to develop calculus, and discovered that white light is made up

of all the colors of the spectrum. These discoveries enabled N. to make major contributions to physics, mathematics, and astronomy.

Ney, Michel (1769-1815) Marshal of France. One of Napoleon's most important generals, he defended the rear during the French retreat from Moscow in 1812. After promising King Louis XVIII that he would stop

Michel Ney

Napoleon after his return from exile in Elba, N. defected and commanded Napoleon's forces at Waterloo. For this, he was condemned for treason and executed.

Nez Percé Native American people of North America. They lived in what are now parts of Idaho, Oregon, and Washington. After 1700 they adopted the horse and became noted breeders, adopting many traits of the Plains Indians. The N. ceded large parts of their territory to the U.S. in 1855, but the gold rushes of the 1860s and 1870s brought large numbers of miners onto their lands. The N. under Chief Joseph battled with U.S. forces in 1877 over a fraudulent treaty signed in 1863, but were overwhelmed.

Ngasaunggyan, Battle of (1277) Battle between the Mongols under Kublai Khan and a Burmese army of the Pagan Dynasty under Naranthihapate. The battle was won by the Mongols.

Ngo Quyen (d.944) Vietnamese patriot. He founded an independent Vietnamese kingdom after having

defeated the Chinese at Haiphong in c.938; *see* Nam Viet.

Ngouabi, Marien (1938-1977) President of the Congo, 1969-1977. A soldier and socialist politician, he helped

Marien Ngouabi

remove President Alphonse Massemba-Debat in 1968 and installed himself as president in 1969. N. established an authoritarian regime that crushed all opposition. He was assassinated in 1977.

Nguyen dynasty Royal house that ruled Vietnam from the 16th century until 1955. Originally, the N. controlled only southern Vietnam, but in the 18th century they expanded their sphere of influence to include Cambodia and northern Vietnam. Emperor Bao Dai (1949-1955) was the last Nguyen ruler of Vietnam.

Nguyen Van Thieu (1923-) President of South Vietnam, 1967-1975. A soldier and politician, he took part in the coup d'état in 1963 that overthrew the Diem regime. When South Vietnam was overrun by the communists in 1975, T. fled to exile in England.

Nibelungenlied Middle High German epic. It originated in southern Germany around 1200. The story revolves around an evil family that possesses a magic but cursed hoard of gold. The N. was the basis of Richard Wagner's operatic tetralogy *Der Ring des Nibelungen*, consisting of *Das Rheingold*, *Die Walküre*, *Siegfried*, and *Die Götterdämmerung*.

Nicaea, Empire of One of the Greek successor states to the Latin Empire of Constantinople, 1204-1261. It was founded by Theodosius I. By preserving Byzantine rituals and customs, N. played an important role in reuniting the Byzantine Empire. Theodosius and his successors expanded their domain and became supreme in Asia Minor. The Emperor Michael VIII captured Constantinople from the Latins and restored the Byzantine Empire in 1261.

Nicaea, First Council of (325) First ecumenical council. It was summoned by the Roman emperor Constantine I to solve the problems raised by Arianism.

Nicaea, Second Council of (787) Seventh ecumenical council. It was summoned by the Byzantine empress Irene to deal with the problem of Iconoclasm. It was the last council accepted by both the Roman Catholic church and the Orthodox Eastern church as ecumenical.

Nicholas I (1796-1855) Czar of Russia, 1825-1855. The son of Paul I, he was an autocratic ruler. A strong nationalist, he mercilessly crushed a

Nicholas I

revolt in Poland in the 1830s. Under Nicholas, Russian law was codified and the country acquired new territories in Armenia and the Caspian and Black Sea areas. He involved Russia in the disastrous Crimean War (1853-1856) and died before the war was completed.

Nicholas II (1868-1918) Last czar of Russia, 1894-1917. The son and suc-

Nicholas II

cessor of Alexander III, he continued his father's policy of repression of the opposition and an aggressive policy abroad. N. was a charming but ineffective leader who could be easily influenced by others. After Russia's defeat in the Russo-Japanese war (1905), a revolution broke out that resulted in the establishment of the Duma and the promulgation of the October Manifesto, that promised a broadening of the right to vote. N., however, curtailed the Duma at every opportunity and attempted to preserve autocratic government. Russia entered World War I against Germany in 1914, and with the czar in command of the army, the course of the war turned against Russia. In 1917 revolution broke out again, and N. was forced to abdicate. He and his wife, the Czarina Alexandra Feodorovna, and their five children were eventually taken into custody and moved to Ekaterinburg, in the Urals. Fearing that counterrevolutionary forces might attempt to liberate the family, the Bolsheviks had them all shot on the night of July 16, 1918. Their bodies were thrown into a pit and burned.

Nicholas Nikolayevich (1856-1929) Russian grand duke and cousin of Czar Alexander III. He was commander of the Russian armies at the start of World War I (1914). Under the influence of Czarina Alexandra Feodorovna and Rasputin, however, Nicholas II removed him in 1915 and relegated him to a lesser command in the Caucasus. In the wake of the Russian Revolution, N. left the country in 1919 and settled in France.

Nicholas of Damascus Greek writer living in the 1st century BC. An adviser to Herod the Great, he moved to Rome after Herod's death. N. wrote a 144-volume history of the world up to his own time.

Nicomedia Ancient city in Asia Minor, Turkey. It was the residence and capital of the kings of Bithynia from 264 BC until it was sacked by the Goths in 258 AD. Diocletian chose N. for his eastern imperial capital, but it was soon superseded by Byzantium (Constantinople).

Nicopolis City near Bucharest, Rumania. There, on September 25, 1396, a Crusader army under the Hungarian King Sigismund was defeated by the Turks.

Niemöller, Martin (1892-1984) German Protestant theologian. He was a submarine commander in World War I. After 1933, N. became a fierce opponent of the Nazis. From 1938 until 1945 he was imprisoned in the Sachsenhausen and Dachau concentration camps. After World War II, he was a leading spokesman of ecumenism, serving as president of the World Council of Churches from 1961 to 1968.

Nien Uprising Rebellion of farmers, smugglers, and army deserters in northern China between 1852 and 1868. The rebels fought the Ch'ing dynasty at a time it was trying to suppress the Taiping Uprising. The Nien rebels used guerrilla tactics, but they lacked an ideological unity and strong leadership and were eventually defeated.

Niepce, Joseph Nicéphore (1765-1833) French chemist. A pioneer of photography, he was the first to produce permanent photographic images. N.'s oldest surviving photo date from 1826-1827.

Nietzsche, Friedrich (1844-1900) German philosopher. He was not a systematic philosopher but more of a moralist who rejected Western bourgeois values and the German state. In their place, he looked to the "superman," the creator of a new morality who would affirm life and its better values. His best-known works are *Thus Spake Zarathustra* (1883-1891) and *Beyond Good and Evil* (1906). Apolog-

Martin Niemöller

ists of Nazism seized on N. to justify their racial doctrines. In doing so, however, they perverted his thought, overlooking his strong individualism and contempt for the German state.

Friedrich Nietzsche

Niflheim In Norse mythology the misty and cold kingdom of the dead ruled by the goddess Hel.

Niger, Pescennius (d.194) Roman emperor, 193-194. Severus, who was also proclaimed emperor by the troops in Pannonia, fought against him at the Battle of Issus, and N. was killed while fleeing.

Night of the Long Knives Name given to a purge in Nazi ranks in 1934. On the night of June 29-30, 1934, the leadership of the SA, the paramilitary organization within the Nazi Party, was systematically murdered on orders from Hitler. Under the leadership of Ernst Röhm, the SA had been challenging the supremacy of the German army as the leading military organization in the state. Hitler, needing army support for his new regime, decided to eliminate the SA as a threat. The beneficiary of the SA's demise was the SS under Heinrich Himmler, which had carried out the executions.

Nightingale, Florence (1820-1910) English nurse. The founder of modern nursing, she achieved international fame during the Crimean War (1853-1856), when she led a unit of some 40 nurses. She was called the "Lady with the Lamp," because she believed a nurse's work was never done. In 1907, N. became the first woman to receive the British Order of Merit.

Nihon-gi Nihon-shoki (Chronicles of Japan) Together with the so-called Kojiki, they are the oldest historical accounts of Japan from its mystical origins until 607. They are written in Chinese.

Nijinsky, Vaslav (1890-1950) Russian ballet dancer and choreographer. One of the greatest dancers of all time, he was note for his jeté and elevation. N. made his debut in 1907 in St. Petersburg and, from 1909, was the star of Diaghilev's Ballet Russe. The first to dance the major parts choreographed by Fokine, N. choreographed *The Rite of Spring* (1913), which caused a sensation. His relationship with Diaghilev was stormy, ending bitterly when N. married. N.'s career ended in 1919, when he went insane. He lived his final years in Switzerland and England.

Nijmegen, Peace of Series of treaties signed in 1678 and 1679. They ended the Dutch Wars (1672-1678) of Louis XIV of France.

Nikanor (c.360-317 BC) Confidant of Alexander the Great. N. accompanied Alexander on his journey to the East and in 318 was commander of the Kassandros fleet. He died in battle.

Nike In Greek mythology, the goddess of victory. The figure of Nike is a popular subject in art, often being represented as winged and carrying a palm branch or wreath.

Nikeforus I (d.811) Byzantine emperor, 802-811. N. fought against the Bulgarian Prince Krum and died in the conflict, after which his head was used by Krum as a cup.

Nikeforus II Phocas (912-969) Byzantine emperor, 963-969. He was proclaimed emperor by the army after the death of Roman II. N. captured Crete and northern Syria from the Arabs and also conquered part of the Bulgarian Empire.

Nikeforus III Botaniates (d.1081) Byzantine emperor, 1078-1081. He governed his Byzantine kingdom with Turkish support. N. was deposed by Alexius I Commen, who was proclaimed emperor in 1081.

Nikias (d.413 BC) Athenian statesman and general. In 421, he concluded the peace treaty with Sparta and, with Alcibiades and Lamachos, assumed authority over the Athenian campaign in Sicily. It was there that he was taken prisoner and killed.

Nikolsburg Town in southern Moravia. Armistice agreements ending the Franco-Austrian War (1805) and the Austro-Prussian War (1866) were signed at Nikolsburg.

Nile, Battle of the (1798) Battle in which British Admiral Horatio Nelson defeated the French fleet off Abu Qir, Egypt, thus blocking French advances in the Middle East.

Nimitz, Chester William (1885-1966) American admiral. He became (1942) commander of the U.S. Pacific fleet during World War II and developed the U.S. "island-hopping" strategy in the war against Japan. In 1945 he became chief of naval operations. N. retired from active duty in 1947 but served on a UN commission (1949) seeking to resolve the Kashmir dispute.

Nin, Anaïs (1903-1977) American writer. Born in France, she came to the U.S. as a child. N. was an early patient of Jung, and her writing often deals with the subconscious. Her most famous work is her multivolume diary.

Anaïs Nin

Ninhursag Mesopotamian goddess of Adab and Kisj. She was said to possess the power to make rocky ground fertile.

Niniveh Ancient city, capital of the Assyrian Empire. On the banks of the Tigris River, N. was made capital of the empire by King Sennacherib in the beginning of the 7th century BC. In 612 BC, it was captured and destroyed by the Medes and the Chaldeans.

Niobid Painter (c.475-450 BC) Anonymous Greek painter of red figure vases, named after the Niobiden crater (mixing vessel). It depicts Hercules, the Argonauts, Apollo, and Artemis with the Niobids. Other vessels by this painter have also been found.

Nippur Ancient city in Mesopotamia. It was well known as early as 2500 BC because of its temple to the god Enlil. More than 40,000 clay tablets found at N. give evidence about Sumerian civilization, especially trade and commerce of the time.

Nisa Ancient city in Greece. Founded by Arsaces I (reigned from c. 250-211 BC), it was the first capital city of the Parthians. Mithradates later changed its name to Mithradatkirt.

Nishapur City in Iran. It was founded in the 3rd century by the Sassanids and was an important cultural center from the 9th to the 13th centuries. N. was largely destroyed by Genghis Khan. The poet Omar Khayyam was buried in N.

Nisibis Byzantine town. It was the site of a 5th-century theology school where Greek and Arabic texts were studied.

Nissaba Semitic goddess of grass, grain, and reeds, and the goddess of writers.

Nithard (c.790-844) French historical writer. The grandson of Charlemagne, he wrote about the death of Charlemagne (814) and the battle between his grandsons (830-843).

Nitria (Wadi Natrun) Region of Egypt, flatlands between Alexandria and Cairo containing salt lakes. Salt was harvested there as early as ancient times. Fifty Coptic monasteries were once located in this area, four of which still remain.

Nivardus Monk who lived in Ghent during the 12th century. He was the writer of the Latin poem "Isengrinus."

Nivelle, Robert Georges (1856-1924) French general. He served in China, Algeria, and on the western front during World War I. N. succeeded Pétain

Robert Georges Nivelle

in 1916 at Verdun and later succeeded Joffre as commander in chief. In 1917, his offensive in the north failed, after which he was dismissed.

Nix Evil spirit in Germanic mythology. N. was supposed to be half man and half fish and be able to make itself invisible and take on any form.

Nixon, Richard Milhous (1913-1994) 37th president of the U.S., 1969-1974. Elected to the U.S. House of Representatives (1946) as a Republican from California, N. quickly made a reputation as a partisan anticommunist in the Hiss case. In 1950 he was elected to the Senate and two years later was selected by Eisenhower to be his vice-presidential running mate. N. served as vice-president for two terms and in 1960 was nominated for president by the Republican Party. Narrowly losing to John F. Kennedy, N. retired from public life. He was defeated for governor of California in 1962 but was renominated for president in 1968, narrowly winning election in a three-way race. N. gradually

(1969-1973) ended U.S. involvement in Vietnam and improved relations with the Soviet Union and Communist China. He was overwhelmingly reelected in 1972, but his second term was marred by the Watergate scandal and by revelations of other wrongdoing committed during his presidency. Facing impeachment for obstructing the Watergate investigation, N. resigned the presidency on August 9, 1974.

Nizza, Treaty of Pact signed in 1538 between Francis I of France and Emperor Charles I, following mediation by Pope Paul III.

Nkrumah, Kwame (1909-1972) President of Ghana, 1960-1966. A leader of the anticolonial movement against Great Britain and a proponent of pan-Africanism, K. led his country to independence in 1957. His regime became increasingly authoritarian, and in 1966 he was deposed while on a visit to China. He spent his remaining years in exile in Guinea.

NKVD Acronym for People's Commissariat for Internal Affairs, the Soviet secret police. It functioned under this name from 1934 until 1943 and was responsible for operating the forced labor camps. The NKVD played a leading role in the Stalinist purges of the late 1930s.

Nobel, Alfred Bernhard (1833-1896) Swedish chemist and inventor. His family manufactured various kinds of

Richard Milhous Nixon

Alfred Bernhard Nobel

explosives, and in 1867, N. invented a compound that he named dynamite. Inclined toward pacifism, N. always had serious reservations about his family's industry. On his death he left a fund for the granting of annual awards. Known now as the Nobel Prizes, they were first established in physics, chemistry, physiology, medicine, literature, and international peace.

Nobile, Umberto (1885-1978) Italian pilot and engineer. N. built the airship Norge, which he and Amundsen flew over the North Pole to Alaska (1926). During a second expedition (1928) his airship Italia crashed. A number of people died during the rescue attempts, and N. was held liable and dismissed.

Nogi, Maresoeke (1849-1912) Japanese general. He fought in the war with China and in 1896 became governor of Formosa. During the Russo-Japanese war of 1905 war he captured Port Arthur and was victorious at Mukden.

Noguchi, Hideyo (1876-1928) Japanese-American bacteriologist who, in 1913, discovered the bacteria that causes syphilis.

Nokrashi Pasha (1888-1948) Egyptian statesman. Originally a member of the Wafd Party, he became the leader of the Saadist group in 1937. He served as prime minister a number of times and was murdered in 1948 by the Muslim Brotherhood.

Nola Town in southern Italy. It was an important center of early Christianity. In 14 AD, the Emperor Augustus died in N.

Nördlingen Town in southern Germany. It was the site of an imperial victory in the Thirty Years War (1634) that led to France's entry into the war a year later.

Norfolk, Thomas Howard, 3rd duke of (1473-1554) English nobleman. An important figure during the reign of Henry VIII, he supported Henry's marriage to N.'s niece Anne Boleyn (1533) but then presided at her trial and execution in 1536. N. was instrumental in the downfall of Thomas Cranmer. He lost influence after the execution (1542) of another niece, Catherine Howard, Henry's fifth wife.

Thomas Howard Norfolk

N. was arrested for high treason in 1546 but escaped execution because of the king's death. He remained a Catholic throughout his life, and after 1553 served Queen Mary I.

Noriega, Manuel Antonio (1938-) Panamanian leader. He became head of the country in 1983 after the death of Omar Torrijos and pursued a strident anti-American policy. After the U.S. invasion of Panama in 1990, N. was taken into custody and removed to the U.S., where he was tried, convicted, and imprisoned for drug trafficking.

Norman Conquest Period in English history following the defeat at the battle of Hastings in 1066 of King Harold of England by William, duke of Normandy, who became William I. A Norman aristocracy was imposed on the English, and the new Norman elite brought with it Norman feudal customs. William, however, consolidated his position by preserving existing Anglo-Saxon administrative systems, which then functioned to serve the centralized monarchy. The blending of Norman and Anglo-Saxon gave English feudalism its unique character.

Normandy Campaign Allied invasion of Europe during World War II. It began on June 6, 1944, with an amphibious assault along the Normandy coast of France by a huge land, air, and naval force from England. The campaign in Normandy lasted until August, 1944, by which time the Allies

Manuel Antonio Noriega

had broken deeper into France and liberated Paris.

Norns *See* Fates.

Norodom Sihanouk (1922-) King of Cambodia, 1941-1955, 1993- . In 1955 he abdicated in favor of his father and became premier. He was deposed (1970) in a rightist coup led by Lon Nol. After five years of exile in China, he returned to Cambodia when the communist Khmer Rouge won control in 1975. S. served as head of state (1975-76) but was subsequently placed under house arrest. While in exile in 1982, S. allied himself

Norodom Sihanouk

with the Khmer Rouge to oppose the Vietnamese-imposed Cambodian government. After the signing of the UN-sponsored peace treaty (1991), he returned to Cambodia and opposed the Khmer Rouge. He became head of state in 1991 and, under a new constitution, king once again in 1993.

North Atlantic Treaty Organization (NATO) Military alliance established in 1949 between the U.S. and Western European states to defend Europe against Soviet aggression. After the Warsaw Pact was disbanded in 1991, N. concentrated on political and military cooperation. NATO troops drawn from the U.S. and a number of European countries were sent into the Bosnian conflict in 1995 to serve as peacekeepers.

North German Federation Federal state formed in 1866 from all German states north of the Main River. It was under the leadership of the King William of Prussia (later Emperor William I of Germany), with Bismarck as chancellor. After the southern German states were admitted to the federation in 1870-1871, it became the new German empire.

Northern Wars Wars between the Scandinavian states in the 16th-18th centuries: 1st N. (1563-1570) Between Denmark and Sweden. It ended with the Peace of Stettin; 2nd N. (1611-1613) The Kalmar War, between Denmark and Sweden, with fighting also against Poland and Russia. Denmark lost its power in northern Europe; 3rd N. (1643-1645) Denmark lost again to Sweden, which was supported by the Dutch; 4th N. (1655-1660) Between Sweden and Poland, Russia, Denmark, and the Republic. It ended by the Peace of Copenhagen and Oliva; 5th N. (1674-1679) Between Sweden and Brandenburg, France, Denmark, and the Republic. It ended with the Peace of St. Germain-en-Laye and Fontainbleau; 6th N. (1700-1721) The Great Northern War between Sweden and Russia, Denmark, Poland, Saxony, Prussia, Hanover, and other countries. In 1701, Charles XII of Sweden defeated the Russians at Narva. Later, he was defeated by Peter the Great at Poltava. In 1720-1721 the various Treaties of Stockholm and the Treaty of Nystadt were signed, ending the conflict.

Northumberland, Henry Percy, 1st Earl of (1342-1408) English nobleman. He fought in France in the Hundred Years War. N. supported King Henry IV in the usurpation of 1399 but rebelled against him in 1403. His son died in battle in 1403 near Shrewsbury, after which N. submitted to Henry. N. revolted again in 1405, fled to France and Scotland, and was killed in battle in 1408 after invading England from the north and attempting to recruit followers.

Northumberland, John Dudley, Duke of (1502?-1553) English nobleman. He supported Somerset (1547) as protector during the reign of the child-king Edward VI. He turned against Somerset (1549), however, and then ruled completely unopposed. After Edward's death (1553), N. attempted to put his daughter-in-law, Lady Jane Grey, on the throne over Mary Tudor, Edward's half-sister. Unpopular with the people, he was deserted by the army, and his plan failed. Mary succeeded as Mary I, and N. was arrested for high treason and executed along with Lady Jane Grey.

Northumbria Anglo-Saxon kingdom in England. It was created in the 7th century by joining Bernicia and Deira. In the 9th century, the Danes invaded and later it was ruled by King Edward of Wessex.

Noske, Gustav (1868-1946) German socialist politician. In 1918, N. put down the sailors' mutiny in Kiel and in 1919, as minister of defense in the Weimar regime, suppressed the communist Spartacist rebellion. Forced out of office in the wake of the monarchist Kapp putsch (1920), he became governor of Hanover. N. was dismissed by the Nazis in 1933. Interred in a concentration camp in 1944 as a suspect in the plot to kill Hitler, he was released in 1945 by Soviet troops.

Nostradamus, Michel (1503-1566) French doctor and astrologer. His oblique and symbolic prophesies

Michel Nostradamus

Gustav Noske

were published under the title Centuries (1555).

Notger, Bishop of Liège (972-1008) Founder of the principality of Liège. He turned Liège into a strong fortified town and, as an ally of the German emperor, kept the aristocracy in check. N. was noted for his support of church construction throughout Lorraine.

Notium, Battle of *See* Lysandros.

Nouri es-Said (1888-1958) Iraqi statesman. During World War I, he collaborated with the Arabian resistance against Turkey and later became the most powerful politician in Iraq. He was murdered on July 14, 1958, during a coup d'état.

Novalis (1772-1801) German romantic poet. Born Friederich von Hardenberg, he is considered one of the great German romantic poets. His major work was the novel Heinrich von Ofterdingen, published a year after his death. A collection of his poetry, *Hymns to the Night* (1800), is a deeply religious expression of his grief over the death of his young lover.

Novara Town in northern Italy. During the Italian struggle for independence, Charles Albert of Savoy was defeated at Novara (1849) by the Austrians under the command of Radetzky.

Novaya Zemyla Islands in the Arctic Ocean, part of Russia. They were probably discovered by Novgorodians in the 11th or 12th century. They have been used by the Soviets for nuclear testing and other scientific purposes.

November Revolution Uprisings that occurred in Germany in November 1918 in the wake of the German surrender in World War I. The uprisings led to the collapse of the German empire and to the delaration (November 9) of a republic.

Novotny, Antonin (1904-1975) President of Czechoslovakia, 1957-1969. A founding member of the Czech communist party, he came to power in the 1950s, first as general secretary (1953) then as president (1957). A strong supporter of the Soviet line, he ruled repressively until 1968, when a liberal majority in the party replaced

Novalis

him as general secretary with Alexander Dubcek. A year later, N. was forced to resign as president.

Noyon Town in northern France. Charlemagne was crowned King of the Franks at N. in 768. It was also the site of an unsuccessful German offensive (June, 1918) during World War I.

Noyon, Treaty of Pact signed in 1516 between France and Spain during the Italian Wars. Under its terms, Naplcs was returned to Spain, and Milan to France.

Nubians Inhabitants of the ancient state of Nubia, in northeast Africa. At its height, Nubia extended from the First Cataract of the Nile, near Aswan, south to Khartoum, in the Sudan. The kingdom came under the influence of Egypt for the first time in the 20th century BC.

Numa Pompilius Legendary second king of Rome, 715-673 BC. Roman ceremonial law and religious rights have been ascribed to him.

Numa Pompilius

Numantia Ancient own in northern Spain. It was a center of Celtiberian resistance to Roman conquest and fell to the Roman Scipio Aemilianus only in 133 BC, after an eight-month siege.

Numeiry, Jafa Muhammad an- (1930-) Sudanese soldier and politician. In 1969, he became prime minister after a revolt, but was himself overthrown in 1971 in a communist coup d'état. He soon organized a counter-coup, after which he persecuted communists. In 1983, N. adopted a number of

measures (for example, a revised legal system) that made Sudan an Islamic country. He was deposed by the army in 1985.

Numerian, Marcus Aurelius Emperor of Rome, 283-284. In 282, he participated in a military campaign against Persia and was murdered on the way back to Rome. The commander of his bodyguard, Diocles (later the Emperor Diocletian), was appointed his successor.

Numidia Ancient kingdom in northern Africa. Covering an area that is now Algeria and parts of Tunisia, N. was part of the Carthaginian empire. After Carthage's defeat by Rome in the Punic Wars (201 BC), N. became a separate entity and entered into a flourishing cultural and political period. N. fought Rome under Jugurtha and lost much of its independence. Under Caesar (c.46 BC), it was incorporated into Rome.

Numitor Legendary king of Alba Longa and grandfather of Romulus and Remus.

Nuraghi Prehistoric stronghold on the island of Sardinia, in the Mediterranean. At the site are a series of round towers and walls that date from c.7000-6500 BC.

Nureddin Mahmud (Nur ad-Din) (1118-1174) Ruler of Syria, 1145-1174. He defeated the Seljuk Turks in Asia Minor and fought the Crusaders. N. was considered a just and fair ruler.

Nuremberg Laws Series of laws promulgated at the Nazi Party Congress in 1935. They deprived German Jews of their civil liberties and forbade intermarriage between Jews and non-Jews.

Nuremberg Trials International war crimes trials held in Nuremberg, Germany, beginning in 1945. At the first trial (November 1945-October 1946), the leading figures of the Nazi regime were tried. Eleven were executed, three were acquitted, and the remainder sentenced to prison terms for war crimes and crimes against humanity.

Nureyev, Rudolf (1938-1993) Russian ballet dancer. He made his debut in 1958 as a soloist in the Kirov Ballet

Nuzi Site in ancient Mesopotamia. It is known for the c.4000 cuneiform tablets (15th-14th century BC) found there. The texts reveal much about ancient laws and customs of the Horims.

Nyerere, Julius Kambarage (1921-) President of Tanzania, 1964-1985. Educated in Scotland, he founded the Tanganyika African National Union (1954) and worked for the independence of his country from Great Britain. N. became prime minister in 1961 and president after the country became a republic. He was the architect of the union of Tanganyika and Zanzibar (1964) as Tanzania. N. was a supporter of East African regional cooperation.

Rudolf Nureyev

in Leningrad. N. defected to the West in 1961 while on tour in Paris. He was one of the leading classical ballet dancers of his generation, noted for his athletic grace and fiery temperament. In the 1970s, he danced frequently with the English ballerina Dame Margot Fonteyn. N. also served as artistic director of the Paris Opera Ballet (1983-1989).

Nut Ancient Egyptian goddess of the heavens. She is frequently pictured with her hands and feet on earth and the curve of her body forming the vault of heaven. N. is the wife and sister of the earth-god Geb and the mother of Isis and Osiris.

Julius Kambarage Nyerere

Nymphenburg, Treaty of (1741) Pact in which Spain promised to support Charles Albert of Bavaria in his attempt to become Holy Roman Emperor.

Nystadt, Treaty of (1720) One of the pacts that ended the war between Sweden and Russia; *see* Northern Wars.

Nut

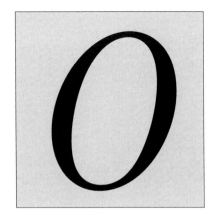

Obote, Apollo Milton (1925-) President of Uganda, 1966-71, 1980-1985. He founded the Uganda People's Congress in 1960, served as prime minister (1962-1966), and then led a revolution and installed himself as president. O. was deposed by Idi Amin in 1971 and fled to exile in Tanzania. After Amin's ouster in 1980, O. returned to Uganda and became president once more. He was accused of corruption and overthrown again in 1985.

Obregón, Alvaro (1880-1928) President of Mexico, 1920-1924. A planter and a general, he supported the revolution against Porfirio Diáz. In 1920, O. helped oust Venustiano Carranza when the latter attempted to assume dictatorial powers. A reformer, O. became president in 1920 and began to enact a program of agrarian and educational reform. He fought a long and bitter fight with the Church, and in 1928, shortly after he was chosen president again, he was assassinated by a fanatical Catholic.

Obrenovic, Michael (1823-1868) Prince of Serbia, 1839-1842, 1860-1868, the son of Milos Obrenovic. M. succeeded his brother Milan in 1839 but was deposed in 1842 by Karageorge. He returned to power on his father's death (1860) and pursued a policy of modernizing Serbia. Under his rule, the last Turkish garrisons withdrew from Serbian fortresses. M. was assassinated in 1868.

Obrenovic, Milan (1854-1901) Prince (1868-1882) and King (1882-1889) of Serbia, the grandnephew of Milos Obrenovic. At the Congress of Berlin (1878), he secured European recognition of the full independence of Serbia from the Ottoman Empire. In 1882, with Austrian support, he proclaimed himself King Milan I of Serbia. Because of heavy taxation, a pro-Austrian policy, and a scandal-ridden private life, he was highly unpopular. He abdicated in 1889 in favor of his son Alexander.

Obrenovic, Milos (1780-1860) Prince of Serbia, 1817-1839, 1858-1860. An illiterate farmer, he fought the Turks under Karageorge, whom he probably later killed. He was named prince by the national assembly, and his title was confirmed by the sultan. O. abdicated in 1839 favor of his son Milan. Milan, however, died the same year, and another son, Michael, was deposed in 1842. Karageorge then ruled until 1858, when O. was recalled by the Serbian parliament. He died two years later.

O'Brien, William Smith (1803-1864) Irish nationalist politician. An advocate of separation from Great Britain, O. helped form the Irish Confederation and in 1848, in Tipperary, led a revolt against British authority. The revolutionaries were quickly defeated by a small police force. O. was sentenced to death for high treason but the sentence was commuted to exile in Tasmania. He remained there until 1854, when he returned to Ireland. Pardoned in 1856, he withdrew from politics for the remainder of his life.

Obol *See* Drachme.

Ochab, Edward (1906-1989) President of Poland, 1964-1968. A member of the Politburo, he opposed Boleslaw Bierut, the Stalinist party leader, whom he succeeded as first secretary in March 1956. In 1964 O. became president.

Octavia, Claudia (42-62 AD) Roman woman. The daughter of Emperor Claudius I and Messalina, she was married to Nero in 53 AD. He rejected her in 62 in favor of Poppaea Sabina and had her exiled to the island of Pandateria and murdered.

Octavia Minor (69-11 BC) Roman woman. The wife of Mark Anthony, she attempted to mediate between Octavian and Anthony during the civil war. Anthony divorced her in 32 BC for Cleopatra, after which O. retired from public life.

Octavian Earlier name of the Roman Emperor Augustus from the death of Julius Caesar until 27 BC.

Octavius, Caius (d.58 BC?) Roman statesman, father of the Emperor Augustus. He was governor of Macedonia in 60 BC and was married to one of Julius Caesar's nieces.

October Revolution Term referring to the Bolshevik seizure of power in Russia on November 7, 1917 (October 25 on the Russian calender).

Oda Nobunaga (1534-1582) Japanese general and statesman. A member of the Fujiwara clan, he deposed the shogun Joshijaki (of the Ashikaga clan) and became the highest authority in Japan. O. forged contacts with the West and committed suicide after a revolt against him.

Odenathus, Septimius (d.267) King of Palmyra. An ally of Rome, he led Roman and Palmyrean troops against Persia from 262-267 and captured Mesopotamia. He and his son were murdered in 267. Soon after his death his second wife Zenobia brought Palmyra to ruin; *see* Zenobia.

Oder-Neisse Line New border established between Germany and Poland in 1945 at the conclusion of World War II. The boundary, which followed the Oder and Neisse rivers from the Baltic Sea to the Czech border, was

Claudia Octavia

agreed upon at the Yalta and Potsdam conferences between the Soviet Union, the U.S., and Great Britain. The line placed considerable amounts of former eastern German land into Polish hands and led millions of German refugees to flee to the West.

Odin Norse god. Also called Woden, he is the most important god in ancient Scandinavian mythology. O. was the god of war and death and gathered those who died in battle around him in Valhalla.

Odoacer (c.435-493) Germanic king. A mercenary in the service of Rome, he defeated the Roman Emperor Orestes in 476. He was then elected emperor by the army and deposed Orestes's son Romulus Augustus. In 488, Zeno, the Roman Emperor of the East, sent the Ostrogoths under Theodoric into Italy to expel O. In 493, O. agreed to share power with Theodoric. At a banquet celebrating the agreement, O. and his son were murdered on orders of Theodoric, who then proclaimed himself master of Italy.

O'Donnell, Leopoldo (1809-1867) Spanish general and statesman. O. was governor-general of Cuba from 1844-1848, after which he played an important role in Spanish politics. Together with Espartero, O. ended the reign of Maria Cristina in 1854 and served several times as prime minister.

Odoric of Pordenone (c.1286-1331) Italian missionary. He spent three years as a missionary in Peking and wrote an account of his travels that later became famous.

O'Duffy, Eoin (1892-1944) Irish soldier. He took part in the Easter uprising of 1916. O. was the leader of the fascist "blue shirts" and during the 1930s fought for Franco in the Spanish Civil war.

Odysseus *See* Homer.

Oebaid Allah al-Mahdi Founder of the Fatimid royal family in North-Africa. O. ruled from 909-934 and was venerated as the Mahdi.

Offa (d.796) King of Mercia, 757-796. He was the most important Anglo-Saxon king before Alfred the

Offa

Great. O. introduced a coinage that for centuries was the basis of English currency. He had sufficient stature to negotiate with Charlemagne. They concluded a trade agreement (the first in English history) and discussed a marriage between their children. Between 784 and 796 the earthwork known as Offa's Dyke was built between Wales and Mercia.

O'Higgins, Bernardo (1778-1842) South American revolutionary, ruler of Chile, 1817-1823. One of the major figures of the Chilean independence movement, he became the nation's leader after defeating the Spanish at Chacabuco. His economic and social reforms aroused much opposition, however, and in 1823 he was overthrown and exiled to Peru, where he lived the remainder of his life.

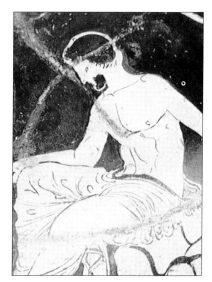
Odysseus

Ohrid Town in Macedonia. It stands on or near the ancient Greek colony of Lychnidos, which was founded in the 3rd century BC. In the 9th century O. was incorporated into the first Bulgarian empire and became the political and cultural center of Bulgaria.

Ojeda, Alonso de (c.1466-1515?) Spanish mariner and explorer. He took part in Columbus's second voyage and in 1499 explored the northeastern coast of South America. He became governor of a colony in northern South America in 1508, but came into conflict with the Indians. He apparently sought aid in Hispaniola, but his actions are his arrival are obscure, and there is no record of him after 1515.

O'Kelly, Sean Thomas (1882-1966) President of Ireland, 1945-1959. A strong nationalist, he was one of the founders of Sinn Fein. O. was imprisoned for a year because of his part in the Easter uprising of 1916.

Okinawa Island in the western Pacific, a part of Japan. It was one of the last hurdles for the Americans during World War II prior to the projected invasion of Japan. The island surrendered to the U.S. army and the marines on June 21, 1945, after 11 weeks of bloody fighting. O. remained under U.S. military control until 1972, when it was returned to Japan. U.S. bases remained on the island but became a contentious issue between the U.S. and Japan.

Olaf I (c.963-1000) King of Norway, 995-1000. His early life is shrouded in mystery and legend. O. overthrew Haakon and became king of Norway in 995. He attempted to convert the country to Christianity by force, and ordered Leif Ericsson to bring Christianity to Greenland. O. was defeated and then killed at the battle of Svolder while fighting a combined Danish-Swedish force. After his death, Norway was divided between Denmark and Sweden.

Old Kingdom Golden Age in Egyptian history, between c.2575-2130 BC. During this period, the power of the king was absolute and the great pyramids were built. Famous kings of the Old Kingdom included Snefroe, Cheops, and Chefren. During the 5th Dynasty, pyramid-mausoleums were

Eoin O'Duffy

relatively small, and every king built a sun temple dedicated to Ra. Central authority started to crumble during the 6th Dynasty and continued into the 7th and 8th Dynasties, after which a period of starvation and civil war ensued.

Old World Term that sometimes refers to the countries and regions that flourished in ancient times, for example, Mesopotamia, Egypt, Asia Minor, Greece, and Rome.

Old Testament Christian name for the Hebrew Bible, which serves as the first portion of the Christian Bible.

Johan van Oldenbarneveldt

Oldenbarneveldt, Johan van (1547-1619) Dutch statesman. He helped William the Silent in the struggle for Dutch independence from Spain. From 1586 on, as advocate of Holland, he controlled the domestic and foreign affairs of the United Provinces. He negotiated a twelve-year truce with Spain (1609) despite the objections of Maurice of Nassau. Favoring the power of the States-General, O. increasingly clashed with the nobles

and the house of Orange. Eventually, his enemies triumphed, and he was imprisoned and beheaded in 1619.

Oléron, Law of Maritime law codified in the 12th century and promulgated by Louis IX.

Oliva, Treaty of Pact signed in 1660 ending the war between Sweden and Poland; *see* Northern Wars.

Olivarez, Gaspar de Guzmá án y Pimental (1587-1645) Spanish statesman. He became the chief minister of Philip IV in 1621. An honest official, he attempted to root out corruption. He did not repudiate Spanish subservience to Austria, however, and during his tenure, Spain became more involved in the Thirty Years War. O.'s desire to centralize government control led to the loss of Portugal in 1640 and to oppressive measures. His unpopularity led to his fall in 1643.

Olivetti, Camillo (1868-1943) Italian industrialist who founded the first typewriter factory in 1908.

Olivier (c.1170-1227) German Crusader. Between 1214 and 1216 he preached the Crusade in Brabant and Utrecht. O. took part in the Fifth Crusade and wrote about his experiences in the Historia Damiatina.

Ollivier, Émile (1825-1913) French statesman. A member of the liberal opposition to Napoleon III after 1857, he sought to gain reforms through constitutional means. Growing public discontent forced Napoleon to ask O. to form a government in 1870. His administration enacted sweeping constitutional reforms, but O. became a victim of the ill-fated Franco-Prussian War of 1870-1871, which he reluctantly supported. After the defeat of France, he was forced to resign. O. spent three years in exile before returning to France to write an account of his service in government.

Olmecs Ancient Mexican Indian peoples. They occupied the lowlands areas of Veracruz and Tabasco. O. culture, which is usually dated from c.500 BC to 1200 AD, was a highly developed agriculturally. The O. left behind huge sculptured heads, some weighing more than 20 tons. O. discoveries have been found at La Venta and Tres Zapotes.

Olmetz City in Moravia. A treaty was signed there in 1850 between Prussia and Austria that dissolved the German Union and restored the German Confederation headed by Austria. The city today is Olomouc, Czech Republic.

Olybrius, Flavius Anicius (d.472) Roman Emperor of the West, 472. From 455 he was supported from Rome by Gaiseric as pretender to the throne. Ricimer made him Roman Emperor of the West in 472, but he died shortly thereafter.

Olympia Center for the worship of Zeus in ancient Greece. It was the site of the Olympic Games.

Olympias (c.375-316 BC) Mother of Alexander the Great and wife of Philip II of Macedon. She quarreled with Antipater, whom Alexander had designated as regent in Macedon. After Alexander's death, Antipater's son Cassander captured O. at Pydna and had her executed.

Olympic Games Principal athletic meetings of ancient Greece. They were held in the summer every four years at Olympia. The Olympic Games were at their height in the 5th and 4th centuries BC. They became professionalized under the Romans and were finally discontinued in the 4th century AD.

Omar Khayyam (1048-1131) Persian poet and scholar. O. wrote a scholarly treatise on algebra and made changes in the calendar. His fame as scientist,

Émile Ollivier

however, has been eclipsed by his popular Rubaiyat, a collection of verse quatrains that express O.'s hedonistic philosophy.

Omar Pasha (1806-1871) Turkish army commander in the Balkans. A Croat named Michael Latas, he converted from Christianity to Islam and became the supreme commander of the Turkish army. He fought successful campaigns in the Balkans and in the Crimean War (1853-1856).

Omdurman City in the Sudan. Kitchener decisively beat the followers of the Mahdi near O. on September 2, 1898.

Omri King of Israel, c.884-872 or 876-869 BC. He moved his capital from Tirzah to Samaria, which then became the chief city of Israel.

Onassis, Aristotle (1906-1975) Greek shipbuilder and financier. He bought his first ships in Canada

Aristotle Onassis

(1932) and expanded his business until it was the largest privately-owned fleet in the world. O. achieved notoriety through his marriage (1968)

to Jacqueline Kennedy, the widow of President John F. Kennedy.

Onna-daigaku Japanese tradition regarding the conduct and position of women in relation to their husbands and relatives. Until the start of the 20th century, the O., which subordinated women to men, remained the standard for the traditional education of girls.

Ostend Company Trading company founded in 1722 under the sponsorship of Charles VI, duke of Lorraine. It was given a monopoly in trade with Africa and the West and East Indies and had the exclusive right right to found colonies in these regions.

Opimius, Lucius Roman statesman and consul. In 121 BC, he led the Optimates against the Grachs. O. was convicted of accepting bribes from Jurgurtha in 110 BC and went into exile.

Opium Wars Two wars, 1839-1842 and 1856-1860, the first between Great Britain and China and second between Great Britain and France against China, over the opening of China to trade with the West. When China refused to allow the import of opium, mainly run by the British East India Company, the British used the event as a pretext for attacking a number of Chinese ports. The Chinese, unable to withstand modern arms, were forced to capitulate and allow increased Western trade. The conflict of 1856-1860 resulted in the opening of additional ports and increased Western influence in the affairs of China.

Oppenheimer, Joseph Süss (c.1695-1738) Financier and favorite of Charles Alexander, duke of Württemberg. A Jew, he became the victim of anti-semitic agitation and was hanged after a trial.

Oppenheimer, J. Robert (1904-1967) American physicist. During World War II, he was the director (1942-1945) of the Manhattan project in Los Alamos, New Mexico, which developed the first atomic bomb. After the war, O. was a strong advocate of the civilian and international control of atomic energy. During the McCarthy era he came under fire as a "security risk" for his views on nuclear weapons, but he remained as director of

the Institute for Advanced Studies at Princeton University.

J. Robert Oppenheimer

Oprichniki Special corps established in 1565 by Czar Ivan IV (Ivan the Terrible) of Russia. Responsible to him alone, the O. were used to diminish the influence of the boyars through land confiscation and murder.

Oquendo, Antonio de (1577-1640) Spanish admiral. Commander of the fleet from 1613, he suffered a heavy defeat at Downs against the Dutch (1639).

Oradour-sur-Glane Town in France. During World War II, it was the site of a massacre by the SS (June 10, 1944) in which the entire civilian population of 642 was murdered in retaliation for the killing of a German soldier. The remains of the town, which was burned, have been preserved as a memorial.

Orange, House of Name of the Dutch royal family. They were descended in the male line from William of Orange's eldest brother, Jan the Elder, whose son William Charles Henry Friso became hereditary governor of all Netherlands provinces in 1747. His grandson, William I, founded the royal dynasty in 1814.

Oranienburg City in Germany, near Berlin. It was the site of one of the earliest Nazi concentration camps (established 1933).

Örebro, Treaty of Pact signed between England and Sweden on the June 18, 1812, which confirmed the termination of Sweden's alliance with Napoleon.

Orellana, Francisco de (c.1490-1546) Spanish conquistador and explorer. He was one of the commanders under Pizarro in Peru and in 1541-1542 was the first to journey through South America by crossing the Andes from Quito and then floating down the Amazon. His tale of having seen long-haired female warriors (which were probably men with long hair) gave the river its name.

Philip I of Orléans

Orendel Middle High German poem (c.1180-1190). It concerns Prince Orendel who, after many adventures, manages to bring Christ's robe to Trier.

Orestes (?476) Roman general. He had his son, Romulus Augustulus, proclaimed Roman Emperor of the West in 475. O. was killed in 476 during a revolt by Odoacer and his son was deposed.

Organization of American States (OAS) International organization created in 1948. It includes almost all the republics of the Western Hemisphere, with the exception of Cuba, which was expelled in 1962. The O.'s mission is to promote peace, justice, and hemispheric solidarity, and to advance economic development.

Oribasius (AD 325-403) Greek physician. He accompanied Julianus Apostata on numerous campaigns. O's greatest work is the Synagogae, a compilation drawn from the works of Greek physicians.

Orléans, Charles of (1391-1465) French prince and poet. The nephew of King Charles VI, he was the son of Louis of Orléans. O. was captured by the English at the battle of Agincourt (1415) and spent 25 years in England. Philip the Good of Burgundy mediated his release, which took place in 1440 after a ransom had been paid. Back in France, he devoted the remainder of life to writing poetry.

Orléans, Louis of (1372-1407) French nobleman. The brother of King Charles VI, he was the monarch's chief counselor from 1388 to 1392. When Charles went insane, O. attempted to gain power but was thwarted by Philip the Bold of Burgundy and then by Philip's successor, John the Fearless. O. was murdered at the behest of John, and his killing precipitated the civil war between the Armagnacs and the Burgundians.

Orléans, Louis II of *See* Louis XII.

Orléans, Philip I of (1640-1701) Brother of King Louis the XIV. A notorious libertine, he remained at court but had almost no influence on affairs of state.

Orléans, Philip II of (1674-1723) Regent of France (1715-1723) during the minority of Louis XV. The son of Philip I of Orléans, O. sought to restore the influence of noble councils, which had been suppressed under Louis XIV. In foreign affairs, O.

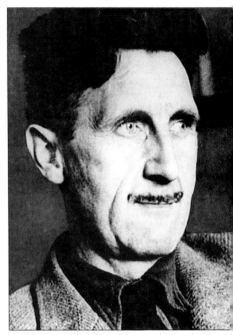

George Orwell

rejected Spain in favor of closer ties with England and the Netherlands.

Orléans, Philip IV of (1747-1793) French revolutionary, The great-grandson of Philip II of Orléans, he had a seat in the States-General and was one of the nobles who joined the third estate in 1789. He returned from a year in exile in England, became a member of the Convention, and, after exchanging his title for the name Philippe Egalité, voted for the execution of King Louis XVI. O.'s contacts with Danton sealed his fate in 1793, and he was guillotined during the Reign of Terror. His son became King Louis Phillipe.

Orlov, Aleksey Grigoryevich, Count (1737-1808) Russian nobleman. He and his brother Grigori conspired to put Catherine II on the throne. O. may have been the actual murderer of Czar Peter III. With the aid of the English, his fleet defeated the Turkish fleet in 1770 during the Russo-Turkish War.

Orlov, Grigori Grigoryevich, Count (1743-1783) Russian nobleman. He and his brother Aleksey conspired to put Catherine II on the throne and to kill Czar Peter III. One of the first lovers of Catherine, he was later supplanted by other favorites, including Potemkin.

Orlov, Nicholai Alekseyevich, Prince (1827-1885) Russian diplomat and soldier during the Crimean war. In 1861 he compiled a report advocating the abolition of corporal punishment in the military.

Orsini, Felice (1819-1858) Italian revolutionary. He was a supporter of Mazzini in 1849 and was banished from Italy after the revolution failed. Because Napoleon III had, in his eyes, betrayed the cause of Italian freedom, O. made a failed assassination attempt in 1858. He was executed after a trial.

Orwell, George (1903-1950) British novelist and essayist. In 1936, he took part in the Spanish Civil War on the Republican side and was wounded. O. is most famous for his satirical novels *Animal Farm* (1945) and *1984* (1949). The latter is a prophetic work that describes the dehumanization of humans in a mechanistic, totalitarian world.

Oscar Name of two kings of Sweden and Norway. Oscar I ruled Norway and Sweden from 1844-1859. Oscar II, the younger son of Oscar I, ruled from 1872 until 1907. In 1905, Norway completely severed its union with Sweden, and O. relinquished the Norwegian throne.

Oschoforia Ancient Greek harvest festival celebrated in October in honor of Dionysus.

Osiris Ancient Egyptian god of the underworld. He was the son of the sky goddess Nut and the earth god Geb. The worship of O. was one of the great cults of ancient Egypt. O. was identified with the creative forces of nature and the imperishability of life.

Osman Nuri Pasha (1837-1900) Turkish field marshal. He distinguished himself in the Russo-Turkish war (1877-1878), during which he defended the town of Pleven, Bulgaria, before surrendering to the Russians. O. served for many years as minister of war.

Osnabrück, Peace of *See* Münster, Treaty of.

Ossietzky, Carl von (1889-1938) German journalist. A well-known pacifist, he was the editor of the antimilitar-

ist weekly Weltbühne. After the takeover by the Nazis in 1933, he was sent to a concentration camp. While imprisoned, O. was awarded the 1935 Nobel Peace Prize. The Germans protested and prohibited all German citizens from accepting future Nobel prizes. O. died in 1938 while still imprisoned.

Oster, Hans (1888-1945) German soldier. During World War II, he was a member of the resistance against the Nazis. After the attempt on Hitler's life on July 20, 1944, he was arrested and executed.

Ostermann, Andrei Ivanovich, count (1686-1747) Russian diplomat. A German by birth, he served Czar Peter I in various positions in the diplomatic service. O. concluded the Treaty of Nystadt (1721), which ended the

Osiris

Northern War between Sweden and Russia. He was able to maintain his positions under a number of czars who followed Peter, and during the brief regency of Anna Leopoldovna, he virtually ruled Russia. After Czarina Elizabeth ascended to the throne (1741), however, he was sentenced to death. The sentence was reprieved and O. was banished to Siberia for the remainder of his life.

Osterman-Tolstoi, Alexander (1770-1837) Russian general, the grandson of Count Andrei Osterman. He fought in the wars against Napoleon's armies at Eylau, Friedland, Borodino, and Bautzen.

Ostia Ancient city in Italy. Located at the mouth of the Tiber River, it served as the harbor of Rome and a transshipment point for grain. Its ruins are an excellent example of the layout of an ancient Italian city.

Ostracism Method of banishing a public figure in ancient Greece. It was introduced c.508 BC by Klisthenes. In Athens and other cities of Greece, banishment of up to 10 years occurred by popular vote (more than 6,000 votes) of a citizen considered dangerous to the state.

Ostroleka City in Poland, north of Warsaw. There, on the May 26, 1831, a Polish revolt was definitively defeated by the Russian army.

Oswald, Saint (c.604-641) King of Northumbria, 633-641. He sought to convert his country to Christianity and died in the struggle against the heathens at Maserfeldt. O. is venerated as a saint in Great Britain.

Otho, Marcus Salvius (32-69 AD) Roman emperor, 69 AD. He was a friend of Nero, who stole his wife, Poppaea Sabina. After the death of Nero, O. first supported Galba, but was proclaimed emperor by his soldiers in 69. In a battle at Cremona, O. was defeated by Vitellius's troops, after which he committed suicide.

Otranto City on the southern coast of Italy. It was originally a Greek settlement and later became an important port under the Romans. During World War II, an Italian naval squadron was routed (July 9, 1940) by a smaller English force off Otranto.

The Ottoman Turks

The Ottomans were a Turkish people who settled in Asia Minor during the 12th and 13th centuries. They developed a great empire that expanded into Europe and lasted until the early 20th century. Europeans greatly feared the Ottoman Turks and sometimes referred to them as "the scourge from the east."

3

1

2

4

1. The Janissaries were the elite troops of the Ottoman monarch, the sultan. *See* Janissaries.
2. A painting of the Ottoman siege of Vienna in 1683. It lasted for two months, until the Turks were driven off by a coalition of European armies headed by King John III of Poland (John Sobieski). *See* John III.
3. The interior of the Blue Mosque in Istanbul. Built in the early 17th century, it was modeled on the Hagia Sophia, also in Istanbul.
4. A portrait of Sultan Muhammad IV, who reigned from 1648 to 1687. He was more interested in hunting than in politics, and during his reign Ottoman power declined.

Otto II (955-983) Holy Roman Emperor, 973-983, and German king, 961-983. He was the son and successor of Otto I, who had him crowned co-regent emperor in 967. O. fought on all fronts of his empire but was eventually beaten by the Arabs in southern Italy.

Otto III (980-1002) Holy Roman Emperor, 996-1002, and German king, 983-1002. He was the son and successor of Otto II. Until 996 O. was under the regency of his mother Theo-

Otto III

phano and his grandmother Adelheid of Burgundy. He then ruled with an iron fist from Rome, where he first had his cousin Bruno (Gregory V) and then his tutor Gerbert of Aurillac (Sylvester II) elected pope. In 1001 discontented Romans rioted and forced Otto to flee. He died as he was preparing to attack the city.

Otto IV of Brunswick (c.1175-1218) Holy Roman Emperor, 1209-1215, and German king. O. was elected king after the death of Emperor Henry VI. Civil war ensured as his election was contested. In 1209 he came into conflict with the Pope Innocent II when he insisted on trying to dominate Italy. He was defeated in battle (1214) by Philip II of France at Bouvines after which he lost all authority. Frederick of Hohenstaufen was then elected emperor, and in 1215, the pope declared Otto deposed.

Otto I (1848-1916) King of Bavaria, 1886-1913. Although insane from 1872 on, he succeeded his brother, Louis II, in 1886 under the regency of his uncle Luitpold. He was removed by an act of the Bavarian parliament in

1913 and replaced by his cousin, the son of Luitpold, who became King Louis III.

Ottoman Empire Vast state founded in the late 13th century by the Ottoman Turks. It was ruled by the descendants of Osman I (1258-1324) until its dissolution in 1918. At its peak in the late 17th century, it extended from southeastern Europe and north Africa in the west across all of the Middle East as far as Persia.

Oudenaarde Town in Belgium, on the Schelde River. A major battle was fought there on July 11, 1708, during the War of the Spanish Succession. The French under Vendôme were beaten by Eugene of Savoy and the Duke of Marlborough at O.

Overlord Code name for the Allied invasion of Normandy (June 6, 1944) during World War II.

Ovid (Publius Ovidius Naso) (43 BC-18 AD) Latin poet. He enjoyed early fame as a poet and was known to the Emperor Augustus. For some unknown reason, he was exiled to the Black sea region in 8 AD, where he ultimately died. O. wrote erotic and mythological poems. His love poems sing the praises of his mistress and give instructions on how to get and keep a lover. His masterpiece is *Metamorphoses*, a collection of myths woven together in a harmonious artistic whole.

Owens, Jesse (1913-1980) American athlete, a track star. An African-American, O. won four gold medals at the 1936 Olympic Games in Berlin,

Otto IV

upsetting his Nazis hosts's Aryan-superiority theories. His records in various remained unbeaten for some 20 years.

Oxenstierna, Count Axel Gustafsson (1583-1654) Swedish statesman. O. became chancellor in 1612 and administered the country during Gustavus II's absences. O. was the most important supporter of Gustav Adolf II and his spouse Queen Christina. While she was a minor (1632-1644), O. was the de factor ruler of Sweden. He followed a cautious foreign policy and distinguished himself with his extensive domestic reforms. O. was the author of the 1634 constitution that centralized power.

Oxenstierna, Count Bengt Gabrielsson (1623-1702) Swedish statesman, son of Count Axel Oxenstierna. He represented his father as the Swedish emissary at the 1648 peace negotiations to end the Thirty Years War. He later served the Swedish crown in a variety of diplomatic missions.

Oxford, Provisions of Plan of government reform forced upon King Henry III by his barons in 1258. The plan set up a council of nobles to advise the king and to keep check on the various branches of government. Divisions among the nobles themselves (the Barons' War, 1263-1267), however, enabled Henry to evade and then repudiate the provisions of the plan.

Oxyrhynchus Archaeological excavation site in Egypt. Some of the largest finds of papyruses, dating from Ptolemaic, Greek, and Roman times, were discovered in O. Many of the documents contain works of well-known Greek authors as well as theological and legal texts.

Özal, Turgut (1927-1993) Turkish politician, founder of the Motherland Party. Gaining a majority in parliament in 1983, O.'s government strove to reduce the influence of the military in Turkish affairs. The Motherland Party lost its majority in 1991.

Ozawa, Jisaburo (1886-1966) Japanese admiral. He took part in the Battle of Leyte Gulf (1944) during World War II and was the supreme commander of the Japanese fleet from May 1945 until the Japanese surrender in September of that year.

Otto I

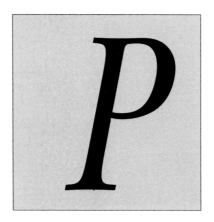

P

Paardekraal Town in South Africa. It was the site of a demonstration by thousands of Boers in 1880 that marked the beginning of the first Boer War.

Pachacamac Ancient Peruvian god, later associated by the Incas with the creator-god Viracocha.

Pachacuti Yupanqui *See* Incas.

Pachomius, Saint (290-346) Egyptian monk. A hermit, he was one of the earliest founders of monastic community life. P. established a monastery in Tabennisi around 320, of which he became the abbot.

Paderewski, Ignace Jan (1860-1941) Polish pianist, composer, and statesman. He was a brilliant, internationally known concert pianist and a Polish patriot. P. briefly headed Polish governments in 1919 and in 1940-1941, the latter in exile during World War II. He devoted much of his personal wealth to the service of Poland and spent his final years pleading the cause of Poland, which was under Nazi occupation. He died in the United States in 1941.

Pagan Ruined city in Burma. It is one of the major archaeological sites of Southeast Asia, with the remains of more than 800 Buddhist temples and pagodas dating from the 11th-13th centuries. P. was sacked by the Mongols in 1287, but many of its shrines, which show a strong Indian influence, survived. The site is still a place of Buddhist pilgrimage.

Paganini, Niccolò (1782-1840) Italian violinist and composer. A legend during his lifetime, P. extended the range of violin virtuosity through the use of harmonics and other devices. His compositions include his violin concertos and the 24 caprices.

Painlevé, Paul (1863-1933) French mathematician and statesman. As a mathematician, he made important contributions in the field of differential equations. He entered politics in 1910 and was briefly premier in 1917, during World War I. He served as premier again in 1925 and was minister of war (1925-1929) and minister of aviation (1930-1931, 1932-1933).

Paisley, Ian (1926-) Northern Irish religious and political leader. A Protestant and a fierce anti-Catholic, he has fought all efforts that would secure the rights of the Catholic minority in Ulster. P. advocates the complete integration of Northern Ireland into the United Kingdom.

Paladins The high-ranking knights and courtiers at the court of Charlemagne. The word has also come to mean a knightly person defending the interests of others.

Palatine The seven hills of the ancient city of Rome.

Palaeologus Greek dynasty that ruled the Byzantine Empire from its restoration in 1261 to its conquest by the Turks in 1453.

Palestine Historic region of the Middle East, comprising parts of Israel, Jordan, and Egypt. It is also referred to as the Holy Land. The name is derived from the word meaning "land of the Philistine."

Palestine Liberation Organization (PLO) Coordinating organization for Palestinian refugees, founded in 1964. It called for the establishment of in independent state of Palestine in what was then the state of Israel. The

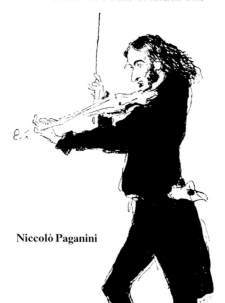

Niccolò Paganini

PLO sponsored acts of terrorism against Israel, but in 1993, it renounced terrorism and agreed to Israel's right to exist. In return, the Israeli government began turning over the civil administration of a limited number of areas on the West Bank and in Gaza to PLO authorities. Under the long-time leadership of Yassir Arafat, the PLO emerged in the 1990s as a supporter of negotiations with Israel in return for limited Palestinian self-rule.

Palestrina, Giovanni Pierluigi (c.1525-1594) Italian composer. In 1551 he became master of the Julian Chapel Choir in the Vatican. He

Giovanni Pierluigi Palestrina

served as well as choirmaster of the Cathedral of St. John Lateran. P. composed more than 105 masses as well as madrigals, motets, and other forms of music.

Palikao, Charles Cousin-Montauban, count of (1796-1878) French general. he fought in Algeria from 1831 and took Abd al-Kadir prisoner in 1847. In 1860 he led the Franco-British expedition to China (where he captured Beijing). P. was prime minister for a month in 1870 under the regency of Empress Eugénie. When the Second Empire was overthrown in 1871, he fled to Belgium.

Palme, Olof (1927-1986) Swedish politician. A Social Democrat, he was prime minister from 1969 until 1976. In 1982, he became prime minister again, this time heading a minority

Pacific Ocean Cultures

It was only in the 18th century that European explorers discovered that the many islands of the Pacific were inhabited. These Pacific islanders were obviously related to the peoples living in Southeast Asia, but they had developed distinctive cultures.

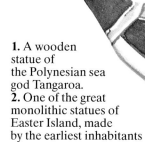

1. A wooden statue of the Polynesian sea god Tangaroa.
2. One of the great monolithic statues of Easter Island, made by the earliest inhabitants of Polynesia.
3. An emu made of painted wood.
4. During his second voyage of discovery, James Cook arrives at Malekula, one of the New Hebrides. *See* James Cook.
5. The migrations across the Pacific.

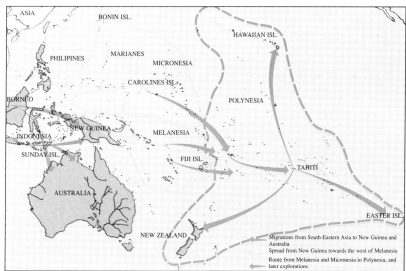

Migrations from South-Eastern Asia to New Guinea and Australia
Spread from New Guinea towards the west of Melanesia
Route from Melanesia and Micronesia to Polynesia, and later explorations

government. P. was assassinated in 1986.

Palmyra Ancient city in Syria. The Romans controlled it after 30 AD. By the 3rd century, Septimius Odenathus had built it into a strong, autonomous state. After his death, the city began to decline, and it eventually fell to the Arabs in the 7th century. It was later sacked by Tamerlane, and its ruins remained untouched until the 17th century.

Pan (Roman: Faunus) Greek god of fertility. He was usually depicted with horns and the legs of a goat. P. was supposed to be able to make flocks of sheep fertile.

Pan

Panda (d.1873) King of the Zulus. He was recognized by the Boers in 1840 after he had rebelled against his brother, Dingaan.

Pangalos, Theodorus (1878-1952) Greek general and politician. After a coup, P. became prime minister in 1925 and dictator in 1926. Soon thereafter, he was overthrown and imprisoned.

Panipat, Battle of *See* Lodi dynasty.

Pankhurst, Emmeline (1858-1928) English feminist who fought for woman suffrage. In 1903, she founded the Women's Social and Political Union, which struggled for women's suffrage using such militant tactics as hunger strikes in prison. During World War I, she shifted her energies to war causes, and when the war ended, she moved to Canada and gave up her feminist pursuits. P. returned to England in 1926 and died two years later while running for a seat in Parliament as a Conservative.

Pannonia Ancient Roman province. It covered parts of what are now Hungary, Austria, and Croatia. P. was permanently subjugated in 9 AD by Tiberius and subdivided into the provinces Pannonia and Dalmatia. It was abandoned by the Romans in 395.

Pansa, Caius Vibius (d.43 BC) Roman general and statesman. A follower of Caesar, he fought Mark Antony's legions at Mutina and was killed in battle.

Pan-Slavism Movement for the political and cultural unity of all Slavs. Originating in the 17th century, it eventually focused on the liberation of the Slavs in the Hapsburg and Ottoman Empires and on the primacy of Russia as the leading Slavic nation.

Pantheon Round temple in ancient Rome, a place for the worship of all the gods of the Roman Empire. It was built in 27 BC, and after 609 AD became a Christian church.

Paoli, Pasquale (1726-1807) Corsican patriot. He was the leader of the resistance (1750s-1760s) against Genoa and later against France. A tireless fighter for Corsican independence, P. struggled unsuccessfully against France during the French Revolution but was never able to secure Corsica's freedom.

Papa Doc *See* Duvalier.

Papadopoulos, Georgios (1919-) Greek soldier. He led a coup against the elected civilian government in 1967 and became president in 1973.

Georgios Papadopoulos

On November 25th of that year, however, the junta he headed was overthrown and a civilian government restored. P. was arrested, tried, and sentenced to death, but the sentence was commuted to life imprisonment.

Papal States Independent territory under the temporal rule of the papacy from 754 until 1870. Although the territory varied in size at different times in history, it generally encompassed the regions of Latium, Umbria, Marche, and eastern Emilia-Romagna on the Italian peninsula. The remaining territories under papal control fell to a unified Italy in the 1860s. When Rome itself came under the control of the Italian government in 1870, Pope Pius IX refused to accept the loss of his lands and retreated inside the Vatican. Until 1929, popes refused to recognize the loss of their territories and remained prisoners inside the Vatican after their elections. In 1929, Italy and the Holy See negotiated the Lateran Treaty, in which the papacy recognized the loss of the Papal States in return for the creation of Vatican City, an independent, papal-controlled state within the city of Rome.

Papen, Franz von (1879-1969) German political leader. A member of the Catholic Center Party, he became chancellor in 1932 and played an important part in the deal-making that brought Hitler to power in 1933. P. served Hitler as vice-chancellor and narrowly escaped being assassinated in the 1934 purge. He was sent abroad, first as ambassador in Austria, where he helped arrange the *Anschluss,* and from 1939 to 1944 as ambassador to Turkey. He was acquitted of war crimes at the Nuremberg trials in 1946 but was sentenced to hard labor (1947) by a German court. In 1949 the sentence was rescinded.

Franz von Papen

Pappenheim, Gottfried Heinrich, Count zu (1594-1632) German

Gottfried Heinrich Pappenheim

cavalry officer. During the Thirty Years War, P. fought under command of the Catholic League and the Holy Roman Emperor. His horsemen became notorious for their cruelty in battle. P. participated in a number of key engagements, and died from injuries suffered at the Battle of Lützen.

Paraguay Wars Conflict that took place between 1865 and 1870 between Paraguay and the armies of Brazil, Uruguay, and Argentina. By the end of the war, Paraguay was devastated and most of its male population killed. The conflict is also called the War of the Triple Alliance.

Parcae *See* Fates.

Paris, Treaty of (1763) Treaty that ended the Seven Years' War between England, France, and Spain.

Paris, Treaty of (1783) Treaty that ended the American Revolutionary War.

Paris, Treaty of (1814) Treaty that ended the war against Napoleon by the Allies (the sixth coalition war).

Paris, Treaty of (1815) Treaty that ended the seventh coalition war between Napoleon and the Allies.

Paris, Treaty of (1856) Treaty that ended the Crimean War.

Paris, Treaty of (1898) Treaty that ended the Spanish-American War.

Paris, Treaty of (1947) Summary of the peace treaties signed between the Allies and Italy, Bulgaria, Finland, Hungary, and Rumania (World War II allies of Germany).

Paris, Treaty of (1995) Treaty that ended the civil war in the former Yugoslavia between the Serbs, Croats, Bosnian Serbs, and Bosnian Muslims.

Paris Treaties (1954) Series of agreements that led to the recognition of the Federal Republic of Germany (West Germany) and that provided for the continued stationing of allied troops in West Germany.

Parma City in northern Italy. It was founded in 183 BC by the Romans. During the Middle Ages, P. belonged to the Lombard Union. In 1545, Pope Paul III made it a duchy, and between 1735 and 1748 it was part of Austria. After periods of rule by France, P. reverted to Italy in 1861.

Parmenion (c.400-330 BC) Macedonian general. He served Philip II and Alexander the Great. During Alexander's campaign to the East, P.'s son was executed for being part of a suspected conspiracy against Alexander. P. was then also put to death by Alexander out of fear of revenge.

Parthenon Doric temple of the goddess Athena on the Acropolis in Athens.

Parthians Peoples from Persia who founded an empire c.250 BC that extended from Mesopotamia in the west as far east as Indus Valley. Partly because of their control of China and India's caravan trade with the West, the P. became involved in several wars with Rome during the 1st century BC. The last of the Parthian monarchs was defeated by Ardashir (*see* Sassanids) in AD 226.

Parti Social Français *See* Rocque.

Partition of Poland Partition of Polish land between Russia, Prussia, and Austria. Poland was partitioned in 1772, 1793, and 1795, an initiative of the Russian Czarina Catherine II. The last partition resulted from the 1794 Polish uprising under Kosciuszko.

Pascal, Blaise (1623-1662) French scientist and religious philosopher.

He founded the modern theory of probability, and, in physics, studied barometric measurements and the equilibrium of fluids (Pascal's Law). P. came eventually to oppose the rationalism of Descartes and advocated the need for a mystic faith in order to understand the universe. His religious writings were posthumously published.

Blaise Pascal

Paschal II (d.1118) Pope, 1099-1118. An Italian named Ranieri, he became involved in the investiture controversy with emperors Henry IV and Henry V, and for a short time was held captive by Henry V.

Pasha Title formerly used in Turkey

Pasha

293

and Egypt for the highest ranking civil servants and military officials.

Pasic, Nikola (1845-1926) Serbian politician. He was one of the founders of the modern Yugoslavia.

Passarowitz, Treaty of Pact signed in 1718 ending the war between the Ottoman Empire on the one hand and Austria and Venice on the other.

Passau, Treaty of. *See* Maurice, duke of Saxony.

Passchendaele Town in Belgium where British troops under Haig mounted an offensive against the Germans (July-November 1917) during World War I. The British troops gained little ground and suffered 300,000 casualties.

Louis Pasteur

Pasteur, Louis (1822-1895) French chemist. His work with bacteria led to the germ theory of infection. P's. research also led to the development of the process known as pasteurization. His technique of vaccination against anthrax was successfully administered against rabies in 1885. P. founded the Pasteur Institute in Paris in 1888 as a research and teaching center for the study of contagious diseases.

Pathet Lao Laotian communist liberation movement founded in 1950 to expel the French from Laos. They had obtained absolute power in 1975 with the communist victory throughout Southeast Asia.

Patricians Members of the privileged class in ancient Rome. In the early period of the republic, only P. were allowed to hold civil and religious offices. From the 6th century BC, however, the lower class, the plebs, struggled for equality and were gradually able to assume more and more offices. The nobiles eventually evolved: a ruling-class aristocracy drawn from both P. and plebs. Caesar and Augustus came from P. families, but they promoted plebs to the P. class.

Patton, George Smith (1885-1945) American general during World War II. A tank commander, he participated in the North African campaign (1942-1943), and, after the invasion of Normandy (1944), was given command of the Third Army. P. was military governor of Bavaria for a brief time in 1945. He died in a road accident in Germany.

Paul, Alice (1885-1977) American feminist. She was an early leader in the movement that eventually gave women the right to vote (1920). A militant, she helped found the National Woman's Party in 1916. P. submitted the first version of the Equal Rights Amendment (ERA) to Congress in 1923.

Paul, Saint (d.64? - 67? AD) Apostle of the Gentiles. He was born a Jew named Saul and was a tentmaker by profession before being baptized as a Christian. The sources for his life are the Acts of the Apostles and the Pauline Epistles of the New Testament. The Christian faith today, whether Roman Catholic or Protestant, is the view of Christ and his life and teachings as put forth by P.

Paul I (1754-1801) Czar of Russia, 1796-1801. Son of Catherine II, he sought to undo her policy of empowering the nobility and create a centralized state. Dissatisfaction with his rule led to a conspiracy on the part of the military and the nobility, which

his son and successor, Alexander, was aware of but did nothing to prevent. In 1801 the czar was overthrown and murdered.

Paul I (1901-1964) King of the Hellenes, 1947-1964. He succeeded his brother, George II, as the Greek king after World War II. P. pursued a pro-Western policy during his reign. After his death, his son Constantine reigned briefly until the abolition of the Greek monarchy in 1967.

George Smith Patton

Paul III (1468-1549) Pope, 1534-1549. Born Alessandro Farnese, he was a shrewd diplomat and a reformer. During his reign, the Catholic Reformation began. The Council of Trent was convened in 1545 to reform the church, and the pope gave his support to reforming groups like the Jesuits. P. was a great supporter of the arts. He had Michelangelo continue to paint *The Last Judgment* in the Sistine Chapel and to complete the dome of St. Peter's.

Paul III

Paul IV (1476-1559) Pope, 1555-1559. Born Gian Pietro Carafa, he worked as pope to further the Inquisition and to rid the Church of worldliness and corruption. He came into conflict with Philip II of Spain, after which Alba marched into Rome in 1557 and forced the pope to make peace.

Paul V (1552-1621) Pope, 1605-1621. Born Camillo Borghese, he was an expert in canon law. As pope, P. attempted to enhance the power and prerogatives of the papacy, often at the expense of local clergies. During his reign, St. Peter's was completed.

Paul VI (1897-1978) Pope, 1963-1978. Born Giovanni Battista Montini, he served most of his church career in the Vatican secretariat of state. As pope, he reconvened the Second Vatican Council begun by his predecessor, John XXIII. P. was generally a conservative pope who upheld traditional church teachings on birth control and the priesthood. He visited the Holy Land in 1964, becoming the first pope in 150 years to leave Italy.

Paulus, Friedrich (1890-1957) German field marshal during World War II. He commanded the ill-fated 6th Army at Stalingrad (1943). After its defeat, he was imprisoned by the Soviets and made radio broadcasts urging the Germans to surrender. Released in 1953, he spent his final years in communist East Germany.

Pauperization Marxist theory that predicted the inevitable worsening of workers' living conditions, leading to their support of a communist revolution.

Pausanias (d.470 BC) Spartan general. In 479 BC, he defeated the Persians at Plataea. P. was unjustly accused a number of times of treason with the Persians but was acquitted. In 470 he was accused of planning a coup in Sparta. To escape prosecution, he took refuge in a temple, where he was left to starve to death.

Pavelich, Ante (1889-1959) Croatian politician. He was the leader of the Ustashi, an anti-Serbian fascist organization that collaborated with the Nazis during World War II. P. led Croatia (1941-1945) as a German

Ante Pavelich

vassal state in which Serbs and Jews were mercilessly persecuted. He subsequently lived in exile in Argentina and Spain.

Pavia City in northern Italy. During the Italian wars, the French King Francis I was defeated and captured (1525) by Emperor Charles near Pavia.

Peace Corps American overseas volunteer program, begun (1961) during the administration of President John F. Kennedy. Volunteers serve for usually two years and work in such areas as education, agriculture, and health care.

Peace of Augsburg Treaty between Roman Catholic and Protestant German rulers (1555) under which they agreed to respect each other's religion.

Peacock Throne Throne of the Iranian shah, named after its decoration in the shape of an opened peacock's fan.

Pearl Harbor American naval base on the island of Oahu, Hawaii. It was bombed by the Japanese on December 7, 1941, precipitating the U.S. entry into World War II.

Peary, Robert (1856-1920) American Arctic explorer. In 1909 he became the first person to reach the North Pole.

Pedro II (1825-1891) Emperor of Brazil, 1825-1889. He became emperor as an infant on the abdication of his father, Pedro I. During his long

reign, Brazil enjoyed peace and growing prosperity. Although P. remained popular, discontent among the wealthy planter class and the church grew in the latter years of his reign. In 1889, a bloodless coup overthrew the monarchy, and P. was exiled to Europe, where he spent the remaining two years of his life.

Pedro the Cruel (1334-1369) King of Castile and León, 1350-1369. His rule was challenged by his half-brother, Henry. With the help of Edward the Black Prince, P. won a victory at the Battle of Nájera (1367). Two years later, however, he was defeated and killed.

Peenemünde Town in Germany. During World War II, it was a research and production center for the German rocket program that produced the V1 and V2 rockets used to terrorize London.

Pelopidas (d.364 BC) Theban general. He fought the Spartans in a number of battles before joining Epaminondas to defeat them again at Leuctra in 371 BC. With Epaminondas he joined in the invasion of the Peloponnesus (370-369) and Macedonia (368). His life was written about by Plutarch.

Peloponnesian League Alliance formed around 500 BC between Sparta and the remaining Peloponnesian states. Designed to protect against Persian aggression, it was dissolved in 366 BC.

Peloponnesian War Decisive struggle in ancient Greece between Sparta and Athens, 431-404 BC. It started in 431 BC, when the Athenians supported Corcyra against Corinth. It came to an end in 404 BC, when Athens was captured by the Spartans under Lysander, who installed an oligarchic government (the Thirty Tyrants). The war destroyed Athens as a political power and left Sparta dominant for the next thirty years. The primary source for the P. is the historian Thucydides.

Penn, William (1644-1718) English quaker. He was the founder (1682) of the colony of Pennsylvania.

William Penn

Pentagon Papers Secret government report, commissioned by Secretary of Defense Robert McNamara in 1967, to examine American involvement in Vietnam. It was leaked to the *New York Times* in 1971 by Daniel Ellsberg, a former Pentagon official who had become disillusioned with the war. The publication of parts of the P., which revealed government miscalculation and deception surrounding America's entry into the conflict, enraged President Nixon. He ordered a series of measures, some of which were illegal, to stop the leaks, and many of these were later used in impeachment proceedings against Nixon in 1974 for abuse of power.

Pepin II of Heristal (d.714) Mayor of the palace of the Frankish kingdom of Austrasia, 680-714. The father of Charles Martel, P. made himself the ruler of all Frankish kingdoms except Aquitaine, thus laying the foundations for the empire of his descendants, the Carolingian mayors and kings.

Pepin the Short (c.714-768) First Carolingian king of the Franks, 751-768. He was the second son of Charles Martel and the father of Charlemagne. After 741, P. was mayor of the palace with his brother Carloman. He deposed the last Merovingian king Childeric III in 751 and had himself crowned king. Before his death, he divided his kingdom between his sons Charlemagne and Carloman. His defense of Rome against the Lombards and the resulting cession of lands to the papacy led to the foundation of the Papal States.

Perdiccas (d.413 BC) King of Macedonia from c.450 BC. In the Peloponnesian War, he alternately supported Athens and Sparta.

Perdiccas (c.365-321 BC) Macedonian general. One of Alexander the Great's generals, he fought with Alexander in the East. After Alexander's death (323 BC), P. attempted to hold the empire together as regent, but was opposed by others of the Diadochi and was eventually murdered by his own officers.

Peres, Shimon (1923-) Prime minister of Israel, 1984-1986, 1995-1996. He emigrated to Israel from Europe in 1934 and became involved trade union activity. P. became Labor party leader in 1977. In 1984, he formed a cabinet of national unity with Yitzhak Shamir's right wing Likud Front, serv-

Pepin the Short

Shimon Peres

ing as prime minister until 1986. When Labor returned to power under Yitzhak Rabin in 1993, P. became foreign minister. He and Rabin began negotiations with the PLO for the return of parts of the West Bank to Palestinian control. P., Arafat, and Rabin were jointly awarded The 1994 Nobel Peace Prize. He became prime minister again when Rabin was assassinated in 1995 until Netanyau was elected prime minister in 1996.

Pergamum Ancient city of Asia Minor, in present-day Turkey. It was a center of Hellenistic civilization after the breakup (4th century BC) of the Macedonian empire. The city is known for its sculpture, the most famous work being an altar dedicated to Zeus dating back to 200 BC. The rulers of P. built a famous library whose specialty was the use of parchment. P. was reconstituted as a province of Asia under the Roman Empire.

Pericles (c.495-429 BC) Athenian statesman. In 461 BC, after the death of Ephialtes, P. became leader of the democratic party and therefore of Athenian politics. He advanced democracy and turned Athens into a center of the arts and sciences. P. was one of the leaders in the events that led to the Peloponnesian War (431-404 BC). His celebrated funeral oration at the end of the first year of war, as reported by Thucydides, was an appeal to Athenian pride and patriotism.

Perkins, Frances (1880-1965) Secretary of Labor during the administration of President Franklin D. Roosevelt. She was the first woman to hold a Cabinet position.

Perón, Juan Domingo (1895-1974) President of Argentina, 1946-1955, 1973-1974. A professional soldier, he rose to prominence in the 1940s by building a coalition consisting of the labor unions, nationalists, and the Church. His movement, Peronism, called for land reform and was highly popular. P.'s political hold on Argentina was enhanced by the enormous popularity of his wife, Eva Perón. When she died of cancer at 33 in 1952, P.'s grip on Argentina began to weaken. He was overthrown in 1955 and went into exile in Paraguay and then Spain. The Peronist movement, however, remained a potent force in Argentine politics, as did the cult of Eva Perón. In 1973, P. was permitted to return and was elected president. He died in 1974 after less than a year in office and was succeeded by his wife, Isabel Martínez de Perón.

Perovskaya, Sofia (1853-1881) Russian revolutionary. She was hanged for her role in the assassination of Czar Alexander II in 1881.

Perret, Auguste (1874-1954) French architect. His most famous work is the

Pericles

church at Raincy, near Paris, built in 1922-1923. P. is considered one of the most important French architects of his generation.

Perry, Matthew Calbraith (1794-1858) American naval officer. He headed an American expedition to Japan in 1853-1854 that resulted in the Japanese opening their ports to the outside world.

Persepolis Ancient city if Persia. It was the ceremonial capital of the Achaemenid Empire under Darius, Xerxes, and their successors. In 330 BC, the city was captured and destroyed by Alexander the Great's forces.

Perseus (c.212-166 BC) Last king of Macedonia, 179-168 BC. He was defeated at Pydna by the Romans under Aemilius Paullus and died in captivity.

John Joseph Pershing

Pershing, John Joseph (1860-1948) American general. He fought in the Spanish-American War (1898) and led the punitive U.S. expedition against Pancho Villa in Mexico (1916-1917). After the U.S. entry into World War I (1917), P. was appointed head of the American Expeditionary Force in France, molding it into an efficient combat organization in a short period of time. After the war he served as army chief of staff (1921-1924).

Persian Gulf War (1991) Conflict between Iraq and an international coalition led by the United States. It

was precipitated by Iraqi's invasion and annexation (1990) of neighboring Kuwait. An international force was formed to eject Iraq from Kuwait, which was accomplished early in 1991 after six weeks of heavy air raids on Iraq and a ground war lasting only four days.

Persian Wars *See* Greek-Persian Wars.

Pertinax, Publius Helvius (126-193 AD) Roman emperor, 193. A general, he was proclaimed Emperor by the Praetorian Guard following the death of Commodus the previous year. After only three months, he was murdered by one of his soldiers.

Pétain, Henri Philippe (1856-1951) French general. A hero of World War I, P. became (1940) head of state of the Vichy government, which collaborated with the Germans during World War II. In 1945, after the war ended, he was tried for treason and sentenced to death. The sentence was commuted to life in prison by De Gaulle. Pétain, in his 90s, spent his final years in a military fortress on the island of Yeu.

Peter the Great (Peter I) (1672-1725) Czar of Russia, 1682-1725. The son of Czar Alexis, he was proclaimed czar jointly with Ivan V in 1682 and took over sole authority in 1696. After a long journey to Western Europe, P. returned to Russia and initiated a program of westernization. In foreign affairs, he consciously pursued an expansionist policy. P. was involved in the Northern War and defeated the Swedish king Charles XII at Poltava. He founded the city of St. Petersburg. P. was a ruthless leader who believed his subjects had to be brought against their will into the modern world.

Peter II (1715-1730) Czar of Russia, 1727-1730. A grandson of Peter the Great, he became czar at the age of 12 on the death of the Czarina Catherine I. He died of smallpox at the age of 15 and never ruled as an adult.

Peter III (1728-1762) Czar of Russia, 1762. A grandson of Peter the Great, he succeeded on the death of the Czarina Elizabeth. In 1745, P. married Sophie of Anhalt-Zerbst, who later became Czarina Catherine II. As czar, P. immediately made peace with Frederick the Great of Prussia, but he

soon fell victim of a conspiracy by the Orlov brothers, one of whom was Catherine's lover. Alleged to be mentally unstable, P. was forced to abdicate by the imperial guards on Catherine's orders. She was proclaimed czarina, and, a few days later, P. was assassinated by his guards.

Henri Philippe Pétain

Peter the Great

Petrarca, Francesco (Petrarch) (1304-1374) Italian poet and humanist. He is one of the great figures of Italian literature. P. perfected the sonnet form and is considered by some to be

The Persians

The Persians first came to live
on the Iranian plateau in c.1500 BC.
By the 6th century BC, they had
established a strong state. For more
than three centuries, they ruled
er an extensive empire. In 331 BC,
however, they were decisively
beaten by Alexander the Great, and
period of domination by Greek
rulers followed.

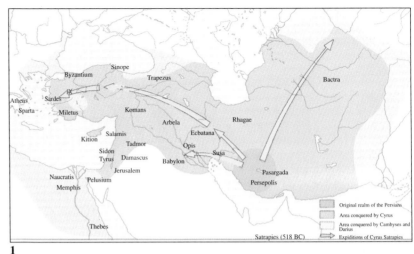

1

2

3

4

5

6

1. Map of the great expansion
of the Persian realm. *See* Cyrus;
Cambyses; Darius I.
2. One of the famous reliefs in Darius
I's palace in Susa, depicting a
winged bull. *See* Darius I; Susa.
3. The grave of Cyrus the Great, king
of the Persians from c.555 BC to
529 BC. *See* Cyrus; Persepolis; Croesus.
4. Persian soldier on a frieze in the
palace of Artaxerxes I in Susa.
See Artaxerxes; Susa.
5. Coin of Cyrus the Younger, who
led a rebellion against King
Artaxerxes II in 401 BC that is
described in the *Anabasis* of
Xenophon.
See Cyrus the Younger.
6. Handle of a gold cup shaped like
a winged chamois, dating from
the 5th century BC. *See* Achaemenids;
Alexander the Great; Darius III.

the first modern poet. His lyric poems, in particular those for his beloved Laura, supplanted the image of the medieval woman as a spiritual symbol and replaced it with a portrait of a modern woman. Through his interest in classical Greece and Rome and his wide correspondence, he helped spread the Renaissance.

Peutinger map Map created in 1265. It was a copy of a Roman map of the world from the 4th century, depicting the then-known world from Britannia to Indonesia.

Pham Van Dong (1906-) Vietnamese political leader. In 1941, he and Ho Chi Minh founded the Vietminh. P, served as premier of North Vietnam from 1954-1976 and as premier of the united Vietnam from 1976-1981.

Pharao Title of the kings in ancient Egypt.

Pharisees Jewish sect in the days of Christ. Its members sought to follow the teachings of Moses as faithfully as possible.

Phidias (c.490-430 B.C.) Greek sculptor. Among his works are the *Athena Parthenos* (Acropolis), the *Zeus* (Olympia), and the sculptures on the façade of the Parthenon.

Philae Former island in the Nile River near the Aswan Dam. It was submerged by the waters of Lake Nasser after the construction of the dam. P. was noted for its temple dedicated to Isis, built during the era of the Ptolemies. After the Christianization

Francesco Petrarca

of Egypt, an Isis cult continued on P. as late as Justinian's time. Most of the monuments on the island were removed in the 1960s before it was submerged.

Philastre (d.AD 397) Bishop of Brescia, 385-391. His work, *Diversarum haereseon liber,* which discussed numerous kinds of heresy, inspired Augustine.

Philip I (Philip the Handsome) (1478-1506) Spanish King of Castile, 1506. He was married Joanna, the daughter of Ferdinand and Isabella, who succeeded her parents as queen of Castile in 1504. P. was able to gain the right to co-rule with her in 1506 but died shortly therafter.

Philip II (382-336 BC) King of Macedon, 359-336 BC. He was the father of Alexander the Great. P. expanded his kingdom, subjecting neighboring peoples to Macedonian rule and defeating the Greek army near Chaironeia in 338.

Philip II (Philip Augustus) (1165-1223) King of France, 1180-1223.

Philip II (Augustus)

During his reign, the power of the centralized French monarchy was consolidated and the territory of France was more than doubled.

Philip II (1527-1598) King of Spain, 1556-1598. He was at constant odds with France, and his marriage to Mary

Philip II (King of Macedon)

I of England drew that country into the conflict. When the English supported the Dutch rebellion against Spain, P. sent his Armada (1588) to invade England but was ignominiously defeated. Spanish colonial ventures flourished during his reign, partly to meet P.'s incessant need for gold to finance his undertakings.

Philip II (King of Spain)

Philip IV (Philip the Fair) (1268-1314) King of France, 1285-1314. He strengthened the monarchy and increased the royal revenues during his reign. P. quarreled with the papacy throughout his reign, and in 1309 forced the popes to relocate to Avignon (the Babylonian captivity).

Philip IV (1605-1665) King of Spain, Naples, and Sicily, 1621-1665. Disinterested in governing, he left the affairs of state to the duke of Olivarez. During his reign, Spain continue to decline politically and economically.

Philistines Non-semitic people who settled in Palestine c.1300 BC and were frequently at odds with the Israelites. They controlled the iron supplies of the region as well as the political organization of urban areas.

Philopoemen (c.252-182 BC) Greek general. He was commander of the Achaean League. P. defeated the Spartans several times but was captured by the rebellious Messenians and executed.

Philotas (c.360-330 BC) Macedonian nobleman, the son of Parmemion. A commander of Alexander the Great's bodyguard, he was accused of conspiracy and executed in 330 BC.

Phoenicia Ancient territory between the Lebanese mountains and the Mediterranean. The main towns were Sidon and Tyrus. As early as c.1500 BC, the Phoenicians colonized parts of Cyprus, Sicily, and southern Spain. They also founded Carthage, which soon became even more powerful than P. itself and finally succumbed to the Romans (*see* Punic Wars). P. was a trading nation, and Phoenicians sailed around Africa (*see* Necho II) and brought tin from England. In P. the alphabetical script was developed.

Phrygians Inhabitants of Anatolia, where they settled having come from Europe after 1200 B.C. Their empire and its capital, Gordium, prospered in the 8th century. The Cimmerian invasion put an end to their rule.

Piaf, Edith (1915-1963) French cabaret singer. Born Edith Giovanna Gassion, she began singing at 15. Although small in stature (she was called the "Little Sparrow"), P. was possessed of a powerful and distinctive voice. She became famous for her emotional performance of songs such as *Milord, La vie en rose,* and *Non, je ne regrette rien.*

Edith Piaf

Piasts Polish dynasty of dukes and kings. They ruled from c. 850-1370 and were succeeded by the Jagiello dynasty.

Piave River in northern Italy. It was the site of a decisive defeat by the Allies (1918) of the Austrian army during the World War I.

Picasso, Pablo (1881-1973) Spanish artist. He was a painter, sculpture, and graphic artist, and one of the foremost figures in twentieth-century art. P. had his first exhibition at the age of 16. After a blue and a pink period, he painted *Les Demoiselles d'Avignon* in 1907, a radical departure from pre-

Pablo Picasso

vious artistic conventions and considered the most important work of Cubism. P.'s work is done is a many different mediums and is extensive and varied. One of his most well-known paintings is *Guernica*, which was inspired by the bombing of the Spanish town of the same name during the Spanish Civil War in the late 1930s.

Pichegru, Charles (1761-1804) French general, commander of the French army that invaded the Netherlands during the French Revolutionary Wars. He was later a proponent of the reinstatement of the monarchy and was forced to flee to England. P. returned to France in 1803 as part of a royalist conspiracy and was arrested. He was found dead in his cell in 1804 under suspicious circumstances.

Pierce, Franklin (1804-1869) 14th president of the U.S., 1853-1857. He

Philosophers

All human societies have had philosophers, people who seek wisdom, hoping to get a grasp of ultimate reality.
Over the centuries many schools of thought on the great problems of life and the universe have developed. This page shows a few of the great thinkers.
See the separate entries on each person.

1

2

3

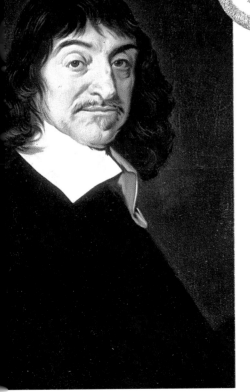

4

5

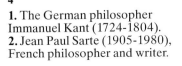

3. The French philosopher
François Marie Arouet de Voltaire
(1694-1778) depicted
in his study.
4. René Descartes, French philosopher
and mathematician (1596 - 1650).
5. The Russian revolutionary
and anarchist Mikhail Bakunin
(1814-1876).

1. The German philosopher
Immanuel Kant (1724-1804).
2. Jean Paul Sarte (1905-1980),
French philosopher and writer.

served in the U.S. House of Representatives and the Senate before fighting in the Mexican War. Although a Northerner, he had proslavery views and was nominated for president by the Democratic Party in 1852. He defeated the Whig candidate, General Winfield Scott. During his administration, the Senate ratified the Gadsden Purchase and passed the Kansas-Nebraska Act. P.'s opposition to the Civil War made him a detested figure, and he died in obscurity.

Franklin Pierce

Pietà Type of sculpture dating from the 14th century depicting a mourning Mary holding the body of Christ after his descent from the Cross. The most famous P. is Michelangelo's (1499) in the St. Peter's Basilica in Rome.

Pilgrims Group of English dissenters from Anglicanism who fled from England to the Netherlands in 1608 and in 1620 sailed to North America aboard the *Mayflower*. There, along the coast of the future state of Massachusetts, they founded the Plymouth Colony.

Pillnitz Town in Germany. There, in 1791, a conference was held between Emperor Leopold II and Frederick William II of Prussia, about possible action against revolutionary France. Their offer to restore Louis XVI to his throne helped precipitate the French Revolutionary Wars.

Pilsudski, Józef (1867-1935) Polish statesman. He was exiled to Serbia in 1887 because of his part in a plot against Czar Alexander III. P. was one of the founders of the Polish Socialist Party. During World War I, he fought against the Russians for a free Poland and in 1918 became the first president of the Polish Republic. P. was a virtual dictator of Poland, regardless of the government position he held. He was at various times president, premier, or war minister, but he remained the principal figure in Poland during the 1920s and 1930s.

Pinckney's Treaty (1795) Agreement between the U.S. and Spain establishing commercial relations and fixing the southern boundary of the U.S. at the 31st parallel. Negotiated by Thomas Pinckney, it also gave the Americans free navigation rights on the Mississippi River.

Pinochet, Augusto (1915-) President of Chile, 1973-1990. A general, he led the military coup that overthrew the government of President Salvador Allende in 1973. As head of a junta, he ruled Chile with an iron hand, ruthlessly suppressing all opposition. In 1988 he submitted to a referendum to extend his term of office and lost. The presidency then reverted to civilian control, although P. retained the powerful position of head of the military.

Pisa, Council of (1409) Convocation of the Roman Catholic Church, called to end the Great Schism. The council deposed the two men claiming to be the legitimate pope—Gregory XII in Rome and Benedict XIII in Avignon—and elected Cardinal Pietro Pilarghi, who took the name Alexander V. Gregory and Benedict refused to step down, however. The Pisa meeting established the precedent of the supremacy of church councils.

Pisistratus (d.527 BC) Athenian soldier and statesman. He became undisputed leader of Athens after 560 BC and laid the foundation for Athens as a world power. When he died, he left an established order to his sons Hippias and Hipparchus.

Piso, Calpurnius (d. 65 AD) Roman nobleman. He led of a conspiracy against Nero in 65 AD. After being discovered, P. and his fellow conspira-

tors, including Seneca, were forced to commit suicide.

Pitt, William, 1st earl of Chatham (1708-1778) British statesman. He served George II and George III in a number of posts, including prime minister (1756-1761; 1766-1768). P. laid the foundation of British colonial empire. He is sometimes referred to as the Great Commoner or William Pitt the Elder.

Augusto Pinochet

Pitt, William (1759-1806) British statesman. The son of William Pitt, earl of Chatham, he became a member of the House of Commons in 1781. P. became prime minister in 1783 at the age of 24 and served in that post until 1801. He was seen as the personifica-

William Pitt

tion of Britain's struggle against revolutionary France. In 1804, P. again became prime minister and a leading figure in the battle against Napoleon. The defeat of Britain's allies by Napoleon at Austerlitz (1805) allegedly hastened his death. He is sometimes known as William Pitt the Younger.

Pius II (1405-1464) Pope, 1458-1464. Born Enea Silvio Piccolomini, he was a classical humanist and the only pope who ever wrote an autobiography. P. condemned the conciliar theory of church authority, and he quarreled frequently with Louis XI of France, who intervened in Church affairs. After a futile attempt to motivate the Christian world to go on a crusade against the Turks, he embarked alone. He died in the port of Ancona.

Pius V, Saint (1504-1572) Pope, 1566-1572. Born Michele Ghislieri, he directed the Inquisition prior to his elevation to the papacy. After his election, he saw to it that the decrees of the Council of Trent were carried out, thus placing himself at the heart of the Catholic Reformation. In 1570, P. excommunicated Elizabeth I of England. He was canonized in 1712.

Pius VII (1740-1823) Pope, 1800-1823. Born Barnaba Chiaramonti, he signed a concordat with Napoleon that reestablished the Church in France following the French Revolution. Napoleon forced him to come to France to consecrate him as emperor, only to seize the crown out of the pope's hands and crown himself. When the French took the Papal States (1809), P. excommunicated Napoleon, who thereupon took the pope prisoner and transported him to Fontainebleau. After Napoleon's downfall (1814), P. returned to Rome in triumph. Despite his treatment by Napoleon, P. gave the fallen emperor's family refuge in Rome and interceded with the British to lighten Napoleon's punishment. As a result of his courage and generosity, P. was highly popular with the people.

Pius IX (1792-1878) Pope, 1846-1878. Born Giovanni Maria Mastai-Ferretti, he began his pontificate as a liberal but became a conservative after being driven from Rome for two years following the 1848 revolution. P. never accepted the loss of the Papal States to the new kingdom of Italy, and

Pius IX

from 1870 on he refused to leave the Vatican. He convened the first Vatican Council (1854), which enunciated the doctrines of papal infallibility and the Immaculate Conception. P.'s reign was the longest in history.

Pius X, Saint (1835-1914) Pope, 1903-1914. Born Giuseppe Sarto, he attempted to improve relations with the kingdom of Italy by lifting the ban on Catholics' participation in political life. A strong conservative, he condemned the Modernist heresy and recodified the canon law. P. was widely revered in his lifetime because of his humble background and his love for the poor. He was deeply distressed at the outbreak of World War I in Europe, and many believe that his death was hastened by the anguish he felt over the coming of war. He was canonized in 1954 by Pope Pius XII.

Pius XI (1857-1939) Pope, 1922-1939. Born Achille Ratti, he served as Vatican librarian and nuncio to Poland before being made a cardinal and archbishop of Milan in 1921. As pope, he negotiated the Lateran Treaty (1929) with Italy, which ended the long quarrel over the Papal territories and established Vatican City as an independent state. P. increasingly opposed Mussolini and fascism in general and denounced dictatorships around the world.

Pius XII (1876-1958) Pope, 1939-1958. Born Eugenio Pacelli, he was Pius XI's secretary of state before being elected pope. A cautious diplomat, he maintained Vatican relations with all belligerents during World War II. After the war, P. was severely criticized for not speaking out against the Nazi persecution of the Jews. In postwar Italy, the pope staunchly opposed the Communist Party and excommunicated Italian Catholics who were communists. Vatican relations with Iron Curtain countries were nonexistent during his pontificate, and persecution of Catholics in these countries was severe. P. served the longest of any twentieth-century pope.

Pizarro, Francisco (1475-1541) Spanish conquistador. After serving in

Francisco Pizarro

Panama he set off on an expedition to Peru, were he conquered the Inca Empire between 1531 and 1533. P. was murdered by the followers of his former colleague, Diego de Almagro.

Plantagenet The most influential royal dynasty in England during the Middle Ages. It was founded by Geoffrey, count of Anjou, the father of Henry II, and is sometimes known as the Angevin dynasty. Henry II was the first Plantagenet to rule England. The dynasty ruled from 1154-1485.

Plastiras, Nikolaos (1883-1953) Greek general and republican statesman. A participant in the 1922 revolution, he attempted a number of coups that failed in the 1930s. During World War II, P. was a leader of the Greek resistance. After the war he served a number of times as prime minister.

Plataea Area of ancient Greece, in Boeotia. In 479 BC, the Greeks under the Spartan Pausanias won a tremendous victory near P. over the Persian armies under Mardonius.

Plato (427-347 BC) Greek philosopher. He was a pupil of Socrates and built on his ideas. P. saw society as being divided into three classes: the artisan class (farmers and workers), the military class, and the wise class (philosophers). In the ideal situation, each class fulfills its role in order for justice to prevail. In a series of dialogues and conversations he sought to understand the harmonious of nature and construct a comprehensive philosophy that addressed the issues of living and knowing.

Plebeians The general population in ancient Rome. Unlike the patrician class, they at first enjoyed no political rights. After 500 BC, however, the P. gradually began to receive more and more rights, until the distinction between P. and patricians had become all but meaningless by the time of Caesar. They are also called Plebs.

Plebs *See* Demos.

Plekhanov, Georgi Valentinovich (1857-1918) Russian revolutionary and political theoretician. In 1883 he helped found the first social democratic organization in Russia. P. played an important role in the Second International and after 1903 gradually became an opponent of the Bolsheviks in the Russian Social Democratic Party. He fled to Finland in 1918 after the Bolshevik revolution.

Pléven, René (1901-) French politician. Between 1944 and 1954 he served in a number of ministerial posts, including premier. A supporter of European unity, he lost office after De Gaulle returned to power in 1958.

He served as minister of justice (1969-1973) under Pompidou but lost his seat in the French National Assembly in 1973.

PLO *See* Palestine Liberation Organization.

Plutarch (c. 46-119 AD) Greek historian. He made a number of trips to Rome and Egypt before returning to Greece, where he became a priest in the temple of Apollo at Delphi. His most famous work is *The Parallel Lives*, in which the lives of leading Greeks and Romans are described side by side. An early translation of the work greatly influenced Shakespeare, who incorporated many of Plutarch's subjects into his plays.

Podgorny, Nikolai Viktorovitch (1903-1983) Soviet politician. In 1964 he was a member of the group that overthrew Khrushchev. P. served as president of the presidium after 1965, traveling widely and enhancing the position of head of state. After 1977, he fell into disfavor and disappeared from public life.

Pogrom Russian term for "destruction." It has come to mean an organized massacre of Jews.

Poincaré, Raymond (1860-1934) President of France, 1913-1920. A conservative nationalist, he favored harsh treatment of Germany after World War I and felt that the Treaty of

Versailles was too lenient. In 1922, he became prime minister, and when Germany failed to meet a reparations payment, P. ordered the occupation of the Rhineland (1923). He resigned in 1924 after an election defeat, but was prime minister again from 1926 until 1929, after which he returned from public life.

Point Pleasant, Battle of *See* Lord Dunmore's War.

Poissy, Colloquy of Conference of Roman Catholic and Protestant officials in 1561, initiated by Catherine de' Medici. Its purpose was to bring about a peaceful reunion of the two branches of Christianity, but it failed because of both parties' refusal to compromise. The Wars of Religion ensued in 1562.

Poitiers Town in central France. Charles Martel definitely halted the Moors' northern advance near P. in 732. During the Hundred Years War (1356), Edward the Black Prince defeated the French army at P., capturing King John II and his son, Philip the Bold of Burgundy.

Polis *See* Demos.

Polisario Front Liberation movement in the Western Sahara, begun in 1975 and directed against Morocco and Mauritania.

Polish Corridor Strip of German land awarded to Poland in the Treaty of Versailles in 1919. It provided Polish access to the sea but cut off East Prussia from the rest of Germany. The city of Danzig was part of the P. In the years 1919-1939, the P. was a constant source of friction between Germany and Poland. During World War II it was absorbed back into Germany, but it became a permanent part of Poland again after 1945.

Polish Succession, War of the (1733-1738) Conflict that broke out after the election of Stanislas Leszczynski, father-in-law of Louis XV of France, as king of Poland. France, Spain, and Sardinia fought against Russia and Austria, who supported the election of the elector of Saxony as Augustus

Plantagenet

Georgi Valentinovich Plekhanov

III. After a provisional peace in 1735, a final peace treaty was signed in Vienna in 1738. Leszczynski relinquished the Polish throne and in return received the duchy of Lorraine. Augustus III retained on the throne in Poland. The peace settlement also resulted in a series of complicated dynastic reshufflings in Europe.

Politburo Central governing body of the Communist Party in the Soviet Union. It was created in 1917 shortly before the Russian Revolution. The P., which varied in size anywhere from 18 to 21 members, was a party organization, but, in fact, it governed the Soviet Union.

Polo, Marco *See* Marco Polo.

Polk, James K. (1795-1849) 11th president of the U.S., 1845-1849. He served in the U.S. House of Representatives (1825-1839) and was governor of Tennessee (1839-1841) before being nominated by the Democratic Party for president in 1844. More territory was added to the U.S. during P.'s term of office than at any other time except during the Jefferson administration. Texas became part of the Union shortly before P. became president, and Oregon was added as a result of a treaty with Britain. The Mexican War was fought (1846-1848) during P.'s presidency, and the Mexican Cession was added to the U.S. P. did not pursue renomination and died three months after leaving office.

Poltava City in the Ukraine. At Poltava, Sweden, under Charles XII, was defeated (1709) by the Russians during the Great Northern War.

Polycrates (d.522 BC) Tyrant of Samos. Through piracy and indiscriminate warfare, he ruled the eastern Mediterranean. P. was murdered by the Persians.

Pompadour, Marquise de (1721-1764) Born Jeanne Antoinette Poisson, she was the daughter of a French tax collector and the mistress of King Louis XV from 1745 to 1750. P. exercised some influence on the king, urging him to pursue an alliance with Austria. She remained his confidante until her death.

Pompeii City of ancient Rome, near Naples and at the foot of Mt. Vesuvius, a volcano. In 79 AD, P. and nearby Herculaneum were buried after an eruption of Vesuvius. The ashes from the eruption preserved the cities with astonishing completeness. They began to be excavated in 1748 and have become a detailed source of daily life in ancient Rome.

Pompey (106-48 BC) Roman general. His soldiers called him Magnus (the Great). P. fought against pirates and King Mithridates VI, and between 67 and 62 BC annexed Syria and Palestine and began the reorganization of the east into the Roman Empire. In 60 BC, P. formed the First Triumvirate with Crassus and Caesar. He later disagreed with Caesar, which led to the civil war in 49 BC. After his defeat at Pharsala (48 BC), P. fled to Egypt, where he was murdered.

Pompeius, Sextus (67-35 BC) Roman soldier. A son of Pompey, he continued to fight against Caesar after the death of his father. When Caesar died, P. became commander of the Roman fleet. He then fought the Second Triumvirate (*see* Augustus) from Sicily, but was eventually defeated by Agrippa at Naulochus (36 BC). He fled to Asia Minor, where he was captured and murdered.

Pompidou, Georges (1911-1974) President of France, 1969-1974. As aide to De Gaulle during World War II, he became a banker before being appointed premier by De Gaulle in 1962. He was dismissed in 1968 in the wake of riots and strikes, but after De Gaulle's resignation in 1969, P. was

Marquise de Pompadour

elected president with the support of the Gaullist party. As president, he reversed France's opposition to British entry into the Common Market. He died in office in 1974.

Poniatowski, Jozéf (1763-1813) Polish general and marshal of France. A nephew of King Stanislas II, he defended Warsaw against the Prussians and the Russians in 1794. P. later fought with Napoleon during the Russian campaign (1812) and died during the Battle of the Nations at Leipzig.

Sextus Pompeius

Poniatowski, Stanislas Augustus (Stanislas II) (1732-1798) King of Poland, 1764-1795. As an ambassador in St. Petersburg, P. became the lover of Czarina Catherine II, who supported his nomination as king of Poland. During his reign, he was completely dependent on Russia. P. was forced to abdicate in 1795 after the third partition liquidated Poland. He spent the remainder of his life in Russia.

Stanislas Augustus Poniatowski

Pontius Pilate Roman procurator of Judaea (c.AD 26-36) under Tiberius. He attempted to evade responsibility at Jesus's trial because of his fear of the power of the high priests. According to legend, he committed suicide in Rome.

Pope, Alexander (1688-1744) English poet. One of the greatest poets and English verse satirists, he wrote descriptive poetry early in his career. He later did magnificent, although inaccurate, translations of Homer written in heroic couplets. Late in his life, P. turned to writing moral poems and scathing satires of literary incompetents and the English nobility. His most ambitious work is *Moral Essays* (1731-1735).

Poppaea Sabina (d.65 AD) Roman empress, the wife of Nero. Originally married to Otho, she became the lover of Nero, whom she married in 62 AD. P. influenced Nero to have his mother and former wife killed. Legend says that Nero personally killed her.

Popular Front for the Liberation of Palestine Palestinian terrorist group, founded in 1967 by George Habash. The P. split from the PLO in 1974.

Popularus *See* Optimates.

Porsenna King of the Etruscans from Clusium. He is supposed to have unsuccessfully besieged Rome in 507 BC at the request of the exiled Tarquinius Superbus.

Port Arthur City in China, know called Lü-Shun. The site of a Russian naval base (1898-1905), it was attacked by the Japanese in 1904, resulting in the Russo-Japanese War. The city passed to Japan under the Treaty of Portsmouth (1905). P. was under joint Chinese-Soviet administration from 1945 to 1955, at which time it reverted to the control of China.

Port Elliott, Treaty of *See* Seattle.

Portsmouth, Treaty of (1905) Agreement that ended the Russo-Japanese War. Japan acquired Korea as a result of the treaty. It was negotiated by President Theodore Roosevelt, who was awarded the Nobel Peace Prize for his efforts in ending the conflict.

Porus (d.318 BC) King in the north of India. In 325 BC, he was defeated by Alexander the Great, who allowed him to retain his throne. P. was killed in 318 BC by a Macedonian.

Postumus, Marcus (d.268 AD) Roman general. After 259 AD he established an independent empire and

Alexander Pope

was a rival emperor of Gallienus in the west. Gallienus tried to oust him, but to no avail. P. was eventually murdered by his own troops.

Potemkin, Grigori Aleksandrovich (1739-1791) Russian general and statesman. He was a lover of Czarina Catherine II, who made him (1787) commander in chief of the army and the fleet during the Russo-Turkish War. P. urged Catherine to attempt to break up the Ottoman Empire and replace it with a Christian empire. He played an important role in the annexation of the Crimea in 1783, and served as its governor.

Grigori Aleksandrovich Potemkin

Potsdam Conference (July-August 1945) Meeting between Churchill, Stalin, and Truman in Potsdam, Germany, immediately following the end of World War II in Europe. They discussed issues relating to postwar Europe as well as the Soviet entrance into the war against Japan. During the meeting, Churchill was defeated for reelection in Great Britain and was replaced at the conference by the new prime minister, Clement Attlee.

Pound, Ezra Loomis (1885-1972) American poet and essayist. He is one of the most influential poets of the twentieth century. P. lived much of his lived in Europe, and his poetry increasingly reflected political preoccupations. During World War II he made propaganda broadcasts for fascist Italy. Back in the United States after the war, he was accused of treason but was deemed to be mentally

Ezra Loomis Pound

incompetent and was placed in a mental institution from 1946 to 1958. He returned to Italy after being released and died there in 1972. One of P.'s most important works is the epic *Cantos* (1925-1960), a sprawling, eclectic poem that weaves together myth, legend, ballads, and economic and political jargon in an attempt to relive the history of civilization.

Powell, Colin (1937-) American general. A career soldier with experience in Vietnam and later in Washing-

Colin Powell

ton, P. was appointed national security adviser to President Ronald Reagan in 1987. In 1989, he was named chairman of the joint chiefs of staff by President George Bush, thus becoming the first African American to hold the highest military rank in the U.S. P. retired from the army in 1993. Highly popular, he was pressed to seek the Republican presidential nomination in 1996 but declined to run.

Praetorians Bodyguards of the Roman emperors. Through their position of power they often invested or deposed emperors. In 312 they were abolished by Constantine the Great.

Pragmatic Sanction of 1549 Decree of Emperor Charles V in which the hereditary succession in the Dutch Provinces was established.

Pragmatic Sanction of 1713 Decree of Emperor Charles VI. It determined that the Hapsburg countries would remain under one ruler and allowed his daughter, Maria Theresa, to ascend the throne.

Prague, Peace of (1635) Pact signed during the Thirty Years War between the emperor and the elector of Saxony and most of the German princes.

Prague, Treaty of (1866) Agreement that ended the Austro-Prussian War.

Praguerie Revolt in 1440 of the French high nobility joined by the crown prince, the future Louis XI, against King Charles VII. The name is an allusion to an uprising of the Hussites in Prague. The revolt was quickly suppressed and the participants treated leniently.

Praxiteles (4th century BC) Greek sculptor. His work is known almost exclusively through Roman copies. P.'s sculpture is characterized by the exquisite beauty of the human form. Some experts believe that his *Hermes and Dionysus*, found in Olympia, is an original.

Presley, Elvis (1935-1977) American popular singer. In the late 1950s he was wildly popular as much for his sexually charged gyrations on stage as for his singing and mastery of rock music. P. sang country and western, rock, and rhythm and blues and made a number of films. In his latter part of

his career he performed frequently in Las Vegas. In the years following his death at 42, P. became even more of a cult figure, with adoring fans visiting his home, "Graceland," as a shrine.

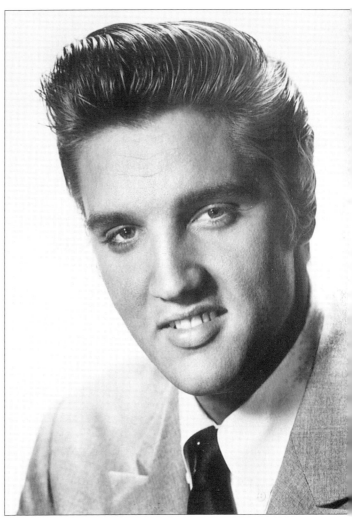

Elvis Presley

Pressburg, Treaty of (1805) Agreement that ended the war between France and Austria and which ceded territories to Napoleon.

Preston Town in England, near Liverpool. During the English Civil War, the Royalists were overwhelmingly (1648) defeated near P. by Cromwell.

Pretorius, Andries Wilhelmus Jacobus (1799-1853) Boer leader. In 1838, he won a battle at Blood River against the Zulus. Two years later he led the final battle against the Zulu king Dingaan at Magono. In 1848 P. led a party of Boers across the Drakensberg and established the nucleus of the South African republic. The city of Pretoria is named in his honor.

Prim y Prats, Juan (1814-1870) Spanish general and statesman. After a military career, he became leader of the liberal opposition against Queen Isabella in 1865. He staged an uprising that failed in 1866, but at the end of 1868, he conquered large parts of Spain and expelled Isabella. After having a new king invested, he was murdered by political opponents.

Primo de Rivera, José Antonio (1903-1936) Spanish politician, son of Miguel Primo de Rivera. In 1932, he founded the fascist Falange. P. was executed by the Republicans at the beginning of the Spanish Civil War.

Primo de Rivera, Miguel (1870-1930) Spanish general and politician. P. led a coup in 1923 and established a mili-

Miquel Primo de Rivera

tary dictatorship. His regime remained unstable because to resistance from both the left and the right. When the army no longer supported him, he was forced to retire in 1930. He died the same year in Paris.

Princip, Gavrilo (1894-1918) Serbian political agitator. A native of Bosnia, P. shot and killed the Austrian archduke Francis Ferdinand and his wife in Sarajevo on June 28, 1914. The assassinations triggered the outbreak of World War I.

Probus, Marcus Aurelius (d.282 AD)

Roman emperor, 276-282. He secured the northeastern frontiers of the Roman Empire fighting against the barbarians in Gaul and Illyria. P. was murdered by mutinous troops.

Prohibition Period from 1920 to 1933 in the U.S. during which the manufacture and sale of alcoholic drinks was prohibited. The law was largely ignored, leading to a rise in organized crime's control of the liquor trade.

Prokofiev, Sergei Sergeyevich (1891-1953) Russian composer and pianist. A student of Rimsky-Korsakov, he lived in the U.S. for as short period before settling in Paris (1922-1933). He returned to the Soviet Union in 1933. P. wrote seven symphonies, five piano concertos, two violin concertos, as well as ballet and chamber music. His operas include the popular *Love for Three Oranges* (1921) and the epic *War and Peace* (1946). P. early style was deliberately harsh, but his later works employed a more simplified popular idiom. He used distinctive and varying rhythmic devices and was a master of orchestration.

Protagoras (c.490-421 BC) Greek (Athenian) philosopher. A Sophist, he stated that "Man is the measure of all things" and that truth or moral values are relative. He was exiled in 415.

Prusias (d.192 BC) King of Bithynia. He ruled from c.257 BC. P. came into conflict with Rome because he offered asylum to the escaped Hannibal.

Przewalski, Nicolai Mikhailovich (1839-1888) Russian explorer. He explored Tibet and discovered the breed of wild horses there (1879), which are named after him.

Psammetichus I (d.610 BC) King of ancient Egypt. he founded the XXVI Dynasty (*see* Saïs), which brought a new era of prosperity to Egypt, and drove the Assyrians, his former benefactors, out of Egypt. Much of Saitic art is based on art from the Ancient Kingdom.

Psammetichus III King of ancient Egypt, 526-523 BC. He was defeated by the Persian king Cambyses at Pelusium and later killed. Cambyses subsequently conquered Egypt.

Sergei Sergeyevich Prokofiev

Ptolemy I (Ptolemy Soter) (d.284 BC) King of ancient Egypt, the first ruler of the Macedonian dynasty. He was originally a general of Alexander the Great; *see* Diadochi. In 323 BC, P. became satrap of Egypt and in 305 BC he adopted the title of king and made the country a Hellenistic kingdom. He founded the great library at Alexandria.

Ptolemy I

Ptolemy II (Ptolemy Philadelphus) (c.308-246 BC) King of ancient Egypt, 285-246 BC. The son of and successor to Ptolemy I, he won great

Presidents of the United States

1

2

3

5

6

1. Mount Rushmore National Memorial in the Black Hills of South Dakota, where the faces of the American presidents Washington, Jefferson, Lincoln, and Theodore Roosevelt are carved out of the rock.

2. George Washington (1732-1799). After the American Revolution against the British, he was elected the 1st president of the United States in 1789 and served until 1797.

3. Woodrow Wilson (1856-1924). The 28th president (1913-1921), he fought hard for his vision of a peaceful world. *See* Fourteen Points; Versailles, Treaty of.

4. Franklin Delano Roosevelt (1882-1945). The 32nd president (1933-1945), he was a great leader and a master politician. "FDR" was elected president four times.
See also New Deal; Pearl Harbor; World War II.

5. Herbert Hoover (1874-1964). The 31st president (1929-1933), he became unpopular because he was unable to end the Great Depression that began in 1929.
See Great Depression.

6. James Monroe (1758-1831). The 5th president (1817-1825), he proclaimed the Monroe Doctrine, which declared the New World off-limits to further European colonization.
See Adams, John Quincy.

Protestantism

1

The protests of Martin Luther, John Calvin, Huldreich Zwingli, and other critics of the Roman Catholic Church had an enormous impact. Their ideas and doctrines spread throughout much of Europe and brought on the Protestant Reformation. Europe became divided between Catholics and Protestants. Religious wars followed, and social revolution nearly broke out in Germany.

2

4

5

1. The interior of the cathedral in Geneva, which was stripped completely of its statues and images at the time of Calvin.
See Calvin, John; Reformation.
2. German farmers plunder their churches, while Luther (standing in the middle) tries to stop them.
See Luther, Martin; Reformation.
3. Zürich, Switzerland, in the 16th century, when it was an important center of the Reformation.
4. Holy Roman Emperor Charles V is handed the Confession of Augsburg, a Protestant manifesto, in 1530.
5. Martin Luther translates the Bible into German, so that everybody could read it. *See* Luther, Martin.

3

victories in Syria against the Seleucids. P. worked to make Alexandria a great cultural center, and he built a canal from the Nile to the Red Sea.

Ptolemy IV (Ptolemy Philopator) (c.238-205 BC) King of ancient Egypt. Egyptian (i.e., Macedonian) pharaoh. In 217 BC, he won a victory over the Seleucid Antiochus III at Raphia.

Ptolemy XI (Ptolemy Auletes) (d. 51 BC) King of ancient Egypt. The father of Cleopatra VII, his misrule caused the Alexandrians to overthrow him in 58 BC. He was reinstalled on the throne with the help of the Romans.

Puccini, Giacomo (1858-1924) Italian operatic composer. His works are among the most popular in the repertory. A master of the stage, P. composed melodramatic operas filled with soaring, unforgettable melody. Among his most performed pieces are the masterpieces *La Bohème* (1896), *Tosca* (1900), and *Madama Butterfly* (1904).

Pueblo affair International incident between the United States and North Korea. It began on January 23, 1968, when an American naval vessel, the *Pueblo*, was seized off the coast of North Korea. The ship and its crew were handed back to the U.S. on December 23, 1968.

Pugachov, Yemelyan Ivanovich (c.1742-1775) Russian peasant leader. Claiming to be the murdered Czar Peter III, he raised an army drawn from the disaffected lower classes, announced the abolition of serfdom, and overran parts of the Volga region. The rebels lacked leadership, however, and were eventually defeated. P. was captured and beheaded. The revolt led Czarina Catherine II to institute various administrative reforms.

Punic Wars Three wars between Rome and Carthage. When they ended, Carthage was destroyed and Rome was the great power of the Mediterranean region.
1st P. (264-241 BC) It was fought over the possession of Sicily and Corsica. The final victory was the sea battle of the Aegean Islands.
2nd P. (218-201 BC) It began with the capture of Saguntum by Hannibal

Ptolemy II

(219). His campaign through Italy resulted in a catastrophic Roman defeat near Cannae, but ended with his own defeat near Zana (202 BC). *3rd P.* (149-146 BC) It was a war over economic supremacy, which ended in the siege and destruction of Carthage.

Purishkevich, Vladimir (1870-1920) Russian reactionary politician. He was part of the the conspiracy that killed Rasputin in 1916.

P'u-i (1906-1970) Last Chinese emperor, 1908-1912. In 1932, under Japanese rule, he became the puppet regent and then emperor in Manchukuo. He was taken prisoner of war by the Russians in 1945. P. lived his final years in Communist China, where he worked as a gardener.

Purcell, Henry (c.1659-1695) English composer. Considered the first great native English composer, he wrote chamber and church music, music for royal occasions, songs, and an opera, *Dido and Aeneas* (1689). P. invigorated English music by melding French and Italian elements into a distinctly English baroque style.

Pydna Town in ancient Macedonia. There, in 168 BC, the Romans under Aemilius Paulus won a final victory over the Macedonian king Perseus, thus destroying the kingdom of Macedon.

Pyramids, Battle of the Battle won by Napoleon (1798) and his expeditionary army against the Mamelukes in Egypt.

Pyrenees, Peace of the (1659) Agreement that ended the protracted (1648-1659) conflict between France and Spain that continued in the wake of the Treaty of Westphalia. It marked the rise of France as the major European power and established a mar-

riage contract between Louis XIV of France and the infanta Marie Thérèse, the daughter of Philip IV of Spain.

Pyrrhus (319-272 BC) King of Epirus, in Asia Minor. He supported the town Tarentum against Rome (281 BC) and defeated the Romans in 280 BC at Heraclea and in 279 BC at Asculum. His victories cost him so many men that his forces were weakened, hence the origin of the term "Pyrrhic victory." After a stalemated battle in 275 BC near Beneventum, he withdrew to Greece, where he faced additional defeats. He was stoned to death by angry mobs in the streets of Argos, where he had fled.

Pyrrhus

Pythagoras (c.580-500 BC) Greek philosopher. He is known for the mathematical theorem that was named after him. P. philosophy taught the transmigration of souls and the theory that numbers constitute the only true nature of things.

Pythia Priestess at the oracle of Delphi. She transmitted the oracles of Apollo to the people. The oracles were often vague. Once, a king who intended to invade another country consulted P. and the god replied, "A large realm will then be razed to the ground." The king then commenced the invasion and saw his own country destroyed.

Pythian Games Games held every four years in ancient Greece in honor of the Greek god Apollo in Delphi from 582 BC until the 4th century AD. They included competitions in music, poetry, athletics and chariot driving.

Pythagoras

311

Qadiriyah Mystical Islamic sect that was established by Abd al-Qadir al-Ghilani (1077-1166).

Qajar *See* Lotf Ali Khan Zand.

Qin dynasty Dynasty that ruled China (265-420) after the period of the Three Kingdoms. The Great Wall of China was begun during this period.

Quakers

Quadi Suebic people who lived in central Europe between the 1st and 5th centuries AD. They traveled through Europe with the Huns under Attila and later intermingled with the Ostrogoths.

Quadruple Alliance (1814) Alliance between Great Britain, Austria, Prussia, and Russia to contain France's expansionism under Napoleon I and maintain the status quo in Europe.

Quaestor Civil servant in the Roman Empire who investigated criminal cases. Later the post entailed management of imperial finances.

Quakers Common name for the followers of the Religious Society of Friends, founded in England in 1648. Originally a term of derision, the word described the physical reaction of quaking that some adherents underwent during religious services. The Q. were vigorously persecuted. After 1681 many migrated to the United States and found refuge in Pennsylvania; *see* Penn.

Quatre-Bras Village in Belgium. There, French troops under Ney were stopped in 1815 by the British under Wellington in one of the battles of the Waterloo campaign.

Quebec Conferences Two conferences held in Quebec during World War II. The first (August 1943) was attended by Roosevelt, Churchill, and the foreign minister of China and discussed strategy in the China theater as well as future military operations in France. The second (September 1944) was attended by Roosevelt and Churchill and discussed strategy in Europe and the postwar status of Germany.

Quebec, battle of *See* Montcalm.

Quetzalcoatl (the feathered snake) Ancient god of water and fertility of the Toltecs, Aztecs, and other Mexican peoples.

Quetzalcoatl

Quiberon Peninsula in Brittany, France. During the Seven Years War, the French fleet was defeated and destroyed by the English in the Bay of Q. on November 20, 1759.

Quintilian (c.35-96 AD) Roman rhetorician and writer. He was Hadrian's tutor. His work *Institutio oratoria* (12 volumes) is an important contribution to the history of education. Q. had enormous influence during in antiquity and during the Renaissance.

Quirinal One of the seven hills of Rome. A papal palace built on the hill served (1870-1946) as the residence of the Italian king and is now the home of the president of Italy.

Quisling, Vidkun (1887-1945) Norwegian fascist. He helped prepare the way for the German invasion in 1940 and served as puppet ruler of Norway until the end of World War II in 1945. After the war he was tried for high treason and shot. From his name comes the word *quisling*, meaning traitor.

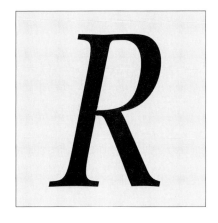

Ra Egyptian sun god and creator. His holy city was Heliopolis. The kings of the 5th Dynasty called themselves sons of R. and elevated him to imperial god.

Rabelais, François (c.1483-1553) French writer. He is one of the great comic geniuses in world literature. R.'s main works are about Gargantua and Pantagruel. Comic satires about the giants, they also contain serious discussion of philosophy and politics. His works were often denounced as obscene, but R. enjoyed the patronage of Francis I and was protected by his friendship with Cardinal Jean du Bellay.

Rabenhaupt, Charles Baron von Sucha (1602-1675) German in the service of the Netherlands. In 1692, he led the defense of Groningen against the troops of Münster.

Rabin, Yitzhak (1922-1995) Prime minister of Israel, 1974-1977, 1992-1995. He was chief of staff during the Six-Day War (1967) and succeeded

Yitzhak Rabin

Golda Meir as prime minister in 1974. A scandal involving an overseas bank account drove him from office in 1977. He later served as minister of defense (1984-1988) during the time when the Palestinian *intifada* broke out on the occupied West Bank. R. returned to office as prime minister following the Labor Party's 1992 victory. He quickly concluded the peace agreement with the PLO, agreed to in Washington on September 13, 1993. The agreement gave the PLO limited autonomy in the Gaza strip and in Jericho and provided a mechanism for gradual return of other West Bank areas to Palestinian self-rule. R., Arafat, and Shimon Peres were awarded the 1994 Nobel Peace Prize. R. was assassinated in 1995 by an Israeli who opposed peace with the Palestinians.

Rachmaninoff, Sergei Vassilievich (1873-1943) Russian composer and pianist. One of the premier pianists of his generation, R. as a composer is known for his piano concertos, piano pieces, symphonies, and songs. His music is darkly emotional and romantic and reflective of a late-nineteenth-century Russian idiom. R. fled Russia in 1917 and in the mid-1930s settled in the United States.

Jean Racine

Racine, Jean (1639-1699) French playwright. With Corneille, he is considered the most important author of French classical drama. R. derived much of his material from classical Greek and Roman sources. His most famous play is *Phèdre* (1677).

Raczkiewicz, Wladyslaw (1885-1947) Polish politician. He was Poland's prime minister in exile during World War II (1939-1945).

Radascu, Nicolai (1874-1953) Romanian statesman. He was imprisoned in a concentration camp after 1941, but became prime minister following an antifascist coup against Antonescu (1944). R. was forced to flee from the communists in 1945.

Radbod (679-719) Frisian king. He was defeated at Dorestad in 689 by Pepin II, the Frankish mayor of the palace, but retained some of his power and managed to expand his influence after 714.

Radegunda (d.587) Wife of the Merovingian king Chlotarius I, who had captured her (c.531). She left him to become a nun and became one of the first Merovingian saints.

Joseph Radetzky von Radetz

Radetzky von Radetz, Joseph, Count (1766-1858) Austrian field marshal. He won a famous victory at Custozza and Novara during the war against Sardinia (1848-1849). R. was governor-general of the Austrian possessions in Italy until 1857. The elder Johann Strauss composed the *Radetzky March* in his honor.

Radic, Stjepan (1871-1928) Croatian politician. He opposed Croatian participation in Yugoslavia following World War I, fearing Serbian dominance. R. reached a temporary compromise with the government and served briefly (1925-1926) as Yugoslav minister of education. He was shot dead in parliament.

Radoslavov, Vasili (1854-1929) Bulgarian politician. He served as prime minister between 1913-1918 but was forced to flee after World War I.

Raeder, Erich Johann Albert (1876-1960) German admiral. He was commander in chief of the German fleet from 1928 until his resignation in 1943, during World War II. At the Nuremberg trials (1946) he was sentenced to life imprisonment but was released in 1955.

Raetia Roman province that formed parts of modern-day Austria, Switzerland, and Germany. It was inhabited by Celts and Illyrians and was conquered by the Romans c.15 BC.

Raffles, Sir Thomas Stamford (1781-1826) English colonialist. He was one of the founders of the British Empire in the Far East. R. was governor of Java during the years 1811-1816 (after the Dutch East Indies were captured by the British) and founded Singapore in 1819. He was noted for his liberal attitude toward colonial native peoples and for his suppression of the slave trade.

Ali Akbar Hashemi Rafsanjani

Rafsanjani, Ali Akbar Hashemi (1934-) Iranian politician. A follower of Ayatollah Khomeini. R. was imprisoned several times during the 1970s for his opposition to the Shah. After the Iranian revolution (1979) he

became a member, and in 1980 chairman, of the Revolutionary Council. In 1988, he was appointed interim supreme commander and in 1989 president of Iran.

Raglan, Fitzroy James Henry Somerset, 1st Baron (1788-1855) British general. He was a long-time aide to Wellington and lost an arm at the battle of Waterloo. R. was the British commander during the Crimean War (1853-1856) and was criticized because of slow military progress. He died before the end of the war.

Ragnarok (final battle) The end of the world in Norse mythology, when the gods and mankind will be destroyed by snowstorms and demons.

Sir Thomas Stamford Raffles

Rainey, Joseph Hayne (1832-1887) African-American legislator. Born a slave, he was the first black person to serve (1869-1879) in the U.S. House of Representatives, where, as a Republican from South Carolina, he was an advocate of rights for blacks, Indians, and Chinese.

Rais, Gilles de (1404-1440) Marshal of France. He fought with Joan of Arc against the English at Orléans. R. later retired to his estate, where he ritualistically murdered hundreds of people, most of them young boys. The character of Bluebeard was modeled on him. R. was tried for his crimes, which he confessed to, and executed.

Rajah Indian prince or chief. A powerful rajah is called maharajah, which means great king.

Rajneesh, Aharya (1931-1990) Indian guru, famous for his ashram in Poona, to which thousands of westerners flocked in the 1970s to become his followers (*sanyasins*).

Rajputs People in northwest India. They are predominantly Hindus, although there are some Muslims. The R. founded their own empire in the 7th century and were conquered by the Mughals in 1616.

Rákóczi, Ferenc (1645-1676) Hungarian nobleman. With his father-in-law, Zrínyi, he led a Hungarian-Croat revolt against the Hapsburgs. After the failure of the revolt, Zrínyi was beheaded. R., however, was pardoned.

Raleigh, Sir Walter (c.1554-1618) English explorer and soldier. A favorite courtier of Elizabeth I, he organized the expedition that attempted to settle the Roanoke Colony in North America in the 1580s. R. at times fell out of favor with the queen and was imprisoned in the Tower. One of his most dramatic explorations was to the Guyana region of South America in 1595 in search of El Dorado. R. achieved a great success for England over Spain in 1596 when he plundered the Spanish fleet at Cádiz. After Elizabeth's death, R. fell into disfavor

Sir Walter Raleigh

with her successor, James I, who suspected R. of opposing his accession to the throne. Eventually, he was executed, years after being accused of treason.

Rallis, George (1918-) Greek politician. He was a partisan during World War II and the civil war. R. was prime minister of Greece from 1980-1981.

Rama Title of the Thai kings. The first R. was Khameng, who ruled c.1290-1318. Khameng maintained diplomatic relations with China and conquered Cambodia.

Ramadan Ninth month of the Muslim year. The first revelation of the Koran is commemorated during R. In this month, all Muslims are required to fast during the day.

Ramayana Classical Sanskrit epic of India. Written after the 3rd century BC, it relates how Rama was disinherited by his father Dasaratha of Ayodhya in favor of Bharata, the son of his second wife. He was banished to the forest, but eventually accepted the throne of Ayodhya. The main characters of the epic are still worshiped in India.

Ramazan dynasty (c.1352-1610) Turkoman royal family that ruled in Cilicia. The R. were recognized by the Egyptian Mamelukes, but they were eventually defeated by the Ottoman Empire.

Ramesseum Ramses II's temple of the dead on the western bank of the Nile, opposite ancient Thebes, Egypt. It is dedicated to the chief god Amon and to the king. The battle against the Hittites at Kadesh is depicted on the walls of the R.

Ramillies Village in Belgium. There, in 1707, during the War of Spanish Succession, the English-Dutch-Danish army under Marlborough won a resounding victory over the French under the Duke of Villeroy. The victory enabled the allies to overrun the Spanish Netherlands.

Ramiro I (d.1063) King of Aragón, 1035-1063. The son of Sancho III of Navarre, he fought the Moors of Saragossa and died fighting the Castilians at Graus.

Ramses I (d.1314 BC) King of the Egyptian 19th Dynasty and father of the field officer Seti, who ruled after him as Seti I. R. was enthroned when very old, after a career as a general for King Horemheb, the founder of the dynasty.

Ramses II

Ramses II (d.1225 BC) Egyptian king, 1292-1225 BC. He fought the famous battle at Kadesh against the Hittites, with whom he later made peace. R. was a great patron of architecture. Under him, Egypt acquired great splendor. R. is probably the king of exile mentioned in the Old Testament.

Ramses III (d.1167 BC) Egyptian king, c.1198-1167. He repelled a large invasion by the Sea Peoples and fought the Libyans several times.

Ranjit Singh (1780-1839) Founder and maharajah of the Sikh kingdom of Punjab (1801-1839). After capturing Lahore (1799), he established himself as the leading Sikh chieftain. After his death, the realm disintegrated and by 1849 had fallen to British control.

Rankin, Jeannette (1880-1973) American pacifist and legislator. In 1916, she became the first woman elected to Congress. During the one term she served, R. voted to oppose U.S. entry into World War I. In 1940, she was elected again to Congress and a year later cast the sole vote opposing U.S. entry into World War II. Rankin remained a staunch feminist and pacifist throughout her entire life, spending her final years opposing the Vietnam War.

Rapacki Plan Proposal (1957) for a nuclear-free zone in Europe. It was named after Poland's minister of foreign affairs, Adam Rapacki.

Rapallo, Treaty of (1922) Signed by the Soviet Union and Germany, in which the Soviet Union relinquished its rights to reparations for the effects of the First World War and Germany recognized the Soviet Union.

Raphael (Raphael Sanzio) (1483-1520) Italian Renaissance painter. his art represents the highest expression of harmony and balance found in Renaissance painting. R. is not seen as an innovator, but as an artist who summarized the accomplishments of his age. He was commissioned by the Pope Leo X, his patron, to paint a number of rooms in the Vatican, and also he made paintings such as the Sistine Madonna. After 1514, R. was also the chief architect of the Vatican.

Raphael

Rashtrakuta Indian royal family that ruled the Decca kingdom c.755-975. Their capital was Ellora.

Rasjid, Ar- (d.1672) Founder of the Moroccan Alawite Empire (1666) following the collapse of the Sadid dynasty. In 1669 he occupied Marrakesh.

Rasjid ad-Din (d.1192) Syrian leader of the Assassins. He is remembered for the number of failed assassination attempts on Saladin.

Rasputin (1872-1916) Russian monk. Born Grigori Yefimovich Novitsj, he became an influential adviser to the Czarina Alexandra in 1908. His religious fervor, sexual debauchery, and powerful influence over the czarina made him a detested figure. In 1916 he was assassinated by a group of noblemen, who threw his bullet-riddled corpse into the Neva River.

Rassiid Dynasty in Yemen named after al-Kasim ar-Rassi, a descendant of Ali, who died in Mecca in 860. The R. ruled until 1230.

Rastafarianism Religious cult among black Jamaicans. It venerates Haile Selassie as a god and teaches that blacks will eventually be redeemed and return to Africa. R. practices the ritual use of marijuana.

Rasulids (1229-1454) Islamic royal family in Yemen. They flourished after the Ajjobids left the Arabian peninsula. Riots in Mecca induced Mameluke intervention, and in the 16th century the R. realm was incorporated into the Ottoman Empire.

Ravel, Maurice (1875-1937) French composer. He was a leading exponent of Impressionism in French music. Although his style is fluid and post-Wagnerian, R.'s compositions adhere to classical forms. His *Boléro* (1928) is one of his most popular and well-known pieces. R. also composed piano compositions, two piano concertos, and ballet music, and did a famous orchestration of Moussorgsky's *Pictures at an Exhibition* (1922).

Ravenna City in Italy. It dates back to Roman times and was the capital of the Roman Empire of the West (5th century) after the barbarian invasions. In the 6th-8th centuries it was part of the Ostrogoth Empire under Theodoric and later the Byzantine Empire. Ravenna is famous today for its mosaics, which date back to the Roman and Byzantine periods.

Ray, Man (1890-1976) American painter and photographer. Between 1921 and 1940, R. exhibited in Paris and was a founder of the Dada movement. R. worked in many mediums, producing paintings, drawings, graphic art, collages, constructions, photographs, and films.

Raymond IV (c.1038-1105) Leader of the First Crusade. Known as Raymond of St. Gilles, Count of Toulouse and Marquis of Provence, he organized and led the First Crusade. He participated in the taking of Jerusalem (1099) and died at Tripoli, which was then formed into a country by his descendants.

Razin, Stenka (c.1630-1671) Russian Cossack leader. He led a peasants' revolt against the government (1670-1671) but was defeated at Simbirsk and drawn and quartered. R. is a mythical figure among Russians and has been celebrated in song and legend.

Reagan, Ronald (1911-) 40th president of the U.S. He started his career as a radio announcer and a film actor in the 1930s. R. was governor of California (1967-75) and soon became the darling of conservatives because of his photogenic appeal and proven vote-getting abilities. He challenged Presi-

Ronald Reagan

dent Gerald Ford for the Republican presidential nomination in 1976 and lost narrowly. R. won the presidential election in 1980 and was reelected overwhelmingly in 1984. Under R. cuts in domestic spending were enacted, but defense spending increased dramatically, and by the time he left office (1989), the nation faced a serious budget deficit. His most important foreign-policy achievement was the signing of an arms control agreement with Gorbachev (1987).

Realpolitik German word coined during Bismarck's era. It means politics based on material and practical con-siderations rather than on ethical or moral objectives.

Réaumur, René Antoine (1683-1757) French physicist and zoologist. One of the foremost scientists of the 18th century, he invented the alcohol thermometer and the Réaumur temperature scale, in which the boiling point of water is 80 degrees. R. is also known for his extensive study of insects, and for his work proving that coral is an animal, not a plant.

René Antoine Réaumur

Reconquista Recapturing of Spain from the Moors. The R. started in the 11th century (though traditionally it starts in c.718) and ended in 1492 with the conquest of Grenada.

Reconstruction Period in U.S. history after the Civil War (1865-1877). During R. the defeated South was occupied by federal troops. R. ended in 1877 when Rutherford B. Hayes became president. The Republicans agreed to pull out of the South and allow Southern whites to resume political control (thus abandoning the freed slaves). In return, Hayes, a Republican, was declared the winner of the disputed 1876 presidential election.

Red Army Army of the Soviet Union. It was founded in 1918 by Trostky from the so called Red Guards of the factories. During Stalin's purges, the leadership of the R. was decimated, but it revived during World War II and enjoyed its greatest triumph in the defeat of Nazi Germany in 1945.

Red Army Faction (Baader-Meinhof Gang) West German terrorist organi-

Rasputin

zation. Led by Andreas Baader and Ulrike Meinhof, it carried out robberies, arson, and kidnappings between 1968-1977. In 1977 the principal members were sentenced to life imprisonment. Most of the leadership eventually committed suicide while in prison.

Red Cloud (1822-1909) Native American chief of the Oglala Sioux. He led the Indian rebellion against the Bozeman Trail, a road through the Indian reservations of the east to the gold fields of Colorado and Montana. The Bozeman Trail was abandoned in 1868. R. was deposed as chief in 1881 and spent his later years on the Pine Ridge Reservation in South Dakota.

Red Guards Organized groups, mainly students, who were charged by Mao Zedong with combating "revisionism" during the Cultural Revolution in China (1960s). During their rampage, lives and careers were destroyed, the traditional Communist Party was attacked, and many of the countries cultural artifacts were ruined. They were disgraced and disbanded after the death of Mao and the arrest of his widow and the "Gang of Four."

Red River Campaign (1864) Union attempt during the American Civil War to sail up the Red River and open the way to Texas. The Union forces were beaten at Sabine Crossroads by the Confederates.

Redl, Alfred (1864-1913) Head of

Alfred Redl

military intelligence in Austria, 1907-1912. He was unmasked as a Russian spy and committed suicide in 1913.

Reform Bills (1832, 1867, 1884-1885) British laws that liberalized representation in the Parliament. The new laws took into account the growing urbanization of the nation and extended the franchise for the first time since the 17th century.

Reforma, La (1854-1876) Mexican political program under Juárez. One of its main elements was confiscation and redistribution of land owned by the Roman Catholic Church. Porforio Diaz' coup in 1876 ended the reforms.

Reformation Religious revolution in Europe during the 16th century. Starting with Luther's struggle against indulgences, it became a mass movement against the abuses in the Roman Catholic Church. The R. led to the division of Christianity into Roman Catholic and Protestant branches; *see* Calvin, Hus, Zwingli.

Regulus, Marcus Atilius (d.250 BC) Roman general. In the First Punic War, he won a naval battle against the Carthaginians in 256 BC, but was captured the following year. He was allowed to return to Rome to present the Carthaginians' peace terms but then voluntarily return to Carthage, where he died in captivity.

Rehnquist, William H. (1924-) 16th chief justice of the United States, 1986-. He was appointed as associate justice on the Supreme Court in 1971 by President Richard Nixon and was elevated to chief justice in 1986 by President Ronald Reagan.

Rehoboam *See* Israel, tribes of.

Reichstag fire Fire in the Reichstag in Berlin (February 27, 1933). The Nazis used it as an excuse to pass the Enabling Act, which suspended democratic government and allowed them to rule by decree. After a show trial, a Dutchman, Marinus van der Lubbe, was sentenced to death for starting the fire.

Reichswehr The German army during the Weimar Republic. According to the provisions of the Treaty of Versailles the R. could not exceed 100,000 men.

Remagen Town in Germany. There, during World War II (March 8, 1945), the American army made its first crossing of the Rhine River on a the bridge the Germans had failed to blow up.

Remarque, Erich Maria (1898-1970) German-American writer. His experiences in World War I led him to write his most memorable work, *All Quiet on the Western Front* (1929), which is a realistic picture of the horrors of war. The Nazis banned his books, and R. emigrated to the U.S. in 1938.

Rembrandt Harmenszoon van Rijn (1606-1669) Dutch painter. The greatest master of the Dutch school, he was a also multitalented artist who liked to

Rembrandt Harmenszoon van Rijn

draw and etch, but became famous for his paintings, among which are the *Night Watch* (1642), the *Staalmeesters* (c.1662) and the *Jewish Bride* (c. 1665). R.'s portraits are also of great importance and go far beyond the conventions of the times. He was dogged by bad luck in his later life, when commissions flagged and he was forced to sell his possessions.

Renaissance Period in Western civilization between the Middle Ages and modern times. It was a time of enormous creativity in art, literature, and science. The R. appeared at different times in Europe. In Italy, especially in Florence and Siena, it began around 1300 and then spread across Western Europe. The R. was characterized by the pursuit of individuality. The Medieval preoccupation with the afterlife was supplanted by the Renaissance philosophy that life should be lived on earth. Classical antiquity was often looked to for inspiration and so experienced a R. (rebirth); *see* Leonardo da Vinci; Michelangelo; Raphael.

Renard, Charles (1847-1905) French soldier. He built *La France*, the first navigable airship, in 1884 and made the maiden flight that same year.

Republican Party Younger and more conservative of America's two major political parties. In was organized in 1854 to oppose the extension of slavery. Its first successful presidential candidate was Abraham Lincoln in 1860.

Rerum novarum Encyclical promulgated by Pope Leo XIII in 1891. It enumerated the social teachings of the Roman Catholic Church and stressed the duty of the state to help the needy.

Resjef (the burner) West Semite god of the underworld and the plague.

Revels, Hiram (1822-1901) African-American politician and educator. He was the first black elected to the U.S. Senate, winning a election as a Republican from Mississippi in 1870 to fill the seat once held by Jefferson Davis. R. fought for equality for blacks and for the restoration of full civil liberties for ex-Confederates. After his term, he headed a small agricultural college in Mississippi.

Revere, Paul (1735-1818) American Revolutionary War patriot. He became a hero for his legendary ride across the Massachusetts countryside in April 1775 warning of approaching British troops. He was immortalized in the poem "Paul Revere's Ride," by Longfellow.

Revolutionary Tribunal Court during the Reign of Terror in France. It served (1793-1795) exclusively to eliminate political adversaries. There was no right of appeal and the only sentence was death.

Rex (king) Highest administrator of Rome between 753-509 BC. The R. was originally chosen by the people.

Reza Shah Pahlavi (1877-1944), Shah of Iran, 1925-1941. An army officers he seized power starting in 1921 and had himself declared shah in 1925. R. began the modernization of Iran. In 1941, the Russians and British occupied the country, fearing R.'s rapprochement with the Germans. R. was exiled to South Africa, where he died.

Rhine, Confederation of (1658-1667) Union of a large number of German states to preclude involvement in armed conflict.

Rhine Union Confederation (1806-1813) of German kings and states under the auspices of Napoleon.

Rhineland, Remilitarization of Occupation of the Rhineland by Hitler's army on March 7, 1936. Under the Treaty of Versailles, the Rhineland had to be free of German troops up to 50 kilometers inland. By remilitarizing the territory, Hitler proved he could violate the Treaty of Versailles without repercussions from the British or French.

Rhodes, Cecil John (1853-1902) English industrialist and colonist. He went to South Africa as a young man and made a fortune in diamond mining. R. was an aggressive believer in

Cecil John Rhodes

British colonial rule in South Africa. He entered Cape Colony parliament in 1881 and by 1890 was virtual dictator of the colony. He was eventually forced out of office by the British Parliament because of misdeeds, and he spent his later years developing the colony of Rhodesia, which was named after him; *see* Jameson raid.

Ribaut, Jean (c.1520-1565) French colonist. He founded a Huguenot colony in Florida, returned to Europe and was imprisoned briefly in England under Elizabeth I, and was murdered as a heretic by the Spaniards when they wiped out his colony.

Joachim von Ribbentrop

Ribbentrop, Joachim von (1893-1946) Foreign minister of Germany under Hitler. He helped negotiate the Molotov-Ribbentrop Pact in 1939. R. was tried as a war criminal at Nuremberg and hanged in 1946.

Rice mother (Me posop) In the various Indonesian cultures, the goddess from whom rice developed.

Richard II (1367-1400) King of England, 1377-1399. The son of Edward the Black Prince, he was a minor when he ascended the throne. In 1381, R. repressed a peasant revolt led by Wat Tyler. He negotiated an armistice with France in 1389 and in the early 1390s enjoyed a relatively quiet rule. In 1397, however, his behavior began to change, and he became tyrannical and unpredictable. In 1399, Henry, the banished son of John of Gaunt, returned to England and raised an army against R. while the latter was in Ireland. The king was forced to abdicate and Henry was declared King Henry IV. R. spent his final year in Pontefract Castle, where he either starved himself or was murdered.

Richard III (1452-1485) King of England, 1483-1485. The youngest son of Richard of York and the brother of Edward IV (1483), he became regent to Edward V in 1483. R. soon had Edward and his younger brother declared illegitimate, and they were placed in the Tower and almost certainly murdered on R.'s orders. He then had himself proclaimed Richard III. R. died at the Battle of Bosworth Field (1485), fighting his opponent Henry Tudor (Henry VII). R. was the last of the York line of kings, and his death ended the War of the Roses. He was a complex ruler who had good intentions, but his negative image has been reinforced by Shakespeare's *Richard III.*

Richard Lionheart (1157-1199) King of England, 1189-1199. In Western sources R. is often portrayed as a legendary king. However, he spent only 6

Richard Lionheart

Richard II

months of his entire reign in England. After his coronation, he began the Third Crusade with Frederick Barbarossa. He failed to capture Jerusalem and spent much of the remainder of his life fighting in Europe. R. died in a minor engagement in France.

Richelieu, Armand-Jean du Plessis, Duke of (1585-1642) French statesman and cardinal from 1622. In 1624, R. became Louis XIII's chief minister and gradually became the highest authority in France. R. ended the influence of the Huguenots and successfully combated supremacy of the Spanish Hapsburg through intervention in the Thirty Years War.

Richelieu, Louis François Armand du Plessis, Duke of (1696-1788) French soldier and statesman. A cousin of Cardinal Richelieu, he fought in the War of Austrian Succession and the Seven Years War. R. enjoyed significant political influence under Louis XV.

Richemont, Arthur, Count of (1393-1458) Brother of John V, Duke of Brittany. R. fought for the French king Charles VII from 1425 and helped drive the English from France during the Hundred Years War.

Richter, Charles Francis (1900-1985) American seismologist. He devised the Richter scale (1935), which measures the amount of energy released during an earthquake.

Richthofen, Manfred, Baron von (1892-1918) German aviator during World War I. He shot down more than 80 enemy planes during the First World War. R.'s nickname, "Red Baron," refers to the red color of his Fokker airplane. He was shot down in combat in 1918.

Ricimer, Flavius (d.472) Roman general. He deposed Emperor Avitus in 456 and thereafter remained the most powerful figure in the West Roman Empire. R. successfully combated the Vandals and the Ostrogoths.

Rickover, Hyman (1900-1986) American admiral. He was the driving force behind the development of nuclear powered naval vessels in the period after World War II; *see* Nautilus.

Matthew Bunker Ridgway

Ridgway, Matthew Bunker (1895-1993) American general. R. conducted the first large-scale American airborne landing during World War II. R. replaced General Douglas MacArthur as supreme commander in Korea in 1951, and in 1952-1953 he was made supreme commander of NATO forces.

Riefenstahl, Leni (1902-) German film director. Her fame rests on two films: *The Triumph of the Will* (1935), a documentary of the Nazi Party rally in Nuremberg in 1934, and *Olympiad* (1936-1938), a documentary about the 1936 Olympics in Berlin. Both films extended the artistic range of documentaries and are considered landmarks of the genre. R., however, used her art in the service of the Nazis and has remained a controversial and even ostracized figure since the end of World War II.

Rif War (1919-1926) War between the Spanish and the Berber tribes in the Rif Atlas under Abd el-Krim. The Spanish had acquired the Rif mountain range in the Treaty of Fez (1912) but only managed to defeat the Berbers with the help of the French.

Riga City in Latvia. It became (1201) the seat of the Livonian Brothers of the Sword under Bishop Albert of Livonia and was a member of the Hanseatic League from 1280. The city was part of Poland in 1581 and Sweden in 1621. After the Treaty of Nystadt in 1721, it reverted to Russia. R. was part of the Soviet Union (Latvian SSR) until 1991, at which time Latvia became independent, with R. as its capital.

Riga, Treaty of *See* Russian-Polish war.

Rigault de Genouilly, Charles (1807-1873) French admiral. He played a leading role in the French conquest of Indochina during the 1850s.

Rikken Seiyukai Leading Japanese political party between 1900 and 1940, founded by Ito Hirobumi. The party was incorporated into the military Taisei Jokusankai, which started the war with the U.S. in 1941.

Rimsky-Korsakov, Nikolay Andreyevich (1844-1908) Russian composer. He was one of a group of nationalist composers ("The Five") that included Moussorgsky, Borodin, Balakirev, and Cui. His works include piano pieces, choral works, the symphonic poem *Schererezade* (1888) and the fairy-tale opera *Le Coq d'Or* (1909).

Nikolay Andreyevich Rimsky-Korsakov

Rio Branco law Law in Brazil (1871) that freed the children of slaves after their 21st birthday. In 1888, slavery was abolished altogether in Brazil.

Rio Salado, Battle of (1340) Invading Saracens were defeated at R. by the Castilian Portuguese army under Alfonso XI of Castile and Alfonso IV of Portugal.

Risjis In Brahmanism, the visionaries who compiled the Vedic hymns.

Risorgimento Period of cultural nationalism and political activism in Italian history that led to the country's unification. Partly as a result of Napoleon's defeat of the Austrians and Garibaldi's conquests, Italian unity was attained in 1870 when the last of the Papal territories in and around Rome were taken.

Ritter, Johann Wilhelm (1776-1810) Scientist who discovered ultraviolet rays in 1801.

Robert I (c.865-923)

Rivera, Diego (1886-1957) Mexican painter. He was inspired by native Mexican folk art and by the idealism embodied in revolutionary communism. R.'s heroic murals adorn many buildings in Mexico, including the National Palace and the Palace of Cortez at Cuernevaca.

Rivoli Village in Northern Italy. There, on January 14, 1797, the Austrians were decisively beaten by Napoleon and Masséna.

Roanoke Island Island off the coast of North Carolina. On R., colonists dispatched by Raleigh founded (1585) the first English settlement in North America.

Robert I (c.865-923) French king, 922-923. The count of Paris and duke of Francia, R. was proclaimed king by the aristocracy in 922, but died at the Battle of Soissons against Charles the Simple.

Robert I (Robert the Magnificent) (d.1035) Duke of Normandy. He was the father of William the Conqueror. He died while on a pilgrimage to Jerusalem. R. is often identified with the legendary Robert the Devil.

Robert II (Robert the Pious) (970-1031) King of France, 996-1031. The son of Hugh Capet, he ruled jointly with his father from 987-996. As king, R. attempted to strengthen the royal authority and secured Burgundy (1015) for the crown.

Robert II (c.1054-1134) Duke of Normandy. He was the eldest son of William the Conqueror. R. succeeded his father as Duke of Normandy upon the

Diego Rivera

The Roaring Twenties

The decade after World War I was a time of profound change. A new phenomenon, mass popular culture, spread from the United States to Europe. Some countries in the West enjoyed widespread prosperity. The twenties, however, also witnessed the emergence of extremist movements and great unrest: for example, the rise of Adolf Hitler and his Nazis in Germany, and a large-scale but unsuccessful general strike in Great Britain.

1

2

1. America prospered, and many people could afford to buy the Model T Fords which were produced in unprecedented numbers. *See* Ford, Henry.
2. Approximately three million people participated in the General Strike of 1926 in Britain. The strike failed, however, as the British government made sure that vital services continued to function.
3. One of the major international issues in the 1920s was the question of the reparations that Germany was required to pay as a result of its defeat in World War I. Pictured is a 1930 conference at which the reparations questions was discussed.
See Dawes Plan; Versailles, Treaty of.
4. During the twenties Hollywood, California, became the center of the film industry. One of its early stars was Charlie Chaplin.
5. In 1923, Adolf Hitler attempted a coup in Munich that failed. He was sent to prison for a short time, and while there he wrote *Mein Kampf*.
See Hitler, Adolf; *Mein Kampf*, Eisener Hall Putsch.

3

4

5

latter's death in 1087. R. came into conflict with his brothers William II and Henry I, both of whom became kings of England. Henry, R.'s younger brother, assumed the crown while R. was on the First Crusade. In 1106. R. was captured by Henry and spent the rest of his life in captivity.

Robert II (1316-1390) King of Scotland, 1371-1390. He rebelled (1363) against the authority of his uncle, David II, when David recognized Edward III as his successor. R. succeeded peacefully to the throne after David's death in 1371. He was the first Stuart king of Scotland.

Robert III (Robert of Bethune) (1247-1322) Count of Flanders. The eldest son of Gwijde of Dampierre, he and his father fought for the independence of Flanders from France. From 1300-1305 he and his family were the prisoners of the French king; *see* Louis of Nevers.

Roberts, Frederick Sleigh, 1st Earl Roberts of Kandahar (1832-1914) British field marshal. He fought during the Indian Mutiny and became famous for the relief of Kandahar during the second Afghan War (1878-1880). After 1885 he commanded all British fores in India. R. helped strengthen British forces during the Boar War in South Africa. In the early 1900s he became a proponent of compulsory military service in Britain.

Robespierre, Augustin de (1763-1794) Brother of Maximilien Robespierre. Toppled from power, he died on the guillotine at the end of his political career in 1794.

Robespierre, Maximilien François Marie Isidore de (1758-1794) French revolutionary. He was one of the leading figures of the French Revolution. R. became leader of the Jacobins, and after the fall of the Girondists he was a leading figure in the Committee of Public Safety. He pressed for the execution of Louis XVI. In the spring of 1794, R. had the Hébertists and Dantonists liquidated and was dictator during the Reign of Terror. On July 27, 1794, he was arrested in the Con-

vention as forces of the right joined the Plain. The following morning, R. was executed without trial.

Roc Legendary giant bird in Arab tales. Is mentioned by Marco Polo and was the subject of a search by Khublai Khan.

Roccasecca, Battle of Battle in the war for Naples (1411) in which Louis II of Anjou defeated the Angevin Ladislas Durazzo.

Rochambeau, Jean Baptiste Donatien de Vimeur, Count (1725-1807) French general. After 1780, he was the commander of the French contingent of troops that fought against the British in North America and forced Cornwallis to surrender at Yorktown.

Rochester, Henry Wilmot Baron (c.1612-1658) English general. A confidant of Charles II, he saved the after the Battle of Worcester (1651), which ended the English Civil War. R. also led the failed revolt at Marston Moor.

Rockefeller, John D. (1839-1937) American businessman and philanthropist. He founded (1870) the Standard Oil Company, turning it into a giant trust that controlled almost all of the U.S. oil industry. During his lifetime, he gave away some $550 million, much of it through the Rockefeller Foundation.

Rocque, François de la (1885-1946) French officer in the fascist parties

**Maximilien François
Marie Isidore de Robespierre**

Croix de Feu (Cross of Fire) and Parti Social Français whose speech in 1934 was the immediate cause of Daladier's resignation. He took part in the Vichy government but was imprisoned by the Germans.

Rocroi Site in northeastern France where Spanish troops under De Melo were heavily defeated (1643) during the Thirty Years War by the French under Condé.

Roderick (d.711) Last Visigothic king in Spain. In 711 he was beaten by the Arabs at Jerez de la Frontera and drowned in the Guadalete River.

Auguste Rodin

Rodin, Auguste (1840-1917) French sculptor. He is considered one of the most important sculptors in history. R.'s work varies in style, some of it being polished while other pieces are extremely rough, seemingly barely to have emerged from their original material. Among his most well-known works are *The Thinker* (1879-1900), *The Kiss* (1886), and his monument to Balzac (1897).

Rodney, George Brydes Rodney, 1st Baron (1719-1792) British admiral. He fought successfully against the French (Seven Years War) and the Spanish. In the latter part of his career, he saw action in the West Indies, where he captured the island of St. Eustatius (1781).

Roger of Antioch (d.1119) Norman ruler from 1112. During the Crusades, he defeated the Seljuks when they invaded Syria (1115). In the struggle for Aleppo, R. was killed in the Battle of the Field of Blood.

Roggeveen, Jacob (1659-1729) Dutch navigator. He explored for the West-India Company and discovered (1722) Easter Island in the Pacific.

Röhm, Ernst (1887-1934) Nazi leader. He was the head of the SA, the Nazi paramilitary organization that helped Hitler achieve power. Hitler had R. and the top SA leadership

Ernst Röhm

assassinated in 1934 in order to eliminate the threat they posed to the primacy of the German army.

Rojas Pinilla, Gustavo (1900-1975) President of Colombia, 1953-1957. The head of the armed forces, he achieved power (1953) in a coup that ousted President Lauréano Gómez. P. rule the country as a brutal dictatorship and was himself ousted by the military in 1957. He attempted a political comeback in 1970 but narrowly lost the presidential election.

Rök Stone Swedish runic inscription from the 9th century. It makes possible reference to Theodoric the Great.

Rokossovsky, Konstantin (1896-1968) Soviet field marshal. In 1942, he led the defense of Moscow and played an important part in the victory at Stalingrad. R., of Polish origin, was installed (1949) by Moscow as commander of the Polish army, Polish minister of defense, and deputy prime minister. After Gomulka came to power (1956), Polish nationalism reasserted itself, and R. was recalled to the Soviet Union. He also served as Soviet deputy defense minister between 1956 and 1958.

Roland Frankish general and margrave of Brittany. He was Charlemagne's commander on the Breton border and accompanied him on an expedition against the Saracens. He died in 778 at Roncevaux in the battle against the Basques. In legend he is the hero of the medieval Charlemagne cycle of *chanson de geste*.

Rolls, Charles Stewart (1877-1910) English car manufacturer. The Rolls-Royce is named after him. R. was also the first Englishman to make a nonstop round-trip flight across the English Channel.

Roman Catholicism Branch of Christianity that acknowledges the pope in the Vatican as its supreme leader.

Roman Empire Historic area of the Mediterranean dominated by the Romans. The empire existed from c.27 BC to 476 AD. Prior to then, Rome was a kingdom (753-509 BC) and a republic (509-27 BC).

Roman Republic Political entity founded in Italy by the French army (1798). The French were driven from Italy by the Austrian-Italian armies in 1799, but Rome was recaptured by Napoleon in 1809.

Romanesque Art Architectural style in Western Europe between 1000-1200. Romanesque churches appear sober and solid and often contain stone barrel vaults. Their shape was inspired by early Christian basilicas, and their walls are often decorated by frescoes.

Romanones, Alvaro de Figueroa y Tor-

res, Count of (1863-1950) Spanish statesman. After 1901 he served in a number of ministries, and following the end of World War I (1918), he was prime minister. R. was forced out of office in 1923 after the coup by Primo Rivera.

Romanov Ruling dynasty of Russia from 1613 until the Russian Revolution of 1917.

Romanov

Romans Term applied to the original inhabitants of ancient Rome. Later, during the Empire, "Romans" meant people who had Roman citizenship, even if they did not live in Rome proper.

Rommel, Erwin (1891-1944) German field marshal. During World War II, he was supreme commander of the German troops in North Africa. A brilliant tactician, he put up a great fight when, after stiff resistance, he was finally defeated in 1943. He later held high command positions on the Western Front in Europe. R. was forced to

The Roman Catholic Church under Criticism

1

In the 15th century, the Roman Catholic Church had become very worldly and, in the opinion of some, decadent and corrupt. Popes lived like great lords, the selling and buying of ecclesiastical offices had become a normal practice, and there was a lively trade in indulgences, or pardons for sin. Religious thinkers who held to a more strict vision of religion began to protest, and their protests led to major changes within the Church.

4

2

3

1. An indulgence, printed around 1450 in Mainz. By buying an indulgence, a person could obtain pardon for having sinned. The Church earned an enormous amount of money by selling indulgences.

2. Martin Luther protested what he felt were the Church's abuses of power and violations of true Christianity. In 1520, Pope Leo X wrote a bull ordering that all Luther's writings be burned. In response, Luther burned the bull on December 10, 1520. *See* Luther, Martin.

3. An example of the splendors of papal life: Michelangelo painted the Last Judgment on the walls of the Sistine Chapel on the commission of Pope Clement VII. *See* Clement VII; Michelangelo.

4. Cardinal Albrecht of Brandenburg in his office. To gain the revenue needed to buy his position as archbishop, he authorized the sale of many indulgences.

5. Huldreich Zwingli was another reformer and critic of the Roman Catholic Church. He rejected the veneration of saints, priestly celibacy, fasting, and the lavish decoration of churches. *See* Zwingli, Huldreich.

5

The Romans

The Roman Empire was the most powerful and extensive civilization of the ancient world. Its capital was the city of Rome in Italy.
The Romans conquered very large areas of Europe, North Africa, and the Middle East.
The empire in the West lasted more than five centuries until Germanic tribes conquered Rome in the late 5th century AD.
In the East, as the Byzantine Empire, it continued until 1453, when the Turks captured Constantinople.

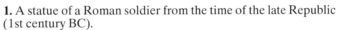

1. A statue of a Roman soldier from the time of the late Republic (1st century BC).
2. A Roman gold coin with a portrait of Julius Caesar as a young man. *See* Caesar.
3. The Triumphal Arch of Emperor Constantine the Great (ruled 324-337 AD) in Rome. *See* Constantine I.
4. A statue of Emperor Augustus (ruled 29 BC-14 AD), showing him as the leader of the Roman army. *See* Augustus.
5. A fragment of the interior decoration of the *Domus Aurea,* the "Golden House," in which Emperor Nero (ruled 54-68 AD) lived. *See* Nero.

6

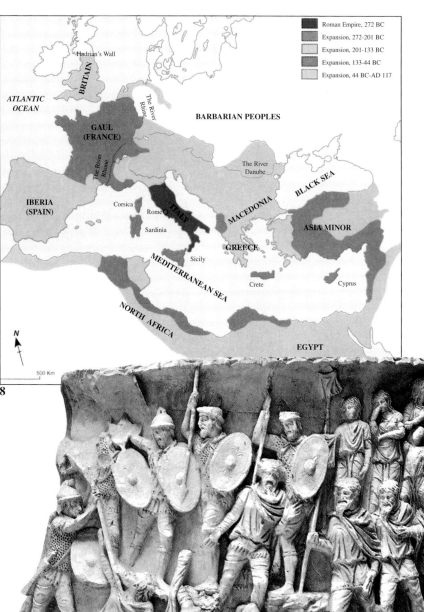

8

7

10

9

6. A relief depicting Emperor Hadrian (ruled 117-138 AD). The relief is a detail of the Triumphal Arch that was built in his honor in Rome. *See* Hadrian.

7. Hadrian's Wall, built by the emperor in the north of England to defend the empire against attacks from the Picts.

8. The expansion of the Roman Empire up to the reign of Emperor Trajan (98-117 AD).

9. A relief depicting the decapitation of barbarians by Roman soldiers.

10. Roman women painted on a mural in Pompeii, city in Italy that was destroyed by a volcanic eruption in 79 AD.

Map legend:
- Roman Empire, 272 BC
- Expansion, 272-201 BC
- Expansion, 201-133 BC
- Expansion, 133-44 BC
- Expansion, 44 BC-AD 117

commit suicide in 1944 for his alleged role in the attempted assassination of Hitler (July 20, 1944).

Romulus Augustus (d.c.476) Last Roman emperor of the West, 475-476. He was appointed (475) to the throne by his father Orestes but was deposed by Odoacer after his father's death in 476.

Romulus and Remus In Roman legend, the two founders of Rome (753 BC). They are symbolized by two children suckled by a wolf. Romulus became king of Rome after murdering Remus.

Ronin Wandering, masterless samurai during the Muromatsji and Tokugawa periods.

Röntgen, Wilhelm Conrad (1845-1923) German physicist. In 1895, he discovered the X-ray and in 1901 received the Nobel Prize for Physics.

Roosevelt, Eleanor (1884-1962) American humanitarian, wife of President Franklin D. Roosevelt. The niece of President Theodore Roosevelt, she grew up in a wealthy New York family. In 1905 she married Franklin D. Roosevelt, a distant cousin. After her husband was stricken with polio (1921), R. became involved in Democratic Party, serving as her husband's "eyes and ears" during his long convalescence. After Roosevelt's election as president (1932), she became an activist First Lady, traveling widely and promoting New Deal programs and equality for African Americans. R. continued her interest in humanitarian causes after her husband's death (1945), serving as a U.S. delegate to the United Nations. She remained an important figure within the Democratic Party until her death in 1962 at age 78.

Roosevelt, Franklin Delano (1882-1945) 32nd president of the U.S., 1933-1945. The son of James and Sara Delano Roosevelt, he entered New York state Democratic Party politics in 1910 and served (1913-1921) as assistant secretary of the navy under Woodrow Wilson. He was the unsuccessful 1920 Democratic vice-presidential nominee. In 1921, R. was stricken with polio, and his career in politics seemed over. Even though he never walked again, R. returned to

Erwin Rommel

politics and was elected (1928) governor of New York. In 1932 he was elected president. His reform program, the New Deal, for the first time actively involved the federal government in regulating the economy and in providing for the welfare of average people. R. decided to run for an unprecedented third term in 1940 as war engulfed Europe and threatened U.S. neutrality. After U.S. entry into World War II (1941), the remainder of R.'s time as president was consumed with the war. He was reelected to a fourth term in 1944, but his health had begun to fail, and he died five months later (April 12, 1945) at age 63.

Roosevelt, Theodore (1858-1919) 26th president of the U.S., 1901-1909. His overnight fame as a Rough Rider in the Spanish-American War propelled him into the governorship of New York and the 1900 Republican vice-presidential nomination. On the assassination of President William McKinley (1901), R., at 42, became the youngest American president. R. expanded the powers of the presidency, using the office to press for a wide variety of domestic reforms, including the breaking up of the trusts. In foreign policy, he acquired the Panama Canal Zone and promoted an aggressive U.S. presence in the world based on a powerful navy. He ran for president again in 1912 on the Bull Moose ticket after unsuccessfully trying to wrest the Republican nomination from his hand-picked successor,

William Howard Taft. After his defeat. R. remained active in Republican politics and was the presumptive nominee in 1920. He died, however, at 60 in 1919.

Theodore Roosevelt

Root, Elihu (1845-1937), American statesman. He served as secretary of war (1899-1904) and as secretary of state (1905-1909) under President Theodore Roosevelt. R. concluded the Root-Takahira agreement (1908), under which both nations agreed to maintain the status quo in the Pacific and uphold the Open Door Policy in China. He served (1909-1915) as a U.S. senator from New York, and in 1912 won the Nobel Peace Prize for his work on behalf of international peace.

Rorke's Drift, Battle at *See* Isandhlwana, Battle at.

Rory O'Connor (d.1198) Last high king of Ireland. He was forced to submit as a vassal to Henry II of England. Although he retained the title of high king, his power declined and he retired to a monastery in 1191.

Rosas, Juan Manuel de (1793-1877) Argentine politician. He was dictator of Argentina from 1835-1852. R.'s domestic policies were brutally repressive. In foreign affairs, he attempted to dominate neighboring countries, incurring the wrath of great Britain, France, and the United States. A coalition of, among others, Brazil and Uruguay ended his reign of terror after his defeat at Caseros (1852). He spent the remainder of his life in exile in England.

Juan Manuel de Rosas

Rosenberg, Alfred (1893-1946) Nazi political leader. He was one of the principal formulators of Nazi racial theory. R. was hanged in 1946 after the Nuremberg trials.

Roses, Wars of the Name of the wars waged between 1455-1485 in England between two aristocratic parties: the supporters of the Lancasters (the red rose was their emblem) and the Yorks (the white rose). The conflict ended in 1485 (Battle of Bosworth), followed Henry Tudor's uniting both claims by descent and marriage. He ascended the throne as Henry VII, the first Tudor monarch to govern England.

Rosetta Stone Stone slab with Egyptian inscriptions found by Napoleon's troops in 1799. The stone is inscribed in hieroglyphics, demotic script (the script in daily use from the 7th century BC), and Greek. Because the Greek on the stone could be read, it gave scholars the key to deciphering the hieroglyphics.

Ross, Betsy (1752-1836) American seamstress. A flag maker during the American Revolution, she was supposed to have sewn the first American Stars and Stripes. This legend, however, is now believed to be untrue.

Ross, Sir John (1777-1856) British arctic explorer. In 1831 he discovered the magnetic North Pole in Boothia Peninsula.

Rossbach Village in central Germany. There, on November 5, 1757, the imperial army and the French suffered a heavy defeat during the Seven Years War at the hands of the Prussians under Frederick the Great.

Rossini, Gioacchino (1792-1868) Italian operatic composer. A master of the Italian opera buffa, he composed *The Italian Girl in Algiers* (1813), *The Barber of Seville* (1816), and *Cinderella* (1817), among other comic masterpieces. His other operas include *Semiramide* (1823) and *William Tell* (1829). R. suddenly stopped composing operas at 37 years of age. For the remainder of his life, he wrote only occasional songs and piano pieces and a setting of the *Stabat Mater* (1842).

Rothschild Prominent European banking family. Meyer Amschell R. (1743-1812), the son of a money changer in the Jewish ghetto of Frankfurt, laid the foundations for the family's fortune through his service as the financial agent of the landgrave of Hesse-Kassel. Succeeding generations established bank branches throughout Europe and became the creditors for many European governments. In the 19th century the family was politically influential. In 1822 all five R. brothers were created barons by Emperor Francis I of Austria. With the emergence of modern banking and more sophisticated forms of state financing, the influence of the R. receded.

Rough Riders Nickname of the 1st Regiment of U.S. Cavalry Volunteers. It was formed at the start of the Spanish-American War (1898) by Leonard Wood and Theodore Roosevelt. Its exploits were highly publicized during the short war with Spain and became a springboard for Roosevelt's rise to the presidency three years later.

Roundheads Derisive name used for the supporters of the parliament during the English Civil War. Those loyal to King Charles I wore long-haired wigs and were known as Cavaliers, whereas the Puritan parliamentarians were mocked because of their short haircuts.

Rousseau, Jean Jacques (1712-1778) Swiss-French philosopher. His thought has had an unparalleled influence on politics, literature, and education. One of his core concepts is that man is by nature good and therefore corrupted by society. Freedom, in his view, is the submission to wisdom as expressed in the general will. Politically, R. was a foe of absolutism, and his doctrine of popular sovereignty had profound impact on French revolutionary thought. His *Confessions* are still widely read.

Jean Jacques Rousseau

Roxana (d. 311 BC) Wife of Alexander the Great. The daughter of the Bactrian king Oxyartes, she married Alexander in order for him to consolidate his position in Persia. After his death, she and his posthumous son, Alexander IV, became involved in the war with the Diadochi. They were imprisoned by Cassander and later killed.

Roxolans Scythian people to the north of the Black Sea. They fought together with the Scythians in the Crimea in 107 BC against Mithradates of Pontus.

Rozwi Karanga realm in southern Africa (*see* Zimbabwe) founded by Changamire Dombo I (ruled 1684-1695), who ousted the Portuguese. In the early 19th century, R. fell to colonizers.

Ruben *See* Israel, tribes of.

Rubens, Peter Paul (1577-1640) Flemish painter. His large and mythical works included scenes of abductions and battles, with nude figures in various poses. R. also painted superb religious works and explored other subjects such as landscapes, portraits, and representations of animals. He studied in Italy, and the influence of the Italians is obvious, but his work is mainly characterized by a Flemish zest and, even in his religious works, an almost pagan joy. Rubens was wealthy and propagated his works through a vast studio-school in which apprentices mimicked his art. Almost everything that came out of his workshop bears the mark of his genius.

Rubicon Stream near Rimini, in northern Italy. It was the boundary between ancient Italy and Cisalpine Gaul. In 49 BC, Caesar disobeyed the senate and crossed the R. in pursuit of Pompey, thus precipitating civil war. The event gave rise to the expression, "crossing the Rubicon," which means taking an irreversible action.

Rudolf I (Rudolf of Hapsburg) (1218-1291) German king, 1273-1291. He was the first king of the Hapsburg dynasty.

Rudolf I

Peter Paul Rubens with his wife Isabella

Rudolf II (1552-1612) Holy Roman emperor, 1576-1612. The son and successor of Maximilian II, he was a learned man but was unfit to rule because of depression and bouts of insanity. His turbulent reign was a prelude to the Thirty Years War.

Rudolf (1858-1889) Archduke and crown prince of Austria-Hungary, son of Emperor Francis Joseph. He committed suicide with his mistress Maria Vetsera at Mayerling.

Rugi German tribe who migrated from Norway to Pomerania c.100 AD and later entered Austria with the Huns. Together with the Ostrogoth Theodoric, the R. invaded Italy, but they were defeated by Odoacer in 487.

Ruhr Industrial and coal-mining region in western Germany. It was occupied in January 1923 by Belgian and French troops when the German government failed to meet reparations payments called for in the Treaty of Versailles, which ended World War I.

Rundstedt, Karl Rudolf Gerd von (1875-1953) German field marshal.

He served both on the eastern and the western fronts during World War II. In 1944 he launched the German counteroffensive known as the Battle of the Bulge, which unsuccessfully attempted to drive German forces as far as Antwerp. After the war, he was held for trial as a war criminal, but he was released in 1949 because of illness.

Runes Ancient characters used in Teutonic, Scandinavian, and Anglo-Saxon inscriptions. The oldest R. date back to c.250 AD. The 24 signs of the alphabet were used up until c.600 in Scandinavia. In addition to being a script, R. were also magical symbols. After the onset of Christianity, R. were reviled as pagan symbols.

Rupert, Prince (1619-1682) Count palatine of the Rhine. The son of Frederick the Winter King, king of Bohemia, and Elizabeth, a daughter of James I of England, he was raised in the Netherlands. He fought on the royalist side in the English Civil War but was ordered to leave England after a disagreement with Charles I. After the reinstatement of the English monarchy (1660), he became a close

Rudolf II

Russian Czars of the 17th Century

The Russian Empire
was founded at the end of the
15th century by Ivan IV, the Great.
He and his successors succeeded
in rapidly expanding Russia
during the following centuries by
conquering Polish, Turkish,
and other territories.

1

2

3

4

1. The crowns of Michael
Romanov, the czar who came
to power in 1613. *See* Romanov.
2. Czar Alexis, the son of
Michael Romanov and father of Peter
the Great. *See* Peter the Great.
3. Czar Peter the Great wanted to
make Russia into a proper European
state. He forbade the nobility
to wear beards, and this picture
shows one having his beard cut off.
See Boyars; Peter the Great.
4. Peter I, the Great of Russia in a
late 17th-century painting.
See Peter I, the Great
5. In 1703 Peter the Great founded
a new capital city, St. Petersburg, that
he wanted to be a "window"
on Europe.

5

Prince Rupert

adviser to Charles II and an admiral of the English fleet. R. played an important role in the Dutch wars.

Rurales Police force instituted by Juárez in 1861 to reduce banditry in Mexico. They were abolished in 1914.

Rurik (d.879) Semi-legendary warrior. He is considered the founder of the princely dynasty of medieval Russia.

Rush-Bagot Agreement Pact concluded between the U.S. and Great Britain regulating the number of warships on the U.S.-Canadian frontier. It established the precedent of peaceful resolution of U.S.-British disputes, and it demilitarized the U.S.-Canadian frontier and inaugurated a policy of peace between the United States and Canada.

Ruska, Ernst (1906-1988) German engineer. He invented the electron microscope and was awarded the Nobel Prize for Physics in 1986.

Russian Civil War Conflict that lasted from 1918-1921 between the newly founded Bolshevik regime and those seeking to overthrow it; *see* Wrangel.

Russian Orthodox Church Principle Christian denomination of Russia, In 1054, a schism developed between the Christian church in the East and Rome. One of the churches that developed as a result in the East was the R. The church suffered under the Soviet system but was never obliterated. It enjoyed a revival under Gorbachev and after the collapse of the Soviet Union (1991).

Russian Revolution Cataclysmic upheaval in Russia (1917) that overthrew the czarist regime and ushered in the communist Soviet Union; *see* Lenin.

Russo-Finnish War Conflict between Finland and the Soviet Union (1939-1940). The Soviets, taking advantage of their nonaggression pact with Germany, made territorial demands on the Finns, who resisted. In the short war, the Finns at first repulsed the Soviets but in the end were no match against their larger opponent. The postwar settlement forced the Finns to give some territorial concessions, as demanded, to the Soviets.

Russo-Japanese War Conflict between Russia and Japan (1904-1905). The conflict arose out of rival designs on the part of Russia and Japan over Manchuria and Korea. The Russians were humiliated on the battlefield and in the Peace of Portsmouth, negotiated by President Theodore Roosevelt. Japan, on the other hand, achieved recognition as a world power and began its imperialistic phase in Asia leading ultimately to World War II.

Russo-Polish War (1919-1920) Conflict between Russia and Poland. It began when the Polish leader Pilsudski occupied Kiev. His forces were soon driven back to the outskirts of Warsaw by the Russians. A peace agreement was signed March 18, 1921, in Riga, Latvia.

Russo-Turkish Wars Series of conflicts between Russia and Turkey (1676-1878). At their root was Russia's desire to acquire territories in and around the Black Sea.

Rustamid Kingdom (761-909) Algerian kingdom that resisted the Abbasids. The realm collapsed after the capture of its capital, Tahart, by the Fatamids.

Rutherford, Ernest (1871-1937) British physicist. In 1899, he discovered and named alfa and beta radiation. R. also provided the first description of the atom. He won the 1908 Nobel Prize in Chemistry

Ruthwell, Cross of 8th-century cross from Dumfrieshire, Scotland, containing English runic inscription. It depicts six guttural sounds in contrast with Scandinavian runic script, which contain only two.

Ruyter, Michiel Adiaanszoon de (1607-1676) Dutch admiral. In 1665, he became admiral of the Dutch fleet. He achieved great victories against the English in the Medway (1667) and against the English and French in the third Dutch War (1672-1678). In 1676, R. was sent to the Mediterranean to support the Spanish against the French. He was mortally wounded in Syracuse.

Michiel Adiaanszoon de Ruyter

Rye House conspiracy Failed attempt (1683) to assassinate King Charles II of England and his Roman Catholic brother, the duke of York (later James II). Although the actual conspirators were minor figures, a number of leading Whigs who had worked to exclude James from the succession, including Lord William Russell, were executed on flimsy evidence.

Rykov, Aleksey Ivanovich (1881-1938) Bolshevik politician. A member of the politburo (1922-1930), he supported Stalin against Trotsky, Zinoviev and Kamenev, but was himself executed in the purges of 1938 after a public trial for treason.

Ernest Rutherford

Ryswick, Treaty of Pact that ended (1697) the War of the Grand Alliance. France was forced to accept almost all the conditions set by England, the Republic of the Netherlands, Spain, and the German emperor.

SA (*Sturmabteilung*) National Socialist paramilitary movement. Founded in 1921, it eventually grew to more than 2 million members by the early 1930s. Under the leadership of Ernst Röhm, the S. demanded a greater role in the National Socialist state and represented a threat to the regular army. Hitler ordered the top SA leadership murdered on June 30, 1934, and thereafter the organization played a subordinate role to the SS, founded by Himmler.

Sá, Mem de (d.1572) Portuguese colonial ruler in Brazil from c.1557. He was the founder of Rio de Janeiro.

Saba Pre-Islamic kingdom in southwest Arabia (c.12th century BC). It was wealthy because of its trade in spices and agricultural products. S. was conquered by the Arabs in the 7th century BC.

Sabbatai Zevi (1626-1676) Jewish mystic who believed himself to be the Messiah. The founder of the Sabbatean sect, he proclaimed the year 1666 as the millennium and attempted to land in Constantinople (Istanbul) with his followers. He was taken prisoner, however, and adopted Islam in order to save his life. The Sabbatean movement survived into the 18th century.

Sabbath Jewish holy day of rest, lasting from sunset on Friday until the start of the following night (Genesis 1:5).

Saberth (d.616/617) First Christian king of the kingdom of the East Saxons (Essex). He followed his uncle Aethelbert I in converting to Christianity and is thought to have founded Westminster Abbey.

Sabines Ancient people of Italy. They lived in the Apennines northeast of

Muhammad Anwar al-Sadat

Rome. The S. colonized part of southern Italy and mixed with the Latins. According to tradition, the S. women were seized and raped by the followers of Romulus. Rome was involved in a number of wars with the Sabines, but by 290 BC they had been subdued and became Roman citizens.

Sabratha Carthaginian trading station (4th century BC) in northern Africa. After the fall of Carthage in 146 BC, S. became Roman. The city was governed by the Vandals in the 5th century and fell into ruins after it was conquered by the Arabs in 643.

Sacajawea (c.1784-1812) Shoshone Indian woman who served as a guide and interpreter during the Lewis and Clark expedition (1804-1806).

Sacco-Vanzetti Case Murder case in the U.S. during the 1920s involving two self-professed Italian-immigrant anarchists. The case drew worldwide attention because of the anti-immigrant, anti-radical emotions it aroused in the United States. S. and V. were executed in 1927 and were thought by many to be innocent of the crime of murder. Forensic studies in the 1960s, however, concluded that S. had probably committed the murder.

Sachs, Hans (1494-1576) German poet. The leading *meistersinger* of the Nuremberg school, he was also a shoemaker and guild master. He is estimated to have produced more than 6,000 works, including fables and farces, Shrovetide stories, comedies, and songs.

Sadat, Muhammad Anwar al- (1918-1981) President of Egypt, 1970-1981. An army officer, he became President of Egypt in 1970 on the death of Nasser. S. waged war against Israel in 1973 but wanted to negotiate a settlement. His historic visit to Israel (1977) became a turning point in the political situation in the Middle East and led in a peace treaty between the two countries (1979) and the return of territories taken by Israel during the Six-Day War (1967). S. and Israeli leader Menachem Begin received the Nobel Peace Prize in 1978. His agreement with Israel as well as his pro-American stance alienated fanatical Muslims in Egypt, and he was assassinated in 1981 by fundamentalist soldiers while watching a parade.

Donatien Alphonse François Sade

Sade, Donatien Alphonse François, Comte of (1740-1814) French writer. He is more commonly known as the marquise de Sade. S. spent more that 27 years in prison because of his writings and his licentious life style. He believed that because sexual deviation existed in nature, it was therefore natural. The term *sadism*—the inflicting of pain for sexual pleasure—is derived from his name.

Sadi dynasty *See* Mali, Kingdom of.

Sadova *See* Königgrätz.

Safavid dynasty (1502-1736) Descendants of the Iranian founder Safi ad-Din (1253-1334). The dynasty introduced Shiite Islam to Iran and defeated the Turks (1603), after which Baghdad was captured. They also drove the Portuguese from Hormuz island (1602 and 1622).

Saffavids (9th century) Iranian dynasty founded by Ya'qub as-Saffar. They conquered parts of India but were defeated by the Samanids at Balkh during a campaign to reach Baghdad (900).

Sagasta, Práxedes Mateo (1825-1903) Spanish statesman. He served seven times as prime minister of Spain between 1871 and 1902. S. helped oust Isabella II (1868). He granted autonomy to Cuba in 1897 but was unable to prevent U.S. intervention and the defeat of Spain in the Spanish-American War (1898), for which he was generally blamed.

Saguntum Ancient city in Spain. An ally of Rome, it was attacked by the Carthaginians under Hannibal (219 BC), leading to the outbreak of the Second Punic War. S. was reconquered by Rome in 214 BC.

Said ibn Sultan (1791-1856) Lord of Muscat and Oman from 1806. In 1840 he shifted his capital to Zanzibar, in east Africa, where he introduced the cloves that became the foundation of the island's economy.

Saigon, Treaty of Agreement in 1862 between France and the last independent emperor of Vietnam, Tu-Duc, in which France was ceded Saigon and parts of Cochin China.

Saint Albans Town north of London, England. There, during the Wars of the Roses, Richard of York defeated a royal army (1455) and Warwick and Edward IV were defeated by the Lancasters (1461).

Saint Augustine City in Florida. Founded in 1565 by the Spanish explorer Pedro Menéndez de Avilés, it is the oldest city in the United States. S. remained a Spanish colony until 1819, when it was purchased by the United States under the Adams-Onís Treaty.

Saint-Exupéry, Antoine de (1900-1944) French writer. His work reflects his love of freedom of action and of the

Antoine de Saint-Exupéry

Práxedes Mateo Sagasta

open skies. His most famous work is the *Le Petit Prince* (*The Little Prince*) (1943), which is read by children as well as adults. S. was a pilot for the Allies during World War II and was killed in action.

Saint-Germain, Treaty of (1570) Pact that ended the first phase of the French Wars of Religion.

Saint-Germain, Treaty of (1679) Pact that ended the third of the Dutch wars.

Saint-Germain, Treaty of (1919) Treaty that ended the war between Austria and the Allies at the end of World War I.

Saint Helena Island in the South Atlantic Ocean. It was discovered by the Portuguese in 1502, belonged to Holland from 1633 to 1673, and has been British since then. In 1815, Napoleon was exiled on S., and he died there in 1821.

Saint Peter's Church Principal church of Roman Catholicism. The largest church in the Christian world, it is located in Vatican City. The present structure was built between 1506-1626 on the site of a 4th-century St. Peter's built by Constantine. Raphael and Michelangelo were among S.'s architects, and Bernini designed the piazza and colonnade. In the grottoes beneath the church are the tombs of St. Peter and other popes.

Saint-Quentin Town in northern

France. It has a long history of sieges and battles. At S., the Spaniards defeated the French in a siege during the Wars of Religion (1577). During the Franco-Prussian War (1870), the Germans defeated the French at S. In World War I, the French were defeated again (1914) by the Germans near S.

Saint-Saëns, Charles Camille (1835-1921) French composer, pianist, and organist. He was organist at the Madeleine for many years, and he com-

Charles Camille Saint-Saëns

posed in almost every form. S.'s Third Symphony with organ and piano became particularly famous and well-liked. Other works include the symphonic poem *Danse macabre* (1875) and the opera *Samson et Dalila* (1877).

Saints, Battle of the Battle in the Caribbean (1782) between the British and French fleets near Guadaloupe. The British won and consolidated their position in the Caribbean as a result.

Sais Ancient city of Egypt, in the Nile delta. It became the capital of a united Egypt under King Psamtik (Psammetichus I) from 664 BC.

Sakaliba Name for Slav slaves taken from Germany to Spain during the Moorish era in Spain.

Sakharov, Andrei Dimitriyevich (1921-1989) Soviet physicist, dissident, and human rights activist. He helped develop the hydrogen bomb (1950) and warned Khrushchev in 1958 about the dangers of atmospheric nuclear testing. In 1970, S. founded the Committee for Human Rights in the Soviet Union, for which he was awarded the Nobel Peace Prize in 1975. His human rights activities brought him into conflict with the regime, and he was sentenced to internal exile in Gorky. In 1986, S. was allowed to return to Moscow at Gorbachev's request.

Sakoku Japanese term for "closed country." S. was the policy of the Tokugawa shoguns, who attempted to shut off the country from the outside world.

Saladin (c.1137-1193) Muslim warrior. He was the Ayyubid sultan of Egypt. A respected general and fair ruler, S. seized power in Egypt in 1171. From Syria, he then became the greatest opponent of the Frankish crusaders in Palestine. After 1187, S. conquered Acre, Jaffa, Beirut, and Jerusalem, and eventually came into conflict with his legendary opponent, Richard Lionheart. In 1192, S. came to an agreement with the Crusaders, leaving them a small strip of land along the coast. S. effectively ended the Crusades. He also built numerous mosques and was a patron of literature.

Salamis Ancient port city on Cyprus. There, Ptolemy I of Egypt was defeated in a battle at sea by Demetrius Poliocretes. St. Paul visited S. on his first missionary journey.

Salamis Island off the coast of Attica, Greece. Near S., the Persian fleet was destroyed by the Greeks under the Athenian Themistocles in 480 BC.

Salazar, António de Oliveira (1889-1970) Portuguese politician. He was appointed prime minister in 1932, and from that time until 1968 ruled Portugal as a dictator. S. allowed the Allies to use the Azores as a base during World War II, and after the war, he spent considerable resources attempting to hold onto Portugal's colonial empire in Africa. After suf-

fering a stroke in 1968, he was replaced by Marcello Caetano.

Salem Town in Massachusetts. It as the site of the Salem witch trials in 1692.

Salghurids Turkmen-Iranian dynasty in Fars (1148-1270). They were subservient to the Il-Khanids and the Seljuks. Abish Khatun, the last of the S. monarchs, was a woman. After her rule, the Il-Khans took over the kingdom.

Salian dynasty Dynasty that ruled Germany from 1027 to 1125, starting with Conrad II and ending with Henry V.

Salic Law of Succession Rule in certain noble families in Europe that prevented women or their descendants from succeeding to the titles or offices in the family. It was practiced in France and Spain (at times) and parts of Germany. Because the Guelphs followed Salic law, the union of Great Britain and Hanover, begun when the elector of Hanover became George I in 1714, had to be discontinued when Victoria ascended the British throne in 1837.

Salih Christian tribe in Arabia (5th-7th century). They captured the area to the south of Damascus in c.400 and maintained diplomatic relations with the Byzantine Empire.

Salih Ayub (d.1249) Last of the Ayyubids (after 1239). During the Seventh Crusade, Louis IX of France invaded Egypt and S. was killed.

António de Oliveira Salazar

Salisbury, Thomas de Montagu, Count of (1388-1428) English general. He fought against France in the Hundred Years' War and was seriously wounded at the siege of Orléans.

Salitis Founder of the 15th Dynasty of Egypt (the Hyksos kings), which conquered a large part of Egypt and made Avaris the capital.

Sallust (c.86-34 BC) Roman historian. A partisan of Caesar, he served as governor of Numidia. S.'s works include a description of the Jugurthine War (41-40 BC). As a historian, his writings are archaic and inaccurate, but he provided vivid character sketches of important people.

SALT *See* Strategic Arms Limitation Talks.

Sam Saen Thai (1356-1417) Monarch of the Lan Xang kingdom in Laos, 1373-1417.

Samaria Ancient city in Palestine. It was built by Omri in the 9th century BC. In 721 BC, it was conquered by Assyria and later rebuilt by Herod the Great. The city gives its name to the Samaritans, descendants of non-Jewish people who settled there after 721 BC. Samaritans believed themselves to be the only true descendants of Abraham and Moses.

Samnites Ancient peoples who lived in central Italy. Their country was Samnium. The S. fought several wars with the Romans but were only defeated by Sulla in 82 BC. The survivors were sold into slavery or Romanized.

Samori Touré (c.1830-1900) Leader of a Muslim kingdom in West Africa. He waged war against the French during the 1880s and 1890s and was arrested in 1898 and exiled to Gabon.

Samothrace Greek island in the Aegean Sea. A member of the Delian League around 425 BC, it came under Macedonian rule in 340 BC. In 170 BC, the Romans imprisoned the last king, Perseus. S. was then Turkish until Greece took possession after World War I. The famous statue *Nike of Samothrace* was discovered there in 1863.

Sampson, Deborah (1760-1827) American female soldier. She enlisted

Andrei Dimitriyevich Sakharov

as "Robert Shurtleff" in the American Revolutionary War and fought and was wounded. In 1783, her true identity was revealed, and she was dismissed.

Samuel (d.1014) Czar of West Bulgaria from 980. After the Battle of Belitsa, in which S. was defeated by the Byzantine Emperor, Basilius II (1014), the latter had 15,000 Bulgarian prisoners of war blinded and sent back to S., who went into shock and died shortly thereafter.

Samurai Japanese knightly warrior class. They originated in the 12th century and lived according to the code of bushido (the life of a warrior), which prescribed courage, loyalty, and honor.

San Francisco Conference Meeting held from April 25 to June 26, 1945, to draw up the United Nations' charter.

San Jacinto, Battle of (1836) Last important military engagement (1836) between the Texans and the Mexicans in the Texan war for independence. Although greatly outnumbered, the Texans inflicted heavy casualties on the Mexicans and took the Mexican president, Santa Ana, prisoner. Santa Ana agreed to give Texas its independence in return for his release.

San Martín, José de (1778-1850) South American revolutionary. From 1812, S. fought against Spanish rule and liberated Chile and Peru. After personal talks with Simón Bolívar, he withdrew and retired to France, where he died in poverty.

José de San Martín

San Stefano Village near Constantinople. There, in 1878, a peace treaty was signed ending the war between Russia and Turkey. As a result, Turkey's power in the Balkans was curtailed.

Sanatescu, Constantine (1885-1947) Romanian army officer. After an antifascist coup against Antonescu, he became the first prime minister in 1944. However, he was forced to resign by the communists.

Sancherib (d.681 BC) King of Assyria, 705-681 BC. He was the son and successor of Sargon II. S. founded the new capital of Nineveh, conquered large parts of Syria and Palestine, and destroyed Babylon in 689 BC. He was murdered by two of his sons.

Sand Creek Site of massacre in Colorado (1864) of Cheyenne Indians by Colonel John Chivington and his Colorado Volunteers. Despite the fact that they had come to make peace, the Indians, under their leader, Battle Kettle, were indiscriminately slaughtered.

Sandino, Augusto César (1895-1934) Nicaraguan general and revolutionary. From 1926, he fought vigorously against the American marines and the National Guard of Nicaragua. He was killed by Somoza's forces in 1934 after being tricked into coming to a meeting, where he was seized. The leftist Sandinista movement that began in the 1970s took its name from him.

Sandwich, Edward Montagu, 1st Earl of (1625-1672) English admiral. He served during the Commonwealth, but with the collapse of the Protectorate, he supported the Restoration. S. helped escort Charles II back to England and played an influential role in his government. He was killed in battle during the Dutch wars.

Sanhedrin Ancient Jewish religious institution that served as a court during the Hellenic-Roman era. There were probably two Sanhedrin, one political and civil, the other religious. The religious Sanhedrin existed as late as 425 AD.

Sankin kotai System instigated (1635) by the Tokugawa shogun whereby influential landowners were required to spend in the capital of Edo. On leaving for their rural estates, they left their families behind as hostages.

Sans-culottes (French for "without knee breeches") Derisive term given by the French aristocracy to the lower classes during the French Revolution. The name derived from the fact that the aristocracy wore knee breeches, while common people wore long trousers.

Sanskrit Indo-European language. Already used in India c.1800 BC, it was the classical standard language of ancient India and is particularly known through many works of poetry. S. is still much studied today.

Antonio López de Santa Ana

Santa Ana, Antonio López de (1794-1876) Mexican general and politician. He fought the Texans in 1836 and was

Edward Montagu Sandwich

briefly captured. S. also fought in the Mexican War (1846-1848). Politically, his career took a number of turns, and he was was intermittently dictator of Mexico from 1833 to 1855. He was finally toppled and exiled for life, but Juarez allowed him to return in 1874.

Santiago de Cuba City in Cuba. It was the site of a decisive engagement of the Spanish-Amercan War (1898). A combined naval-infantry action blockaded and attacked the city. When the Spanish fleet trapped in the harbor attempted to escape, it was destroyed by the Americans.

Santos, Lucia dos Portuguese shepherdess supposed to have seen a vision of the Virgin Mary at Fatima in 1917. Fatima has since become a famous place of pilgrimage.

Sanusi (Senussi) Islamic brotherhood in northern Africa. The order was founded in Mecca in 1837 and took root in Africa in the late 19th and early 20th centuries. It opposed French expansion in Africa and later came to oppose the Italians in Libya. The leader of the S. became King Idris I of Libya in 1951.

Saoshans In Zoroastrianism, the savior of the world and opponent of evil at the last judgment. S. is the posthumous son of Zoroaster.

Saracens Terms commonly used in Medieval times to designate Arabs.

Sarajevo City in Bosnia-Herzegovina. The Slavs established themselves there in the 6th-7th century. S. was conquered by the Turks in the 15th century and was under Austro-Hungarian rule from 1878-1918. On June 28, 1914, Francis Ferdinand, the heir to the throne of Austria-Hungary, was assassinated in S., triggering the the outbreak of World War I. The city was under siege (1992-1995) during war in the former Yugoslavia and suffered great damage.

Sarapis Ancient Egyptian whose cult flourished during the reign of Ptolemy I. He was originally a god of the underworld and was later associated with the sun.

Saratoga City in New York. It was the site of a decisive American victory (1777) during the Revolutionary War. The British general Burgoyne and his armed troops surrendered to the Americans after several engagements. The victory ended the British plan to split the colonies along the Hudson River, and it encouraged the French to enter the conflict on the side of the Americans.

Sardanapalus In Greek tradition, the last king of Assyria, who lived in great luxury and died by setting his palace on fire during the fall of Nineveh in 612 BC. The identity of S. is a mystery. The legend does not fit the details of the life of Assurbanipal.

Sardes Capital of the kingdom of Lydia in Asia Minor. It was the political and cultural center of Asia Minor from c.650-550 BC. Destroyed and burned by the Greeks in 499 BC at the beginning of the Ionian uprising against Persia, it later passed to the Romans and became a center of early Christianity. S. was destroyed by Tamerlane (14th century), and its ruins were not discovered until 1958.

Sargon King of Akkad in Mesopotamia, c.2340-2305 BC. He founded a large kingdom in Mesopotamia, Syria, and Anatolia and was the first monarch to field a standing army. His dynasty, which spread Semitic and Sumerian civilization, lasted 160 years.

Sargon

Sargon (d.705 BC) King of Assyria, 722-705 BC. He was presumably a son of Tiglath-Pileser III and succeeded to the throne after the murder of Shalmaneser V. S. initiated many campaigns against Syria, Israel, Urartu, and Chaldaea. He was the founder of the new Assyrian empire and ruled from the Mediterranean Sea to the Persian Gulf. S. built the stronghold of Dur Sharrukin (Khorsabad).

Sarmatia Ancient area between the Vistula and the Carpathian Sea. The term is also used to refer to the area along the Danube and across the Carpathian Mountains where the Sarmatians, who originally lived in the area near the Don River, were driven by the Huns in the 2nd century. Related to the Scythians, the Sarmatians were assimilated with the Germans in the 3rd century.

Jean Paul Sartre

Sartre, Jean Paul (1905-1980) French writer and existential philosopher. In his major work, *Being and Nothingness* (1943), he emphasized individual responsibility and freedom in a lonely and meaningless universe. His plays express his philosophy and were successful as stage adventures. S.'s later writings reveal an increasing interest in Marxism. He refused the Nobel Prize for Literature in 1964 on the grounds that it bestowed too much influence on one writer.

Sassanids Iranian dynasty of monarchs from the expulsion of the Parthians (224) up to the arrival of the

Satan's Witches and Magicians

Although witches and magicians are commonly regarded as a late medieval phenomenon, the persecution of people suspected of witchcraft was more common in the late 16th and 17th centuries.

1

3

2

1. Witches casting a spell to bring rain. Medieval illustration from 1489.
2. Miniature from a medieval treatise on witchcraft (ca.1467), on which Satan's servants worship their lord, who is depicted as a billy-goat.
3. The witch's stool in Oudewater, the Netherlands, where alledged witches were weighed in order to determine whether they were guilty of sorcery.
4. Engraving from 1833, depicting a magician's room that is filled with symbols of the occult arts.
5. According to popular belief, witches gathered at night to worship the devil. This is an 18th-century picture of a witches' Sabbath.
6. Having started in ca. AD 1300, the persecution of witches reached a climax in the 16th and 17th centuries. This graphic indicates the number of accused witches in northern France in the period 1351-1790.

4

5

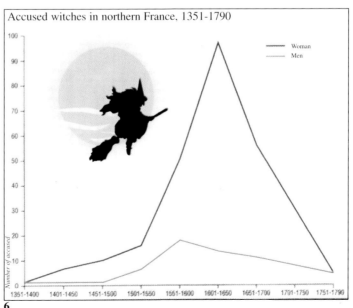

6

Accused witches in northern France, 1351-1790

Arabs (651). Important monarchs were Sapor I (241-272), who took the Roman Emperor Valerianus prisoner at Edessa, and Sapor II (310-379), who successfully fought against Constantine II and Julianus Apostata. Under the S., the ancient Zoroastrianism was reinstated as the state religion.

Satrap Governor of a province of the ancient Persian kingdom. The system was instituted under Darius I. Alexander the Great revised it, replacing Persians with Macedonians and drastically reducing powers of the satraps, including their power to hire mercenaries.

Satsuma uprising Rebellion in Japan in 1877, led by Saigo Takamori (1827-1877), against the central government after the Meiji Restoration. After some initial successes, the rebels suffered an overwhelming defeat at the hands of the imperial armies at Shiroyama.

Saturn Roman god of seeds and sowing. His festival, the Saturnalia, was a holiday in December in which gifts were exchanged and masters and peasants ate at the same table. The day Saturday is derived from S.

Sauckel, Fritz (1894-1946) Nazi politician. He was responsible for the conscript labor program that imported millions of foreigners into Germany to work in factories. S. was a defendant at the Nuremberg Trials (1945-1946), where he was found guilty of crimes against humanity and hanged.

Sauerbruch, Ferdinand (1875-1951) German surgeon. During World War I, responding to the battlefield injuries he treated, S. created (1916) the first artificial limbs.

Saul First king of Israel, c.1021-1000 BC. He strengthened his kingdom, fought the Philistines, but committed suicide after a lost battle. His successor was David.

Savannah City in Georgia. It was held by the British (1778-1782) during the American Revolution. Sherman occupied the city (1864) during the Civil War but did not sack or burn it. As a result, S. retains much of its early architecture, which is a tourist attraction.

Savimbi, Jonas Malheiro (1934-) Angolan guerrilla leader. After Angolan independence (1975), he continued to fight the governing MPLA with his Unita movement. A peace agreement with the government was signed in 1991.

Savonarola, Girolamo (1452-1498) Italian preacher and religious reformer. He became unpopular by openly criticizing the extravagance of the nobility and clergy in Florence. His call for a return to a true religion alienated Pope Alexander VI, who ordered him to stop preaching. S. refused and called Alexander a false pope. Eventually the citizens of Florence tired of his rigidity. S. was soon betrayed and burned at the stake on Alexander's orders.

Savoy Conference (1661) Meeting of 12 Anglican bishops and 12 Puritan clergy in Savoy Palace (London) to revise the Book of Common Prayer. The conference was a failure, and the Puritans left the Anglican Church over this issue.

Savoy, House of Dynasty that ruled Italy from 1861 to 1946; *see* Victor Amadeus; Victor Emmanuel.

Saxe, Maurice, Count of (1696-1750) Marshal of France. Of German-Polish noble heritage, he entered the service of France in 1720 and led the French during the War of the Austrian Succession. He won the Battle of Fontenoy (1745) and in 1747 invaded Holland and captured the fortified city of Bergen op Zoom at the Battle of Laufeld (near Maastricht). S. was one of the great generals of his age. Among his descendants was George Sand.

Saxe-Coburg-Saalfeld, Friedrich Josias, Prince of (1737-1815) General serving in the Austrian army. He fought in the Turkish War (1791) and in 1793 became commander in chief of the Austrian army against France. S. won the victory at Neerwinden, but on June 26, 1794, he suffered a defeat at Fleurus against the French led by Jourdan.

Saxons Germanic tribe in northwest Germania. Around 450 AD, part of the tribe went to England with the Angles. The remaining S. later fought against Charlemagne but were defeated and absorbed into his empire.

Girolamo Savonarola

They then accepted Christianity and their lands became part of the territories that later formed the modern Germany.

Sayf ad-Dawlah (916-967) Arabic Hamdanid monarch of Northern Syria. From 950, he continually waged war against the Byzantine Empire, which captured his capital city of Aleppo in 962 S. defeated the Byzantines in 964.

Sayyid dynasty (c.1414-1451) Indian dynasty of Delhi thought to have descended from the prophet Muhammad.

Scarlatti, Alessandro (1660-1725) Italian composer and conductor. He was a leader of the Neapolitan School, which helped establish the conventions of the *opera seria*. His work includes 115 operas and some 700 chamber cantatas.

Scarlatti, Domenico (1685-1757) Italian composer. The son of Alessandro Scarlatti, he was a harpsichord virtuoso. His fame as a composer rests on his more than 550 harpsichord sonatas.

Schacht, Hjalmar (1877-1970) German financier. A conservative, he supported the Nazis after 1931 and became minister of economy (1934) when Hitler came to power. He quarreled with Goering and opposed German rearmament because it would cause inflation. In 1944 he was arrested and placed in a concentration camp because of his alleged part in the plot on Hitler's life. After being acquitted at the Nuremberg Trials, he returned to private banking.

Scheel, Walter (1919-) West German statesman. A Free Democrat, he served as foreign minister under Willy Brandt before being elected president of West Germany (1974-1979).

Friedrich von Schiller

Schiller, Friedrich von (1759-1805) German dramatist and poet. One of the great German literary figures, he studied law and medicine before turning to writing. His play *Die Räuber* (1782) was a popular attack on political tyranny. In 1789, he settled in Jena, where he completed a trilogy about

Domenico Scarlatti

Wallenstein. In 1799, S. moved to Weimar, the home of his great friend Goethe. There, he wrote many plays, including *Mary Stuart* and *William Tell* (1804). In addition, he is known for an articles and ballads. His "Ode to Joy" was used by Beethoven in the finale of the Ninth Symphony. S. greatly influenced the German romantic poets and is ranked as one of the great figures of modern German literature.

Schleich, Carl Ludwig (1859-1922) German physician. He developed local anesthesia and first applied it in 1894.

Schleicher, Kurt von (1882-1934) German general and politician. The last chancellor (1932-1933) of the Weimar Republic, he tried to prevent Hitler from achieving power. S. and his wife were murdered during the purge of June 30, 1934.

Schliemann, Heinrich (1822-1890) German archaeologist. After having made a fortune in business, he devoted himself to his dream of rediscovering Troy, which he did in fact find. S. was not a trained archaeologist, but was assisted by the archaeologist Wilhelm Dörpfeld. Among his excavations were Mycenae, Ithaca, and Boeotia.

Schmalkaldic League Alliance (1531) of German Protestant princes and cities created to defend their religion and independence from the threats of the Holy Roman Emperor Charles V. The main members were Bremen, Magdeburg, the monarchs of Saxony and Hesse, Hamburg, Frankfurt, and the duke of Württemberg. Under the protection of the S., the Reformation spread throughout much of Germany. The S. was dissolved after the Schmalkaldic War.

Schmalkaldic War (1546-1547) War between the Schmalkaldic League and Holy Roman Emperor Charles V. Charles caused the poorly organized members of the league to submit and defeated the monarchs of Saxony and Hessen in the Battle of Mühlberg (1547).

Schmidt, Helmut (1918-) West German statesman. A Social Democrat, he served as defense minister and finance minister before succeeding Willy Brandt as chancellor in 1974. S.

sought to improve relations with East Germany and the Soviet Union. He left office in 1982.

Helmut Schmidt

Schoenberg, Arnold (1874-1951) Austrian composer. His major impact on music was in the abandonment of tonality and the development of a 12-tone, serial technique of composition. As a theorist, he strongly influenced Berg and Webern. His early works, such as *Verklärte Nacht* (1899) and *Gurrelieder* (1901-1902) expanded the chromatic style of Wagner and Mahler. His later works were highly contrapuntal and much thinner in texture. S.'s masterpiece is his unfinished opera, *Moses and Aron* (1932-1951). He moved to the U.S. in 1933 and taught at the University of California at Los Angeles.

Schopenhauer, Arthur (1788-1860) German philosopher. He considered

Arthur Schopenhauer

himself the true successor of Kant. S. was a pessimist who saw the world as nothing but unsatisfied wants and needs, and pleasure as simply the absence of pain. According to him, the only escape was through the renunciation of desire.

Schubert, Franz (1797-1828) Austrian composer. Although not widely recognized during his lifetime, he composed an enormous number of compositions, including more than 600 songs (for example, the song cycles *Die schöne Müllerin* [1823] and *Die Winterreise* [1829]), chamber and piano music, and nine symphonies. S. is now widely seen as one of the major composers of the 19th century. His songs represent the height of romantic lyricism.

Franz Schubert

Schumann, Robert (1886-1963) French statesman. After World War II, he held numerous ministerial posts, including finance minister and premier. S. worked to advance European unity and in 1951 was a force behind the formation of European Coal and Steel Community, the first step toward the creation of the European Community.

Schumann, Robert Alexander (1810-1856) German composer. A leader of the romantic movement, S. composed songs, music for piano (for example, *Kinderszenen, Carnaval*, and the *Sym-phonic Etudes*), four symphonies, and concertos. His wife, Clara Schumann, was a noted pianist and composer.

Schuschnigg, Kurt von (1897-1977) Austrian statesman. He became federal chancellor after the assassination of Dollfuss (1934). S. successfully resisted Hitler's attempts to incorporate Austria into the Third Reich until losing the support of Mussolini. In 1938 he was forced to resign and Austria was aborbed into Germany (*Anschluss*). S. was imprisoned in a concentration camp until 1945. After his release, he moved to the U.S. and settled in Missouri.

Schutsbund Socialist paramilitary organization in Austria between World Wars I and II. It often fought against the right-wing Heimwehr.

Schütz, Heinrich (1585-1672) German composer. A pupil of Gabrielli, he was the director of music at the Dresden court. Most of his works that survive were written for the church. S.'s choral style, a combination of Venetian influences and German polyphony, influenced Handel and Bach.

Schwarzenberg, Karl Philipp, Fürst zu (1771-1820) Austrian field marshal. He led the Austrian forces that accompanied Napoleon (1812) on his campaign in Russia. The following year, after Austria had joined the allies against Napoleon, S. commanded the victorious forces at Leipzig (1813).

Schweitzer, Albert (1875-1965) French-German physician. He became famous through his work with

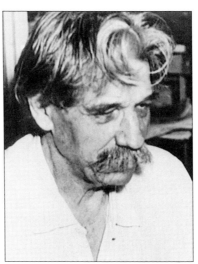

Albert Schweitzer

leprosy patients in Lambarene in Gabon. S. was awarded the Nobel Peace Prize in 1952. He was also a noted theologian as well as a composer and organist.

Scipio, Publius Cornelius (d.c.211 BC) S. was consul in 218 BC. He was defeated by Hannibal at the Ticino River during the Second Punic War. He died in the battle against the Carthaginians in Spain. S. was the father of Scipio Africanus Major.

Publius Cornelius Scipio

Scipio Africanus Major (c.234-183 BC) Roman general. The son of of Publius Cornelius Scipio, he assumed command in Spain after the death of his father. S. landed in North Africa in 204 BC and defeated Hannibal in 202 BC at Zama. He was named Africanus after the country he conquered.

Scipio Africanus Minor (c.185-129 BC) Roman general. The son of Lucius Aemilius Paullus, he was adopted by the eldest son of Scipio Africanus Major. As a young man, he fought with his father at Pydna (168 BC) and became consul in 147 BC. In 146 BC, he destroyed Carthage, bringing an end to the Third Punic War. In 133 BC, S. captured Numantia in Spain. On his return to Rome, he openly attempted to destroy the Gracchan reforms and was found dead in his bed under mysterious circumstances.

Scone Village in Scotland. It was the repository of the Coronation Stone and the site of the coronation of Scottish kings from Kenneth I to Charles II.

Sir Walter Scott

Scott, Sir Walter (1771-1832) Scottish writer. He mainly wrote historical novels that are set partly in the Middle Ages in Scotland. His best known work is *Ivanhoe* (1819). Considered the founder the the historical novel, Scott excelled in the creation of mood and scene.

Scottsboro Case Legal case in Alabama in which nine black youths were found guilt of guilty of raping two white women in 1931. Over the next few years the convictions were gradually overturned, and the case became a symbol of racial injustice in the South.

Scribonia Roman aristocrat who married the future Emperor Augustus in 40 BC. She was repudiated by Augustus soon after the birth of her daughter Julia.

Scythians Ancient peoples living in the area to the north of the Black Sea bounded on the west by the Danube River and on the east by China. They flourished from the 8th to the 4th centuries BC and were nomadic conquerors and skilled horsemen. The S. had no written language.

SEATO *See* South East Asia Treaty Organization.

Sebastian (1554-1578) King of Portugal, 1557-1578. He was fiercely religious and was imbued with a desire to fight the Muslims in North Africa. In 1578 he was killed in battle in Morocco. His uncle, Henry, succeeded him and was the last Portuguese king before the Spanish took control of the country.

Sebastian, Saint (d.3rd cent.) Roman Christian martyr. Little is known of his life. He was allegedly a member of the Praetorian Guards and was ordered tortured and killed by bow and arrow when the emperor discovered he was a Christian. S. supposedly recovered, after which he was beaten to death. S. was a favorite subject of Renaissance painters.

Sebastopol (Sevastopol) Russian port city on the Black Sea. It was besieged (1854-1855) by a French-British army during the Crimean War. The Russians sank the fleet and eventually evacuated the city.

Sebetwane (d.1851) King of the Kololo tribe in southern Africa. He led his people to Barotseland during the Mfecane and ruled them justly. Livingstone met S. at Barotseland in 1851.

Seckmet Egyptian lion goddess of war. She was associated with Ptah of Memphis.

Second Front Allied front in western Europe during World War II, opened with the invasion of Normandy, in France, in June 1944. It was termed the "second" front since the Soviets had already been battling the Germans on the ground since June 1941.

Second Empire Period between 1852-1870 when Napoleon III ruled France.

Second World War *See* World War II.

Sedan Town in France. It was the site of the decisive defeat of the French by the Germans (1870) during the Franco-Prussian War. S. was also the location of the German breakthrough in the invasion (1940) of France during World War II.

Sedgemoor Site in the south of England. There, in 1685, King James II's army defeated a force raised by the duke of Monmouth, illegitimate son of Charles II, who was attempting to overthrow James. Monmouth was later executed.

Seeckt, Hans von (1866-1936) German general. He played an important role in the German victories on the eastern front during World War I. S. was the head of the Reichswehr (1920-1926) and built it into an efficient nucleus of a larger army. During his tenure, he was able to secure weapons from the Soviet Union that were prohibited under the Treaty of Versailles. S. was later an adviser to Chiang Kai-shek in China.

Hans von Seeckt

Segesta Ancient city of Sicily. It was the city of the Elymi, thought to be descendants of the Trojans. Under Hannibal, S. was an ally of Carthage, but it allied itself with the Romans at the time of the First Punic War.

Ségou City in Mali. It was the capital of the Bambara kingdom in the 17th and 18th centuries. S. was pillaged by an Islamic army under Al-Hajj Umar in 1861 and never regained its former glory.

Seianus, Lucius Aelius (D.31 AD) Roman general. A favorite of Tiberius, he was commander of the Praetorian Guard from 26 AD. Tiberius eventually had him executed for high treason.

Sekigahara, Battle of *See* Ishida Mitsunari.

Selangor Civil War (1867-1873) War between Malaysian chiefs over the ownership of tin mines in Selangor. The conflict led to British expansion in the area and to S. becoming a British protectorate in 1874.

Seleucia Ancient city in Mesopotamia. Founded by Seleucus I (4th century BC), it replaced Babylon as the center of commerce in the Tigris valley. S. declined after the Seleucids moved their capital to Ctesiphon. In 164 BC the city was burned by the Romans.

Seleucids Dynasty founded by Seleucus I, king of ancient Syria, one of the Diadochi. The S. were in power in Syria from 312-64 BC. Their kingdom stretched from Thrace to the Indian border.

Seleucus I (Seleucus Nicator) (d.280 BC) King of ancient Syria. A general of Alexander the Great, he became governor of Babylonia in 321 BC. Thereafter, he founded a large kingdom and from 305 BC bore the title of king. His domain expanded to Syria (301 BC) and Asia Minor. S. was opposed in India by Chandragupta.

Seleucus I

Selim I (1467-1520) Ottoman sultan, 1512-1520. He conquered part of Persia, Syria, Egypt, and Arabia. A ruthless tyrant, S. was also a superb administrator who expanded Ottoman power to its greatest heights.

Selim II (1524-1574) Ottoman sultan, 1566-1574. During his rule, the Turkish fleet was defeated at Lepanto (1571) by the Christians. Although the Ottoman Empire retained supremacy in the Mediterranean, Lepanto represented the first challenge to Ottoman power by Christians.

Selim III (1761-1808) Ottoman sultan, 1789-1807. He signed the Peace of Jassy with the Russians in 1792, ending the Russo-Turkish War. S. was a reformer who tried to modernize the Turkish navy along European lines and curb the Janissaries. He joined the war against France after Napoleon's invasion of Egypt in 1798. A revolt of the Janissaries forced him to abdicate in 1807, and he was strangled a year later after a failed attempt to restore him to his throne. S.'s reforms came too late to prevent the decay of Ottoman power.

Selinis Ancient city in Sicily. Founded by Dorian Greeks in the 7th century BC, S. was an ally of Syracuse against Carthage. The city was twice invaded and twice destroyed by the Carthaginians (409 and 250 BC).

Seljuks Turkmen tribe that was converted to Islam in c.1000. The S. ruled Asia Minor in the 11th and 12th centuries.

Seminoles *See* Five Civilized Tribes.

Semiramis Mythical queen of Assyria and Babylonia. She was supposed to be a woman of great beauty who enjoyed a long reign then disappeared in the form of a dove. The legend may be connected to the real Sammu-

Selim I

ramat, the wife of Shamsi-Adad V and the regent of Assyria from 810 to 805 BC.

Semmelweis, Ignaz (1818-1865) Hungarian physician. He discovered the antiseptic treatment of wounds and the method of effectively combating puerperal fever.

Ignaz Semmelweis

Sempach Town in Switzerland. It was the site of a battle (1386) in which the Swiss Confederation defeated the Austrians under Leopold III of Tirol, who was killed.

Sen Rikyu (1522-1591) Japanese man who raised the tea ceremony, initiated by the 15th-century monk, Shuko, to a national art.

Sena Dynasty that governed Bengal in the 11th-12th centuries. Founded by Hemantasena, the dynasty was overwhelmed by the Turk Muhammad Khalji. The Muslims gained then supremacy in the region.

Sendero Luminoso (Shining Path) Peruvian Marxist guerrilla movement. Founded in 1970, it was still creating problems for the government in the 1990s.

Seneca (c.4 BC-65 AD) Roman philosopher, dramatist, and statesman. He was a tutor of Nero, and with Burrus virtually ruled Rome for a short period. S. was a Stoic, and his writings expound the Stoic philosophy. His dramas were meant to be read, not performed, and were influential as late as the Renaissance. S. fell out of favor with Nero's wife and was eventually ordered to commit suicide.

Seneca Falls Convention Meeting (1848) in Seneca Falls, New York, that marked the beginning of the women's rights movement in the U.S. The Seneca Falls Declaration of Sentiments included a demand for the right of women to vote.

Seneffe Town in Belgium. It was the site of a victory (1674) by the French under Louis II de Condé over the Dutch, and of a later victory by the French (1794) over the Austrians.

Seneschal Courtier in charge of the court under the early kings of France. It later became the term for an official who was in charge of maintaining law and order in a specific area.

Senigallia Gallic kingdom in Italy, on the Adriatic Sea. Founded in the 6th century BC, it became the Roman province of Sena Gallia in 289 BC. S. was papal territory between 1631 and 1860.

Senlis Town near Paris. There, in 1815, the French under Kellerman fought against the Prussians under von Bülow.

Sepoy Rebellion (Indian Mutiny) (1857-1858) Rebellion in British India by soldiers in the Bengal army of the British East India Company. (Sepoys is the name of native soldiers.) It developed into a wider rebel-

Seneca

Saint Sergius I

lion against British rule in India and led to the abolition of the East Indian Company and to direct rule by the British crown.

Septuagint (Latin for 70) Greek translation of the Old Testament made by Hellenistic Jews in Alexandria, c.250 BC. According to legend, 72 scholars did the translation in 72 days. The S. version is still used in the Greek Orthodox Church. It was translated from texts that are now lost.

Serapeion Library in Alexandria, Egypt. Built by Christians in 390, it was destroyed in 641, when the Arabs occupied the city.

Serbia Former state of Yugoslavia. It became independent after a war of liberation against the Turks (starting in 1804). S.'s championship of Pan-Slavism led to conflict with Austria-Hungary, a conflict that triggered World War I. S. was a constituent republic of Yugoslavia under Tito and became (with Montenegro) the core of the post-Tito Yugoslavia. It heavily supported the Bosnian Serbs in the war in Bosnia-Herzegovina in the 1990s.

Serbo-Bulgarian War (1885-1886) Conflict between Serbia and Bulgaria of the question of Eastern Rumelia. Serbia, which claimed Eastern Rumelia, objected to Bulgaria's annexation of the region. The Serbs were defeated in battle, however, and the boundaries remained unchanged in the peace that followed.

Serbo-Turkish War (1876-1878) War in which Serbia and Montenegro fought for independence from the Ottoman Empire. A Russian threat after a Turkish advance in the direction of Belgrade led to the truce of 1878.

Serfdom Condition of semibondage in which peasant laborers were attached to the manor and required to perform duties for the lord. S. was known in Greek and Roman times, but it is mainly associated with the Middle Ages in Europe. It was not abolished in Russia until 1861.

Sergius I, Saint Pope, 687-701. He successfully resisted Emperor Justinianus' attempts to weaken the supremacy of Rome. S. was an ardent restorer of Roman churches and was highly popular with the people.

Sergius II Pope, 844-847. He crowned Louis II, son of Lothair, as king of the Lombards and was unable to stop the Saracens from plundering Rome in 846.

Sergius II

Sertorius, Quintus (c.123-72 BC) Roman general. He helped local Spanish peoples in their rebellion against Rome. S. was never defeated but was eventually murdered by Perperna, one of his own officers.

Servilia (1st century BC) Lover of Julius Caesar for 20 years and the mother of Marcus Brutus, who later murdered Caesar.

Servius and Bacchus (d.303 AD) Roman Christian soldiers of Emperor Maximin. They are among the first martyrs whose authenticity can be verified.

Servius Tullius Monarch thought to be the sixth Etruscan or Latin king of Rome, 578-534 BC.

Sesostris I (d.1926 BC) King of ancient Egypt. The second ruler of the 12th Dynasty, he was the son and successor of Amenemhet I. S. organized the administration in Egypt, conquered Nubia, and conducted a campaign against the Libyans.

Sesostris III (d.1840 BC) King of ancient Egypt. He was the son and successor of Sesostris II. S. conducted campaigns against Nubia and southern Palestine and erected forts to secure the southern and northeastern borders of Egypt.

Sesostris III

Sestertius *See* Denarius.

Set Egyptian god of evil. In Egyptian myth, he murdered his brother Osiris; *see* Osiris.

Seti I (d.c.1290 BC) King of ancient Egypt. The son and successor of Ramses I, he restored Egyptian rule in Syria-Palestine and came into conflict with the Hittites there. S. had temples built at Abydos and Thebes and a tomb in the Valley of the Kings at Thebes.

Setthathirat (1534-1571) King of the Lao princedom of Lan Xang. He made Vientiane the capital in 1560 and became an ally of Thailand against Burma. S. successfully repelled a Burmese invasion in c. 1565.

Settlement, Act of Law passed by the British Parliament in 1701. It provided that if King William III and Princess (later Queen) Anne died without heirs, the British crown would pass to Sophia, electress of Hanover, a granddaughter of King James I, and her heirs. When Queen Anne died in 1714 without an heir, the crown passed to Sophia's son, the elector George, who became King George I. Through this act, the House of Hanover came to rule Great Britain.

Seven Days battles Week-long series of battles (1862) during the American Civil War. The Confederate counteroffensive near Richmond, Virginia, ended the Peninsular campaign of the Union army.

Seven Years War (1756-1763) Worldwide conflict fought in Europe, North America, and India. France, Austria, Russia, Saxony, Sweden, and Spain were on one side, and Prussia, Great Britain, and Hanover were on the other. Complex in origin, the conflict involved the colonial rivalry of Great Britain and France and the Prussian-Austrian struggle for dominance in Europe. The treaties of Paris and Hubertusburg ended the war. Great Britain emerged as the dominant colonial power, with France losing most of its overseas empire. In Europe, Prussia emerged as the main power.

Seven Weeks' War *See* Manteuffel, Edwin.

Severus, Marcus Aurelius Alexander (208-235) Roman emperor, 222-235. The nephew and successor of Heliogabalus, he was an enlightened ruler who ended persecution of the Christians during his reign. S. was killed in a mutiny of his troops while in Germany.

Severus, Lucius Septimius (146-211) Roman emperor, 193-211. The successor to Pertinax, he first restored order in Rome and throughout the empire, and then eliminated the pretenders Pescennius Niger and Clodius Albinus. S. waged war against the Parthians and in 208 went on a campaign to Britannia, where he died in

Lucius Septimius Severus

York after an illness. He was a patron of new building in Rome. During S.'s reign, the Arch of Septimius Severus, in the Old Forum, was built.

Sèvres, Treaty of Pact at the end of World War I between the Allies and the Ottoman Empire. It liquidated the Ottoman Empire and virtually abolished Turkish sovereignty.

Seward, William Henry (1801-1872) American statesman. A governor of New York and U.S. senator, and a strong voice against slavery, S. lost the 1860 Republican presidential nomination to Abraham Lincoln. He was appointed secretary of state by Lincoln and served in that post from 1861 to 1869. An able diplomat, he purchased Alaska from Russia in 1867.

Seyss-Inquart, Arthur (1892-1946) Austrian Nazi. As acting chancellor, he proclaimed (1938) the *Anschluss*. In 1940, Hitler appointed him Nazi high commissioner for the occupied Netherlands. S. was tried at Nuremberg (1946) and executed.

Arthur Seyss-Inquart

Sforza Italian royal house that governed the Duchy of Milan from 1450 to 1535. They rose from the peasantry and assumed military positions in Milan, from which they built their power. Unlike the Medici in Florence, the Sforzas were warriors, not bankers. Under their rule, Milan expanded and prospered.

Sforza, Carlo, Count of (1872-1952) Italian statesman. He was a prominent diplomat and minister but went into exile after Mussolini came to power in 1922. After World War II, S. served as foreign minister (1947-1951) and was a supporter of European unity.

Shaftesbury, Anthony Ashley Cooper, 1st Earl of (1621-1683) English statesman. Originally a supporter of Cromwell, he switched and helped arrange the Restoration. Under Charles II, he took up high positions, yet later became one of the staunchest opponents of the king over the issue of Roman Catholicism. Shaftesbury supported Monmouth over James II. In 1682 he was indicted for treason and fled to Holland, where he died the following year.

Shah Alam II (1728-1806) Mughal emperor of India, 1759-1806. He did not occupy Delhi until 1771. In 1788, the Afghan Rohillas captured Delhi and blinded S. Subsequently, he remained under British protection.

Shah Jahan (1592-1666) Mughal emperor of India, 1628-1658. The son and successor of Jahangir, S. expanded his empire and reinstated Islam. He is particularly known for building the Taj Mahal. In 1657, he became ill and was deposed (1658) and imprisoned by his son Aurangzeb.

Shah Shoja (1780-1842) King of Afghanistan, 1803-1810 and 1839-

Sforza

1842. Between the two periods of his rule, S. attempted to regain the throne with the aid of the British. He succeeded in the First Afghan War, but when the British withdrew, S. was murdered.

Shahrir, Sutan (1909-1966) Prime minister of Indonesia, 1945-1947. He lost influence because of his criticism on Sukarno and was imprisoned between 1962 and 1965.

Shahrukh Son of the Timur Lenk. He ruled during the period 1405-1447. S. was killed in a campaign against the Turkmen.

Shaka (Chaka) (c.1787-1828) Leading Zulu chief, 1818-1828. He founded a large Zulu kingdom in what is now Natal with the help of a 40,000-man army he had created. S. was murdered by his half-brother, Dingaan.

Shakespeare, William (1564-1616) English dramatist and poet. He is considered one of the greatest playwrights in history. Born in Stratford-upon-Avon, S. lived in London between 1584 and 1610. S. wrote comedies (examples include *The Taming of the Shrew, A Midsummer Night's Dream, As You Like It*), tragedies (*Hamlet, Romeo and Juliet, Julius Caesar, Macbeth, Othello, King Lear*) and historical dramas (*Henry VI*, parts 1-3, *Richard III, Richard II, Henry IV*, parts 1-2). S.'s characters are complex human beings imbued with both good and evil, and his plays address the span of moral issues facing man.

Shalmaneser I (d.1290 BC) King of ancient Assyria. The son and successor of Adad-Nirari I, he expanded his kingdom to the north and to the south and restored the temple at Assur.

Shalmaneser III (858-824 BC) King of Assyria. The son and successor of Ashurnasirpal II, He expanded his kingdom into Syria-Palestine, where he came into conflict with Israel and Damascus. S. built a large ziggurat at Calah.

Shalmaneser V (d.721 BC) King of Assyria. The son and successor of Tiglat-Pileser III, he laid siege to the Israeli capital of Samaria but died in the battle.

Shamash Semitic sun god, one of the

greatest deities of ancient Middle Eastern religions. S. was called Utu in Sumerian civilization.

Shamash

William Shakespeare

Shamash-shum-ukin (7th century BC) Crown prince of Babylonia, the son of Esarhaddon of Assyria. In 685, he revolted against his younger brother Ashurbanipal of Assyria, who eventually defeated him. S.'s capital, Babylon, was destroyed and he was killed in his palace.

Shamir, Yitzhak (1915-) Prime minister of Israel, 1983-1984, 1986-1992. A member of the right-wing Herut party, he became prime minister after the resignation of Menachem Begin in 1983. In 1984, S. became foreign minister in a unity cabinet under Shimon Peres, and two years be prime minister again at the head of the Likud coalition. S. encouraged Jewish settlement in the occupied territories and adamantly refused to negotiate with the Palestinians. His hard-line position created strains with the United States and led, in part, to the defeat of Likud in the elections of 1992.

Shamshi-Adad I King of Assyria in the first half of the 18th century BC. An influential ruler and builder, he attempted to expand his kingdom, but in doing so clashed with Hammurabi of Babylonia.

Shamshi-Adad V King of Assyria, 824-810 BC. The son and successor of Shalmaneser III, he revived a centralized power in the kingdom. S. was married to Sammuramat.

Shariah Islamic laws codified in the 8th-9th century. They contain regulations concerning religious, political, social, and personal life.

Sharon, Ariel (1928-) Israeli soldier and politician. He commanded parachute brigades in the Sinai in during the 1956 war. S. served as minister of agriculture (1977-1981) under Menachem Begin, where he concentrated on colonizing the occupied territories. As minister of defense in 1981, he planned the Israeli invasion of Lebanon and was criticized for the brutality of his tactics.

Sharpeville incident Massacre of black demonstrators (March 21, 1960) by the South African police at Sharpeville in which 69 people were killed. The incident focused worldwide attention on South Africa's racial policies and galvanized opposition within the country.

Shaw, George Bernard (1856-1950) Anglo-Irish playwright and critic. S. revolutionized the stage in Victorian England by writing plays propelled by vigorous ideas and, at times, cutting satire. A socialist, S. frequently criticized the church and social injustice in his writings. His most well-known work is probably *Pygmalion* (1913), which satirized the English class system and which became world famous in the musical version, *My Fair Lady*. S. was awarded the Nobel Prize for Literature in 1925.

George Bernard Shaw

Shawnee *See* Lord Dunmore's War.

Shelley, Percy Bysshe (1792-1822) English poet. He is considered one of the great romantic poets. S. frequently wrote poems about the beauty of nature, such as *Ode to a Skylark* and *The Cloud*. His masterpiece is *Prometheus Unbound* (1818-1819), which is patterned after the ideas of Plato. S. drowned while on a boat trip.

Shen Nung (28th century BC) Mythical Chinese emperor with a bull's head. According to legend, he spoke three days after his birth and ploughed a field at the age of three.

Shenute (c.360-450) Egyptian Coptic saint. The abbot of the White Monastery near Atripe, he reintroduced communal monastic life in Egypt.

Sheridan, Philip Henry (1831-1888) American Union general. During the Civil War he laid waste (1864) to the Shenandoah Valley, and in 1865 blocked Lee's retreat from Appomattox. S. conducted military operations against the Indians after the Civil War. After Sherman's retirement (1884) he became head of the army.

Sherman, William Tecumseh (1820-1891) American Union general. He is remembered for "Sherman's March" through Georgia and South Carolina (1864), in which the Union forces sacked and burned everything in their path. S. helped create the tactics of "total" war against civilians as well as military targets. After Grant, he was the most important Union general. S.

William Tecumseh Sherman

Percy Bysshe Shelley

was the head of the army after the Civil War.

Sheshonk I King of ancient Egypt, c.945-924 BC. The founder of the 22nd Dynasty, he captured Jerusalem and enlarged the temple at Karnak. S.'s remains were found in 1938 in his burial chamber at Tanis.

Shiites Members of one of the great branches of Islam (the other being the Sunnis, who are the majority). Shiism developed during a schism that arose in the Umayyad dynasty and may be said to be a Persian variation of Islam. S. reject the oral tradition of Islam and differ from the Sunnis on matters of law and ceremony. S. also adhere much more strongly to theocratic forms of government, for example in Iran, which is the center of world Shiism. Significant Shiite communities are also found in Iraq and parts of the Arabian peninsula.

Shimabara Rebellion Large-scale uprising (1637-1658) by Japanese Roman Catholics at Nagasaki. They were subjugated by a Dutch gunboat, after Japan effectively sealed itself off from external influences.

Shimonoseki, Treaty of (1895) Agreement concluding the first Sino-Japanese War. The treaty imposed harsh territorial losses on China, including Korea and Taiwan, and forced the Chinese to open five more treaty ports to foreign trade.

Shostakovich, Dmitri (1906-1975) Russian composer. He wrote chamber music, fifteen symphonies, and a satiric opera, *The Nose*, based on a story by Pushkin. He lived in the Soviet Union all his adult life and was in and out of favor at various times during the Stalin years.

Shroud of Turin Cloth in Turin that is thought by some to have been Jesus's shroud. After extensive study in 1989, it was determined that the S. dates from the 13th or 14th century.

Shuysky, Vasily Ivanovich, Prince (1552-1612) Russian nobleman who was named czar (1606-1610) after the murder of a false Dmitri. He ruled as Vasily IV but was forced to resign when rioting broke out in Moscow after Poland declared war.

Sibelius, Jean (1865-1957) Finnish composer. The founder of the Finnish national musical tradition, he was greatly inspired by Finnish folklore. S.'s music is broodingly romantic and melancholy and often expresses a

Jean Sibelius

mystical love of nature. In addition to chamber music, a violin concerto, and works for the piano, he composed tone poems and seven symphonies. His *Finlandia* is the Finnish national anthem.

Sicilian Vespers Rebellion (1282) by Sicilians against the Angevin French domination. It erupted in Palermo at the start of Vespers on Easter Monday,

1282, and spread throughout the island. Almost all the French on the island were massacred. Sicily then passed to the house of Aragón, while southern Italy remained under Angevin control.

Sidi el Barrani Town on the northwest coast of Egypt. During World War II, the British, under Wavell, defeated (1940) the Italians at S.

Siegfried Line Popular name for the German western frontier during World War II.

Sieyès, Emmanuel Joseph (1748-1836) French statesman. A clergyman before the French Revolution, he became a leading figure after 1789. S. formulated the famous tennis court oath that marked the formation of the national assembly. He survived the Reign of Terror and became a member of the Directory in 1799. S. was a supporter of Napoleon and was exiled (1815) to Belgium after Napoleon's downfall.

Sigismund (1368-1437) Holy Roman Emperor, 1433-1437. The son of Emperor Charles IV, S. was also king of Hungary and from 1419, king of Bohemia. The Council of Constance was convened on his initiative in 1413, to end the Great Schism. Because he allowed the execution of Jan Hus, S. was despised in Bohemia. In subsequent wars with the Hussites, S. suffered numerous setbacks, but he eventually accepted a compromise that allowed him to assume (1436) the Bohemian crown.

Sigismund I (1467-1548) King of Poland, 1506-1548. He struggled with the Polish nobles in order to centralize power and build an army capable of defending Poland form outside threats. S. waged a long war with Russia, which invaded Poland in 1531 and 1535.

Sigismund II Augustus *See* Augustus I of Poland.

Sigismund III (1566-1632) King of Poland, 1587-1632, and King of Sweden, 1592-1599. The son of John III of Sweden, he reunited the Vasa and Jagiello dynasties. S. was defeated in 1598 by his Protestant uncle, Charles IX, at Stångebro and deposed the following year as king of Sweden. He

Emmanuel Joseph Sieyès

invaded Russia in 1610 and took Moscow, but was repelled by 1612.

Sikorski, Wladyslaw (1881-1943) Polish general and statesman. In the 1920s, he held various governmental positions, including chief of staff, prime minister, and minister of war. In 1928, he was dismissed from the government after a disagreement with Pilsudski. S. was recalled in 1939 after the German invasion of Poland, and during World War II served as prime minister and commander in chief of the Polish government in exile. He died in a plane crash in Gibraltar in 1943.

Silesian Wars Three conflicts (1740-1742, 1744-1745, and 1756-1762) between Frederick II of Prussia and Maria Theresa of Austria over the possession of Silesia.

Silvester II (c.945-1003) Pope, 999-1003. Born Gerbert of Rheims, he was the first French pope. S. was noted for the brilliance of his intellect. He defended the rights of the papacy and attacked nepotism and other forms of corruption. Although overshadowed politically by the Holy Roman Emperor, S. maintained contacts with the major leaders of his day.

Simeon I (c.863-927) Ruler of Bulga-

Wladyslaw Sikorski

ria, 893-927. The son of Boris I, he unsuccessfully besieged Constantinople several times. S. had himself proclaimed czar of the Bulgarians in 925. During his reign, the first Bulgarian empire achieved its greatest power.

Simeon II (1937-) Czar of Bulgaria, 1943-1946. The son of Boris III, he ascended to the throne in 1943 at the age of 6, but fled in 1946 when Bulgarians abolished the monarchy and became a communist state.

Simeon *See* Israel, Tribes of.

Sinn Fein (Gaelic for "we, ourselves") Irish nationalist movement striving for a united Ireland. It was founded in 1899 by Arthur Griffith. The term Sinn Fein today refers to the political wing of the Irish Republican Army.

Sino-Indian War Conflict (1962-1963) between India and China following a number of border skirmishes that started in 1959. China invaded India and defeated an Indian army before withdrawing after a ceasefire.

Sino-Japanese War, First Conflict (1894-1895) between China and Japan over Korea. It broke out following an uprising in Korea that received military support from both countries. As a result of the Treaty of Shimonoseki (1895), Japan gained hegemony over Korea and annexed the Pescadores Islands.

Sino-Japanese War, Second Conflict (1937-1945) between China and Japan. Japan's motive in attacking China was territorial expansion. The civil war between nationalists and communists in China was temporarily suspended as the warring parties formed a united front against Japan. The war ended with the Japanese defeat in World War II (1945).

Sioux Wars Series of battles (1854-1890) between Sioux Indians and white settlers and soldiers. The Sioux were a confederation of nine tribes that lived in the northern Plains. The last engagement of the conflict was the battle of Wounded Knee (1890), the final encounter between the American Indians and the U.S. military.

Sitting Bull (c.1831-1890) Native American chief, leader of the Sioux.

He encouraged the Sioux to resist forced settlement on reservations. In 1876, S. defeated a U.S. army unit under General Custer at Little Bighorn. After fleeing to Canada, he returned on a promise of amnesty and during the 1880s worked in Buffalo Bill's Wild West Show. He continued to encourage Indian resistance to white encroachment and was an advocate of the ghost dance. He was shot and killed by army officers in 1890 while allegedly resisting arrest.

Sitting Bull

Six Day War Conflict (1967) between Israel on the one hand and and Egypt, Jordan, and Syria on the other. As a result of an Egyptian blockade of Gulf of Aqaba, the massed Arab troops on Israel's borders, and the withdrawal of a UN force that had kept Israel and Egypt apart, a potentially dangerous military situation arose for Israel. In a preemptive strike, Israel attacked first and occupied the Sinai desert, the West Bank of the Jordan (including the Jordanian portion of Jerusalem), and the Golan Heights. The Sinai was returned to Egypt in stages during the early 1980s as part of the Egyptian-Israeli peace treaty. Portions of the West Bank were turned over to Palestinian civil authority in the early 1990s.

Sixtus IV (1414-1484) Pope, 1471-1484. Born Francesco della Rovere, he was embroiled in the political turmoil on the Italian peninsula throughout his pontificate. S. agreed to the establishment of the Spanish Inquisition but opposed its excesses. He was a patron of the Vatican Library, created the Sistine Chapel, and did much to beautify the city of

Rome. S.'s nephew, Giuliano della Rovere, became Pope Julius II.

Sixtus V (1521-1590) Pope, 1585-1590. Born Felice Peretti, he was one of the major figures of the Catholic Reformation well before he became pope. S. restored order in the Papal States, reorganized the Roman Curia, and did much to beautify the city of Rome. He fixed the number of cardinals at a maximum of 70, a figure that remained in effect until the pontificate of John XXIII in the early 1960s.

Skylax of Karianda (6th century BC) Greek explorer. He led an expedition in c.515 BC to find the source of the Indus River in India and wrote about his experiences. His was the first description of India by a Westerner.

Slanski, Rudolf (1901-1952) Czech politician. He was general secretary of the Czech Communist Party after World War II and vice president of Czechoslovakia from 1951. After a show trial for treason, he was executed in 1952.

Slave Coast Coastal region of Western Africa around the Gulf of Guinea. It was the starting point of the huge slave trade from Africa to the Americas.

Slavs Largest ethnic and linguistic groups of European peoples belonging to the Indo-European linguistic family. The main divisions are West Slavs (Czechs, Poles, Slovaks), South Slavs (Serbs, Croats, Slovenes, Bosnians, Montenegrins, Bulgars, Macedonians), and East Slavs (Great Russians, Ukrainians, and Belorussians).

Sixtus V

Sluis Site in Zeeland, Flanders, where in 1340, during the Hundred Years War, the English fleet inflicted a severe blow on the French. In 1603, the Italian/Spanish admiral, Frederico de Spinola, died in a naval battle at Sluis.

Smith, Alfred E. (1873-1844) American politician. Dubbed the "Happy Warrior" by Franklin D. Roosevelt, S. served four terms as a reform governor of New York. He was the 1928 Democratic nominee for president, but he lost overwhelmingly to Herbert Hoover. Smith later broke with Roosevelt after the latter became president and spent his final years opposing the New Deal.

Smith, John (1580-1631) English soldier and colonist. He helped establish Jamestown, Virginia, as the first permanent English colony in North America. S. treated the Indians harshly, and during his absence in 1609 they wiped out the colony. His later story of how Pocahontas saved his life may be a fabrication, although it remains a popular legend.

Smuts, Jan Christiaan (1870-1950) South African military officer and statesman. He was a Boer by birth as well as a British citizen. S. fought against the British in Boer War but later concluded that cooperation with Britain was essential for South Africa. He was a cabinet minister several times (1919-1924) before serving as prime minister (1939-1948). He spent much of World War II in London, where he helped create the United Nations. S.'s party lost (1948) to the Nationalists, whose racial views were more extreme than his.

Soares, Mario (1924-) Portuguese politician. A socialist, he was imprisoned and exiled a number of times under the Salazar regime. After the 1974 revolution, he returned to Portugal. S. was prime minister several times between 1976 and 1985. He was elected president in 1986 and was reelected in 1991.

Sobibor Town in Poland. Located west of Lublin, it was the site of a Nazi extermination camp built in 1942-1943. Approximately 250,000 people were murdered at S. during World War II.

Sobk (Sebek) Egyptian crocodile god, originally a god of fertility and later associated with Re (Sebek-Re). The major cult sites were the Fayyum and Kawn Umbu.

Sobieski *See* Jan III of Poland.

Socialism (derived from the Latin word *socius,* meaning sharer) General term for political and economic theory that advocates a collective or government ownership of the means of production and the distribution of goods. It contrasts with capitalism, which believes in private property. Socialistic theory developed in the late 18th and early 19th centuries as a reaction to the excesses of the Industrial Revolution. What S. is or is not has been a subject of intense debate throughout much of the 20th century. Russian communism was often seen as a radical form of socialism, while democracies in Western Europe often considered themselves practitioners of "democratic" socialism.

Socrates (c.469-399 BC) Greek philosopher who lived in Athens. Knowledge of S. and his ideas comes mainly through his disciple Plato and through Xenophon. S. developed a new way of approaching knowledge, which put man in a central position. S. saw the universe as purposively mind-ordered. His technique consisted of increasing people's understanding by means of simple answers and questions. S. was charged with not believing in the gods and corrupting the young. He was condemned to commit suicide by drinking poison hemlock, a death described with great drama by Plato.

Mario Soares

Sokölli, Mehmed Pasha (1508-1579) Turkish statesman. He became grand vizier in 1565 and brought the Ottoman empire to the height of its power.

Solebay, Battle of Naval engagement (1672) in which the English fleet under the Duke of York was defeated by De Ruyter, thus preventing the English from landing in Holland.

Socrates

Soleure, Treaty of (1579) Pact by which Michel Roset, Calvin's successor in Geneva, gained the support of France against Savoy.

Solferino Town in Italy. The Austrian army was defeated (1859) at S. by a French and Sardinian army in the war for Italian independence.

Solidarity Polish trade union and democracy movement. It was founded by Lech Walesa, a shipyard worker, in 1980, but was declared illegal by the communist government between 1981-1989. In June 1989 free elections were held in Poland for the first time since the World War II, and S. achieved a huge majority.

Solomon (d.c.932 BC) King of Israel, c.972-932 BC. The son of King David and Bathsheba, he built the first Hebrew temple at Jerusalem. His reign was largely peaceful, and he is legendary for his wisdom, however in his old age he became more despotic. At the end of his rule, he had to fight against an uprising of his son and successor Jeroboam. The biblical account of S. is considered fairly complete. Proverbs and Ecclesiastes are ascribed to him, an the Song of Solomon bears his name.

Solomon (1045-1087) King of Hungary, 1063-1074. The son of Andreas I, he became king with the support of Holy Roman Emperor Henry IV. S. was toppled in 1074.

Solon (c.630-560 BC) Athenian philosopher and statesman. He became chief archon in 594 BC and instituted a series of reform. S. abolished serfdom in Attica and opened the assembly to all freemen. He also introduced a more human code of law to replace Draco's laws. S.'s reforms became the basis of the Athenian state.

Solon

Solzhenitsyn, Aleksandr Isayevich (1918-) Russian author. In 1945, while still in the military, he was sentenced to 8 years hard labor for criticizing Stalin in a letter. His first novel, *One Day in the Life of Ivan Denisovich*, appeared in 1962 and was based on his life in the prison camp. His novels *The First Circle* (1964) and *Cancer Ward* (1966) were also exposés of the Soviet system that alarmed authorities and led to his further persecution. S. was awarded the Nobel Prize for Literature in 1970 but was not allowed to accept it by the Soviet government. In 1974 he was expelled after his book, *The Gulag Archipelago*, a historical study of the Stalinist camp system, was published in the West. S. lived most of his exile in the U.S. and was allowed to return to Russia in 1994.

Somerset, Edward Seymour, 1st Duke of (c.1506-1552) Protector of England. The brother of Queen Jane Seymour, he became powerful after his sister's marriage to Henry VIII (1536). After Henry's death (1547), he made himself protector of England during the minority of his nephew, King Edward VI. S. was an able administrator and military man, but he created many enemies and was eventually brought down by the earl of Warwick. He was imprisoned, released, then arrested again and beheaded in 1552.

Somme, Battle of the French-British offensive during World War I (July-November 1916) commanded by Joffre and Haig. Little territory was gained, but the battle cost the lives of more than 600,000 Allied troops and some 650,000 Germans.

Song of Igor's Campaign Earliest great poetic work in Russian literature. An anonymous work, it describes the unsuccessful campaign of Igor Svyatoslavitch (1150-1202), grand duke of Novgorod Severskiy, against the nomadic Polovtsy.

Sophists Originally itinerant teachers in Greece (5th and 4th centuries BC). The Sophists (wise men) taught the art of persuasion (rhetoric) and were considered experts in defending indefensible and false statements. The word *sophist* later became synonymous with intentionally deceptive reasoning. Among the most noted Sophists were Protagoras and Gorgias.

Sophocles (c. 496-406 BC) Greek tragic dramatist. He and Pericles were

Aleksandr Isayevich Solzhenitsyn

Sophocles

the strategists behind the Athenian war against Samos. Later he devoted his life entirely to writing. S. wrote mainly tragedies, of which *Antigone, Electra,* and *Oedipus Rex* are the best known.

Sophocles, Themistocles (1860-1949) Greek politician. A fierce anti-communist, he served as prime minister from 1945-1946 and from 1947-1949.

Sorge, Richard (1895-1944) German journalist and intelligence agent. From his post in Tokyo, S. passed on virtually all German and Japanese military secrets to Moscow between 1934-1941. He was finally unmasked and hanged.

Soto, Hernando de (c.1497-1542) Spanish conquistador and explorer. He and Pizarro carried out expeditions to Peru and parts of North America from 1539. S. discovered and explored the Mississippi River region.

Soubise, Benjamin de Rohan, Seigneur de (1583-1642) French general. He was the leader of Huguenots between 1620-1629.

Soubise, Charles de Rohan, Prince of (1715-1787) French general and field marshal of France from 1758. A favorite of the Marquise de Pompadour and the Comtesse Du Barry, he

South America before Columbus

We know that South America was populated with many different peoples before the sixteenth century, when the Spanish arrived, but we know very little about them. Most of these peoples could not write and left only artifacts and structures.

1

1. Monolith of Quebradillas in Colombia.
It is probably a funerary monument.
2. An anthropomorphic vase, made in Ecuador.
3. A ritual knife of the Chimus in north Peru, bearing a portrait of the god Naym Lap.
See Chimus.

2

3

351

4. The ruins of Machu Picchu, once a major city of the
Inca Empire. *See* Incas; Machu Picchu.
5. An Inca vase in the shape of a puma. *See* Incas.
6. A Peruvian mummy, dating from between 1000 and 900 BC.
7. Painted pottery from Tiahuanaco in Bolivia.
8. Gold vase made by the Quimbayas, who lived in Colombia.

fought in the Seven Years War but was defeated by Frederick II of Prussia at Rossbach.

Soulouque, Faustin (c.1782-1867) Emperor of Haiti, 1849-1859. A former slave, he declared himself emperor as Faustin I. His rule was cruel and corrupt, and his court was a caricature of Napoleon's. He was brought down by a revolution led by Nicholas Fabre Geffrard.

South East Asia Treaty Organization (SEATO) Alliance founded in 1954. The member states (Great Britain, France, Australia, New Zealand, the Philippines, the U.S., Pakistan, and Thailand) are committed to the peaceful settlement of disputes among themselves and to collective security in the Western Pacific. The alliance was founded as a bulwark against Chinese communist expansionism in Asia.

South Moluccans Inhabitants of the Moluccas (Spice Islands), Indonesia. Some groups of S. fought for independence from Indonesia and staged terrorist attacks in Europe during the 1970s to dramatize their cause. They were unsuccessful.

Soviet Russian word for council. The original soviets were revolutionary committees of factory workers organized during the 1905 revolution by the Socialists. During the 1917 revolution, soviets of workers, peasants, and soldiers were established throughout the country, and they were soon controlled by the Bolsheviks.

Soviet Union (Union of Socialist Soviet Republics) Former Communist constituent republic in eastern Europe and Asia, with Moscow as the capital. S. was founded in 1922, when the Russian Soviet Republic united with Belorussia, Ukraine, and Transcaucasia. It was abolished on January 1, 1992, after the collapse of communism throughout eastern Europe. Some of the constituent republics were united during the transitional period in the Commonwealth of Independent States (CIS).

Spa, Conference of (July 1920) Conference in Belgium following World War I at which the Allies accepted a German proposal for reparations payments.

Faustin Soulouque

Spanish-American War Conflict between the U.S. and Spain (1898). The Americans used the revolt against Spanish rule in Cuba as a pretext to declare war. The Spanish were quickly defeated, and as a result of the war, the U.S. acquired a colonial empire that included Puerto Rico, Guam, and the Philippines.

Spanish Civil War Conflict in Spain (1936-1939) between republicans and nationalists. The republicans, who generally supported democratic institutions, were backed by France and Russia and volunteers from the West, but they were seriously divided. The nationalists received aid from Nazi Germany and fascist Italy. Under Franco's leadership they were victorious, inaugurating a 30-year period of dictatorship in Spain. Over a million lives were lost during the war.

Spanish Fury See Fury.

Spanish-Peruvian War Conflict (1866) between Peru and Spain. It began after an attack by Peruvian laborers on Basque immigrants at Talambo, Peru (1864). The Spanish fleet then occupied a number of important offshore Peruvian islands, but a coalition of Chile, Peru, Ecuador, and Bolivia declared war on Spain and defeated the Spanish fleet at Callao.

Spanish Succession, War of the Last of the European wars caused by the efforts of Louis XIV to extend French power. It involved a complex dispute over the succession to the throne of Spain in which France, the Holy Roman Emperor, and Bavaria all laid claims. The war eventually established the principle of the balance of power between states and ended the influence of dynastic considerations in negotiations in European affairs.

Sparta City state of ancient Greece, in the Peloponnesus. It flourished from the 7th century BC, when it became increasingly militaristic and was run on a caste system. The Spartans ruled the native inhabitants (helots), who did all menial work in S. The Spartans were a martial people. They ruled the Peloponnesus through the Peloponnesian League, which they dominated. During the Persian Wars, S. fought alongside Athens, but after that conflict, the rivalry with Athens sharpened. The Peloponnesian War (431-404 BC) wrecked Athens. S. prospered under the Romans and was devastated by the Goths in 395 AD; *see* Peloponnesian League; Peloponnesian War.

Spartacus (d.71 BC) Thracian gladiator. From 73 BC, he was the leader of a slave revolt in Italy. After several victories with his 90,000-man army, he was defeated by Crassus. More than 6,000 surviving slaves were then crucified along the road connecting Rome and Capua.

Spee, Maximilian, Count von (1861-1914) German admiral. He fought in the waters off South America at the start of World War I and went down with his flagship, *Scharnhorst*. The World War II pocket battleship *Graf Spee* was named after him. After causing great damage in the South Atlantic, it was trapped by the British in the harbor of Montevideo, Uruguay (1939), where it was scuttled by its crew.

Speer, Albert (1905-1981) Nazi armaments minister in World War II. He began as Hitler's architect and was appointed head of arms production in 1942. S. was sentenced to 20 years in prison at the Nuremberg Trials (1946). After his release in 1966, he lectured and wrote about his experiences in Hitler's entourage and in prison.

Spengler, Oswald (1880-1936) German cultural philosopher. He is

Albert Speer

Sports

Sports have been important to people throughout history. Every country has its own favorite sport, and national teams are treated like heroes when they win. Millions of people play sports themselves, and even more are enthusiastic spectators of sporting events.

1

2

1. The procession at the opening of the 1988 Olympic Games at Seoul.
2. After hitting the ball, this baseball-player starts running to reach a base. Baseball is the most populair sport in the U.S.A.
3. The celebration, with flowers and a medal, of Carl Lewis, champion of the 100 meters event at the 1984 Olympic Games in Los Angeles.
4. A Japanese sumo wrestling match.
5. A street soccer match in Zambia.
6. "Tossing the Caber" is one of the competitions during the traditional Highland Games in Scotland.

4

5

6

3

known mainly for his work *The Decline of the West* (1918-1922), in which he states that all human civilizations go through similar evolutionary periods of birth, prosperity, and inevitable decline. According to S., the West was now in a period of irreversible decay. He supported German dominance of Europe, but he refused to accept Nazi racial theories and was ostracized as a result.

Spillbergen, Joris van (1568-1620) Dutch explorer. He went on expeditions to West Africa, New Guinea, Brazil, and the East Indies. From 1614-1617, he circumnavigated the globe via the Straits of Magellan.

Spinola, Ambrogio (1569-1630) Spanish general. Born in Genoa, he entered the service of Spain and fought in the Netherlands against Maurice of Nassau in 1562. In 1604 he captured Ostend, but he is especially known for his taking of Breda in 1625, an event immortalized by Velásquez.

Spinoza, Benedict (1632-1677) Dutch philosopher of Portuguese-Jewish origin. He lived a simple life as a lens grinder, first studying the Hebrew bible. His independence of thought, however, eventually led to his excommunication from the Jewish community (1656). S. reworked some of Descartes writings. His own philosophy was rational and deductive. As a pantheist, he believed God and Nature were one, not separate. S. believed that knowledge was essential in order to be free. His writings, almost all of which were published after his death, greatly influenced later German thinkers, including Lessing, Herder, and Goethe.

Splendid Isolation Term used to describe 19th-century British desire to be involved as little as possible in world affairs. The call for S. was increased as a result of the Crimean War (1853-1856).

Spurs, Battle of the (1302) Battle in which the Flemish, in their struggle for independence, defeated Philip IV's army of French noblemen. The battle received its name from the spurs taken from the fallen French knights by the victors.

SS (*Schutzstaffel*) Nazi paramilitary organization. It was founded in 1925

Oswald Spengler

Benedict Spinoza

as Hitler's personal bodyguard, but rapidly expanded under Heinrich Himmler into an elite army. The SS carried out the assassinations of leading SA members in 1934 and effectively replaced that organization as the Nazi Party's armed unit. They later controlled the concentration camps and were responsible for the murder of millions of European Jews. Armed SS units (called *Waffen SS*) fought alongside the regular army during engagements in World War II.

Staël, Germaine de (1766-1817) French-Swiss woman of letters. Born Anne Louise Germaine Necker, she was the daughter of Jacques Necker and the wife of the Baron Staël-Holstein. S. was a central figure in Revol-

Germaine de Staël

utionary France under the Directory, where her salon was a meeting place for powerful figures. S. was banished from France in 1803 because of her opposition to Napoleon. Her book *De l'Allemagne* (1810) was banned by Napoleon because he felt it compare German culture too favorably with French culture. Madame de Staël returned to France in 1815 after the downfall of Napoleon.

Stalin, Joseph (1879-1953) Soviet dictator. A Georgian, his birth name was Dzhugashvili. As a young revolutionary, he adopted the name Stalin ("man of steel") around 1913. In 1922 he became secretary general of the communist party central committee, a position that allowed him eventually to control the party apparatus. After the death of Lenin in 1924 he gradually amassed the power of both the party and state. During the 1930s, S. instituted a series of purges that eliminated all real or imagined opposition in the state and the military, seriously weakening the latter. S. led the Soviet Union during the critical days of World War II, rallying the nation from the edge of defeat. He died in 1953, apparently shortly before instituting a new series of purges and anti-Jewish actions. At the 1956 party conference, S. was denounced by Khrushchev for his excesses and his cult of personality. Although generally reviled since then as a murderer of millions, S. still has supporters within Russia.

Stalingrad City in the Soviet Union, site of a great and decisive battle (August 1942-February 1943) in World War II between the German and Soviet armies. The defeat of the German army marked the turning point of the war.

Stambuliski, Alexander (1879-1923) Bulgarian statesman. He forced the resignation of Czar Ferdinand and after 1919 served as prime minister. An agrarian reformer, S. ruled as a dictator and was overthrown and killed (1923) in a military coup.

Stamp Act Legislation passed by the British Parliament (1765) requiring stamps to be purchased and used on most documents in the North American colonies. The colonists rejected the act and called the Stamp Act Congress in protest, the first united colonial action against Great Britain. With the act widely ignored, it was repealed in 1766.

Joseph Stalin

Stanislas I

Stanislas I (Stanislas Leszcynski) (1677-1766) King of Poland, 1704-1709, 1733-1735. A nobleman by birth, he was elected king with the help of Charles XII of Sweden, who had deposed King Augustus II. After the battle of Poltava (1709), however, he was forced to flee and Augustus was restored. S. married one of Louis XV of France's daughters in 1725 and with his help became king of Poland again in 1733 upon Augustus's death. In 1735 pressure from the Russians and Austrians forced him to relinquish the throne, and he returned to France, where he was made duke of Lorraine.

Stanislas II *See* Poniatowski.

Stanley, Sir Henry Morton (1841-1904) Anglo-American journalist. Born John Rowlands, he is known principally for his journey to Africa for the New York *Herald* in search of Livingstone, whom he found in 1871. S. made additional journeys and discoveries in Africa and advanced the cause of British colonial rule. Although an American, he became a British citizen, was elected to Parliament, and was knighted in 1899.

Starhemberg, Ernst Rüdiger, Count von (1638-1701) Austrian general. He was the garrison commander who successfully defended Vienna during the Turkish siege of 1683.

Starhemberg, Ernst Rüdiger, Prince von (1899-1956) Austrian politician. He took part in Hitler's beer-hall putsch (1923) but later turned against him and supported Dollfuss. He was the leader of the Heimwehr, a fascistic Austrian militia. In 1936, S. was fired as vice-chancellor by Schuschnigg and later fought with the Free French against Nazi Germany. He lived in exile in Argentina from 1942 to 1955 before being allowed to return to Austria.

Starhemberg, Guido, Count von (1657-1737) Austrian field-marshal. He fought with distinction in the Turkish wars and in the War of the Spanish Succession.

Staten van Dordt (1572) Meeting of a number of Dutch towns where William of Orange was recognized as leader of the resistance against Spain and as legitimate stadtholder.

Stauffenberg, Klaus Schenk, Count von (1907-1944) German military officer. S. planted the bomb used in the failed attempt to assassinate Hitler on July 20, 1944. he was quickly captured and executed the same evening.

Stavisky, Serge Alexandre (1886-1934) French swindler of Russian descent. His death led to a national scandal because the suspicion arose that he had been murdered to hide his connections to high-ranking government officials. After a general strike Prime Minister Daladier was forced to resign. The Stavisky affair discredited parliamentary democracy in France.

Ernst Rüdiger Starhemberg

St. Clair, Arthur (1734-1818) American general. During the American Revolution, he vacated Fort Ticonderoga (1777) without a fight. He later served as governor of the Northwest Territory, where he fought a number of unsuccessful battles against the Indians before being relieved (1802) by President Thomas Jefferson.

Steenkerke Battle site in Flanders, where the French under Luxembourg defeated the allied armies under William III on August 3, 1692, during the War of the Grand Alliance.

Stein, Karl, Freiherr vom and zum (1757-1831) Prussian statesman. As a minister in the Prussian government, he instituted a number of major reforms, including the abolition of serfdom and the increase in the power of local government. S.'s reforms turned Prussia into a modern state.

Stephen I (977-1038) First king of Hungary, 1001-1038. Hungary achieved independence under his rule, and he was canonized in 1083.

Stephen II (d.757) Pope, 752-757. During his reign, Pepin the Short, through the Act of Donation, ceded the Duchy of Rome to the pope, thus laying the foundation for the Papal States.

Stephen (c.1097-1154) King of England, 1135-1154. He was the nephew of King Henry I, whom he succeeded in 1135. In the struggle against the followers of Henry's daughter Mathilda, S. had to recognize her son, Henry Plantagenet, as successor to the throne in 1135.

Stephenson, George Robert (1781-1848) English inventor who built the first steam locomotive used in railroads.

Stern Gang Jewish terrorist organization that carried out attacks on Arabs and the British in Palestine. When Israel was founded (1948) the S. was disbanded.

Stilicho, Flavius (c.365-408) Roman general. A Vandal by birth, he was effectively the ruler of the Roman Empire in the West from 394. In 401-402 S. stopped Alaric from marching into Italy, but he could not stop the Vandal and Alan invasions in Gaul.

When the Italian army revolted against him, Emperor Honorius had him murdered.

Flavius Stilicho

Stoicism Ancient Greek philosophical school. Founded by Zeno (c.300 BC), S. teaches that virtue is the highest good in life. Only by putting aside passion and indulgence and preforming one's duty can man achieve true happiness. S. was influential in the Roman period, when Epictetus,

George Robert Stephenson

Seneca, and the Emperor Marcus Aurelius were adherents.

Stolypin, Piotr Arkadevich (1862-1911) Prime minister and minister of the interior of Russia, 1906-1911. He sought to met the threat of revolution through a combination of brutal suppression as well as agrarian reform. Through his reforms, S. hoped to create a class of small land owners loyal to the czar. At the same time, he had hundreds of radicals executed. S. was assassinated by a revolutionary.

Stradivarius violin

Stone Age Term that covers three prehistoric periods in Europe: the Old S. (Paleolithic period), the Middle S. (Mesolithic period), and the Young S. (Neolithic period). During the Paleolithic period, which lasted until c.12000 BC, people used stones and tools and were hunter-gatherers. The cave paintings of Altamira and Lascaux date from this period. The Mesolithic period lasted from c.12000-4000 BC. In this time people started living in huts, specialized in fishing, and developed the art of pottery. The first microliths were carved, small shards of flint, fashioned into scrapers and arrowheads. In the Neolithic period (until c.2000 BC), settlements increased in size and number and people started specializing in agriculture and animal husbandry. The dead began to be buried in megalithic tombs.

Stonehenge Megalithic monument in Wiltshire, England. Its original purpose is still not understood. S. consists of three concentric circles, the first traces of which are from c. 3100 BC, while the extant structure dates from c.1600 years later.

Stradivarius, Antonius (Antonio Stradivari) (1644-1737) Italian violin builder. He was a pupil of Niccoló Amati of Cremona. S.'s violins (dated between 1679-1736) are regarded as the epitome of violin construction.

Strafford, Thomas Wentworth, 1st Earl of (1593-1641) English statesman. He at times opposed Charles I, but later supported him. In 1640 he was prosecuted by the Long Parliament for the so-called army plot, by which the king was supposed to move against the Parliament. A bill of attainder against S. was passed, and the king reluctantly signed it and agreed to S.'s execution.

Strategic Arms Limitation Talks (SALT) Negotiations between the U.S. and the Soviet Union on arms limitations. The SALT I treaty (1972) limited the growth of strategic offensive weapons; SALT II (1979) regulated launching methods, including long distance bombers and rockets.

Strasbourg, Oath of (842) Oath sworn by Charles the Bald (later Holy Roman Emperor Charles II) and Louis the German in solidifying their alliance against their brother Lothair I. The version used by Louis is often considered the oldest known example of French.

Strauss, Johann the Elder (1804-1849) Austrian conductor and composer. He wrote many waltzes and marches, of which the *Radetzky March* is the most famous.

Strauss, Johann the Younger (1825-1899) Austrian conductor and composer. The son of Johann Strauss, he is called the "Waltz King" because of his copious output (more than 500 waltzes). The most famous are the *Blue Danube* (1866) and *Tales from the Vienna Woods* (1868). S. also composed successful operettas, including the popular *Die Fledermaus* (1873).

Strauss, Richard (1864-1949) German composer. He achieved fame as a young composer with his tone poems, including *Don Juan* (1888), *Till Eulenspiegel's Lustige Streiche* (1895), *Also Sprach Zarathustra* (1895), and *Ein Hel-*

Richard Strauss

denleben (1898). S. was one of the most successful opera composers of the 20th century. Among his works in this genre are *Salome* (1905), *Elektra* (1909), both of which shocked audiences because of their content and daring music, and *Der Rosenkavalier* (1911). His most successful operatic ventures were done in collaboration with his librettist, Hugo von Hofmannsthal. S. composed well into his 80s. Among the compositions of his later life are the opera *Capriccio* (1942) and the *Four Last Songs* (1948).

Stravinsky, Igor (1882-1971) Russian-American composer. Considered one of the century's great composers, S. revolutionized modern music. His first compositions of note, *The Firebird* (1910) and *Petrouchka* (1911), were written for Diaghilev's Ballet Russe in Paris. The work that drew the most attention, however, was *The Rite of Spring* (1913), which used primitive rhythms and harsh disso-

Igor Stravinsky

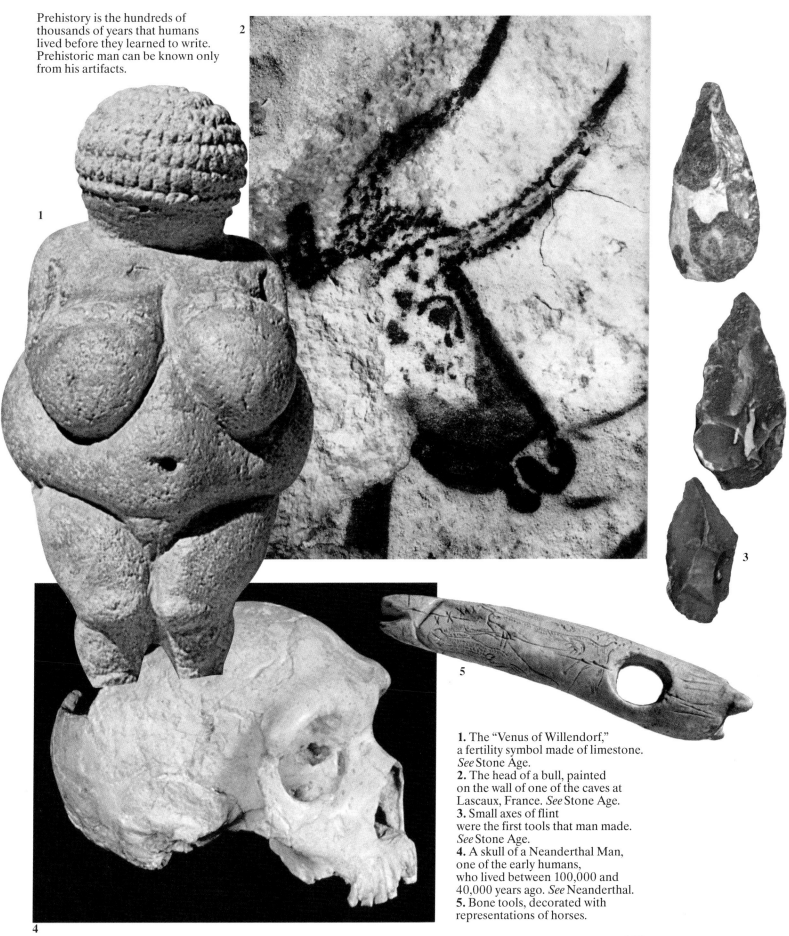

Prehistory is the hundreds of thousands of years that humans lived before they learned to write. Prehistoric man can be known only from his artifacts.

1. The "Venus of Willendorf," a fertility symbol made of limestone. *See* Stone Age.
2. The head of a bull, painted on the wall of one of the caves at Lascaux, France. *See* Stone Age.
3. Small axes of flint were the first tools that man made. *See* Stone Age.
4. A skull of a Neanderthal Man, one of the early humans, who lived between 100,000 and 40,000 years ago. *See* Neanderthal.
5. Bone tools, decorated with representations of horses.

359

nance. Its premier caused a riot, but it was soon recognized as a masterpiece. S. composed in different styles and genres. During the 1920s, some of his works (*Oedipus Rex*, for example) adhere to a neoclassical style, but by the 1950s some of his works had gone to full serialism (*Septuor*). S.'s influence on 20th-century music is great. He revitalized the rhythms of European music, and he used new orchestral colors in his compositions.

Streicher, Julius (1885-1946) Nazi leader. He took part in the beer-hall putsch in 1923 and served as publisher of the anti-semitic periodical, *Der Stürmer*. S. was convicted of war crimes at the Nuremberg Trials (1946) and hanged.

Streltsy Bodyguards of the Russian czars. They were founded by Ivan the Terrible c.1550 but were abolished by Peter the Great in 1698.

Stresa, Conference of Discussions between Great Britain, France and Italy (1935) about the German threat after Hitler had reintroduced the draft in Germany.

Gustav Stresemann

Stresemann, Gustav (1878-1929) German statesman. He was minister of foreign affairs from 1923-1929. S. strove for rapprochement with Great Britain and France while attempting to relieve Germany of the harshest provisions of the Treaty of Versailles. He helped win respect for Germany as a powerful nation, negotiating its entrance into the League of Nations (1926). In 1926 he and Aristide Briand received the Nobel Peace Prize. S.'s premature death was considered a calamity by all but the most extreme elements in Germany.

Stroessner, Alfredo (1912-) Paraguayan soldier and politician. A member of the conservative Colorado Party, he established a right-wing dictatorship after a coup in 1954. In 1989 he was deposed by the army and fled abroad.

Struensee, Johann Friedrich, Count of (1737-1772) Danish politician. A German by birth, he was the personal physician to the insane King Christian VII of Denmark and effectively ruled the country from 1768. S. imposed industrial, agrarian, and educational reforms, but his authoritarianism alienated the Danish nobles. In 1772 he was arrested on a charge of adultery with the queen and executed.

Stuart Dynasty that ruled Scotland from 1371-1707, England from 1603-1707 (with the exception of the Commonwealth period, 1649-1660), and Great Britain from 1707-1714.

Stuart, Charles Edward (1720-1788) Pretender to the English throne. He was the son of James Stuart, the "Old Pretender." Known as "Bonnie Prince Charlie" and the "Young Pretender," S. attempted to win the throne for his father but was defeated at Culloden in Scotland in 1745. James Stuart died in 1766. After his defeat at Culloden, S. spent the rest of his life on the continent.

Sture, Sten (Sten Sture the Elder) (c.1440-1503) Regent of Sweden. He defeated the Danes at Brunkerberg (1471) in a victory that gave hope for permanent independence from Denmark, but in 1497 he was forced to resign and the union of Denmark and Sweden was recognized in the Union of Kalmar. He became regent again in 1501.

Sturm und Drang (German for "Storm and Stress") Movement in German literature that flourished the end of the 18th century. The movement revolutionized literature in its stress on subjectivity and on the theme of the young genius in rebellion against traditional society. Goethe's *The Sorrows of the Young Werther* (1774) was the most representative Sturm und Drang novel.

Stuyvesant, Peter (c.1610-1672) Dutch Colonial administrator. He rose in the West India Company's ranks to become governor of Curaçao. S. was the autocratic director general of the colony New Netherland from 1647-1664. After a surprise English attack (1664) S. handed the colony over to England.

Sublime Porte From the 18th century the name for the grand vizier of Istanbul's residence and the government of the Ottoman Empire.

Submarine warfare Attacks carried out by submarines on enemy shipping. During World War I (1914-1918), the German navy sank 4,837 ships in an attempt to impose an economic stranglehold on Great Britain. The German policy of unrestricted submarine warfare was one of the contributing factors that eventually drew the United States (1917) into the conflict. Submarine warfare also took place in the Atlantic during World War II, but the major threat of German submarines was eliminated by 1943 through a combination of better detection equipment, protected convoys, and air surveillance.

Sucre, Antonio José de (1795-1830) South American revolutionary. Born

Antonio José de Sucre

in Venezuela, he took part in the South American wars of independence as one of Simon Bolívar's deputy commanders. S. helped found the republic of Bolivia and was that country's first president in 1826. Unhappy in the position, he resigned in 1828 and returned to his home in Quito, Ecuador. S. was killed (1830) by unknown men while riding on horseback in the mountains near Quito.

Sudetenland (Czech *Sudety*) German name for region of northwestern Czechoslovakia that was historically the home of numerous ethnic Germans. Hitler demanded that Czechoslovakia cede the region to Germany in 1938, and the seizure of the S. was ratified by the Munich Agreement between Germany, Great Britain, France, and Italy. In 1945, at the end of World War II, Czechoslovakia recovered the S., and the entire German population was expelled.

Suebi Germanic tribe, who lent their name to Schwaben in southern Germany. Some of the S. migrated to Spain with the Vandals, where they settled in c.450.

Suez Canal Canal in Egypt connecting the Mediterranean Sea and the Red Sea. Some 100 miles long, it was built between 1859-1866 under the auspices of the French engineer Ferdinand De Lesseps.

Suez Crisis International crisis that arose after the nationalization of the Suez Canal by Egyptian President Gamel Abdel Nasser in 1956. Shortly thereafter, Israel invaded the Sinai and broke through to the Suez Canal. Although Egypt rejected intervention, French and British troops landed near the Suez Canal on November 5, 1956. A UN force eventually replaced the French and British, and with UN help, the canal was cleared of war wreckage and reopened. Egypt agreed to reimburse member nations of the previous Canal Authority for their losses that resulted from nationalization.

Suger of Saint-Denis (1081-1151) French statesman and cleric. The abbot St. Denis, he was also an important financial adviser to Louis VI and Louis VII. While Louis VII was away on a crusade (1147-149), S. served as regent.

Suharto

Suharto (1921-) President of Indonesia since 1968. An army general, he fought against the Dutch in the late 1940s in the war of independence. An opponent of Sukarno's pro-Chinese communist policies, S. crushed an attempted Communist coup in 1965. He succeeded Sukarno as president in 1968 and implemented a pro-Western, pro-business policy.

Sukarno (1901-1970) Indonesian nationalist statesman and the first president of Indonesia. He cooperated with the Japanese during World War II while still fighting for Indonesian independence. On August 17, 1945, he proclaimed Indonesia a republic and became its president in 1949. In 1962, S. assumed dictatorial powers, declaring himself (1963) president for life. His policies became more pro-Communist, provoking a military coup in 1965 in which Suharto assumed power. S. was stripped of his title of president for life and placed under house arrest for the remainder of his life.

Sulayman I (Sulayman the Magnificent) (1494-1566) Ottoman sultan, 1520-1566. The son and successor of Selim I, he continued his father's conquest of the Balkans and the Mediterranean. He conquered Belgrade in 1521, defeated the Hungarians at Mohács in 1526, and reached the outskirts of Vienna in 1529. S. instituted numerous legal, educational, and military reforms, and was a lavish patron of literature and the arts.

Sulla, Lucius Cornelius (138-78 BC) Roman general and statesman. S. dis-

tinguished himself in the war against Jugurtha. In 88 he became consul and was made commander in the war against Mithradates VI of Pontus. Because Marius assumed command, S. first had to combat him. After a rapid peace with Mithradates, he returned to Rome to neutralize Marius, who had come to power. S. ruled as dictator from 82.

Lucius Cornelius Sulla

Sukarno

Sumerians People who founded a civilization along the lower Euphrates and Tigris rivers in southern Mesopotamia. Sumerian civilization was fully developed by 3000 BC. Largely agricultural, it also had a well-developed communal life and sophisticated urban centers. S. are credited with developing the cuneiform system of writing. The S. as a nation disappeared with the rise of Babylonia under Hammurabi (c.1900 BC).

Sun Yat-sen (1866-1925) Chinese statesman. He founded the Guomindang (Nationalist People's Party) in 1905. S. led the revolution of 1911-

Sun Yat-sen

1912 against the emperor and became the first president of China. After his death he was succeeded by his brother-in-law, Chiang Kai-shek. S.'s widow, Soong Ch'ing-ling, became a prominent figure in the Chinese Communist government.

Sunnis Adherents of the main branch of Islam. S. make up about 85 percent of all Muslims. Unlike the Shiites, the other main branch of Islam, they accept the historic order to succession of the first four successors of Muhammad, and they believe in the oral traditions of Islam. S. are found almost all over the Middle East and Africa, with Shiites concentrated in Iran and parts of Iraq.

Surrealism Artistic movement dedicated to the representation of imagination as revealed in dreams and the subconscious and free of traditional conventions. Dali and Magritte are examples of surrealistic painters, while Cocteau and Desnos are considered surrealistic writers.

Susa Ancient city in Iran. It was the capital of the Elamite empire c.3000 BC and was destroyed by the Assyrians in 639 BC. S. flourished during the Achaemenian period (5th-4th century BC), when the Persians kings established their winter residence here. The city was later Hellenized and played an important role during the Roman Empire. The Code of Hammurabi was discovered in S.

Suvorov, Aleksandr Vasilyevich Count (1729-1800) Russian general. He achieved many victories against the Turks during the Seven Years War (1756-1763). In 1799 S. became commander in chief of the Russo-Austrian army, and was victorious against the French in Italy. Never defeated in battle, he is considered one of the great modern generals. His willingness to allow his army to plunder gave Russian troops a bad name throughout Europe.

SWAPO (South West Africa People's Organization) Namibian independence movement that fought against South African occupation with the support of Communist Cuba. In 1989, S. won the elections, and in 1990 Namibia became independent, with SWAPO leader Nujama as president.

Sweers, Isaac (1622-1673) Dutch admiral. He served under De Ruyter and Cornelis Tromp. S. distinguished himself during the voyage to Chatham (1667) and in the naval battles at Schoonevelt and Kijkduin (1673), where he he was killed.

Swift, Jonathan (1667-1745) Anglo-Irish author. He is famous for his book *Gulliver's Travels* (1726), which is a merciless satire of human follies.

Swiss Guards Papal bodyguards established by Pope Julius II in 1506. They still serve as guards at the entrance to Vatican City and the papal palaces. Their uniforms may have been designed by Michelangelo.

Syagrius (d.486) Last Roman governor of Gaul. He ruled from 464 in the area of Soissons, where he was ultimately defeated by Clovis in 486.

Symbolism Literary school that originated in France in the late 19th century. Its primary exponent was Baudelaire. Symbolists reacted against naturalism and realism and sought to convey impressions rather than direct statements of reality.

Sykes-Picot Agreement Pact signed (1916) between Great Britain and France on the division of the Ottoman Empire and the future of Arab independence.

Syracuse City in Sicily. The town was founded by the Corinthians in c.730 BC and was an important power in the Mediterranean between the 5th and the 3rd centuries BC.

Svyatopolk the Cursed *See* Yaroslav the Wise.

Szczecin, Treaty of Pact that ended (1570) the Three Crowns War between Denmark and Sweden.

Jonathan Swift's *Gulliver's Travels*

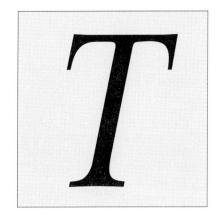

Ta Yu (Yu the Great) Chinese cultural hero, founder of the semi-legendary Hsia Dynasty (c.2200 BC).

Tacitus, Marcus Claudius (c.200-276) Roman emperor, 275-276. He was elected by the senate to succeed Aurelian, but was murdered by his own soldiers after a victory over the Goths in Asia Minor.

Marcus Claudius Tacitus

Taft, Robert Alphonso (1889-1953) American political leader. The son of William Howard Taft, he was elected to the U.S. Senate in 1938. He was a staunch opponent of the New Deal and an isolationist. Although he later supported U.S. entry into the UN, he remained critical of most of the Truman administration's foreign policy. He attempted to win the Republican presidential nomination in 1952 but was defeated by Dwight D. Eisenhower.

Taft, William Howard (1857-1930) 27th president of the U.S., 1909-1913, and 10th chief justice of the U.S., 1921-1930. He was the only person to occupy both the highest executive and judicial offices in the country. T.

served as secretary of war under President Theodore Roosevelt and was his hand-picked successor in 1908. The two soon quarreled, however, as Roosevelt accused T. of abandoning progressive principles. Roosevelt challenged Taft on the third-party Progressive ticket in 1912, thus dividing the Republican vote. After his defeat for reelection, T. taught law at Yale. He was named chief justice in 1921 by President Warren Harding.

Taginae, Battle of (552) Battle in which the Ostrogoths under Totila were vanquished by Narses with an army of approximately 30,000 men.

Taharqa (d.663 BC) King of ancient Egypt, the last ruler of the 25th Dynasty. He fought against the Assyrians to retain control of Egypt and was defeated by Esarhaddon, who conquered Memphis in 671. T. was again defeated in another campaign against Ashurbanipal, Esarhaddon's son, and fled to Nubia.

Tahirid (821-873) Dynasty in Khorasan (Iran) that owed allegiance to the Abbasid caliph. They extended their empire as far as India.

Taiping Rebellion Rebellion (1850-1864) by a group, called the Taiping, whose political creed contained elements of Protestantism. Seeking to topple the Manchu dynasty, they captured Nanking and made it their capital. The Western powers, fearing a loss of trade, intervened and assisted in crushing the rebellion. Some 20 million people died during the course of the uprising.

Taira Tadamori (1096-1153) Japanese samurai who served at the imperial court and made his Taira clan the most powerful in Japan.

Taira clan Powerful clan (11th century) at the Japanese imperial court. The T. were defeated in the naval battle of Dannoura in 1185.

Taisei Jokusankai *See* Rikken Seiyukai.

Taisha Reign name of the Emperor Yoshihito of Japan (1912-1926). He was the son of Mutsuhito, the Emperor Meiji, and the father of Hirohito, who succeeded him as emperor and led Japan during World War II.

Taj Mahal Mausoleum in Agra in India built by the Muhgal emperor Shah Jahan for his deceased wife between 1630-1652. It is considered one of the most beautiful buildings in the world.

Talat Pasha, Mehmed (1874-1921) Turkish politician. Leader of the Young Turks, he had absolute power from 1913-1918 and was responsible for the deportation of the Armenians. T. was assassinated in 1921.

Charles Talbot

Talbot, Charles, Duke of Shrewsbury (1660-1718) English nobleman. He secured Bristol and Gloucester for William III when the king assumed the throne (1688) during the Glorious Revolution.

Talent *See* Drachme.

Talikota, Battle of Battle (1565) in which the Hindu state of Vijayanagar was defeated by the Islamic army of the Decca empire.

Talleyrand-Périgord, Charles Maurice de (1754-1838) French statesman. Ordained as a clergyman, he was active in politics beginning in the

French Revolution. Appointed minister of foreign affairs by the Directory, T. later served Napoleon but grew increasingly alienated by the emperor's ambitions. In 1814 he worked for the return of the Bourbons and played a significant role in the Congress of Vienna. T.'s last service was for Louis Philippe as ambassador to London (1830-1834). Although regarded by some as an opportunist, T. worked consistently for a peaceful and stable Europe.

Talmud Vast compilation of the Oral Laws of the Jews. It consists of the Mishna (text of the Oral Laws, in Hebrew) and the Gemara (a kind of commentary on the Mishna, in Aramaic). The T. is the accepted authority for Orthodox Jews.

Tambo, Oliver Reginald (1917-1993) South African political leader. He and Nelson Mandela started the first black law practice in Johannesburg in 1952. T. was deputy president of the African

Oliver Reginald Tambo

National Congress (ANC) from 1958. When the ANC was banned in 1960, he fled the country. Returning to South Africa in 1990, T. was elected (1991) national chairman of the ANC.

Tamerlane (Timur Lenk) (1336-1405) Mongol conqueror said to descend from Genghis Khan. He became emir of Trans-Oxania in c. 1366 and conquered large areas in India, Persia, and the Mediterranean, leaving behind a trail of death and destruction.

Tammuz Mesopotamian god of fertility.

Charles Maurice de Talleyrand-Périgord

Tampico, Battle of Battle (1829) in which the Mexican general and dictator Santa Anna defeated the Spaniards.

Tanagra, Battle of Battle (437 BC) in which the Thebans were defeated by the Spartans during in the Peloponnesian War.

Tancred (1076-1112) One of the leaders in the First Crusade. T. participated in the conquest of Jerusalem in 1099 and was later regent of the Norman kingdom Antioch and Edessa (1104-1108). He subsequently made extensive conquests in Cilicia and northern Syria.

Tanis Ancient city of Egypt, in the Nile Delta. It was the capital city of 21st Dynasty under Smendes. Excavations beginning in the 1860s and continuing into the 20th century uncovered several temples and a royal necropolis.

Tannenberg Village in East Prussia. The Germans inflicted a severe defeat at T. on the invading Russian armies in the opening days of World War (1914).

Tantia Topi (1819-1859) Leader of the Sepoy Rebellion. He was the most successful guerrilla fighter against British rule in India during the 19th century.

Tanuma Okitsugo (1719-1788) Ruler of Japan during the Tokugawa period. He promoted foreign trade, but was ultimately held responsible for various failures in the empire. He lost his

powers after the death of his Tokugawa patron Ieharu.

Tanzimat (Turkish for "reorganization") Measures undertaken to modernize the Ottoman Empire between 1839-1876. They included such reforms as the implementation of legislation based on the French system.

Tarakanova, Yelizaveta Alekseyevna (c.1745-1775) Russian adventuress who claimed she was the daughter of the unmarried Empress Elizabeth. Catherine II had her imprisoned in St. Petersburg.

Taraori, Battles of Battles that took place (1191-1192) near Delhi, India, between Prthviraja, the Rajput maharaja of Delhi, and the Islamic Muhammad of Ghur, who had invaded Delhi in 1192/1193. Within 20 years, northern India was conquered by the Muslims.

Tariq ibn Ziyad (d.c.720) Berber leader who, after landing at Gibraltar in 711, defeated the Visigoth King Roderick and conquered two-thirds of Spain for the Muslims.

Tarquinius Priscus According to tradition, the fifth king (of Greek heritage) of Rome. T. ruled from 616-578 BC.

Tarquinius Superbus King of Rome, 534-510 BC. He was the son of T. Priscus. During his reign, Etruscan influence reached its height.

Tashkent, Treaty of Pact (1966) that ended the Indian-Pakistan War of 1965.

Tasman, Abel Janszoon (1603-1659) Dutch navigator. He served in the Dutch East India Company and between 1642-1644 circumnavigated Australia twice, proving that the country was not linked to Antarctica. During his first voyage he discovered Tasmania, which he named Van Diemensland.

Tartars (Tatars) Turkic-speaking peoples living in Eurasia. They number some 6 million and are mainly Sunni Muslims.

Tauroggen, Convention of Agreement (1812) between the Prussian General Yorck and the Russian army. Under its terms, Yorck declared his troops' neutrality, thus allowing the Russians to continue their pursuit of Napoleon's forces.

Tausen, Hans (1494-1461) Danish religious reformer. He studied with Luther in Wittenberg and brought the Reformation to Denmark.

Tay Soy *See* Le dynasty.

Taylor, Zachary (1784-1850) 12th president of the U.S., 1849-1850. An army officer, he fought in the War of 1812 and campaigned against the Seminole Indians. T. won fame as a hero in the Mexican War with his decisive victory at the battle of Buena Vista (1847). Nominated as the Whig candidate for president, he was elected in 1848. Although a Southerner by birth, T. as president was a strong supporter of the free-soil principle. He was opposed to the Compromise of 1850 but died (July 9, 1850) before it was fully enacted. His successor, Millard Fillmore, supported the Compromise, thus temporarily averting a sectional crisis.

Tawaret (The Great) Egyptian hippopotamus goddess of fertility and birth.

Tchaikovsky, Peter Ilyich (1840-1893) Russian composer. A passionate Romantic, and one of the most popular composers in history, he is famous for his ballet music (*Swan Lake, The Sleeping Beauty, The Nutcracker*) as well as for his six symphonies, symphonic poems, piano

Peter Ilyich Tchaikovsky

concertos, and violin concerto. Of his numerous operas, *Eugene Onegin* (1879), based on a Pushkin story, is the most famous and has become the Russian national opera.

Teapot Dome Scandal in U.S. history in the early 1920s during the administration of President Warren G. Harding. Teapot Dome, Wyoming, was the site of government oil reserves that were put aside by President Woodrow Wilson for use by the navy. Harding's secretary of the interior, Albert Fall, leased the reserves to a private businessman in return for cash payments. He was later convicted of bribery. T. came to symbolize the corruption that was widespread during Harding's term (1921-1923) of office.

Tecumseh (c.1768-1813) Leader of the Shawnee tribe of Native Americans. He urged all Indians to collectively resist ceding land to white settlers and succeeded in uniting many Native American tribes. In 1811 an army of Native Americans was defeated at Tippecanoe, in Indiana, effectively ending the Indians' military movement against the U.S. T. became an ally of the British in the War of 1812 and died in the Battle at the Thames (Canada) in 1813.

Tedder, Arthur William Tedder, 1st Baron (1890-1967) British air marshal. During World War II, he played a significant role in determining Allied strategy in North Africa and the Mediterranean. After the war, he served as chancellor of Cambridge University.

Teheran, Conference of Meeting (1943) in Teheran, Iran, between Roosevelt, Churchill, and Stalin at which the second front in Europe was discussed.

Tekakwitha, Kateri (Catherine Tekakwitha) (1656-1680) Native American woman who converted to Roman Catholicism. As a result of her conversion, she was forced to flee from her tribe. T. entered a monastery in Canada and lived a holy life. The process for her canonization was begun in the 1930s.

Telemann, Georg Philipp (1681-1767) German composer and organist. He wrote more than 600 overtures as well as cantatas, chamber music,

and operas. A representative of the Hamburg school, he was more popular in his time than Bach.

Telipinus (16th century BC) Hittite king, c.1525-1500 BC. He was the last king of the Hittites during the Old Empire.

Tell, William Legendary Swiss hero. A 14th-century tale describes T.'s resistance to Austrian rule under the cruel Hapsburg regent Gessler. There is no evidence that he ever really existed. T. was immortalized in a play by Schiller and an opera by Rossini.

Teller, Edward (1908-) American physicist. He was a leading researcher and was instrumental in the development and testing of the first hydrogen bomb (1952).

Temple Prison tower in Paris. Louis XVI and his family were confined there during the French Revolution. The T. was demolished in 1811.

Sir William Temple

Temple, Sir William (1628-1699) English statesman and author. He arranged the Triple Alliance (1668) as well as the marriage of stadtholder William III to Princess Mary, the daughter of the future James II. Jonathan Swift was T.'s secretary and edited his works after T.'s death.

Ten Commandments In the Bible, the summary of the divine law given to Moses on Mt. Sinai. They occupy a major position in Judaism, Christianity, and Islam.

Ten Thousand Immortals Personal bodyguard to the king of the Achaemenid empire. They were always replenished after a battle to number exactly 10,000 men.

Ten-day's Campaign (1831) Dutch military campaign against the Belgians. The Belgians were defeated, but they achieved their separation after French and English intervention.

Tenji Tenno (c.625-672) Japanese emperor, 668-672. He centralized government and implemented a new tax system. T.'s expedition to aid Korea was defeated by the Chinese invaders.

Tenochtitlán Capital of the Aztec empire. Founded in the 14th century, it is on the site of what is currently Mexico City.

Teotihuacán Ancient commercial and religious city in central Mexico. It was built c.400 BC by an unknown Indian culture and was destroyed by the Toltecs probably around 900 AD. Covering some 7 square miles, it is the largest preserved site of urban ancient America.

Teplitz, Treaty of (1813) Agreement between Austria, Prussia, and Russia detailing the terms of their alliance against Napoleonic France.

Ter Heyde Village on the south coast of the Netherlands. There, the English fleet under Admiral Monck fought against the Dutch on August 10, 1653. The Dutch Admiral Tromp was killed during the battle.

Terauchi, Hisaichi (1879-1946) Japanese field marshal. He was appointed war minister after a military coup d'état in 1936. During World War II, T. commanded the Japanese invasion of the Philippines, the Dutch East Indies, Malaya, and Burma. He was in charge of the construction of the infamous Burma railway, which used prisoners of war as slave laborers and for which he was indicted for crimes against humanity. T. died, however, before his trial.

Terminalia Feast at the end of the Roman year (February 23) during which neighbors decorate a border rock (termin) and make sacrifices to the god of the same name.

Terror, Reign of (1793-1794) Period during the French Revolution. It was essentially a war dictatorship, created to preserve the Revolution and the republic when it appeared that they were under grave threat from invading foreign powers and the uprising among royalists in the Vendée. Power was centralized in the Committee of Public Safety, which carried out many executions, including those of the former king and queen.

Tet Offensive North Vietnamese and Vietcong attacks (1968) throughout South Vietnam during the Vietnam War. The targets of the coordinated offensive were South Vietnamese urban centers and U.S. military installations. Although the T. was not a military success, it turned out to have a devastating psychological effect on the U.S., which then gradually started to pull out of the war.

Tetzel, Johann (c. 1465-1519) German monk and preacher. His preaching of an indulgence for the construction of St. Peter's in Rome ignited the wrath of Luther, who then posted his 95 theses.

Johann Tetzel

Teutoburger Wald Hills in northwest Germany. Three Roman legions led by Varus were destroyed there by the Germans under Arminius in the year 9 AD.

Teutonic Order Order of German knights founded in the Holy Land in 1189. Originally an order that cared for sick and wounded crusaders, it developed into a military organization with the status of a sovereign power, active in the Baltic and elsewhere. After a defeat at Tannenberg in a battle (1410) against the Poles and Lithuanians, its power began to wane.

Teutons Germanic tribe that moved south with the Cimbris and was destroyed by a Roman army led by Marius at Aquae Sextiae (Aix-en-Provence) in 102 BC.

Tewkesbury, Battle at Battle at "Bloody Meadow," near T., in which Edward IV of York defeated the Lancastrians during the Wars of Roses.

Tezcatlipoca *See* Xiuhtecuhtli.

Thames, Battle at the Engagement (1813) during the War of 1812, in Ontario, Candada, on the Thames River. The American general William Henry Harrison pursued a British and Indian army into Canada following their defeat at Detroit. The British were defeated and the Indian leader Tecumseh was killed in the battle, thus ending his Indian confederation and guaranteeing American supremacy in the Northwest.

Thamugai Ancient Roman city in Algeria. It was founded by Trajan in 100 AD to safeguard Numidia. T. was destroyed by Berbers in the 6th century.

Thapsus, Battle of Engagement (46 BC) near Carthage in which the Scipio and the Numidians were defeated with the loss of 10,000 men in the civil war between Pompey and Julius Caesar (49-46). Their defeat marked the end of opposition to Caesar in Africa.

Thatcher, Margaret Hilda (1925-) Prime minister of Great Britain, 1979-1990. A Conservative, she was the first woman to hold the office of prime minister. T. was noted for her uncompromising views, especially concerning economic reform. She sought to revive British capitalism and make

Margaret Hilda Thatcher

Britain competitive in world markets. Accordingly, she fought the labor unions and effectively reduced their influence in British politics. Equally determined when it came to foreign affairs, she led Britain to victory in the Falklands War (1982). T.'s unpopular tax policies and hard-line demands concerning the European Union led the Conservative party to force her resignation in 1990.

Thebes City in ancient Greece, settled originally by Mycenaeans. During the Peloponnesian War, T. fought with Sparta against Athens. In the Corinthian War, T. fought against Sparta and thereby gained hegemony over Greece for a brief period in the 4th century BC (*see* Epaminondas). T. was destroyed (336 BC) by Alexander the Great after an uprising against the Macedonian garrison located there.

Thebes City in ancient Egypt. It flourished during the time the Theban family established the 11th Dynasty (c.2100 BC). It was a center of the worship of the god Amon. At T. is the Valley of the Tombs, a splendid necropolis carved into the cliffs on the west bank of the Nile. The city was sacked by Ashurbanipal's Assyrians in 663 BC and gradually rebuilt, although it never regained its former splendor.

Themistocles (c.524-459 BC) Athenian statesman. T. was a leading political figure in Athens from 493. In 480 BC, in order to defend Athens from the invading Persians, he ordered the city evacuated. The Persian fleet was then defeated at Salamis. T. eventually lost power and was exiled. He spent his final years living comfortably in Persia.

Theodora I (c.508-548) Byzantine empress. She probably was an actress before marrying the Emperor Justinian I in 525. T. had a great influence on state policy. A stronger figure than Justinian, she saved the throne during the Nika revolt.

Theodora III (981-1056) Byzantine empress. She was the daughter of Constantine VIII. In 1050, after the death of her sister Zoe, who had confined her to a convent, T. ruled with her brother-in-law Constantine IX. After his death, she was sole ruler until she died in 1056.

Theodoric I (d.451) King of the Visigoths from 419. He fought with Aetius against the Huns and was killed in a battle at Cata Fields while fighting against Attila.

Theodoric II (d.466) King of the Visigoths from 453. The son of Theodoric I, he became king after his brother, King Thorismund, was murdered. T. recognized the supremacy of the Romans. He was murdered by his brother Eurik.

Theodoric III (d.691) Merovingian king. The son of Chlotar II, he became King of Neustria in 672, but was eventually forced to cede power to his mayor of the palace, Pepin II.

Themistocles

Theodoric the Great (c.454-526) King of the Ostrogoths from 471. Under the nominal command of the East Roman Emperor Zeno, T. advanced into Italy and conquered Ravenna by 493. He then proclaimed himself king of Italy. The 33 years of his reign were marked by peace and prosperity. T. respected Roman law and institutions, and he supported the building of roads and monuments. His tomb is one of the finest monuments in Ravenna.

Theodora I

Theodosius I (Theodosius the Great) (347-395) Roman Emperor of the East, 379-392, and then of the entire empire, 392-395. In 382, he conquered the Visigoths, who were plundering the Balkans, and incorporated many of them into his army. T.'s reign was notable for events that occurred in the church. He crushed the Arian heresy by recognizing the Nicene Creed as the only true confession of faith at the Council of Constantinople, and he forbade heathen cults in

The Thirties World Economic Crisis

As the decade of the 1920s neared its end, there were some signs that the great prosperity of the twenties would not last forever. The end of the great stock market boom came on Thursday, October 24, 1929, when prices on the New York Stock Exchange began a sharp decline. The decline heralded many years of high unemployment and general economic depression.

1. Many business and political leaders asserted that "conditions were fundamentally sound," but the Wall

Market in Panic as Stocks Are Dumped in 12,894,600 Share Day; Bankers Halt It

1

2

4

3

5

Street Crash indicated that the good times were over. *See* Black Thursday.
2. On Wall Street, crowds of businessmen wait for news on the day of the crash.
3. Even before the Crash, America's farmers had been suffering hard times. After the Crash, things got even worse. With crop prices low and credit hard to get, millions of farmers had to give up their farms and look for other work. Many never found it. This painting by Grant Wood gives a good idea of the general atmosphere of gloom.
4. The economic depression was worldwide. In London thousands of unemployed people participated in an enormous demonstration on February 5, 1933.
5. Nominated for president of the United States by the Democratic Party in 1932, Franklin Delano Roosevelt believed that vigorous governmental efforts were needed to combat the Great Depression. Critical of President Herbert Hoover's limited response to the crisis, Roosevelt promised the American people a "New Deal." In November he was elected in a landslide. *See* Hoover, Herbert; New Deal; Roosevelt, Franklin Delano.

392. On his death the empire remained divided between East and West, with his son Arcadius becoming emperor in the East, and his Honorius coemperor in the West.

Theodosius II (401-450) Roman emperor of the East, 408-450. The Grandson of the Emperor Theodosius I, he succeeded his father Arcadius as Roman emperor of the East. The first imperial civil code, later named Codex Theodosianus in his honor (438), was written during his reign. T. preferred theology and astronomy to government and left much of the affairs of state to his sister Pulcheria.

Theophilus (d.842) Byzantine emperor from 829 and the last one to oppose icon worship. T. fought against the advancing Arabs and lost the Battle of Dazimon (838).

Theramenes (d.c.404 BC) Athenian statesman. He was sent to negotiate with Sparta during the Peloponnesian War and was accused of treachery because of the amount of time spent in Sparta. T. was one of the Thirty Tyrants, but his liberal policy brought him into conflict with Critias, who forced him to drink poison.

Theresienstadt Nazi concentration camp in Czechoslovakia during World War II. To outside observers (especially the Red Cross), it was presented as an ideal "model camp" for Jews. In fact, its inmates were shipped to the gas chambers at Auschwitz.

Thermidor Eleventh month on the French Revolutionary calendar. The coup d'etat of 9 Thermidor (July 27, 1794) brought down Robespierre and ended the Reign of Terror.

Thermopylae Mountain pass in central Greece. At T. the Spartan King Leonidas and his followers were killed by the Persians under Xerxes in 480 BC. The Romans also defeated Antioch III there in 191 BC.

Theron Tyrant who ruled Acragas (Agrigento), Sicily, between 488-472 BC. He and his father-in-law defeated the Carthaginians at Himera in 480 BC.

Theudis (d.548) Ostrogoth leader. He was appointed regent to Amalaric, the

Theodosius I

under-age heir to the Visigoth empire, by Theodosius I. Amalaric died in 531 and was succeeded by T, who was murdered (548) by the usurper Theudigesil.

Thiers, Adolphe (1797-1877) French statesman. He served in various ministerial posts under Louis Philippe, including premier, but his aggressive foreign policy alienated the king. After 1863, T. was the leader of the opposition to Napoleon III. He opposed the Franco-Prussian War and became president (1871-1873) of the Third Republic after the French defeat. He crushed the rebellion of the Commune of Paris (1871) and generally pursued a conservative economic policy as president. T. alienated both monarchist and the left and was forced

Adolphe Thiers

to resign in 1873. He was also a historian, although his works today are seen as somewhat superficial endorsements of the French Revolution and Napoleon.

Third Reich Name given by Hitler to his regime. The term was supposed to suggest the continuation of the (first) Holy Roman Empire and the (second) German Empire.

Third Republic State proclaimed in France in 1870 in the wake of the Franco-Prussian War and lasting until the German invasion of 1940 during World War II. There were fifty different cabinets in the 1871-1914 period. Although political disunity ended temporarily during World War I (1914-1918), the postwar period was highly unstable. The Third Republic ceased to exist when the Germans occupied France in June 1940. When the Germans were driven out of France in 1944, the Fourth Republic was established.

Third World Developing countries of Africa, Asia, and Latin America. The term First World is applied to the the highly industrialized countries of Western Europe and North America, and to Japan. The term Second World has come to mean Central and Eastern Europe, including Russia.

Thirty Years War European war fought mainly in Germany between 1618 and 1648. Although there were shifting alliances and local peace treaties throughout the length of the conflict, the T. may be seen as a struggle between the German Protestant princes and foreign powers on the one hand against the Holy Roman Empire of the Hapsburgs and the Catholic princes on the other. The war ended with the Peace of Westphalia (1648). The T. was a huge calamity that devastated Germany for centuries. It also resulted in the break-up of the Holy Roman Empire and the decline of the Hapsburgs.

Thököly, Imre (1656-1705) Hungarian nobleman, leader of the Hungarian movement for independence from the Austrians. T. fought against the Turks at Vienna in 1683, but he later allied with them in his struggle against the Holy Roman Emperor. When the Turks negotiated a settlement with the emperor, the agreement

Thoth

required that T. be imprisoned near Constantinople. Hungary passed to the emperor (1699), and T. spent the remainder of his days imprisoned by the Turks.

Thomas à Becket, Saint (1118-1170) English martyr. The son of a Norman merchant, he was appointed chancellor by King Henry II in 1155. A strong supporter of the king, T. was named archbishop of Canterbury in 1162. He then took on his new role and forcefully defended the interests of the church even when they conflicted with the state, which angered the king. He was murdered in Canterbury cathedral by knights who felt they were carrying out the king's wishes. The king, however, was forced to do penance at T.'s tomb because of public outcry

Saint Thomas à Becket

over the murder. T. was canonized in 1173, and his burial site became a place of pilgrimage until it was destroyed on the orders of Henry VIII in the 1530s.

Thomas à Kempis (d.c.1380) German monk. He is considered the traditional author of the great devotional work, *The Imitation of Christ*. A manuscript of this work dating from 1424 has been preserved.

Thomas Aquinas, Saint (1225-1274) Italian philosopher and theologian. He is the greatest figure of Scholasticism, declared by Pope Leo XIII to be the official Catholic philosophy. The author of some some 100 works, T.

Saint Thomas Aquinas

studied with Albertus Magnus in Cologne between 1248-1252 and was a professor of theology in Paris.

Thor Norse god of thunder. He was often depicted as a red-bearded warrior god armed with a magical hammer and iron gloves. T. was a protector of both warriors and peasants.

Thorez, Maurice (1900-1964) French communist politician. T. was secretary general of the French Communist party from 1930 and was a faithful follower of Stalin. After the outbreak of the World War II he fled to Moscow. Although he helped build the French Communist party into a major political force after the war, he was discredited after the revelations of Stalin's atrocities.

Thoth Egyptian god of magic and wisdom, credited with inventing astronomy and writing. T. is often represented as an ibis-headed man or a baboon.

Thousand and One Nights (Arabian Nights) Collection of tales and fairy stories in Arabic, considered one of the masterpieces of world literature.

Thrace Greek name for the area in the Balkans that borders on Aegean Sea south of the mouth of the Danube River. It consists of parts of northeastern Greece, southern Bulgaria, and European Turkey. T. became a Roman province in 46 AD.

Thrasybulus (d.388 BC) Athenian general and statesman. He expelled the Thirty Tyrants in 403 BC and restored democracy to Athens.

Three Emperors' League Informal alliance (1872) between Austria-Hungary, Germany, and Russia pledging mutual support in the event of an external attack. The T. was weakened by the rivalry between Austria-Hungary and Russia in the Balkans, and it lapsed in 1887, giving way to Franco-Russian rapprochement in the Triple Entente.

Throckmorton Plot (1583) Failed conspiracy between the Catholic aristocrat Francis T. (1554-1584) and France and Spain to overthrow the Protestant Queen Elizabeth I and place Mary Tudor on the English throne. He was tortured and confessed, and was executed.

Thucydides (d.422 BC) Athenian statesman. Between c.449-443 BC, he succeeded Cimon as leader of the aristocratic party and opponent of Pericles, but he was ultimately exiled.

Thucydides (c.460-400 BC) Greek historian. He is considered one of the greatest ancient historians. He was unsuccessful as a strategist in war between Athens and Sparta, after which he retired and devoted himself to writing. His main work is his incomplete *History of the Peloponnesian War*. T.

was the first objective historian. Accurate and impartial, his writing details events as results of the actions of men, not of fate.

Thugga Ancient Roman city in North Africa, in Tunisia. It is famous for a Punic mausoleum (2nd century BC) and for numerous ancient ruins that still survive. Its current name is Dougga.

Thugs Religious sect in India devoted to the goddess Kali and to the robbery and strangulation of well-to-do victims. The T. would carry out their murders only in the fall of each year. Their members led respectable lives the remainder of the year. The British decided to eliminate the T., and by 1850 they had been all but wiped out through mass arrests and executions.

Thule Name given by the ancients to the northernmost point of the world. It has been variously identified with Iceland, Norway, and the Shetland Islands.

Thurn, Heinrich Matthias, Count von (1567-1640) Protestant nobleman and leader of the uprising in Bohemia in 1618. In 1620 he entered the service of King Gustav Adolph of Sweden and was captured briefly by Wallenstein in 1632.

Thutmose I King of ancient Egypt, c.1493- 1482 BC (18th Dynasty). The brother-in-law of Amenhotep I, he led his armies against Syria, Palestine, and Nubia.

Thutmose III (d.1426 BC) King of ancient Egypt, 1479-1426 BC (18th Dynasty). Originally overshadowed by his stepmother and regent, Hatshepsut, he developed into a powerful king after her death. He conquered Syria and Palestine and defeated the kingdom of Mitanni. T. built numerous temples along the Nile and is buried in the Valley of the Kings at Thebes.

Tiananmen Square Public square in Beijing, China, where the army crushed student demonstrations for democratic reforms (June 3-4, 1989). Estimates on the number killed range from 300 to 7,000.

Tiberius (42 BC- 37 AD) Emperor of Rome, 14-37 AD. He was the son of

Tiberius

Livia, the third wife of Emperor Augustus, and was adopted by the emperor in 4 AD and recognized as his successor. T. became emperor in 14 AD and reigned competently. He retired to the island of Capri in 23 AD and ruled by correspondence. In the latter part of his reign he became more tyrannical, having a number of former trusted associates put to death.

Ticonderoga *See* Montcalm.

Thutmose III

Tientsin, Treaty of Agreement concluded in 1858 between China and Great Britain, France, the U.S., and Russia, in which the Chinese agreed to allow foreign countries access to their

Thucydides

country. When the Chinese emperor did not recognize the T., Peking was occupied in 1860.

Tiepolo, Giovanni Battista (1696-1770) Italian painter. He worked in Venice, where he painted the ceilings of many palaces and churches and many altar pieces. He also worked for Louis XV of France and George III of England. Among his works is the ceiling of archbishop's palace in Würzburg, Germany (1750).

Tiglat-Pileser I King of ancient Assyria, c.1115-1077 BC. He restored the empire and fought many wars in which the Phoenician coastal cities were forced to pay tribute.

Tiglat-Pileser III King of ancient Assyria, 746-727 BC, and as Pulu, king of Babylon between 729-728 BC. T. brought about great changes, particularly in Syria and Palestine. He was an excellent administrator and is considered a major figure in Assyrian history.

Tigranes (c.140-55 BC) King of Armenia, 95-55 BC. He fought against the Romans in alliance with his father-in-law, Mithradates VI of Pontus. They were defeated by Lucullus (69 BC) and by Pompey (66), after which T. was forced to pay tribute to Rome.

Tilsit, Treaty of Agreement (1807) that ended the fourth (coalition) war between France and Russia against Prussia. Prussia was forced to relinquish all of its territory west of the Elbe River to France and its Polish provinces to the grand duchy of Warsaw. It was also forced to join the war against Great Britain.

Timur Lenk *See* Tamerlane.

Timoshenko, Semyon Konstantinovich (1895-1970) Soviet marshal. He led the Soviet invasions into Poland and Finland in 1939. Between 1943-1945, T. was in charge of the Ukrainian front, which advanced toward Germany through Rumania.

Tintoretto (c.1518-1594) Venetian painter. Born Jacopo Robusti, his work reflects the influence of Michelangelo. T. was a master in the use space, perspective, and light in his paintings. A superb example of his

Tintoretto

work is *The Last Supper,* in the Church San Giorgio Maggiore in Venice. T. is considered one of the great painters in the Venetian tradition.

Alfred von Tirpitz

Tirpitz, Alfred von (1849-1930) German admiral. He helped build the German navy into a powerful force second only to that of Great Britain. T. was an early advocate of submarines, and during World War I he strongly supported the policy of unrestricted submarine warfare.

Tiso, Josef (1887-1947) Slovakian fascist politician. In 1938, he became prime minister of Slovakia. A supporter of Hitler, T. persecuted the Jews of Slovakia and was hanged as a war criminal after the end of World War II.

Tissaphernes (d.395 BC) Persian satrap of Sardes (Asia Minor). He helped King Artaxerxes II defeat his younger brother Cyrus the Younger, and intervened in the Peloponnesian War in support of Sparta.

Titanic British passenger liner said to be unsinkable. The T. sank on her maiden voyage from Southampton to New York after colliding with an iceberg on the evening of April 14-15, 1912. Because the ship lacked sufficient lifeboats, more than 1,500 of the 2,200 people on board were drowned. The disaster led to the establishment of an iceberg patrol in the Atlantic and to strict regulations concerning lifeboats on passenger liners.

Tito, Josip Broz (1892-1980) Yugoslav leader. A Communist, he led the partisan forces fighting the Germans during World War II. By the war's end (1945), T. was virtual dictator of Yugoslavia. In the early years of his regime he ruthlessly eliminated any opposition, but his economic policies gradually became more relaxed from Communist orthodoxy. T. pursued an autonomous line from Moscow, which led at time to hostile relations. He placed Yugoslavia in the non-aligned camp while at the same time hoping to receive loans from the West. After his death, the Yugoslav federation gradually disintegrated as the consitutent republics declared independence and as warfare broke out.

Todleben, Franz (1818-1884) Russian general. During the Crimean War (1853-1856), he led the defense of Sebastopol. He also served with distinction in the Russo-Turkish War of 1877-1878.

Todt, Fritz (1891-1942) German engineer. From 1940-1941 he was Hitler's minister of armaments and, as the founder of the Todt Organization, was responsible for the construction of the Atlantic Wall. He died in an airplane crash and was succeeded by Albert Speer.

Togliatti, Palmiro (1893-1964) Italian Communist politician. He lived in exile in the Soviet Union when Mussolini was in power and returned to Italy (1945) after World War II. T. became the Italian Communist party leader and made it one of the largest Communist parties in Western Europe. Although he never broke with Moscow, T. supported more autonomy for Western European Communist parties from the Soviet Union.

Josip Broz Tito

Togo, Heihachiro (1846-1934) Japanese naval commander in chief. He is famous for his victories during the Russo-Japanese War at Port Arthur and the Tsushima Strait (1905). T. built the Japanese navy and is considered Japan's greatest naval hero.

Tojo, Heideki (1884-1948) Japanese general and politician. He became prime minister in 1941 and was the leading advocate of war with the United States. He resigned in 1944 after the fall of Saipan. T. was a believer in fighting to the last man, and he unsuccessfully attempted suicide in 1945. He was tried, convicted, and executed as a war criminal (1948) by the victorious Americans.

Tokugawa Japanese noble family of shoguns that ruled from 1603-1867. Ieyasu (1543-1616) was the first T. to rise to power after the death of Hideyoshi Toyotomi in 1598. His position was reinforced in 1600 after the battle of Sekigahara.

Toledo, Fadrique Alvarez (1529-1583) Spanish general. The son of the Duke of Alba, he led a number of campaigns in the Netherlands. After being defeated at Alkmaar in 1573, he returned to Spain, where he was imprisoned for several years.

Tolstoy, Leo Nikolaievich (1828-1910) Russian author. He is considered one of the greatest writers in history. T. was born at Yasnaya Polyana of noble parentage and fought in the Crimean War. Early in life he began to question authority and the bases of civilization, and by middle age was a believer in non-resistance to evil and in a life of Rousseauian simplicity. His belief in abandoning earthly good (he distributed his wealth among the poor) led to an estrangement from his family. In 1901 he was excommunicated by the Russian Orthodox Church for refusing to recognize its authority. His most famous works include his epic masterpiece *War and Peace* (1862-1869) and *Anna Karenina* (1873-1876).

Toltecs Ancient Indian people of Mexico. They founded an empire with Tula as its capital on the Mexican plains c. 900 AD. Until the destruction of Tula in the 12th century, the T. ruled in Central Mexico. The Mayan reli-

Heideki Tojo

gion contains a number of T. elements, for example human sacrifice. The invading Chitimecs finally destroyed the T. in the 12th century.

Tonkin Gulf Resolution (1964) Congressional resolution that granted President Lyndon B. Johnson authority to take any necessary war measures against the North Vietnamese during the Vietnam War. It stemmed out of an alleged attacks by North Vietnamese patrol boats against U.S. naval vessels in the Gulf of Tonkin. It later years, the occurrence of the incident was doubted.

Topa Yupanqui *See* Incas.

Tordesillas, Treaty of Treaty (1494) between Spain and Portugal dividing

Leo Nikolaievich Tolstoy

the non-Christian world into spheres of influence. The demarcation line was the meridian 370 miles to the west of Cape Verdes, which gave Portugal Brazil and Africa, and Spain all of the New World.

Tories Name for supporters of the Great Britain's Conservative Party. The term was originally a derogatory label applied to the supporters of the duke of York (later James II). The T. supported Catholicism and James's right to succeed to the throne. They were opposed at the time by the predominantly Protestant Whigs.

Torrington, Arthur Herbert, Earl of (1647-1716) English admiral. He fought against the Dutch and Barbary pirates and played an important role in the Glorious Revolution of 1688. In 1690, T. was commander in chief of the Anglo-Dutch fleet that lost the battle at Beachy Head (1690).

Lennart Torstensson

Torstensson, Lennart (1603-1651) Swedish general. He commanded King Gustaf Adolf's armies in the Thirty Years War. He is remembered for transforming the artillery into a mobile army unit.

Totila (d. 552) Last king of the Ostrogoths, 541-542. He gave the slaves their freedom and land to the farmers. T. conquered most of Italy but was defeated and killed when the Byzantine Emperor Justinian sent Narses against him in 552. After T.'s defeat, the Byzantines controlled Italy.

Tourville, Anne Hilarion de Cotentin, Count of (1642-1701) French admiral. In 1767 he fought against the Dutch, who were commanded by De Ruyter. T. defeated an Anglo-Dutch fleet at Beachy Head (1690) but lost the battle of La Hogue in 1692. He is considered one of the great naval strategists of his time.

François Dominique Toussaint L'Ouverture

Toussaint L'Ouverture, François Dominique (c.1743-1803) Black Caribbean freedom fighter. A freed slave, T. rose to general in the French army and became President of Saint-Domingue. T. eventually became an obstacle to Napoleon's colonial ambitions in the Western Hemisphere. The emperor had him captured in 1802 and taken to France, where he died in a dungeon the following year.

Toutates (Celtic: god of the people) Celtic god. People were sacrificed to T. by being hung upside down in a barrel of beer.

Trafalgar Cape in the south of Spain

where, in 1805, a decisive naval battle took place between the British fleet led by Horatio Nelson (who was killed in the battle) and the Franco-Spanish fleet commanded by Villenueve. The French and Spanish were defeated, thus crippling French naval power and making an invasion of England impossible.

Trajan (53-117 AD) Roman emperor, 98-117 AD. Born in Spain, he succeeded Nerva and was the first emperor born outside Italy. T. was an able administrator at home and pursued a vigorous foreign policy abroad. He defeated Dacia in two wars (101-102) and (105-106) as well as the Parthians. T. was succeeded by Hadrian.

Transcontinental Railroad Railway line that connected (1869) the Atlantic and Pacific coasts of the U.S. It opened officially when the Union Pacific and the Central Pacific lines were joined at Promontory Point, Utah.

Trasimene, Lake Body of water near Perugia, in central Italy. There Hannibal defeated a Roman army commanded by Caius Flaminius in 217 BC.

Treblinka Village in Poland. A Nazi death camp was built near T. during World War II, at which some 730,000 people, most of whom were Jews, were killed.

Trent, Council of 19th ecumenical council of the Roman Catholic Church. It met in Trent, Italy, intermittently between 1545 and 1563. The canons and decrees of T., which were issued as reform measures to counter the Protestant Reformation, in essence created the modern Roman Catholic Church.

Tribune One of various offices in ancient Rome. A representative of the plebeians (from the 5th century BC), the T. had the right to veto measures in the Roman Senate.

Trichardt, Louis (1783-1838) South African leader. He was one of the first leaders of the Great Trek.

Trinh family *See* Mac.

Triple Alliance, War of the *See* Paraguay wars.

Trajan

Triumvirate (Latin for "three people") Ruling commission of three men in ancient Rome. The first T. was formed in 60 BC by Pompey, Crassus, and Caesar, the second in 44 BC by Octavian, Antony, and Lepidus.

Trocadero Fort near Cadiz, Spain. It was seized by French supporters of Ferdinand VII in 1823, ending the Spanish revolution that had started in 1820.

Trochu, Louis (1815-1896) French general. He commanded the defense of Paris during the Franco-German war in 1870. He became head of state of the new government on September 4, 1870, but resigned after the armistice in 1871.

Trojan War In Greek mythology, the war between the Greeks and the Trojans. The war was started by the kidnapping of Helen of Sparta by Paris of Troy. The war ended when Troy was invaded by the Greeks through the use of a large wooden horse that sneaked Greeks within the city walls. The last years of the T. are described in Homer's *Iliad*.

Tromp, Maarten Harpertszoon (1597-1653) Dutch admiral. He defeated the Spanish fleet at Dungeness in 1639, thereby ending Spain's dominance of the sea. During the first Anglo-Dutch War, T. was killed in the battle of Terheyde.

Trotsky, Leon (1878-1940) Russian Communist revolutionary. Originally named Lev Davidovich Bronstein, he was one of the founders of the Soviet Union. He was first minister of foreign affairs under Lenin and then became minister of war during the civil war, during which time he built the Red Army from the tattered remnants of the czarist military. After Lenin's death, Stalin took control of the party apparatus, and by 1925 had T. dismissed from his government posts. He was expelled from the party and exiled in 1929. Settling in Mexico, T. continued to challenge the Stalinist regime through his writings. He was assassinated in 1940 by an agent of Stalin's who had been planted in his entourage.

Trujillo Molina, Rafael (1891-1961) President of the Dominican Republic, 1930-1938, 1942-52. A ruthless dictator, he maintained power even after leaving the office of the presidency. Although his regime was repressive, the country made considerable material progress during his years in power. T. was assassinated in 1961.

Truman, Harry S. (1884-1972) 33rd president of the U.S., 1945-1953. Born in Missouri, T. served in World War I and entered Missouri politics after working as a farmer and small businessman. He was a U.S. senator (1935-1944) before being selected to run as Roosevelt's vice-presidential running mate in 1944. He succeeded to the presidency on April 12, 1945, on Roosevelt's death. T. presided over the end of World War II, making the decision to drop the atomic bomb on Japan. During his administration the Marshall Plan and NATO were created. His domestic program, dubbed the Fair Deal, continued the New Deal

Leon Trotsky

policies of Roosevelt. T. won reelection in 1948 against what were thought to be unfavorable odds. Most of his second term was consumed by the Korean War.

Truman Doctrine American plan (1947) for resistance to worldwide Communist expansion. President Harry Truman stated that U.S. policy would be to aid any country seeking to resist communism or the Soviet Union. Congress then passed $400 million in aid to Greece and Turkey.

Truth, Sojourner (c.1797-1883) African-American abolitionist and feminist. Born as a slave named Isabella Baumfree, she escaped (1827) to live with a Quaker family in New York. She changed her name to Sojourner Truth in 1843 and became a powerful orator against slavery. Traveling widely throughout New England and the Midwest, she joined in the crusade for equal rights for women in 1850. T. visited Lincoln in the White House in 1864 and spent her later years trying to improve the conditions of African Americans living in Washington, D.C.

Tserklaes, Jan (1559-1632) Flemish commander of the Spanish and imperial armies during the Thirty Years War. He achieved a decisive victory over the Protestants in 1620. T. succeeded Wallenstein as commander in chief of the imperial armies in 1630, but was defeated by the Swedish King Gustav Adolf.

Tsushima Group of islands between Korea and Japan. There, the Japanese fleet defeated the Russian fleet on May 27-28, 1905, during the Russo-Japanese War.

Tu Duc *See* Saigon, Treaty of.

Tubants Germanic tribe that settled along the lower Rhine and were absorbed by the Franks. The name of the region Twente in the Netherlands is derived from the T.

Tubman, Harriet (c.1821-1913) African-American abolitionist. An escaped slave, she was called the "Moses of her people" because of her numerous trips to the South to lead more than 300 slaves to freedom via the network known as the Underground Railroad. During the Civil War she was a nurse and a scout and

spy for the Union in Florida and the Carolinas.

Tudor Dynasty that ruled England and Scotland between 1485-1603. *See* Henry VIII; Elizabeth I.

Tukhachevsky, Mikhail Nikolayevich (1893-1937) Soviet marshal. He fought in World War I and then with the Bolsheviks in the Russian Civil War. At the start of Stalin purges, T. was executed after a show trial for alleged collaboration with the Germans.

Jan Tserklaes

Tukulti-Ninurta I King of ancient Assyria, c.1238-1197 BC. He added Armenia to his empire and also conquered Babylon. T. was murdered by one of his sons.

Tullius, Servius (6th century BC) Sixth king of Rome and successor to Traquinius Priscus.

Tullus Hostilius (7th century BC) Third king of Rome, 673-642 BC. He conquered Alba Longa and built the Curia Hostilia, which housed the Roman senate.

Tunis *See* Carthage.

Tupac Amaru (c.1742-1781) Indian leader in the uprising against Spain in Peru in 1780. Baptized with the name José Gabriel Condorcanqui, he fought for reforms to improve the lives of the Indians. Claiming to be a descendant of the Incas, he took the name T. when he began his revolt in 1780. He was regarded with reverence by the Indians, but he was captured by the Spaniards and executed. Tupamaros, urban guerillas operating in South America in the 1970s, named themselves after T.

Turenne, Henri de La Tour d'Auvergne, Vicomte de (1611-1675) Marshal of France. The grandson of William of Orange, he served under Frederick Henry and was one of the

Henri de La Tour d'Auvergne
Turenne

most important generals in the army of Louis XIV. T. conquered the Spanish at Dunkirk (1658), which led to the Peace of the Pyrenees. He was victorious in many battles after 1672, including the defeat of the Germans in the war for the Alsace.

Turin, Treaty of (1381) Pact that granted almost all of Dalmatia, which belonged to Venice, to Louis I of Hungary.

Desmond Mpilo Tutu

Turnhout Town in Belgium. It was the site of a battle in which Maurice of Nassau defeated the Spanish in 1597. Two centuries later (1789), the Dutch beat the Austrians under Van Mersch near T.

Tushratta (14th century BC) Last king of the Mitanni Empire. He was an ally of the Egyptian pharaohs Amenhotep III and Amenhotep IV. T. extended his empire by conquering Assyria, but was defeated by the Hittites.

Tutankhamen (14th century BC) King of ancient Egypt (18th Dynasty). His grave was found virtually intact in the Valley of the Kings at Thebes by Howard Carter in 1922.

Wat Tyler

Tutu, Desmond Mpilo (1931-) South African Anglican archbishop. He became the first black archbishop in South Africa. As a prominent opponent of apartheid, T. was arrested a number of times by the regime. He received the Nobel Peace Prize in 1984.

Twelve Years' Armistice Agreement signed (1609) at Antwerp during the Eighty Years' War. It freed the Northern Provinces from Spanish control.

Tyler, John (1790-1862) 10th president of the U.S., 1841-1845. He served as a U.S. representative, governor of Virginia, and U.S. senator. Although a Democrat, he became (1840) the Whig nominee for vice-president on the ticket headed by William Henry Harrison. Harrison was elected but died after only 30 days in office, at which time T. became the first vice-president in U.S. history to succeed to the presidency. He spent almost all of his term vetoing Whig measures and was not renominated in 1844. T. supported Southern secession during the Civil War.

Tyler, Wat (d.1381) Leader of the Peasant's Revolt in England. His demands were granted by Richard III in London on June 14, 1381, but he was mortally injured by the Lord Mayor of London the following day and the revolt was brutally put down.

Tyre *See* Phoenicia.

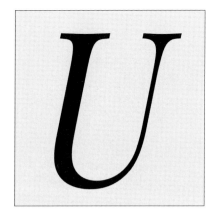

U2 incident International incident involving the U.S and the Soviet Union. On May 1, 1960, an American U2 spy plane was shot down over the Soviet Union and its pilot, Gary Francis Powers, was captured. Khrushchev used the event to scuttle a conference in Paris with President Dwight D. Eisenhower.

Ubii Germanic people who lived east of the Rhine. In 38 BC, they were attacked by the Suevians, after which they were taken by Agrippa to the left bank of the Rhine. The U. were allies of the Romans, and in 50 AD, their capital became Oppidium Ubiorum de Colonia Agrippinensis (the present Cologne).

Ucciali, Treaty of (1889) Treaty between the Ethiopian Emperor Menelik II and Italy, in which Italy acquired part of Ethiopia in exchange for money and weapons. A misunderstanding concerning the treaty led to a conflict and to Ethiopia being declared an Italian protectorate.

Ugandan martyrs Twenty-two African saints who died as martyrs for Christianity during the rule of Mwanga of Baganda in 1885-1886.

Ugarit Ancient city of Syria, on the Mediterranean coast. It flourished in the period from c.1450-1200 BC, when it was part of the Ugarit kingdom. The city was later invaded by the Phoenicians. U. was excavated beginning in 1929.

Uhse, Bodo (1904-1963) German writer. An opponent of the Nazis, he fought in the Spanish Civil War on the republican side. He describes the conflict in his novel, *Leutnant Bertram* (1944).

Uighur Turkic-speaking people who live mainly in western China. They rose to prominence in the 7th century and converted to Islam in the 13th century.

Uilenspiegel, Tijl (Till Eulenspiegel) Legendary German peasant-clown who was first referred to in books at the end of the 15th century. U. was a debaucher who was continually playing practical jokes and up to no good. The character may have been based on a certain Dyl from Lower Saxony, who died in Mölln in Lauenburg in c.1350.

Ukemochi no kami Goddess of food in the Japanese religion of Shinto.

Ulbricht, Walter (1893-1973) East German communist politician. He lived in exile in the Soviet Union from 1933-1945 and fought in the Spanish Civil War. In 1960, he became chairman of the East German State Council and was responsible for building of the Berlin Wall. He was forced to resign in 1971.

Walter Ulbricht

Ullr (Old Norse for "the Magnificent") Great archer and cross-country skier in Old Scandinavian mythology who supports warriors in battle.

Ulm, Battle of (1805) Battle in Germany in which Napoleon defeated an Austrian army and took a large number of prisoners.

Ulrika Eleonora (1688-1741) Sister of the Swedish King Charles XII. After her brother's death, U. had herself proclaimed queen but abdicated in 1720 in favor of her husband Frederik I.

Ulster Northernmost of the historic provinces of Ireland. Large numbers of Scots and Protestant Englishman settled there beginning in the 17th century. In the 19th century many Roman Catholic workers were settled there, but the Protestant population opposed unification with the Irish Free State. The province remains a part of Great Britain but has been torn by sectarian violence.

Tijl Uilenspiegel

Ulster Volunteer Force Right-wing Protestant group founded in 1966 to combat the Irish Republican Army (IRA) through counter-terrorist activities.

Umar I (c.581-644) 2nd caliph. He succeeded Abu Bakr in 634. During his reign, Islam expanded into Persia, Syria, and Egypt. U. laid the administrative foundation for the empire, including a system of fixed taxes. He was murdered by a Persian slave.

Umayyads Dynasty of caliphs that ruled Arabia from 661-750, first with Baghdad and later with Damascus as their capital. A grandson of the last Umayyad caliph of Damascus, Abd ar-Rahman, founded the Muslim realm of Cordoba in Spain in 756. The U. built a brilliant civilization that reached its peak under Abd ar-Rahman III.

Umberto I (1844-1900) King of Italy, 1878-1900. A soldier by training, he was increasingly influenced by conservative advisers who supported the Triple Alliance. U. was assassinated in Monza and was succeeded by his son, Victor Emmanuel III.

Umberto I

Umbria Region of central Italy. It was conquered by the Romans in the 4th century BC. The Umbrians also inhabited Etruria but were expelled from that area.

Unas (24th century BC) Last king of the 5th Dynasty of the Egyptian Old Kingdom. He is remembered for the texts, which were supposed to protect him in the afterlife, that are engraved on his pyramid.

Uncle Sam Name for the U.S. government. The term was first used in the War of 1812. Its origin is uncertain. The character of U. is represented as a tall, thin man with a white goatee and top hat. His trousers and top hat are in the colors of the American flag.

Underground Railroad Network of abolitionists who helped slaves escape from the South in the years before the Civil War and travel north to Canada.

Undine Supernatural being referred to in German literature. She was a water spirit with the appearance of a beautiful woman but could only get a soul by marrying a mortal.

Unetice culture Central European Bronze Age culture (c. 2100-1700 BC), named after a burial ground near U. Characteristics of the U. are decorated daggers and earrings made from gold thread.

Ungern-Sternberg, Roman Fyodorovitch (1885-1921) Russian Cossack general. Nicknamed the "Mad Baron," he fought against the Bolsheviks after 1917. Following his victory at Oerga (1921), he ordered the slaughter of the defenders. U. was eventually captured and executed by the Bolsheviks.

United Irishmen, Society of Irish political organization founded in 1791. It fought for Irish independence with the assistance of French revolutionaries. An uprising in 1798 did not, however, have sufficient French support and was put down ruthlessly.

United Nations International organization dedicated to the peaceful resolution of world conflict. It was founded in 1945 in the wake of World War II and was the successor organization of the League of Nations.

Universal Declaration of Human Rights Declaration of the most important fundamental human rights, ratified by the United Nations in Paris in 1948.

Upanishads Scriptures of Hinduism. They form the last section of the literature of the Veda and were composed c.900 BC. Of the 112 U., about 13 date from the Vedic period. The remainder are sectarian works. The U.

Uncle Sam

are not a systematic compilation but are are derived from a variety of sources. They contain allegorical information about diverse subjects, including death and rebirth.

Ur Ancient city of Sumer, in Mesopotamia. The first traces of civilization dating from c.2500 BC were unearthed at U. by the British archaeologist C. Leonard Woolley beginning in 1922.

Urabi Pasha (1938-1911) Egyptian nationalist officer. He came into conflict with the British over the Suez Canal and was defeated by them in a battle at Tell al-Kabir. U. was exiled to Ceylon until 1901.

Urartians People of the ancient kingdom of Armenia, centered in eastern Turkey. Urartu reached its peak in the 8th century BC, at which time its power extended as far as the Black and Caspian seas. The kingdom was plundered (c.714 BC) and subdued by the Assyrian King Sargon II.

Understanding the Universe

Stars and planets have
always puzzled people, and attempts
to understand the night sky are as old
as mankind itself. This fascination
resulted in many fanciful stories but
also eventually in space travel.

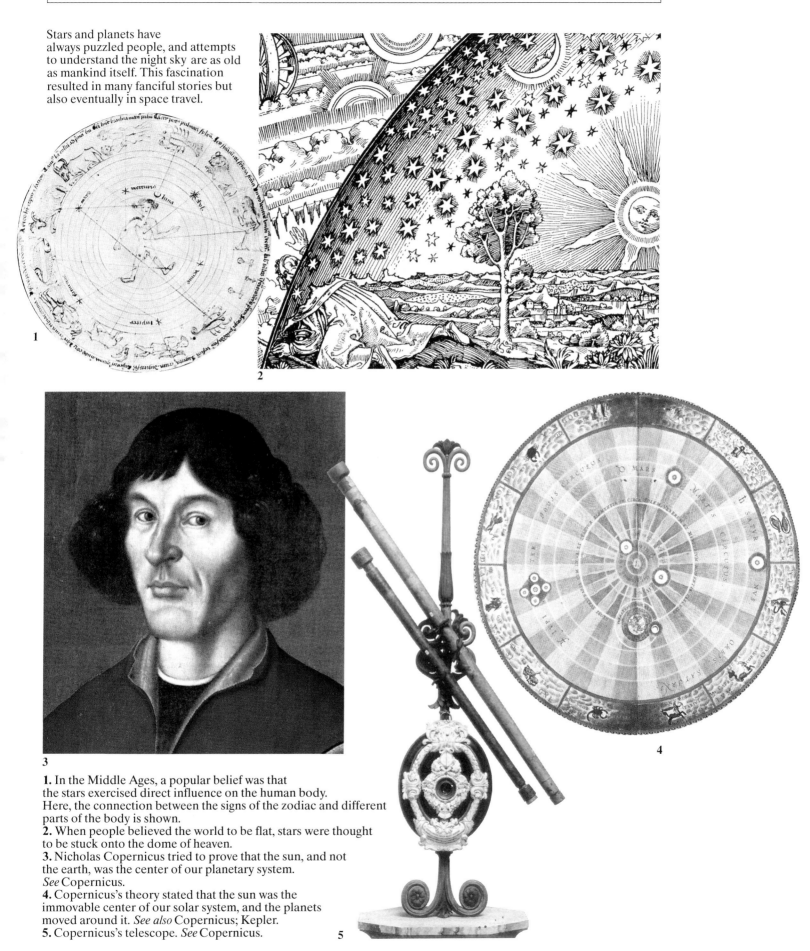

1. In the Middle Ages, a popular belief was that
the stars exercised direct influence on the human body.
Here, the connection between the signs of the zodiac and different
parts of the body is shown.
2. When people believed the world to be flat, stars were thought
to be stuck onto the dome of heaven.
3. Nicholas Copernicus tried to prove that the sun, and not
the earth, was the center of our planetary system.
See Copernicus.
4. Copernicus's theory stated that the sun was the
immovable center of our solar system, and the planets
moved around it. *See also* Copernicus; Kepler.
5. Copernicus's telescope. *See* Copernicus.

379

Universities in Early Europe

In the early Middle Ages, schools at cathedrals or monasteries were the only places a person could get a good education. With the growth of cities in the 13th century, a new institution developed: the university.

1. Abélard (1079-1142) was one of the great teachers in Paris. His love for Héloise ruined his career. *See* Abélard.
2. A picture used in the study of medicine.
3. Before the invention of printing, the only way to make textbooks available was to copy them by hand.
4. The works of Aristotle were the basis of much education in the Middle Ages and Renaissance. For a long time, they were available only in Arabic. *See* Aristotle.
5. A group of Parisian students, depicted on a relief at the Notre-Dame Cathedral in Paris.
6. European universities established in the Middle Ages before 1500. The data refer to the year of foundation.

Urban II

Urban II (c.1042-1099) Pope, 1088-1099. A Frenchman born Odo of Lagery, he was barred from Rome until the antipope was expelled in 1093. U. called numerous councils and preached the First Crusade.

Urban V (1310-1370) Pope, 1362-1370. A Provençal born Guillaume de Grimoard, he tried in vain to have the papal seat moved back to Rome from Avignon. U. was a patron of the arts who founded universities in Cracow and Vienna.

Urban VI (c.1318-1389) Pope, 1378-1389. Born Bartolomeo Prignano, he alienated the cardinals who elected him by his tyrannical behavior. They, in turn, elected an antipope, Clement VII, whose choice created the Great Schism. U. had five cardinals murdered and was probably insane. His election, however, is considered canonical.

Urban VIII (1568-1644) Pope, 1623-1644. Born Maffeo Barberini, he reigned during the Thirty Years War in Europe. U. tried unsuccessfully to unite the Catholic monarchs but is known for his liturgical reforms and for his condemnation (and later pardoning) of Galileo.

Urbi et Orbi (Latin for "to the city and to the world") Papal blessing, usually given to the crowds in St. Peter's square at Christmas and Easter.

Uriburu, José Félix (1868-1932) Argentine military leader. He came to power in 1930 following a coup d'état.

Urnammu (21st century BC) King of the ancient city of Ur. He was the founder of the third Ur dynasty and ruler of Sumeria and Akkad. U. is remembered for his code of laws, which preceded Hammurabi's by some 300 years.

Urquiza, Justo José de (1801-1870) Argentine general. He was victorious over the tyrant Juan Manuel de Rosas at Monte Caseros and became president of the Argentine confederation (1854-1860). Troops from Buenos Aires attempted to oust him, and he suffered a defeat at Pavón in 1861, after which he retired to his home province. He was assassinated in 1870.

Urraca (c.1078-1126) Queen of Leon and Castile, 1109-1126. In 1109 she married Alfonso I of Aragón, but the marriage was marred by warfare caused by Alfonso's attempts to confiscate U.'s lands. The marriage was annulled in 1114, and U. recovered most of her lands with the help of her son by her first marriage. That son succeeded her as Alfonso VII.

Uruk (Erech) Ancient city of Sumer, in Mesopotamia. A thriving city of southern Mesopotamia and a major religious center, U. was the home of Gilgamesh and is mentioned in the Bible.

Uskoks Slavic people who, in the 15th century, were driven out of Bosnia by the Turks. With Austrian support, they

Urban VIII

waged war against Venice, which grew into a full-scale war between Austria and Venice (1615).

U Thant (1909-1974) Burmese statesman. Between 1957 and 1961 he was Burma's United Nations representative, and between 1962-1971 he served as UN secretary general.

Uthman (c.574-656) 3rd caliph, 644-656. A son-in-law of Muhammad, he was selected caliph after the murder of Umar. U. recognized only one official version of the Koran and destroyed all other versions. He was murdered by a mob in Medina in 656.

Utica Ancient city in North Africa (founded c.8th-7th century BC). The most important city after Carthage, U. sided with Rome in the Third Punic War and became the capital of the Roman province of Africa after the fall of Carthage.

Utrecht, Peace of (1713) Agreement that ended the War of the Spanish Succession. Portugal, Prussia, and Savoy agreed to peace, but Charles VI fought on until 1714. As a result of the treaty, Philip of Anjou remained King of Spain but had to surrender significant territories. The southern Low Countries came under the rule of the Hapsburgs. The Peace of U., in effect, put an end to French expansion and signaled the rise of the British empire.

Utrecht, Union of (1579) Alliance between Holland, Zeeland, Utrecht and the main Brabant and Flemish cities (excluding Brussels). Its purpose was to continue the conflict against Philip II of Spain. Groningen, Drenthe, and Friesland joined at a later date.

Utu *See* Shamash.

Uxmal Ancient city of Mexico, in the Yucatan. It flourished between 600-900 and was a major center of Mayan civilization. The site today has numerous points of architectural interest, including the great pyramid and the governor's palace.

Uzbeks Turkic-speaking people, named after Uzbek (14th century), who founded a realm to the east of the Caspian sea. Although he was a khan of the Golden Horde, Uzbek was tolerant of Western missionaries.

The United Nations

The United Nations (UN) organization was founded by the victorious Allied powers in 1945, shortly after the end of World War II. Its main purpose is to maintain peace in the world. Initially the UN had 51 members; today it has 185 members. Since its foundation, the UN has intervened many times to resolve or at least bring about a truce in many conflicts, and has given humanitarian aid to the victims of wars and disasters.

1

2

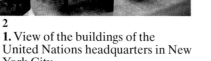

3

1. View of the buildings of the United Nations headquarters in New York City.
2. The Security Council of the UN at work discussing a problem.
3. Boutros Boutros-Ghali, the present UN secretary-general.
4. UN peacekeeping troops in action in Bosnia.

4

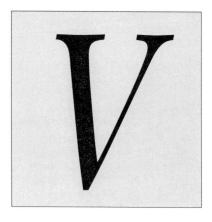

Vaca, Alvar Nuñez Cabeza de (c.1490-1557) Spanish explorer. He and his party wandered after a shipwreck for eight years through the American Southwest and reported their findings when they returned to Mexico.

Vakataka Indian dynasty, founded by Vindhyasakti (3rd century). The V. were allies of the Gupta dynasty and were famous as patrons of the arts and sciences. Their last prince was Prthvisena.

Valdés, Francisco (d.1580) Spanish soldier. He fought in the Schmalkaldic War and came to the Netherlands with Alva. V. led the siege of Leiden (1573-1574) and took part in the siege of Maastricht (1579).

Valdivia, Pedro de (c.1500-1554) Spanish conquistador. In 1540, he left Pizarro to conquer Chile, of which he became governor. He founded Santiago and numerous other settlements on his march south. V. was killed by Indians.

Valens, Flavius (c.328-378) Roman emperor of the East, 364-378. He fought against the Parthians and the Visigoths, but was defeated and killed in a battle against the latter at Adrianople.

Valentinian I (321-375) Roman emperor of the West, 364-375. He was chosen by the army as successor to Jovian. V. defended the empire's borders by building fortifications. He was a supporter of education and, although a Christian himself, was tolerant of pagans.

Valentinian III (419-455) Roman emperor of the West, 425-455. During his reign, large parts of the empire were lost to the Vandals and the Saxons. Real power was in the hands of his general, Aetius, but V. murdered him in 454 and was himself assassinated the following year.

Valera, Eamon de (1882-1975) Irish statesman. Born in the U.S., he moved to Ireland as a child. From 1904, V. was member of the nationalist movement. Strongly anti-British throughout his career, he took part in the Easter Uprising (1916), for which he was sentenced to death, but was pardoned because he was a U.S. citizen. He was prime minister many times between 1932-1959. During World War II he kept Ireland neutral, refusing to allow the British to use southern Irish ports. V. became president of the Irish Republic in 1959 and held that office until 1973.

Valerian (d.260) Roman emperor, 253-260. V. reigned with his son Gallien, whom he appointed coregent. V. persecuted the Christians and fought against the Goths and Persians. He was captured by the latter and died in captivity.

Valerian

Valerius, Marcus Messalla Corvin (64 BC-8 AD) Roman general. he fought in the Battle at Philippi on the side of Brutus and Cassius. He later served Octavian at the battle at Actium.

Valhalla In Norse mythology, Odin's hall for slain heroes. The dead warriors were brought to V. by the Valkyries.

Valley Forge (Pennsylvania) Site of Washington's winter encampment (1777-1778) of the Continental army during the American Revolution. The extreme hardship suffered by the troops became a legend of heroism and patriotism.

Valley of the Tombs Site in Egypt, on the west bank of the Nile River opposite Karnak. It is famous for the rock tombs of the kings of the 18th-20th dynasties.

Valmy Village in northeastern France. It was the site of the first important engagement (1792) of the French Revolutionary Wars. The battle, between French and Prussian forces, revealed the superiority of French artillery.

Valois French royal house that ruled from 1328 to 1589. They were a branch of the Capetian dynasty.

Van Buren, Martin (1782-1862) 8th president of the U.S. 1837-1841. He was a leader of the Democratic Party in New York State, where he was elected governor in 1828. A loyal supporter of Andrew Jackson, he served as secretary of state (1829-1831) and as vice-president (1833-1837). V. was elected president in 1836, defeating the Whig candidate William Henry Harrison. His presidency was clouded by economic depression, and he lost the 1840 election to Harrison. V., who always strongly opposed to the extension of slavery, was nominated for president in 1848 on the Free-Soil Party ticket but lost.

Van Gogh, Vincent (1853-1890) Dutch postimpressionist painter. He spent much of his life in Paris and Arles. Most of his works are strongly colored, highly personal evocations of nature (*Starry Night*, 1889) or moody depictions of human society (*Night Café*, 1888). During his life, he sold only one painting. Today, however, he is perhaps one of the most widely known painters. V. was a passionate artist and a severely troubled personality. He committed suicide at 37.

Vandals Germanic tribe. In the fifth century BC, they migrated to the Oder region from Jutland. In the early 400s, the V. moved into Gaul, where the Franks refused to allow them to stay, and then over the Pyrenees into Spain. Shortly thereafter, they crossed to North Africa, where they founded a pirate state on the old site of Carthage. The V. plundered Rome in 455. In 533, they were defeated overwhelmingly by an army under Belisarius, who was working for the Byzantine emperor. With this defeat, the V. ceased to exist as a nation.

Vandegrift, Alexander Archer (1887-1973) American naval officer. In World War II, he was the first to lead a large-scale offensive against the Japanese at Guadalcanal (1942).

Vanderbilt, Cornelius (1794-1877) American railroad magnate. Known as "Commodore Vanderbilt," he made a fortune in shipping before gaining control of the New York Central Railroad. V. expanded his railroad empire in the 1870s and connected Chicago and New York by rail.

Vanir In Norse mythology, the gods of riches and fertility.

Varanasi (Benares) City in India. It is the holiest city of the Hindus, who call in Kasi. Located on the Ganges River, V. was conquered by the Afghans, who surrendered it to the British in 1776. Along the banks of the river are ghats, or flights of steps, that Hindus descend in order to bathe in the sacred river.

Vargas, Getúlio (1883-1954) Brazilian statesman, president of Brazil, 1930-1945, 1951-1954. He exercised dictatorial control but was popular with the masses. In 1945 the military overthrew V. He was elected president again in 1950 and took office the following year. In 1954, under threat of impeachment, he resigned and committed suicide.

Vargas, Juan de (16th century) Spanish lawyer. V. came to the Netherlands with Alva, where he became one of the most infamous members of the Council of Troubles.

Varna City in Bulgaria. It was the site of a battle (1644) in which the Turks under Murad II defeated a Crusader army sent by Pope Eugene IV.

Varus (d.9 AD) Roman general. He was proconsul of Africa and governor of Syria. In 9 AD, he commanded three legions that were destroyed by Arminius in the Teutoburg Forest in Germany. V. committed suicide as a result of the defeat.

Vasa Dynasty that ruled Sweden from 1523-1818 and Poland from 1587-1668. In Poland they were known as the Waza dynasty.

Vasari, Giorgio (1511-1574) Italian

Getúlio Vargas

architect, writer, and painter. He built the Uffizi in Florence (from 1560). V. is also remembered for an amusing book he wrote about Italian artists of the Renaissance.

Giorgio Vasari

Vassal In feudalism, someone who received a fief from his master, usually land, in exchange for services.

Vassy massacre (1562) Massacre of unarmed Huguenots by the duke of Guise, which signaled the start of the French Religious Wars.

Vasubandhu (4th century) Indian Buddhist philosopher. He believed that everything exists in consciousness, and that there is no objective reality. A few of his philosophic works in Sanskrit have survived.

Vatican Council, First (1869-1870) 20th ecumenical council of the Roman Catholic Church. Summoned by Pope Pius IX, it enunciated the doctrine of papal infallibility.

Vatican Council, Second (1962-1965) 21st ecumenical council of the Roman Catholic Church. Popularly called Vatican II, it was summoned by Pope John XXIII and continued under his successor, Pope Paul VI. Its purpose was the spiritual renewal of the church and a reconsideration of its role in the modern world. One of V.'s major reforms was the vernacularization of the liturgy.

Vatin, Publius (1st century BC) Roman tribune. As a tribune of the people, he helped form of the first triumvirate (60 BC). In 54 BC, he was defended by Cicero against a bribery charge. According to tradition, V. had no moral values.

Vauban, Sébastien la Prestre de (1633-1707) French fortress builder. He built some 30 forts, including the one at Metz.

Veda (Sanskrit for "knowledge") Oldest scriptures (c.1500-1200 BC) of Hinduism. They form the basis of Hindu philosophy and theology.

Veer, Gerrit de (1570-1598) Dutch navigator. He accompanied Heemskerck and Barentz on journeys to the north.

Veii Etruscan city. A threat to the ascension of Rome, V. was captured by the Roman Camillus in 396 BC after a ten year siege.

Velasquez, Diego (1460-1523) Spanish conquistador. He accompanied Columbus on his second voyage (1493) to America. V. later became governor of Cuba and founded Havana.

Veldeke, Heynric van (12th century) Dutch poet. He was a prominent lyrical poet who had an influence on both German and Dutch literature.

Vendée uprisings Peasant uprisings against the French Revolution that took place in the Vendée from 1793-1796. Later uprisings in the Vendée (1815, 1832) were smaller in scope and had royalist backings.

Vendôme, Louis Joseph de Bourbon, duke of (1654-1712) Marshal of France. He served Louis XIV during the War of the Spanish Succession and led the campaign in the southern Low Countries. In 1708, he lost the battle of Oudenarde against Marlborough and Eugene of Savoy.

Venizelos, Eleutherios (1864-1936) Greek statesman. Born in Crete, he became premier for the first time in 1910 and led Greece through the Balkan Wars. He was a strong supporter of the Allied cause in World War I against the pro-German king, Constantine I. V. fought to make Greece a republic into the 1920s, when Constantine finally abdicated. Fearing a restoration of the monarchy, he attempted an uprising in 1935, which failed. V. fled to France, where he died.

Ventris, Michael George Francis (1922-1956) British linguist. In 1952, he deciphered Linear B, which was a Mycenaean script. His theory, now accepted by scholars, was that Linear B was an archaic form of Greek.

Venus *See* Aphrodite.

Venus

Vercellae City in Italy, in the Po valley. The Cimbri were defeated at V. (101 BC) by the Romans under Marius.

Vercingetorix (d.46 BC) King of the Arveni in Gaul and leader of the Gallic uprising against Roman rule. After initial successes, V. was taken prisoner by Caesar in Alesia and killed after Caesar's triumphal march into Rome.

Giuseppe Verdi

Verdi, Giuseppe (1813-1901) Italian composer. He is the foremost composer of Italian opera. V.'s works are one of the mainstays of opera repertory throughout the world. Among the most popular are *Rigoletto* (1851), *Il Trovatore* (1853), and *La Traviata* (1853), and the operas of his later years, including *Aïda* (1871), *Otello* (1887), and *Falstaff* (1893). He also composed a requiem (1874) and several sacred compositions.

Verdugo, Francisco (1537-1595) Spanish general. He took part in the siege of Haarlem (1573). In 1581, he conquered Steenwijk and Zutphen for the Spanish, but was eventually beaten by Maurice of Nassau, who captured Groningen (1594).

Verdun Town in France. The site of a major fortification, V. was the location of the longest and bloodiest battle (1916) of World War I. Some 700,000 French and German soldiers died in the battle of attrition.

Verdun, Treaty of (843) Agreement that divided Charlemagne's kingdom between his three grandsons, the sons of Louis the Pious.

Vergil (70 BC-19 BC) Roman poet. His *Aeneid*, a national epic relating the adventures of Aeneas, is one of the greatest long poems in history. V. is the dominant figure in Latin literature,

and his influence continued through the Middle Ages up to Dante, who acknowledged V.'s greatness.

Verhuell, Carel (1764-1845) Dutch admiral. He took part in the battle of Doggerbank and was naval minister under Louis Napoleon from 1806-1810. V. remained faithful to Napoleon after 1813. His name appears on the Arc de Triomphe in Paris.

Verne, Jules (1828-1905) French writer. He is the creator of the modern science fiction genre. Well-known works include *Twenty Thousand Leagues Under the Sea* (1870) and *Around the World in 80 Days* (1873). V. anticipated with remarkable accuracy many of the scientific and technological advances made in the 20th century.

Verres, Gaius Cornelius (c.115-43 BC) Roman governor. In 80 BC, he was a legate in Asia Minor where he was involved in extortion. V. was also involved in criminal activities while governor of Sicily (73-71) and was eventually exiled to Massilia, where he was killed on the orders of Marc Antony.

Versailles, Treaty of (1871) Agreement that ended the Franco-Prussian War.

Versailles, Treaty of (1919) Agreement that ended World War I.

Verus, Lucius Aurelius (136-161) Roman emperor. In 138, he was adopted by Antoninius Pius and was chosen emperor by his son and successor, Marcus Aurelius in 161. He died during a campaign against the Marcomanni.

Vervins, Peace of (1598) Treaty between Philip II of Spain and Henry IV of France. It ended the French Wars of Religion by obliging Philip to withdraw his troops from France.

Jules Verne

Verwoerd, Hendrik Frensch (1901-1966) South African politician. As prime minister from 1958, he was a supporter of total apartheid. He was assassinated in 1966.

Vespasian (9-79 AD) Roman emperor, 69-79 AD. In 67, he was legate in Palestine, where he subdued the Jewish uprising. In 69, V. was proclaimed emperor by the legions in Alexandria and Judea. He restored the state's finances and brought about a period of prosperity and building, including the construction of the Colosseum in Rome. V. left his son Titus to prosecute the war against the Jews. He destroyed Jerusalem and returned to Rome in triumph. Titus succeeded V. as emperor.

Vespasian

Vespucci, Amerigo (1454-1512) Florentine navigator and merchant.

Vergil

Between 1499-1502, V. made several journeys on behalf of Spain and Portugal to America, which is named after him.

Amerigo Vespucci

Vestal Virgins Servants in a small temple in Rome who tended the flame burning in honor of Vesta, the goddess of the home and family life. They were chosen when they were children and served 30 years, during which time they were forbidden to marry. The V. had great influence in Rome.

Via Dolorosa Road that Jesus is said to have taken from the court of Pilate in Jerusalem to Golgotha, where he was crucified.

Vichy government Pro-German puppet government (1940-1944) in France during World War II. Its capital was Vichy.

Victor Amadeus I (1587-1637) Duke of Savoy. He succeeded his father Charles Emanuel and married the daughter of Henry V of France.

Victor Amadeus III (1726-1796) King of Sardinia, 1773-1796. He suc-

ceeded his father Charles Emmanuel III. He declared war on France in 1792, but four years later Bonaparte forced him to accept an armistice.

Victor Emmanuel II (1820-1878). King of Sardinia, 1849-1861, and first king of a united Italy, 1861-1878. He consolidated the Italian nation on the peninsula of Italy throughout his reign, including the acquisition of the papal states in 1870. In 1871 he made Rome the capital of Italy.

Victor Emmanuel III (1869-1947) King of Italy, 1900-1946, the son and successor of Umberto I. He supported Italy's joining the Allies in World War I, but after the war, he was unable to control in the internal chaos within Italy. V. asked Mussolini (1922) to form a government, and under fascism, the king's influence declined. V. opposed Italian participation World War II as a German ally. In 1943, he had Mussolini arrested and appointed Badoglio prime minister. Unpopular because of his long association with Mussolini, V. abdicated (1946) in favor of his son, Umberto II, who reigned briefly until the republic was declared. V. died in exile in Egypt.

Victoria (1819-1901) Queen of Great Britain and Ireland, 1837-1901, and Empress of India,1876-1901. She was the daughter of the Duke of Kent, a brother of George IV, and the niece of William IV, her predecessor. V. married her cousin Albert of Saxe-Coburg-Gotha in 1840 and had a large family, many of whose members

Victoria, Queen of Great Britain and Ireland

Victor Emmanuel II

joined other European royal families through marriage. V. presided over Great Britain at the height of its industrial and imperial power. Although not imaginative, she was diligent and highly moral, and her reign restored the prestige to the crown that had been lost under the dissolute rule of her uncles. V. reigned longer than any British monarch (64 years) and gave her name to an age.

Victoria (1840-1901) Empress of Germany, 1888. The oldest daughter of Queen Victoria of England, she married (1858) the Prussian crown prince Frederick William. In 1888, she became Empress of Germany and queen of Prussia, but her husband, Emperor Frederick III, died after only three months on the throne. V.'s son was Emperor William II.

Videla, Jorge Rafaél (1925-) Argentine military officer. Following a coup d'état, he became head of a military junta (1976). After the collapse of the military in the wake of the Falklands War, V. and others were tried for their role in the human rights violations committed after the coup. He was condemned to life imprisonment but received a pardon in 1990.

Vidocq, Eugène François (1775-1857) French chief of police. After an early life of crime, he was appointed (1809) to the Paris police force. In the fight against crime, he used former criminals as spies. V. wrote a multi-volume memoir of his experiences.

Vienna, Congress of (1814-1815) International conference called to remake Europe after the downfall of Napoleon. It was presided over by Metternich, the chief Austrian negotiator. The Congress of V. represented an effort to deal with Europe's affairs as a whole. Although the territorial settlements ultimately did not last, the Congress was a significant step in European cooperation.

Vienna, Treaty of (1689) Agreement concluded against France between the Holy Roman Emperor, England, the States General, Spain, Savoy, and several German principalities. Its objective was to restore the treaties of Münster and the Pyrenees and to arrange the Spanish succession.

Vienna, Treaty of *See* Lombardy-Venetian Kingdom.

Vienne, Council of (1311-1312) 15th ecumenical council of the Roman Catholic Church. It was summoned by Pope Clement V at the behest of the French king, Philip IV, who used the forum to dissolve the Knights Templar.

Viet Cong Communist insurgents in South Vietnam. They were first supported and then directed by North Vietnam.

Viet Minh Communist-led nationalist coalition in Vietnam that opposed the French and the Japanese in Indochina. Founded by Ho Chi Minh in

Jorge Rafaél Videla

1941, it was absorbed (1951) into the Communist Party of North Vietnam.

Vietnam War (1955-1975) War fought primarily in South Vietnam between that country's government, backed by the U.S., and communist insurgents supported and directed by North Vietnam. American involvement increased after the French defeat in 1954. Under Presidents Kennedy and Johnson, American military support rose eventually to some 540,000 men. U.S. policy changed, however, after the Tet offensive (1968), and under President Nixon, American troops were gradually withdrawn (1973). Two years later, the North Vietnamese conquered the south and incorporated it into a greater Vietnam. The Vietnam War was the only conflict the U.S. ever lost.

Vigos Harbor town on western coast of Spain. On October 23, 1702, an English-Dutch fleet destroyed a Franco-Spanish fleet off V.

Vikings Scandinavian warriors who raided the coasts of Europe and the British Isles from the 9th-11th centuries. They controlled the sea routes and ventured as far as Greenland and North America. The V., also called Norsemen, settled permanently in France and gave their name to the French area of Normandy. Under Knut the Great (1016-1035), Denmark and England were temporarily united. The Swedish V. traveled toward Eastern Europe and founded the kingdom that included Novgorod and Kiev, which created the foundations of the Russian czarist empire. In c.1000 most V. were converted to Christianity.

Villa, Francisco (Pancho Villa) (1877-1923) Mexican revolutionary. He was a gang leader and a revolutionary who fought against Porfirio Diaz and Huerta. In 1920 he surrendered in exchange for a hacienda, where he was later murdered. V. was a folk hero in northern Mexico, where he was considered a kind of Robin Hood.

Villafranca, Treaty of (1859) Agreement after the battle of Solferino between Napoleon III and the Austrian emperor Francis Joseph.

Villanovan culture Early Iron Age culture (c.1100-700 BC) in Italy. The name is derived from the town of Vil-

lanova, near Bologna, where the excavations were made in the mid-1850s. The V. were predecessors of the Etruscans.

Villars, Claude Louis Hector, Duke of (1653-1734) Marshal of France. He fought in the War of the Spanish Succession. At Malplaquet, he fought against Eugene of Savoy and Marlborough (1709) and was defeated. In 1714, he held talks with Eugene and negotiated the Peace of Rastatt.

Claude Louis Hector Villars

Villèle, Jean Baptiste Séraphin Joseph, Count of (1773-1854) French statesman. As prime minister (1822-1828), he stabilized the country's finances but led a reactionary regime that suppressed freedom of the press and favored ultra-royalist causes. He was defeated in elections in 1828 and resigned.

Villeroi, François de Neufville, Duke of (1644-1730) Marshal of France.

The Vikings

The Vikings, also known as the Norsemen, were Scandinavian sea warriors. For about 200 years, starting in the 9th century, they raided the coasts of Britain and continental Europe and were greatly feared. Some Vikings settled in the places they raided. They also sailed west, to Greenland and North America. *See* Leif Ericson; Vikings.

1

2

3

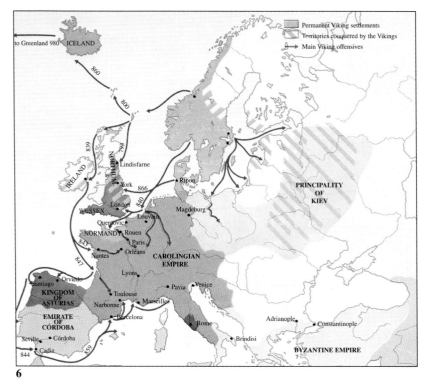

4

5

1. A Viking stone inscribed with runes.
2. A reconstruction of a Viking ship, a so-called drakar.
3. A photograph of the remains of a Viking cemetary in Iceland.
4. A Viking helmet.
5. A set of chess pieces, made by Vikings who settled on the Orkney Islands.
6. A map of the routes the Vikings followed in their European raids.

Permanent Viking settlements
Territories conquered by the Vikings
Main Viking offensives

to Greenland 980 ICELAND
860
800
IRELAND 839
NORTHUMBRIA 794
Lindisfarne
York 866
Ripon
London 840
WESSEX
Quentovic Louvain Magdeburg
NORMANDY Rouen
843 Paris
Nantes Orleans
847 CAROLINGIAN
Lyons EMPIRE
Santiago Orviedo
KINGDOM OF ASTURIAS Pavia Venice
Toulouse
EMIRATE OF CÓRDOBA Narbonne Marseilles
Barcelona Rome
Seville Córdoba
Cadiz 859
844

PRINCIPALITY OF KIEV

Adrianople Constantinople

Brindisi

BYZANTINE EMPIRE

6

French general. He fought with little success during the Spanish War of Succession. In 1706, he suffered a great defeat at the hands of Marlborough at Ramillies but retained Louis XIV's favor. In the latter part of his life he fell out of royal favor and was exiled from court.

Villon, François (1431-c.1463) French medieval poet, one of the early great poets of France. V. was a vagabond and criminal in his early life, and killed a man in 1455. Some of his early works are ballads composed in thieves' jargon. Although he wrote in a medieval form of verse, the content of V.'s poems is intensely personal and emotional. His works were rediscovered in the 19th century, with translations done by Swinburne and Rossetti.

François Villon

Vimeiro Battle site in Portugal. The French armies under Junot were defeated (1808) by the English under Wellesley (the later Duke of Wellington) at V.

Viminale One of the seven hills on which Rome is built.

Leonardo da Vinci

Vinci, Leonardo da (1452-1519) Italian painter, scientist, sculptor, and architect. His versatility and power make him the supreme Renaissance genius. Between 1482-1499, Leonardo resided at the court of Sforza in Milan. After the occupation of Milan by the French (1499), he went to Mantua and Venice and settled in Florence until 1506, where he designed a mural in the Palazzo Vecchio. In 1512, he served Giuliano de Medici, a brother of Pope Leo X. Leonardo had one of the most brilliant human minds. As well as many drawings and sculptures, he studied, among other things, the human body, hydraulics, and optics, and designed such diverse machines as dredgers and aircraft. His most famous paintings include *Last Supper* and the celebrated *Mona Lisa.*

Viracocha Inca god of creation.

Viriathus (d.139 BC) Leader of the Lusitani. From 147-139 BC, he successfully fought against the Romans. He was persuaded to make peace, but in 139 the Romans renewed the war

and bribed emissaries of V. to kill him. With his death, Lusitani resistance collapsed.

Vishnu One of the main gods of Hinduism and protector of the world.

Vitellius, Aulus (15-69 AD) Roman emperor, 69. He was proclaimed emperor by the legions in Lower Germany. His generals defeated his rival, Otho, in northern Italy, but V. was defeated by Vespasian and was murdered in Rome.

Vitoria City in Spain. In 1813, at V., the French under Joseph Bonaparte were completely routed by Wellington in the decisive battle of the Peninsular War against the French.

Vittorio Veneto Town in northern Italy. It was the site of the Italian victory (1918) in World War I over the Austrians, leading to the Austrian surrender.

Vivaldi, Antonio (1678-1741) Italian composer. He was a master of baroque

Vishnu

violin music and the concerto grosso. Although he wrote 46 operas, he is remembered mainly for his instrumental music, which included sonatas, concerto grossos, and concertos for oboe, flute, and violin. One of his most famous pieces is *The Four Seasons*.

Antonio Vivaldi

Vizier Title used by the Umayyad as an alternative for the title *katib* (writer). Under the Ottoman sultans, the V. was the acting representative of the sultan.

Vladimir I (c.956-1015) Grand Duke of Kiev, 908-1015. In c.987, he renounced paganism and made Greek Orthodox Christianity the religion of his people. He is an Orthodox saint.

Vladimir II (1053-1125) Grand Duke of Kiev, 1113-1125. During his reign, he enacted social legislation and increased the power and territories of his realm.

Vladislav IV (Ladislaus IV) (1595-1648) King of Poland, 1632-1648. The son of the Swedish king Sigismund III, he fought in the Polish-Russian wars (1617-1618, 1632-1634). V. died in 1648 during a campaign against insurgent Cossacks.

Vlassov, Andrei (1900-1946) Soviet general. During World War II, he was taken prisoner by the Germans, who appointed him leader of several divisions of Russian prisoners of war who were forced to fight on the German side from 1944. After the war, V. was executed for high treason in the Soviet Union.

Vo Nguyen Giap (1909-) Vietnamese general. During World War II, he fought against the Japanese and the French. In 1954, Giap won the decisive victory against the French at Dienbienphu that ended the French colonial empire. In the Vietnam War, Giap was the major strategist of the campaign against the South Vietnamese and Americans.

Vojvoda Title of a Slavic army leader or duke. In Poland and Russia, V. was the title given to regional governors.

Vologases I (1st century AD) Parthian king from 54-63 AD. He fought against the Roman armies under Corbulo but capitulated to Nero in 66 AD.

Vologases IV (1st century AD) Parthian king. He fought against Septimus Severus who conquered areas of his kingdom.

Volsci People who settled in the Latium region of Italy c.500 BC. They were not conquered by the Romans until 304 BC.

Voltaire, François Marie Arouet de (1694-1778) French philosopher, writer, and historian. He was one of the great geniuses of the Enlightenment. Between 1750-1753, V. resided at the court of Frederick the Great. In his writings, he attacked the Roman Catholic Church and the French court and advocated a humanitarian and tolerant government. In 1791, during the French Revolution, he was reburied in the Panthéon in Paris.

Volunteer Corps Paramilitary organizations that were established in Germany immediately after World War I. They consisted mainly of former soldiers and were opposed to the Weimar Republic. Many members of the V. later became members of the SA.

Voortrekkers Participants in the Great Trek in South Africa, which started in 1838.

Voroshilov, Kliment Yefremovich (1881-1969) Soviet marshal and politician. He fought in the Russian Civil War and was the People's commissar of defense from 1925-1940. He was involved in purges within the army and became vice-president in 1940. V. was chairman of the Supreme Soviet from 1953-1960. Because of his connection with Stalin, he lost his party posts under Khrushchev.

Vorster, Balthazar Johannes (1915-1983) South African politician. He became prime minister after the death of Verwoerd in 1966. V. was infamous for his policy of relocating blacks into homelands. He served also as president of South Africa but had to resign in 1979 because of a financial scandal.

Vrindaban Town in India. It is a popular pilgrim site for Hindus because of its association with the god Krishna. The Red Temple (1590) is situated in V.

Vulcanus *See* Hephaistos.

Vulgate Oldest extant version of the whole Bible. It is the official Latin version of the Catholic Church.

V-rockets German drone rockets fired on during World War II. They were the prototypes of modern missiles. Some 3,000 were fired against England, most after 1944.

François Marie Arouet de Voltaire

Waardgelders Mercenary troops recruited mainly by the cities of Holland and Utrecht in the 16th and 17th centuries. They were disarmed by Maurice of Nassau and dismissed by the States General.

Wafd Egyptian political party founded by Sa'd Zaghlul in 1919. The W. espoused Egyptian independence as well as social and political reforms. In 1924, it won 190 of the 214 seats in parliament. The party was disbanded in 1978.

Wagner, Richard (1813-1883) German composer. His operas represent the pinnacle of German romanticism. W. exerted enormous influence on 19th- and 20th-century composers. His long, complex, and demanding

Richard Wagner

operas are standard pieces of the modern operatic repertory. Among the most famous are *Tannhäuser* (1845), *Lohengrin* (1850), the tetralogy, *Der Ring des Nibelungen* (1853-1874), *Tristan und Isolde* (1857-1859), and *Parsifal* (1877-1882). Wagner built a theater in Bayreuth, which still

operates today, for the performance of his works.

Wagram Town in Austria. It was the location of a battle where the Austrians under Archduke Charles were defeated by Napoleon in 1809.

Wahhabis Reform movement in Islam. Founded by Abd al-Wahab (1703-1792) in Arabia, the W. strove for a return to the pure Islam that existed in the time of Muhammad. The Saudi Arabian royal family are W.

Wakf Arabic foundations, the profits of which were made available to the community by the deceased owners.

Walcourt Town in Belgium. There, Waldeck defeated the French under d'Humières in 1689.

Waldeck, Georg Friedrich, Count (1620-1692) German commander in chief in the service of the Netherlands from 1665. As supreme commander, W. was victorious over the French in 1689, but was defeated by Luxembourg at Fleurus on July 1, 1690.

Waldemar (1243-1302) King of Sweden, 1250-1275. The successor of Erik, he was defeated by his brothers at Hofwa in 1274 and fled to Norway.

Waldemar I (Waldemar the Great) (1131-1182) King of Denmark, 1157-1182. The son of Duke Canute Lavard, he conquered the island of Rügen in 1169 and was devoted to Christianity. He codified Danish law and conquered territory in Norway.

Waldemar II (1170-1241) King of Denmark, 1202-1241. The successor of his brother Canute, he conquered Estonia after 1219 and made a significant contribution to Danish jurisprudence.

Waldenses Protestant religious sect founded in medieval times. It was named after the merchant Valdès, who converted to a life of poverty and preached in Lyons from 1170. The W., who rejected church hierarchy, indulgences, and the mass, and advocated a life of simple poverty, were relentlessly persecuted in France.

Waldheim, Kurt (1918-) President of Austria, 1986-1992 and secretary general of the United Nations, 1972-

1980. After his service at the UN, he returned to Austria and ran for president. Prior to his election, however, it was discovered that he had probably been involved as an army officer in Nazi atrocities in Greece. He was elected president and served out his term, but most nations of the world refused to deal with him in his official capacity.

Walesa, Lech (1943-) President of Poland, 1990-1995. An electrician by profession, he was a founder of the Solidarity trade union movement at the Lenin Shipyard in the city of Gdansk. His calls for democracy led to his imprisonment by the communist regime in 1981, but he was released in 1982. After the collapse of communism in Poland, W. was elected president (1990). He was defeated for reelection in 1995 and returned to his job as an electrician in Gdansk.

William Wallace

Wallace, William (c.1270-1305) Scottish national hero. He succeeded John Baliol as leader of the Scots in 1296. W. fought against Edward I of England with varying success, but was eventually taken prisoner and executed.

Wallenstein, Albrecht Wenzel Eusebius von (1583-1634) Imperial general in the Thirty Years War. W. was involved in the fight against the Hungarians as early as 1604. In 1620, he suppressed the Bohemian rebellion (1618-1623) after his victory on White Mountain. He was appointed supreme commander of the imperial forces (1626), but was dismissed in 1630 (until 1632). He lost the Battle of Lützen (1632) against the Swedes and was murdered in 1634 after being deposed by Emperor Ferdinand II.

Albrecht Wenzel Eusebius von Wallenstein

Walpole, Robert (1676-1745) English statesman. W. entered the House of Commons in 1701. He was secretary of war from 1708 to 1711 and from 1713 to 1714. As leader of the Whigs from 1713, he became powerful after the accession of King George I in 1714. As First Lord Treasurer, Walpole was the virtual leader of the government from 1722 to 1742. He is often described as the first prime minister of Great Britain because of the evolution of cabinet responsibility during his ministry.

Walther von der Vogelweide (c.1170-1230) German court poet, probably of knightly birth. He wrote many love poems. After 1210 he fought for Otto IV and Frederick II, whose vassal he became. He supported Frederick's crusade in his *Elegy* (1228).

Wang Ching-wei (1884-1944) Chinese politician. A leader of the Kuomintang, he was pushed aside by Chiang Kai-shek and the death of Sun Yat-sen. W. collaborated with the Japanese occupation forces in China and headed a puppet regime.

Wannsee Conference Meeting of high-ranking Nazi officials held in the Wannsee section of Berlin in January 1942. The conference formalized the plans for the extermination of the Jews of Europe.

War of the Allies (90-89 BC) War between the Romans and the Italic tribes that had remained loyal to Rome during the Second Punic War. The tribes revolted when the civic rights that had been promised as their reward were never granted. The revolting tribes were defeated, but all inhabitants of Italy living south of the Po River were given civic rights.

Warhol, Andy (1930?-1987) American artist, photographer, and film maker. He was the leading exponent of the Pop-Art movement. W.'s imagery came from the world of commonplace objects, for example, his paintings of Campbell's soup cans (1962). He produced hundreds of films in his "factory" in New York and influenced a large following of young avant-garde artists.

Warlords Commanders of private armies who controlled a large part of China between 1916 and 1928. Many of them were later subordinated to the

Robert Walpole

Kuomintang, but some warlords in the west of China maintained power until the establishment of the Communist government in 1949.

Warsaw Pact Alliance between the Soviet Union, Poland, East Germany, Czechoslovakia, Rumania, Bulgaria, Hungary, and Albania, formed in 1955 as a counterforce to NATO.

Wartburg Medieval castle at Eisenach in eastern Germany. Luther resided there from May 1521 to March 1522.

Wartburg Contest Poetry contest between court poets. It was held at the court of Herman von Thüringen at the Wartburg and included Walther von der Vogelweide and Wolfram von Eschenbach.

Richard Beauchamp Warwick

Warwick, Richard Beauchamp, Earl of (d.1439) English statesman. Under King Henry V, W. was appointed governor of Normandy, where he presided at the trial of Joan of Arc.

Warwick, Richard Neville, Earl of (1428-1471) British statesman, known as the "Kingmaker." He supported the Yorkists during the War of the Roses. After imprisoning Henry VI, he set Edward of York on the throne in 1461, but they later became enemies. W. was killed in the battle of Barnet against Edward.

Washington, Booker Taliaferro (1856-1915) African-American educator. The son of a black slave mother and white father, he taught at the Hampton Institute before being chosen (1881) to develop a normal school for African Americans in Tuskegee, Alabama. The Tuskegee Institute, which emphasized industrial training and economic independence, became one of the leading black educational institutions in the U.S. W. believed that African Americans should strive for economic self-sufficiency before social equality, views that came under bitter attack by W. E. B. Du Bois.

Washington, George (1732-1799) 1st president of the U.S., 1789-1797. The father of American independence, W. was a well-to-do plantation owner from Virginia. In 1775, he was appointed commander in chief of the colonial troops during the Revolutionary War. Although not a great military strategist, W. was an inspirational leader universally recognized for his integrity and dignity. After presiding over the Constitutional Convention (1787), he was chosen the first president of the U.S., taking office in New York City on April 30, 1789. W. established all of the major precedents that governed the conduct of the presidency and its relationship to the other branches of government. Although he abhorred political parties, his administration witnessed the emergence of the first two-party system in America. W. declined to run for a third term, thus establishing a precedent that was observed until 1940.

Watergate Scandal Political scandal (1972-1974) that occurred during the administration of President Richard Nixon. It was named after the Watergate apartment complex in Washington, DC, where a burglary of the Democratic Party's headquarters oc-
curred in 1972. The burglars were found to have connections to Nixon's reelection campaign. After denying knowledge of the business, Nixon made attempts to cover up the affair, as was later implicated by tapes of conversations with aides made on a secret system in place in his office. Facing im- impeachment, he resigned (August 9, 1974). The W. was a major constitutional crisis that brought into question the powers of the presidency and the relationship of the Congress to the Executive.

Waterloo Village near Brussels where Napoleon was decisively defeated (June, 1815) by the allied armies under Wellington and Blücher.

James Watt

Watt, James (1736-1819) Scottish physicist. He is best known for inventing the steam engine, the driving force behind the Industrial Revolution.

Wavell, Archibald Percival Wavell, 1st Earl (1883-1950) British field marshal. Serving in France during World War I, he was appointed commander in chief of the land forces in the Middle East in 1939. He defeated the Italians in Ethiopia in 1940. W. was appointed British commander in chief in Southeast Asia in 1941. He was viceroy of India from 1943-1947.

George Washington

Wayne, John (1907-1979) American film actor. Born Marion Michael Morrison, he was one of Hollywood's most durable stars. W. appeared in more than 40 films, most of them Westerns or war movies. Among them are *The Big Trail* (1930), *Stagecoach* (1939), and *Rio Bravo* (1959).

John Wayne

Weber, Carl Maria von (1786-1826) German Romantic composer. Although he composed many works for piano, masses, and cantatas, his first opera, *Der Freischütz* (1821), is his most famous work.

Webern, Anton von (1883-1945) Austrian composer. He was a pupil of Schoenberg. W. composed relatively few pieces in his lifetime, most of them 12-tone compositions devoid of traditional harmony. His best known works include *Fünf Lieder* (*Five Songs*) (1908). Near the end of World War II, Webern was accidentally killed by a sentry during the occupation of Germany.

Josiah Wedgwood

Wedgwood, Josiah (1730-1795) British pottery maker. W. made various discoveries in the field of pottery production and is famous for his pottery's cameo-like, neoclassical decoration, which he copied from the Roman Portland Vase.

Weimar, Constitution of (1919) Constitution of Germany that created a democratic republic (the so-called Weimar Republic) following World War I.

Weizmann, Chaim (1874-1952) Is-

Chaim Weizmann

raeli statesman. He was president of the World Zionist Organization for many years. W. was elected the first president of Israel in 1949.

Welf (Guelf) Dynasty of landowners in Italy and Germany, rivals of the Hohenstaufens. In the 1130s, the Welf Henry the Proud attempted to become Holy Roman Emperor but lost the battle with Conrad von Hohenstaufen.

Welles, Orson (1915-1985) American motion-picture and stage actor, director, and writer. He achieved national recognition in 1938 with his radio broadcast of an adaptation of H.G. Wells' *War of the Worlds*. The realism of the alleged invasion from outer space created panic across the country. W.'s most critically acclaimed film is *Citizen Kane* (1939), which he starred in, produced, and directed.

Wellington, Arthur Wellesley, 1st Duke of (1769-1852) British soldier and statesman. After a long stay in India, W. was sent to Portugal in 1808 as commander in chief of the army and fought the French successfully there. After the return of Napoleon in 1815, W. was appointed commander in chief of the allied forces, which were victorious at Waterloo. In politics, he served briefly as prime minister

(1828-1830) and in a number of ministeries in the 1830s.

Wenceslaus (1361-1419) Holy Roman Emperor and German king, 1378-1400, and King of Bohemia, 1378-1419, as Wenceslaus IV, and king of the Romans from 1376. Although gifted, he was a drunkard and unable to influence events in Germany. W. ruled mainly in Bohemia. He was deposed as Holy Roman Emperor in 1400.

Wenzel, Duke of Luxembourg (1337-1383) He married Johanna of Brabant in 1354 and the two were recognized as duke and duchess of Brabant in 1356. W. lost the battle against Louis of Male, Count of Flanders.

Wessel, Horst (1907-1930) Nazi SA member. He was the writer of the lyrics to the Nazi party song. W. was murdered by political opponents and became a martyr of the movement.

Westerbork Town in the Netherlands. It as the site of a Nazi deportation camp from which more than 100,000 Dutch Jews were sent to Auschwitz and Sobibor.

Western Schism Period from 1378-1417 when there was a division in the Roman Catholic Church and two (later three) popes were installed. The Council of Constance restored unity.

Westphalia, Peace of Treaties that brought an end to the Thirty Years War. They were signed in Osnabrück and Münster on October 24, 1648. The treaties were between France, the German emperor, and Sweden on the one hand and Spain and the Netherlands on the other. Switzerland and the Netherlands became independent and France emerged as the most important power in Europe at the expense of the Holy Roman Empire and Spain.

Westkapelle Town in the Netherlands. A Flemish-French army under Guy and John of Dampierre was defeated (1253) at W. by the Dutch under Floris.

Westminster, Statute of (1931) Treaty of free association of former British

colonies within the Commonwealth, united by ties to the British crown.

Westminster, Peace of See Anglo-Dutch Wars.

Westmoreland, William Childs (1914-) American general. He fought in France (1944) and in the Korean War. W. was appointed commander of U.S. forces in Vietnam in 1964. He was responsible for the buildup of American forces and the the strategy of "search-and-destroy." W. was replaced after the 1968 Tet Offensive.

Western Roman Empire Empire created in 395 by the division of the Roman Empire (see Theodosius). The fall of the Western Roman Empire in 476 marks the end of the period known as Ancient History.

Westrozebeke Town in Flanders. The army of Ghent, under Phillipe of Artevelde, was defeated (1382) at W. by Louis of Male, who was supported by King Charles VI.

West wall See Siegfried line.

Weyden, Roger van der (c.1400-1464) Flemish painter in Brussels. His *Descent from the Cross* (Louvain, c.1435/1440) is world-renowned. Weyden also worked abroad, including for the Medicis in Florence.

Roger van der Weyden

William Childs Westmoreland

Maxime Weygand

Weygand, Maxime (1867-1965) French general. He served as Marshal Foch's chief of staff during World War I. In May 1940, W. succeeded Gamelin as commander in chief of the French army in the midst of the German invasion of France. After the capitulation on June 12, 1940, he served as minister of defense in the Vichy government and governor-general of Algeria. W. was imprisoned (1942-1945) by the Germans but was nonetheless charged with collaboration after the war. He was pardoned in 1948.

Whigs *See* Tories.

Simon Wiesenthal

Whitby, Synod of (c.664) Synod of the Anglo-Saxon Church in which the decision was made to follow the Roman liturgy rather than Celtic rituals.

Whittington, Richard (d.1423) English merchant and financier of Henry IV and Henry V. W. was lord mayor of London three times between 1397 and 1420.

Whittle, Sir Frank (1907-) British design engineer. In 1937, Whittle designed a jet engine for an airplane and developed it with the support of the RAF. His Gloster-Whittle jet plane flew for the first time in 1941. It was not used during the war.

Whymper, Edward (1840-1911) English mountain climber and illustrator. He was the first to climb (1865) the Matterhorn in Switzerland.

Widukind Commander of the Saxons in the battle against Charlemagne. He subjugated them in 785 and forced them to convert to Christianity. W. probably died between 804 and 812.

Wiesenthal, Simon (1908-) Austrian publicist. He has devoted his life to searching for Nazi war criminals. A Jew, W. was held in several concentration camps between 1941-1945. He opened the Jewish Documentation Center in Vienna in 1961, which seeks to document wartime atrocities.

Wilberforce, William (1759-1833) English antislavery advocate. A member of Parliament, he was successful in getting the slave trade banned in the British West Indies in 1807. Slavery in the British Empire was abolished shortly after his death.

Wilhelmina (1880-1962) Queen of the Netherlands, 1890-1948. She was the daughter of King William III of the Netherlands and succeeded him at the age of 10. W. married Henry, Duke of Mecklenburg-Schwerin, in 1901 and gave birth to a daughter, Juliana, in 1909. While in London (1940-1945) during World War II, W. was a source of inspiration to the Dutch resistance movement. Extremely popular, she abdicated in 1948 in favor of Juliana.

William (1882-1951) Crown prince of Germany, the eldest son of Emperor William II. He fought at Verdun in World War I and in 1918 went into exile in the Netherlands with his father. He was allowed to return to Germany in 1923 after renouncing any claims to the throne.

William I (1797-1888) Emperor of Germany, 1871-1888, and King of Prussia, 1861-1888. He was the second son of Frederick William III of Prussia. From 1858, W. was regent for his mentally ill brother, Frederick William IV, whom he succeeded in 1861. William was proclaimed emperor of Germany in 1871. He ruled together with Bismarck, despite regular differences of opinion. W.'s reign was important because it was the period in which a united Germany emerged as a world power. He was succeeded by his son, Frederick III, in 1888.

William II (1859-1941) Emperor of Germany, 1888-1918. He was the son

Willem II (1859-1941)

The Wild West

1

Many stories we hear today about the American "Wild West" —with its cowboys, Indians, and gold miners—has at best little connection with real history. Still, there was a time in which many people went to seek their fortunes in the West of the United States. This movement of people often led to conflict with the local population, the Native Americans or American Indians.

2

3

4

1. A settlement of gold miners in the valley of the Klondike River, near Alaska.
2. An 1885 print of a cowboy chasing a steer that has left the herd during a cattle drive.
3. A drawing of a Sioux Indian village in the West.
4. A c.1890 photograph of a Cree Indian squaw standing outside her tepee with her papoose on her back.
5. An 1871 print showing a train crossing the American West. The buffalo are stampeding in the face of a prairie fire.

5

397

William

of Frederick III and the English princess Victoria (daughter of Queen Victoria). William succeeded his father as German emperor in May 1888. He forced Bismarck to resign in March 1890. His love of military display and his impulsiveness were character traits that affected many of his policies. World War I demonstrated his poor political and military skills. With the defeat of Germany (1918), W. fled to the Netherlands, where he abdicated, thus ending the Hohenzollern dynasty's rule of Germany. He lived in exile at Doorn until his death in 1941.

was crowned king at Westminster in 1066.

William II (William Rufus) (1056-1100) King of England, 1087-1100. He was the son of William I. W.'s rule was brutal. He recovered a large part of Normandy from his brother and was killed while hunting.

William I (d.1222) Count of Holland and Zeeland and son of Floris III. Supported by the Frisians, W. rebelled against his brother, Dirk VII. After 1203, he battled his cousin Ada and her husband Lodewijk of Loon. W. was a member of the crusade to Damietta.

William III (1285-1337) Count of Holland and Zeeland from 1304, and Count of Hainault. He married Johanna of Valois, and his daughters were married to Edward III of England and to the German emperor, Louis of Bavaria. W. played an important role in the formation of an anti-French coalition at the beginning of the Hundred Years War.

William II (1056-1100)

William IV (1318-1345) Count of Holland and Zeeland and son of William III. W. won fame in the Crusades in the Holy Land and against the Lithuanians. He was killed in a battle against the Frisians at Warns.

William I (William the Silent) (1533-

William I (c.1028-1087)

William I (William the Conqueror) (c.1028-1087) King of England, 1066-1087. The duke of Normandy from 1035, W. landed on the south coast of England in 1066, where he defeated Harold, Edward the Confessor's successor, at Hastings. William

William I (1533-1584)

1584) Prince of Orange and stadt-holder of the Netherlands. He was the son of William the Rich. Philip II appointed him stadtholder of Holland, Zeeland and Utrecht in 1559. However, after William was declared an outlaw by Philip II, he defended himself in his famous *Apologie* (1580). The following year he renounced his allegiance to the king. W. was murdered in Delft in 1584 and was succeeded by his son, Maurice.

William III (1650-1702) King of England, 1689-1702. He was the son of William II, prince of Orange. W. was proclaimed stadtholder of Zeeland and Holland in 1672. He married Princess Mary, the daughter of James, duke of York (later king James II), in 1677. W. became the English king in 1689 in the wake of the Glorious Revolution. W. was an able soldier and astute politician. His reign was of enormous constitutional significance for England.

William V Batavus (1748-1806) Prince of Orange and Nassau, stadtholder of the Dutch Republic and a son of Prince William IV. He ruled under the regency of Brunswijk until he became of age in 1766. In 1795, W. fled to England, where he led the resistance against the French. Napoleon offered him compensation in the form of property in Germany in 1802, which he refused.

William I (1772-1843) First king of the Netherlands, 1815-1840. He was the son of Prince William V of Orange. W. fought the French but was forced to flee to England after the French invasion in 1795. He became king of the Netherlands in 1815. His rule was autocratic. W. did not recognize Belgium until 1839, when he became Grand Duke of Luxembourg. He abdicated in 1840 and was succeeded by his son, William II.

William II (1792-1849) King of the Netherlands, 1840-1849. He was the son of William I. After receiving military training in 1811, W. served as Wellington's aide-de-camp. He fought at Quatre-Bras and Waterloo in 1815. In 1816, he married Anna Pavlovna, the sister of Czar Alexander I. W. succeeded his father as king of the Netherlands in 1840. Although he generally resisted the liberal movement, the king allowed liberal con-

William III (1650-1702)

stitutional changes to be made in 1848.

William I (William the Bad) (1120-1166) King of Sicily, 1154-1166. He was the son of king Roger II of Sicily. W.'s rule was tyrannical. He recovered southern Italy from rebellious vassals and supported Pope Adrian IV against Frederick Barbarossa.

William II of Dampierre (1225-1251) Eldest son of William of Dampierre and Margaretha of Constantinople. He was recognized as the heir of Flanders in 1246. W. participated in the seventh Crusade with Louis IX in 1248. After his death (in a joust in Flanders), he was succeeded by his younger brother, Guy Dampierre.

William Clito of Normandy (d.1128) Great-grandson of Boudouin V of Flanders and grandson of William the Conqueror. W. was appointed as Count of Flanders by King Louis VI of France in 1127. He died in the battle of Aalst fighting against his rival Diederik of Alsace.

William of Gulik (the Elder) (c.1268-1297) Eldest son of William of Gulik

and Mary of Dampierre. He fought for Flanders against Philip IV of France in 1297. W. lost the battle of Bulskamp and soon after died of his wounds.

William of Gulik (the Younger) (c.1275-1304) Youngest son of William of Gulik and Mary of Dampierre. He gave up his studies at Bologna to help the Flemish fight Philip IV. W. led the army of Bruges in the battle of the Spurs. He died later that year in the battle of Mount Pevelen against the French.

William the Rich (1487-1559) Count of Nassau-Katzenelnbogen. William was the fourth son of Count John V, whose German possessions he inherited in 1516. In 1531, he married Juliana von Stolberg, with whom he had eleven children, including William of Orange and John the Old.

Wilson, Woodrow (1856-1924) 28th president of the U.S., 1913-1921. He was the son of a minister who was educated at Princeton and John Hopkins University, where he received a PhD in political science. W. taught at Princeton and became its president before entering politics. In 1910, he

Woodrow Wilson

Famous Woman

Although the history of the world may often seem to be an affair of men, great women have held power as well.
Below are some examples:

1. Queen Elizabeth of England (1533-1603), sometimes called "the Virgin Queen," made England a powerful nation. *See* Elizabeth I of England, Leicester, Raleigh.
2. Cleopatra (69-30 BC), Queen of Egypt. After losing the Battle of Actium, she took her own life. *See* Cleopatra, Actium, Marc Antony.
3. Maria Theresa (1717-1780), Queen of Hungary and Bohemia, Archduchess of Austria. *See* Seven Years' War, Frederick the Great, War of Austrian Succession.
4. Catherine II the Great (1729-1796), Czarina of Russia. Under her rule, Russia became a more powerful nation.

was elected governor of New Jersey, and in 1912 was elected president on the Democratic ticket. W. instituted a number of progressive reforms, including the Federal Reserve system. He was reelected in 1916. W.'s second term was consumed by American involvement in World War I. W. negotiated the Treaty of Versailles (1919) but was unable to convince Congress to ratify it. He spent his final year in office as an invalid after a stroke in 1919.

Winchester Largest settlement in England around 200 BC (Iron Age). It was conquered by the Romans in 44 AD, who called it Venta Belgarum. In Saxon times, Winchester was the capital of Wessex and the residence of King Alfred the Great (848-899). William the Conqueror made Winchester as well as London capital of the kingdom, and was crowned in both cities.

Windsor Name of the British royal family since 1917.

Wingate, Orde Charles (1903-1944) British military officer. He was renowned for his military operations during World War II with the so-called Chindits (Indian Chinese) behind the Japanese front lines in Burma in 1943. W. died in a plane crash during a second operation.

Sergei Yulyevich Witte

Witte, Sergei Yulyevich, Count (1849-1915) Russian-Dutch entrepreneur. Witte was appointed minister for transport in Russia in 1892 and also finance minister a few months later.

Women's Rights

The modern movement for the emancipation of women started in the second half of the 19th century in England and gradually spread to most of the rest of the world. Equal rights for men and women began to be considered an important element of democracy. Consequently in most Western countries women acquired the right to vote, the ability to obtain an education equal to that of men, and other rights. Many people feel, however, that women still have not been truly liberated.

1

2

1. Emmiline Pankhurst, who formed the Women's Social and Political Union in Great Britain, was arrested in 1914 after having tried to present a petition on women's rights to the King.
2. A demonstration of suffragettes, women campaigning for the right to vote, in Washington, DC in 1913.
3. During World War I in Europe, women were employed in factories doing work previously done by men. This led to considerable public sympathy for the women's suffrage movements.
4. Prime Minister Benazir Bhutto of Pakistan, the first woman to govern an Islamic country.

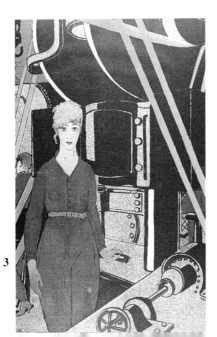
3

4

His efforts to expand the Russian railway network include the construction of the Trans-Siberian Railroad.

Thomas Wolsey

Witzleben, Erwin von (1881-1944) German field marshal. He was commander in chief on the western front between 1941 and 1942. W. played a crucial role in the plot to assassinate Hitler in 1944. He was arrested and executed for his role in the conspiracy.

Wodan Germanic god. The English word "Wednesday" illustrates the relationship between Wodan and Mercury. Both were associated with the realm of the dead.

Woeringen Town north of Cologne, on the Rhine River. John I of Brabant won a decisive victory at W. over Reinald of Guelders and the latter's allies during the war over the Duchy of Limburg.

Wolfram von Eschenbach (c.1170-1220) German poet who wrote in Middle High German. His most famous work is *Parzival* (1200-1210).

Wolsey, Thomas (1474-1530) English cardinal and statesman. A favorite of Henry VIII, he was lord chancellor from 1515. W. fell out of grace when the pope refused to annul the marriage of Henry VIII and Catherine of Aragon. He was arrested and died when taken to the Tower.

Wonders of the World Seven Wonders of the ancient world are the pyramid of Cheops, the hanging gardens of Semiramis in Babylon, the temple of Artemis at Ephesus, the statue of Zeus at Olympia (Greece), the tomb of Mausolus at Halicarnassus, the Colossus of Rhodes, and the Pharos, a lighthouse on an island near Alexandria.

Worcester Town near Gloucester, in the east of England. Parliamentary troops led by Cromwell gained a decisive victory at W. over the army of the future Charles II, who subsequently fled to France.

World War I Conflict (1914-1918) between Germany, Austria-Hungary, Bulgaria, and Turkey (Central Powers) on the one side and Serbia, Russia, France, Belgium, Great Britain, Japan, Italy, and the U.S. (Allied Powers) on the other. War broke out on July 28, 1914, after the assassination of the Austrian Archduke Franz Ferdinand in Sarajevo. Russia was forced to sign the disadvantageous Treaty of Brest-Litovsk on March 3, 1918. The Allied victory became reality on November 11, 1918, when an armistice was concluded with Germany. In 1919, the Treaties of Versailles, Saint-Germain and Neuilly ended of the war against Germany, Austria, and Bulgaria. The Treaties of Trianon and Sèvres with Hungary and Turkey followed in 1920.

World War II Conflict (1939-1945) between the Axis Powers (Germany, Italy and Japan, joined later by Bulgaria, Romania, Hungary and Finland) and the Allied Powers (primarily Britain, France and other Western European countries, joined later by the U.S., Russia and many other nations). The war began on September 1, 1939, when Germany invaded Poland. The German invasion of Western Europe began in May 1940. Germany and Finland invaded the Soviet Union on June 22, 1941. The turning point in that campaign was the battle for Stalingrad (1942-1943). The Japanese attack on Pearl Harbor on December 7, 1941, brought the U.S. into the war. In 1943, the Germans and Italians were driven out of North Africa. The Allied invasion of Normandy began on June 6, 1944, after which Germany suffered more and more losses until the end of September. The bitter battle for Germany itself was fought in the winter of 1944-1945. Germany capitulated on May 7, 1945, but Japan did not surrender until September 2, 1945, after the atomic bombings of Hiroshima and Nagasaki.

Worms, Edict of (1521) Order of the Diet that outlawed Luther as well as anyone who read his works.

Wörth Town in the Alsace. The French suffered a defeat at W. against the German armies in 1870.

Wounded Knee Battle site in South Dakota in the United States. It was the location of the last armed encounter (1890) between the U.S. military and the Indians. W. marked the end of armed Indian resistance.

Wrangel, Karl Gustav count (1613-1676) Grand marshal of Sweden, 1664-1676. He fought against the Poles on the side of King Karl X Gustav. In his capacity as admiral, he fought against the Dutch on the Sont in 1658, but lost the battle.

Wrangel, Pyotr Nikolayevich, Baron (1878-1928) Russian general. In 1920, Wrangel succeeded Denikin as the commander in chief of the White Army in southern Russia. He scored several victories, but was eventually defeated by the more powerful Red Army forces. W. fled to Western Europe via Turkey.

Wright brothers American inventors who created one of the first functioning airplanes. On October 17, 1903, Orville and Wilbur Wright made the first motorized flight in history in a plane they had designed themselves.

Wulfila (Ulfilas) (c.311-382) Visigoth bishop. He translated the Bible into Visigothic, the so-called *Codex Argenteus*, called "Argenteus" because of the silver color of the script on purple parchment.

Wurmser, Dagobert, Count of (1724-1797) Austrian field marshal. Wurmser was victorious over the French at

World War I

After a half-century of general peace in Europe, the increasingly tense international situation exploded in 1914.
All the great powers of the world eventually became involved in what turned out to be the most violent, bloody, and extensive war the world had yet experienced.

1

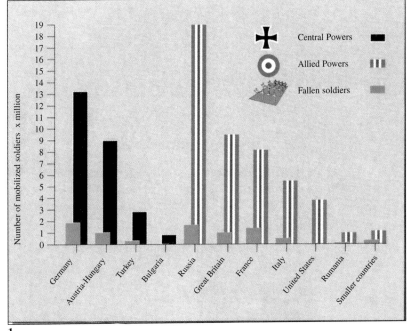

2

1. The number of soldiers mobilized and killed during World War I. *See* World War I.
2. The assassination in Sarajevo on June 28, 1914, of Archduke Franz Ferdinand, the heir to the Austro-Hungarian throne, precipitated World War I. *See* World War I; Franz Ferdinand; Sarajevo.
3. The bombing of Verdun, a French town that suffered four years of fierce battle. Half a million men died in the battlefields of Verdun. *See* Verdun; Joffre; Falkenhayn.
4. In 1917 the United States entered World I. Here, on April 2, 1917, President Wilson asks Congress for a declaration of war against Germany. *See* World War I; Submarine War; Wilson.

3

4

5

6

7

8

5. German Emperor William II between his two generals Hindenburg (left) and Ludendorff, who were expected to win a German victory at the Marne. *See* William II; Hindenburg; Ludendorff; Marne.

6. Germany used these gigantic cannon against the French. *See* World War I.

7. German troops enter the Russian city of Kiev. *See* World War I; Brest-Litovsk, Treaty of.

8. World War I was mainly a war of trenches, in which soldiers sometimes lived for months on end. *See* World War I.

9. World War I ended in November 1918, when the Germans asked for an armistice. The Treaty of Versailles that was signed in 1919 created many problems later on. *See* World War I; Versailles, Treaty of; Clemenceau; Lloyd George.

9

World War II

In the 1930s aggressive right-wing movements came to power in Japan and Germany. These countries—and their ally Italy, where fascists had taken over in 1922—soon began threatening their neighbors. By the end of the 1930s, World War II had begun. It turned out to be even more destructive than World War I and became the most horrible war in history.

2

1

3

4

1. Adolf Hitler, the leader of the German Nazis, during a military parade. *See* World War II; Hitler; Nazism.
2. German troops enter Prague, Czechoslovakia, on March 15, 1939. *See* Hitler; Nazism.
3. At the French village of Compiègne, where Germany had signed the armistice ending World War I in 1918, France surrendered to Germany in June 1940 during World War II. *See* Pétain; Compiègne.
4. Hiroshima, Japan, after the United States dropped the first atomic bomb on it on August 6, 1945. A second atomic bomb was dropped on Nagasaki three days later, and within a week Japan surrendered. *See* Hiroshima; Nagasaki; Truman; World War II.

5

6

5. The German bombing of Rotterdam, the Netherlands, in 1940.
6. American troops in battle on a Pacific island.
7. German soldiers advance toward Moscow in late 1941.
See World War II.
8. The British general Bernard Montgomery. He defeated the Germans led by Rommel in North Africa and participated in the liberation of France, Belgium, and the Netherlands. *See* Montgomery; Rommel.
9. Entrance gate to the death camp at Auschwitz, where hundreds of thousands, perhaps millions, of Jews were killed by the Germans.
See Concentration camp; Auschwitz; Nazism.

8

7 9

Mannheim in 1795. In 1797, he was forced to relinquish the city of Mantua, which he had defended since 1796, to Napoleon.

Wyatt, Sir Thomas (c.1521-1554) English conspirator, son of the poet, Sir Thomas Wyatt. In 1544, W. was involved in a conspiracy against the proposed marriage of Queen Mary and Philip II of Spain. He entered London with a force of supporters, but the city refused to rise against the queen. W. was arrested and hanged.

Sir Thomas Wyatt

Wycliffe, John (c.1330-1384) English church reformer. He opposed the secular power and hierarchy of the Church both orally and in writing. W.'s ideas greatly influenced Hus and contributed to the developments that led to the Reformation. He was protected by the court until the Peasants' Revolt in 1381, for which he was held responsible. Although condemned as a heretic, he was allowed to live undisturbed in retirement.

John Wycliffe

Xanthippe Wife of Socrates. According to legend, Xanthippe was notorious for her sharp tongue and her fighting spirit.

Xantippos (5th century BC) Father of Pericles. In 479 BC, X. led the Athenian army to victory during the naval battle of Mycale.

Xanthus Ancient city of Lycia (in present-day Turkey). In 540 BC, X. was besieged by the Persians. The Lycians burned their wives, children, possessions, and servants and then launched a suicide attack.

Xavier, St. Francis (1506-1552) Roman Catholic missionary. A Jesuit, his missionary work took him to India and Japan. He died in 1552 off the Chinese coast, waiting to be allowed into China. X. was canonized in 1622.

Xenocrates (4th century BC) Greek philosopher. X. headed the Academy founded by Plato between 339-314 BC.

Xenophanes (c.560-478 BC) Greek philosopher. He founded his own (Eleatic) school of philosophy and taught about the unity and indivisible nature of things.

Xenophon (c.431-350 BC) Greek historian and military official. After the battle of Cunaxa in 401 BC, X. led the defeated Greek mercenary army back to Greece, which he described in the *Anabasis*. X. is also known for his *Hellenica* (a historical work that begins where Thucydides left off) and works about his teacher Socrates.

Xerxes (c.519-465) King of Persia, 486-465 BC. In 480 BC, he bridged the Hellespont and invaded Greece by land and by sea. Although he succeeded in destroying Athens, his fleet was defeated by the Greeks near Salamis.

Xipe Totec (Our Lord the Flayed One) Pre-Columbian god of spring and renewed fertility, worshiped in ancient Mexico. He was depicted wearing a flayed human skin.

Xiuhtecuhtli Aztec god of fire and creator of all life.

Xochicalco Ancient Toltec city in Mexico. It was a major trading center. The oldest traces of construction date back to the 8th and 9th centuries. The ruins of the city also show numerous fortifications that reflect the arrival of the Spaniards.

Xochiquetzal Aztec goddess of beauty and sexual love. Originally the wife of Tlaloc, the god of rain, she was abducted by Tezcatlipoca, the god of night, and installed as the goddess of love.

XYZ Affair (1797-1798) Scandal caused by three French agents attempting to offer bribes to Americans who were negotiating a treaty with France. A U.S. delegation that had set out to France to protect American naval trade was approached by three French agents (dubbed X, Y, and Z), who suggested that a bribe be paid before any further negotiations could be conducted. The affair nearly resulted in a war between the U.S. and France.

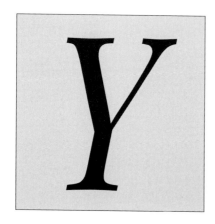

Yad Vashem Israeli national institute devoted to research on the Holocaust and the commemoration of its victims. Located in Jerusalem, it was founded in 1953.

Yadava Dynasty (12th-14th century) Hindu kingdom in central India that flourished under Singhana (1210-1247). The last Yadava monarch was Ramacandra, who ruled until 1309. The kingdom was annexed by the Khalji empire in 1317.

Yagoda, Genrikh Grigoryevich (1891-1938) Soviet secret police chief. Y. became a member of the Cheka in 1919. Stalin appointed him head of the NKVD in 1934 but had him executed in 1938.

Yahweh Hebrew word for God. It is actually a vocalization of the Hebrew letters for YHWH, since devout Jews do not spell out God's name.

Yahya Khan, Aga Muhammad (1917-1980) Pakistani military commander in chief. Yahya deposed president Ayub Khan and assumed power in Pakistan in 1969. The pressure for autonomy for Eastern Pakistan (later Bangladesh) contributed to his fall in 1971.

Yalta, Conference of (February 1945) Meeting between Roosevelt, Stalin, and Churchill held in Yalta, a resort in the Crimea, toward the end of World War II. The conference dealt with the ending of the war and power relationships in postwar Europe.

Yama Lord of Death in Indian mythology.

Yamagata, Aritomo (1838-1922) Japanese general and political leader. Y. built up the Japanese army and favored Japanese expansion in Asia. From the 1880s until his death, he held several high civilian posts and supported a stronger military.

Yamamoto, Isoroku (1884-1943) Japanese admiral. Y. planned the Japanese attack on Pearl Harbor (December 7, 1941) that brought the U.S. into World War II. He was killed when his plane was shot down in 1943.

Yamani, Ahmed Zaki (1930-) Saudi-Arabian politician. Yamani was appointed Minister for Oil Affairs by crown prince Faisal in 1962. He

Ahmed Zaki Yamani

played a major political role during the 1970s and 1980s, but was removed from office in 1986.

Yamasee War (1715-1716) War between British colonists in South Carolina and the Yamasee tribe, caused by a territorial dispute. Some 90 colonists were killed. Some other tribes allied themselves to the Yamasees. After being defeated, the Y. migrated to Florida.

Yamashita, Tomoyuki (1885-1946) Japanese general. During World War II, Y. captured Singapore (1942) from the British and drove the Americans from Bataan and Corregidor in the Philippines (1942). He was defeated by MacArthur when the Americans returned to the Philippines (1945). After the war he was tried and hanged for war crimes.

Yang Hsiu-chi'ng (d.1856) Chinese leader of the Taiping Rebellion who claimed to be the Son of God. He

Isoroku Yamamoto

achieved major military successes, including the capture of Nanking, but grew too powerful and was executed in Nanking.

Yang Yen (727-781) Chinese administrator during the Tang dynasty. He introduced a new taxation system that also assessed rich landowners. The system survived until 1949.

Yaroslav I the Wise (980-1054) Grand Prince of Kiev, 1019-1054. He defeated Svyatopol the Cursed, one of his brothers, who had already killed three other brothers. In 1043, Y. staged an abortive campaign against Constantinople.

Tomoyuki Yamashita

Young Turks

Yazdegerd I (5th century) King of the Sassanian Empire from 390- 420. He put an end to the persecution of Christians in his kingdom and maintained friendly relations with the Roman and Byzantine Empires.

Yazdegerd II (5th century) King of the Sassanian Empire from 438 to 457, successor of Bahram V (son of Yazdegerd I). He persecuted both Christians and Jews and fought a brief war against Rome.

Charles Yeager

Yeager, Charles (1923-) American test pilot, the first to fly faster than the speed of sound (1947).

Yeltsin, Boris Nikolayevich (1931-) Russian political leader. Y. became head of the Communist Party in Moscow (1985) and was initially a supporter of Mikhail Gorbachev. He later quarreled with Gorbachev, and after resigning from the party was elected president of Russia (1990). Y. successfully opposed the attempted Communist coup (August 1991) and was instrumental in bringing about the end of the Soviet Union (December 1991). His presidency was troubled, however, by the difficulties of democratizing Russia after 70 years of Communist rule, economic prob-

lems, and a bloody war in the Chechenya region, which attempted to secede from Russia.

Yenan City in China, in northern Shensi province. It was the end point of the Chinese Communists' Long March (1934-1935) and served as their capital for most of the period from 1936-1949.

Yeomanry Volunteer forces formed in England in 1794. They reached a strength of approximately 45,000 troops in the wars against France. The yeomen fought in the Boer War, World War I (Gallipoli), and in Palestine.

Yggdrasill World tree in Norse mythology, with a crown reaching up into the heavens. The image of a tree as the center of the universe occurs in many forms and many religions.

Yolande of Flanders (d.1219) Empress of Constantinople. Her son, Baldwin II, was the last emperor of the Latin Empire of Constantinople.

Yom Kippur War (1973) Conflict between Israel on one side and Egypt and Syria on the other. It began on October 6, the Jewish holy day of Yom Kippur, when Egypt and Syria suddenly attacked Israeli positions. The Egyptians initially gained ground in the Sinai but were eventually driven back across the Suez Canal. On the Syrian front, the Israelis advanced towards Damascus. A cease-fire went into effect on October 23.

Yorck von Wartenburg, Johann Ludwig, Count (1759-1830) Prussian field marshal. He was the commander of a Prussian section of Napoleon's army during the campaign in Russia. Later he fought on the side of the Allied powers against Napoleon.

York City in England. It was the site of the Evora fort, built by the Romans on the Ouse River in 71 AD. Y. became an Anglo-Saxon city and the capital of the kingdom of Northumbria in 406. The city was conquered by the Danes in 867 and renamed Yorvik.

York, Frederick Augustus, Duke of (1763-1827) English field marshal. He was a son of King George III. As the military commander in chief, Y. he introduced major reforms to modernize the army.

York, Rowland (d.1588) English army officer in the service of the Dutch army. A Roman Catholic, Y. surrendered a fortification near Zutphen to

Boris Nikolayevich Yeltsin

the Spaniards in 1587 and, later, another one near Deventer. He eventually chose to side with the Spaniards. In 1591, the Dutch disinterred his corpse in order to exhibit it to the public.

Yoshida, Shigeru (1878-1967) Japanese diplomat and political leader. After serving as ambassador to Italy and Britain in the 1930s, S. opposed Japan's war against the U.S. and was arrested in 1944. After the end of World War II, he was prime minister five times between 1946 and 1954.

Young Plan (1929) Plan drawn up by the American Owen D. Young (1874-1962) to make Germany's World War I reparations a financial, rather than a purely political, matter.

Young Turks Revolutionary movement in the Ottoman Empire under Ahmed Riza (1859-1930). Aided by

409

Youth Cultures of the Late 20th Century

In the prosperous societies of the Western world in the 20th century, youth cultures developed for the first time. With ample amounts of leisure time and money to spend, young people made heroes out of entertainment personalities—especially from the movies and rock music worlds—and used them to identify with one another.

2

1

3

5

6

7

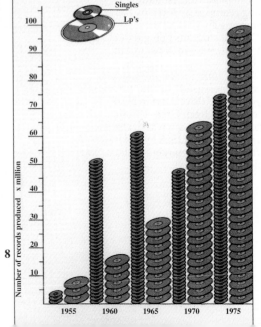

8

4

1. The Woodstock, New York, rock music festival held in the summer of 1969. It became a legendary event in the youth culture.
2. A group of typical "punkers" of the late 20th century, with their hair dyed in bright colors, wearing ripped jeans, piercings, and anarchy-signs.
3. The British rock star Mick Jagger at a concert. *See* Jagger, Mick.
4. The American entertainment personality Madonna became enormously successful. She was so often imitated that Madonna-look-alike contests were organized.
5. Graffiti started as spraying slogans or curse words on private and public buildings, but later developed into an art form in itself.
6. Empty buildings are sometimes occupied by young people protesting against the large numbers of homeless. Here, squatters are being removed by force by the police (Amsterdam 1993).
7. College students being inducted into a fraternity in Amsterdam in 1970.
8. The production of phonograph records increased enormously from the 1950s on, as can be seen on this graphic from Great Britain. There, as well as anywhere else in Europe and the U.S.A., youngsters form the largest market for the record industry's products.

the army, the Y. deposed Sultan Abdul Hamid II (1876-1909) in 1909, and put their candidate Mehmet V Reshad (1875-1918), the sultan's brother, in his place. This action initiated the reform period of the Young Turks (1908-1918). After World War I, their influence declined rapidly.

Youssef, Salah ben (1910-1961) Tunisian nationalist and co-founder, with Bourguiba, of the separatist Néo-Destour Party in 1934. He became a member of the government in 1950. In 1958, Y. was sentenced to death in absentia by the Tunisian government on charges of conspiracy. He was assassinated some years later.

Youssouf Bey (1810-1866) French general. Born Joseph Vantini, he established a police force made up of Algerians in the city of Algiers, from which the spahis (French mounted desert troops) were recruited later. Y. commanded a Turkish army during the Crimean War.

Ypres Town in Belgium. It was the scene of heavy fighting in World War I. The names of 58,000 British military dead are recorded on the Menen Gate in Y.

Ypsilanti, Alexander (1792-1828) Greek military officer. He fought against Napoleon (1813) and was severely wounded. At the beginning of 1821, Y. led a Greek revolt that was

soon crushed by the Turks near Dragatsani.

Yuan Mongolian dynasty that ruled China from 1260-1368.

Yuan Shikai

Yuan Shikai (1859-1916) Chinese general and politician. Although exiled in 1908, Y. was allowed to return to China in 1911 to put down a revolt against the government. In 1912, he became president of the Republic of China, and was appointed dictator for life in 1915.

Yüeh-chih Chinese nomadic tribe from Central Asia. They were driven to Bactria in the 1st century, where they assumed power and extended their rule to India (c.128-450).

Alexander Ypsilanti

Zadruga Family community in the Balkans characterized by communal land ownership.

Zaghlul Pasha, Saad (1860-1927) Egyptian politician. He became prime minister of Egypt in 1924, but was forced to resign by the British. They also prevented him from being prime minister after his Wafd party won the 1926 elections.

Saad Zaghlul Pasha

Zahedi Fazullah (1897-1963) Iranian general and politician. In 1942, Z. was exiled to Palestine and India by the British for his pro-German views. He became chief of police in Iran in 1949 and led a coup d'état in 1953 that toppled Mossadegh and allowed Shah Muhammad Reza Pahlavi to regain power.

Zama Site in North Africa where Hannibal was defeated by Scipio Africanus (202 BC) with the loss of 20,000 lives. The Romans lost 1,500 men.

Zand dynasty *See* Lotf Ali Khan Zand.

Zannekin, Nicolas (d.1328) Flemish rebel leader in a peasant uprising against Louis of Nevers. Z. captured Nieuwpoort and Veurne, but failed to take Ghent and Oudenaarde (1325). The peasants were defeated by the French in the battle of Kassel.

Zapata, Emiliano (1879-1919) Mexican revolutionary. He defended the rights of tenant farmers who were being exploited by the landowners and the government. After the defeat of his ally Pancho Villa, Z. lost much support, and he was ultimately murdered. Rebellious Indians named the armed rebellion against the central government early in 1994 after him.

Zapotecs Indian people related to the Maya. Monte Alban in Mexico was their religious center.

Zara, Battle of (1346) Engagement in which the Venetians defeated Louis I of Hungary.

Zara, Treaty of (1358) Agreement by which Venice had to cede its Dalmatian cities to Hungary after losing the war against Louis I of Hungary.

Zasulich, Vera (1849-1919) Russian socialist. She was a member of the Mensheviks (minority) in opposition to Lenin.

Zebrzydowski Rebellion (1606-1607) Failed uprising of the Polish Catholic aristocracy led by Mikolai Z. against Sigismund III of Poland. The rebels were defeated at Guzow but granted amnesty in 1609.

Zealots Jewish political and religious faction that rebelled against the Romans (66-73). The rebellion ended when the mountaintop fortress, Masada, was captured.

Zebulon *See* Israel, Tribes of.

Zecharia (Zachary) Prophet at the end of the Babylonian exile. Under the command of Zerubbabel, Z. participated in the return to Jerusalem.

Zend Avesta Holy scriptures of Zoroastrianism. The Avesta consists of fragmentary and much-corrupted texts, while the Zend is commentary on them.

Zeno

Zeno (d.491) Byzantine emperor, 474-491. He was continually engaged in wars with the Barbarians, including Theodoric, who became king of Italy in 489.

Zenobia, Septimia (d.c.274) Empress of Palmyrac. 267-272. She captured Syria and Egypt (269), and Asia Minor at Bithynia (270), which forced the Romans to react. In 271, Aurelian recaptured Asia Minor and took Palmyra. Z. was confined to her home for the rest of her life.

Zeppelin, Ferdinand, Count von (1838-1917) German aviation pioneer. He built the airships named after him. The first flight in an airship was made in 1900. During World War I, zeppelins played an important role in reconnaissance and bombardments, but they proved to be too vulnerable for extensive use in combat.

Zeus Greek ruler of the gods and lord of the universe. The Roman counterpart is Jupiter.

Zhu Enlai (Chou En-lai) (1898-1976) Chinese communist leader. Z. became one of the leaders of the Communist Party during the civil war and was prime minister and minister of foreign affairs concurrently between 1949-1958. He relinquished the foreign affairs post in 1958 but retained the prime ministership for the remainder of his life. Urbane and sophisticated, he survived all of the upheavals within the party and was largely responsible for the opening to the West in the early 1970s.

Zhu De (1886-1976) Chinese general and member of the Communist Party from 1922. Z. led the Long March with Mao Zedong. He fought against the Japanese during World War II and was commander in chief of the armies that fought against the Kuomintang.

Zhukov, Georgi Konstantinovich (1896-1974) Soviet marshal. He was responsible for the first major Soviet victory during World War II, when he forced the Germans to retreat from Moscow in December 1941. He was also involved in the battle for Stalingrad and Battle at Kursk. Z.'s forces captured Berlin in the spring of 1945.

Zhung Lu (1836-1903) Chinese general. He was largely responsible for training and arming the Chinese army along Western lines.

Zia ul-Haq, Muhammad (1924-1988) Pakistani general. Z. led the military coup against Prime Minister Bhutto in 1977 and had him executed in 1979. He became president in 1978 and banned other political parties until 1984. In the last years of his rule, Bhutto's daughter, Benazir, emerged as a formidable opponent of Z. He was killed in airplane crash in 1988 that was probably the work of saboteurs.

Zeus

Ziggurat Form of pyramidal temple common to the Sumerians, Babylonians, and Assyrians. The Mayans also built temples with similar forms in Central America.

Zimbabwe (Bantu for "stone dwelling") Ruined stone complex in southeastern Zimbabwe. The ruins are the remains of the Karanga culture (11th-15th century). The prosperity of Z. was closely related to gold mining and trade with the East African coastal cities.

Muhammad Zia ul-Haq

Zimmermann note Secret telegram sent by the German foreign minister Arthur Zimmermann to the German ambassador in Washington in 1917. It said that in the event of war with the U.S., Germany should urge Mexico to enter World War I as a German ally in return for the possession of Texas, Arizona, and New Mexico. The telegram was intercepted by the British, who sent it to President Woodrow Wilson. Wilson released the contents to the public, thus helping turn American public opinion even more against Germany.

Zimrilim (18th century BC) King of Mari. After Mari was conquered by the Assyrians, Z. sought refuge from the King of Aleppo, his father-in-law. After the Assyrians were driven away, Z. resumed the throne, only to be deposed by his former ally, Hammurabi of Babylon, in 1760 BC.

Zinoviev, Grigori Yevseyevich (1883-1936) Russian revolutionary and a close associate of Lenin. After the

1917 revolution he was party leader in St. Petersburg and became a member of the Politburo in 1919. Stalin expelled him and his allies from the party in 1927. He was executed after a highly publicized show trial in 1936.

Zionism Movement to found a Jewish national state in Palestine. Z. was largely cultural until Theodor Herzl founded the World Zionist Congress in 1897.

Zouaves Originally the Kabyle bodyguards of Berber kings. After they entered French military service in 1830, the Kabyle disappeared from the French Z. corps and were replaced by Frenchmen. Papal Z. were Belgian and French volunteers in papal service. The Z. participated in the Franco-German war.

Zog I (1895-1961) King of Albania, 1928-1939. After the Italian invasion in 1939, he fled to Great Britain. Albania became a communist state in 1945.

Emile Zola

Zola, Emile (1840-1902) French author. Z. was an exponent of the naturalist movement. He described in minute and at times sordid detail the decline of a family in the 20-volume

Les Rougon-Macquart (1871-1893). Z. believed in social reform and wrote many anti-Catholic pieces. His writing in defense of Dreyfus (1898) led to his prosecution for libel and his exile in England. He returned to France a few months later after a general amnesty.

Zoroaster (Zarathustra) (c.628-551 BC) Religious teacher and prophet in ancient Persia. He was the founder of Zoroastrianism.

Stefan Zweig

Zosimus (d.418) Greek pope who succeeded Innocent I in 417. He was unable to pursue Innocent's Roman-centralist policies and became embroiled in the religious crisis against Pelagianism.

Zoutman, Johan Arnold (1724-1794) Dutch admiral. He fought (1781) in the battle at the Dogger Bank during the Fourth Anglo-Dutch war.

Zrinyi Dalmatian royal family that controlled virtually all of Croatia in the 13th and 14th centuries. One of their most prominent members was Miklos, viceroy of Croatia between 1542-1561, who played a significant role in defending the Szigetvar fortress against Sulayman I.

Zuiderzee, Battle of the (1573) Engagement in which the Gueux led by Dirksz defeated a Spanish fleet commanded by Boussu.

Zurich, Treaty of *See* Lombardy-Venetian Kingdom.

Zweig, Stefan (1881-1942) Austrian author. Z. moved to England in 1938 at a time when his books were being burned in Nazi Germany. His famous works include *The World of Yesterday* (1943) which described his time, *The Tide of Fortune* (1941), and *Beware of Pity* (1938). He and his wife migrated to Brazil, where they committed suicide in 1942.

Zwentibold (871-900) King of Lorraine, 895-900. He was the illegitimate son of Arnulf of Carinthia. Z. was killed during an uprising of rebellious vassals.

Zwingli, Huldreich (Ulrich) (1484-1531) Swiss Protestant reformer. Z., a follower of Luther, brought the Reformation into Switzerland in 1525. This led to a civil war in which the Catholic cantons fought against the Protestant ones. Z. died of the injuries he suffered in the battle at Kappel am Albis.

Huldreich Zwingli

Illustration Credits

Ancient Art & Architecture Collection, London, U.K. 12a; 38d; 43b; 79c; 96c; 190a; 255b; 283a; 342b; 383a (photos Ronald Sheridan); 61c (photo Allan Eaton); 75d (photo John P. Stevens); 148b.

AKG Berlin, Germany 122a; 156e; 237a; 247a; 261b; 266a; 377a; 398a.

AKG London, U.K. 9c; 13b; 15c; 27e; 39b; 40a; 41b; 43a; 44a; 46abd; 48b; 54a; 56d; 57abc; 60b; 61b; 61e (photo Michael Teller); 70ac; 73b; 74bc; 75bc; 85b; 94b; 95b; 99bd; 106b; 108b; 109b; 113abcde; 114abcde; 121a; 126a; 128a; 131b; 137b; 141a (© 1997 DACS, Marc Chagall *The Blue Cock* 1955/60); 141b; 141c (© 1997 DACS, Henri Matisse *Dance* 1909/10, Les Héritiers de Matisse, State Hermitage St. Petersburg); 142abc; 145b; 148c; 149ab; 153b; 154a; 157c; 158a; 161a; 164ab; 165b; 172b; 179b; 182d; 189b; 192acde; 192b (photo by Erich Lessing); 204a; 205ac; 209c; 210a; 211b; 259b; 271a; 275c; 276b; 278b; 279b; 280ab; 292c; 293a; 301cde; 304b; 306b; 307a; 308b; 312a; 315b; 317ab; 318a; 320c; 322a; 329ab; 331a; 332a; 333b; 336a; 340c; 341b; 344b; 350c; 353b; 355b; 357b; 358ac; 363a; 366a; 369b; 372ab; 373c; 377b; 378b; 384a; 386a; 389b; 392c; 395c; 396a; 388ad; 398b; 406e; 410a; 411c; 414c. AKG London/AP 153a;

Allsport U.K., London, U.K. 354a (photo Gray Mortimore); 354d (photo Simon Bruty); 355a.

ANP Foto, Amsterdam, The Netherlands 25d (photo Frans Vanderlinde); 85a; 86b; 95e; 410bf; 410e (photo Ruud Hoff); 411a. ANP Foto/Allsport U.S.A., Pacific Palisades, U.S.A. 354b (photo Otto Greule). ANP Foto/Topham Picture Source, Edenbridge, U.K. 382ac.

Ann Ronan at Image Select International, London, U.K. 11a; 15ab; 19a; 27a; 33bc; 35ab; 38a; 44bd; 44c (courtesy of the Nobel Foundation); 51b (courtesy of the Nobel Foundation); 59c; 62b; 65b; 79a; 80b; 92c; 93ab; 94a; 97a; 98a; 99a; 100a; 103a; 104b; 105b; 106a; 115ab; 179acde; 120ab; 121b; 125b; 128c; 143b; 146b; 152a; 158c; 161c; 162b; 174a; 181abcd; 182abc; 196a; 203a; 252a; 261c; 262a; 263b; 267abc; 268a; 290b; 292a; 293c; 301a; 306c; 313b; 316b; 337ade; 339b; 339c; 346b; 348a; 362b; 363b; 365a; 379abcde; 385b; 394a; 396b. Ann Ronan/E.P. Goldschmidt & Co., Ltd 279a.

B&U International Picture Service, Amsterdam, The Netherlands 337c;

Bibliothèque Nationale, Paris, France 5a.

K. Brouwer, Amsterdam, The Netherlands 248e.

Explorer Archives, Paris, France 225a; 226b; 387a.

Hessisches Landesmuseum, Darmstadt, Germany 133e.

Ton van der Heyden, Naarden, The Netherlands 27b; 28d; 325c; 235b.

Hulton Getty Collection, London, U.K. 86a; 95a; 177b; 199c; 206b; 251b; 253a; 283b; 295a; 319b; 383b; 395a; 408ac.

Image Select International, London, U.K. 9d; 10b; 14b; 18cd; 19c; 22ab; 25a (photo Eric Bouvet); 25be; 25c (photo David Barret); 26b (photo Alain Morvan); 27c (photo Paul Hanny); 29e (photo Art Seitz); 30b; 38bc; 39a; 46c (photo Ferry); 46e (photo Oswald); 47ac; 48c; 49a (photo G. de Keerle); 49b; 50a; 51c (photo Abbas); 54bc; 55b (photo J.C. Bourbault); 56ac; 59ab; 62a; 69a; 72c; 73a (photo William Stevens); 75a; 85cd (photo D. Simon); 86c (photo Woodson); 86d (photo Brad Markel); 99c (photo Alexandre Figour); 102a; 104a; 110a; 110b (photo Bouvet-Hires-Merillon); 113d (photo Hoaqui); 117bc; 119c; 126b; 127ab; 128b; 131a; 132a; 133a (photo Daniel Simon); 133b; 134c; 134d (photo Jacek Marczewski); 135a; 138a; 143a; 146a (photo Mingasson); 150b (photo Daniel Simon); 159a (photo Noel Quidu); 159b; 160b; 163b (photo Frederic Reglain); 164c; 168a (photo by Carlos Angel); 171b; 173a; 176a; 177c; 178a (photo Georges Merillon); 178c; 183c; 184a; 189d (photo Benami); 189e (photo Mattison); 193c; 194a (photo Giles Basignac); 196b (photo Alexis Duclos); 199b; 200c (photo Livio Anticoli); 202b; 204b (photo Christian Vioujard); 207a (photo A. Zamur); 208ab; 208c (photo G. Uzan); 209a; 209b; 211a (photo Patrick Piel); 213b; 216b; 219a; 221c (photo Jacana-R. Konig); 221d; 251a; 255a (photo William Stevens); 246a; 260b; 265a; 266 (photo Kaku Kurita); 271b; 272a; 274b (photo J. Martinengo); 276a; 277ac; 278a (photo Gilles Mermet); 278c (photo Patrick Aventurier); 281a; 281b (photo Abbas); 285a (photo Eric Brissaud); 285b; 290a; 292b (photo R. Depardon); 295b; 296a (photo Francis Apesteguy); 300b; 300c (photo Hugues-Vassal); 301b (photo Sas-Rey-Rodicq); 302ab; 303b; 307b (courtesy of 20th Century Fox Films); 307c (photo Brad Markell); 312b; 313c; 314a; 314b (photo Alexis Duclos); 316c (photo Kennerly); 318b; 319c; 320b; 323a; 331c; 332b; 334a (photo Alain Morvan); 335abc; 339a (photo Guis); 339d; 340b; 341a; 344a; 346a; 347bc; 349b (photo R. Gaillarde); 354c; 358b (photo Gifford); 360a; 364b (photo Ken Oosterbroek); 365b; 367a (photo G. de Keerle); 371c; 376a (photo Cilo); 376c; 378a; 382b (photo Vogel); 382d (photo Noel Quidu); 385a; 386b (photo P. Lovelace); 389a; 390a; 391ab; 392b; 395b; 401c; 401d (photo Chip Hires); 402a; 404de; 408a (photo Gavin Smith); 409a (photo Zimberoff); 409b (photo Georges Merillon); 410c (photo Giboux); 411b; 413a (photo Chip Hires). Image Select/Atlantiola 387b. Image Select/B&U International Picture Service, Amsterdam, The Netherlands 11d; 16b; 89a; 148a; 202a; 284a; 394b. Image Select/Exley Publishers 154c. Image Select/Ford 138c. Image Select/NASA 65a; 70b. Image Select/Sestini Agency 47b. Image Select/Xinhua 27d; 80c.

India Office Library, London, U.K. 273c.

Koninklijke Bibliotheek Albert I, Brussels, Belgium 337b.

Hugo Maertens, Ghent, Belgium 8a.

Mary Evans Picture Library, London, U.K. 30a; 55a; 91b; 95cd; 109a; 122b; 130a; 134e; 183d; 188a; 215a; 247b; 253a; 286b; 313a; 320a; 333ac; 342a; 343ab; 348b; 373b; 381b; 401c.

Museé du Louvre, Paris, France 193a.

National Archaeological Museum, Athens, Greece 61d.

Henk Oostenrijk, Utrecht, The Netherlands 66b.

Point Studios, Ghent, Belgium 6a; 410d.

Popperfoto, Northampton, U.K. 11b; 13a; 45a; 92b; 132b; 138b; 252b; 274a; 286a; 294a; 346c; 373a; 407a; 412b.

Robert Harding Picture Library, London, U.K. 156c.

Spaarnestad Fotoarchief, Haarlem, The Netherlands 189a; 401ab.

Spectrum Colour Library, London, U.K. 29acf; 29bd (photos G.R. Richardson); 134b; 354e.

Trinity College Library, Cambridge, U.K. 258a.

Trip, Surrey, U.K. 134c (photo Eric Smith); 177a; 189c (photo S. Hhapiro); 388c (photo G. Spencely).

Wellcome Institute, London, U.K. 179f.

M. Wijnings, Breda, The Netherlands 352a.

All other illustrations:
Salvat S.A., Barcelona, Spain and/or H.D. Communication Consultants B.V., Hilversum, The Netherlands.

JAN 1 2 1998